wxPython in Action

*wx**Python in Action***

NOEL RAPPIN
ROBIN DUNN

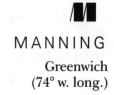

MANNING

Greenwich
(74° w. long.)

Manning Publications Co.   Copyeditor: Elizabeth Martin
209 Bruce Park Avenue   Typesetter: Denis Dalinnik
Greenwich, CT 06830 Cover designer: Leslie Haimes

ISBN 1-932394-62-1

Printed in the United States of America
1 2 3 4 5 6 7 8 9 10 – VHG – 10 09 08 07 06

To every Jane and Joe Programmer,
chained to their computer, burning the midnight oil,
striving to make a dream come true

brief contents

PART 1   INTRODUCTION TO WXPYTHON 1

    1 ▪ Welcome to wxPython   3

    2 ▪ Giving your wxPython program a solid foundation   29

    3 ▪ Working in an event-driven environment   56

    4 ▪ Making wxPython easier to handle with PyCrust   83

    5 ▪ Creating your blueprint   116

    6 ▪ Working with the basic building blocks   146

PART 2   ESSENTIAL WXPYTHON 183

    7 ▪ Working with the basic controls   185

    8 ▪ Putting widgets in frames   224

    9 ▪ Giving users choices with dialogs   258

   10 ▪ Creating and using wxPython menus   293

   11 ▪ Placing widgets with sizers   323

   12 ▪ Manipulating basic graphical images   356

PART 3 ADVANCED WXPYTHON 391

13 ▪ Building list controls and managing items 393

14 ▪ Coordinating the grid control 425

15 ▪ Climbing the tree control 460

16 ▪ Incorporating HTML into your application 485

17 ▪ The wxPython printing framework 504

18 ▪ Using other wxPython functionality 521

contents

preface   xix
acknowledgments   xxii
about this book   xxiv

PART 1   INTRODUCTION TO WXPYTHON 1

1   *Welcome to wxPython   3*

1.1   Getting started with wxPython   5

1.2   Creating the bare-minimum wxPython program   7
*Importing wxPython   9 ▪ Working with applications
and frames   11*

1.3   Extending the bare-minimum
wxPython program   12

1.4   Creating the final hello.py program   15

1.5   What can wxPython do?   17

1.6   Why choose wxPython?   19
Python programmers   19 ▪ wxWidget users   20 ▪ New users   20

1.7 How wxPython works 21

The Python language 21 ▪ *The wxWidgets toolkit 22*
Putting it together: the wxPython toolkit 25

1.8 Summary 27

2 *Giving your wxPython program a solid foundation* 29

2.1 What do I need to know about the required objects? 30

2.2 How do I create and use an application object? 31

Creating a wx.App subclass 31 ▪ *Understanding the application*
object lifecycle 34

2.3 How do I direct output from a wxPython program? 35

Redirecting output 35 ▪ *Modifying the default redirect*
behavior 37

2.4 How do I shut down my wxPython application? 38

Managing a normal shutdown 38 ▪ *Managing an emergency*
shutdown 39

2.5 How do I create and use the top-level window object? 39

Working with wx.Frame 40 ▪ *Working with wxPython IDs 42*
Working with wx.Size and wx.Point 43 ▪ *Working with*
wx.Frame styles 44

2.6 How do I add objects and subwindows to a frame? 47

Adding widgets to a frame 47 ▪ *Adding a menubar, toolbar,*
or status bar to a frame 49

2.7 How can I use common dialogs? 51

2.8 What are some common errors with application objects
and frames? 53

2.9 Summary 54

3 *Working in an event-driven environment* 56

3.1 What terminology do I need to understand events? 57

3.2 What is event-driven programming? 58

Coding event handlers 60 ▪ *Designing for event-driven*
programs 61 ▪ *Event triggers 62*

3.3 How do I bind an event to a handler? 63

Working with the wx.EvtHandler methods 65

3.4 How are events processed by wxPython? 68

Understanding the event handling process 69 ▪ *Using the Skip() method 75*

3.5 What other event properties are contained in the application object? 77

3.6 How can I create my own events? 77

Defining a custom event for a custom widget 78

3.7 Summary 81

4 **Making wxPython easier to handle with PyCrust 83**

4.1 How do I interact with a wxPython program? 84

4.2 What are the useful features of PyCrust? 86

Autocompletion 87 ▪ *Calltips and parameter defaults 88 Syntax highlighting 89* ▪ *Python help 90* ▪ *Command recall 91* ▪ *Cut and paste 92* ▪ *Standard shell environment 93* ▪ *Dynamic updating 94*

4.3 What do the PyCrust notebook tabs do? 95

Namespace tab 95 ▪ *Display tab 97* ▪ *Calltip tab 97 Session tab 98* ▪ *Dispatcher tab 98*

4.4 How can I wrap PyCrust around my wxPython application? 99

4.5 What else is in the Py package? 104

Working with the GUI programs 104 ▪ *Working with the support modules 105*

4.6 How can I use modules from the Py package in my wxPython programs? 112

4.7 Summary 115

5 **Creating your blueprint 116**

5.1 How can refactoring help me improve my code? 117

A refactoring example 118 ▪ *Starting to refactor 121 More refactoring 122*

5.2 How do I keep the Model and View separate in my program? 126

What is a Model-View-Controller system? 126 ▪ *A wxPython model: PyGridTableBase 128* ▪ *A custom model 136*

5.3   How do you unit-test a GUI program?   140

*The unittest module   140 ▪ A unittest sample   141
Testing user events   143*

5.4   Summary   145

6   *Working with the basic building blocks   146*

6.1   Drawing to the screen   148

How do I draw on the screen?   148

6.2   Adding window decorations   155

*How do I add and update a status bar?   155 ▪ How do I include
a submenu or checked menu?   158 ▪ How do I include
a toolbar?   161*

6.3   Getting standard information   165

*How do I use standard file dialogs?   165 ▪ How do I use a
standard color picker?   169*

6.4   Making the application look nice   170

*How do I lay out widgets?   170 ▪ How do I build an
about box?   178 ▪ How do I build a splash screen?   180*

6.5   Summary   181

PART 2   ESSENTIAL WXPYTHON 183

7   *Working with the basic controls   185*

7.1   Displaying text   186

*How do I display static text?   186 ▪ How can I get the user to
enter text?   189 ▪ How do I change the text without
user input?   192 ▪ How do I create a multi-line or styled
text control?   193 ▪ How do I create a font?   196 ▪ Can I have
styled text if my platform doesn't support rich text?   197 ▪ What if
my text control doesn't match my string?   198 ▪ How do I respond
to text events?   199*

7.2   Working with buttons   199

*How do I make a button?   200 ▪ How do I make a button with
a bitmap?   201 ▪ How do I create a toggle button?   202
What's a generic button, and why should I use one?   203*

7.3 Entering and displaying numbers 205

*How do I make a slider? 205 ▪ How can I get those
neat up/down arrow buttons? 208 ▪ How can I make
a progress bar? 210*

7.4 Giving the user choices 211

*How do I create a checkbox? 211 ▪ How can I create a group of
radio buttons? 212 ▪ How can I create a list box? 216 ▪
Can I combine a checkbox and a list box? 219 ▪ What if I want
a pull-down choice? 220 ▪ Can I combine text entry
and a list? 221*

7.5 Summary 222

8 Putting widgets in frames 224

8.1 The life of a frame 225

*How do I create a frame? 225 ▪ What are some different
frame styles? 227 ▪ How do I create a frame with extra style
information? 230 ▪ What happens when I close a frame? 232*

8.2 Using frames 234

*What are the methods and properties of wx.Frame? 234
How do I find a subwidget of a frame? 237 ▪ How do I create a
frame with a scrollbar? 238*

8.3 Alternative frame types 242

*How do I create an MDI frame? 242 ▪ What's a mini-frame
and why would I use it? 244 ▪ How do I make a
non-rectangular frame? 245 ▪ How can I drag a frame
without a title bar? 248*

8.4 Using splitter windows 250

*Creating a splitter window 250 ▪ A splitter example 251
Changing the appearance of the splitter 253 ▪ Manipulating
the splitter programmatically 254 ▪ Responding
to splitter events 255*

8.5 Summary 256

9 Giving users choices with dialogs 258

9.1 Working with modal dialogs 259

*How do I create a modal dialog? 259 ▪ How do I create an
alert box? 261 ▪ How do I get short text from the user? 264*

How can I display a list of choices in a dialog? 266 ▪ *How can I display progress?* 267

9.2   Using standard dialogs   269

How can I use a file picker? 269 ▪ *How can I use a font picker?* 273 ▪ *How can I use a color picker?* 275 *Can I allow the user to browse images?* 277

9.3   Creating a wizard   278

9.4   Showing startup tips   281

9.5   Using validators to manage data in a dialog   282

How do I use a validator to ensure correct data? 282 ▪ *How do I use a validator to transfer data?* 286 ▪ *How do I validate data as it is entered?* 288

9.6   Summary   291

10   **Creating and using wxPython menus   293**

10.1   Creating Menus   294

How do I create a menu bar and attach it to a frame? 295 *How do I create a menu and attach it to the menu bar?* 295 *How do I add items to a pull-down menu?* 297 ▪ *How do I respond to a menu event?* 301

10.2   Working with menu items   303

How do I find a specific menu item in a menu? 303 ▪ *How do I enable or disable a menu item?* 306 ▪ *How do I associate a menu item with a keyboard shortcut?* 307 ▪ *How do I create a toggle menu item with a checkbox or radio button?* 311

10.3   Sprucing up your menus   313

How do I create a submenu? 313 ▪ *How do I create a pop-up menu?* 315 ▪ *How can I create fancier menus?* 317

10.4   Usability guidelines for menus   319

Keeping menus uniform in length 319 ▪ *Creating logical item groups* 319

10.5   Summary   321

11   **Placing widgets with sizers   323**

11.1   What's a sizer?   324

11.2   Basic sizers with the grid sizer   326

What is a grid sizer? 327 ▪ *How do you add or remove children from a sizer?* 329 ▪ *How do sizers manage the size and*

*alignment of their children? 331 ▪ Can I specify a minimum size
for my sizer or its children? 334 ▪ How do sizers manage the
border around each child? 336*

11.3 Using the other sizer types 337

*What's a flex grid sizer? 337 ▪ What's a grid bag sizer? 341
What's a box sizer? 345 ▪ What's a static box sizer? 349*

11.4 Can I see a real-world example of sizers in action? 350

11.5 Summary 354

12 **Manipulating basic graphical images 356**

12.1 Working with images 357

*How do I load images? 357 ▪ What can I do with
an image? 361 ▪ How can I change cursors? 364*

12.2 Dealing with device contexts 367

*What is a device context, and how can I create one? 367
How do I draw to a device context? 371 ▪ How do I draw images
to the context? 376 ▪ How can I draw text to the context? 379*

12.3 Graphics manipulation 381

*How do I manage the foreground drawing pen? 381
How do I manage the background drawing brush? 384
How can I manage logical and physical device coordinates? 385
What color names are predefined? 387*

12.4 Summary 388

PART 3 ADVANCED WXPYTHON 391

13 **Building list controls and managing items 393**

13.1 Building a list control 394

*What is icon mode? 394 ▪ What is small icon mode? 395
What is list mode? 396 ▪ What is report mode? 397
How do I create a list control? 398*

13.2 Managing items in a list 400

*What is an image list and how do I add images to it? 400
How can I add and delete items from a list? 402*

13.3 Responding to users 405

*How can I respond to a user selection in a list? 405 ▪ How can
I respond to a user selection in a column header? 407*

13.4 Editing and sorting list controls 411

How can I edit a label? 411 ▪ *How can I sort my list? 413*
How can I learn more about list controls? 416

13.5 Creating a virtual list control 420

13.6 Summary 423

14 *Coordinating the grid control 425*

14.1 Creating your grid 426

How do I create a simple grid? 426 ▪ *How do I create a grid with*
a grid table? 429

14.2 Working with your grid 432

How do I add and delete rows, columns, and cells? 432
How do I manage the row and column headers of a grid? 433
How can I manage the size of grid elements? 436
How can I manage which cells are selected or visible? 440
How do I change the color or font of a grid cell? 442

14.3 Custom renderers and editors 445

How do I use a custom cell renderer? 445 ▪ *How do I edit*
a cell? 449 ▪ *How do I use a custom cell editor? 450*

14.4 Capturing user events 455

How can I capture user mouse selections? 455 ▪ *How can I*
capture user keyboard navigation? 457

14.5 Summary 458

15 *Climbing the tree control 460*

15.1 Creating tree controls and adding items 461

How do I add a root? 463 ▪ *How do I add more items*
to the tree? 463 ▪ *How do I manage items? 464*

15.2 What styles control the display of the tree control? 465

15.3 Sorting elements of a tree control 467

15.4 Controlling the image for each item 468

15.5 Navigating the tree programmatically 471

15.6 Managing the tree selection 472

15.7 Controlling which items are visible 473

15.8 Making a tree control user editable 477

15.9   Responding to other user events from a tree control   478

15.10   Using a tree list control   480

15.11   Summary   482

16 Incorporating HTML into your application   485

16.1   Displaying HTML   486

How can I display HTML in a wxPython window?   486
How can I display HTML from a file or URL?   488

16.2   Manipulating the HTML window   490

How can I respond to a user click on an active link?   490
How can I change an HTML window programmatically?   491
How can I display the page title in a frame's title bar?   493
How can I print an HTML page?   495

16.3   Extending the HTML window   496

How does the HTML parser work?   496 ▪ How can I add
support for new tags?   498 ▪ How can I support other
file formats?   501 ▪ How can I get a more fully featured
HTML Widget?   502

16.4   Summary   503

17 The wxPython printing framework   504

17.1   How do I print in wxPython?   505

Understanding the printout lifecycle   506 ▪ Print framework
in action   507 ▪ Working with wx.Printout methods   511

17.2   How do I display the print dialog?   512

Creating a print dialog   512

17.3   How do I display the page setup dialog?   515

Creating a page setup dialog   515 ▪ Working with page
setup properties   516

17.4   How do I print something?   518

17.5   How can I perform a print preview?   519

17.6   Summary   520

18 Using other wxPython functionality   521

18.1   Putting objects on the clipboard   522

Getting data in the clipboard   522 ▪ Manipulating data
in the clipboard   523 ▪ Retrieving text data from the

clipboard 524 ▪ The clipboard in action 524 ▪ Passing other data formats 526

18.2 Being the source of a drag and drop 527

Dragging in action 529

18.3 Being the target of a drag and drop 530

Using your drop target 531 ▪ Dropping in action 533

18.4 Transferring custom objects 534

Transferring a custom data object 534 ▪ Retrieving a custom object 535 ▪ Transferring an object in multiple formats 535

18.5 Setting timed events using wx.Timer 536

Generating EVT_TIMER events 536 ▪ Learning other timer uses 539

18.6 Creating a multithreaded wxPython application 539

Working with the global function wx.CallAfter() 540 Managing thread communication with the queue object 543 Developing your own solution 543

18.7 Summary 544

index 545

preface

The wxPython part of the story actually begins in 1995, with Harri Pasanen and Robin Dunn. Robin, who is one of the co-authors of the book, wrote the following about the history of wxPython, and we decided that it was a story better told in his own voice than paraphrased:

In 1995 I was working on a project that needed a GUI to be deployed on HP-UX systems, but my boss also wanted to show something at a trade show on his Windows 3.1 laptop in a few weeks' time. So I started searching for a cross platform C++ GUI toolkit to do a prototype with. In those days it wasn't easy without Google, but I found that there were several commercial alternatives available (none of which is still available today) and lots of toolkits with freely available source.

While evaluating each of the free toolkits for my immediate needs and deciding which of the commercial offerings would be best for our long-term needs, I ran into the term "Python bindings" on the wxWidgets website (in this case "binding" refers to the connection between the Python language and the wxWidgets toolkit). Full of curiosity at how one would "bind" a software toolkit to a reptile (I had never heard of the Python language up to this point), I clicked on the link, and the next link, and the next, until I finally ended up at the Python 1.2 Tutorial document. Three hours later I was converted from being the local C++ guru to a Python evangelist bugging all the developers in the immediate vicinity and showing them the cool new thing I had discovered.

Instead of working on my prototype, I started working with Harri Pasanen in Finland to advance the Python bindings for wxWidgets, otherwise known as wxPython 0.2, with some help from Edward Zimmerman. The mailing list announcement of that release is archived here: (http://www.google.com/ groups?selm=PA.95Jul27032244%40ok.tekla.fi&oe=UTF-8). We got it to be functional enough that I could build the prototype for my boss using Python, but wxPython was a nightmare to maintain and to enhance because everything (C++ extension module code, Python proxy modules, build system, etc.) was done by hand, and little changes or enhancements to wxWidgets would often require changes to several places in wxPython code to add the support for the enhancement or fix to wxPython. When it reached many tens of thousands of lines of code it became very awkward and fragile to continue working in that manner. Add to that the fact that there was no central source code repository (this was also before SourceForge's time) so we were emailing code changes to each other—you can get an inkling of the difficulties involved.

About that time, I had to start doing "real" work again as my main project was building up from a gleam in the eye to a full-force development project with several developers under my control with design meetings and deadlines, and I found myself fully back in the C++ world again, although I was able to use Python for some of the build and test scripts for the project. Harri wasn't able to spend any time on it either, so wxPython development slowed to less than a crawl and eventually stopped.

In 1997 I discovered SWIG (Simple Wrapper and Interface Generator), and realized that it could help with all the maintenance issues that had pained us in the wxPython project. In three or four weeks of spare time using SWIG, I almost completely reimplemented everything in wxPython that had taken several weeks of full-time work on my part and several months of part-time work for Harri doing it by hand. After getting sidetracked on another project for a while, I discovered that wxWidgets 2.0 was in active develop-ment, but had a whole new architecture, so I had to do it all again. But this time the new architecture simplified things enough that it took only about a week's worth of spare time! So in the summer of 1998 the first "modern ver-sion" of wxPython was released and has been in active development ever since. The first announcement is archived here: (http://groups.yahoo.com/group/python-announce-list/message/95).

The rest is, as they say, history. It's important to note that SWIG is allowing me to easily create and maintain literally hundreds of thousands of lines of code, so much of the credit for the vastness of wxPython's feature set deserves to go to David Beazley and the other developers contributing to that project.

With this book, we hope to share with you our excitement about wxPython, a toolkit that is truly unique in the ease that it brings to GUI application development. We wrote it with the goal of creating a useful resource for both the novice and the pro.

acknowledgments

Our work on this book has been aided by a number of people, in ways both obvious and subtle.

Patrick O'Brien was instrumental in getting this project off the ground and Marjan Bace, our publisher at Manning Publications, gave us the chance to make it happen. Jackie Carter was our first editor at Manning and Lianna Wlasiuk came in at a crucial juncture, and, like a great bullpen pitcher, earned the save. We would like to thank our production team at Manning and everyone who worked behind the scenes on the book, especially our copyeditor Elizabeth Martin and our typesetter Denis Dalinnik. Big thanks also to our agent Laura Lewin for her help and understanding.

We've benefited a great deal from the generosity of programmers worldwide in creating the technologies used in this book. First on that list is the crew who developed the wxWidgets foundation of wxPython: Julian Smart, Vadim Zeitlin, Robert Roebling, and the rest of the core wxWidgets team, as well as many contributors. Of course, without Guido van Rossum and other members of the Python language development team, there would be no "Python" in "wxPython." A large part of this book was written using the jEdit text editor and the images were manipulated using the GIMP.

Thanks also to the many reviewers who looked at the manuscript in its various stages of development and added their valuable insight along the way. They helped make this a better book: Alex Martelli, Dave Brueck, Christopher Bailey,

Mike Stok, Jean Baltus, Thomas Palmer, Jack Herrington, Peter Damoc, Nick Coghlan, Pim Van Heuven, John Paulson, Ian Brown, Stefan Neis, Chris Mellon, Kevin Ollivier, and Doug Tillman. Special thanks to Clint Howarth who was our technical proofreader.

Noel Rappin   My wife, Erin, makes my life better every day. Thank you for your strength, your intelligence, and your love. I also want to thank my parents Donna and Donnie and my sister Michelle for supporting me fully and completely. Matt Cohen helped this effort by entertaining me via IM while I was trying to write. Finally, I want to thank my daughter Emma, who is now old enough to be excited to see her name in a book, and my son Elliot, in anticipation of the day he will also be glad to see his name.

Robin Dunn   I'd like to thank my wife, Malaura, and my children, Jordyn, Myka, Samuel, and Christian, for their patience, understanding, and love. You make it worth the effort to get past all the difficulties of life. I'd also like to thank the many wonderful members of the wxPython user community whose praise and excitement have helped me to stay motivated and have helped me to take wxPython from an interesting toy to a very useful tool that thousands of developers all around the world love and depend upon. And finally, many thanks go to Mitch Kapor, John Anderson, David Surovell, and others at the Open Source Applications Foundation for believing in the Open Source concept, the potentials of wxPython, and especially for believing in my capabilities and funding my work on wxPython for several years.

about this book

Who should read this book?

Naturally, we'd love everybody to read this book. If you are reading this in the bookstore, trying to decide whether to purchase it, we say, go for it! Buy one for the people next to you too—they'll thank you later.

That said, we did have certain assumptions about you, the reader, in mind as we wrote this book. We assume that you don't need us to explain the basics of the Python programming language. We present a lot of Python code in this book. We think Python code is pretty easy to understand, but we want to let you know up front that we don't have a tutorial on Python basics. If you'd like a Python tutorial, we recommend Manning's *The Quick Python Book*, by Daryl Harms and Kenneth McDonald.

We also assume that you are at least familiar with the basic terms describing graphical interface objects, and have at least some familiarity with graphical interfaces from a user's perspective. More advanced user interface concepts, or less familiar user interface display elements, will be described as they come up.

We do not assume that you have any prior knowledge of wxPython. If you do have prior experience with wxPython, we expect that you'll still be able to find new information here, or, at the very least, you'll find this book to be a more useful resource than the existing online documentation.

How this book is organized

We've divided *wxPython In Action* into three parts. The first part is an introduction to wxPython concepts, a tutorial on how to get started with wxPython, and some information on wxPython best practices. The chapters in part 1 are:

Chapter 1, Welcome to wxPython
In this chapter, we introduce wxPython, explain to you why it's the greatest thing since sliced bread, and give some background on the technologies used to create wxPython.

Chapter 2, Giving your wxPython program a solid foundation
The two most important objects in wxPython are discussed. Every application must have an application object and a top-level window. This chapter will show you how to start a wxPython program, and how to manage its lifecycle.

Chapter 3, Working in an event-driven environment
Like all GUI toolkits, control in wxPython is managed by events. This chapter discusses how events are handled, and how you can use them as hooks to drive your functionality.

Chapter 4, Making wxPython easier to handle with PyCrust
PyCrust is a Python shell written in wxPython that contains many advanced and useful features. Not only can you use PyCrust for your wxPython development, you can wrap your program inside it for debugging purposes, and you can reuse the PyCrust components in your own applications.

Chapter 5, Creating your blueprint
This chapter discusses best practices in three areas that are often difficult for GUI programmers. We show how to use refactoring to improve the structure and maintainability of your code. The Model/View/Controller design pattern is explored, and we'll show you how to unit test our GUI code to minimize errors.

Chapter 6, Working with the basic building blocks
This chapter is a bridge between parts one and two. Building on the basic ideas already shown, we give hints of some of the features discussed in parts 2 and 3 as we build a sketchpad application.

Part 2 begins the more detailed portion of the book. The chapters in part 2 take a look at the most commonly used parts of wxPython. This includes a tour of the basic widget set, a look at standard frames and dialogs, and information on drawing and layout. The chapters in part 2 are:

Chapter 7, Working with the basic controls

This chapter covers the API for the basic widget set, including text fields, buttons, list boxes, and the like.

Chapter 8, Putting widgets in frames

All your wxPython widgets will be inside a frame or a dialog. In this chapter we cover how frames work, what kind of frames there are, and how to manage widgets within a frame.

Chapter 9, Giving users choices with dialogs

Dialogs behave slightly differently than frames. We cover how modal dialog boxes work, as well as the standard predefined wxPython dialogs. We'll also show you how to use wxPython validators to help mange the data in a dialog.

Chapter 10, Creating and using wxPython menus

Most windowed applications have a menu. We'll show you how to add menus to the menu bar, and menu items to a menu. Specialized menus, such as checkboxes, and radio menus will also be covered. We'll also discuss keyboard shortcuts and some usability guidelines for using menus effectively.

Chapter 11, Placing widgets with sizers

In wxPython, sizers are used to spare you the drudgery of placing your widgets manually. There are several useful sizers that are part of wxPython, and we'll show you how to use them, and what kind of layout is best suited to each.

Chapter 12, Manipulating basic graphical images

The most basic purpose of any UI toolkit is to draw lines and shapes to the screen. In wxPython, there is a rich set of drawing tools available for your use. There is also a powerful abstraction called a device context which allows you to draw to a target without caring whether the target is a window, a printer, or a file.

Part 3 contains a detailed look at more advanced portions of wxPython. It starts with a description of the three most complex wxPython widgets, and continues with a discussion of various print and display mechanisms, closing out with a tour of useful items that didn't quite earn their own chapter. The chapters in part 3 are:

Chapter 13, Building list controls and managing items

The wxPython list control gives you the ability to display lists "explorer-style," in icon mode, list mode, or multi-column report mode. You can also customize sort behavior, and allow users to edit list entries.

Chapter 14, Coordinating the grid control

If you want something that looks like a spreadsheet, the wxPython grid control is a full-featured widget that will meet your needs. It allows full control over the display and behavior of the grid, and allows for complete customization.

Chapter 15, Climbing the tree control

The wxPython tree control allows for compact display of hierarchical data, including, but not limited to a directory tree or class hierarchy. You can also allow the user to edit entries on the fly.

Chapter 16, Incorporating HTML into your application

Within wxPython, you can use HTML to simplify the display and printing of styled text. The HTML engine inside wxPython can also be customized to fit your special needs.

Chapter 17, The wxPython printing framework

Printing is managed from a wxPython application through several dedicated print, print data, and print preview objects. In this chapter, we explore how all of them work together.

Chapter 18, Using other wxPython functionality

In this chapter, we cover some important features that are not quite long enough to justify a chapter on their own, including cut and paste, drag and drop, and multithreading.

How to use this book

How you use this book will depend on your wxPython knowledge. We designed this book to be useful for both experts and novices, but we expect that different parts of the book will have more or less resonance for users at different levels.

If you are a wxPython beginner, you definitely want to start in part 1. Chapters 1–3 will give you a solid grounding in wxPython concepts, and chapter 6 will give you a nice overview of the steps in building a reasonably sized program. Chapter 5 will introduce you to some methods for making your code easy to manage, and chapter 4 will have some tools to help you debug and write wxPython applications. As you start writing your own wxPython programs, you'll also start using the API discussions in part 2—we tried to organize them by functionality to make it easy to find useful topics.

If you are already familiar with wxPython, you'll probably be spending most of your time in parts 2 and 3. However, we recommend you take a spin through part 1 as well. If you aren't familiar with PyCrust, then chapter 4 will be new to you, and we think you might get something useful out of chapter 5 as well. You'll find discussion of more complex widgets in part 3, and you'll also see that the code samples in that section tend to be longer and more integrated than in the other sections.

The examples in this book were written against Python version 2.3.x—we don't think we included any of the new 2.4 language features—and wxPython 2.5.x. The 2.6.x release of wxPython came out too late for coverage in this book; however, it was largely a bug fix release, numbered for compliance with wxWidgets.

There is one other point that we need to make before we begin. This book is not intended to be a complete reference to every nook and cranny of wxPython. We expect that it will be a useful reference to the features that you are most likely to need to know about, but it is not 100% feature-complete. In the interests of time and space, we had to choose some elements to focus on and others, well, not to. For instance, there are a number of wxPython features inherited from the C++ wxWidgets toolkit that are replicated in the standard Python library—we chose not to cover those features. Also, if you are working in a Windows operating system whose name includes a date in the 1990s, you'll probably find that some features don't work exactly as described in some cases and we didn't have the space to enumerate all of those exceptions. Finally, there were some features of the core widgets set that we determined were either not often used or that we did not have the space to do justice.

Typographical conventions

The following conventions are used throughout the book:

- Courier typeface is used in all code listings.
- *Italics* are used to introduce new terms.
- **Courier Bold** is sometimes used to draw your attention to a section of code.
- Code annotations are used when directing your attention to a particular line of code. Annotations are marked with bullets, such as ❶.
- Courier typeface is used in text for code words, wxPython class and method names, or snippets of Python code.

Code downloads

Source code for all of the examples used in this book is available for download from the publisher's website at www.manning.com/rappin.

Where to get more help

Although we tried to be as comprehensive as possible, we couldn't possibly anticipate all the uses and issues you might have using wxPython. The main wxPython website at http://www.wxpython.org has some resources that you might visit

for insight into your problem. The official online documentation is at http://www.
wxpython.org/docs/api/. A collaborative wiki site is available at http://wiki.wxpy-
thon.org/, and there are mailing lists that you can subscribe to at http://www.wxpy-
thon.org/maillist.php.

Author Online

Help is also available from the Author Online forum, a private web discussion
board run by Manning Publications. You are encouraged to use this forum to
make comments about the book, ask technical questions, and receive help from
the authors and other readers. Use your browser to navigate to www.man-
ning.com/rappin to take advantage of this free service. The forum's welcome
page gives you all the information you need to sign up and get going.

The Author Online forum is one of the ways Manning remains committed to
readers. The authors' participation in the forum is voluntary and without a
specified level of commitment. The forum is a great way to share ideas and
learn from each other. The Author Online forum will remain accessible from
the publisher's website as long as the book is in print.

about the title

By combining introductions, overviews, and how-to examples, the *In Action*
books are designed to help learning and remembering. According to research in
cognitive science, the things people remember are things they discover during
self-motivated exploration.

Although no one at Manning is a cognitive scientist, we are convinced that for
learning to become permanent it must pass through stages of exploration, play,
and, interestingly, retelling of what is being learned. People understand and
remember new things, which is to say they master them, only after actively
exploring them. Humans learn in action. An essential part of an *In Action* guide
is that it is example-driven. It encourages the reader to try things out, to play
with new code, and explore new ideas.

There is another, more mundane, reason for the title of this book: our readers
are busy. They use books to do a job or to solve a problem. They need books that
allow them to jump in and jump out easily and learn just what they want just
when they want it. They need books that aid them "in action." The books in this
series are designed for such readers.

about the cover illustration

The figure on the cover of *wxPython in Action* is a "Soldat Japonais," a Japanese soldier. The illustration is taken from a French travel book, *Encyclopedie des Voyages* by J. G. St. Saveur, published in France in 1796. Travel for pleasure was a relatively new phenomenon at the time and travel guides such as this one were popular, introducing both the tourist as well as the armchair traveler to the inhabitants of other regions of France and abroad.

The diversity of the drawings in the *Encyclopedie des Voyages* speaks vividly of the uniqueness and individuality of the world's towns and provinces just 200 years ago. This was a time when the dress codes of two regions separated by a few dozen miles identified people uniquely as belonging to one or the other. The travel guide brings to life a sense of isolation and distance of that period and of every other historic period except our own hyperkinetic present.

Dress codes have changed since then and the diversity by region, so rich at the time, has faded away. It is now often hard to tell the inhabitant of one continent from another. Perhaps, trying to view it optimistically, we have traded a cultural and visual diversity for a more varied personal life. Or a more varied and interesting intellectual and technical life.

We at Manning celebrate the inventiveness, the initiative, and the fun of the computer business with book covers based on the rich diversity of regional life two centuries ago, brought back to life by the pictures from this travel guide.

Part 1

Introduction to wxPython

We start right off by introducing you to wxPython in chapter 1, "Welcome to wxPython," which explains how wxPython came to be, and what makes it so great that you should drop everything and start using it. We'll show a little bit of sample code, some cool screenshots, and contrast wxPython with its wxWidgets parent project. In chapter 2, "Giving your wxPython program a solid foundation," we discuss the two objects required in all wxPython applications. The first, the application object, manages the event loop and oversees the application lifecycle. The second, the top-level window, is the focal point of user interaction with your program. We'll show you how to use both, and offer troubleshooting tips.

In chapter 3, "Working in an event-driven environment," we'll focus on the wxPython event cycle, covering what events are and how they are generated. We'll take a detailed run through the process by which an event is associated with the code that should be generated in response. You'll also see how to create your own custom events. Chapter 4, "Making wxPython easier to handle with PyCrust," is an introduction to the PyCrust interactive shell, as well as the related Py package of useful applications. We'll show you how to wrap your own application in a PyCrust shell for easier debugging, and also how to use the Py objects as part of your applications.

In chapter 5, "Creating your blueprint," we'll discuss important general issues with the creation of user interface code. We'll show ideas about how to keep your code clean and easy to maintain. We'll also show how wxPython can be used as part of the Model/View/Controller design pattern. The chapter finishes with a discussion of how to unit-test wxPython applications. In chapter 6,

"Working with the basic building blocks," we'll put it all together to build a sketch application showing several useful pieces of wxPython functionality. By the end of this first part of the book, you should have a solid grounding in wxPython and be ready to face the more reference-oriented material in the rest of the book.

Welcome to wxPython

1

This chapter covers

- Getting started with wxPython
- Creating a minimum wxPython program
- Importing wxPython
- Learning the Python programming language
- Putting it all together

Here's a simple wxPython program. It creates a window with one text box that displays the position of the mouse pointer. Counting white space, it's about 20 lines long.

Listing 1.1 A working wxPython program in a mere 20 lines

```
#!/bin/env python
import wx
class MyFrame(wx.Frame):

    def __init__(self):
        wx.Frame.__init__(self, None, -1, "My Frame", size=(300, 300))
        panel = wx.Panel(self, -1)
        panel.Bind(wx.EVT_MOTION,  self.OnMove)
        wx.StaticText(panel, -1, "Pos:", pos=(10, 12))
        self.posCtrl = wx.TextCtrl(panel, -1, "", pos=(40, 10))

    def OnMove(self, event):
        pos = event.GetPosition()
        self.posCtrl.SetValue("%s, %s" % (pos.x, pos.y))

if __name__ == '__main__':
    app = wx.PySimpleApp()
    frame = MyFrame()
    frame.Show(True)
    app.MainLoop()
```

(handwritten annotations: "parent / id", "title", "(10, 12)", "(40, 10)", "32")

What can we say about the program in listing 1.1? It's very short, for one thing. Admittedly, it doesn't do a whole lot, but still, creating a window, populating it, getting it to respond to mouse events—that's not bad for 20 lines. It's not an exaggeration to say this example could easily be three or four times longer in some, more caffeinated, programming languages. Figure 1.1 shows the running program.

The code sample is quite readable. Even if you don't know the details of Python or wxPython, if you have any experience with interface programming you likely have a sense of what words like `Frame`, `__init__`, `EVT_MOTION`, `TextCtrl`, and `Main-Loop` mean. The indentation might seem a bit weird

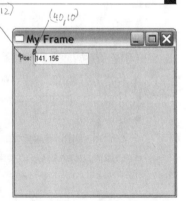

Figure 1.1 Our first wxPython program, showing the position of the mouse

if you aren't used to Python (where are all those closing braces, anyway?), and you probably don't know what all the arguments mean (what's with those -1s?), but you could quite easily come to some rough understanding of the code without much help.

In this book, we'll show you why wxPython is one of the easiest, most powerful ways of building a real graphical user interface (GUI) program that there is. Most toolkits that make the building of the interface itself easier (such as a Visual Basic style tool) don't have an implementation language with the clarity, flexibility, and power of Python. Most of the toolkits that have the functionality of wxPython force you to use a language that is ill-suited to rapid development. You'll find wxPython right in the sweet spot, where you get the maximum bang for your development buck. Even better, wxPython is an open-source project, with both the source code and the binary installations distributed under a license that allows it to be freely used in both commercial and open source development.

By the time you've reached the end of this book, you'll know how to build a state-of-the-art GUI using the wxPython toolkit. You'll be able to create and manipulate common interface elements such as buttons and menus, as well as less common ones such as trees and HTML editors. So there's quite a bit of ground for us to cover. In this chapter, we'll get you started with wxPython, and discuss what wxPython does and why you might choose it for your programming needs.

A good interface allows the user to access the functionality of the application as simply and cleanly as possible, with a stylish look that is attractive to the users. A bad interface can keep users from finding the functionality in the program, and can even cause people to assume that a perfectly working program is malfunctioning. In wxPython, you can create the interface you want with less effort than you'd expect.

1.1 Getting started with wxPython

We're going to start by working on a real wxPython program, albeit a simple one. We won't create anything complicated, yet. For now, we're going to lead you step-by-step through the process of creating your very first wxPython program. Let's begin by making sure you've got everything installed. Table 1.1 shows everything you'll need in order to run wxPython.

Once the installations are complete, get ready to type. We're going to create a program that displays a single image file. This will happen in three steps:

1 We'll start with the bare minimum required for a working wxPython program.

2 We'll make that code more structured and sophisticated.

3 We'll end with a version that can display the wxPython logo.

Table 1.1   Everything you'll need to run wxPython on your own computer

Tool	Notes
The right operating system	This is an easy one—you have a lot of options. Specifically, you must be running one of the following: • Any Microsoft Windows 32-bit operating system—meaning anything from Windows 98 onward (and you can get it going under Windows 95 if you must, but you'll need to download some extras). • Any Unix or Linux system capable of running the Gnome Toolkit (GTK). • A Macintosh running Mac OS X 10.2.3 or higher.
The Python programming language	Available for download at www.python.org. Any version 2.3 or higher will work. Many Linux distributions include a version of Python, as does Mac OS X 10.3 or higher. Even so, you might still want to download the latest version.
The wxPython Toolkit	Available for download at www.wxpython.org. There are different versions, depending on your operating system and Python version. Be sure to download the runtime installer that matches your platform, Python version, and Unicode preference. Download the packages for the demos and documentation as well. If you've installed other software on your system, you should find that installing the wxPython packages works very similarly. Again, recent versions of Mac OS X and some Linux distributions already include wxPython, but you should download the latest version if you can.
A text editor	We recommend an editor that recognizes Python syntax and can do things like colorize the code to make it more readable. Most of the popular editors have support for Python code, so use the editor you prefer. If you have no strong feelings for any particular editor, try IDLE, the integrated development environment included with Python, which includes a source code editor, interactive shell, debugger, and other tools. The Python web site has a list of Python-aware editors at www.python.org/editors.

Figures 1.2, 1.3, and 1.4 illustrate what the final program will look like, depending on your platform.

**Figure 1.2
Running** `hello.py`
on Windows

Figure 1.3
Running `hello.py`
on Linux

Figure 1.4
Running `hello.py`
on Mac OS X

1.2 Creating the bare minimum wxPython program

Let's begin with the simplest possible wxPython program that will run successfully. Create a file named "bare.py" and type in the following code. Remember, in Python, the spacing at the start of each line is significant.

```python
import wx                                          complete, minimal          *

class App(wx.App):

    def OnInit(self):           # application initialization
        frame = wx.Frame(parent=None, title='Bare')
        frame.Show()
        return True

app = App()
app.MainLoop()
```

There's not much to it, is there? Even at only eight lines of code (not counting blank lines) this program might seem like a waste of space, as it does little more than display an empty frame. But bear with us, as we'll soon revise it, making it something more useful.

The real purpose of this program is to make sure you can create a Python source file, verify that wxPython is installed properly, and allow us to introduce more complex aspects of wxPython programming one step at a time. So humor us: create a file, type in the code, save the file with a name "bare.py," run it, and make sure it works for you.

The mechanism for running the program depends on your operating system. You can usually run this program by sending it as a command line argument to the Python interpreter from an operating system prompt, using one of the following commands:

```
python bare.py
```

```
pythonw bare.py
```

Figures 1.5, 1.6, and 1.7 show what the program looks like running on various operating systems.

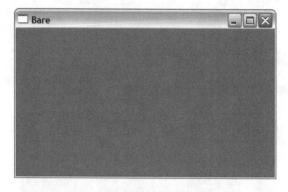

Figure 1.5
Running `bare.py` on Windows.

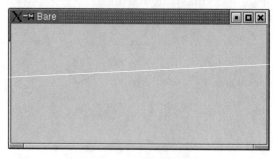

Figure 1.6
Running `bare.py` on Linux.

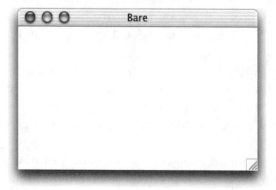

Figure 1.7
Running `bare.py` on Mac OS X.

JARGON:
IT LOOKS
LIKE A
WINDOW...
When most people look at this running program, they see something they would call a "window." However, wxPython does not call this a window. It calls this a "frame." In wxPython, "window" is the generic term for any object that displays on the screen (what other toolkits might call a "widget"). So, a wxPython programmer will often refer to objects such as buttons or text boxes as "windows." This may seem confusing, but the usage dates to the earliest days of the original C++ toolkit, and it's unlikely to change now. In this book, we'll try to avoid the use of window as a generic term, because it's confusing and also because it's the name of a big product from a major corporation. We'll use widget as the generic term. When we're specifically referring to the operating system of similar name, we'll do it with a capital "W."

While this bare-minimum program does little more than create and display an empty frame, all of its code is essential; remove any line of code and the program will not work. This basic wxPython program illustrates the five basic steps you must complete for every wxPython program you develop:

1 Import the necessary wxPython package   wx

2 Subclass the wxPython application class   wx. App , but p 4 ?

3 Define an application initialization method

4 Create an application class instance

5 Enter the application's main event loop

Let's examine this bare minimum program step-by-step to see how each one was accomplished.

1.2.1 *Importing wxPython*

The first thing you need to do is import the main wxPython package, which is named wx:

```
import wx
```

Once that package is imported, you can refer to wxPython classes, functions, and constants using the wx package name as a prefix, like this:

```
class App(wx.App):
```

OLD STYLE
IMPORTS
During the writing of this book the name of the wxPython package changed. Since the old naming convention is still supported, you will probably encounter wxPython code written in the old style. So, we'll digress briefly to explain the older style and why it was changed. The old

package name was `wxPython` and it contained an internal module named `wx`. There were two common ways to import the needed code—you could import the `wx` module from the `wxPython` package:

```
from wxPython import wx #DEPRECATED—DON'T DO THIS ANY MORE
```

Or, you could import everything from the `wx` module directly.

```
from wxPython.wx import * #DEPRECATED—DON'T DO THIS ANY MORE
```

Both import methods had serious drawbacks. Using the second method of `import *` is generally discouraged in Python because of the possibility of namespace conflicts. The old `wx` module avoided this problem by putting a `wx` prefix on nearly all of its attributes. Even with this safeguard, `import *` still had the potential to cause problems, but many wxPython programmers preferred this style, and you'll see it used quite often in older code. One downside of this style was that class names began with a lowercase letter, while most of the wxPython methods begin with an uppercase letter—the exact opposite of the normal Python programming convention.

However, if you tried to avoid the namespace bloat caused by `import *` by doing `from wxPython import wx`, you now had to type "wx" twice for each class, function, or constant name—once as the package prefix and once as the "normal" prefix, such as `wx.wxWindow`. This got old fast. Many wxPython programmers saw this dilemma as a wart that should be removed, and eventually, it was. If you're interested, you can search the wxPython mailing list archives to read more of the details surrounding this change.

✳ One more thing to know about importing wxPython: you must import `wx` before you import anything else from wxPython. In general, the order of imports in Python is irrelevant, meaning you can import modules in any order. However, wxPython, although it looks like a single module, is actually a complex set of modules (many of which are automatically generated by a tool called the Simplified Wrapper and Interface Generator, or SWIG) that wrap the functionality provided by the underlying wxWidgets C++ toolkit (we'll discuss wxWidgets in more detail in section 1.7). When you import the `wx` module for the first time, wxPython performs some initialization that is vital to other wxPython modules. As a result, some of the wxPython subpackages, such as the `xrc` module, might not work properly unless the `wx` module has already been imported:

SWIG

```
import wx            # Always import wx before
from wx import xrc   # any other wxPython packages,
from wx import html  # just to be on the safe side.
```

This requirement applies only to the wxPython modules; you can still import other Python modules as you always have, and those modules can be imported before or after the wxPython modules. For instance, this example is valid:

```
import sys
import wx
import os
from wx import xrc
import urllib
```

1.2.2 Working with applications and frames

Once you've imported the wx module, you can create your application and frame objects. Every wxPython program must have one application object and at least one frame object. These objects will be discussed in detail in chapter 2. For now, you just need to know that the application object must be an instance of wx.App or of a subclass you define where you declare an OnInit() method. The OnInit() method will be called by the wx.App parent class when your application starts.

Subclass the wxPython application class

Here is how we defined our wx.App subclass:

```
class MyApp(wx.App):

    def OnInit(self):
        frame = wx.Frame(parent=None, id=-1, title="Bare")
        frame.Show()
        return True
```

We named our class "MyApp," which is a common convention, but any valid Python class name would do.

The OnInit() method is where you'll most often create frame objects. But you won't usually directly create instances of wx.Frame as we did here. Instead, you'll define your own wx.Frame subclass the same way we defined our own wx.App subclass. (You'll see an example in the next section.) We'll explore frames in detail in the next chapter, so for now we'll simply point out that the wx.Frame constructor accepts several parameters. Of the three we supplied, only the first is required, while the rest have default values.

Invoking the Show() method makes the frame visible. If we had left that out, the frame would have been created, but we wouldn't be able to see it. We can toggle the frame's visibility by calling Show() with a Boolean parameter:

```
frame.Show(False)    # Make the frame invisible.
frame.Show(True)     # True is the default parameter value.
frame.Hide()         # Equivalent to frame.Show(False).
```

Define an application initialization method

Notice that we didn't define an __init__() method for our application class. In Python, this means that the parent method, wx.App.__init__(), is automatically invoked on object creation. This is a good thing. If you define an __init__() method of your own, don't forget to call the __init__() of the base class, like this:

```
class App(wx.App):

    def __init__(self):
        # Call the base class constructor.
        wx.App.__init__(self)         #    super (App, self), __init__ ()
        # Do something here...
```

If you forget to do so, wxPython won't be initialized and your OnInit() method won't get called.

Create an application class instance and enter its main event loop

The final step is to create an instance of the wx.App subclass, and invoke its Main-Loop() method:

```
app = App()
app.MainLoop()
```

That's it. Once the application's main event loop processing takes over, control passes to wxPython. Unlike procedural programs, a wxPython GUI program primarily responds to the events taking place around it, mostly determined by a human user clicking with a mouse and typing at the keyboard. When all the frames in an application have been closed, the app.MainLoop() method will return and the program will exit.

1.3 Extending the bare-minimum wxPython program

We showed you a bare-minimum wxPython program to give you a comfortable start, but something that small isn't useful for anything but discussion. By oversimplifying the code, we produced a Python program that was easy to understand, but difficult to extend—which is not how we would encourage you to create serious wxPython programs.

So now we're going to enhance this minimal program until it has a reasonable amount of functionality, incorporates common Python programming standards, and can serve as a proper foundation for your own programs. Listing 1.2 shows the next iteration, which we named spare.py.

Listing 1.2 The spare version of our minimal program.

```
#!/usr/bin/env python          ❶

"""Spare.py is a starting point for a wxPython program."""          ❷

import wx

class Frame(wx.Frame):          ❸
    pass

class App(wx.App):

    def OnInit(self):
        self.frame = Frame(parent=None, title='Spare')          ❹
        self.frame.Show()
        self.SetTopWindow(self.frame)          ❺     # method of wx.Frame
        return True

if __name__ == '__main__':          ❻
    app = App()
    app.MainLoop()
```

This version is still quite small, only 14 lines of code, but we added several important items that get us closer to what we would consider good, solid code.

❶ The first line in the file is now a *shebang* line. It looks like a Python comment, which it is, but on some operating systems, such as Linux and Unix, the shebang tells the operating system how to find the interpreter that will execute the program file. If this program file was then given executable privileges (using the chmod command, for example) we could run the program from the operating system command line by simply supplying the program name:

```
% spare.py
```

The shebang line is a convenience for Unix and Mac OS X users and is simply ignored on other platforms. Even if you aren't using one of those systems, it's polite to include it on a script that might be executed cross-platform.

❷ We added a module *docstring* (documentation string). When the first statement in a module is a string, that string becomes the docstring for the module and is stored in the module's __doc__ attribute. You can access the docstring in your code, some development environments, and even the Python interpreter running in interactive mode:

```
>>> import spare
>>> print spare.__doc__
Spare.py is a starting point for simple wxPython programs.
>>>
```

Docstrings are but one example of Python's powerful introspection capabilities, and we will encourage you to provide them for modules, classes, methods, functions, and any other place that Python supports. Python development tools, such as PyCrust, are able to use the docstring to provide useful information to a developer while you are coding.

❸ We changed the way we created the frame object. The "bare" version of this program simply created an instance of the wx.Frame class. In the "spare" version we defined our own Frame class as a subclass of wx.Frame. At this point it hasn't made any difference to the final results, but you'll want your own Frame class if you want anything interesting, such as text, buttons, and menus, to appear in your frame. Introducing your own custom Frame class now sets the stage for future iterations. In fact, once your Frame class becomes complicated, you'll probably want to move it into its own module and import it into your main program.

❹ We added a reference to the frame instance as an attribute of the application class instance. Again, we're setting the stage for things to come, as well as demonstrating how easy it is to add attributes to Python classes. It makes no difference that the attribute is a reference to a complex, graphical object, such as a frame. To Python, an object is an object is an object.

❺ Inside the OnInit() method we called the App class's own SetTopWindow() method, passing it our newly created frame instance. We didn't have to define the SetTopWindow() method because it was inherited from the wx.App parent class. It's an optional method that lets wxPython know which frame or dialog should be considered the main one. A wxPython program can have several frames, with one designated as the top window for the application. In this case the choice was easy since we have but one frame.

❻ The final addition to the program represents a common idiom in Python programs used to test whether the module is being run as a program or was imported by another module. We do that by examining the module's __name__ attribute:

```
if __name__ == '__main__':          # module is being executed as a program
    app = App()
    app.MainLoop()
```

If the module was imported, its __name__ attribute will be the same as its filename (without the extension), like this:

```
>>> import spare                     # File:   ...\spare.py
>>> spare.__name__
'spare'
>>>
```

But if the module is being executed, rather than imported, Python overrides the default naming convention and sets the module's __name__ attribute to '__main__', giving us the chance to have the module behave differently when executed directly. We take advantage of this feature by creating an application instance and entering its main event-loop only if the module is being executed as a program.

If we didn't perform this test, and created an application instance even when this module was imported, it could conflict with code in the module doing the importing—especially if the importing module has already started the wxPython event loop. It would also be quite difficult to test (especially since there can only be one application instance active at one time in a wxPython program, and once we enter the event loop, control passes to wxPython.) By not starting our own application when the module is imported, we make our frame and app classes readily available to other Python programs, facilitating the reuse of existing code.

1.4 *Creating the final hello.py program*

Now that you've got the basics under your belt, let's create the final version of the program we showed at the beginning of this chapter. Create a file named hello.py and enter in the code shown in listing 1.3.

Listing 1.3   The final hello.py

```python
#!/usr/bin/env python          ❶  Shebang

"""Hello, wxPython! program."""    ⟵  Docstring describes the code

import wx    ⟵  Import the wxPackage
                              ❷  wx.Frame subclass
class Frame(wx.Frame):    ⟵
    """Frame class that displays an image."""

    def __init__(self, image, parent=None, id=-1,    ❸  Image parameter
                 pos=wx.DefaultPosition,
                 title='Hello, wxPython!'):
        """Create a Frame instance and display image."""
        temp = image.ConvertToBitmap()
        size = temp.GetWidth(), temp.GetHeight()   # tuple        ❹
        wx.Frame.__init__(self, parent, id, title, pos, size)     Displaying
        self.bmp = wx.StaticBitmap(parent=self, bitmap=temp)      the image
                          ❺  wx.App subclass
class App(wx.App):    ⟵
    """Application class."""

    def OnInit(self):                              Image handling  ❻
        image = wx.Image('wxPython.jpg', wx.BITMAP_TYPE_JPEG)
        self.frame = Frame(image)    # create instance of Frame,
                                       supplying image obj
```

```
            self.frame.Show()
            self.SetTopWindow(self.frame)
            return True

    def main():                              ⑦  main()
        app = App()                              function
        app.MainLoop()

    if __name__ == '__main__':               ⑧  Import vs.
        main()                                   execute
```

❶ The shebang line allows this program to be an executable script under Linux and other Unix-like operating systems.

❷ Defining a custom Frame class that subclasses wx.Frame lets us more easily control the Frame's contents and appearance.

❸ We added an image parameter to our Frame's constructor. This value is provided by our application class when it creates a Frame instance. As long as we can pass the required values to wx.Frame.__init__(), there's no reason we can't add more parameters to our subclass's constructor.

❹ We're going to display the image in a wx.StaticBitmap control, which requires a bitmap. So we convert the image to a bitmap. We also create a size tuple, using the width and height of the bitmap. The size tuple is supplied to the wx.Frame.__init__() call, so that the frame size matches the bitmap size.

❺ Defining a wx.App subclass with an OnInit() method is a minimum requirement for any wxPython application.

❻ We create an image object, using a wxPython.jpg file stored in the same directory as hello.py. You can get this file from the Manning web site, or substitute one of your own. A more sophisticated version of this program would accept the name of a file from the command line. We pass our image object as a parameter when we create the frame.

❼ The main() function creates an application instance and starts the wxPython event loop.

❽ Checking if this module is the main module allows it to be used in two different ways: run from the command line or imported by another module.

What happened when you ran your version of hello.py? Did you see a frame sized to match the graphic you provided? If not, brush yourself off and try again. If so, congratulations! You're ready to move on to the next exciting steps.

But before you rush into the next chapter, we're going to talk about wxPython a little more broadly, what it's capable of, and how it came to be. If that doesn't interest you, feel free to jump to the next chapter and continue coding—the rest of the introduction will still be here.

1.5 What can wxPython do?

Nearly all of your interface needs can be filled by wxPython. In this section, we'll show you what some of the wxPython toolkit looks like, using pictures from elements of the wxPython demo application. Figure 1.8 is a composite image showing all the basic widgets you'd expect: buttons, checkboxes, a combo box, menus, list box, a spinner control, text controls and radio buttons.

Figure 1.9 shows less common, but very useful widgets, including a slider control, an editable list box, a time selector, a toolbar, a notebook control, a tree list control, and an analog clock.

The grid control is one of wxPython's most flexible widgets, allowing custom rendering and editing of cells. Figure 1.10 shows an example of many of the features of the grid control.

And that's not all—you also get a quite fully featured HTML-rendering widget that you can use for static styled text, as the base of a simple web browser, as a help system, or anything else you might want to display HTML for. An example is shown in figure 1.11.

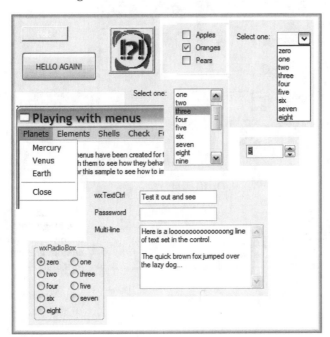

Figure 1.8
A sampling of basic user interface controls, including menus, list boxes, and text controls.

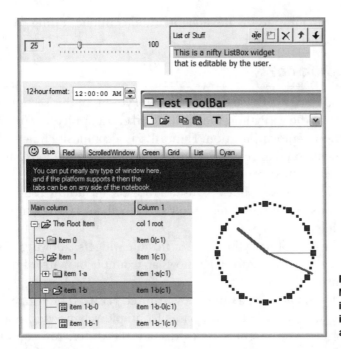

Figure 1.9
More advanced
interface controls,
including a tree list
and an analog clock.

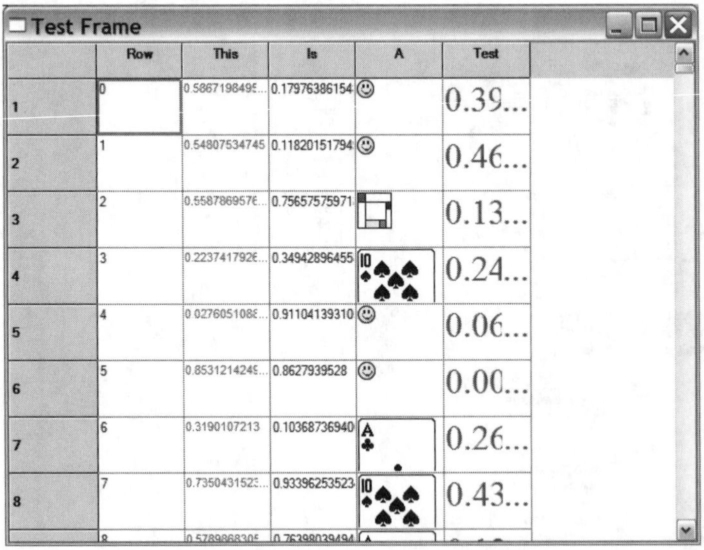

Figure 1.10
The mega-grid
example, showing
custom grid cell
rendering.

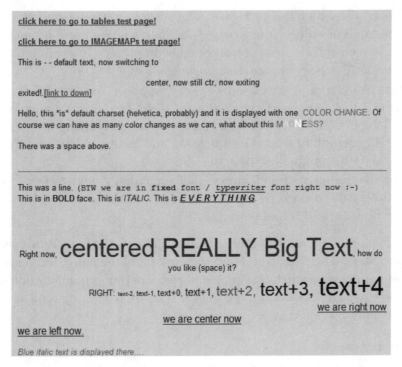

Figure 1.11 The wx.HTMLWindow, showing some of the HTML rendering capability.

We've only just scratched the surface. The wxPython library also includes tools for image animation. You also get clipboard and drag-and-drop support, support for MIME types and audio, all the standard dialogs offered by your system, the ability to specify an interface definition in an XML file, full control over the layout of your windows, and more.

1.6 Why choose wxPython?

The most powerful benefit of wxPython depends on your needs and expertise. While we think that all user interface (UI) programmers would benefit from using wxPython, the specific features that are most helpful will vary from case to case.

1.6.1 Python programmers

If you are already a Python programmer, you've probably noticed that Tkinter, the interface toolkit distributed with Python, has some problems:

- Tkinter is based on the Tk toolkit, which is somewhat out-of-date in terms of the kinds of widgets it supports. By default, it doesn't support more complex widgets such as tree controls or tabbed windows. It also doesn't have a particularly rich set of predefined dialogs.
- The Tk toolkit does not use native widget support, resulting in an application that looks foreign on all platforms. In wxPython, dialogs and widgets will look like those that are standard on the underlying operating system. Your Tk user will find that buttons, fonts, and menus all look slightly different from what might be expected.
- Many programmers find Tkinter itself somewhat clunky to work with. In particular, the process by which events are translated to actions in wxPython is more flexible and powerful.

You'll find that wxPython solves these problems. The toolkit in wxPython is vastly more complete and extensive than that of Tkinter and the native widget support means your application will look at home in your operating system. Additionally, the Python language support is more fluid in wxPython, making for a somewhat nicer programming experience.

1.6.2 *wxWidget users*

If you are already using wxWidgets, then what wxPython has to offer you is the Python language itself. With its clear syntax, dynamic typing, and flexible object model, Python can improve your productivity dramatically. Python has a very extensive standard library that is easily incorporated into your application, and Python programs tend to be shorter and less error-prone than C++ programs. There are also a number of Python-only additions to the wxWidgets tool set.

1.6.3 *New users*

If you're not currently using either Python or wxWidgets, you're in for a real treat, since you'll get the benefit of both the extensive toolkit and the Python language. If you are currently working in Java/Swing, you'll probably find wxPython less complex and easier to use, and the Python language significantly less verbose than Java. If you are currently using a single-platform C++ toolkit like the Microsoft Foundation Classes (MFC), then you'll appreciate the cross-platform nature of wxPython. In order to follow the examples in this book, however, some Python familiarity is helpful. If you need to get started on Python itself, try *The Quick Python Book*, by Daryl Harms and Kenneth McDonald, or the web site www.diveintopython.org.

In the next section, you'll learn about the component pieces of wxPython: the Python language itself, and the wxWidgets toolkit. You'll also learn about the rationale and implementation of wxPython itself.

1.7 How wxPython works

In the previous section, we talked about what wxPython can do. In this section, we'll take a closer look at how wxPython works. Internally, wxPython is a wrapper or interface for a popular C++ interface toolkit called wxWidgets. The wxWidgets project has a long history and is the source of most of the functionality of wxPython. Using wxPython allows you to get the benefits of the wxWidgets toolkit, while being able to use Python rather than C++.

The wxPython toolkit is the combination of two distinct pieces of software, which have over 25 years of development between them. In addition, the wxPython toolkit itself was the result of a significant amount of work. To make wxPython go, a tool called SWIG is used to generate wrapper functions, or *glue code*, which allow a Python program to use the C++ wxWidgets library just as if it were any old Python library. Although SWIG does a lot of the work, there's still some hand-tooling needed to make the wxPython objects look and act like other Python objects. There have also been several additional widgets written directly in wxPython that are not available in the C++ version of the tool—you'll encounter several of them along the way in this book.

In this section we will provide a brief overview of the Python programming language and the wxWidgets C++ toolkit. It is the combination of Python's ease of use and wxWidgets' range of functionality that gives wxPython its unique power.

1.7.1 The Python language

Python is a programming language which is easily able to handle both the scripting tasks normally associated with Perl and the full-scale application development normally associated with C++ or Java. Using a simple, elegant, concise, syntax and a clean, consistent, semantic model, Python allows programmers to easily combine simple pieces to make a complex whole.

Throughout the rest of this book, it's assumed that you have a good working knowledge of Python, and are familiar with basic concepts such as how Python implements objects and classes. You don't need to be a Python expert to read this book, but ordinary Python language constructs are not explained in the discussion of the wxPython examples. If you need more background information on Python, the Python web site contains an excellent tutorial and other documentation at www.python.org/doc.

One important Python feature is the interactive interpreter, which can be very helpful in exploring the language and in debugging programs. If Python is installed and on your path, you can access the interpreter by entering `python` at a command prompt. You'll then see `>>>`, which is the Python command prompt. From there, you can enter any Python expression, and its value will be displayed on the screen. For example:

```
$ python
Python 2.3.3c1 (#50, Dec  4 2003, 21:27:34) [MSC v.1200 32 bit (Intel)] on
    win32
Type "help", "copyright", "credits" or "license" for more information.
>>> 2 + 2
4
>>> 10 / 3
3
>>> zip(['a', 'b', 'c'], [1, 2, 3])
[('a', 1), ('b', 2), ('c', 3)]
>>>
```

In this short session, I did a couple of simple arithmetic functions, then used the Python built-in function `zip()`, to combine two lists into an associated list. You can do anything from the interpreter that you can do in a standalone Python program, including import modules, define functions, and define classes.

1.7.2 *The wxWidgets toolkit*

The other base component of wxPython is the wxWidgets toolkit. At base, wxWidgets is a GUI framework implemented in C++, which means it is a set of C++ classes that encapsulate a wide range of features. Although the primary use of wxWidgets is for UI applications, it also contains useful features for C++ programmers including C++ implementations of data structures not supported in ANSI C++, such as strings and hashtables, as well as interfaces for system features like sockets and threads. Since these features and others are already available in the Python language or standard library, wrappers for these wxWidgets classes are not provided in wxPython and you should use the Python equivalents instead. For the most part wxPython only provides wrappers for the GUI classes in wxWidgets. The goal of wxWidgets is to allow a C++ program to compile and run on all supported platforms with only minor changes to the source from platform to platform, and a reasonably consistent look and feel between the platforms.

Here's a sample C++ wxWidgets program, taken from Robert Roebling's tutorial on the wxWidgets site. This creates a blank window with a two-element menu, Quit and About. This is being shown primarily for comparison with the Python examples we'll be seeing throughout the book.

Listing 1.4   A simple Hello World program in C++ wxWidgets

```cpp
#include "wx/wx.h"

class MyApp: public wxApp {
    virtual bool OnInit();
};

class MyFrame: public wxFrame {
public:
    MyFrame(const wxString& title, const wxPoint& pos,
            const wxSize& size);
    void OnQuit(wxCommandEvent& event);
    void OnAbout(wxCommandEvent& event);
    DECLARE_EVENT_TABLE()
};

enum {
    ID_Quit = 1,
    ID_About,
};

BEGIN_EVENT_TABLE(MyFrame, wxFrame)
    EVT_MENU(ID_Quit, MyFrame::OnQuit)
    EVT_MENU(ID_About, MyFrame::OnAbout)
END_EVENT_TABLE()

IMPLEMENT_APP(MyApp)
```

 # This macro sets up a default main() which
 # handles the initialization

```cpp
bool MyApp::OnInit() {
    MyFrame *frame = new MyFrame("Hello World", wxPoint(50,50),
            wxSize(450,340));
    frame->Show(TRUE);
    SetTopWindow(frame);
    return TRUE;
}

MyFrame::MyFrame(const wxString& title, const wxPoint& pos,
        const wxSize& size)
    : wxFrame((wxFrame *)NULL, -1, title, pos, size) {
    wxMenu *menuFile = new wxMenu;
    menuFile->Append( ID_About, "&About..." );
    menuFile->AppendSeparator();
    menuFile->Append( ID_Quit, "E&xit" );
    wxMenuBar *menuBar = new wxMenuBar;
    menuBar->Append( menuFile, "&File" );
    SetMenuBar( menuBar );
    CreateStatusBar();
    SetStatusText( "Welcome to wxWidgets!" );
}
```

// CTOR

```
void MyFrame::OnQuit(wxCommandEvent& WXUNUSED(event)) {
    Close(TRUE);
}

void MyFrame::OnAbout(wxCommandEvent& WXUNUSED(event)) {
    wxMessageBox("This is a wxWidgets Hello world sample",
        "About Hello World", wxOK | wxICON_INFORMATION, this);
}
```

If you're familiar with C++, you probably noticed that something is missing. Usually, C++ programs have a function named `main()` which is the starting point for the program. In wxWidgets, the macro `IMPLEMENT_APP(MyApp)` automatically sets up a default `main()` which manages initialization of the wxWidget program.

As with most cross-platform interface kits, the classes and methods visible to the programmer are actually proxies for a set of subclasses. Typically there is a subclass for each platform that wxWidgets runs under, and the subclass specific to the current platform is automatically used. As of this writing, these are the most significant supported platforms:

- Microsoft Windows
- Mac OS
- Gnome Toolkit (GTK+), which is applicable on most modern Unix systems

For each platform, wxWidgets attempts to use native widgets and features where applicable, and generally tries to emulate the native look and feel. In this way, wxWidgets avoids the "least common denominator" problem that cross-platform toolkits frequently have.

If you are familiar with any other large-scale object-oriented interface toolkit, such as MFC or Java Swing, the basic structure of wxWidgets should feel largely similar. One difference from some toolkits is that wxWidgets does not make a class distinction between widgets that can contain other widgets and ones that can't. (The way that, for example, Java Swing has a `JComponent` and `JContainer` class). The mechanism for adding child widgets is built into the `wxWindow` base class so that it is potentially available to all widgets, whether or not they are typically thought of as containers. Typically, though, widgets that are not containers prevent you from using this behavior (you can't put a dialog box inside a button, for example).

Development of wxWidgets goes back farther than you might think. The project was begun in 1992 by Julian Smart, at the University of Edinburgh's Artificial Intelligence Applications Institute. Smart was trying to build an application that could run on both Unix and Windows, and the existing commercial toolkits were prohibitively expensive, so he wrote his own. The name wxWidgets refers to the two original platforms—"w" for Microsoft Windows and "x" for Unix X server. The original version was written in terms of MFC, for the Windows version, and XView on Unix, but that quickly gave way to more general libraries for each platform as XView was replaced by the Motif toolkit, and MFC was replaced with direct calls to the Windows API. In 1997, the entire system was built with a more flexible API, and the GTK+ version became the standard Unix port soon after. The Macintosh port came on board the next year. More recent developments in the wxWidget side include a Unix library which is not dependent on a pre-existing toolkit, and ports for handheld systems.

Python is not the only language which has a binding library for wxWidgets, although it has the largest user community of the group. The wxWidgets web site links to projects with support for Ada, Basic, C#, Eiffel, Euphoria, Haskell, Java, JavaScript, Lua, Perl, and Ruby, although we make no claims for the robustness or level of support of any of those ports.

1.7.3 *Putting it together: the wxPython toolkit*

While both Python and wxWidgets are pretty great on their own, they combine to create an even greater whole, like peanut butter and chocolate. The flexibility of the Python language makes wxPython much easier to develop in than its C++ counterpart, while the native C++ code of wxWidgets gives the Python GUI both the speed and native look and feel it would otherwise lack. Table 1.2 gives a sample of some issues that are difficult to manage in C++ but easy, if not trivial, in Python.

Table 1.2   Developing in C++ versus developing in wxPython

C++ environment	wxPython environment
Memory management handled by programmer	Memory management handled by Python
Static typing makes polymorphism difficult	Dynamic typing makes polymorphism easy
Program reflection very limited	Program reflection easy, allowing for powerful abstraction
Unable to use functions as arguments easily	Functions can be passed around like any other variable
Compilation cycle needed before each run	Program interpreted at runtime

Here is an example of how the two tools interact. In the previous section, we showed you a "hello world" example in C++ wxWidgets. Listing 1.5 shows the same example translated basically line-by-line into wxPython.

Listing 1.5 A simple Hello World program in wxPython

hello_world.py (handwritten)

```python
import wx

class MyApp(wx.App):

    def OnInit(self):
        frame = MyFrame("Hello World", (50, 60), (450, 340))
        frame.Show()
        self.SetTopWindow(frame)
        return True

class MyFrame(wx.Frame):

    def __init__(self, title, pos, size):
        wx.Frame.__init__(self, None, -1, title, pos, size)
        menuFile = wx.Menu()
        menuFile.Append(1, "&About...")
        menuFile.AppendSeparator()
        menuFile.Append(2, "E&xit")
        menuBar = wx.MenuBar()
        menuBar.Append(menuFile, "&File")
        self.SetMenuBar(menuBar)
        self.CreateStatusBar()
        self.SetStatusText("Welcome to wxPython!")
        self.Bind(wx.EVT_MENU, self.OnAbout, id=1)
        self.Bind(wx.EVT_MENU, self.OnQuit, id=2)

    def OnQuit(self, event):
        self.Close()

    def OnAbout(self, event):
        wx.MessageBox("This is a wxPython Hello world sample",
            "About Hello World", wx.OK | wx.ICON_INFORMATION, self)

if __name__ == '__main__':
    app = MyApp(False)
    app.MainLoop()
```

Handwritten annotations in margins:
- hello_world.py
- @32
- 33 : using __init__()
- also 35-6
- 40
- title, pos, size (over the MyFrame line)
- par, id (over the wx.Frame.__init__ line)
- # redirect 36
- menu : appended to menu bar
- menu bar
- menu items, appended to menu

There are two high-level things that we'd like to point out about the wxPython example compared to the wxWidgets C++ one (beyond merely the difference between the two languages).

First, notice that wxPython does not have the automatic macro for creating a main starting point, and must do so explicitly at the end of this module.

Second, the mechanism for associating events with the code to be executed is different between the two programs. Since Python allows functions to be passed easily around as objects, the wxPython program can use the relatively straightforward wx.Bind() methods to do the associating dynamically at runtime. The C++ program must use the DECLARE_EVENT_TABLE and BEGIN_EVENT_TABLE macros, which do the binding statically at compile time and are somewhat more awkward.

Beyond those changes, the two programs are quite similar line by line—we find the Python version more readable, though. As you'll see, Python becomes more of an advantage in larger programs, due to its simpler syntax, automatic memory management, and so forth. At this point it's worth mentioning that wxPython did not come about by accident. It was developed to fill a specific need for a cross-platform rapid development environment. It has prospered and advanced because of the continued efforts of programmers who need rapid GUI development.

Development of wxPython and wxWidgets continues. Ongoing projects include support for mobile devices and better multimedia support. The most current version of wxPython is available at www.wxpython.org.

1.8 Summary

- You can create a minimal wxPython program in less than 10 lines of code. Most wxPython programs are much longer than 10 lines, and are typically divided into separate modules, each containing customized subclasses of wxPython classes, and, hopefully, plenty of docstrings.

- Most of the wxPython toolkit is accessed through the wx package which you access using the import wx statement. Every wxPython program must have an application object—an instance of a wx.App subclass that defines an OnInit() method. Most wxPython programs will have one or more frames—instances of subclasses of wx.Frame. A frame is the large, movable, resizeable window-like container that appears on screen, often with a menu, status bar, tool bars, and other widgets. Control of your program passes to wxPython when you call your application's MainLoop() method.

- Within wxPython are all the basic widgets you would expect, plus common dialogs, a wide variety of more complex widgets, HTML rendering, spreadsheet-style grids, and so forth. The wxWidgets toolkit that wxPython is based on is a C++ framework with a large list of features. It is a cross-platform toolkit, with most support for Microsoft Windows, Unix GTK+, and the Mac OS. The basic unit of a wxWidgets application is the window, meaning any item that can be drawn to the screen.

- The wxPython toolkit is a combination of the Python programming language and the wxWidgets toolkit and can be downloaded at www.wxpython.org. It combines a very extensive interface toolkit with an easy-to-use scripting language. It offers productivity gains and useful features for any programmer, including existing Python or wxWidgets programmers.

- The wxPython version of the toolkit is a wrapper around wxWidgets containing bindings which allow Python language constructs to interact with the C++ framework. These bindings are largely created from the SWIG tool, from a long list of descriptions of how Python objects and C++ objects relate to each other.

Now it's time to do some wxPython coding. The next chapter starts you off with writing some code, and the remainder of part 1 explores the most important concepts of wxPython. Let's go!

2

Giving your
wxPython program
a solid foundation

This chapter covers
- Creating application objects
- Directing output from a wxPython program
- Shutting down a wxPython application
- Creating and using top-level window objects
- Adding objects and subwindows to a frame

The foundation of a house is a concrete structure that provides a strong base for the rest of the construction. Your wxPython program also has a foundation, made up of two required objects that support the rest of your application. These are the *application object* and the *top-level window object*. Using these objects properly will give your wxPython application a strong base to start with, and will make the job of constructing the rest of your application easier.

In this chapter, you will work with the application object to customize global aspects of your program, including initialization, redirecting output, and shutdown. You will use window objects in various styles, and put together basic widget combinations. You will also use simple default dialog boxes to get user information. At the end of the chapter, we'll help you diagnose and troubleshoot common problems with usage of application and top-level window objects.

2.1 What do I need to know about the required objects?

Let's start with a description of the two foundation objects. The application object manages the main event loop, which is the heartbeat of your wxPython program. The event loop will be covered in detail in chapter 3. For now, it is enough to say that it is the application object's job to start the main event loop. In addition, the application object has the final chance to respond to any events which are otherwise ignored by your application. Without the application object, your wxPython application cannot run.

The top-level window object generally manages the most important data and controls and presents them to the user. For example, in a word-processing program, the main window is the display of the document, and will likely manage at least some of the data for the document (depending, of course, on the exact architecture of your application). Similarly, the main window of your web browser both displays the page you are looking at and manages that page as a data object.

Figure 2.1 gives a basic schematic of the relationship between the two foundation objects and the rest of your application.

As this diagram shows, the application object "owns" both the top-level window and the main event loop. The top-level window manages the components in that window, and any other data objects you assign to it. That window and its components trigger events based on user actions, and receive event notifications to make changes in the display. In the next sections, we'll discuss the application and top-level window objects in more detail.

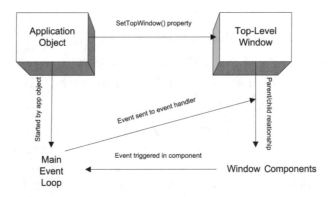

Figure 2.1 **A schematic of the basic wxPython application structure, showing the relationship between the application object, the top-level window, and the main event loop**

2.2 *How do I create and use an application object?*

Every wxPython application needs exactly one application object. The application object must be an instance of the class wx.App, or a custom subclass thereof. The primary purpose of the application object is to manage the main event loop behind the scenes. This event loop responds to windowing system events and dispatches them to the appropriate event handler. The application object is so important to the management of a wxPython process that you cannot create any wxPython graphical objects until after your program has instantiated an application object.

The parent wx.App class also defines a few properties which are global to the entire application. Much of the time, that's all the functionality you'll need from your application object. A custom application subclass can be used if you need to manage other global data or connections (such as a database connection). In some cases, you might also want to extend the main event loop for more specialized error or event handling. However, the default event loop will be suitable for nearly all wxPython applications that you will write.

2.2.1 *Creating a wx.App subclass*

Creating your own subclass of wx.App is so simple that it's often a good idea to create one when you start your application even if you don't need any custom functionality. That way, you'll have the subclass if you need it later. To create and use a wx.App subclass, you need to perform four steps:

1 Define the subclass.

2 Write an `OnInit()` method within the subclass definition.

3 Create an instance of the class in the main section of your program.

4 Call the `MainLoop()` method of the application instance. This method transfers program control to wxPython.

We saw the `OnInit()` method in chapter 1. It's called by the wxPython system when the application is started and before the main event loop begins. This method takes no parameters and returns a boolean value—if the return value is `False`, then the application will exit immediately. In most cases, you'll want to hardwire `True` as the result of this method. Exiting might be the proper way to handle certain error conditions, such as the absence of a required resource.

Because the `OnInit()` method exists, and is part of the wxPython framework, any initialization needed for your custom class is typically managed there, and not in the Python `__init__` special method. If you decide that you need an `__init__` method for some reason, you must call the `__init__` method of the parent class in that method, as in the following.

```
wx.App.__init__(self)
```

Typically, you'll create at least one frame object within the `OnInit()` method, and you'll also call the `Show()` method of that frame. You may optionally specify that the frame is the top window for the application by calling the method `SetTopWindow()`. The top window is used as the default parent for dialogs that are created without a parent—it's essentially the main window of your program. We'll discuss the top-level window in section 2.5.

When to omit a wx.App subclass

You aren't required to create your own `wx.App` subclass. You usually will want to do so to be able to create your top-level frame in the `OnInit()` method. But there is nothing stopping you from creating the frame outside of the application definition in some other part of calling script—the most common alternate place is the `__main__` clause. The only restriction is that your `wx.App` instance has to have been created first. Generally, it is only a good idea to avoid creating a `wx.App` subclass if there's just one frame in the system, and therefore the application setup is trivial. In such a case, wxPython provides the convenience class `wx.PySimpleApp`. The class provides a skeleton `OnInit()` method, and is defined as follows:

```
class PySimpleApp(wx.App):                    35: stdout, stderr to a window

    def __init__(self, redirect=False, filename=None,
                 useBestVisual=False, clearSigInt=True):
        wx.App.__init__(self, redirect, filename, useBestVisual,
                 clearSigInt)


    def OnInit(self):
        return True
```

It doesn't get much simpler than that. A sample usage of wx.PySimpleApp might look like this:

```
if __name__ == '__main__':
    app = wx.PySimpleApp()
    frame = MyNewFrame(None)
    frame.Show(True)
    app.MainLoop()
```

In the first line of this snippet, you create the application object as an instance of wx.PySimpleApp(). Since we're using the wx.PySimpleApp class, we don't have a custom OnInit method, so we define a frame in the second line of the snippet—since it has no parent specified, it's a top-level frame. (Obviously, the MyNewFrame class needs to be defined somewhere.) The third line of the code shows the frame, and the last line calls the application main loop, and we're good to go.

As you can see, using wx.PySimpleApp allows you to run your wxPython program without creating your own custom application class. You should only use wx.PySimpleApp if the application is, well, simple, and doesn't need any other global parameters.

NOTE *Naming Conventions*—While wxPython does a fantastic job of simplifying a complex C++ toolkit, the C++ origins of the tool do leak through in spots. One of the most noticeable examples of the C++ heritage has to do with naming conventions. In Python, method names usually use the lower_case_ separated_by_underscores or the lowerCaseInterCap style. However, the C++ convention which wxWidgets uses for methods is the UpperCaseInterCap style. This can be jarring if you are used to the Python style. For consistency's sake, it is recommended that you use the wxWidgets style in your wxPython classes. (Of course, you'll need to use it if you want to override wxWidgets methods).

Also note that the wxPython classes use explicit Get and Set methods for properties. That's more of a C++ style because most Python programs wouldn't define special accessor methods for simple cases.

The data members of the C++ classes are private—in most cases you must access the data of a wxPython class by using the access methods, you cannot use bare attribute names.

2.2.2 *Understanding the application object lifecycle*

The lifecycle of your wxPython application object begins when the application instance is created and ends just after the last application window is closed. This does not necessarily correspond to the beginning and ending of the Python script that surrounds your wxPython application. The script may choose to do some activity before creating the wxPython application, and may do further cleanup after the application MainLoop() exits. All wxPython activity, however, must be performed during the life of the application object. As we've mentioned, this means that your main frame object cannot be created until after the wx.App object is created. (This is one reason why we recommend creating the top-level frame in the OnInit() method—doing so guarantees that the application already exists.)

As figure 2.2 shows, creating the application object triggers the OnInit() method and allows new window objects to be created. After OnInit(), the script calls MainLoop(), signifying that wxPython events are now being handled. The application continues on its merry way, handling events until the windows are closed. After all top-level windows are closed, the MainLoop() function returns to the calling scope and the application object is destroyed. After that, the script can close any other connections or threads that might exist.

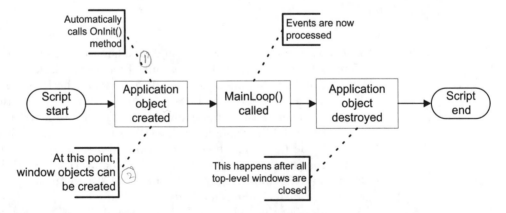

Figure 2.2   Major events in the wxPython application lifecycle, including the beginning and ending of both the wxPython application and the script which surrounds it

One reason to be aware of the main application life cycle is that, while active, a wxPython application will take control of certain system functions, such as the standard output streams. We'll discuss how to direct output in the next section

2.3 *How do I direct output from a wxPython program?*

All Python programs can output text via two standard streams: the standard output stream, `sys.stdout`, and the standard error stream `sys.stderr`. An ordinary Python script directs the standard output streams back to the console from which the script was launched. However, when your application object is created you can decide to have wxPython take control of the standard streams and redirect the output to a window instead. This redirect behavior is the default behavior for wxPython under Windows. In Unix systems, however, where there is more likely to be an actual console window, wxPython does not control the standard streams by default. In all systems the redirection behavior can be explicitly specified when the application object is created. We recommend taking advantage of this feature and always specifying redirect behavior to avoid any problems from different behavior on different platforms.

2.3.1 *Redirecting output*

If wxPython is controlling the standard streams, then text sent to the streams via any mechanism—including a print statement or a system traceback—is redirected to a separate wxPython frame. Text sent to the streams before the wxPython application begins or after it ends is, of course, processed normally. Listing 2.1, demonstrates both the application lifecycle and the `stdout`/`stderr` redirection.

Listing 2.1   A sample startup script showing output stream redirection

```python
#!/usr/bin/env python

import wx
import sys

class Frame(wx.Frame):

    def __init__(self, parent, id, title):
        print "Frame __init__"
        wx.Frame.__init__(self, parent, id, title)

class App(wx.App):
```

```
        def __init__(self, redirect=True, filename=None):
     (1) print "App __init__"    # to console
            wx.App.__init__(self, redirect, filename)

        def OnInit(self):
     (2) print "OnInit"    <── Writing to stdout
            self.frame = Frame(parent=None, id=-1, title='Startup')  <── Creating
            self.frame.Show()                                             the frame
            self.SetTopWindow(self.frame)
     (4) print >> sys.stderr, "A pretend error message"    <── Writing to stderr
            return True

        def OnExit(self):
            print "OnExit"    # displays (to window) too fast to see

if __name__ == '__main__':
        app = App(redirect=True)          ❶ Text redirection starts here
   (5) print "before MainLoop"
        app.MainLoop()              ❷ The main event loop is entered here
   (6) print "after MainLoop"    # to console
```

❶ This line creates the application object. After this line, all text sent to `stderr` or `stdout` can be redirected to a frame by wxPython. The arguments to the constructor determine whether this redirection takes place.

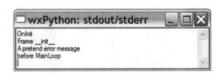

Figure 2.3 The `stdout/stderr` window created by Listing 2.1

❷ When run, this application creates a blank frame, and also generates a frame with the redirected output, as shown in figure 2.3. Notice also that both `stdout` and `stderr` messages get directed to the window.

After you run this program you'll see that your console has the following output:

```
App __init__
after MainLoop
```

The first line is generated before the frames are opened, the second line is generated after they close.

By looking at both the console and the output frame, we can trace the application lifecycle.

The first bubble in figure 2.2—Start Script—corresponds to the first lines run from the script's `__main__` clause. The transition to the next bubble comes immediately in the line marked ❶. The instantiation of the instance calls the method wx.App.__init__(). Then control goes to OnInit(), which is automatically called by wxPython. From there, the program jumps to the wx.Frame.__init__(), which is run when the wx.Frame instance is instantiated. Finally, control winds back to the __main__ clause, where MainLoop() is invoked, corresponding to the third bubble in figure 2.2. After the main loop ends, then wx.App.OnExit() is called by wxPython, transitioning to the fourth bubble, and then the rest of the script finishes out the process.

"Wait a minute," you say, "the message from OnExit() didn't display in either the window or the console." As we'll see, the message does display in the wxPython frame, but it does so right before the window is closed, so that it's nearly impossible to capture in a screen shot.

The quickly vanishing OnExit() message is a symptom of a larger issue with the output frame. Although it's a useful feature during development, you don't necessarily want the error stream frame popping out in a user's face at run time. Furthermore, if an error condition happens during the OnInit() method, it gets sent to the output frame, but the error causes the application to exit, since OnInit() will return a False value in case of an error condition. The result is that the line of text is displayed but disappears far too quickly to be seen.

2.3.2 *Modifying the default redirect behavior*

In order to modify this behavior, wxPython allows you to set two parameters when creating the application. The first parameter, redirect, causes output to be redirected to the frame if it is True. If the value is False, output stays at the console. If the redirect parameter is True, then the second parameter, filename, can also be set. If so, output is redirected to a file with that name, rather than to the wxPython frame. Therefore, changing the wx.App creation at annotation ❶ in listing 2.1 to:

```
app = App(False)
```

causes all of the following output to go to the console:

```
App __init__
OnInit
Frame __init__
A pretend error message
before MainLoop
OnExit
after MainLoop
```

Notice that the OnExit() message is displayed here. Changing the line to:

```
app = App(True, "output")
```

will cause all the redirected lines to be sent to a file named output. The App
init and after MainLoop messages will still be sent to the console, however,
because they occur outside of the time period where the wx.App object has control
of the streams.

2.4   How do I shut down my wxPython application?

When the last top-level window in your application is closed by the user, the
wxPython application exits. By top-level, we mean any frame without a parent,
and not just the frame designated using the SetTopWindow() method. This
includes any frames created by wxPython itself. For instance, in listing 2.1, the
application does not exit until *both* the main frame and the output redirection
frame are closed, even though only the main frame is registered using SetTop-
Window(), and even though the application doesn't explicitly create the output
redirect frame. To trigger a shutdown programatically, you can call Close() on all
top-level windows.

2.4.1   *Managing a normal shutdown*

During the shutdown process, wxPython takes care of deleting all its windows and
freeing their resources. You have one hook into the exit process to perform your
own cleanup. If defined, the OnExit() method of your wx.App subclass is called
after the last window closes but before wxPython's internal cleanup. You can use
this method to clean up any non-wxPython resources you've created (a database
connection, for example). Even if the application is closed with wx.Exit(), the
OnExit() method is still triggered.

   If for some reason you want the application to continue after the last window
closes, you can change the default behavior using the wx.App method SetExitOn-
FrameDelete(flag). If the flag parameter is set to False, the program will continue to run even after the last window closes. This means that the wx.App
instance will continue to live, and the event loop will continue to process events.
You could, for example, then create all new top-level windows. The application
will remain alive until the global function wx.Exit() is explicitly called.

   A further subtlety is that wxPython will not trigger the shutdown process
before the main loop is even entered. Specifically, if you open a dialog in your
OnInit() method, you can close it without fear that wxPython will interpret that
as closing your last top-level window and shut itself down.

2.4.2 *Managing an emergency shutdown*

You can't always close your program in a controlled way. Sometimes, you need to end the application immediately and you don't care that your program cleans up after itself fully. For example, a critical resource may have closed or become corrupted. If the system is shutting down, you may not be able to do all the cleanup.

There are two mechanisms for exiting your wxPython application in an emergency situation. You can call the `wx.App` method `ExitMainLoop()`. This method explicitly causes the main message loop to break, causing the control to leave the `MainLoop()` function. This will generally end the application—it's effectively equivalent to closing all the top-level windows.

You can also call the global method `wx.Exit()`. Neither method is recommended for normal use because it may cause some cleanup functions to be skipped.

Sometimes, your application will need to shut down due to an event outside of its control. An example of this is when the underlying operating system is about to shut down or log the user off. In that case, your application gets one shot at cleanup to save documents or close connections or whatever. If your application binds an event handler for the `wx.EVT_QUERY_END_SESSION` event, then that event handler is called when wxPython is notified of the shutdown. (We'll show how to bind events to handlers later in the chapter, and in more detail in chapter 3.) The event parameter is a `wx.CloseEvent`. The close event may allow the application to veto the shutdown. Use the event method `CanVeto()` to find out. The application can make its veto known by calling the event method `Veto()`. You might want to do this if you cannot successfully save or close all resources. The default handler for the `wx.EVT_QUERY_END_SESSION` event calls the `Close()` method of the top-level windows, which will in turn send the `wx.EVT_CLOSE` event to the top-level windows giving you another chance to control the shutdown process. If any of the `Close()` methods returns `False` then the application attempts to veto the shutdown.

2.5 How do I create and use the top-level window object?

A top-level window object is a widget (usually a frame) that is not contained by another widget in your application—it's what a typical user would point to and say, "That's the program." The top-level window object is usually the main window of your application and contains widgets and interface objects that the user interacts with. As we have seen, the application exits when all top-level windows are closed.

Your application must have at least one top-level window object. The top-level window object is usually a subclass of the class wx.Frame, although it can also be a subclass of wx.Dialog. Most of the time, you will define custom subclasses of wx.Frame for use in your application. However, there are a number of pre-defined wx.Dialog subclasses that provide many of the typical dialogs that you might encounter in an application.

There's some naming confusion here, due to overloading of the word top. A generic "top-level" window is *any* widget in your application that doesn't have a parent container. Your application must have at least one of these, but it can have as many as you'd like. Only one of these windows, however, can be explicitly blessed by wxPython as the main top window by using SetTopWindow(). If you do not specify a main window with SetTopWindow, then the first frame in the wx.App's top-level window list is considered to be the top window. So, explicitly specifying the top window is not always necessary—you don't need to if, for example, you only have one top window. Repeated calls to SetTopWindow() will replace the current top window—an application can only have one top window at a time.

2.5.1 *Working with wx.Frame*

In wxPython parlance, a frame is the name given to what a GUI user normally calls a window. That is to say, a frame is a container that the user can generally move freely around on the screen, and which often includes such decorations as a title bar, menubar, and resize targets in the corners. The class wx.Frame is the parent class of all frames in wxPython. There are also a few specialized subclasses of wx.Frame that you use. This section will give an overview of the wx.Frame family—enough for you to get started using them. A more complete description of the wx.Frame class will be presented in chapter 8.

When you create subclasses of wx.Frame, the __init__() method of your class should call the parent constructor wx.Frame.__init__(). The signature of that constructor is as follows.

```
wx.Frame(parent, id=-1, title="", pos=wx.DefaultPosition,
        size=wx.DefaultSize, style=wx.DEFAULT_FRAME_STYLE,
        name="frame")
```

This constructor takes several parameters. In normal use, however, at least some of the defaults are reasonable options. We will see parameters similar to this constructor again and again in other widget constructors—it's a very similar pattern in wxPython. Table 2.1 describes each of the parameters.

Remember, these are the parameters as passed to the parent constructor method, wx.Frame.__init__(). The argument signature of the constructor to your

Table 2.1   Parameters of the `wx.Frame` constructor method

Parameter	Description
parent	The parent window of the frame being created. For top-level windows, the value is None. If another window is used for the parent parameter then the new frame will be owned by that window and will be destroyed when the parent is. Depending on the platform, the new frame may be constrained to only appear on top of the parent window. In the case of a child MDI window, the new window is restricted and can only be moved and resized within the parent.
id	The wxPython ID number for the new window. You can pass one in explicitly, or pass -1 which causes wxPython to automatically generate a new ID. See the section "Working with wxPython ID" for more information.
title	The window title—for most styles, it's displayed in the window title bar.
pos	A `wx.Point` object specifying where on the screen the upper left-hand corner of the new window should be. As is typical in graphics applications, the (0, 0) point is the upper left corner of the monitor. The default is (-1, -1), which causes the underlying system to decide where the window goes. See the section "Working with wx.Size and wx.Point" for more information.
size	A `wx.Size` object specifying the starting size of the window. The default is (-1, -1), which causes the underlying system to determine the starting size. See the section "Working with wx.Size and wx.Point" for more information.
style	A bitmask of constants determining the style of the window. You may use the bitwise or operator (`|`) to combine them when you want more than one to be in effect. See the section "Working with wx.Frame styles" for usage guidelines.
name	An internal name given to the frame, used on Motif to set resource values. Can also be used to find the window by name later.

class can, and often will, be different. This allows you to conveniently ensure default values for your own frame by not allowing them to be modified by a call to your constructor. For example, you might want your frame class to always be a 300 pixel square. In that case, you probably wouldn't have a `size` argument in your class constructor, but would just explicitly pass (300, 300) to the `wx.Frame.__init__()` method. Listing 2.2 shows a frame class that does not allow any of the attributes of the window to be passed as an argument.

Listing 2.2   A frame subclass which sets its own defaults

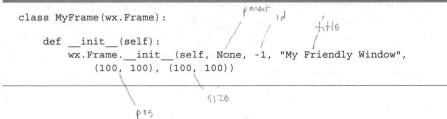

```
class MyFrame(wx.Frame):

    def __init__(self):
        wx.Frame.__init__(self, None, -1, "My Friendly Window",
            (100, 100), (100, 100))
```

In listing 2.2, the __init__() method of MyFrame does not take any arguments. This means that MyFrame users cannot override the hardwired arguments that MyFrame.__init__() passes to the superclass wx.Frame.__init__(). Remember that a determined user of your class can always change the default values by calling setter methods after the frame is instantiated.

2.5.2 *Working with wxPython IDs*

Table 2.1 lists the *wxPython ID* number of the new frame. ID numbers are a feature of all widgets in wxPython, and it's worth a few paragraphs to explain how they work. Every widget in a wxPython application has a window identifier. The ID numbers must be unique within each frame, but you can reuse ids between frames. We recommend, however, that you try to have your ID numbers be unique across your application, to prevent errors and confusion when processing events. However, there are few standard predefined ID numbers in wxPython, which have specific meanings within parts of the code (for example, wx.ID_OK and wx.ID_CANCEL are assumed to be the ID numbers of the OK and Cancel buttons in a dialog box). It's usually not a problem to reuse standard ID numbers in your application as long as you use them in the manner expected. The ID number is usually the second parameter in the constructor of a wxPython widget object, after the parent widget. The most important use of ID numbers in wxPython is to create a unique relationship between an event that happens to a specific object and a function which is called in response to that event. Using a duplicate ID can cause the wrong function to be triggered in response to an event.

There are three ways to create the ID numbers used by a widget:

1 Explicitly pass a positive integer into the constructor
2 Get wxPython to create IDs for you using the wx.NewId() function
3 Pass either the global constant wx.ID_ANY or -1 to a widget constructor

Explicitly choosing the ID

First and most straightforwardly, you can explicitly pass a positive integer into the constructor—that number becomes the widget's ID. If you pass a specific number, it is your responsibility to make sure that you do not duplicate ID numbers within a frame or reuse one of the predefined constants. You can ensure that wxPython does not use your explicit ID elsewhere in the application by calling the global function wx.RegisterId(). To prevent your program from duplicating wxPython

IDs, you should avoid using ID numbers between the global constants wx.ID_LOWEST and wx.ID_HIGHEST.

Using the global NewID() function

However, ensuring the uniqueness of ID numbers can become burdensome quickly. You can instead get wxPython to create ids for you using the wx.NewId() function:

```
id = wx.NewId()
frame = wx.Frame.__init__(None, id)
```

Using a constant to say 'I don't care'

Alternately, you can pass either the global constant wx.ID_ANY or -1 to many widget constructors, and then wxPython will generate the new ID for you. Then you can use the GetId() method if you need the ID later on:

```
frame = wx.Frame.__init__(None, -1)
id = frame.GetId()
```

There's no particular functional difference between the styles.

2.5.3 Working with wx.Size and wx.Point

The list of wx.Frame constructor arguments (table 2.1) also referenced the classes wx.Size and wx.Point. These two classes will be used frequently in your wxPython programming. Because of that, some Python-specific shortcuts have been added to the classes.

The wx.Size and wx.Point classes are quite similar both in their wxWidgets method list and in how they are represented in wxPython. The wx.Point class, surprisingly enough, represents a point or position. The constructor takes two arguments for the *x* and *y* values of the point. The values both default to zero if not set:

```
point = wx.Point(10, 12)   # init        Change in 1 line via point = Set (11, 13)
```

To set both dimensions in one line, use the function Set(x,y). To retrieve them both at once, use Get(), which returns the two values as a Python tuple. Unlike most wxWidgets classes, wx.Point has functionality defined to retrieve the x and y values as simple Python properties such that the *x* and *y* values are accessible like ordinary Python attributes:

```
x = point.x
y = point.y
```

In addition, wx.Point instances can be transparently added, subtracted, and compared just like other Python objects. For example:

```
x = wx.Point(2, 3)
y = wx.Point(5, 7)
z = x + y
bigger = x > y
```

In a `wx.Point` instance, the attributes are expected to be integers. If you need floating-point coordinates, you can use the class `wx.RealPoint`, which works much the same way as `wx.Point`.

The `wx.Size` class is almost identical to `wx.Point`, except that the instance variables are named `width` and `height` instead of x and y. Otherwise, it has the same attribute and operator features defined.

When a `wx.Point` or `wx.Size` instance is needed anywhere in your wxPython program—for example, in the constructor for another object—you do not need to create the instance explicitly. Instead, you can pass a Python tuple to the constructor, and wxPython will implicitly create the `wx.Point` or `wx.Size` instance:

```
frame = wx.Frame(None, -1, pos=(10, 10), size=(100, 100))
```

This works not just in constructors for other objects, but also anyplace where a `wx.Point` or `wx.Size` is expected by a wrapped C++ method or function call. You can even write something like this, if you so desire:

```
frame.SetPosition((2, 3))
```

2.5.4 *Working with wx.Frame styles*

The `wx.Frame` constructor takes a bitmask as a `style` parameter. Every wxPython widget object takes a similar `style` parameter, although the exact values that are defined are different for each type of widget. This section will discuss the styles used for `wx.Frame`. At least some of this is applicable to other wxPython widgets. The widget definitions in part 2 will discuss styles applicable to each class.

WHAT'S A BITMASK? A bitmask is a way of compactly storing information about system attributes that is especially useful when there are a limited number of attributes with boolean values and the values are more or less mutually independent. In wxPython, bitmasks are used to manage a number of different attributes throughout the framework, most notably style information.

In a bitmask, the individual attributes are assigned constant values corresponding to powers of two, and the value of the bitmask is the sum of all the attributes which are "turned on". In binary notation, the power of two system guarantees that each attribute corresponds to a single bit in the total sum, allowing all of the attribute state to be compactly stored in a single integer or long value. For example, if attribute a=1, b=2, c=4, and d=8, then any combination of the group has a unique sum that can be stored in an integer. The pair a and c would be 5 (binary 0101), while b, c, and d would be 14 (binary 1110). In wxPython, the attributes have symbolic constants, so you don't need to worry about the individual bit values.

Styles are defined for all wxPython widgets by passing a bitmask to the style parameter of the constructor. Some widgets also define a SetStyle() method, allowing you to change the style after the widget is created. All the individual style elements that you might use have a predefined constant identifier (such as wx.MINIMIZE_BOX). To add multiple styles together, you use the Python bitwise OR operator, |. For example, the constant wx.DEFAULT_FRAME_STYLE is defined as a combination of basic style elements:

```
wx.MAXIMIZE_BOX | wx.MINIMIZE_BOX | wx.RESIZE_BORDER |
wx.SYSTEM_MENU | wx.CAPTION | wx.CLOSE_BOX
```

To remove individual style bits from a composed style, you use the bitwise exclusive or (XOR) operator, ^. For example, to create a window that is based on the default, but which is not resizable by the user, you could do this:

```
wx.DEFAULT_FRAME_STYLE ^ (wx.RESIZE_BORDER | wx.MINIMIZE_BOX |
wx.MAXIMIZE_BOX)
```

It is highly recommended that you use the default style on top-level frames so that the user can easily recognize them as being top level. At the very least, you need to ensure that there is some way for a top-level frame to be closed. This is most easily done by including the wx.SYSTEM_MENU style. Also be aware that by inadvertently using a bitwise AND (&) operation, instead of a bitwise OR, you can easily wind up with no styles chosen, resulting in an unbordered frame that you cannot move, resize, or close. This is, of course, not recommended.

Table 2.2 has a listing of the most important styles for wx.Frame.

Table 2.2   Some of the most commonly used style parameters for wx.Frame

Style	Description
wx.CAPTION	Adds a title bar on the frame, which displays the frame's Title property.
wx.CLOSE_BOX	Instructs the system to display a close box on the frame's title bar, using the system defaults for placement and style. Also enables the close item on the system menu if applicable.

continued on next page

Table 2.2   Some of the most commonly used style parameters for `wx.Frame` *(continued)*

Style	Description
wx.DEFAULT_FRAME_STYLE	As you might expect from the name, this is the default if no style is specified. It is defined as `wx.MAXIMIZE_BOX` | `wx.MINIMIZE_BOX` | `wx.RESIZE_BORDER` | `wx.SYSTEM_MENU` | `wx.CAPTION` | `wx.CLOSE_BOX`.
wx.FRAME_SHAPED	Frames created with this style can use the `SetShape()` method to create a window with a non-rectangular shape.
wx.FRAME_TOOL_WINDOW	Makes the frame look like a toolbox window by giving it a smaller titlebar than normal. Under Windows a frame created with this style does not show in the taskbar listing of all open windows.
wx.MAXIMIZE_BOX	Adds a maximize box on the frame, using the system parameters for the look and placement of the box. Also enables maximize functionality in the system menu if applicable.
wx.MINIMIZE_BOX	Adds a minimize box on the frame, using the system parameters for the look and placement of the box. Also enables minimize functionality in the system menu if applicable.
wx.RESIZE_BORDER	Adds a resizable border to the frame.
wx.SIMPLE_BORDER	A plain border without decoration. May not work on all platforms.
wx.SYSTEM_MENU	Adds the system menu (with close, move, resize, etc. functionality, using system look and feel) and the close box to the window. The availability of resize and close operations within this menu depends on the styles `wx.MAXIMIZE_BOX`, `wx.MINIMIZE_BOX` and `wx.CLOSE_BOX` being chosen.

The next four figures show a few common frame styles.

Figure 2.4 was created with `wx.DEFAULT_STYLE`. Figure 2.5 is a frame created using the non-resizable style combination shown in the previous code snippet.

Figure 2.4   A frame created with the default style

Figure 2.5   A frame created to be non-resizable. Notice the lack of minimize/maximize buttons.

Figure 2.6 uses `style=wx.DEFAULT_FRAME_STYLE | wx.FRAME_TOOL_WINDOW.`

Figure 2.6   A toolbar frame, with a smaller title bar and no system menu

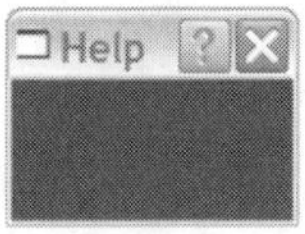

Figure 2.7   A frame with a help button

Figure 2.7 uses the extended style `wx.help.FRAME_EX_CONTEXTHELP`, which is described in chapter 8.

Now that we've seen how to create `wx.Frame` objects, we'll start to show how to make them useful, by adding additional widgets inside the frame.

2.6 How do I add objects and subwindows to a frame?

We've described how to create `wx.Frame` objects, but as yet the frames are not very interesting. For one thing, they are empty. In this section, we'll show you the basics of inserting objects and subwindows inside your frame for the user to interact with.

2.6.1 Adding widgets to a frame

Figure 2.8 shows a custom frame subclass called `InsertFrame`. When the close button is clicked, the window will close and the application will end.

Listing 2.3 defines the `wx.Frame` subclass shown in figure 2.8. Not all of the concepts in this snippet have been covered yet, so don't worry if some things are not clear.

Figure 2.8   The `InsertFrame` window is an example demonstrating the basics of inserting items into a frame.

Listing 2.3   The `InsertFrame` code

```python
#!/usr/bin/env python

import wx

class InsertFrame(wx.Frame):
    def __init__(self, parent, id):
        wx.Frame.__init__(self, parent, id, 'Frame With Button',
                size=(300, 100))
        panel = wx.Panel(self)      # Creating the panel
        button = wx.Button(panel, label="Close", pos=(125, 10),
```

Adding the button to the panel ❷

❶ **Creating the panel**

```
                size=(50, 50))
        self.Bind(wx.EVT_BUTTON, self.OnCloseMe, button)      ◄──❸  Binding
        self.Bind(wx.EVT_CLOSE, self.OnCloseWindow)    ◄─┐          the button
                                                         │          click event
    def OnCloseMe(self, event):         Binding the window  ❹
        self.Close(True)                    close event

    def OnCloseWindow(self, event):
        self.Destroy()

if __name__ == '__main__':
    app = wx.PySimpleApp()
    frame = InsertFrame(parent=None, id=-1)
    frame.Show()
    app.MainLoop()
```

subwidgets

The __init__ method of the `InsertFrame` class creates two subwindows ❶, ❷.
The first is a `wx.Panel`, which is essentially a plain container for other windows
and has little functionality of its own. The second is a `wx.Button`, which is an
ordinary button. Next, the button click event and the close window event are
bound to the function that will be executed when the event takes place ❸, ❹.

✳✳   In most cases, you will create a single `wx.Panel` instance the same size as your
`wx.Frame` to hold all of the contents of your frame. Doing so keeps the custom
contents of the window separate from other elements such as the toolbar and status bar. In addition, on Windows operating systems, the default background color
of a `wx.Frame` is not standard (it's gray, not white), while a `wx.Panel` will have a
white background by default (assuming you haven't changed your system's color
and theme settings). The `wx.Panel` class also enables traversal of the elements
inside via the tab button, which `wx.Frame` does not.

If you are familiar with other UI toolkits, it may seem strange that you do not
need to explicitly call an add method to insert a subwindow into a parent.
Instead, in wxPython you just specify the parent window when the subwindow is
created, and the subwindow is implicitly added inside that parent object, as is
done in listing 2.3 ❷.

You might also wonder why the `wx.Button` in listing 2.5 is created with an
explicit position and size, while the `wx.Panel` is not. In wxPython, if a frame is created with just a single child window, then that child window (in this case, the
`wx.Panel`) is automatically resized to fill the client area of the frame. This automatic resizing will override any position or size information for the child—even if
a position or size had been specified for the panel, it would have been ignored.
This automatic resizing only happens for a single element if it is within frames or

dialogs. The button is a child of the panel, not the frame, so its specified size and position are used. If a size and position had not been specified for the button, it would have been placed in the default position, which is the upper left corner of the panel, with its size based on the length of the label.

Explicitly specifying the size and position of every subwindow can get tedious quickly. More importantly, it doesn't allow your application to reposition objects gracefully when the user resizes a window. To solve both of these problems, wxPython uses objects called *sizers* to manage complex placement of child windows. Sizers will be covered briefly in chapter 7 and in more detail in part 2.

2.6.2 *Adding a menubar, toolbar, or status bar to a frame*

Often, an application window will have one or more of three special subwindows—a menubar at the top, a toolbar below that, and a status bar at the bottom. This is so common that wxPython provides special shortcut methods for the creation of toolbars and status bars (and menus aren't that hard either). Figure 2.9 shows a sample frame with a menubar, toolbar, and status bar.

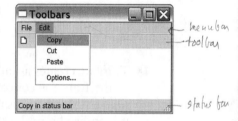

Figure 2.9   A sample frame with menubar, toolbar, and status bar

Listing 2.4 shows the __init__ method which decorates a plain window with all three subwindows. Again, this is just an overview, and the classes in question will be covered in more detail in chapter 7 and later in part 2.

Listing 2.4   Creating toolbars

```python
#!/usr/bin/env python

import wx
import images

class ToolbarFrame(wx.Frame):

    def __init__(self, parent, id):
        wx.Frame.__init__(self, parent, id, 'Toolbars',
                size=(300, 200))
        panel = wx.Panel(self)
        panel.SetBackgroundColour('White')
        statusBar = self.CreateStatusBar()
        toolbar = self.CreateToolBar()
        toolbar.AddSimpleTool(wx.NewId(), images.getNewBitmap(),
                "New", "Long help for 'New'")
        toolbar.Realize()
        menuBar = wx.MenuBar()
```

❶ **Creating the status bar**

❷ **Creating the toolbar**

❸ **Adding a tool to the bar**

<— **Creating a menubar**

❹ **Preparing the toolbar for display**

Expanded : 113

```
menu1 = wx.Menu()
menuBar.Append(menu1, "&File")
menu2 = wx.Menu()
menu2.Append(wx.NewId(), "&Copy", "Copy in status bar")
menu2.Append(wx.NewId(), "C&ut", "")
menu2.Append(wx.NewId(), "Paste", "")
menu2.AppendSeparator()
menu2.Append(wx.NewId(), "&Options...", "Display Options")
menuBar.Append(menu2, "&Edit")
self.SetMenuBar(menuBar)

if __name__ == '__main__':
    app = wx.PySimpleApp()
    frame = ToolbarFrame(parent=None, id=-1)
    frame.Show()
    app.MainLoop()
```

⑤ Creating two individual menus

⑥ Creating individual menu items

Attaching the menu to the menubar

Attaching the menubar to the frame

❶ This line creates a status bar, which is an instance of the class wx.StatusBar. As far as the frame is concerned, it's a subwindow placed at the bottom of the frame whose width is the same as the width of the frame, and whose height is determined by the underlying operating system. The purpose of the status bar is to display text set by various events in the application. The text size and font of the status window are also set by the underlying system.

❷ Creates an instance of wx.ToolBar, which is a container of command buttons automatically positioned at the top of the frame.

❸ There are two methods to add tools to your toolbar, this line shows the one with fewer arguments, AddSimpleTool(). The arguments are an ID, a bitmap, short help text to display as a tooltip for the item, and longer help text to be displayed in the status bar for the item. (Don't worry about where the bitmap is coming from at the moment.) Although the tool as displayed on the toolbar will look like a button, in terms of the event system, it behaves more like a menu item, which makes it easy for a tool to act as an exact duplicate for an item in your menubar. Specifically, pressing the tool button triggers the same kind of wxPython event as the menu item, meaning that both can be responded to by the same method.

❹ The Realize() method tells the toolbar to calculate where the buttons should be positioned, and is required if the toolbar has any tools added that depend on the toolbar's dynamic positioning because they do not specify their own size or position explictly.

❺ Creates a wx.Menu object, which represents a single menu on the bar. (We created two of them, but only so that we could take a screen shot of the pull-down without covering the toolbar icon.)

6 Creates the individual menu items, with the arguments representing an ID, the text of the item, and the text displayed on the status bar when the menu is moused over. The "&" indicates the character to be chosen for a menu accelerator.

In addition to using widgets in your frames, you'll also communicate with users via standard dialogs, which is made easy using wxPython's predefined dialog functions.

2.7 How can I use common dialogs?

The wxPython library provides a rich set of predefined dialog boxes that you can use to give your application a consistent, familiar look and feel. In this section, we'll discuss three basic ways to get information from a user in a dialog:

1. Message dialog   *wx. Message Dialog*   51
2. Text entry   *wx. Text Entry Dialog*   52
3. Choosing from a list   *wx. Single Choice Dialog*   53

There are many other standard dialogs in wxPython, including a file picker, a color picker, progress dialog, print setup, and a font picker. These will be discussed in chapter 9. *259*

Sending a message without using Western Union

The most basic mechanism for communicating with the user is wx.MessageDialog, which is a simple alert box. The wx.MessageDialog can be used as both a simple OK box, or as a yes/no dialog. The following snippet shows the yes/no behavior:

```
dlg = wx.MessageDialog(None, 'Is this the coolest thing ever!',
                       'MessageDialog', wx.YES_NO | wx.ICON_QUESTION)
result = dlg.ShowModal()
dlg.Destroy()
```

The resulting dialog looks like figure 2.10, and the signature for the constructor is:

```
wx.MessageDialog(parent, message,
        caption="Message box",
        style=wx.OK | wx.CANCEL,
        pos=wx.DefaultPosition)
```

where parent is a parent window, or None if the dialog should be top-level. The message is the string which appears in the dialog, and the caption is the string that appears in the dialog's title bar. The style parameter is

Figure 2.10 A message dialog, configured for a yes/no response

a bitmask which covers the buttons and icons displayed in the dialog, The pos parameter takes either a wx.Point or Python tuple, and allows you to specify the position of the dialog on the display, if you so desire.

The ShowModal() method displays the dialog as a modal frame, meaning that no other window in the application will respond to user events until the dialog is closed. This method is common to all dialogs. The return value of ShowModal() is an integer, signifying the result of the dialog. In this case, the result corresponds to the button pressed by the user. For a wx.MessageDialog, it will be one of the following constants: wx.ID_YES, wx.ID_NO, wx.ID_CANCEL, or wx.ID_OK.

The style bits can be combined to manage the buttons displayed, with the legal values being wx.OK, wx,CANCEL, or wx.YES_NO. Style bits can also be used to set the icon displayed on the window, which is one of wx.ICON_ERROR, wx.ICON_EXCLAMATION, wx.ICON_INFORMATION, and wx.ICON_QUESTION.

Just a single line of text, please

If you need to get a single line of text from the user, then you can use the class wx.TextEntryDialog, as follows. This snippet creates the dialog, and retrieves the entered value if the user exits with a click on the OK button:

```
dlg = wx.TextEntryDialog(None, "Who is buried in Grant's tomb?",
  'A Question', 'Cary Grant')
  if dlg.ShowModal() == wx.ID_OK:
      response = dlg.GetValue()
```

Figure 2.11 shows what the dialog looks like in use.

The parameters of the wx.TextEntryDialog constructor are, in order, a parent window, the text caption inside the window, the text caption for the outside of the window (which defaults to "Please enter text"), and a default value for the user entry field (which defaults to the empty string). There is also a style argument which defaults to wx.OK | wx.CANCEL. You can use the style attribute to display the dialog without a cancel box, by passing only the value wx.OK. As with the wx.MessageDialog, the ShowModal() method returns the ID of the button pressed. The GetValue() method contains the value the user entered into the text field (there's a parallel SetValue() method that allows you to change the field programmatically).

Figure 2.11   A text entry dialog

Choose from the following list

If, instead of all the freedom that comes with being able to enter any thing that enters his head, you want the user to only be able to select a choice from a provided list, you can use the wx.SingleChoiceDialog class. A simple usage is shown here:

```
dlg = wx.SingleChoiceDialog(None,
        'What version of Python are you using?',
        'Single Choice',
        ['1.5.2', '2.0', '2.1.3', '2.2', '2.3.1'],
if dlg.ShowModal() == wx.ID_OK:
    response = dlg.GetStringSelection()
```

Figure 2.12 shows the resulting dialog box. The parameters are similar to the text entry dialog, except that instead of passing a string default text, you pass a list of strings that are displayed in the list. There are two ways that you can get the returned selection. The method GetSelection() returns the index of the user selection, while GetStringSelection() returns the actual string selected.

Figure 2.12 The `SingleChoiceDialog` **window, allowing a user to choose from a predefined list**

2.8 *What are some common errors with application objects and frames?*

There are a few errors that can happen in the creation of your wxPython application object or initial top-level window that can be difficult to track down, especially if you are seeing the error for the first time. The errors listed here are the kind of thing where the error message is not necessarily completely descriptive of the actual problem, or where the error can be difficult to diagnose the first time you see it. These are all fairly common errors for new wxPython programmers.

Here is a troubleshooting guide for some of the most common symptoms:

Symptom   *Error message at startup saying "unable to import module wx."*

Cause—The wxPython module is not in your PYTHONPATH. This means wx.Python may not have been correctly installed. Alternately, if there is more than one version of Python on the system, wxPython may have been installed against a different one than the one you are using.

Solution—Determine which Python version or versions are installed on the machine you are using. On a Unix system, the command `which python` should tell you the default installation. On a Windows system, you may have to go into the folder options dialog and see what application `.py` files are assigned to. If wxPython is correctly installed for that Python version, it puts itself in the `<python-home>/Lib/site-packages` subdirectory. You will likely need to install or reinstall wxPython.

Symptom   *The application crashes immediately on startup, or a blank window is displayed, followed immediately by an application crash.*

Cause—A wxPython object is created or used before the creation of the `wx.App`.

Solution—Create the `wx.App` object immediately on starting your script.

Symptom   *My top-level windows are created and immediately close. The application exits immediately.*

Cause—The method `wx.App.MainLoop()` was not called.

Solution—Call the `MainLoop()` method after all your setup is complete.

Symptom   *My top-level windows are created and immediately close. The application exits immediately, and I did call `MainLoop()`.*

Cause—An error in your application's `OnInit()` method, or some method called by it (such as a frame `__init__()` method).

Solution—An error before `MainLoop()` is called can trigger an exception that exits the program. If your application is set to redirect `stdout` and `stderr` to windows, then those windows will not display long enough for you to see the error. Create your application object with the `redirect=False` option to allow you to see the error message. See the section "Redirecting Output" for more details.

2.9 Summary

- The foundation of a wxPython program is based on two required objects: an application object and the top-level window. Every wxPython application needs to instantiate one instance of `wx.App`, and have at least one top-level window.

- The application object contains the `wx.App.OnInit()` method, which is called on startup. This method is the preferred place to initialize frames and other global objects. A wxPython application normally shuts down when all of its top-level windows have closed, or when the main event loop is otherwise exited.

- The application object also controls where wxPython directs textual output. By default, wxPython redirects `stdout` and `stderr` to a special window. This behavior can make it hard to troubleshoot startup errors. Luckily, it's no trouble at all to change this behavior to allow wxPython to send error messages to a file or console window.

  35-6

- A wxPython application usually has at least one subclass of `wx.Frame`. A `wx.Frame` object can be created in multiple styles using the `style` parameter. Every wxWidgets object, including frames, has an ID, which can be explicitly assigned by the application or generated by wxPython. Subwindows are the meat of a frame, inserted into a frame by creating the subwindow with that frame as a parent. Usually, a frame contains a single `wx.Panel` and further subwindows are placed in the panel. A frame's single subwindow is automatically resized when the parent frame resizes. Frames have explicit mechanisms for managing a menubar, toolbar, and status bar.

  44

- Although you'll use frames for anything complex, when you want to simply get quick information from a user, you can show the user a standard dialog window. There are standard dialogs for many tasks, including an alert box, simple text entry, and entry from a list.

Now that we've talked about the foundation of a wxPython program in terms of the required data objects, we'll start to talk about the basic blocks of a wxPython program as it manages the flow of control while running. In the next chapter, we'll talk about events and the event loop.

Working in an
event-driven environment

This chapter covers

- Programming in an event-driven environment
- Binding an event to a handler
- Processing events using wxPython
- Defining other application object event properties
- Creating custom events

Event handling is the fundamental mechanism that makes wxPython programs work. A program that works primarily via event handling is called *event driven*. In this chapter, we will discuss what an event-driven application is, and how it differs from a traditional application. We'll provide an overview of the concepts and terminology involved in GUI programming, covering the interaction between the user, the toolkit, and the program logic. We'll also cover the lifecycle of a typical event-driven program.

An *event* is something that happens in your system which your application can respond to by triggering functionality. The event can be a low-level user action, such as a mouse move or key press, or a higher level user action given a specific meaning by wxPython because it takes place inside a wxPython widget, such as a button click or a menu selection. The event can also be created by the underlying operating system, such as a request to shut down. You can even create your own objects to generate your own events. A wxPython application works by associating a specific kind of event with a specific piece of code, which should be executed in response. The process by which events are mapped to code is called event handling.

This chapter will show what an event is, how you write code to respond to an event, and how the wxPython system knows to invoke your code when the event is triggered. We'll also show you how to add custom events to the wxPython library, which contains a listing of standard events for user and system activities.

3.1 What terminology do I need to understand events?

This chapter contains a lot of terminology, much of which begins with the word *event*. Table 3.1 is a quick reference guide to the terms we'll be using.

Table 3.1   Event terms

Term	Definition
event	Something that happens during your application that requires a response.
event object	The concrete representation of an event in wxPython including data attributes that encapsulate the specifics of the event. Events are represented as instances of the `wx.Event` class and its subclasses, such as `wx.CommandEvent` and `wx.MouseEvent`.

continued on next page

Table 3.1   Event terms *(continued)*

Term	Definition
event type	An integer ID that wxPython adds to every event object. The event type gives further information about the nature of the event. For example, the event type of a `wx.MouseEvent` indicates whether the event is a mouse click or a mouse move.
event source	Any wxPython object that creates events. Examples are buttons, menu items, list boxes, or any other widget.
event-driven	A program structure where the bulk of time is spent waiting for, or responding to, events.
event queue	A continuously maintained list of events that have already occurred, but have not yet been processed.
event handler	A written function or method that is called in response to an event. Also called a *handler function* or *handler method*.
event binder	A wxPython object that encapsulates the relationship between a specific widget, a specific event type, and an event handler. In order to be invoked, all event handlers must be registered with an event binder.
`wx.EvtHandler`	A wxPython class that allows its instances to create a binding between an event binder of a specific type, an event source, and an event handler. Note that the class `wx.EvtHandler` is not the same thing as an event handler function or method defined previously.

[handwritten margin notes: binder: encapsulates relationship: widget (event source), event type, handler; a separate event binder for each event type; Bind(binder, handler, widget) "fills in" the info in O's]

We hope this table will keep you from getting your event handlers mixed up with your event binders. Please refer to this table throughout the chapter as necessary. We'll begin with a general overview of event-driving programming, and then we'll discuss the specifics of how everything is managed in wxPython.

3.2   *What is event-driven programming?*

An event-driven program is mainly a control structure that receives events and responds to them. The structure of a wxPython program (or of any event-driven program) is fundamentally different from that of an ordinary Python script. A typical Python script has a specific starting point and a specific ending point, and the programmer controls the order of execution using conditionals, loops, and functions. The program is not linear, but its order is often independent of user action.

From the users perspective, a wxPython program spends much of its time doing nothing. Typically, it is idle until the user or the system does something to

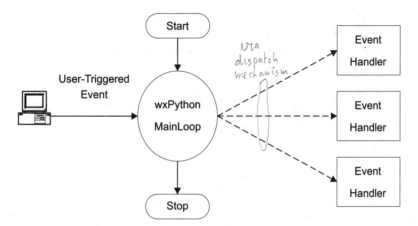

Figure 3.1 A schematic of the event handling cycle, showing the life of the main program, a user event, and dispatch to handler functions.

trigger the wxPython program into action. The wxPython program structure is an example of an event-driven program architecture. Figure 3.1 shows a simple diagram outlining the major parts of an event-driven program.

Think of the main loop of an event-driven system as analogous to an operator at a customer service call center. When no calls are coming in, the operator is, as they say, standing by. Eventually, an event occurs, such as the phone ringing. The operator initiates a response process, which involves talking to the customer until the operator has enough information to dispatch the customer to the proper respondent for her call. The operator then waits for the next event.

Although each event-driven system is somewhat different, there are many similarities between them. The primary characteristics of an event-driven program structure are as follows:

- After the initial setup, the program spends most of its time in an idle loop, where it does little or no information processing. Entering into this loop signifies the beginning of the user-interactive part of the program, and exiting the loop signifies its end. In wxPython, this loop is the method `wx.App.MainLoop()`, and is explicitly invoked in your script. The main loop is automatically exited when all top-level windows are closed.

- The program contains events that correspond to things that happen in the program environment. Events are typically triggered by user activity, but can also be the result of system activity, or arbitrary code elsewhere in the program. In wxPython, all events are instances of the class `wx.Event` or one of its subclasses. Each event has an event type attribute (see table 3.1) that allows different kinds of events to be distinguished. For example, a mouse up and mouse down event are both delivered as instances of the same class, but have a different event type.

- As part of the idle loop, the program periodically checks to see whether anything requiring a response has happened. There are two mechanisms by which an event-driven system may be notified about events. The more popular method, used by wxPython, posts the events to a central queue, which triggers processing of that event. Other event-driven systems use a polling method, where possible raisers of events are periodically queried by the central process and asked if they have any events pending.

- When an event takes place, the event-based system processes the event in an attempt to determine what code, if any, should be executed. In wxPython, native system events are translated to `wx.Event` instances and then given to the method `wx.EvtHandler.ProcessEvent()` for dispatching out to the proper handler code. Figure 3.3 presents a basic overview of the process. The component parts of the event mechanism are event binder objects and event handlers, both defined in table 3.1. An event binder is a predefined wxPython object. There is a separate event binder for each event type. An event handler is a function or method that takes a wxPython event instance as an argument. An event handler is invoked when the user triggers the appropriate event.

Next, we'll discuss more details about wxPython, beginning with the basic unit of event response, the event handler.

3.2.1 Coding event handlers

In your wxPython code, events and event handlers are managed on a widget-by-widget basis. For example, a button click is dispatched to a particular handler based on the button that was clicked. In order to bind an event from a specific widget to a specific handler method, you use a binder object to manage the connection. For example,

```
self.Bind(wx.EVT_BUTTON, self.OnClick, aButton)
```

uses the predefined event binder object `wx.EVT_BUTTON` to associate a button click event on the object `aButton` with the method `self.OnClick`. The `Bind()` method is a method of `wx.EvtHandler`, which is a parent class of all display objects. Therefore, the example line of code can be placed in any display class.

Even as your wxPython program appears to be waiting passively for an event, it's still doing something. Specifically, it's running the method `wx.App.Main-Loop()`, which is basically an infinite `while` loop. The `MainLoop()` can be translated into oversimplified Python pseudocode as:

```
while True:
    while not self.Pending():          @ 77
        self.ProcessIdle()
    self.DoMessage()
```

In other words, if there is no message pending, do some idle processing until a message comes in, then dispatch the message to the appropriate event-handling method.

3.2.2 *Designing for event-driven programs*

The event-driven nature of a wxPython program has several implications for designing and coding. Since there is no longer an assumption about when events happen, the programmer cedes much of the control of the program to the user. Most of the code in your wxPython program is executed as the direct or indirect result of an action taken by the user or the system. For example, saving work in your program happens after the user selects a menu item, presses a toolbar button, or invokes a special key combination. Any of these events can trigger a handler which saves the user's work.

Another consequence of an event-driven architecture is that the architecture is often somewhat spread out. The code that is called in response to an event is usually not defined by the widget that triggered the event. Or to clarify, there's nothing in the nature of the binding between an event and its handler that requires them to have any relationship at all. For instance, the code called in response to a button click doesn't have to be part of the definition of the button, but can be in the button's enclosing frame, or any other location. When combined with a solid object-oriented design, this architecture can lead to loosely coupled, highly reusable code. You'll find that the flexible nature of Python makes it particularly easy to reuse common event handlers and structures between different wxPython applications. On the other hand, the uncoupled nature of an event-driven program can make it difficult to follow and maintain. When an event click happens in a button tied to a binder listed in the frame code, and the event invokes a method in a model class, it can be difficult to track it down. (To some extent, this issue is true of all object-oriented programming). In chapter 5, we will discuss code structuring guidelines for event-driven programs.   115

3.2.3 *Event triggers*

In wxPython, most widgets cause higher level events to be fired in response to lower level events. For example, a mouse click within the space of a wx.Button causes the generation of an EVT_BUTTON event, which is a specific type of wx.Command-Event. Similarly, a mouse drag in the corner of a window causes a wx.SizeEvent to be created automatically for you by wxPython. The advantage of these higher level events is that they make it easier for the rest of your system to focus on the most relevant events, rather than getting bogged down in tracking every mouse click. For example, saying that a mouse click is a button activation makes it clear that a particular click has contextual meaning in the system, whereas another mouse click may not contain contextual meaning. Higher level events can also encapsulate more useful information about the event. As you create your own custom widgets, you can define your own custom events to manage this process for you.

Events are represented within wxPython by objects. Specifically, event objects in wxPython are instances of the class wx.Event, or one of its subclasses. The parent wx.Event class is a relatively small abstract class consisting of getters and setters for a few properties common to all events, such as EventType, EventObject, and Timestamp. Different subclasses of wx.Event each add further information. For example, wx.MouseEvent contains information about the exact location of the mouse as the event happened, and information about which mouse button was clicked, if any.

There are several different subclasses of wx.Event in wxPython. Table 3.2 contains a list of some of the event classes you will most often encounter. Remember, one event class can have multiple event types, each corresponding to a different user action.

Table 3.2   Important subclasses of wx.Event

Event	Description
wx.CloseEvent	Triggered when a frame closes. The event type distinguishes between a normal frame closing and a system shutdown event.
wx.CommandEvent	Triggered by a wide variety of simple interactions with widgets, such as a button click, menu item selection, or radio button selection. Each of these separate actions has its own event type. Many more complex widgets, such as the list or grid controls, define subclasses of wx.CommandEvent. Command events are treated differently by the event handling system than by other events.

continued on next page

Table 3.2 Important subclasses of wx.Event *(continued)*

Event	Description
wx.KeyEvent	A key press event. The event types distinguish between key down, key up, and complete key press.
wx.MouseEvent	A mouse event. The event types distinguish between a mouse move and a mouse click. There are separate event types depending on which button is clicked and whether it's a single or double click.
wx.PaintEvent	Triggered when a window's contents need to be redrawn.
wx.SizeEvent	This event is triggered when a window is resized, and typically results in a change to the window layout.
wx.TimerEvent	Can be created by the wx.Timer class, which allows periodic events.

Typically, event objects do very little on their own, but instead, need to be passed to the relevant event handler method or methods using an event binder and an event processing system.

3.3 How do I bind an event to a handler?

Event binders consist of instances of the class wx.PyEventBinder. A predefined instance of wx.PyEventBinder is provided for all of the event types supported, and you can create your own event binders for your custom event types when needed. There is one event binder instance for each event type, which means that multiple binders may correspond to any one wx.Event subclass.[1] This is because event types are more detailed than wx.Event subclasses. For example, the wx.Mouse-Event class has fourteen separate event types, each of which uses the same basic information about the state of the mouse when the event is triggered by a user action (i.e., left click, right click, double click).

In wxPython, names of the event binder instances are global. In order to clearly associate event types with handlers, these names start with wx.EVT_ and correspond to the names of the macros used in the C++ wxWidgets code. When discussing wxPython code, the tendency is to use the wx.EVT_ binder name as a stand-in for the actual event type. As a result, it's worth highlighting that the value of the wx.EVT binder name is not the actual integer code used for event typing that you'd receive by calling the GetEventType() method of a wx.Event instance. Event-type integer codes have an entirely different set of global names, and are not often used in practice.

1 Associated with an event there may be many event types
   Associated with an event type is a single binder

As an example of the wx.EVT names, let's look at the event types of wx.Mouse-Event. As we just mentioned, there are fourteen of them, nine of which cover mouse down, mouse up, or double click events based on the button clicked. Those nine event types use the following names:

```
wx.EVT_LEFT_DOWN
wx.EVT_LEFT_UP
wx.EVT_LEFT_DCLICK
wx.EVT_MIDDLE_DOWN
wx.EVT_MIDDLE_UP
wx.EVT_MIDDLE_DCLICK
wx.EVT_RIGHT_DOWN
wx.EVT_RIGHT_UP
wx.EVT_RIGHT_DCLICK
```

(binders)

 # event types of wx. Mouse Event

Also

WX. EVT-MOTION
WX. ENTER-WINDOW
WX. LEAVE-WINDOW
WX. EVT- MOUSEWHEEL
WX. EVT_MOUSE_EVENTS

Additionally, the type wx.EVT_MOTION is caused by the user moving the mouse. The types wx.ENTER_WINDOW and wx.LEAVE_WINDOW are caused when the mouse enters or leaves any widget. The wx.EVT_MOUSEWHEEL type is bound to the movement of a mouse scroll wheel. Finally, you can bind all mouse events to a single function at one time using the wx.EVT_MOUSE_EVENTS type.

Similarly, the wx.CommandEvent class has 28 different event types associated with it; although several are only for older Windows operating systems. Most of these are specific to a single widget, such as wx.EVT_BUTTON for a button click, and wx.EVT_MENU for a menu item selection. Command events for specific widgets are described with that widget when it is discussed in part 2.

The advantage of this binding mechanism is that it allows wxPython to dispatch events on a very granular basis, while still allowing similar events to be instances of the same class, and to share data and functionality. This makes writing event handlers much cleaner in wxPython than in other interface toolkits.

Event binders are used to connect a wxPython widget with an event object and a handler function. This connection allows the wxPython system to respond to an event on that widget by executing the code in the handler function. In wxPython, any object which can respond to an event is a subclass of wx.EvtHandler. All window objects are a subclass of wx.EvtHandler, so every widget in a wxPython application can respond to events. The wx.EvtHandler class can also be used by non-widget objects, such as wx.App, so event handling functionality is not limited to displayable widgets. To clarify the terminology, saying that a widget can respond to events means that the widget can create event bindings which wxPython recognizes during dispatch. The actual code called by a binder in the event handler function is not necessarily located in a wx.EvtHandler class.

3.3.1 *Working with the wx.EvtHandler methods*

The wx.EvtHandler class defines a number of methods that are not called under normal circumstances. The method of wx.EvtHandler that you will use frequently is Bind(), which creates the event bindings that we've discussed so far. The method signature is:

```
Bind(event, handler, source=None, id=wx.ID_ANY, id2=wx.ID_ANY)
```

The Bind() function associates an event and an object with an event handler function. The event parameter is required, and is a wx.PyEventBinder instance as described in section 3.3. The handler argument, also required, is a Python callable object, usually a bound method or function. The handler must be callable with a single argument, the event object itself. The handler argument can also be None, in which case the event is disassociated from its current handler. The source parameter is the widget that is the source of the event. The parameter is used when the widget triggering the event is not the same as the widget being used as the event handler. Typically, this is done because you're using a custom wx.Frame class as the handler and are binding events from the widgets contained in the frame. The parent window's __init__ is a convenient location for declaring the event bindings. However, if the parent window contains more than one source of button click events (i.e., the OK button and Cancel button), the source parameter is used to allow wxPython to differentiate between them. Following is a specific example of this method:

```
self.Bind(wx.EVT_BUTTON, self.OnClick, button)
```

The call binds a button event from the object named button (and only the object named button) to the OnClick() method of the instance being bound. Listing 3.1, adapted from code displayed in chapter 2, illustrates event binding both with and without a source parameter. You are not required to name your handler methods On<event>, but it is a common convention.

Listing 3.1 Sample event binding both with and without source objects

```
def __init__(self, parent, id):
    wx.Frame.__init__(self, parent, id, 'Frame With Button',
            size=(300, 100))
    panel = wx.Panel(self, -1)
    button = wx.Button(panel, -1, "Close", pos=(130, 15),
            size=(40, 40))
    self.Bind(wx.EVT_CLOSE, self.OnCloseWindow)
    self.Bind(wx.EVT_BUTTON, self.OnCloseMe, button)
```

❶ Binding the frame close event

❷ Binding the button event

```
def OnCloseMe(self, event):
    self.Close(True)

def OnCloseWindow(self, event):
    self.Destroy()
```

❶ This line binds the frame close event to the `self.OnCloseWindow` method. Since the event is both triggered by and bound by the frame, there is no need to pass a source argument.

❷ This line binds the button click event from the button object to the `self.OnCloseMe` method. In this case, the button which generates the event is not the same as the frame which is binding it. Therefore, the button ID must be passed to the `Bind` method to allow wxPython to distinguish between click events on this button and click events from other buttons in the frame.

You can also use the source parameter to identify items even if the item is not the source of the event. For example, you can bind a menu event to the event handler even though the menu event is technically triggered by the frame. Listing 3.2 illustrates an example of binding a menu event.

Listing 3.2   Binding a menu event

```
#!/usr/bin/env python

import wx

class MenuEventFrame(wx.Frame):

    def __init__(self, parent, id):
        wx.Frame.__init__(self, parent, id, 'Menus',
            size=(300, 200))
        menuBar = wx.MenuBar()
        menu1 = wx.Menu()
        menuItem = menu1.Append(-1, "&Exit...")     # append menu item to menu
        menuBar.Append(menu1, "&File")              # append menu to menu bar
        self.SetMenuBar(menuBar)                    # Set menu bar on Frame
        self.Bind(wx.EVT_MENU, self.OnCloseMe, menuItem)
                                                      ↑ source
    def OnCloseMe(self, event):
        self.Close(True)

if __name__ == '__main__':
    app = wx.PySimpleApp()
    frame = MenuEventFrame(parent=None, id=-1)
    frame.Show()
    app.MainLoop()
```

The id and id2 parameters of the Bind() method specify the source of the event using an ID number, rather than the widget itself. Typically, the id and id2 are not required, since the ID of the event source can be extracted from the source parameter. However, at times using the ID directly does make sense. For example, if you are using predefined ID numbers for a dialog box, it's easier to use the ID number than to use the widget. If you use both the id and id2 numbers, you can bind an entire range of widgets to the event with numbers between the two IDs. This is only useful if the IDs of the widgets you want to bind are sequential.

OLDER EVENT BINDING The Bind() method is new in wxPython 2.5. In previous versions of wxPython, the EVT_* name is used like a function object, so that a binding call would appear as follows:

```
wx.EVT_BUTTON(self, self.button.GetId(), self.OnClick)
```

The disadvantage of the older style is that it does not look or act like an object-oriented method call. However, the older style still works in 2.5 (because the wx.EVT* objects are still callable), so you'll still see it in wxPython code.

Table 3.3 lists some of the most commonly used methods of wx.EvtHandler that you may call to manipulate the process of handling events.

Table 3.3 Commonly used methods of wx.EvtHandler

Method	Description
AddPendingEvent(event)	Places the event argument into the event processing system. Similar to ProcessEvent(), but it does not actually trigger immediate processing of the event. Instead, the event is added to the event queue. Useful for event-based communication between threads.
Bind(event, handler, source=None, id=wx.ID_ANY, id2=wx.ID_ANY)	See full description in section 3.3.1.
GetEvtHandlerEnabled() SetEvtHandlerEnabled(boolean)	The property is True if the handler is currently processing events, False if otherwise.
ProcessEvent(event)	Puts the event object into the event processing system for immediate handling.

3.4 *How are events processed by wxPython?*

A key component of an event-based system is the process by which an event that comes into the system is dispatched to the piece of code that is executed in response. In this section, we'll walk through the procedure wxPython uses when processing an incoming event. We'll use a small code snippet as an example

Figure 3.2 A simple window with mouse events

to trace the steps in the process. Figure 3.2 displays a sample window with a single button, which will be used to generate the sample events.

Listing 3.3 contains the code that generated this window. In this code, wxPython events are generated both by clicking the button and by moving the mouse over the button.

Listing 3.3 Binding multiple kinds of mouse events

```
#!/usr/bin/env python

import wx

class MouseEventFrame(wx.Frame):

    def __init__(self, parent, id):
        wx.Frame.__init__(self, parent, id, 'Frame With Button',
                size=(300, 100))
        self.panel = wx.Panel(self)
        self.button = wx.Button(self.panel,
            label="Not Over", pos=(100, 15))
        self.Bind(wx.EVT_BUTTON, self.OnButtonClick,     ❶ Binding the
            self.button)            # bound by frame        button event
        self.button.Bind(wx.EVT_ENTER_WINDOW,
            self.OnEnterWindow)     # bound by button
        self.button.Bind(wx.EVT_LEAVE_WINDOW,            ❷ Binding the mouse
            self.OnLeaveWindow)                            enter event
    def OnButtonClick(self, event):      ❸ Binding the mouse
        self.panel.SetBackgroundColour('Green')  leave event
        self.panel.Refresh()

    def OnEnterWindow(self, event):
        self.button.SetLabel("Over Me!")
        event.Skip()

    def OnLeaveWindow(self, event):
        self.button.SetLabel("Not Over")
        event.Skip()
```

```
if __name__ == '__main__':
    app = wx.PySimpleApp()
    frame = MouseEventFrame(parent=None, id=-1)
    frame.Show()
    app.MainLoop()
```

The MouseEventFrame contains one button in the middle. Clicking on the mouse changes the background color of the frame to green. The mouse click event is bound to the action in line ❶. When the mouse pointer enters the button, the button caption changes, as bound in line ❷. When the mouse pointer leaves the button, the caption changes back, as bound in line ❸.

Looking at the mouse event example raises some questions about event processing in wxPython. In line ❶, the button event triggered by the button is bound by the frame. How does wxPython know to look for a binding in the frame object, rather than the button object? In lines ❷ and ❸, the mouse enter and leave events are bound to the button object. Why can't those events also be bound to the frame? Both of these questions are answered by examining the procedure wxPython uses to determine how to respond to an event.

3.4.1 *Understanding the event handling process*

The wxPython event handling procedure was designed to make it simple for the programmer to create event bindings in what are generally the most obvious places, while ignoring unimportant events. As is often the case in simple design, the underlying mechanism is actually a bit complex. Next, we'll trace the procedure for a button click event and a mouse entering event.

Figure 3.3 displays a basic flow chart of event handling process. Rectangles indicate the start and end of the process, circles indicate various wxPython objects that are part of the process, diamonds indicate decision points, and rectangles with bars indicate actual event handler methods.

The event process begins with the object that triggered the event. Typically, wxPython looks first at the triggering object for a bound handler function matching the event type. If one is found, the method is executed. If not, wxPython checks to see if the event propagates up the container hierarchy. If so, the parent widget is checked, up the hirerarchy, until wxPython either finds a handler function or hits a top-level object. If the event doesn't propagate, wxPython still checks the application object for a handler method before finishing. When an event handler is run, the process typically ends. However, the function can tell wxPython to continue searching for handlers.

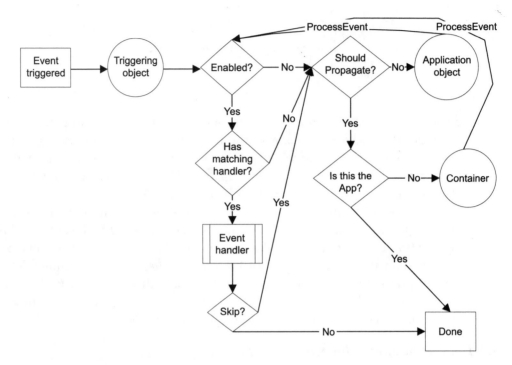

Figure 3.3   Event handling process, starting with the event being triggered, and moving through the steps of searching for a handler

Let's take a closer look at each step of the process. Before discussing each step, we'll display a thumbnail for each relevant part of Figure 3.3.

Step 1 Creating the event

The process starts when the event is created.

Most pre-existing event types are created within the wxPython framework in response to specific user actions or system notifications. For example, the mouse entering event is triggered when wxPython notices a mouse move entering the bounds of a new widget

Figure 3.4   Creation of the event that sends focus to the triggering object

object, and the button click event is created after a left mouse down and left mouse up in the same button.

The event is first handed to the object responsible for creating the event. For a button click, the object is the button, for a mouse enter event, the object is the widget entered.

Step 2 *Determining whether the object is allowed to process events*

The next step of the event handling process checks to see if the responsible widget (the `wx.EvtHandler`) is currently allowed to process events.

A window can be set to allow or disallow event processing by calling the `wx.EvtHandler` method `SetEvtHandlerEnabled(boolean)`. The effect of disallowing event processing is that the widget is completely bypassed in the event process, binding objects associated with the object are not searched for, and the processing in this step goes down the *no* branch.

Enabling or disabling a widget at the event handler level is not the same as disabling the widget at the UI level. Disabling a widget at the UI level is done using the `wx.Window` method `Disable()` and `Enable()`. Disabling a widget in the UI sense means that the user cannot interact with the disabled widget. Usually, the disabled widget is grayed out on the screen to indicate its status. A window that has been disabled at the UI level won't be able to generate any events; however, if it's on the container hierarchy for other events, it still processes events it receives. For the remainder of this section, we'll use enabled and disabled in the `wx.EvtHandler` sense, referring to whether the widget is allowed to process events.

The check for the enabled/disabled state of the initiating object happens in the `ProcessEvent()` method which is called by the wxPython system to start and handle the event dispatch mechanism. We'll see the `ProcessEvent()` method again and again during this process—it's the method in the `wx.EvtHandler` class that actually implements much of the event process depicted in figure 3.3. The `ProcessEvent()` method returns `True` if event processing is complete at the end of the method. Processing is considered complete if a handler function is found for the instance and event combination being processed. The handler function can explicitly request further processing by calling the `wx.Event` method `Skip()`. In addition, if the initiating object is a subclass of `wx.Window`, it can filter the event

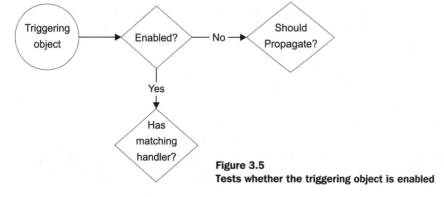

Figure 3.5
Tests whether the triggering object is enabled

using a special object called a *validator*. Validators will be discussed in more detail in chapter 9. 282

Step 3 Locating the binder object

The `ProcessEvent()` method then looks for a binder object that recognizes a binding between the event type and the current object.

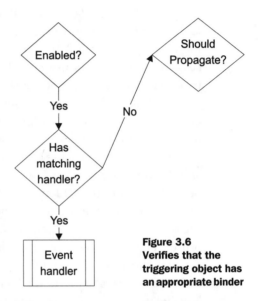

   If a binder isn't found for the object itself, the processing walks up the class hierarchy to find a binder defined in a superclass of the object—this is different than the walk up in the container hierarchy that happens in the next step. If a binder object is found, wxPython calls the associated handler function. After the handler is called, event processing stops for that event, unless the handler function explicitly asks for more processing.

**Figure 3.6
Verifies that the
triggering object has
an appropriate binder**

   In listing 3.3, the mouse enter event is captured, and because there is a defined binding between the button object, the binder object `wx.EVT_ENTER_WINDOW`, and the associated method `OnEnterWindow()`, the method is called. Since we don't bind the mouse button click event, `wx.EVT_LEFT_DOWN`, wxPython would keep searching in that case.

Step 4 Determining whether to continue processing

After calling the first event handler, wxPython checks to see if further processing is requested. The event handler asks for more processing by calling the `wx.Event` method `Skip()`. If the `Skip()` method is called, processing continues and any handlers defined in the superclass are found and executed in this step. The `Skip()` method can be called at any point in the handler, or any code invoked by the handler. The `Skip()` method sets a flag in the event instance, which wxPy-

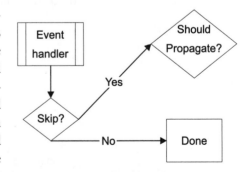

Figure 3.7 The event handler calls `Skip()`, and processing continues

thon checks after the handler method is complete. In listing 3.3 the OnButton-Click() doesn't call Skip(), so in that case the event process is complete at the end of the handler method. The other two event handlers do call Skip() so the system will keep searching for a matching event binding, eventually invoking the default functionality for mouse enter and leave events for the native widget, such as mouse-over events.

Step 5 Determining whether to propagate

Eventually wxPython determines whether the event process should propagate up the container hierarchy to find an event handler. The container hierarchy is the path from a specific widget to the top-level frame, moving from each widget to its parent container, and upward.

If the current object doesn't have a handler for the event, or if the handler called Skip(), wxPython determines if the event should propogate up the container hierarchy. If the answer is No, the process looks once more for a handler, in the wx.App instance, and then stops. If the answer is Yes, the event process starts over using the container of the window currently being searched. The process continues upward until wxPython either finds an appropriate binding, reaches a

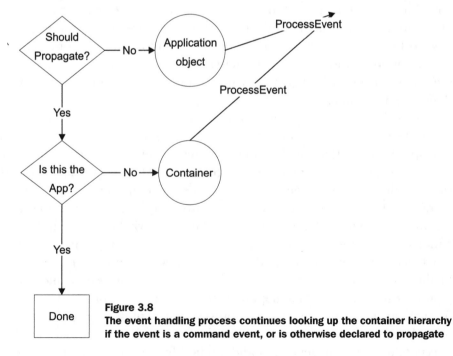

Figure 3.8
The event handling process continues looking up the container hierarchy
if the event is a command event, or is otherwise declared to propagate

top-level frame object with no parent, or reaches a wx.Dialog object (even if the dialog is not top-level). The event is considered to have found an appropriate binding if ProcessEvent() for that object returns True, indicating that processing is complete. The rationale for stopping at a wx.Dialog is to prevent the parent frame from being hit by spurious events coming from dialog boxes that are unrelated and unexpected.

Whether an event should propagate up the container hierarchy is a dynamic property of each event instance, although in practice the default values are almost always the ones used. By default, only instances of wx.CommandEvent, or any subclass thereof, propagate up the container hierarchy. All other events do not.

In listing 3.3, this is where the button click gets handled. Clicking the mouse on the wx.Button generates a wx.EVT_BUTTON type of command event. Since the wx.EVT_ BUTTON is a wx.CommandEvent, after wxPython fails to find a binding in the button object, it looks to the parent, which in this case is the panel. Since there is no matching binding in the panel, the panel's parent, the frame, is checked next. Since the frame does have a matching binding, ProcessEvent() calls the appropriate function, in this case OnButtonClick().

Step 5 also explains why the mouse enter and mouse leave events need to be bound to the button and not to the frame. Since mouse events are not a subclass of wx.CommandEvent, the mouse enter and mouse leave events do not propagate upward to the parent, thus wxPython cannot find a binding from the button's mouse enter event to the frame. If there is a mouse enter or leave event bound to the frame, the event is triggered by wxPython when the mouse enters or leaves the frame as a whole.

Command events are privileged in this way because they are intended to be higher level events indicating that the user is doing something in the application space, rather than in the window system. The assumption is that window system type events are only of interest to the widget that initially receives them, while application-level events may be of interest higher up in the containment hierarchy. This rule does not prevent us from declaring the binding an event anywhere, no matter what object is being bound or what object defines the event handler. For example, even though the mouse click event binding is to the button object, the binding itself is defined inside the frame class, and calls a method of the frame class. In other words, low-level non-command events are typically used for things that happen *to* the widget or for some system level notification, such as a mouse click, key press, paint request, size, or move. On the other hand, command events, such as a mouse click on a button or a list box selection, are typically generated and emitted by the widget itself. For example, button command events are generated after a mouse down and mouse up event on the appropriate widget.

Finally, if the event is not handled after walking through the containment hierarchy, ProcessEvent() is called on the wx.App object for the application. By default, this does nothing, however, you can add event bindings to your wx.App to route events in some non-standard way. For example, if you were writing a GUI builder, you may want events in your builder window to propagate to your code window, even though they are both top-level windows. One way of doing that is to capture the events in the application object and pass them on to the code window.

3.4.2 *Using the Skip() method*

The first handler function found for an event halts processing on that event *unless* the Skip() method of the event is called before the handler returns. Calling Skip() allows additional handler bindings to be searched for, following the rules described in step 4 of 3.4.1, so parent classes and parent windows are searched just as if the first handler didn't exist. In some cases, you want the event to continue processing to allow the default behavior in the native widget to be executed along with your custom handler. Listing 3.4 displays a Skip() example that allows the program to respond to both a left button down event and a button click in the same button.

Listing 3.4 Response to a mouse down and button click at the same time

```python
#!/usr/bin/env python

import wx

class DoubleEventFrame(wx.Frame):

    def __init__(self, parent, id):
        wx.Frame.__init__(self, parent, id, 'Frame With Button',
              size=(300, 100))
        self.panel = wx.Panel(self, -1)
        self.button = wx.Button(self.panel, -1, "Click Me", pos=(100, 15))
        self.Bind(wx.EVT_BUTTON, self.OnButtonClick,        ❶ Binding the button
            self.button)                                         click event
        self.button.Bind(wx.EVT_LEFT_DOWN, self.OnMouseDown)
                          Binding the left button down event ❷
    def OnButtonClick(self, event):
        self.panel.SetBackgroundColour('Green')
        self.panel.Refresh()
```

```
def OnMouseDown(self, event):
    self.button.SetLabel("Again!")
    event.Skip()                    ◁┐  ❸  Skip() ensures
                                            more processing
if __name__ == '__main__':
    app = wx.PySimpleApp()
    frame = DoubleEventFrame(parent=None, id=-1)
    frame.Show()
    app.MainLoop()
```

❶ This line binds the button click event to the `OnButtonClick()` handler, which changes the background color of the frame.

❷ This line binds the left mouse button down event to the `OnMouseDown()` handler, which changes the label text of the button. Since left button down is not a command event, this event must be bound to the button rather than the frame.

When the user clicks the mouse over the button, the left button down event is generated first, by direct interaction with the underlying operating system. Under normal circumstances, the left button down event changes the state of the button such that the subsequent left button up event creates a `wx.EVT_BUTTON` click event. The `DoubleEventFrame` preserves this processing but *only* because of the `Skip()` statement in line ❸. Without the `Skip()` statement, the event processing algorithm finds the binding created in line ❷, and stops before the button can generate the `wx.EVT_BUTTON` event. With the `Skip()` call, event processing continues normally and the button click is created.

In this example, there is nothing particularly special about the choice of `wx.EVT_LEFT_DOWN` and `wx.EVT_BUTTON`. The same situation occurs whenever one handler is found in the same event process as another. For instance, changing the `wx.EVT_LEFT_DOWN` event to another `wx.EVT_BUTTON` event has the same effect. A `Skip()` call is still required for both handlers to be processed.

As far as event handling is concerned, the default behavior is first come, first served. To enable further event processing, you must call `Skip()`. Although this choice is made on a case by case basis, remember that when binding to lower level events like a mouse up/down, wxPython expects to catch those events in order to generate further events. If you don't call `Skip()` in that case, you run the risk of blocking expected behavior; for example, losing the visual notification that a button has been clicked.

3.5 What other event properties are contained in the application object?

To manage the main event loop more directly, you can modify it using some `wx.App` methods. For instance, you may want to start processing the next available event on your own schedule, rather than waiting for wxPython to begin processing. This feature is necessary if you are starting a long procedure, and don't want the GUI to appear to freeze. You won't need to use the methods in this section often, but it's occasionally important to have these capabilities.

Table 3.4 lists the `wx.App` methods you can use to modify the main loop.

Table 3.4 Event main loop methods of `wx.App`

Method Name	Method Description
Dispatch()	Programmatically forces the next event in the event queue to be sent. Used by `MainLoop()`, for example, or in customized event loops.
Pending()	Returns `True` if there are pending events in the wxPython application event queue.
Yield(onlyIfNeeded=False)	Allows pending wxWidgets events to be dispatched in the middle of a long process that might otherwise block the windowing system from displaying or updating. Returns `True` if there were pending events that were processed, `False` otherwise. If `True`, the `onlyIfNeeded` parameter forces the process to yield if there are actually pending events. If the argument is `False`, then it is an error to call `Yield` recursively. There is also a global function `wx.SafeYield()`, which prevents the user from inputting data during the yield (by temporarily disabling user-input widgets). This prevents the user from doing something that would violate the state needed by the yielding task.

Another method for managing events in a custom way is to create your own event types that match the specifics of your application's data and widgets. In the next section, we will discuss how to create your own custom events.

3.6 How can I create my own events?

Although a more advanced topic, this is the most obvious place to discuss custom events. On a first reading, you can probably skip it and come back later. In addition to different event classes supplied by wxPython, you can create your own custom events. You can do this in response to data updates or other changes that are specific to your application, where event instances are required to carry your custom data. Another reason to create a custom event class could be to support a custom widget with its own unique command event type. In the next section, we'll walk through an example of a custom widget.

3.6.1 *Defining a custom event for a custom widget*

Figure 3.9 displays the widget, a panel containing two buttons. The custom event, TwoButtonEvent, is triggered only after the user has clicked both buttons. The event contains a count of how many times the user has clicked on the widget. The idea here is to show how a new command event can be created out of smaller events—in this case, the left button down events on each individual button.

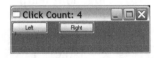

Figure 3.9 **The custom two-button widget. Clicking both buttons in succession triggers a change in the window title.**

To create a custom event:

1. Define the new event class as a subclass of the wxPython class wx.PyEvent. If you want the event to be treated like a command event, create the event as a subclass of wx.PyCommandEvent.^ Like many override situations in wxPython, the Py version of a class allows the wxWidgets system to see that a method written in Python can override the C++ method.

2. Create an event type and a binder object to bind the event to specific objects.

3. Add code that can build instances of the new event, and introduce the instances into the event processing system using the ProcessEvent() method. Once the event is created, you can create bindings and handler methods as you would with any other wxPython event. Listing 3.5 displays the code that manages the widget.

Listing 3.5 Building a custom two-button event widget

```
import wx

class TwoButtonEvent(wx.PyCommandEvent):      # event class
    def __init__(self, evtType, id):
        wx.PyCommandEvent.__init__(self, evtType, id)
        self.clickCount = 0

    def GetClickCount(self):
        return self.clickCount
```

❶ Defining the event

1 wx.CommandEvent   74

binder object

event source
source

event type   *event handler*

```
    def SetClickCount(self, count):
        self.clickCount = count
```
② **Generating an event type**
```
myEVT_TWO_BUTTON = wx.NewEventType()
EVT_TWO_BUTTON = wx.PyEventBinder(myEVT_TWO_BUTTON, 1)
```
    ③ **Creating a binder object**

79   *type*   *80*

```
class TwoButtonPanel(wx.Panel):
    def __init__(self, parent, id=-1, leftText="Left",
            rightText="Right"):
        wx.Panel.__init__(self, parent, id)
        self.leftButton = wx.Button(self, label=leftText)
        self.rightButton = wx.Button(self, label=rightText,
                                    pos=(100,0))
        self.leftClick = False
        self.rightClick = False
        self.clickCount = 0
```
Binding the lower level events **④**
```
        self.leftButton.Bind(wx.EVT_LEFT_DOWN, self.OnLeftClick)
        self.rightButton.Bind(wx.EVT_LEFT_DOWN, self.OnRightClick)

    def OnLeftClick(self, event):     # in response to L-clk on left button
        self.leftClick = True
        self.OnClick()
        event.Skip()
```
⑤ **Skip for more processing**
```
    def OnRightClick(self, event):    # in response to L-clk on right button
        self.rightClick = True
        self.OnClick()
        event.Skip()
```
⑥ **Skip for more processing**
```
    def OnClick(self):          # executed when left, right button pressed... may emit the
        self.clickCount += 1                          two button event
        if self.leftClick and self.rightClick:
            self.leftClick = False                Id of panel
            self.rightClick = False
```
Creating the custom event **⑦**
```
            evt = TwoButtonEvent(myEVT_TWO_BUTTON, self.GetId())
            evt.SetClickCount(self.clickCount)
```
← **Adding data to the event** *(changing event-state)*
```
            self.GetEventHandler().ProcessEvent(evt)
```
← **Processing the event** **⑧** *ie: "emit the event"*
```
class CustomEventFrame(wx.Frame):
    def __init__(self, parent, id):
        wx.Frame.__init__(self, parent, id, 'Click Count: 0',
                          size=(300, 100))
        panel = TwoButtonPanel(self)
```
Binding the custom event **⑨**
```
        self.Bind(EVT_TWO_BUTTON, self.OnTwoClick, panel)
```
binder obj   *handler*   *source is panel*
```
    def OnTwoClick(self, event):
        self.SetTitle("Click Count: %s" % event.GetClickCount())
```
Define an event handler function **⑩**
```
if __name__ == '__main__':
    app = wx.PySimpleApp()
```

```
frame = CustomEventFrame(parent=None, id=-1)
frame.Show()
app.MainLoop()
```

❶ The constructor for the event class declares it a subclass of wx.PyCommandEvent. The wx.PyEvent and wx.PyCommandEvent are wxPython-specific constructs you can use to create new event classes and should be used to bridge the gap between the C++ classes and your Python code. If you try to use wx.Event directly, wxPython cannot see the new methods of your subclass during event processing, because the C++ event handlers do not know about the Python subclass. If you use wx.PyEvent, a reference to the Python instances are saved and later passed to the event handler directly, allowing the Python parts of the code to be used.

❷ The global function wx.NewEventType() is analogous to wx.NewId(); it returns an event type ID that is guaranteed to be unique. This value uniquely identifies an event type for the event processing system.

❸ The binder object is created using the new event type as a parameter. The second parameter is between 0 and 2, and represents the number of wxId identifiers expected by the wx.EvtHandler.Bind() method to determine which object is the source of the event. In this case, there is one ID representing the widget that generates the command event.

❹ To create the new higher level command event, the program must respond to specific user events, for instance, left mouse down on each button object. Depending on which display button is clicked, the events are bound to the OnLeftClick() and OnRightClick() methods. The handlers set a Boolean, indicating that the button has been clicked.

❺ ❻ The Skip() call in this case allows for further processing after the event handler is complete. In this specific case, the new event does not require the skip call; it's dispatched before the handler method completes. However, all left down events need to call Skip() so that the handler does not block the eventual button click event. The button click event is not being handled by this program, but wxPython uses it to draw the button properly during a click. If it's blocked, the user does not get the expected feedback from a button push.

We chose not to bind to the wx.EVT_BUTTON event to show you what happens if you don't call Skip() in cases like this. To see the difference in behavior between these two buttons, comment out either line ❺ or ❻.

❼ If both left and right buttons are clicked, the code creates an instance of the new event. The event type and the ID of the two-button widget are the parameters of the constructor. Typically, a single event class can have more than one event type, although that's not the case in this example.

⑧ The `ProcessEvent()` call injects the new event into the event system for processing, as described in section 3.4.1. The `GetEventHandler()` call returns an instance of `wx.EvtHandler`. In most cases, the returned instance is the widget object itself, but if other `wx.EvtHandler()` methods have been pushed on to the event handler stack, the top item in the stack is returned instead.

⑨ The custom event is bound just like any other event, in this case using the binder object created in line **❸**.

⑩ The event handler function for this example changes the title of the window to display the new click count from the event.

At this point, your custom event can do anything pre-existing wxPython events can do, such as creating different widgets that trigger the same event. Creating events is an important part of the customization of wxPython.

3.7 *Summary*

- A wxPython application uses an event-based flow of control. Most of the application's time is spent in a main loop, waiting for events and dispatching them to the appropriate handler function.

- All wxPython events are subclasses of the class `wx.Event`. Lower level events, such as mouse clicks, are used to build up higher order events, such as button clicks or menu item selections. These higher order events that result from wxPython widgets are subclasses of the class `wx.CommandEvent`. Most event classes are further classified by an event type field which differentiates between events that may all use the same data set.

- To capture the relationship between events and functions, wxPython uses instances of the class `wx.PyEventBinder`. There are many predefined instances of this class, each corresponding to a specific event type. Every wxPython widget is a subclass of `wx.EvtHandler`. The `wx.EvtHandler` class has a method `Bind()`, which is usually called at initialization with an event binder instance and a handler function as arguments. Depending on the type of event, other wxPython object IDs may also need to be passed to the `Bind()` call.

- Events are generally sent to the object that generated them to search for a binding object which binds it to a handler. If the event is a command event, the event propagates upward through the container hierarchy until a widget is found that has a handler for the event type. Once an event handler is found, processing on that event stops, unless the handler calls the `Skip()` method of the event. You can use the `Skip()` method to allow multiple handlers to respond to a single event, or to verify that all the default behavior for the event occurs. Certain aspects of the main loop can be controlled using methods of wx.App.

- Custom events can be created in wxPython, and emitted as part of the behavior of a custom widget. Custom events are subclasses of wx.PyEvent, custom command events are subclasses of wx.PyCommandEvent. To create a custom event, the new class must be defined, and a binder object must be created for each event type managed by the new class. Finally, the event must be generated somewhere in the system by passing a new instance to the event handler system via the ProcessEvent() method.

In this chapter, we've covered the application objects that are most important to your wxPython application. In the next chapter, we'll show you a useful tool, written using wxPython, that will also assist you with wxPython development work.

Making wxPython easier to handle with PyCrust

This chapter covers

- Interacting with a wxPython program
- Reviewing the features of PyCrust
- Wrapping PyCrust around a wxPython application
- Working with PyCrust GUI and support modules
- Interacting with modules from PyCrust in wxPython programs

PyCrust is a graphical shell program, written in wxPython, that you can use to help analyze your wxPython programs.

Why call it PyCrust? When Patrick O'Brien created an interactive Python shell using wxPython, the most obvious name—PyShell—was already in use. PyCrust was chosen instead.

PyCrust is part of a larger Py package that includes additional programs with related functionality including PyFilling, PyAlaMode, PyAlaCarte, and PyShell. The common theme of these programs is the combination of a graphical, point-and-click environment, and wxPython's interactive and introspective runtime features. While each of the Py programs leverage this combination, PyCrust represents the most complete realization of this theme.

In this chapter, we'll show you what PyCrust and its related programs do, and how you can use them to make your work with wxPython flow more smoothly. We'll start by talking about ordinary Python shells, then PyCrust specifically, and finally, we'll cover the remaining the programs in the Py package.

4.1 How do I interact with a wxPython program?

A compelling feature of Python compared to other programming languages is that it can be used in two ways: you can use it to run existing programs written in the Python language, or you can run Python interactively from a command prompt. Running Python interactively is similar to having a conversation with the Python interpreter. You type in a line of code and hit Enter. Python executes the code, responds, and prompts you for the next line. It is this interactive mode that sets Python apart from languages such as C++, Visual Basic, and Perl. Because of the Python interpreter, there is no need to write an entire program in wxPython to do simple things. In fact, you can even use interactive Python as your desktop calculator.

In listing 4.1 we've started Python from the command line and entered some mathematical calculations. Python begins by displaying a few lines of information, followed by its primary prompt (>>>). When you enter something that requires additional lines of code, Python displays its secondary prompt (...).

Listing 4.1 A sample Python interactive session

```
$ Python
Python 2.3.3 (#1, Jan 25 2004, 11:06:18)
[GCC 3.2.2 (Mandrake Linux 9.1 3.2.2-3mdk)] on linux2
Type "help", "copyright", "credits" or "license" for more information.
>>> 2 + 2
```

```
4
>>> 7 * 6
42
>>> 5 ** 3
125
>>> for n in range(5):
...     print n * 9
...
0
9
18
27
36
>>>
```

Interactive Python is not only a good desktop calculator, it is also a great learning tool, because it provides immediate feedback. When in doubt, you can simply launch Python, type in a few lines of throwaway code, see how Python reacts, and adjust your main code accordingly. One of the best ways to learn Python, or to learn how existing Python code works, is to try it interactively.

PyCrust sets the standard for a Python shell

When you work with Python interactively, you work in an environment that is called the Python *shell* which is similar to other shell environments, such as the DOS window on Microsoft platforms, or the bash command line on Unix-based systems.

The most basic of all the Python shells is the one in listing 4.1, which you see when you launch Python from the command line. While it is a useful shell, it is strictly text-based, rather than graphical, and it doesn't provide all the shortcuts or helpful hints that Python is capable of providing. Several graphical Python shells have been developed that provide this additional functionality. The most well-known is IDLE, the Integrated DeveLopment Environment that is a standard part of the Python distribution. IDLE's shell, as seen in figure 4.1, looks much like the command line Python shell, but has additional graphical features such as *calltips*.

Other Python development tools, such as PythonWin and Boa Constructor, include graphical Python shells similar to the one in IDLE. It was the existence of all these shells that prompted the creation of PyCrust. While each tool's shell had some useful features, such as command recall, autocompletion, and calltips, no tool had a complete set of all the features. One of the goals of PyCrust was to support a complete set of all the existing Python shell features.

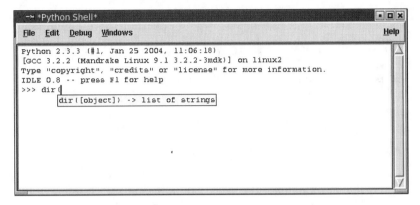

Figure 4.1   IDLE's shell provides calltips for functions and methods

The other motivation for creating PyCrust was that tools written using one GUI toolkit often cannot work with code from a different GUI toolkit. For example, IDLE is written using Tkinter, not wxPython. Until recently, if you tried to import and use a wxPython module from within IDLE's Python shell, you would be caught in a conflict between the event loop for wxPython and the event loop for Tkinter, resulting in a frozen or crashed program.

In effect, the two toolkits fought to have control over the event loop. So if you want runtime introspection features that work with wxPython modules, your Python shell must be written using wxPython. Since there wasn't an existing Python shell that supported a complete feature set, PyCrust was created to fill that need.

4.2   *What are the useful features of PyCrust?*

Now we will look at some of the shell features that PyCrust provides. The PyCrust shell looks familiar because it displays the same information lines and uses the same prompts as the command line Python shell. Figure 4.2 displays an opening PyCrust screen.

You'll notice that the PyCrust frame, which contains a wx.SplitterWindow control, is divided into two sections: the top section looks like the regular Python shell, the bottom section contains a Notebook control that includes a variety of tabs with the default tab displaying information about the current namespace. The top section, the PyCrust shell, has several useful features, discussed in the next few sections.

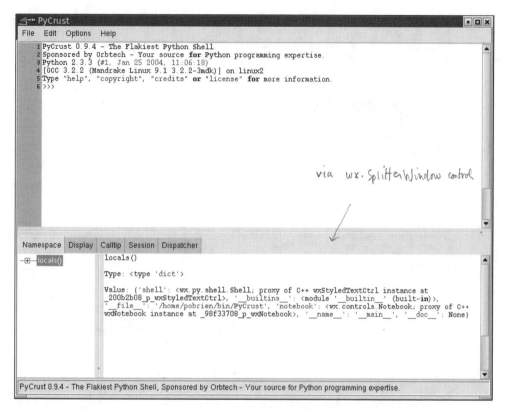

Figure 4.2 **Launching PyCrust reveals a shell and tabbed notebook interface.**

4.2.1 *Autocompletion*

Autocompletion occurs when you type in the name of an object followed by the dot operator. PyCrust displays an alphabetical listing of all known attributes for that particular object. As you enter additional letters, the highlighted selection in the list changes to match the letters you have entered. If the item you want is highlighted, press the Tab key and PyCrust fills in the rest of the attribute name for you.

In figure 4.3, PyCrust is displaying a list of attributes for a string object. This autocompletion list includes all the properties and methods of the object.

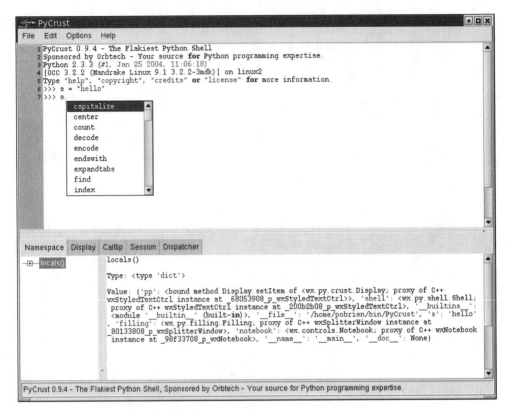

Figure 4.3   The autocompletion feature displays an object's attributes.

4.2.2 *Calltips and parameter defaults*

When you enter a left parenthesis after the name of a callable object, PyCrust displays a calltip window (see figure 4.4) containing information about the arguments that are supplied to the callable, as well as the docstrings for the callable, if defined.

A *callable object* can be a function, method, built-in, or class. All of these can be defined to accept arguments, and may have docstrings that provide information about what the item does, and what kind of value is returned. Displaying this information in a temporary window positioned directly above or below the caret eliminates the need to refer to the documentation. If you know how to use the callable object, ignore the calltip and continue typing.

PyCrust fills in default parameters for the call when you enter the left parenthesis in the Python shell. As this is happening, PyCrust automatically selects the

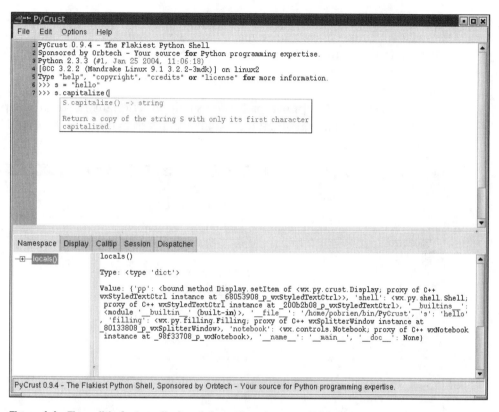

Figure 4.4   The calltip feature displays information about a callable object.

additional text that was created, and subsequent keystrokes are replaced. To retain these parameters, press any of the caret movement keys (such as the arrow keys), and the text is unselected and available for your modifications.

4.2.3 Syntax highlighting

As you enter code into the shell, PyCrust changes the color of the text depending on its significance. For example, Python keywords appear in one color, literal string values in another, and comments in yet another. This provides a visual confirmation that you haven't missed any trailing quotes, or misspelled a Python keyword.

Many of the features of PyCrust are made possible by a very powerful text control distributed with wxPython. The `wx.stc.StyledTextCtrl` is a wxPython wrapper of the Scintilla source code editing component developed by Neil Hodgson. Scintilla (www.scintilla.org) is used by a variety of source code editing applications, including the demo program shipped with wxPython. Although it was a struggle to make a source code editor behave like a wxPython shell, it would have been nearly impossible to create PyCrust without Scintilla.

4.2.4 *Python help*

PyCrust provides full support for Python's help functionality. Python's help function displays information about almost all aspects of Python, as displayed in figure 4.5.

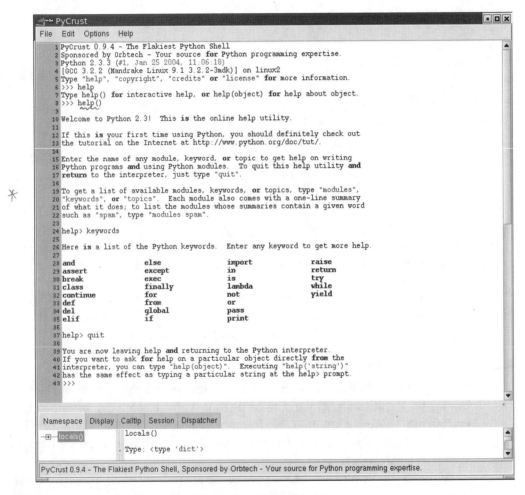

Figure 4.5   Using Python's help function from within PyCrust

Python's help function provides an additional prompt (help). After using help, you can exit the help mode by entering quit at the help prompt, and return to the regular Python prompt.

4.2.5 *Command recall*

There are many ways to avoid typing within the PyCrust shell. Most of them involve capturing something you have previously entered, modifying it if necessary, and sending it to the Python interpreter.

For example, PyCrust maintains a history of all the commands you have entered in the current session. You can recall any previously entered Python commands (single-line or multi-line) from the command history. Table 4.1 displays a list of keyboard shortcuts that relate to this functionality.

Table 4.1 Keyboard shortcuts related to command recall in the PyCrust shell

Key Combination	Result
Ctrl+Up Arrow	Retrieve previous history item
Alt+P	Retrieve previous history item
Ctrl+Down Arrow	Retrieve next history item.
Alt+N	Retrieve next history item
Shift+Up Arrow	Insert previous history item
Shift+Down Arrow	Insert next history item
F8	Command-completion of history item. (Type a few characters of a previous command and press F8)
Ctrl+Enter	Insert new line into multiline command

As you can see, there are separate commands for retrieving and inserting old commands, distinguished by how PyCrust handles the text entered at the current wxPython prompt. To replace what you have entered, use one of the shortcuts that retrieves a history item. To insert an old command at the caret, use one of the shortcuts that inserts a history item.

Inserting a line into the middle of a multi-line command works differently than inserting into a single-line command. To insert a line into a multi-line command, you can't simply press the Enter key, because that sends the current command to the Python interpreter. Instead, press Ctrl+Enter to insert a break in the current line. If you are at the end of the line, a blank line is inserted after the current line. This process is similar to the way you would cut and paste text in a regular text editor.

The final method of recalling a command is to simply move the caret to the command that you want to recall, and press Enter. PyCrust copies that command to the current Python prompt, and repositions the caret at the end. You can then modify the command, or press Enter again and submit the command to the interpreter.

These shortcuts allow you to develop code incrementally, testing your creation every step of the way. For example, you can define a new Python class, create an instance of that class, and see how it behaves. Then you can go back to the class definition, add more methods or edit the existing methods, and create a new instance. By repeating this as often as you need, you can develop your class definition to the point that it is good enough to cut and paste into your program's source code. Which brings us to our next feature.

4.2.6 *Cut and paste*

You may often want to reuse code developed within the shell without having to type it again. At other times, you may find sample code, perhaps from an online tutorial, and you'd like to apply it to a Python shell. PyCrust provides a couple of simple cutting and pasting options, listed in table 4.2.

Table 4.2   Keyboard shortcuts related to cutting and pasting in the PyCrust shell

Key Combination	Result
Ctrl+C	Copy selected text, removing prompts
Ctrl+Shift+C	Copy selected text, retaining prompts
Ctrl+X	Cut selected text
Ctrl+V	Paste from clipboard
Ctrl+Shift+V	Paste and run multiple commands from clipboard

Another feature of pasting is that PyCrust recognizes and automatically strips out the standard Python prompts from any code that is pasted into the PyCrust shell. This makes it easy to copy example code from a tutorial or email message, paste it into PyCrust, and try it without having to do manual cleanup.

At times, when you copy code you may want to remove the PyCrust prompts, such as when copying the code into your source files. Other times you'll want to retain the prompts, such as when you are copying examples into a document, or posting to a newsgroup. PyCrust provides both options when copying text from the shell.

4.2.7 *Standard shell environment*

As much as possible within the wxPython environment, PyCrust behaves the same as the command line Python shell. This includes some unusual situations, such as pickling instances of classes that are defined within a shell session. One area where PyCrust falls short in its ability to duplicate the command line functionality is keyboard interrupts. Once Python code has been entered into the PyCrust shell, there is no way to interrupt the execution of the code. For example, suppose you coded an infinite loop in PyCrust, as in the following:

```
>>> while True:
...     print "Hello"
...
```

After you press Enter, and the code is sent to the Python interpreter, PyCrust stops responding. To interrupt the infinite loop, shut down the PyCrust program. This shortcoming of PyCrust is in contrast to the command line Python shell, that retains the ability to handle a keyboard interrupt (Ctrl+C). From the command line Python shell, you would see the following behavior:

```
>>> while True:
...     print "Hello"
...
Hello
Hello
Hello
Hello
Hello
Hello
Hello
Hello
Hello
Hello
Hello
Traceback (most recent call last):
  File "<stdin>", line 2, in ?
KeyboardInterrupt
>>>
```

The nature of event handling in a GUI environment has made it extremely difficult to devise a solution that allows PyCrust to break out of an infinite loop, or interrupt any long-running sequence of code entered at the shell prompt. A future version of PyCrust may provide a solution to this. In the meantime, keep this behavior in mind. Fortunately, this is the only known difference between PyCrust and the standard command shell. In all other regards, the PyCrust shell works exactly the same as the command line Python shell.

4.2.8 *Dynamic updating*

→ No so! ¹

All of PyCrust's shell features are updated dynamically as you run PyCrust, which means that features such as autocompletion and calltips are available even on objects defined at the shell prompt. For example, take a look at the sessions shown in figures 4.6 and 4.7 where we have defined and made use of a class.

In figure 4.6, PyCrust displays the autocompletion options available for this new class.

In figure 4.7, PyCrust displays a calltip for the newly defined method of the class.

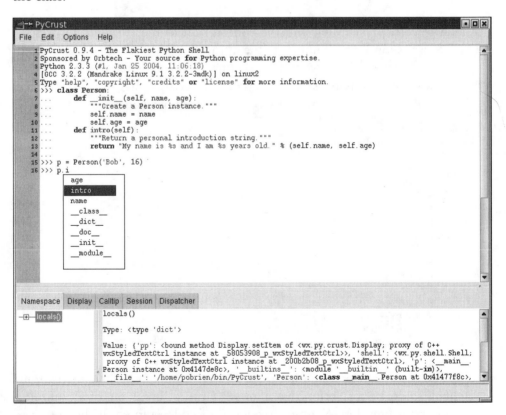

Figure 4.6 PyCrust's autocompletion information is dynamically generated.

¹ Need to close then reopen locals tree ...

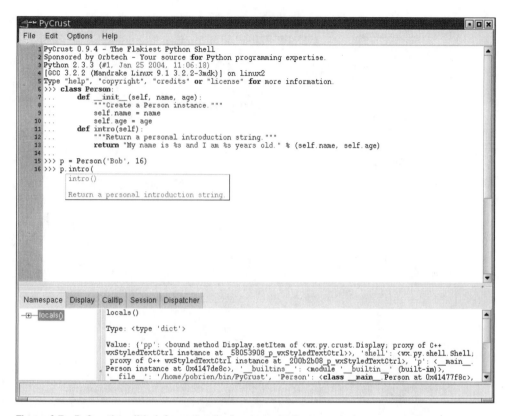

Figure 4.7   PyCrust's calltip information is also dynamically generated

This illustrates the way that PyCrust leverages the dynamic runtime capabilities of Python, which would be impossible in other programming languages that are statically typed and compiled.

4.3 What do the PyCrust notebook tabs do?

On the lower half of the PyCrust interface is a notebook control that includes several tabs with useful information. The tab you see when PyCrust begins is the Namespace tab.

4.3.1 Namespace tab

The Namespace tab, displayed in figure 4.8, is split into two parts, again using the wx.SplitterWindow control. The left-hand side contains a tree control that displays the current namespace, while the right-hand side displays details about the object currently selected in the namespace tree.

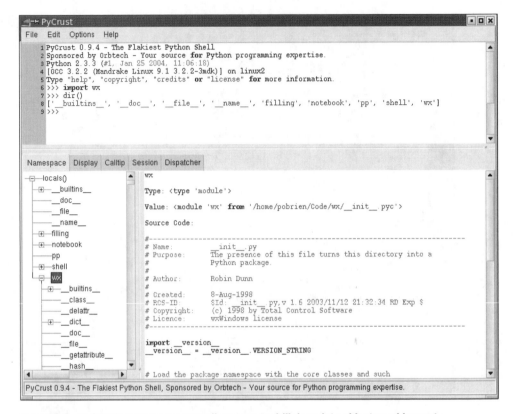

Figure 4.8   PyCrust's namespace tree allows one to drill down into objects and inspect their attributes

The namespace tree presents a hierarchical view of all the objects in the current namespace. These are the items that would be returned if you ran the `locals()` built-in Python function. In figure 4.8, we've imported the wx package and selected it in the namespace tree. The right-hand side displays the name of the selected item, its type, and its current value. If the object has source code associated with it, PyCrust displays that also. In this case, wx is a wxPython package, so PyCrust displays the source code from the `__init__.py` file that resides in the wx directory.

The first line of the display provides a fully qualified object name that you can cut and paste into the PyCrust shell or into your application source code. For example, if you import the `locale` module and drill down into it you can reach the items stored within an `encoding_alias` dictionary attribute of the `locale` module. Once you select one of these items, you can cut and paste its displayed name directly into the PyCrust shell, as in the following:

```
>>> import locale
>>> locale.encoding_alias['en']
'ISO8859-1'
>>>
```

locale.--dict--['locale_encoding-alias']['en']

In this case, PyCrust provided us with a fully qualified name (`locale.encoding_alias['en']`) that used Python's index notation (`['en']`) to reference the specified item in the encoding_alias dictionary. This mechanism also works for lists. If you find something in the namespace tree that you want to reference in your code, PyCrust gives you the exact syntax to fulfill the task.

4.3.2 *Display tab*

pp (obj) ... shows up in display

The Display tab displays a pretty print view of an object. PyCrust has a built-in function, `pp()`, that uses Python's pretty print module (`pprint`) to produce a nicely formatted view of any wxPython object. However, instead of requiring you to explicitly import and use `pprint` repeatedly, the information in the Display tab is updated every time the displayed object is updated.

For example, to see how the contents of a list change as you manipulate it in the shell, you can make the Display tab the current tab, use the `pp()` function within the shell to display your list object, then run the code that modifies your list. Whenever the list changes, the changes are immediately visible in the Display tab.

4.3.3 *Calltip tab*

The Calltip tab displays the contents of the most recent calltip in the Python shell. If you are working with a callable that requires a large number of parameters to be passed to it, select the Calltip tab. When using the wxPython package itself, there are a lot of classes that can have many methods, which may take many parameters. For example, to create a `wx.Button`, you can supply up to eight parameters, one of which is required, while the other seven have default values. The Calltip tab displays the following details about the `wx.Button` constructor:

```
__init__(self, Window parent, int id=-1, String label=EmptyString,
    Point pos=DefaultPosition, Size size=DefaultSize,
    long style=0, Validator validator=DefaultValidator,
    String name=ButtonNameStr) -> Button
```

```
Create and show a button. The preferred way to create standard buttons
is to use a standard ID and an empty label. In this case wxWigets will
automatically use a stock label that corresponds to the ID given. In
addition, the button will be decorated with stock icons under GTK+2.
```

Because the wxPython classes are actually wrappers for C++ classes, the calltip information is based entirely on the docstrings for the class. These have been generated to show both the parameters that can be passed, and the type (int, string, point, etc.) required by the underlying C++ class. That's why the wx.Button constructor calltip appears the way it does. For objects defined completely in the Python language, PyCrust inspects the object to determine the nature of its arguments.

4.3.4 *Session tab*

The Session tab is a simple text control that lists all the commands that are entered in the current shell session. This makes it easy to cut and paste commands for use elsewhere, without having to remove the responses that are returned from the wxPython interpreter.

4.3.5 *Dispatcher tab*

PyCrust includes a module named dispatcher that provides a mechanism to loosely couple objects in an application. PyCrust uses this dispatcher to keep aspects of its interface updated, primarily when commands are sent from the shell to the Python interpreter. The Dispatcher tab (figure 4.9) lists information about signals routed through its dispatching mechanism. It's primarily useful when working with PyCrust itself.

The Dispatcher tab also illustrates how to add another tab to a wx.Notebook control. The source code for the text control that appears on the Dispatcher tab illustrates how the dispatcher module can be used, as in the following:

```
class DispatcherListing(wx.TextCtrl):
    """Text control containing all dispatches for session."""

    def __init__(self, parent=None, id=-1):
        style = (wx.TE_MULTILINE | wx.TE_READONLY |
                 wx.TE_RICH2 | wx.TE_DONTWRAP)
        wx.TextCtrl.__init__(self, parent, id, style=style)
        dispatcher.connect(receiver=self.spy)

    def spy(self, signal, sender):
        """Receiver for Any signal from Any sender."""
        text = '%r from %s' % (signal, sender)
        self.SetInsertionPointEnd()
        start, end = self.GetSelection()
        if start != end:
            self.SetSelection(0, 0)
        self.AppendText(text + '\n')
```

Now that we've seen what PyCrust can do as a standalone Python shell and namespace inspector, let's take a look at some of the ways that you can use PyCrust in your own wxPython programs.

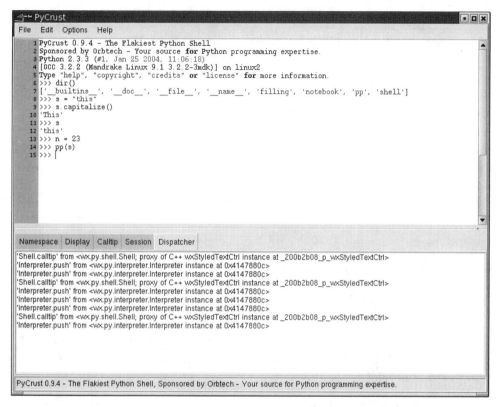

Figure 4.9   Dispatcher keeps PyCrust updated as commands are sent to the Python interpreter.

4.4 *How can I wrap PyCrust around my wxPython application?*

Let's assume that you've used wxPython to create a program, and your program is working, and now you'd like a better understanding of exactly how it works. You've seen the PyCrust features listed earlier in this chapter, and they look like they could be very useful in gaining insights into the functioning of your program. But you'd rather not change your program just to be able to use PyCrust. What do you do?

By passing the name of your program to the PyWrap utility, you can start your program with a PyCrust shell wrapped around it, without changing any of your program. Listing 4.2 displays a program, spare.py, that we are preparing to wrap with PyCrust.

Listing 4.2   The `spare.py` program being prepared for a PyCrust wrapper

```python
#!/usr/bin/env python

"""Spare.py is a starting point for simple wxPython programs."""

import wx

class Frame(wx.Frame):
    pass

class App(wx.App):

    def OnInit(self):
        self.frame = Frame(parent=None, id=-1, title='Spare')
        self.frame.Show()
        self.SetTopWindow(self.frame)
        return True

if __name__ == '__main__':
    app = App()
    app.MainLoop()
```

To run this program with PyCrust wrapped around it, pass the name of the program to PyWrap from the directory where spare.py resides. On Linux, the command line looks like this:

```
$ pywrap spare.py
```

When started, PyWrap attempts to import the module included in the command line. PyWrap then looks inside that module for a wx.App subclass, and creates an instance of that class. After that, PyWrap creates a wx.py.crust.CrustFrame window with a shell, exposes the application object to the PyCrust namespace tree, and starts the wxPython event loop.

The complete source code for PyWrap is provided in listing 4.3. This is an example of how a great deal of functionality can be added to your program with just a small amount of additional code

Listing 4.3   `PyWrap.py` source code

```python
"""PyWrap is a command line utility that runs a python
program with additional runtime tools, such as PyCrust."""

__author__ = "Patrick K. O'Brien <pobrien@orbtech.com>"
__cvsid__  = "$Id: PyCrust.txt,v 1.15 2005/03/29 23:39:27 robind Exp $"
```

```
__revision__ = "$Revision: 1.15 $"[11:-2]

import os
import sys
import wx
from wx.py.crust import CrustFrame

def wrap(app):
    wx.InitAllImageHandlers()
    frame = CrustFrame()
    frame.SetSize((750, 525))
    frame.Show(True)
    frame.shell.interp.locals['app'] = app
    app.MainLoop()

def main(modulename=None):
    sys.path.insert(0, os.curdir)
    if not modulename:
        if len(sys.argv) < 2:
            print "Please specify a module name."
            raise SystemExit
        modulename = sys.argv[1]
        if modulename.endswith('.py'):
            modulename = modulename[:-3]
    module = __import__(modulename)
    # Find the App class.
    App = None
    d = module.__dict__
    for item in d.keys():            # Go thru the items looking for class derived from
        try:                         #                                    wx.App
            if issubclass(d[item], wx.App):
                App = d[item]
        except (NameError, TypeError):
            pass
    if App is None:
        print "No App class was found."
        raise SystemExit
    app = App()
    wrap(app)

if __name__ == '__main__':
    main()
```

After running the PyWrap command, both the simple frame from spare.py and a   ← Not so...
PyCrust frame are displayed.

PyCrust in action

Now let's see what we can do with the spare.py application frame from within the PyCrust shell. Figure 4.10 displays the result. We'll start by importing wx and adding a panel to our frame:

```
>>> import wx
>>> app.frame.panel = wx.Panel(parent=app.frame)
>>> app.frame.panel.SetBackgroundColour('White')
True
>>>
```

Figure 4.10   Using PyWrap to enhance a wxPython program at runtime

The panel that was added to the frame began with a default silver color, then it was changed to white. However, setting the panel background color doesn't immediately change its appearance. Instead, something needs to trigger an event that causes the panel to repaint itself, using its new background color property. One way to trigger such an event is to ask the panel to refresh itself:

```
>>> app.frame.panel.Refresh()
```

Now a white panel is displayed, and we're one step closer to understanding the details of how wxPython actually works.

Next, let's add a status bar:

```
>>> app.frame.statusbar = app.frame.CreateStatusBar(number=3)
>>> app.frame.statusbar.SetStatusText("Left", 0)
>>> app.frame.statusbar.SetStatusText("Center", 1)
>>> app.frame.statusbar.SetStatusText("Right", 2)
```

Notice how the status bar appears within the frame, without changing the outermost dimensions of the frame. Also notice that the text added to each of the three status bar sections appears immediately, and doesn't require a refresh. Now let's add a menu and a menubar:

```
>>> app.frame.menubar = wx.MenuBar()          # create menu bar
>>> menu = wx.Menu()                          # create menu
>>> app.frame.menubar.Append(menu, "Primary") # Add menu labelled "Primary" to menubar
True
>>> app.frame.SetMenuBar(app.frame.menubar)   # set this menu bar on the frame
>>> menu.Append(wx.NewId(), "One", "First menu item")  # append menu item to menu  51
<wx.core.MenuItem; proxy of C++ wxMenuItem instance at
   _d8043d08_p_wxMenuItem>
>>> menu.Append(wx.NewId(), "Two", "Second menu item") # append menu item to menu
<wx.core.MenuItem; proxy of C++ wxMenuItem instance at
   _40a83e08_p_wxMenuItem>
>>>
```

As you manipulate your own wxPython objects in the PyCrust shell, be aware of the impact that the changes have on your running program. Try to answer the following questions. When does the menu actually appear within the frame? What menu attributes can you change while the program is running? Can you add more menu items? Can you remove them? Can you disable them? Exploring all your options interactively should help you better understand wxPython, and provide you more confidence when it comes to writing your actual program code.

Now that we've spent most of the chapter discussing PyCrust itself, we're ready to take a walk through the rest of the Py package components.

4.5   *What else is in the Py package?*

Under the covers, all of the PyCrust programs simply make use of the Python modules included in the Py package, such as shell.py, crust.py, introspect.py, and interpreter.py. These programs are the building blocks that are used to make PyCrust, which you can use separately or together.

Think of PyCrust as representing one way of assembling the bits and pieces of functionality contained within the Py package. PyShell is another way, and PyAla-Mode is a third. In each of these cases, the majority of the underlying code is common to all of them, with only the outermost containers varying. So think of the Py package as a library of modules that you can assemble as you like, wherever you want to display a wxPython shell, a code editor, or runtime introspection information within your program.

Within the Py package, there is a clear separation between modules that provide user interface functionality and those that do not. That separation makes it much easier to use these modules in your own programs. The modules that begin with Py are all end-user GUI programs, such as PyCrust, PyShell, PyAlaMode, and PyAlaCarte. You won't want to import any of these in your programs. The next section describes the end-user modules.

4.5.1   *Working with the GUI programs*

The user-level programs are packages that support modules in different ways. Table 4.3 displays a description of the user-level programs.

Table 4.3   End-user programs included in the Py package

Program	Description
PyAlaCarte	Simple source code editor. Edits one file at a time.
PyAlaMode	Multi-file source code editor. Each file is displayed in a separate notebook tab. The first tab contains a PyCrust splitter window.
PyCrust	Combination of a wxPython shell with a notebook of tabs displaying a variety of runtime information, including a namespace tree viewer.
PyFilling	Simple namespace tree viewer. This program isn't terribly useful on its own. It exists simply as another example of how to use the underlying library.
PyShell	Simple wxPython shell interface, without the additional notebook that appears in PyCrust. Functionally, the wxPython shells in PyShell and PyCrust are identical.
PyWrap	Command-line utility that runs an existing wxPython program alongside a PyCrust frame, allowing you to manipulate the application within the PyCrust shell.

4.5.2 *Working with the support modules*

The support modules provide basic functionality for the end-user programs, and can also be imported into your own programs. These modules are essentially the building blocks used to create the user-level Py programs. Table 4.4 displays a listing of the support modules that are part of the Py package, along with a brief description.

Table 4.4   The Py support modules

Module	Description
buffer	Supports file editing
crust	Contains GUI elements unique to the PyCrust application program
dispatcher	Provides global signal dispatching services
document	The document module contains a very simple Document class, which is a thin wrapper around a file. A document keeps track of various file attributes, such as its name and path, and provides read() and write() methods. The Buffer class delegates these low-level reading and writing operations to a Document instance.
editor	Contains all of the GUI editing components that appear in the PyAlaCarte and PyAlaMode programs
editwindow	The editwindow module contains a single EditWindow class. This class inherits from the wx.stc.StyledTextCtrl (STC) and provides all the features that are common between the three main uses of the STC within the Py package: as a Python shell, as a source code editor, and as a read-only source code displayer.
filling	Contains all the GUI controls that allow the user to navigate the namespaces of objects and display runtime information about those objects
frame	The frame module defines a Frame class that is the base class for all the other frames within the Py package. It has a status bar, icon, and menu that are used by all the other frame classes. The menu items continuously update themselves, based on the current status and context. That way, the menus can be the same across all the programs, and menu items that aren't valid for the current situation are simply disabled.
images	The images module contains the pie icon used by the various Py programs
interpreter	The Interpreter class is responsible for providing autocompletion lists, calltip information, and the keycodes that will trigger the autocompletion feature).
introspect	Provides a variety of introspective-type support functions for things like calltips and command autocompletion

continued on next page

Table 4.4   **The Py support modules** *(continued)*

Module	Description
pseudo	The pseudo module defines file-like classes that allow the Interpreter class to redirect stdin, stdout, and stderr
shell	Contains GUI elements that define the Python shell interface that appears in PyCrust, PyShell, and PyAlaMode
version	This final module is the simplest of them all. It contains a single string variable, named VERSION, that represents the current version or release of Py as a whole.

In the sections that follow, we'll discuss the more complex modules.

The buffer module

The buffer module contains a Buffer class that supports the normal editing of a file. A buffer has methods such as new(), open(), hasChanged(), save(), and saveAs(). The file operated on by a buffer is represented by an instance of the Document class defined in the document module. The actual editing of the file contents takes place via one or more instances of the Editor class defined in the editor module. The buffer acts as a middleman between one or more editors and the actual physical file.

A unique twist to the Buffer class is that each buffer instance has assigned to it its own Python interpreter instance. This feature allows buffers to be used in applications that need to provide autocompletion, calltips, and other runtime help while editing Python source code files. Each buffer interpreter is completely independent, and is updated when the buffer's updateNamespace() method is called. Listing 4.4 displays the source code for this method.

Listing 4.4   The update namespace buffer method

```
def updateNamespace(self):
    """Update the namespace for autocompletion and calltips.

    Return True if updated, False if there was an error."""
    if not self.interp or not hasattr(self.editor, 'getText'):
        return False
    syspath = sys.path              # redefine sys.path, saving
    sys.path = self.syspath         # orig list value
    text = self.editor.getText()
    text = text.replace('\r\n', '\n')
    text = text.replace('\r', '\n')
    name = self.modulename or self.name
    module = imp.new_module(name)
```

```
newspace = module.__dict__.copy()
try:
    try:
        code = compile(text, name, 'exec')
    except:
        raise
    try:
        exec code in newspace
    except:
        raise
    else:
        # No problems, so update the namespace.
        self.interp.locals.clear()          # Remove all items
        self.interp.locals.update(newspace)  # Dict (self.interp locals) now
        return True                          # coincides with dict newspace
finally:
    sys.path = syspath
    for m in sys.modules.keys():
        if m not in self.modules:
            del sys.modules[m]
```

This method compiles the text in the editor using Python's built-in `compile` method, then executes it using the keyword `exec`. If the compilation is successful, the result places a number of variables into the `newspace` namespace. By resetting the interpreter's local namespace with the result of the execution, the interpreter is provided with access to any classes, methods, or variables defined in the editor's buffer.

The crust module

4.3, 100-101

The crust module contains the six GUI elements that are unique to the PyCrust application program. The most general class is `CrustFrame`, which is a subclass of `wx.Frame`. If you review listing 4.1, you can see how the PyWrap program imports `CrustFrame` and creates an instance of it. That's the simplest way to embed a PyCrust frame into your own program. If you want something smaller than an entire frame, you can use one or more of the other classes listed in table 4.5.

Table 4.5   Classes defined in the crust module

Class	Description
Crust	Based on wx.SplitterWindow and containing both a shell and notebook tab with runtime information
Display	Styled text control used to display an object using Pretty Print

continued on next page

Table 4.5   Classes defined in the crust module *(continued)*

Class	Description
Calltip	Text control containing the most recent shell calltip
SessionListing	Text control containing all commands for a session
DispatcherListing	Text control containing all dispatches for a session
CrustFrame	A frame containing a `Crust` splitter window

These GUI elements can be used in any wxPython program to provide useful introspective visualizations.

The dispatcher module

The dispatcher provides global signal dispatching services. That means it acts as a middleman, allowing objects to send and receive messages without having to know anything about each other. All they need to know is the signal (typically a simple string) that is being sent. One or more objects can ask the dispatcher to notify them whenever that signal has been sent, and one or more objects can tell the dispatcher to send that particular signal.

Listing 4.5 is an example of why the dispatcher is so useful. Because all Py programs are built upon the same underlying modules, both PyCrust and PyShell use almost identical code. The only difference is that PyCrust includes a notebook with extra functions, like the namespace tree view, that are updated whenever commands are sent to the interpreter. The interpreter uses the dispatcher to send a signal whenever a command is pushed through it:

Listing 4.5   Code to send a command via the dispatcher module

```
def push(self, command):
    """Send command to the interpreter to be executed.

    Because this may be called recursively, we append a new list
    onto the commandBuffer list and then append commands into
    that. If the passed in command is part of a multi-line
    command we keep appending the pieces to the last list in
    commandBuffer until we have a complete command. If not, we
    delete that last list."""
    command = str(command)  # In case the command is unicode.
    if not self.more:
        try: del self.commandBuffer[-1]
        except IndexError: pass
    if not self.more: self.commandBuffer.append([])
    self.commandBuffer[-1].append(command)
```

```
source = '\n'.join(self.commandBuffer[-1])
more = self.more = self.runsource(source)
dispatcher.send(signal='Interpreter.push', sender=self,
                command=command, more=more, source=source)
return more
```

Various interested parties in the crust and filling modules set themselves up as receivers of this signal by connecting to the dispatcher in their constructors. Listing 4.6 shows the complete source code for the SessionListing control appears in the Session tab in PyCrust:

Listing 4.6   Code for the PyCrust session tab

```
class SessionListing(wx.TextCtrl):
    """Text control containing all commands for session."""

    def __init__(self, parent=None, id=-1):
        style = (wx.TE_MULTILINE | wx.TE_READONLY |
                 wx.TE_RICH2 | wx.TE_DONTWRAP)
        wx.TextCtrl.__init__(self, parent, id, style=style)
        dispatcher.connect(receiver=self.push,
                           signal='Interpreter.push')

    def push(self, command, more):
        """Receiver for Interpreter.push signal."""
        if command and not more:
            self.SetInsertionPointEnd()
            start, end = self.GetSelection()
            if start != end:
                self.SetSelection(0, 0)
            self.AppendText(command + '\n')
```

Notice how SessionListing's receiver (its push() method) ignores the sender and source parameters sent by the interpreter. The dispatcher is very flexible, and only sends along parameters that the receivers are able to accept.

The editor module

The editor module contains all of the GUI editing components that appear in the PyAlaCarte and PyAlaMode programs. If you'd like to include a Python source code editor in your program, use the classes described in table 4.6.

These classes can be used in any program to provide useful code style editing functionality.

Table 4.6   Classes defined in the editor module

Class	Description
EditorFrame	Used by PyAlaCarte to support the editing of one file at a time `EditorFrame` is a subclass of the more general `Frame` class from the frame module.
EditorNotebookFrame	Subclass of `EditorFrame` that extends `EditorFrame` by adding a notebook interface and the ability to edit more than one file at the same time. This is the frame class used by PyAlaMode.
EditorNotebook	The control used by `EditorNotebookFrame` to display each file in a separate tab.
Editor	Manages the relationship between a buffer and its associated `EditWindow`
EditWindow	Text editing control based on `StyledTextCtrl`

The filling module

The filling module contains all the GUI controls that allow the user to navigate the namespaces of objects, and displays runtime information about those objects. The four classes defined in the filling module are described in Table 4.7.

Table 4.7   Classes defined in the filling module

Class	Description
FillingTree	Based on `wx.TreeCtrl`, `FillingTree` provides a hierarchical tree of an objects namespace
FillingText	A subclass of `editwindow.EditWindow`, used to display details about the object currently selected in the FillingTree
Filling	A `wx.SplitterWindow` that includes a `FillingTree` in its left side and a `FillingText` on its right side
FillingFrame	A frame containing a `Filling` splitter window. Double-clicking on an item in the filling tree will open up a new `FillingFrame`, with the selected item as the root of the tree

Using these classes in your own program allows you to easily create a hierarchical tree of a Python namespace. This can be used as a quick data browser if you set up your data as Python objects.

The interpreter module

The interpreter module defines an `Interpreter` class, based on the `Interactive-Interpreter` class of the `code` module from the Python standard library. Besides being responsible for sending source code to Python, the Interpreter class is also responsible for providing autocompletion lists, calltip information, and even the keycodes that trigger the autocompletion feature (typically the dot "." keycode).

Because of this clean division of responsibility, you can create your own subclass of Interpreter and pass an instance of it to the PyCrust shell, instead of the default interpreter. This has been done in a few programs to support custom language variations, while still getting the benefit of the PyCrust environment. For example, one program of this sort allows users to control laboratory equipment from an embedded PyCrust shell. That program uses the forward slash (/) to trigger the autocompletion feature whenever the forward slash appears after a reference to one of the pieces of equipment. The autocompletion options that appear are specific to that piece of equipment, how it was configured, and its current state.

The introspect module

The introspect module is used by the Interpreter and FillingTree classes. It provides a variety of introspective-type support functions for calltips and command autocompletion. The following presents the use of wx.py.introspect to get all of the attribute names for a list object, suppressing those attributes with leading double underscores:

```
>>> import wx
>>> L = [1, 2, 3]
>>> wx.py.introspect.getAttributeNames(L, includeDouble=False)
['append', 'count', 'extend', 'index', 'insert', 'pop',
'remove', 'reverse', 'sort']
>>>
```

The getAttributeNames() function is used by the FillingTree class to populate its namespace hierarchy. One of the best ways to understand the introspect module is to look at the unit tests that it successfully passes. View the test_introspect.py file in the Lib/site-packages/wx/py/tests directory of your Python installation.

The shell module

The shell module contains GUI elements that define the Python shell interface appearing in PyCrust, PyShell, and PyAlaMode. Table 4.8 provides a description of each element. The most general class is ShellFrame, a subclass of frame.Frame. It contains an instance of the Shell class, which is the class that handles the bulk of the work involved in providing an interactive Python environment.

The ShellFacade class was created during the development of PyCrust as a way to simplify things when accessing the shell object itself from within the shell. When you start PyCrust or PyShell, the Shell class instance is made available in

Table 4.8 Classes defined in the shell module

Class	Description
Shell	Python shell based on the `wx.stc.StyleTextCtrl`. `Shell` subclasses `editwindow.EditWindow`, then jumps through many hoops to make the underlying text control behave like a Python shell, rather than a source code file editor
ShellFacade	Simplified interface to all shell-related functionality. This is a semi-transparent facade, in that all attributes of the real shell are still accessible, even though only some are visible to the user from the shell itself.
ShellFrame	A frame containing a `Shell` window

the Python shell. For example, you can call the shell's `about()` method at the shell prompt, as in the following:

```
>>> shell.about()
Author: "Patrick K. O'Brien <pobrien@orbtech.com>"
Py Version: 0.9.4
Py Shell Revision: 1.7
Py Interpreter Revision: 1.5
Python Version: 2.3.3
wxPython Version: 2.4.1.0p7
Platform: linux2
>>>
```

Because the Shell inherits from `StyledTextCtrl`, it contains over 600 attributes. Most of the attributes aren't useful from the shell prompt, so a `ShellFacade` was created to limit the number of attributes that appear in the autocompletion list when you enter shell. at the shell prompt. Now the shell object only displays about 25 of the most useful shell attributes. If you want to use one that isn't included in the autocompletion list, you can enter it and it will get forwarded to the "real" shell, which is stored as an attribute of the facade.

4.6 *How can I use modules from the Py package in my wxPython programs?*

What do you do if you don't want an entire PyCrust frame in your application? What if you just want the shell interface in one frame, and perhaps a namespace viewer in another? And what if you want them to be permanent additions to your program? These alternatives are not only possible, they're also fairly easy. We'll end this chapter with one example of how this can be done.

We're going to revisit the program we created in chapter 2, the one with a menubar, toolbar, and status bar. We'll add another menu with one item that

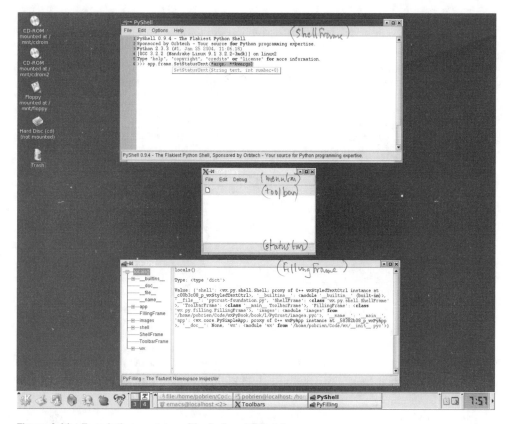

Figure 4.11 Foundation program with shell and filling frames

displays a shell frame, and another item that displays a filling frame. Finally, we'll
set the root of the filling tree to the frame object from our main program. The
results are displayed in figure 4.11.

Listing 4.7 shows the modified source code. (Refer to chapter 2 for an expla-
nation of the original program.) As you can see, only a couple of extra lines of
code were used to add the ability to launch a shell frame and a filling frame, with
each operating on the primary application frame.

Listing 4.7   Foundation program with additional runtime tools

```
#!/usr/bin/env python

import wx
from wx.py.shell import ShellFrame
from wx.py.filling import FillingFrame
```
❶ Importing the
frame classes

```python
import images

class ToolbarFrame(wx.Frame):

    def __init__(self, parent, id):
        wx.Frame.__init__(self, parent, id, 'Toolbars',
                size=(300, 200))
        panel = wx.Panel(self, -1)
        panel.SetBackgroundColour('White')
        statusBar = self.CreateStatusBar()
        toolbar = self.CreateToolBar()
        toolbar.AddSimpleTool(wx.NewId(), images.getNewBitmap(),
                "New", "Long help for 'New'")
        toolbar.Realize()
        menuBar = wx.MenuBar()
        menu1 = wx.Menu()
        menuBar.Append(menu1, "&File")
        menu2 = wx.Menu()
        menu2.Append(wx.NewId(), "&Copy", "Copy in status bar")
        menu2.Append(wx.NewId(), "C&ut", "")
        menu2.Append(wx.NewId(), "Paste", "")
        menu2.AppendSeparator()
        menu2.Append(wx.NewId(), "&Options...", "Display Options")
        menuBar.Append(menu2, "&Edit")

        menu3 = wx.Menu()
        shell = menu3.Append(-1, "&wxPython shell",
                            "Open wxPython shell frame")
        filling = menu3.Append(-1, "&Namespace viewer",
                            "Open namespace viewer frame")
        menuBar.Append(menu3, "&Debug")
        self.Bind(wx.EVT_MENU, self.OnShell, shell)
        self.Bind(wx.EVT_MENU, self.OnFilling, filling)

        self.SetMenuBar(menuBar)

    def OnCloseMe(self, event):
        self.Close(True)

    def OnCloseWindow(self, event):
        self.Destroy()

    def OnShell(self, event):
        frame = ShellFrame(parent=self)
        frame.Show()

    def OnFilling(self, event):
        frame = FillingFrame(parent=self)
        frame.Show()

if __name__ == '__main__':
    app = wx.PySimpleApp()
```

❷ Creating the Debug menu and items

❸ Setting the menu event handlers

❹ The OnShell menu item handler

The OnFilling menu item handler

```
app.frame = ToolbarFrame(parent=None, id=-1)
app.frame.Show()
app.MainLoop()
```

❶ Here we import the `ShellFrame` and `FillingFrame` classes.

❷ As with the previous two menus, we append items to our third menu, the Debug menu, and append it to the frame's menubar.

❸ Binding a function to `wx.EVT_MENU()` allows us to associate a handler with a menu item, so that when the menu item is selected the handler is called.

❹ When the user selects Python shell from the Debug menu, a shell frame is created whose parent is the toolbar frame. When the toolbar frame is closed, any open shell or filling frames is also closed.

4.7 *Summary*

- Toolkits like wxPython are by their very nature large and complex. Interactions between GUI controls are not always intuitive, and the entire process is determined by events, and responses to events, rather than a linear sequence of execution. Using tools like the PyCrust shell can greatly enhance your understanding of this event-driven environment.

- PyCrust is just another Python shell, similar to the shells included with IDLE, Boa Constructor, PythonWin, and other development tools. However, PyCrust was created using wxPython, which is beneficial when you are developing programs with wxPython. In particular, you won't have problems with conflicting event loops, and you can manipulate all aspects of your program at runtime within PyCrust's shell and namespace viewer.

- Because PyCrust is part of the wxPython distribution, it is installed along with wxPython, including all the source code. That makes PyCrust easy to use, and eases the learning curve of figuring out how to provide introspective functionality in your own programs.

- In addition, the modular design of the Py package makes it very easy for you to pick and choose the modules that would benefit your program the most, such as source editing, namespace browsing, or shell functionality.

- PyCrust reduces the learning curve associated with wxPython, and helps you grasp the finer points of your own program's runtime behavior.

In the next chapter, we'll use the knowledge we've learned about wxPython, and provide some practical advice about how to structure your GUI programs without getting tangled in knots.

Creating your blueprint

This chapter covers

- Refactoring and how it improves code
- Separating the Model and View
- Using a Model class
- Unit testing a GUI program
- Testing user events

GUI code has a reputation for being hard to read, hard to maintain, and always looking like spaghetti—long, stringy, and tangled. One prominent Python GUI module (not written with wxPython) includes this note in its comments: "Why is it that GUI code always ends up looking a mess, despite all the best intentions to keep it tidy?" It doesn't have to be that way. There's no particular reason why UI code has to be any harder to write or manage than any other part of your program. In this chapter we'll discuss three techniques for taming your UI code. Since layout code is particularly susceptible to poor structure, we'll discuss *refactoring* the code to make it easier to read, manage, and maintain. Another area where a UI programmer can get tied into knots is the interaction between the display code and the underlying business objects. The *Model/View/Controller* (MVC) design pattern is a structure for keeping display and data separate to allow each to change without affecting the other. Finally, we'll discuss techniques for unit testing your wxPython code. Although all the examples in this chapter will use wxPython, many of the principles are applicable to any UI toolkit—although the Python language and wxPython toolkit make some techniques particularly elegant. The design and architecture of your code is the blueprint of your system. A well thought out blueprint will make your application simpler to build and easier to maintain. The suggestions in this chapter will help you design a solid blueprint for your program.

5.1 How can refactoring help me improve my code?

There are many reasons why bad interface or layout code happens to good programmers. Even a simple UI can require many lines to show all of its elements on the screen. Programmers often try to accomplish this using a single method, and the method quickly becomes long and hard to control. Furthermore, interface code is susceptible to being tweaked and changed constantly, which can wreak havoc unless you are disciplined about managing the changes. Because writing all the layout code can be tedious, an interface programmer will often use a design toolkit that generates code. The machine-generated code is notorious for being awkward and hard to make sense of without using the generation tool.

In principle, it's not hard to keep UI code under control. The key is *refactoring*, or continually improving the design and structure of existing code. The goal in refactoring is to keep the code in a state where it can be easily read and maintained in the future. Table 5.1 contains a description of some of the principles to keep in mind when refactoring. The most basic goal is to remember that somebody is going to have to read and understand your code in the future. Try to make that person's life easier—after all, it might be you.

Table 5.1 A listing of some important principles of refactoring

Principle	Description
No duplication	You should avoid having multiple segments of code with the same functionality. This can become a maintenance headache when the functionality needs to change.
One thing at a time	A method should do one thing, and one thing only. Separate things should be moved into separate methods. Methods should be kept short.
Build shallow nests	Try to keep from nesting code more than two or three levels deep. Deeply nested code is also a good candidate for a separate method.
Avoid magic literals	String and numeric literals should be kept to a minimum. A good way to manage this is to separate literal data from the main portion of your code, and store it in a list or dictionary.

Some of these principles are particularly important in Python code. Because of Python's indentation-based syntax, small, compact methods are very easy to read. Longer methods, however, can be harder to decipher, especially if they are unable to fit on a single screen. Similarly, deep nesting in Python can make it tricky to trace the beginning and ending of code blocks. However, Python is a particularly good language for avoiding duplication, especially because of the ease with which functions and methods can be passed as arguments.

5.1.1 A refactoring example

To show you how these principles work in action, we'll walk you through a refactoring example. Figure 5.1 shows a window that might be used as the front end to a Microsoft Access-like database.

This layout is a little more complex than those we have seen so far, but by the standard of real-world applications, it is still quite simple. Listing 5.1 shows a poorly structured way to produce Figure 5.1. When people talk about UI

Figure 5.1 The sample window for the refactoring example

code being a mess, this is what they mean. Having several problems compressed into a few lines of code may be a bit of an exaggeration, but it's representative of the trouble you can get into in layout code. Certainly, it's representative of the trouble I get into when writing layout code.

Listing 5.1   An un-refactored way to produce figure 5.1

```python
#!/usr/bin/env python                                    # poor version

import wx

class RefactorExample(wx.Frame):

    def __init__(self, parent, id):
        wx.Frame.__init__(self, parent, id, 'Refactor Example',
                size=(340, 200))
        panel = wx.Panel(self, -1)
        panel.SetBackgroundColour("White")
        prevButton = wx.Button(panel, -1, "<< PREV", pos=(80, 0))
        self.Bind(wx.EVT_BUTTON, self.OnPrev, prevButton)
        nextButton = wx.Button(panel, -1, "NEXT >>", pos=(160, 0))
        self.Bind(wx.EVT_BUTTON, self.OnNext, nextButton)
        self.Bind(wx.EVT_CLOSE, self.OnCloseWindow)

        menuBar = wx.MenuBar()
        menu1 = wx.Menu()
        openMenuItem = menu1.Append(-1, "&Open", "Copy in status bar")
        self.Bind(wx.EVT_MENU, self.OnOpen, openMenuItem)
        quitMenuItem = menu1.Append(-1, "&Quit", "Quit")
        self.Bind(wx.EVT_MENU, self.OnCloseWindow, quitMenuItem)
        menuBar.Append(menu1, "&File")
        menu2 = wx.Menu()
        copyItem = menu2.Append(-1, "&Copy", "Copy")
        self.Bind(wx.EVT_MENU, self.OnCopy, copyItem)
        cutItem = menu2.Append(-1, "C&ut", "Cut")
        self.Bind(wx.EVT_MENU, self.OnCut, cutItem)
        pasteItem = menu2.Append(-1, "Paste", "Paste")
        self.Bind(wx.EVT_MENU, self.OnPaste, pasteItem)
        menuBar.Append(menu2, "&Edit")
        self.SetMenuBar(menuBar)

        static = wx.StaticText(panel, wx.NewId(), "First Name",
                pos=(10, 50))
        static.SetBackgroundColour("White")
        text = wx.TextCtrl(panel, wx.NewId(), "", size=(100, -1),
                pos=(80, 50))

        static2 = wx.StaticText(panel, wx.NewId(), "Last Name",
                pos=(10, 80))
        static2.SetBackgroundColour("White")
        text2 = wx.TextCtrl(panel, wx.NewId(), "", size=(100, -1),
                pos=(80, 80))
```

```
        firstButton = wx.Button(panel, -1, "FIRST")
        self.Bind(wx.EVT_BUTTON, self.OnFirst, firstButton)

        menu2.AppendSeparator()
        optItem = menu2.Append(-1, "&Options...", "Display Options")
        self.Bind(wx.EVT_MENU, self.OnOptions, optItem)

        lastButton = wx.Button(panel, -1, "LAST", pos=(240, 0))
        self.Bind(wx.EVT_BUTTON, self.OnLast, lastButton)

    # Just grouping the empty event handlers together
    def OnPrev(self, event): pass
    def OnNext(self, event): pass
    def OnLast(self, event): pass
    def OnFirst(self, event): pass
    def OnOpen(self, event): pass
    def OnCopy(self, event): pass
    def OnCut(self, event): pass
    def OnPaste(self, event): pass
    def OnOptions(self, event): pass

    def OnCloseWindow(self, event):
        self.Destroy()

if __name__ == '__main__':
    app = wx.PySimpleApp()
    frame = RefactorExample(parent=None, id=-1)
    frame.Show()
    app.MainLoop()
```

Let's categorize how this code example works against the principles in table 5.1. On the positive side, there's no deep nesting. On the negative side, the other three ideas listed in table 5.1 aren't followed at all. Table 5.2 summarizes the ways in which refactoring might improve this code.

Table 5.2 Refactoring opportunities in listing 5.1

Principle	Problem in code
No duplication	Several patterns are duplicated repeatedly, including "add a button, and give it an action," "add a menu item and give it an action," and "create a caption/text entry pair."
One thing at a time	This code does several things. In addition to basic frame setup, it creates the menu bar, adds the buttons, and adds the text fields. Worse, the three functions are mixed up through the code, as if late changes were just added at the bottom of the method.
Avoid magic literals	Every button, menu item, and text box has a literal string and a literal point in the constructor.

To give you a general idea of how to fix this code, we'll pull all the button code into a separate method.

5.1.2 *Starting to refactor*

Listing 5.2 contains the code used to create just the button bar in the previous listing. As a first step in refactoring, we've extracted the code to its own method.

Listing 5.2 The button bar as a separate method

```
def createButtonBar(self):
    firstButton = wx.Button(panel, -1, "FIRST")
    self.Bind(wx.EVT_BUTTON, self.OnFirst, firstButton)
    prevButton = wx.Button(panel, -1, "<< PREV", pos=(80, 0))
    self.Bind(wx.EVT_BUTTON, , self.OnPrev, prevButton)
    nextButton = wx.Button(panel, -1, "NEXT >>", pos=(160, 0))
    self.Bind(wx.EVT_BUTTON, self.OnNext, nextButton)
    lastButton = wx.Button(panel, -1, "LAST", pos=(240, 0))
    self.Bind(wx.EVT_BUTTON, self.OnLast, lastButton)
```

With the code separated out like this, it's easy to see what the commonality is between all the button additions. We can factor that portion out into a generic method, and just call the method repeatedly, as shown in listing 5.3:

Listing 5.3 A generic and improved button-bar method

```
def createButtonBar(self, panel):
    self.buildOneButton(panel, "First", self.OnFirst)
    self.buildOneButton(panel, "<< PREV", self.OnPrev, (80, 0))
    self.buildOneButton(panel, "NEXT >>", self.OnNext, (160, 0))
    self.buildOneButton(panel, "Last", self.OnLast, (240, 0))
def buildOneButton(self, parent, label, handler, pos=(0,0)):
    button = wx.Button(parent, -1, label, pos)
    self.Bind(wx.EVT_BUTTON, handler, button)
    return button
```

There are a couple of advantages in following the second example instead of the first. For one thing, the intent of the code is clearer just from reading it—having short methods with meaningful names goes a long way toward signaling intent. The second example also gets rid of all the local variables that are needed just to hold on to IDs (admittedly, you could also get rid of the local variables by hard-wiring the IDs, but that can cause duplicate ID problems). This is helpful because it makes the code less complicated, and also because it almost eliminates the common error of cutting and pasting a couple of lines of code and forgetting to change all the variable names. (In a real application, you might need to store the buttons as instance variables to be able to access them later, but for this example, you do not.) In addition, the buildOneButton() method is easily moved to a utility module and could be reused in other frames or other projects. A toolkit of common utilities is a useful thing to have.

5.1.3 *More refactoring*

Having made a significant improvement, we could stop here. But there are still a lot of *magic literals*—hardcoded constants used in multiple locations—in the code. For one thing, the literal points used for positioning could make the code prone to errors when another button is being added to the bar, especially if the new button is placed in the middle of the bar. So let's go one step farther and separate the literal data from the processing. Listing 5.4 shows a more data-driven mechanism for creating buttons.

Listing 5.4   Creating buttons with data separated from code

```
def buttonData(self):
    return (("First", self.OnFirst),
            ("<< PREV", self.OnPrev),
            ("NEXT >>", self.OnNext),
            ("Last", self.OnLast))

def createButtonBar(self, panel, yPos=0):
    xPos = 0
    for eachLabel, eachHandler in self.buttonData():
        pos = (xPos, yPos)
        button = self.buildOneButton(panel, eachLabel, eachHandler, pos)
        xPos += button.GetSize().width

def buildOneButton(self, parent, label, handler, pos=(0,0)):
    button = wx.Button(parent, -1, label, pos)
    self.Bind(wx.EVT_BUTTON, handler, button)
    return button
```

In listing 5.4, the data for the individual buttons is stored in a nested tuple in the buttonData() method. The choice of data structure and use of a constant method is not inevitable. The data could be stored as a class-level or module-level variable, rather than the result of a method, or it could be stored in an external file. One advantage to using a method is being able to make a relatively simple transition if you wish to store the button data in another location—just change the method so that instead of returning a constant, it returns the external data.

The `createButtonBar()` method iterates over the list returned by `button-Data()` and creates each button from that data. The method now calculates the x-axis position of the buttons automatically as it traverses the list. This is helpful because it ensures that the order of the buttons in the code will be identical to the order on the screen, making the code clearer and less error-prone. If you need to add a button in the middle of the bar now, you can just add the data to the middle of the list and the code guarantees that it will be placed correctly.

The separation of the data has other benefits. In a more elaborate example, the data could be stored externally in a resource or XML file. This would allow interface changes to be made without even looking at the code, and also makes internationalization easier, by making it easier to change text. We're currently still hard-wiring the button width, but that could easily be added to the data method as well. (In reality, we'd probably use a wxPython `Sizer` object, which is covered in chapter 11). Also, with the specifics of the data removed, `createButtonBar` is now well on its way to being a utility method itself, and could easily be reused in another frame or project.

After performing the same steps of consolidating, factoring the common process, and separating data for the menu and text field code, the result is shown in listing 5.5.

Listing 5.5   A refactored example

```
#!/usr/bin/env python

import wx

class RefactorExample(wx.Frame):

    def __init__(self, parent, id):
        wx.Frame.__init__(self, parent, id, 'Refactor Example',
                size=(340, 200))
        panel = wx.Panel(self, -1)
        panel.SetBackgroundColour("White")
        self.Bind(wx.EVT_CLOSE, self.OnCloseWindow)
        self.createMenuBar()              <─┐  Simplified init method
        self.createButtonBar(panel)
        self.createTextFields(panel)

    def menuData(self):       <──  Data for menus
        return (("&File",
```

```
                            ("&Open", "Open in status bar", self.OnOpen),
                            ("&Quit", "Quit", self.OnCloseWindow)),
                 ("&Edit",
                            ("&Copy", "Copy", self.OnCopy),
                            ("C&ut", "Cut", self.OnCut),
                            ("&Paste", "Paste", self.OnPaste),
                            ("", "", ""),
                            ("&Options...", "DisplayOptions", self.OnOptions)))

    def createMenuBar(self):
        menuBar = wx.MenuBar()
        for eachMenuData in self.menuData():
            menuLabel = eachMenuData[0]
            menuItems = eachMenuData[1:]      # list of lists
            menuBar.Append(self.createMenu(menuItems), menuLabel)
        self.SetMenuBar(menuBar)

    def createMenu(self, menuData):
        menu = wx.Menu()
        for eachLabel, eachStatus, eachHandler in menuData:
            if not eachLabel:
                menu.AppendSeparator()
                continue
            menuItem = menu.Append(-1, eachLabel, eachStatus)
            self.Bind(wx.EVT_MENU, eachHandler, menuItem)
        return menu

    def buttonData(self):
        return (("First", self.OnFirst),
                ("<< PREV", self.OnPrev),
                ("NEXT >>", self.OnNext),
                ("Last", self.OnLast))

    def createButtonBar(self, panel, yPos = 0):
        xPos = 0
        for eachLabel, eachHandler in self.buttonData():
            pos = (xPos, yPos)
            button = self.buildOneButton(panel, eachLabel,
            eachHandler, pos)
            xPos += button.GetSize().width

    def buildOneButton(self, parent, label, handler, pos=(0,0)):
        button = wx.Button(parent, -1, label, pos)
        self.Bind(wx.EVT_BUTTON, handler, button)
        return button

    def textFieldData(self):
        return (("First Name", (10, 50)),
                ("Last Name", (10, 80)))
```

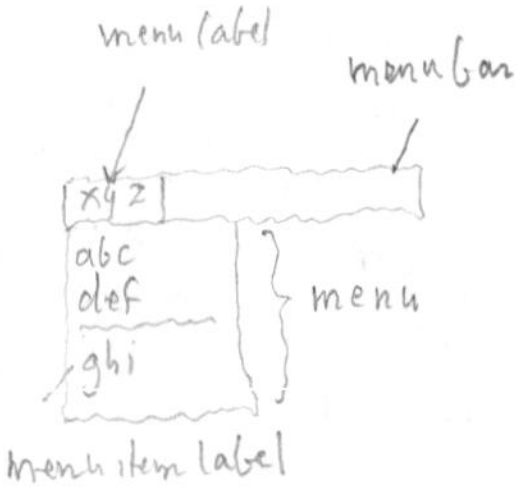

(handwritten annotations: label, status, handler; label; menu items; Menu creation here; menu label; menuBar; menu; menu item label; Button bar data; Create buttons; Text data)

```
def createTextFields(self, panel):
    for eachLabel, eachPos in self.textFieldData():
        self.createCaptionedText(panel, eachLabel, eachPos)

def createCaptionedText(self, panel, label, pos):
    static = wx.StaticText(panel, wx.NewId(), label, pos)
    static.SetBackgroundColour("White")          # eg  First Name
    textPos = (pos[0] + 75, pos[1])
    wx.TextCtrl(panel, wx.NewId(), "", size=(100, -1), pos=textPos)    #

                                                         See p118
    # Just grouping the empty event handlers together
    def OnPrev(self, event): pass
    def OnNext(self, event): pass
    def OnLast(self, event): pass
    def OnFirst(self, event): pass
    def OnOpen(self, event): pass
    def OnCopy(self, event): pass
    def OnCut(self, event): pass
    def OnPaste(self, event): pass
    def OnOptions(self, event): pass
    def OnCloseWindow(self, event):
        self.Destroy()

if __name__ == '__main__':
    app = wx.PySimpleApp()
    frame = RefactorExample(parent=None, id=-1)
    frame.Show()
    app.MainLoop()
```

Create text

The amount of effort involved in moving from listing 5.1 to listing 5.5 was minimal, but the reward is tremendous—a code base that is much clearer and less error-prone. The layout of the code logically matches the layout of the data. Several common ways that poorly structured code can lead to errors—such as requiring a lot of copying and pasting to create new objects—have been removed. Much of the functionality can now be easily moved to a superclass or utility module, making the code savings continue to pay off in the future. As an added bonus, the data separation makes it easy to use the layout as a template with different data, including international data.

The key to successfully refactoring is to keep doing it in small increments as you write your code. Like dirty dishes, poor code can pile up to an overwhelming mess quickly unless you make an effort to clean it up regularly. If you can acquire the mindset that working code is only an intermediate step toward the final goal of well-factored working code, then you can make refactoring part of your regular developing process.

However, even with the refactoring that has been done, the code in listing 5.5 is still missing something important: the actual user data. Most of what your application will do depends on manipulating data in response to user requests. The structure of your program can go a long way toward making your program flexible and stable. The MVC pattern is the accepted standard for managing the interaction between interface and data.

5.2 How do I keep the Model and View separate in my program?

Dating back to the late 1970s and the seminal language *Smalltalk-80*, the MVC pattern is probably the oldest explicitly identified object-oriented design pattern around. It's also one of the most prevalent, having been adopted in one way or another by nearly every GUI toolkit written since then (not to mention a good number of other systems, such as web application frameworks). The MVC pattern is the standard for structuring programs that both manipulate and display information.

5.2.1 What is a Model-View-Controller system?

An MVC system has three subsystems. The *Model* contains what is often called business logic, or all the data and information manipulated by your system. The *View* contains the objects that display the data, and the *Controller* manages the interaction with the user and mediates between the Model and the View. Table 5.3 summarizes the components.

Table 5.3 The components of standard MVC architecture

Component	Description
Model	Business logic. Contains all the data manipulated by the system. This can include an interface to an external store, such as a database. Typically the model exposes only a public API to the other components.
View	Display code. The widgets that actually place the information in the user's view. In wxPython, pretty much anything in the `wx.Window` hierarchy is part of the view subsystem.
Controller	Interaction logic. The code that receives user events and ensures that they are handled by the system. In wxPython, this subsystem is represented by the `wx.EvtHandler` hierarchy.

In many modern UI toolkits, the View and Controller components are somewhat intertangled. This is because the Controller components themselves need to be displayed on the screen, and because often you want widgets that display data to also respond to user events. In wxPython, this relationship is enshrined by the fact that all `wx.Window` objects are also subclasses of `wx.EvtHandler`, meaning they function as both View elements and Controller elements. In contrast, most web-application frameworks have a stricter separation between View and Controller, since the interaction logic happens behind the scenes on the server.

Figure 5.2 shows one rendering of how data and information is passed in an MVC architecture.

An event notification is handled by the Controller system, which dispatches it to the appropriate place. As we saw in chapter 3, wxPython manages this mechanism using the `wx.EvtHandler` method `ProcessEvent()`. In a strict MVC design, your handler functions might actually be declared in a separate controller object, rather than in the frame class itself.

In response to the event, the model objects can do some processing on the application data. When that processing is done, the model sends an update notification. If there is a controller object, the notification is usually sent back to the controller and the controller notifies the appropriate view objects to update themselves. In a smaller system or a simpler architecture, the notification is often directly received by the view objects. In wxPython, the exact nature of the update from the model is up to you. Options include explicitly raising custom wxPython events from the model or controller, having the model maintain a list of objects that receive update notifications, or having views register themselves with the model.

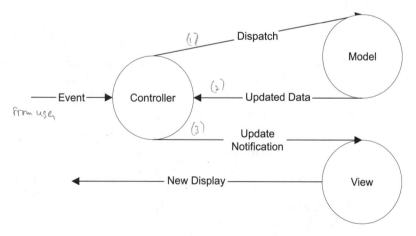

Figure 5.2   The data flow of an MVC request

The key to a successful MVC design is not in making sure that every object knows about every other object. Instead, a successful MVC program explicitly hides knowledge about one part of the program from the other parts. The goal is for the systems to interact minimally, and over a well-defined set of methods. In particular, the Model component should be completely isolated from the View and Controller. You should be able to make arbitrary changes to either of those systems without changing your Model classes. Ideally, you'd even be able to use the same Model classes to drive non-wxPython interfaces, but that would preclude, say, using wxPython events for update notification.

From the View side, you should be able to make arbitrary changes in the implementation of the Model objects without changing the View or the Controller. While the View will depend on the existence of certain public methods, it should never get to see the private internals of the Model. Admittedly, this is difficult to enforce in Python, but one way to help enforcement it is to create an abstract Model class that defines the API that the View can see. Subclasses of the Model can either act as proxies for an internal class that can be changed, or can simply contain the internal workings themselves. The first option is more structured, the second is easier to implement.

In the next section, we'll take a look at one of the Model classes built into wxPython, `wx.grid.PyGridTableBase`. This class makes it possible to use a grid control within an MVC design framework. After that, we'll take a look at building and using a custom model class for a custom widget.

5.2.2 *A wxPython model: PyGridTableBase*

The class `wx.grid.Grid` is the wxPython control for a spreadsheet-style layout of rows and columns. You're probably familiar with the basic concept, but figure 5.3 shows how the wxPython version looks.

The grid control has a lot of interesting features, including the ability to create custom renderers and editors on a cell-by-cell basis, as well as dragable rows and columns. Those features will be discussed in greater detail in chapter 13. In this chapter, we'll stick to the basics and show how to use a model to populate a grid. Listing 5.6 shows the simple non-model way of setting the cell values in a grid. In this case, the grid values are the lineup for the 1984 Chicago Cubs.

A Grid		
	First	**Last**
CF	Bob	Demier
2B	Ryne	Sandberg
LF	Gary	Matthews
1B	Leon	Durham
RF	Keith	Moreland
3B	Ron	Cey
C	Jody	Davis
SS	Larry	Bowa
P	Rick	Sutcliffe

Figure 5.3 **A sample of the wxPython grid control**

Listing 5.6 Populating a grid without models

```python
import wx
import wx.grid

class SimpleGrid(wx.grid.Grid):
    def __init__(self, parent):
        wx.grid.Grid.__init__(self, parent, -1)
        self.CreateGrid(9, 2)
        self.SetColLabelValue(0, "First")      # col label
        self.SetColLabelValue(1, "Last")       # col label
        self.SetRowLabelValue(0, "CF")         # row label
        self.SetCellValue(0, 0, "Bob")
        self.SetCellValue(0, 1, "Dernier")
        self.SetRowLabelValue(1, "2B")         # row label
        self.SetCellValue(1, 0, "Ryne")
        self.SetCellValue(1, 1, "Sandberg")
        self.SetRowLabelValue(2, "LF")
        self.SetCellValue(2, 0, "Gary")
        self.SetCellValue(2, 1, "Matthews")
        self.SetRowLabelValue(3, "1B")
        self.SetCellValue(3, 0, "Leon")
        self.SetCellValue(3, 1, "Durham")
        self.SetRowLabelValue(4, "RF")
        self.SetCellValue(4, 0, "Keith")
        self.SetCellValue(4, 1, "Moreland")
        self.SetRowLabelValue(5, "3B")
        self.SetCellValue(5, 0, "Ron")
        self.SetCellValue(5, 1, "Cey")
        self.SetRowLabelValue(6, "C")
        self.SetCellValue(6, 0, "Jody")
        self.SetCellValue(6, 1, "Davis")
        self.SetRowLabelValue(7, "SS")
        self.SetCellValue(7, 0, "Larry")
        self.SetCellValue(7, 1, "Bowa")
        self.SetRowLabelValue(8, "P")
        self.SetCellValue(8, 0, "Rick")
        self.SetCellValue(8, 1, "Sutcliffe")

class TestFrame(wx.Frame):
    def __init__(self, parent):
        wx.Frame.__init__(self, parent, -1, "A Grid",
                size=(275, 275))
        grid = SimpleGrid(self)      # parent of Grid instance is self, a TestFrame instance

if __name__ == '__main__':
    app = wx.PySimpleApp()
    frame = TestFrame(None)
    frame.Show(True)
    app.MainLoop()
```

In listing 5.6, we have the class SimpleGrid, a subclass of the wxPython class wx.grid.Grid. As mentioned earlier, wx.grid.Grid has oodles of methods that we're going to discuss later. For now, we'll focus on the SetRowLabelValue(), Set-ColLabelValue(), and SetCellValue() methods which are actually setting the values displayed in the grid. As you can see by comparing figure 5.3 and listing 5.6, the SetCellValue() method takes a row index, a column index, and a value, while the other two methods take an index and a value. The row and column labels are *not* considered part of the grid for the purposes of assigning indexes to the cells.

This code directly assigns values to the grid using the setter methods. While this method has an admirable directness, it can become tedious and error-prone on larger grids. And even if we were to create utility methods to ease the burden, the code would still have the problem we saw in the refactoring section of this chapter. The data would be intertwined with the display in a way that would make future modifications to the code—such as adding a column or swapping the data out completely—difficult.

The answer is wx.grid.PyGridTableBase. As with other classes we've seen thus far, the Py prefix indicates that this is a Python-specific wrapper around a C++ class. Like the PyEvent class we saw in chapter 3, the PyGridTableBase class is implemented as a simple Python wrapper around a wxWidgets C++ class specifically for the purpose of allowing Python subclasses to be declared. A PyGrid-TableBase is a model class for a grid. That is, it contains methods that the grid object can use to draw itself, without having to know about the internal structure of that data.

Methods of PyGridTableBase

The wx.grid.PyGridTableBase has several methods, many of which you will not have to deal with. The class is abstract and cannot be instantiated directly. You will have to provide an implementation of five required methods every time you create a PyGridTableBase. Table 5.4 describes the methods.

Table 5.4 Required methods of wx.grid.PyGridTableBase

Method	Description
GetNumberRows()	Returns an integer indicating the number of rows in the grid.
GetNumberCols()	Returns an integer indicating the number of columns in the grid.
IsEmptyCell(row, col)	Returns True if the cell at index (row, col) is empty.

continued on next page

Table 5.4   Required methods of `wx.grid.PyGridTableBase` *(continued)*

Method	Description
GetValue(row, col)	Returns the value that should be displayed at the cell (row, col).
SetValue(row, col, value)	Sets the value associated with (row, col). If you want a read-only model, you still must include this method, but you can have it pass.

ie, subclass of Py GridTable Base

The table is attached to the grid by using the `SetTable()` method of the grid.   ✳
After that property is set, the grid object will call the methods of the table to get
the information it needs to draw the grid. The grid will no longer expect to have
the values explicitly set with grid methods. ← ? *The programmer of the grid will no longer*
expect...

Using a PyGridTableBase

In general, there are two ways to use a `PyGridTableBase`. You can explicitly have
your model class be a subclass of `PyGridTableBase`, or you can create a separate
`PyGridTableBase` subclass that connects to your actual model class. The first
option is easier and makes sense when your data is not very complex. The second
option enforces a stronger separation between the Model and the View, which is
preferable if your data is complex. The second option is also preferred if you have
a pre-existing data class that you want to adapt into wxPython, because you can
create a table without changing the existing code. We'll show an example of both
options in this section.

Using a PyGridTableBase: application-specific subclass

Our first example will use an application-specific subclass of `PyGridTableBase` as
our model. This works because our lineup example is relatively straightforward,
so we can directly incorporate the data into a class derived from `PyGridTableBase`.
We'll set up the actual data in a two-dimensional Python list, and set up the other
methods to read from that list. Listing 5.7 shows the Cubs lineup generated from
a Model class.

Listing 5.7   A table generated from a `PyGridTableBase` **model**

```
import wx
import wx.grid

class LineupTable(wx.grid.PyGridTableBase):

    data = (("CF", "Bob", "Dernier"), ("2B", "Ryne", "Sandberg"),
            ("LF", "Gary", "Matthews"), ("1B", "Leon", "Durham"),
            ("RF", "Keith", "Moreland"), ("3B", "Ron", "Cey"),
```

```
                ("C", "Jody", "Davis"), ("SS", "Larry", "Bowa"),
                ("P", "Rick", "Sutcliffe"))

    colLabels = ("Last", "First")

    def __init__(self):
        wx.grid.PyGridTableBase.__init__(self)

    def GetNumberRows(self):
        return len(self.data)

    def GetNumberCols(self):
        return len(self.data[0]) - 1

    def GetColLabelValue(self, col):
        return self.colLabels[col]

    def GetRowLabelValue(self, row):
        return self.data[row][0]

    def IsEmptyCell(self, row, col):
        return False

    def GetValue(self, row, col):
        return self.data[row][col + 1]

    def SetValue(self, row, col, value):          # grid is RO
        pass

class SimpleGrid(wx.grid.Grid):
    def __init__(self, parent):
        wx.grid.Grid.__init__(self, parent, -1)
        self.SetTable(LineupTable())          ← Table set here

class TestFrame(wx.Frame):          instance of wx.grid.PyGridTableBase
    def __init__(self, parent):
        wx.Frame.__init__(self, parent, -1, "A Grid",
                size=(275, 275))
        grid = SimpleGrid(self)

if __name__ == '__main__':
    app = wx.PySimpleApp()
    frame = TestFrame(None)
    frame.Show(True)
    app.MainLoop()
```

In listing 5.7, we've defined all the required `PyGridTableBase` methods, plus the additional methods `GetColLabelValue()` and `GetRowLabelValue()`. Hopefully you will not be too surprised to learn that these methods allow the table to specify the column and row labels, respectively. As in the refactoring section, the effect of using the model class is to separate the data from the display. In this case, we've also moved the data into a more structured format, which could easily be separated to an external file or resource (a database would be particularly easy to add here).

Using a PyGridTableBase: a generic example

In fact, we're very close to having a generic table that can read any two-dimensional Python list. Listing 5.8 shows what the generic model would look like.

> **Listing 5.8 A generic table for two-dimensional lists**

```
import wx                                         File:   generic table.py
import wx.grid

class GenericTable(wx.grid.PyGridTableBase):

    def __init__(self, data, rowLabels=None, colLabels=None):
        wx.grid.PyGridTableBase.__init__(self)
        self.data = data
        self.rowLabels = rowLabels
        self.colLabels = colLabels

    def GetNumberRows(self):                R
        return len(self.data)

    def GetNumberCols(self):                R          R = requires, as per
        -return len(self.data[0])                                  p 130

    def GetColLabelValue(self, col):
        if self.colLabels:
            return self.colLabels[col]

    def GetRowLabelValue(self, row):
        if self.rowLabels:
            return self.rowLabels[row]

    def IsEmptyCell(self, row, col):       R
        return False

    def GetValue(self, row, col):          R
        return self.data[row][col]

    def SetValue(self, row, col, value):   R
        pass
```

The `GenericTable` class takes a two-dimensional list of data and an optional list of row and/or column headers. It's suitable to be imported into any wxPython program. With a slight change in the data format, we can now use the generic table to display the lineup, as in listing 5.9.

Listing 5.9 The lineup display using the generic table

```
import wx
import wx.grid
import generictable

data = (("Bob", "Dernier"), ("Ryne", "Sandberg"),
        ("Gary", "Matthews"), ("Leon", "Durham"),
        ("Keith", "Moreland"), ("Ron", "Cey"),
        ("Jody", "Davis"), ("Larry", "Bowa"),
        ("Rick", "Sutcliffe"))

colLabels = ("Last", "First")
rowLabels = ("CF", "2B", "LF", "1B", "RF", "3B", "C", "SS", "P")

class SimpleGrid(wx.grid.Grid):
    def __init__(self, parent):
        wx.grid.Grid.__init__(self, parent, -1)
        tableBase = generictable.GenericTable(data, rowLabels,
                colLabels)
        self.SetTable(tableBase)

class TestFrame(wx.Frame):
    def __init__(self, parent):
        wx.Frame.__init__(self, parent, -1, "A Grid",
                size=(275, 275))
        grid = SimpleGrid(self)

if __name__ == '__main__':
    app = wx.PySimpleApp()
    frame = TestFrame(None)
    frame.Show(True)
    app.MainLoop()
```

Using a PyGridTableBase: a standalone Model class

At the risk of being repetitive, there is one more way to use the `PyGridTable-Base` that is worth showing here. This is the second option alluded to earlier, where the data is kept in a separate model class which is accessed by the `PyGrid-TableBase`. Python's self-inspection capabilities are very useful here, allowing you to make a list of the attributes that are displayed in each column and then use the

built-in function `getattr()` to retrieve the actual value. In this case, the model takes a list of elements. Structuring your program with separate model objects has ✗
one big advantage in wxPython. Under normal circumstances, you can only call `SetTable()` once for a grid—if you want to change the table, you need to create a new grid, and that can be annoying. However, if, as in the next example, your `PyGridTableBase` only stores references to instances of your real data class, then you can update the table to new data by just changing the underlying data object in the table.

Listing 5.10 shows the `PyGridTableBase` using a separate data class for the lineup entries we've been displaying—we'll spare you another listing of the frame and data creation itself, as it's quite similar to the previous ones.

Listing 5.10   The lineup display table using a custom data class

```
import wx
import wx.grid

class LineupEntry:              # · data for a row, incl label

    def __init__(self, pos, first, last):   # Now have identifying attributes for
        self.pos = pos                      # row values
        self.first = first
        self.last = last

class LineupTable(wx.grid.PyGridTableBase):    ⟵ The column
                                                 headers
    colLabels = ("First", "Last")     ⟵
    colAttrs = ("first", "last")      ❶ The attribute names
                                          list or tuple
    def __init__(self, entries):
        wx.grid.PyGridTableBase.__init__(self)   ⟵ ❷ Initializing
        self.entries = entries                        the model

    def GetNumberRows(self):
        return len(self.entries)

    def GetNumberCols(self):
        return 2

    def GetColLabelValue(self, col):
        return self.colLabels[col]     ⟵ Reading the value of the header

    def GetRowLabelValue(self, row):
        return self.entries[row].pos     ❸ Reading the row header

    def IsEmptyCell(self, row, col):
        return False
```

R: required, as per 130

R (beside GetNumberRows, GetNumberCols, IsEmptyCell)

len (entries[0]) - 1 (handwritten, near GetNumberCols)

→ # get LineUpEntry instance
→ # apply: getattr (obj, attrname) 1

```
R    def GetValue(self, row, col):
         entry = self.entries[row]
         return getattr(entry, self.colAttrs[col])
```

4 **Reading the attribute value**

```
R    def SetValue(self, row, col, value):
         pass
```

1 This list contains the attributes that need to be referenced to display the values column by column.

2 The model takes a list of entries where each entry is an instance of the `Lineup-Entry` class. (We're not doing any error checking or validation here).

3 To get the row header, we look up the `pos` attribute of the entry in the proper row.

4 The first step here is getting the correct entry based on the row. The attribute is taken from the list in line **1**, and then the `getattr()` built-in is used to reference the actual value. This mechanism is extensible even in the case where you don't know if the name refers to an attribute or a method by checking to see if `<object>.<attribute>` is `callable()`. If it is, then call it using normal Python function syntax, and return that value.

The grid class is an example where wxPython already has a valuable model component to help you structure your application. The next section will discuss how to create model components for other wxPython objects.

5.2.3 *A custom model*

The basic idea behind creating your model objects is simple. Construct your data classes without worrying about how they will be displayed. Then document a public interface for that class which will be accessible to the display objects. Obviously, the size and complexity of the project will determine how formal this public declaration needs to be. In a small project, with simple objects, it's probably enough to do the simple thing and allow the View objects direct access to the attributes of the model. In a more complex object, you may want to define specific methods for this use, or create a separate model class that is the only thing that the view sees (as we did in listing 5.10). 135

You also need some kind of mechanism for allowing the view to be notified of changes in the model. Listing 5.11 shows a simple one—an abstract base class that you can use as the parent for any of your model classes. You can think of this as an analogue to `PyGridTableBase` for use when the display is not a grid.

1   Could do:
entry = getattr (self, "entries") [row]

module: abstractmodel.py

Listing 5.11   A custom model for updating a view

```python
class AbstractModel(object):        # new style class

    def __init__(self):
        self.listeners = []

    def addListener(self, listenerFunc):
        self.listeners.append(listenerFunc)

    def removeListener(self, listenerFunc):
        self.listeners.remove(listenerFunc)

    def update(self):
        for eachFunc in self.listeners:
            eachFunc(self)
```

The listeners in this case are expected to be callable objects which can take `self` as an argument—obviously the actual class of `self` can vary, so your listener might have to flexible. Also, we've set up `AbstractModel` as a Python new-style class, as evidenced by the fact that it is a subclass of `object`. Therefore, this example requires Python 2.2 or higher to run.

How can we use the abstract model class? Figure 5.4 shows a new window, similar to the window we used for the refactoring earlier in this chapter. The window is simple. The text boxes are read-only. Clicking one of the buttons sets the text boxes to display the name of the relevant character.

The program that runs this window uses a simple MVC structure. The button-handler methods change the model, and the model-update structure causes the text fields to change. Listing 5.12 shows this in detail.

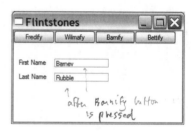

after Barnify button is pressed

Figure 5.4   A simple window showing how models work

Listing 5.12   The MVC program to "Flintstonize" your window

```python
#!/usr/bin/env python

import wx
import abstractmodel              # above

class SimpleName(abstractmodel.AbstractModel):

    def __init__(self, first="", last=""):
```

```
            abstractmodel.AbstractModel.__init__(self)
            self.set(first, last)

        def set(self, first, last):            # doing a set causes an update
            self.first = first
            self.last = last
 @137       self.update()          ❶ Updating

class ModelExample(wx.Frame):

        def __init__(self, parent, id):
            wx.Frame.__init__(self, parent, id, 'Flintstones',
                    size=(340, 200))
            panel = wx.Panel(self)
            panel.SetBackgroundColour("White")
            self.Bind(wx.EVT_CLOSE, self.OnCloseWindow)
            self.textFields = {}
            self.createTextFields(panel)
            self.model = SimpleName()    # create instance    ❷ Creating
            self.model.addListener(self.OnUpdate)                the model
            self.createButtonBar(panel)

        def buttonData(self):
            return (("Fredify", self.OnFred),
                    ("Wilmafy", self.OnWilma),
                    ("Barnify", self.OnBarney),
                    ("Bettify", self.OnBetty))

        def createButtonBar(self, panel, yPos = 0):
            xPos = 0
            for eachLabel, eachHandler in self.buttonData():
                pos = (xPos, yPos)
                button = self.buildOneButton(panel, eachLabel, eachHandler, pos)
                xPos += button.GetSize().width

        def buildOneButton(self, parent, label, handler, pos=(0,0)):
            button = wx.Button(parent, -1, label, pos)
            self.Bind(wx.EVT_BUTTON, handler, button)
            return button

        def textFieldData(self):
            return (("First Name", (10, 50)),
                    ("Last Name", (10, 80)))

        def createTextFields(self, panel):
            for eachLabel, eachPos in self.textFieldData():
                self.createCaptionedText(panel, eachLabel, eachPos)

        def createCaptionedText(self, panel, label, pos):
            static = wx.StaticText(panel, wx.NewId(), label, pos)
            static.SetBackgroundColour("White")
```

```
        textPos = (pos[0] + 75, pos[1])
        self.textFields[label] = wx.TextCtrl(panel, wx.NewId(),
            "", size=(100, -1), pos=textPos,
            style=wx.TE_READONLY)

    def OnUpdate(self, model):
        self.textFields["First Name"].SetValue(model.first)
        self.textFields["Last Name"].SetValue(model.last)

    def OnFred(self, event):
        self.model.set("Fred", "Flintstone")

    def OnBarney(self, event):
        self.model.set("Barney", "Rubble")

    def OnWilma(self, event):
        self.model.set("Wilma", "Flintstone")

    def OnBetty(self, event):
        self.model.set("Betty", "Rubble")

    def OnCloseWindow(self, event):
        self.Destroy()

if __name__ == '__main__':
    app = wx.PySimpleApp()
    frame = ModelExample(parent=None, id=-1)
    frame.Show()
    app.MainLoop()
```

❸ Setting text fields

❹ Button click handlers *... this ... ... model*
These handlers ,
via set()?

(1) change the model
(2) invoke the model
object's update
method. That
finds self.OnUpdate
registered as listener:
it is invoked to
change the view

❶ This line performs the update.

❷ These two lines create the model object, and register the `OnUpdate()` method as a listener. Now that method will be called whenever the update is invoked.

❸ The `OnUpdate()` method itself simply sets the value of the text fields using the model passed around as part of the update. The code could use the `self.model` instance instead (they should be the same object). Using the method argument is more robust in the case where the same code is listening on multiple objects.

❹ The button-click handlers change the value of the model object, which triggers the update.

In an example this small, the model update mechanism may seem overly baroque. There's no reason why the button handlers couldn't directly set the text field values. The model mechanism becomes more valuable, however, when the model class has a more complex internal state and processing. You would be able, for example, to change the internal representation from a Python dictionary to an external database without making any changes in the view.

If you are dealing with an existing class that you cannot or do not want to change, then AbstractModel can be used as a proxy for the existing class in much the same way as the LineupTable is in listing 5.10.

In addition, wxPython contains two separate implementations of similar MVC update mechanisms that have more features than the one described here. The first is the module wx.lib.pubsub, which is quite similar in structure to the AbstractModel class given previously. The model class, called Publisher, allows objects to listen for only specific kinds of messages. The other update system, wx.lib.evtmgr.eventManager, is built on top of pubsub, and has some additional features, including a more elaborate object-oriented design and easy connection and removal of event relationships.

5.3 How do you unit-test a GUI program?

A key advantage of good refactoring and the MVC design pattern is that it makes it easier to validate the performance of your program using *unit tests*. A unit test is a test of a single, specific function of your program. Because both refactoring and the use of an MVC design pattern tend to break your program into smaller pieces, it is easier for you to write specific unit tests targeting individual parts of your program. Unit testing is a particularly useful tool when combined with refactoring, because a complete suite of unit tests allows you to verify that you are not introducing any errors as you move your code around.

A continual challenge in unit testing is how to test UI code. Testing a model is relatively straightforward, as most of the model functionality will not depend on user input. Testing the functionality of the interface itself can be more difficult because the behavior of the interface depends on user behavior that can be hard to encapsulate. In this section we'll show you how to use unit testing in wxPython, particularly the use of manually generated events to trigger behavior during a unit test.

5.3.1 The unittest module

When writing user tests, it's helpful to use a pre-existing test engine to spare you the repetitive task of writing code to run your tests. Since version 2.1, Python has been distributed with the unittest module. The unittest module implements a test framework called PyUnit (a Tkinter based user interface for unittest and some other goodies are available at http://pyunit.sourceforge.net/). A PyUnit module is made up of tests, test cases, and test suites. Table 5.5 defines the three groups.

Table 5.5   The three levels of abstraction in the unittest module

Item	Definition
Test	An individual method called by the PyUnit engine. By convention, the name of a test method begins with `test`. A test method typically executes some code, then performs one or more assert statements to test whether the results are as expected.
TestCase	A class defining one or more individual tests that share a common setup. The class is defined in PyUnit to manage a group of such tests. The `TestCase` class has support for doing common setup before and tear down after each test, ensuring that each test runs separately from the others. The `TestCase` class also defines some special assert methods, such as `assertEqual`.
TestSuite	One or more test methods or `TestCase` objects grouped together for the purpose of being run at the same time. When you actually tell PyUnit to run tests, you pass it a `TestSuite` object to run.

A single PyUnit test can have one of three results: success, failure, or error. Success indicates that the test method ran to completion, all assertions were true, and no errors were triggered. That is, of course, the desirable outcome. Failure and error indicate different problems with the code. A failure result means that one of your assertions returned false, indicating that the code runs successfully, but is not doing what you expect. An error result means that a Python exception was triggered somewhere in the execution of the test, showing that your code is not running successfully. The first failure or error in a single test will end the execution of that test, even if there are more assertions to test in the code, and the test runner will move on to the next test.

5.3.2   A unittest sample

Listing 5.13 shows a sample `unittest` module, in this case, tests for the model example in Listing 5.12.

Listing 5.13   A sample unit test for the model example

```
import unittest
import modelExample
import wx
                                           ❶ Declaring
                                             a test case
class TestExample(unittest.TestCase):
    def setUp(self):          ❷ Set up for each test
        self.app = wx.PySimpleApp()
        self.frame = modelExample.ModelExample(parent=None, id=-1)

    def tearDown(self):    ❸ Tear down after each test
```

```
        self.frame.Destroy()
    def testModel(self):
        self.frame.OnBarney(None)   # None is Event instance
        self.assertEqual("Barney", self.frame.model.first,
                msg="First is wrong")
        self.assertEqual("Rubble", self.frame.model.last)
def suite():
    suite = unittest.makeSuite(TestExample, 'test')
    return suite

if __name__ == '__main__':
    unittest.main(defaultTest='suite')
```

④ Declaring a test

⑤ An assertion that could fail

⑥ Creating a test suite

prefix to identify a test method

⑦ Starting the test

method name

❶ The test case is a subclass of `unittest.TestCase`. The test runner creates an instance of the class for each test, in order to best allow the tests to be independent of each other.

❷ The `setUp()` method is called before each test is run. This allows you to guarantee that each test starts with your application in the same state. In this case, we create an instance of the frame that we are testing.

❸ The `tearDown()` method is called after each test is run. This allows you to do any clean-up necessary to ensure that the system state remains consistent from test to test. Generally this includes resetting global data, closing database connections and the like. In this case we call `Destroy()` on the frame, which forces wxWidgets to exit, and keeps the system in a good state for the next test.

❹ The test method usually begins with the prefix `test`, although that is under your control (see line **❻**). Test methods take no arguments. This method starts by explicitly calling the `OnBarney` event handler method to test behavior.

❺ This line uses the `assertEqual()` method to test that the model object has been correctly changed. The `assertEqual()` method takes two arguments, and the test fails if they are not equal. All PyUnit assertion methods take an optional `msg` argument which is displayed if the assertion fails (the default for `assertEqual()` is almost always useful enough).

❻ This method creates a test suite through the easiest mechanism available, the `makeSuite()` method. The method takes a Python class object and a string prefix as arguments, and returns a test suite containing all the test methods in that class whose names begin with the prefix. There are other mechanisms that allow for more explicit setting of a test suite's contents, but this method is generally all you need. The `suite()` method as written here is a boilerplate template that can be used in all of your test modules.

➐ This line invokes the PyUnit text-based runner. The argument is the name of a method that returns a test suite. The suite is then run, and the results are output to the console. If you wanted to use the GUI test runner, you would change this line to call the main method of that module.

The results of this PyUnit test, run from a console window, are as follows:

```
⊙    One test executed
---------------------------------------------------------------
Ran 1 test in 0.190s

OK
```

This is a successful test. The top line, with the dot, indicates that the one test ran successfully. Each test gets one character in the display, . indicates success, F indicates failure, and E indicates error. Then comes the simple listing of the number of tests and the total time elapsed, and an OK indicating that all tests passed.

On a failure or error, you receive a stack trace showing how Python got to the point of the error. If we were to change the last name test to Fife, for instance, we'd receive the following result:

```
Ⓕ              name of failing method
===============================================================
FAIL: testModel (__main__.TestExample)        assertion, line 18, Failed
---------------------------------------------------------------
Traceback (most recent call last):
  File "C:\wxPyBook\book\1\Blueprint\testExample.py", line 18, in testModel
    self.assertEqual("Fife", self.frame.model.last)
  File "c:\python23\lib\unittest.py", line 302, in failUnlessEqual
    raise self.failureException, \
AssertionError: 'Fife' != 'Rubble'


---------------------------------------------------------------
Ran 1 test in 0.070s

FAILED (failures=1)
```

This indicates the failure in the first line, gives the name of the method that failed, and a traceback showing that the assertion on line 18 failed, and how it failed. You generally need to go a few levels deep in the stack trace to show where the actual failure was; the last line or two of the stack trace is likely to be in the unittest module itself.

5.3.3 *Testing user events*

This test is not a complete test of the system, of course. We could also test that the TextField instances in the frame were updated with the values after the model was updated. That test would be reasonably straightforward. Another test you might want to run would be to automatically generate the button-click event itself, and ensure that the proper handler is called. That test is a little less straightforward. Listing 5.14 shows an example:

Listing 5.14   A sample test by generating a user event

```
def testEvent(self):
    panel = self.frame.GetChildren()[0]
    for each in panel.GetChildren():
        if each.GetLabel() == "Wilmafy":
            wilma = each
            break
    event = wx.CommandEvent(wx.wxEVT_COMMAND_BUTTON_CLICKED, wilma.GetId())
    wilma.GetEventHandler().ProcessEvent(event)
    self.assertEqual("Wilma", self.frame.model.first)
    self.assertEqual("Flintstone", self.frame.model.last)
```

[handwritten annotations: frame / panel / button labelled 'Wilmafy'; programmatically create button press on "Wilmafy" button; set id of event; constant for event type (see wx.py)]

The first few lines of this example find the appropriate button (in this case, the "Wilmafy" button). Since we did not explicitly store the buttons as Python instance variables, we just need to walk through the panel's children list until we find the right button. (You could also do this as a Python list comprehension if you wanted).[1] The next two lines create the wx.CommandEvent to be sent from the button. The single parameter to the creator is wx.wxEVT_COMMAND_BUTTON_CLICKED, a constant for the actual integer event type that is bound to the EVT_BUTTON binder object. (You can find the integer constants in the wxPython source file wx.py). After that, we set the ID of the event to the ID of the Wilmafy button. At this point, the event has all the relevant features of the actual event as it would be created by wxPython. So, we call ProcessEvent() to send it into the system. If the code works as planned, then the model first and last names will be changed to "Wilma" and "Flintstone."

By generating events, you can test the responsiveness of your system from beginning to end. In theory, you could generate a mouse-down and mouse-up event within your button to ensure that the button-click event is created as a response. In practice, this won't work with native widgets because the low level wx.Events aren't translated back into native system events and sent to the native widget. However, a similar process could be useful when testing custom widgets (such as the two-button control in chapter 3). This kind of unit testing can give you confidence in the responsiveness of your application.

[handwritten footnote]
[1] wilma = [for each in panel.GetChildren() if each.GetLabel() == "Wilmafy"][0]

5.4 *Summary*

- GUI code has a bad reputation for being messy and hard to maintain. This can be overcome with a little extra effort, which will pay off when it's time to make changes to your code.

- Refactoring is the improvement of existing code. Some goals of refactoring are to remove duplication, remove magic literals, and create short methods that do only one thing. Continually striving for those goals will make your code easier to read and understand. In addition, good refactoring also make certain types of errors (such as cut-and-paste errors) much less likely.

- Separating your data from your layout code makes both data and layout easier to work with. The standard mechanism for managing this separation is the MVC mechanism. In wxPython terms, the View is the `wx.Window` objects that display your data, the Controller is the `wx.EvtHandler` objects that dispatch events, and the Model is your own code that contains the information to be displayed.

- Perhaps the clearest example of an MVC structure in the core wxPython classes is the `wx.grid.PyGridTableBase`, which is used to model data for display in a `wx.grid.Grid` control. The data in the table can either come from the class itself, or the class can reference another object containing the relevant data. *128 ff*

- You can create your own MVC setup with a simple mechanism for notifying the view when the model has been updated. There are also existing modules within wxPython that will help you do this. *140*

- Unit testing is a useful way to verify the validity of your program. In Python, the `unittest` module is one of the standard ways of executing unit tests. In some packages, unit testing of a GUI is difficult, but wxPython makes it relatively easy to programmatically create events. This allows you to test the event handling behavior of your application from beginning to end.

In the next chapter, we'll show you how to build a small application and how to do several things that will be common to many of the wxPython applications that you will build.

Working with
the basic building blocks

This chapter covers

- Using a device context to draw to the screen
- Adding window decorations to a frame
- Working with standard file dialogs and color pickers
- Laying out widgets and creating a sizer
- Building about boxes and splash screens

Even a simple wxPython program needs to use standard elements such as menus and dialogs. These are the basic building blocks of any GUI application. Using these building blocks, along with fancier widgets like a splash screen, status bar, or about box, provides a more user-friendly environment, and gives your application a professional look and feel. To conclude the first part of the book, we'll guide you through the creation of a program using all of these components. We'll build a simple draw program, then add these building block elements and explain some of the issues in using them. We'll reinforce the fundamental concepts covered in the previous chapters, and at the end you'll have a simple but professional application. This chapter is a middle ground between the basic concepts discussed in the previous chapters and the more detailed discussion of wxPython functionality in parts 2 and 3.

The application we'll build in this chapter is loosely based on the Doodle and Super Doodle samples that are distributed with wxPython in the wxPython/samples directory. It's a very simple draw program that tracks the mouse pointer when the left mouse button is down, and draws a line. Figure 6.1 displays a simple initial sketch window.

Figure 6.1 A simple sketch window, with no further decorations

We chose a sketch sample because it's a fairly simple program that illustrates many of the issues involved in creating more complex applications. Within this chapter, we'll show you how to draw lines on the screen, and add a status bar, a toolbar, and menubar. You'll see how to use common dialogs, such as a file chooser and a color picker. We'll use sizers to lay out complicated widget sets, and we'll add an about box and a splash screen. At the end of the chapter, you'll have created a nice looking sketch program.

6.1 Drawing to the screen

The first job of your sketch program is to draw the sketch lines to the display. Like many other GUI tools, wxPython provides a device-independent set of tools for drawing to various kinds of displays. In the following section we'll discuss how to draw on the screen.

6.1.1 How do I draw on the screen?

To draw on the screen, we use a wxPython object called a *device context*. A device context abstracts a display device, giving each device a common set of draw methods, so that your draw code is the same no matter what kind of device you are targeting. A device context is represented by the abstract wxPython class wx.DC and its subclasses. Since wx.DC is abstract, you'll need to use one of its subclasses for your application.

Using a device context

Table 6.1 displays a field guide to the subclasses of wx.DC and their usage. Device contexts, which are used to draw to a wxPython widget, should *always* be locally created, temporary objects, and should not be kept between method calls in an instance variable, global variable, or other manner. On some platforms device contexts are a limited resource and so holding references to a wx.DC could cause your program to be unstable. Because of the way wxPython uses device contexts internally, there are several subtly different wx.DC subclasses used for drawing in a widget. Chapter 12 will explain these differences in more detail.

Table 6.1 A brief guide to the device context subclasses of wx.DC

Device Context	Usage
wx.BufferedDC	Used to buffer a set of drawing commands until they are complete and ready to draw to screen. This prevents unwanted flicker in the display.
wx.BufferedPaintDC	As wx.BufferedDC but only used within the processing of a wx.PaintEvent. Only create instances of this class temporarily.

continued on next page

Table 6.1   A brief guide to the device context subclasses of `wx.DC` *(continued)*

Device Context	Usage
`wx.ClientDC`	Used to draw on a window object. Use this when you want to draw on the main area of the widget—not the border or any other decoration. The main area is sometimes called the client area, hence the name of this DC. The `wx.ClientDC` class should only be created temporarily. This class is only used outside of the processing of a `wx.PaintEvent`.
`wx.MemoryDC`	Used to draw graphics to a bitmap stored in memory, not being displayed. You can then select the bitmap, and use the `wx.DC.Blit()` method to draw the bitmap to a window.
`wx.MetafileDC`	On Windows operating systems, this device context allows you to create standard windows metafile data.
`wx.PaintDC`	Identical to `wx.ClientDC` except that it is only used within the processing of a `wx.PaintEvent`. Only create instances of this class temporarily.
`wx.PostScriptDC`	Used to write encapsulated PostScript files
`wx.PrinterDC`	Used on Windows operating systems to write to a printer.
`wx.ScreenDC`	Used to draw directly to the screen itself, on top and outside of any windows being displayed. This class should only be created temporarily.
`wx.WindowDC`	Used to draw on the entire area of a window object, including the border, and any other decorations not included in the client area. Non-Windows operating systems might not support this class.

Handwritten annotations in margins: "Use: 163" (next to wx.MemoryDC), "154", "Use 326-7" (next to wx.PaintDC)

Listing 6.1 contains the code for the initial pass of the sketch window displayed in figure 6.1. Because this code shows tricks of drawing to device contexts, we'll annotate it in detail.

Listing 6.1   The initial SketchWindow code

Handwritten annotation: "sketch0.py"

```python
import wx

class SketchWindow(wx.Window):
    def __init__(self, parent, ID):
        wx.Window.__init__(self, parent, ID)
        self.SetBackgroundColour("White")
        self.color = "Black"
        self.thickness = 1
        self.pen = wx.Pen(self.color, self.thickness, wx.SOLID)
        self.lines = []
        self.curLine = []
        self.pos = (0, 0)
        self.InitBuffer()
```

Handwritten annotations: "or: wx.DOT .LONG DASH .SHORT DASH", "Creating a ❶ wx.Pen object", "# no lines yet; just # paint (white) background"

```
        self.Bind(wx.EVT_LEFT_DOWN, self.OnLeftDown)
        self.Bind(wx.EVT_LEFT_UP, self.OnLeftUp)
        self.Bind(wx.EVT_MOTION, self.OnMotion)
        self.Bind(wx.EVT_SIZE, self.OnSize)
        self.Bind(wx.EVT_IDLE, self.OnIdle)
        self.Bind(wx.EVT_PAINT, self.OnPaint)
```

❷ **Linking the events**

Ⓐ 151

374: Similar use of buffer

Ⓑ 370

```
    def InitBuffer(self):
        size = self.GetClientSize()
        self.buffer = wx.EmptyBitmap(size.width, size.height)
        dc = wx.BufferedDC(None, self.buffer)
        dc.SetBackground(wx.Brush(self.GetBackgroundColour()))
        dc.Clear()
        self.DrawLines(dc)
        self.reInitBuffer = False
```

Creating a buffered device context ❸

p361

txt   bitmap

Using the device context ❹

```
    def GetLinesData(self):
        return self.lines[:]

    def SetLinesData(self, lines):
        self.lines = lines[:]
        self.InitBuffer()
        self.Refresh()
```

(0)
```
    def OnLeftDown(self, event):
        self.curLine = []              # Now empty current line
        self.pos = event.GetPositionTuple()
        self.CaptureMouse()
```
❺ **Getting the mouse position**

❻ **Capturing the mouse**

(2)
```
    def OnLeftUp(self, event):
        if self.HasCapture():          # If self.CaptureMouse() was called
            self.lines.append((self.color,
                               self.thickness,
                               self.curLine))
            self.curLine = []
            self.ReleaseMouse()
```
❼ **Releasing the mouse**

When user moves mouse (1) a drawing action self.DrawMotion() is performed

(2) The data involved are saved to permit redrawing of all motions

(1)
```
    def OnMotion(self, event):   # draws a short segment
        if event.Dragging() and event.LeftIsDown():
            dc = wx.BufferedDC(wx.ClientDC(self), self.buffer)
            self.drawMotion(dc, event)
        event.Skip()
            # dc goes out of scope here...
```
❽ **Determining if a drag is ongoing**

txt   bitmap

Creating another buffered context ❾

```
    def drawMotion(self, dc, event):
        dc.SetPen(self.pen)
        newPos = event.GetPositionTuple()
        coords = self.pos + newPos  # (x1,y1,x2,y2)
        self.curLine.append(coords)
        dc.DrawLine(*coords)   # (x1,y1,x2,y2)
        self.pos = newPos
```
❿ **Drawing to device context**

curLine : [(x0,y0,x1,y1),
(x1,y1,x2,y2),
⋮
]

draw ∙ x1,y1
∙ x2,y2

1 means offscreen buffer
2 clear by painting the background

```
def OnSize(self, event):          # invoked when window is resized
    self.reInitBuffer = True      ⑪  Handling a resize event

def OnIdle(self, event):          ⑫  Idle processing      # invoked when "an idle event comes along"
    if self.reInitBuffer:
        self.InitBuffer()
        self.Refresh(False)

def OnPaint(self, event):                                              ⓒ 370
    dc = wx.BufferedPaintDC(self, self.buffer)  ?  ⑬  Handling a paint request    ⓓ 153
                                                                        ⓐ 368
                                                         lines: list of lists like
def DrawLines(self, dc):
    for colour, thickness, line in self.lines:               # [(colour, thickness, [(x₀,y₀,x₁,y₁)
        pen = wx.Pen(colour, thickness, wx.SOLID)   ⑭  Drawing
        dc.SetPen(pen)                                       all lines     (x₁,y₁, x₂,y₂),
        for coords in line:
            dc.DrawLine(*coords)   #        x₁ y₁
                              \ 372          x₀ y₀

def SetColor(self, color):   # recreate pen
    self.color = color
    self.pen = wx.Pen(self.color, self.thickness, wx.SOLID)     lines is a list of 3 tuples.
                                                                The 3rd member of each tuple
def SetThickness(self, num):   # recreate pen                    is a list of 4-tuples,
    self.thickness = num                                        orig. a curline
    self.pen = wx.Pen(self.color, self.thickness, wx.SOLID)

class SketchFrame(wx.Frame):
    def __init__(self, parent):
        wx.Frame.__init__(self, parent, -1, "Sketch Frame",
                size=(800,600))
        self.sketch = SketchWindow(self, -1)      # SketchFrame obj holds onto
                                                  # SketchWindow instance

if __name__ == '__main__':
    app = wx.PySimpleApp()
    frame = SketchFrame(None)
    frame.Show(True)
    app.MainLoop()
```

❶ The wx.Pen instance determines the color, thickness, and style of lines drawn to the device context. Styles other than wx.SOLID include wx.DOT, wx.LONGDASH, and wx.SHORTDASH.   Need to create pen then do dc.SetPen() to use it

❷ This window needs to respond to several different mouse event types in order to draw the sketch. It responds to left mouse button up and down, mouse motion, window resize, and window repaint. It also specifies processing to take place during idle times.   @ 150

❸ The buffered device context is created in two steps: (1) Create the empty bitmap that serves as the offscreen buffer and (2) Create a buffered device context using the offscreen buffer. The buffered context is used to prevent the redrawing of the

1 Yes: take a Window obj here p 370
use: dc = wx.BufferedPaintDC(wx.PaintDC(self), self.buffer) ?

sketched lines from causing screen flicker. Later in this section, we'll discuss the buffered device contexts in more detail.   *clear by painting the background*

❹ These lines issue drawing commands to the device context; specifically, setting the background drawing brush and clearing the device. The wx.Brush object determines the color and style of the background for fill commands.

❺ The event method GetPositionTuple() returns a Python tuple containing the exact position of the mouse click being processed.

❻ The CaptureMouse() method directs all mouse input to the window, even if you drag the mouse outside the border of the window. This call must be negated by calling ReleaseMouse() later in the program.

❼ The ReleaseMouse() call returns the system to the state before the previous CaptureMouse() call. The wxPython application uses a stack to keep track of windows that have captured the mouse, and calling ReleaseMouse() is equivalent to popping that stack. This implies that you need the same number of CaptureMouse() and ReleaseMouse() calls.

❽ This line determines if the motion event is part of a line draw, defined by whether the motion event occurs while the left mouse button is down. Both Dragging() and LeftIsDown() are methods of wx.MouseEvent that return True if the associated condition is true when the motion event occurs.

❾ Since wx.BufferedDC is one of the device contexts that is created temporarily, we need to create another one before we draw the lines. In this case we create a new wx.ClientDC as the main device context, and reuse our instance variable bitmap as the buffer.   *a 4-tuple*

❿ These lines actually use the device context to draw the newly sketched line to the screen. First, we create the coords tuple, which is a combination of the self.pos and the newPos tuples. In this case, the new point comes from the event GetPositionTuple(), and the old point is stored from the last call to OnMotion(). We save that tuple to the self.curLine list, and then use the function call unpack syntax to call DrawLine(), with the elements of the tuple as the arguments. The DrawLine() method takes as parameters (x1, y1, x2, y2), and draws a line from the point (x1, y1) to the point (x2, y2). The frequency with which the motion event occurs and gives the sketch pad a new data point, is dependent on the underlying system speed.

⓫ If the window is resized, we make a note of it by storing a True value in the self.reInitBuffer instance attribute. We don't actually do anything until the next idle event.

⓬ When an idle event comes along, the application takes that opportunity to respond to a resize event, if one (or more) has occurred. The reason we respond in the idle event, rather than the resize event itself, is to allow multiple resize events to occur in quick succession without having to redraw for each one.

⓭ Handling the request for redraw is surprisingly simple: create a buffered paint device context. The real `wx.PaintDC` is created (since we are inside a paint request, we need `wx.PaintDC` and not a `wx.ClientDC` instance), and then the bitmap is blitted to it after the `dc` instance is deleted. More detailed information about buffering is provided in the following paragraphs.

⓮ This is used when the application needs to redraw the lines from the instance data due to a resize (and later due to a load from file). Again, we use the `Draw-Func()` wrapper. In this case, we walk the list of lines stored in the instance variable, recreate the pen for each line (currently all the same—support for changing pen characteristics will be added shortly), and then draw all the coordinate tuples added for that line.

The sketch example uses two special subclasses of `wx.DC` to allow the use of a buffer for drawing. A drawing buffer is an undisplayed area where all your primitive drawing commands can be performed one at a time, and then copied to the screen in one step. The advantage of a buffer is that the user does not see individual drawing commands happening, and thus, the screen refreshes with less flicker. For this reason, buffering is commonly used in animation or in cases where the drawing is made up of several smaller parts.

In wxPython, there are two classes used for buffering: `wx.BufferDC`, usually used to buffer a `wx.ClientDC`; and `wx.BufferPaintDC`, used to buffer a `wx.PaintDC`. Each works essentially the same way. The buffer device context is created with two arguments. The first is a target device context of the appropriate type (for example, in line **⓭** of listing 6.1, it's a new `wx.ClientDC` instance). The second is a `wx.Bitmap` object. In listing 6.1, we create a bitmap using the `wx.EmptyBitmap` function. When draw commands are made to the buffered device context, an internal `wx.MemoryDC` is used to draw to the bitmap. When the buffer object is destroyed, the C++ destructor uses the `Blit()` method to automatically copy the bitmap to the target. In wxPython, the destruction typically occurs when the object drops out of scope. The implication of this is that buffered device contexts are only useful when created temporarily, so that they can be destroyed and do the blit.

For example, in the `OnPaint()` method of listing 6.1, the `self.buffer` bitmap has already been written during the events that built the sketch. The buffered object simply needs to be created, thereby establishing a connection between the existing bitmap and the temporary `wx.PaintDC()` for the window. The method ends, and the buffered `DC` immediately drops out of scope, triggering its destructor, and copying the bitmap to the screen.

Functions of the device context

When using device contexts, remember to use the correct context for the kind of drawing you are trying to do (specifically, remember the distinction between `wx.PaintDC` and `wx.ClientDC`). Once you have the correct device context, then you can do something with it. Table 6.2 lists some of the more interesting methods of `wx.DC`.

Table 6.2 Commonly used methods of `wx.DC`

Function	Description
Blit(xdest, ydest, width, height, source, xsrc, ysrc)	Copies bits directly from a source device context to the device context making the call. The xdest and ydest parameters are the starting point for the copy on the destination context. The next two parameters specify the width and height of the copy area. The source is the source device context, and xsrc and ysrc are the starting point of the copy in the source context. There are further optional parameters to specify a logical overlay function and a mask.
Clear()	Clears the device context by painting the whole thing with the current background brush.
DrawArc(x1, y1, x2, y2, xc, yc)	Draws a circular arc with a start point of (x1, y1) and an end point of (x2, y2). The point (xc, yc) is the center of the circle whose arc is drawn. The resulting arc is filled using the current brush. The function assumes that it will draw a counterclockwise arc from the start point to the end point. There is a related method, `DrawEllipticalArc()`.
DrawBitmap(bitmap, x, y, transparent)	Copies a `wx.Bitmap` object starting at the point (x, y). If transparent is `True`, then the bitmap will be drawn transparently.
DrawCircle(x, y, radius) DrawCircle(point, radius)	Draws a circle centered at the given point with the given radius. There is a related method, `DrawEllipse`.
DrawIcon(icon, x, y)	Draws a `wx.Icon` object to the context, starting at the point (x, y).
DrawLine(x1, y1, x2, y2)	Draws a line from the point (x1, y1) to the point (x2, y2). There is a related method `DrawLines()` which takes a Python list of `wx.Point` objects and connects them.
DrawPolygon(points)	Draws a polygon, given a Python list of `wx.Point` objects. Differs from `DrawLines()` in that the end point is connected to the first point, and that the resulting shape is filled using the current brush. There are optional parameters to set an x and y offset and a fill style.
DrawRectangle(x, y, width, height)	Draws a rectangle whose upper left corner is (x, y) and which has the given width and height. The rectangle is filled.

continued on next page

Table 6.2 Commonly used methods of `wx.DC` *(continued)*

Function	Description
DrawText(text, x, y)	Draws the given string starting at the point (x, y), using the current font. Related functions include `DrawRotatedText()` and `GetTextExtent()`. Text items have separate text foreground and background color properties.
FloodFill(x, y, color, style)	Performs a flood fill starting at (x, y) and using the color of the current brush. The style parameter is optional. The default, `wx.FLOOD_SURFACE`, assumes the color parameter is the surface to flood—it stops when any other color is found. The other value, `wx.FLOOD_BORDER`, assumes the color is the border of the shape to flood, and flooding stops when that color is found.
GetBackground() SetBackground(brush)	The background brush is a `wx.Brush` object, and is used when the `Clear()` method is called.
GetBrush() SetBrush(brush)	The Brush is a `wx.Brush` object and is used to fill any shapes that are drawn on the device context.
GetFont() SetFont(font)	The font is a `wx.Font` object and is used for all text draw operations.
GetPen() SetPen(pen)	The pen is a `wx.Pen` object and is used for all drawing operations that draw a line.
GetPixel(x, y)	Returns a `wx.Colour` object for the pixel at (x, y).
GetSize() GetSizeTuple()	Returns the pixel size of the device context as either a `wx.Size` object or a Python tuple.

This is not an exhaustive list. In the interest of simplicity, several of the more obscure drawing methods were left out, as were text processing and pixel mapping functions. Those methods will be described in chapter 12.

6.2 *Adding window decorations*

While drawing to the screen is an indispensable part of a sketch program, it's far from the only thing necessary to make your application look polished. In this section, we'll talk about common window decorations: the status bar, the menubar, and the toolbar. We'll also discuss these features in more detail in chapter 10.

6.2.1 *How do I add and update a status bar?*

In wxPython, you can add and place a status bar in the bottom of a frame by calling the frame's `CreateStatusBar()` method. The status bar automatically resizes itself when the parent frame resizes. By default, the status bar is an instance of the class wx.StatusBar. To create a custom status bar subclass, attach it to your frame using the SetStatusBar() method, with an instance of your new class as the argument.

To display a single piece of text in your status bar, you can use the SetStatus-Text() method of wx.StatusBar. Listing 6.2 extends the SketchFrame class illustrated in listing 6.1 to display the current mouse pointer position in the status bar.

Listing 6.2 Adding a simple status bar to the frame

sketch1.py

```python
import wx
from example1 import SketchWindow

class SketchFrame(wx.Frame):
    def __init__(self, parent):
        wx.Frame.__init__(self, parent, -1, "Sketch Frame",
                size=(800,600))
        self.sketch = SketchWindow(self, -1)
        self.sketch.Bind(wx.EVT_MOTION, self.OnSketchMotion)
        self.statusbar = self.CreateStatusBar()    # add and place status bar

    def OnSketchMotion(self, event):
        self.statusbar.SetStatusText(str(event.GetPositionTuple()))
        event.Skip()

if __name__ == '__main__':
    app = wx.PySimpleApp()
    frame = SketchFrame(None)
    frame.Show(True)
    app.MainLoop()
```

We've hooked up the status bar by having the frame also capture the wx.EVT_MOTION event of the sketch window. The event handler sets the status text using the data provided by the event. Then it calls Skip() to ensure that the other OnMotion() method is called, otherwise the line won't be drawn.

You can treat the status bar like any other widget by adding objects to it. As a shortcut, if you want to display more than one text element, you can create multiple status text fields in the status bar. To use this functionality, call the method SetFieldsCount() with the number of fields you want; the default, as we've seen, is one. After that, use SetStatusText() as before, but with a second argument specifying the field being set by the method. The field numbers start at zero. If you don't specify a field, the zero field is set by default, which is why the previous example works even though we didn't specify the field.

By default, each of the fields have the same width. However that's not always what you want. To adjust the sizes of the text fields, wxPython provides the method

SetStatusWidth(). The method takes a Python list of integers, which must be the same length as the number of fields in the status bar. The integer list is used to calculate the width of the fields in order. If the integer is positive, it is the absolute fixed width of the field. If you want the field width to change with the frame, indicate that by using a negative integer. The absolute value of the negative integer indicates the relative size of the field; think of it as the number of shares of the total width that field gets. For example, the call statusbar.SetStatusWidth([-1, -2, -3]) results in the rightmost field getting half the width (3 parts out of 6), the center field getting a third of the width (2 parts out of 6), and the leftmost field getting a sixth of the width (1 part out of 6). Figure 6.2 displays the results.

Pos: (609, 213)	Current Pts: 39	Line Count: 4	

Figure 6.2   A sample status bar with the fields getting 1/6, 2/3, and 1/2 of the total width

Listing 6.3 adds support for two more status fields, one which shows the number of points in the current line being drawn, the other shows the number of lines in the current sketch. This listing produces the status bar displayed in figure 6.2.

Listing 6.3   Support for multiple status fields

```
import wx
from example1 import SketchWindow          Sketch2.py

class SketchFrame(wx.Frame):
    def __init__(self, parent):
        wx.Frame.__init__(self, parent, -1, "Sketch Frame",
                size=(800,600))
        self.sketch = SketchWindow(self, -1)
        self.sketch.Bind(wx.EVT_MOTION, self.OnSketchMotion)
        self.statusbar = self.CreateStatusBar()
        self.statusbar.SetFieldsCount(3)
        self.statusbar.SetStatusWidths([-1, -2, -3])   # Relative lengths for the 3 fields

    def OnSketchMotion(self, event):
        self.statusbar.SetStatusText("Pos: %s" %
                str(event.GetPositionTuple()), 0)
        self.statusbar.SetStatusText("Current Pts: %s" %
                len(self.sketch.curLine), 1)
        self.statusbar.SetStatusText("Line Count: %s" %
                len(self.sketch.lines), 2)
        event.Skip()

if __name__ == '__main__':
    app = wx.PySimpleApp()
```

```
frame = SketchFrame(None)
frame.Show(True)
app.MainLoop()
```

The StatusBar class allows you to treat the status fields as a last in/first out stack. Although not useful for the demo application in this chapter, the PushStatusText() and PopStatusText() methods allow you to return to the previous status text after temporarily displaying new text. Both of these methods take an optional field number, so they can be used in the case of multiple status fields.

Table 6.3 summarizes the most commonly used methods of wx.StatusBar.

Table 6.3   Methods of wx.StatusBar

Function	Description
GetFieldsCount() SetFieldsCount(count)	Property for the number of fields in the status bar
GetStatusText(field=0) SetStatusText(text, field=0)	Property for the text displayed in the specified status field. The index of 0 is the default and represents the leftmost field
PopStatusText(field=0)	Pops the text statck of the specified status field, changing the text of that field to the popped value
PushStatusText(text, field=0)	Changes the display of the specified status field to the given text, and pushes that value to the top of the stack for that field
SetStatusWidths(widths)	Takes a Python list of integers and specifies the width of the status fields. A positive number indicates a fixed width in pixels, and a negative number indicates a dynamic share of the width proportional to the absolute value of the number.

In chapter 10, we'll provide more details about status bars. In the meantime, we'll discuss menus.

6.2.2   *How do I include a submenu or checked menu?*

In this section, we'll present two common menu tricks, the submenu and the checked or radio menu. A submenu is a menu which is accessible inside one of the top menus. A checkbox or radio menu is a group of menu items that behaves like a group of checkboxes or radio buttons. Figure 6.3 displays a menubar, including a submenu with radio menu items.

To create a submenu, build it just as you would any other menu, and append it to the parent menu using wx.Menu.AppendMenu().

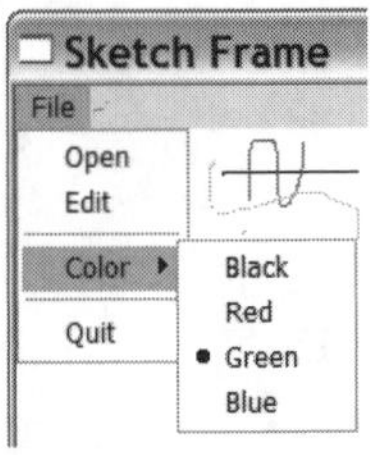

Figure 6.3
A menu that uses a submenu with radio menu items

Menu items with checkbox or radio button decorations can be created either
by using the wx.Menu methods AppendCheckItem() and AppendRadioItem(), or by
passing the kind attribute to the creator for wx.MenuItem one of the following values: wx.ITEM_NORMAL, wx.ITEM_CHECKBOX, or wx.ITEM_RADIO. A checkbox menu
item displays a check that automatically toggles on and off as the item is selected;
you do not have to manually manage that process. The start value of a checked
menu item is off. Radio menu items are implicitly grouped. Consecutive radio
items are considered to be part of the same group (a menu separator will break up
the group). By default, the topmost member of the group is checked, after which
selecting any member of the group automatically transfers the check to that item.
To programmatically check a menu item, use the wx.Menu method Check(id,
bool), where id is the wxPython ID of the item to be changed, and the Boolean
specifies the checked state of the item.

Listing 6.4 adds menu support to the sketch application frame. The menu
functionality here is an evolutionary descendent of the refactored utility code displayed in listing 5.5. In this case, the data format is tweaked to provide submenus,
and the creation code recursively creates a submenu when necessary. Support is
also added for radio and checkbox menus.

Listing 6.4 Menu support for the sketch application

```
import wx
from example1 import SketchWindow                          sketch3.py

class SketchFrame(wx.Frame):
    def __init__(self, parent):
        wx.Frame.__init__(self, parent, -1, "Sketch Frame",
                size=(800,600))
        self.sketch = SketchWindow(self, -1)
        self.sketch.Bind(wx.EVT_MOTION, self.OnSketchMotion)
        self.initStatusBar()                 ◁┐ Note slight
        self.createMenuBar()                 ❶ refactoring

    def initStatusBar(self):
        self.statusbar = self.CreateStatusBar()
        self.statusbar.SetFieldsCount(3)
        self.statusbar.SetStatusWidths([-1, -2, -3])

    def OnSketchMotion(self, event):
        self.statusbar.SetStatusText("Pos: %s" %
                str(event.GetPositionTuple()), 0)
        self.statusbar.SetStatusText("Current Pts: %s" %
                len(self.sketch.curLine), 1)
        self.statusbar.SetStatusText("Line Count: %s" %
                len(self.sketch.lines), 2)
        event.Skip()
```

(handwritten: menu items)

(handwritten: (sub) menu with label & items ✓)

(handwritten: menu items)

```python
def menuData(self):
    return [("&File", (
        ("&New", "New Sketch file", self.OnNew),
        ("&Open", "Open sketch file", self.OnOpen),
        ("&Save", "Save sketch file", self.OnSave),
        ("", "", ""),
        ("&Color", (
            ("&Black", "", self.OnColor,
                wx.ITEM_RADIO),
            ("&Red", "", self.OnColor,
                wx.ITEM_RADIO),
            ("&Green", "", self.OnColor,
                wx.ITEM_RADIO),
            ("&Blue", "", self.OnColor,
                wx.ITEM_RADIO))),
        ("", "", ""),
        ("&Quit", "Quit", self.OnCloseWindow)))]
```

❷ Identifying menu data

```python
def createMenuBar(self):
    menuBar = wx.MenuBar()
    for eachMenuData in self.menuData():
        menuLabel = eachMenuData[0]
        menuItems = eachMenuData[1]        # a tuple
        menuBar.Append(self.createMenu(menuItems), menuLabel)
    self.SetMenuBar(menuBar)
```

(handwritten: # a tuple)

```python
def createMenu(self, menuData):
    menu = wx.Menu()
    for eachItem in menuData:
        if len(eachItem) == 2:
            label = eachItem[0]
            subMenu = self.createMenu(eachItem[1])
            menu.AppendMenu(wx.NewId(), label, subMenu)
        else:
            self.createMenuItem(menu, *eachItem)
    return menu
```

❸ Creating submenus

(handwritten: write to status bar)

```python
def createMenuItem(self, menu, label, status, handler,
                   kind=wx.ITEM_NORMAL):
    if not label:
        menu.AppendSeparator()
        return
    menuItem = menu.Append(-1, label, status, kind)
    self.Bind(wx.EVT_MENU, handler, menuItem)
```

❹ Creating menu items with kind

```python
def OnNew(self, event): pass
def OnOpen(self, event): pass
def OnSave(self, event): pass
```

```
        def OnColor(self, event):
            menubar = self.GetMenuBar()
            itemId = event.GetId()
            item = menubar.FindItemById(itemId)
            color = item.GetLabel()
            self.sketch.SetColor(color)

        def OnCloseWindow(self, event):
            self.Destroy()

    if __name__ == '__main__':
        app = wx.PySimpleApp()
        frame = SketchFrame(None)
        frame.Show(True)
        app.MainLoop()
```

⑤ Handling color change

❶ Now that the __init__ method contains more functionality, we've encapsulated the status bar stuff into its own method. *menu: (label, (items))* *len2* *menu item: (label, status, hdlr[, kind])* *opt* *len=3 or 4*

❷ The format of the menu data is now (label, (items)), where each item is either a list *tuple* (label, status text, handler, optional kind) or a menu with a label and items. To determine whether a subitem of data is a menu or a menu item, remember, menus are length 2, and items are length 3 or 4. In a production system, where the data is more complex, I recommend using XML or some other external format.

❸ If the data piece is of length 2, it's meant to be a submenu, so break it up the same way the top-level was broken up, and recursively call createMenu and append it.

❹ Given the implementation of the menus here, it was easier to add the kind parameter to the wx.MenuItem constructor than to use the special methods of wx.Menu.

❺ The OnColor method is set up to handle the color changes of all the menu items, rather than setting up separate handlers for each item. In this case, the code gets the item id from the event, and uses the FindItemById() method to get the appropriate menu item (notice that this does not require us to maintain a separate hash table of item ids—we're using the menubar as that data structure). This method assumes that the label of the menu item is a wxPython color name, and passes that label to the sketch window, which updates its pen.

6.2.3 *How do I include a toolbar?*

Menu bars and toolbars are often tightly linked, making most or all of the functionality of the toolbar available via a menu item. In wxPython, this similarity is enhanced by the toolbar buttons emitting wx.EVT_MENU events when clicked, making it easy to use the same methods to handle both the menu item selection, and the toolbar click. A wxPython toolbar is an instance of the class wx.ToolBar, and as

we saw in chapter 2, can be created using the Frame method
`CreateToolBar()`. Like a status bar, a toolbar automatically
resizes along with the parent frame. The toolbar is similar to
other wxPython windows in that it can have arbitrary subwindows. Toolbars also contain methods for creating tool buttons. Figure 6.4 displays a portion of the sketch window with a
toolbar replicating the menu functionality we just created.

Figure 6.4 A typical toolbar showing both regular and toggle buttons

As in the menu code, the color bitmaps are radio buttons, and switching one
causes it to appear selected. Rather than duplicate the menu code in listing 6.5,
we'll include new and changed methods of `SketchFrame`.

Listing 6.5 Adding a toolbar to the sketch application

sketch4.py

```python
def __init__(self, parent):
    wx.Frame.__init__(self, parent, -1, "Sketch Frame",
            size=(800,600))
    self.sketch = SketchWindow(self, -1)
    self.sketch.Bind(wx.EVT_MOTION, self.OnSketchMotion)
    self.initStatusBar()
    self.createMenuBar()
    self.createToolBar()

def createToolBar(self):                    # ① Creating the toolbar
    toolbar = self.CreateToolBar()          # Like initToolBar() better
    for each in self.toolbarData():         # each is a 4-tuple: (label, file, help, hdlr)
        self.createSimpleTool(toolbar, *each)
    toolbar.AddSeparator()                  # "disperse" tuple args into 4 sep args
    for each in self.toolbarColorData():
        self.createColorTool(toolbar, each)
    toolbar.Realize()                       # ② Realizing the toolbar

def createSimpleTool(self, toolbar, label, filename,
        help, handler):
    if not label:
        toolbar.AddSeparator()
        return                              # ③ Creating the simple tools
    bmp = wx.Image(filename,
            wx.BITMAP_TYPE_BMP).ConvertToBitmap()
    tool = toolbar.AddSimpleTool(-1, bmp, label, help)   # 164
    self.Bind(wx.EVT_MENU, handler, tool)

def toolbarData(self):
    return (("New", "new.bmp", "Create new sketch",        # Each inner tuple is
                self.OnNew),                               # (label, file, help, hdlr)
            ("", "", "", ""),
            ("Open", "open.bmp", "Open existing sketch",
                self.OnOpen),
```

```
                ("Save", "save.bmp", "Save existing sketch",
                    self.OnSave))
    def createColorTool(self, toolbar, color):
        bmp = self.MakeBitmap(color)
        newId = wx.NewId()
        tool = toolbar.AddRadioTool(-1, bmp, shortHelp=color)
        self.Bind(wx.EVT_MENU, self.OnColor, tool)
    def MakeBitmap(self, color):
        bmp = wx.EmptyBitmap(16, 15)
        dc = wx.MemoryDC()
        dc.SelectObject(bmp)
        dc.SetBackground(wx.Brush(color))
        dc.Clear()
        dc.SelectObject(wx.NullBitmap)
        return bmp
    def toolbarColorData(self):
        return ("Black", "Red", "Green", "Blue")

    def OnColor(self, event):
        menubar = self.GetMenuBar()
        itemId = event.GetId()
        item = menubar.FindItemById(itemId)
        if not item:
            toolbar = self.GetToolBar()
            item = toolbar.FindById(itemId)
            color = item.GetShortHelp()
        else:
            color = item.GetLabel()
        self.sketch.SetColor(color)
```

4 Creating color tools

5 Creating a solid bitmap

6 Changing color in response to toolbar click

1 The toolbar code is similar in setup to the menu code in that it is data-driven. However, in this case, we set up different loops for the typical buttons and for the radio toggle buttons, since they are not nested in the toolbar.

2 The Realize() method actually lays out the toolbar objects within the bar. It must be called before the toolbar is displayed, and it must be recalled if any tools are added or removed from the bar.

3 This method is similar to the creation of menu items. The main difference is that simple toolbar tools require bitmaps. In this case, we've placed three basic bitmaps in the same directory as the sample code. At the end of the method, we hook up the same wx.EVT_MENU event that is used for menu items. For a signature of the AddTool method, providing more specification of tools, see table 6.4.

4 The color tools are created similarly to the simple tools, with just a different method to tell the toolbar they are radio tools. The solid bitmaps are created by the MakeBitmap() method.

❺ This method creates a solid bitmap of the proper size by creating a bitmap, attaching a wx.MemoryDC to it, and clearing the bitmap with the desired color used in the background brush.

❻ A slight addition to the OnColor() method searches the toolbar for the proper tool, and sets the color accordingly. However, one problem with the code as written is that changing the color via the menu item doesn't change the toolbar radio state, and vice versa.

Toolbars do have one piece of event flexibility that menu items don't have. They can generate the event type wx.EVT_TOOL_RCLICKED when the tool is clicked with the right mouse button. Toolbars also have a few different styles that are passed as bitmaps as an argument to CreateToolBar(). Table 6.4 lists some of the toolbar styles.

Table 6.4   Styles of the wx.ToolBar class

Style	Description
wx.TB_3DBUTTONS	Makes the tools display with a 3D look
wx.TB_HORIZONTAL	Default style, lays out the toolbar horizontally
wx.TB_NOICONS	Do not display the bitmaps for each tool
wx.TB_TEXT	The toolbar will show the short help text along with the default bitmaps
wx.TB_VERTICAL	Lays the toolbar out vertically

Toolbars are more complicated than status bars. Table 6.5 displays some of the more commonly used methods.

Table 6.5   Commonly used methods of wx.ToolBar

Function	Description
AddControl(control)	Adds an arbitrary wxPython control widget to the toolbar. Also see the related method InsertControl().
AddSeparator()	Places empty space between tools.
AddSimpleTool(id, bitmap, shortHelpString="", kind=wx.ITEM_NORMAL)	Adds a simple tool button to the toolbar, with the given bitmap. The shortHelpString is displayed as a tooltip. The kind can be wx.ITEM_NORMAL, wx.ITEM_CHECKBOX, or wx.ITEM_RADIO.

continued on next page

Table 6.5 Commonly used methods of `wx.ToolBar` *(continued)*

Function	Description
AddTool(id, bitmap, bitmap2=wx.NullBitmap, kind=wx.ITEM_NORMAL, shortHelpString="", longHelpString="", clientData=None)	Additional parameters for simple tools. The bitmap2 is displayed when the tool is pressed. The `longHelpString` is displayed in the status bar when the pointer is in the tool, and `clientData` can be used to associate an arbitrary piece of data with the tool. There is a related `InsertTool()` method.
AddCheckTool(...)	Adds a checkbox toggle tool, with the same parameters as `AddTool()`.
AddRadioTool(...)	Adds a radio toggle tool, with the same parameters as `AddTool()`. A consecutive, unbroken sequence of radio tools is considered a group for toggling.
DeleteTool(toolId) DeleteToolByPosition(x, y)	Deletes the tool with the given `id`, or which is displayed at the given point.
FindControl(toolId) FindToolForPosition(x, y)	Finds and returns the tool with the given `id`, or displayed at the given point.
ToggleTool(toolId, toggle)	If the tool with the specified `id` is a radio or checkbox, sets the toggle of that tool based on the Boolean toggle argument.

In the next section, we'll show you how to use common dialogs to get information from the user. On most operating systems, you can leverage standard dialogs to provide your user with a familiar interface for common tasks, such as choosing a file.

6.3 Getting standard information

Your application often needs basic information from the user, typically through dialog boxes. In this section, we'll talk about using the standard file and color dialogs for standard user information.

6.3.1 How do I use standard file dialogs?

Most GUI applications must save and load data of some kind or another. For the sanity of both you and your users, having a single, consistent mechanism for choosing files is desirable. Happily, wxPython provides the standard dialog `wx.FileDialog` to insert into your applications for this purpose. Under MS Windows, this class is a wrapper around the standard Windows file dialog. Under an X Window system, this is a similar looking custom dialog. Figure 6.5 displays the file dialog for the sketch application.

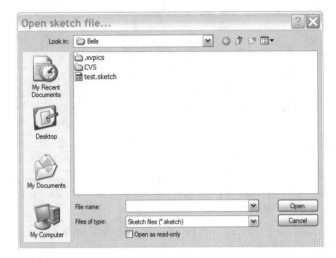

**Figure 6.5
A standard file
dialog for Windows**

✳ The most important method for using the wx.FileDialog is the constructor, which has the following signature.

```
wx.FileDialog(parent, message="Choose a file", defaultDir="",
        defaultFile="", wildcard="*.*", style=0)
```

Table 6.6 describes the parameters of the constructor.

Table 6.6   The parameters of the wx.FileDialog constructor

Parameter	Description
parent	The parent window for the dialog, or None if there is no parent window.
message	The message is displayed in the title bar of the dialog.
defaultDir	The directory that the dialog should start with. If empty, the dialog starts in the current working directory.
defaultFile	The file selected when the dialog opens. If empty, no file is selected.
wildcard	The options for the wildcard filter which allows the user to limit the display to selected file types. The format is <display>|<wildcard>, which may be repeated multiple times to give the user multiple options; for example, "Sketch files (*.sketch)|*.sketch|All files (*.*)|*.*"
style	A bitmask style. Styles are listed in table 6.6.

Table 6.7 lists the style options for the style bitmask.

Table 6.7   Style options for `wx.FileDialog`

Style	Description
wx.CHANGE_DIR	After the user selects a file, the current working directory is changed to that directory.
wx.MULTIPLE	Only applicable for an open dialog, this style allows the user to select multiple files.
wx.OPEN	The style is used for opening a file.
wx.OVERWRITE_PROMPT	Only applicable for a save dialog, this style gives a prompt to confirm the choice if an existing file is selected to be overwritten.
wx.SAVE	The style is used for saving a file.

To use the file dialog, call the `ShowModal()` method on a dialog instance. The method returns either `wx.ID_OK` or `wx.ID_CANCEL`, depending on the button the user clicks to dismiss the dialog. After the selection, use the `GetFilename()`, `Get-Directory()`, or `GetPath()` methods to retrieve the data. Afterwards, it's a good idea to destroy the dialog with the `Destroy()` method.

Listing 6.6 displays the modifications necessary to the `SketchFrame` to support saving and loading. These changes also require the import of the `cPickle` and `os` standard modules. We'll use `cPickle` to convert the list of data from the sketch window to a format that can be written to, and read from, the file.

Listing 6.6   Saving and loading methods of `SketchFrame`

```
def __init__(self, parent):
    self.title = "Sketch Frame"
    wx.Frame.__init__(self, parent, -1, self.title,
            size=(800,600))
    self.filename = ""
    self.sketch = SketchWindow(self, -1)
    self.sketch.Bind(wx.EVT_MOTION, self.OnSketchMotion)
    self.initStatusBar()
    self.createMenuBar()
    self.createToolBar()

def SaveFile(self):
    if self.filename:
        data = self.sketch.GetLinesData()
        f = open(self.filename, 'w')
        cPickle.dump(data, f)
        f.close()
```

❶ Saving the file

```
def ReadFile(self):          ❷  Reading the file
    if self.filename:
        try:
            f = open(self.filename, 'r')
            data = cPickle.load(f)
            f.close()
            self.sketch.SetLinesData(data)
        except cPickle.UnpicklingError:
            wx.MessageBox("%s is not a sketch file."
                    % self.filename, "oops!",
                    style=wx.OK|wx.ICON_EXCLAMATION)

wildcard = "Sketch files (*.sketch)|*.sketch|All files (*.*)|*.*"

def OnOpen(self, event):
    dlg = wx.FileDialog(self, "Open sketch file...",
            os.getcwd(), style=wx.OPEN,
            wildcard=self.wildcard)
    if dlg.ShowModal() == wx.ID_OK:
        self.filename = dlg.GetPath()
        self.ReadFile()
        self.SetTitle(self.title + ' -- ' + self.filename)
    dlg.Destroy()

def OnSave(self, event):          ❹  Saving the file
    if not self.filename:
        self.OnSaveAs(event)
    else:
        self.SaveFile()

def OnSaveAs(self, event):
    dlg = wx.FileDialog(self, "Save sketch as...",
            os.getcwd(),
            style=wx.SAVE | wx.OVERWRITE_PROMPT,
            wildcard=self.wildcard)
    if dlg.ShowModal() == wx.ID_OK:
        filename = dlg.GetPath()
        if not os.path.splitext(filename)[1]:
            filename = filename + '.sketch'
        self.filename = filename
        self.SaveFile()
        self.SetTitle(self.title + ' -- ' +
                self.filename)
    dlg.Destroy()
```

❸ **Popping up the open dialog**

❺ **Popping up the save dialog**

❻ **Ensuring filename extensions**

(handwritten annotations: 150; display₀ · wildcard₀ · display, · wildcard,; view p.166; 'abc.sketch' → ['abc', 'sketch'])

❶ This method writes the file data to disk, given the filename, and uses the cPickle module.

❷ This method reads the file using cPickle. If the file is not of the expected type, it pops up a message box alert to that effect.

❸ The OnOpen() method creates a dialog with the wx.OPEN style, in the current directory. The wildcard string on the previous line allows the user to limit the selection to .sketch files. If the user clicks OK, this method calls the ReadFile() method with the selected path.

❹ If a filename has already been selected for the current data, we save the file, otherwise, we treat it as a save as, and open the save dialog.

❺ The OnSave() method creates a wx.SAVE file dialog.

❻ This line ensures that filenames typed without an extension get the .sketch extension.

In the next section, we'll describe how to use the color picker.

6.3.2 *How do I use a standard color picker?*

It would be useful if the user was allowed to select an arbitrary color in the sketch dialog. For that purpose, we can use the standard wx.ColourDialog provided by wxPython. Use of this dialog is similar to the file dialog. The constructor takes only a parent and an optional data attribute. The data attribute is an instance of wx.ColourData, storing some data associated with the dialog such as the user-chosen color, and the list of custom colors. Using the data attribute allows you to keep the custom colors consistent from one usage to the next.

Using the color dialog in the sketch application requires the addition of a menu item, and a pretty straightforward handler method. Listing 6.7 shows the additions to the code.

> **Listing 6.7   Changes to the** SketchFrame **to display the color dialog**

```
def menuData(self):
    return [("&File", (
                ("&New", "New Sketch file", self.OnNew),
                ("&Open", "Open sketch file", self.OnOpen),
                ("&Save", "Save sketch file", self.OnSave),
                ("", "", ""),
                ("&Color", (
                    ("&Black", "", self.OnColor,
                            wx.ITEM_RADIO),
                    ("&Red", "", self.OnColor,
                            wx.ITEM_RADIO),
                    ("&Green", "", self.OnColor,
                            wx.ITEM_RADIO),
                    ("&Blue", "", self.OnColor,
```

```
                              wx.ITEM_RADIO),
                ("&Other...", "", self.OnOtherColor,
                        wx.ITEM_RADIO))),
            ("", "", ""),
            ("&Quit", "Quit", self.OnCloseWindow)))]

def OnOtherColor(self, event):
    dlg = wx.ColourDialog(self)
    dlg.GetColourData().SetChooseFull(True)      ← Creating color data object
    if dlg.ShowModal() == wx.ID_OK:
        self.sketch.SetColor(dlg.GetColourData().GetColour())  ←┐
    dlg.Destroy()                                Setting color from user input │
```

We've done two things with the color dialog that may not be immediately obvious. The SetChooseFull() method of the color data instance tells the dialog to display with the full palette, including the custom color information. After the dialog is closed, we grab the color data again to get the color. The color data is returned as a wx.Color instance and is suitable for passing back to the sketch to set the color.

6.4 *Making the application look nice*

In this section, we'll discuss issues related to how you give your application that final coat of polish. These range from the serious, such as how you arrange things so that the user can resize the window, to the more trivial, such as how you can display an about box. These topics are covered in more detail in part 2.

6.4.1 *How do I lay out widgets?*

One way to lay out your widgets in your wxPython application is to explicitly specify the position and size of every widget when it is created. Although this method is reasonably simple, over time it has a few flaws. For one thing, because widget sizes and default font sizes differ, it can be very difficult to get the positioning exactly right on all systems. In addition, you must explicitly change the position of each widget every time the user resizes the parent window. This can be a real pain to implement properly.

Fortunately, there's a better way. The layout mechanism in wxPython is called a *sizer*, and the idea is similar to layout managers in Java AWT and other interface toolkits. Each different sizer manages the size and position of its windows based on a set of rules. The sizer belongs to a container window (typically a wx.Panel).

Subwindows created inside the parent must be added to the sizer, and the sizer manages the size and position of each widget.

Creating a sizer

To create a sizer:

1. Create the panel or container that you want to be automatically sized.

2. Create the sizer.

3. Create your subwindows as you would normally.

4. Add each subwindow to the sizer using the sizer's `Add()` method. This is in addition to adding the subwindow to the parent container. When you add the window, give the sizer additional information, including the amount of space to surround the window, how to align the window within the allotted space managed by the sizer, and how to extend the window when the container window resizes.

5. Sizers can nest, meaning that you can add other sizers to the parent sizer as well as window objects. You can also set aside a certain amount of empty space as a separator.

6. Call the method `SetSizer(sizer)` of the container.

Table 6.8 lists the most commonly used sizers available in wxPython. For a more complete description of each particular sizer, see chapter 11.

324

Table 6.8   The most commonly used wxPython sizers

Sizer	Description
wx.BoxSizer	Lays children out in a line. A `wx.BoxSizer` can be either horizontally or vertically oriented, and can contain subsizers in any orientation to create complex layouts. Parameters passed to the sizer when items are added govern how children react when resized along either the main or perpendicular axis of the box.
wx.FlexGridSizer	A fixed two-dimensional grid, which differs from `wx.GridSizer` in that the size of each row and column is set separately based on the largest element in that row or column.
wx.GridSizer	A fixed two-dimensional grid, where each element is the same size—the size needed by the largest element in the sizer. When creating a grid sizer, you fix either the number of columns or the number of rows. Items are added left to right until a row is filled, and then the next row is started.

continued on next page

Table 6.8   **The most commonly used wxPython sizers** *(continued)*

Sizer	Description
wx.GridBagSizer	A two-dimensional grid, based on `wx.FlexGridSizer`. Allows for items to be placed in a specfic spot on the grid, and also allows items to span multiple grid locations.
wx.StaticBoxSizer	Identical to a `wx.BoxSizer`, with the one addition of a border (and optional caption) around the box.

Using a sizer

To demonstrate the use of a sizer, we'll add a control panel to the Sketch application. The control panel contains buttons for setting the color and thickness of the line. This example uses instances of both `wx.GridSizer` (for the buttons) and `wx.BoxSizer` (for the rest of the layout). Figure 6.6 displays the Sketch application with the panel, illustrating how the grid and box layouts appear in practice.

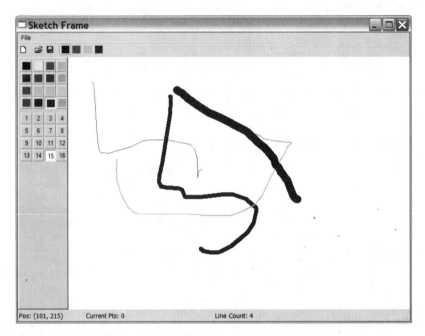

Figure 6.6   The Sketch application with an automatically laid out control panel

Listing 6.8 displays the changes to the Sketch application required to implement the control panel. The discussion in this section will focus on the sizer implementation.

Listing 6.8   Sketch sizer changes in the Sketch Frame

```
def __init__(self, parent):
    self.title = "Sketch Frame"
    wx.Frame.__init__(self, parent, -1, self.title,
            size=(800,600))
    self.filename = ""
    self.sketch = SketchWindow(self, -1)
    self.sketch.Bind(wx.EVT_MOTION, self.OnSketchMotion)
    self.initStatusBar()
    self.createMenuBar()
    self.createToolBar()
    self.createPanel()

def createPanel(self):
    controlPanel = ControlPanel(self, -1, self.sketch)
    box = wx.BoxSizer(wx.HORIZONTAL)     - for vertical stretching        horiz. placement of
    box.Add(controlPanel, 0, wx.EXPAND)                                    control panel, sketch wind
    box.Add(self.sketch, 1, wx.EXPAND)
    self.SetSizer(box)            \  stretch factor (for horiz dim)
```

In listing 6.8, the `createPanel()` method creates the instance of `ControlPanel` (described in the next listing), and puts together the box sizer. The only parameter to the constructor for `wx.BoxSizer` is the orientation, which can be either `wx.HORIZONTAL` or `wx.VERTICAL`. Next, the new control panel and the previously created `SketchWindow` are each added to the sizer using the `Add()` method. The first argument is the object that should be added to the sizer. The second argument is used by `wx.BoxSizer` as a stretch factor to determine how the sizer should resize its children when its own size changes. In the case of a horizontal sizer, the stretch factor determines how the horizontal size of each child changes (the vertical stretching is performed by the box sizer based on the flags in the third argument).

If the stretch factor is zero, the object shouldn't change size no matter what happens to the sizer. If the factor is greater than zero, that is interpreted as a share of the total size relative to the shares of the other children in the sizer (similar to how `wx.StatusBar` manages text field widths). If all children in the sizer have the same factor, they all resize at the same rate and equally share in the space that is left after positioning the fixed size elements. In this case, the 0 for the control panel indicates that the panel should not change horizontal size if the user stretches the frame, while the 1 for the sketch window means that all the size changes are absorbed there.

The third argument to `Add()` is another bitmask flag. Full details on expected flag values will be given later in the chapter. The `wx.EXPAND` value is one of several values that govern how the item changes size across the axis perpendicular to the main axis for a box sizer; in this case, what happens when the frame changes size vertically. Using the `wx.EXPAND` flag directs the sizer to resize the child to completely fill the available space. Other possible options allow the child to be resized proportionally or aligned to a particular part of the sizer. Figure 6.7 should help clarify which parameter governs which resize direction.

The result of these settings is that when you run the frame with this box sizer, any size change in a horizontal direction causes the sketch window to change size, and the control panel remains the same. A size change in the vertical direction causes both subwindows to expand or contract vertically.

The `ControlPanel` class referenced in listing 6.8 uses a combination of grid and box sizers. Listing 6.9 contains the code for that class.

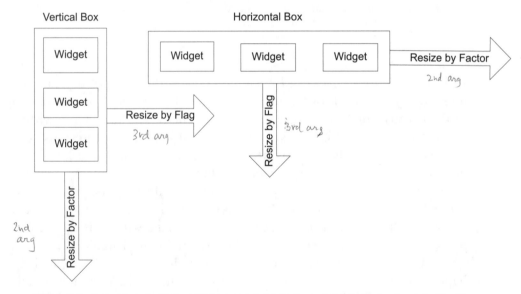

Figure 6.7   A drawing showing which argument determines resize behavior in each direction.

Listing 6.9 The control panel class, using grid and box sizers

```
class ControlPanel(wx.Panel):

    BMP_SIZE = 16
    BMP_BORDER = 3
    NUM_COLS = 4
    SPACING = 4

    colorList = ('Black', 'Yellow', 'Red', 'Green', 'Blue', 'Purple',
             'Brown', 'Aquamarine', 'Forest Green', 'Light Blue',
             'Goldenrod', 'Cyan', 'Orange', 'Navy', 'Dark Grey',
             'Light Grey')
    maxThickness = 16

    def __init__(self, parent, ID, sketch):
        wx.Panel.__init__(self, parent, ID,
                          style=wx.RAISED_BORDER)
        self.sketch = sketch
        buttonSize = (self.BMP_SIZE + 2 * self.BMP_BORDER,
                      self.BMP_SIZE + 2 * self.BMP_BORDER)
        colorGrid = self.createColorGrid(parent, buttonSize)
        thicknessGrid = self.createThicknessGrid(buttonSize)
        self.layout(colorGrid, thicknessGrid)

    def createColorGrid(self, parent, buttonSize):
        self.colorMap = {}
        self.colorButtons = {}
        colorGrid = wx.GridSizer(cols=self.NUM_COLS, hgap=2,
            vgap=2)
        for eachColor in self.colorList:
            bmp = parent.MakeBitmap(eachColor)
            b = buttons.GenBitmapToggleButton(self, -1, bmp,
                    size=buttonSize)
            b.SetBezelWidth(1)
            b.SetUseFocusIndicator(False)
            self.Bind(wx.EVT_BUTTON, self.OnSetColour, b)
            colorGrid.Add(b, 0)
            self.colorMap[b.GetId()] = eachColor
            self.colorButtons[eachColor] = b
        self.colorButtons[self.colorList[0]].SetToggle(True)
        return colorGrid

    def createThicknessGrid(self, buttonSize):
        self.thicknessIdMap = {}
        self.thicknessButtons = {}
        thicknessGrid = wx.GridSizer(cols=self.NUM_COLS, hgap=2,
            vgap=2)
        for x in range(1, self.maxThickness + 1):
            b = buttons.GenToggleButton(self, -1, str(x),
                    size=buttonSize)
```

Handwritten annotations:
- Sketch7.py
- 16 + 2 × 3 = 22 = w
- + self.BMP_SIZE + 2 * self.BMP_BORDER) = 22 = h
- ❶ Creating the color grid
- 163
- @ 176
- id ↦ color
- color ↦ button
- # Use first color in list, # initially
- ❷ Creating the thickness grid

```
        b.SetBezelWidth(1)
        b.SetUseFocusIndicator(False)
        self.Bind(wx.EVT_BUTTON, self.OnSetThickness, b)
        thicknessGrid.Add(b, 0)
        self.thicknessIdMap[b.GetId()] = x          id ↦ n
        self.thicknessButtons[x] = b                n ↦ Button
    self.thicknessButtons[1].SetToggle(True)   # Use thickness 1, init
    return thicknessGrid

def layout(self, colorGrid, thicknessGrid):      ←⅃    ❸ Combining
    box = wx.BoxSizer(wx.VERTICAL)                         the grids
    box.Add(colorGrid, 0, wx.ALL, self.SPACING)
    box.Add(thicknessGrid, 0, wx.ALL, self.SPACING)
    self.SetSizer(box)                           ↖ border
    box.Fit(self)

def OnSetColour(self, event):
    color = self.colorMap[event.GetId()]
    if color != self.sketch.color:
        self.colorButtons[self.sketch.color].SetToggle(False)
    self.sketch.SetColor(color)

def OnSetThickness(self, event):
    thickness = self.thicknessIdMap[event.GetId()]
    if thickness != self.sketch.thickness:
        self.thicknessButtons[self.sketch.thickness].SetToggle(False)
    self.sketch.SetThickness(thickness)
```

❶ The createColorGrid() method builds the grid sizer that contains the color buttons. First, we create the sizer itself, specifying the number of columns as four. Since the column count is set, the buttons will be laid out from left to right, and then down. Then, we take the list of colors, and create a button for each color. Inside the for loop, we create a square bitmap of the proper color, and create a toggle button with that bitmap using one set of generic button widget classes defined in the wxPython library. Then we hook the button up to an event, and add it to the grid. After that, we add it to a few dictionaries to make it easier to relate color, ID, and button in later code. We don't have to specify the button's placement within the grid; the sizer takes care of that for us.

❷ The createThicknessGrid() method is almost identical to the color grid method. In fact, an enterprising programmer might be able to merge them into a common utility function. The grid sizer is created, and the sixteen buttons are added one at a time, with the sizer making sure they line up nicely on the screen.

❸ We use a vertical box sizer to place the grids one on top of the other. The second argument for each grid is 0, indicating that the grid sizers should not change size when the control panel stretches vertically. (Since we already know that the control

@ 175

panel doesn't change size horizontally, we don't need to specify the horizontal behavior.) This example shows the fourth argument to Add(), which is the width of the border to place around the item, in this case specified by the self.SPACING variable. The wx.ALL as the third argument is one of a set of flags that governs which sides to apply the border. Not surprisingly, wx.ALL says that the border should be applied on all four sides of the object. At the end, we call the Fit() method of the box sizer, with the control panel as an argument. The method tells the control panel to resize itself to match the minimum size that the sizer thinks it needs. Typically, you'll call this method as part of the creation of a window that uses sizers, to ensure that the enclosing window is large enough to encompass the sizer.

The wx.Sizer base class contains several methods common to all sizers. Table 6.9 lists the most commonly used methods.

Table 6.9   Methods of wx.Sizer

Function	Description
Add(window, proportion=0, flag=0, border=0, userData=None) Add(sizer, proportion=0, flag=0, border=0, userData=None) Add(size, proportion=0, flag=0, border=0, userData=None)	Adds an item to the sizer. The first version adds a wxWindow, the second a nested sizer. The third version adds empty space which is used as a separator and is subject to the same rules for positioning as a window would be. The proportion argument manages the size amount that the window changes relative to other windows—it's only meaningful for a wx.BoxSizer. The flag argument is a bitmap with many different flags for alignment, border position, and growth. A full list is in chapter 11. The border argument is the amount of space in pixels to place around the window or sizer. userData allows you to associate data with the object, for example in a subclass that might need more information for sizing.
Fit(window) FitInside(window)	Causes the window argument to resize to the sizer's minimum size. The argument is usually the window using the sizer. The FitInside() method is similar, but instead of changing the screen display of the window, only changes its internal representation. This is used for a window inside a scroll panel to trigger scroll bar display.
GetSize()	Returns the size of the sizer as a wx.Size object.
GetPosition()	Returns the position of the sizer as a wx.Point object.
GetMinSize()	Returns the minimum size needed to fully lay out the sizer as a wx.Size object.
Layout()	Programatically forces the sizer to recalculate the size and position of its children. Call after dynamically adding or removing a child.
Prepend(...)	Identical to Add() (all three versions, but the new object is placed at the beginning of the sizer list for layout purposes).

continued on next page

Table 6.9 Methods of `wx.Sizer` *(continued)*

Function	Description
Remove(window) Remove(sizer) Remove(nth)	Removes an object from the sizer. Depending on the version, either a specific object or the nth in the sizer list is removed. If this is done after startup, call `Layout()` after.
SetDimension(x, y, width, height)	Programatically forces the sizer to take the given size, and causes all children to reposition themselves

For more detailed information about sizers and nesting sizers, refer to chapter 11.

6.4.2 *How do I build an about box?*

An about box is a good example of a display dialog that displays more complex information than is possible in a plain message box, but doesn't require other functionality. In this case, you can use `wx.html.HtmlWindow` as a straightforward mechanism to display styled text. Actually, `wx.html.HtmlWindow` is much more powerful than we show here, and includes methods to manage user interaction and rendering in detail. Chapter 16 covers the features of `wx.html.HtmlWindow`. Listing 6.10 displays a class that creates an about box using the HTML renderer.

Listing 6.10 Using `wx.html.HtmlWindow` as an about box

```
class SketchAbout(wx.Dialog):
    text = '''                    # class string attribute
<html>
<body bgcolor="#ACAA60">
<center><table bgcolor="#455481" width="100%" cellspacing="0"
cellpadding="0" border="1">
<tr>
    <td align="center"><h1>Sketch!</h1></td>
</tr>
</table>
</center>
<p><b>Sketch</b> is a demonstration program for
<b>wxPython In Action</b>
Chapter 6. It is based on the SuperDoodle demo included
with wxPython, available at http://www.wxpython.org/
</p>

<p><b>SuperDoodle</b> and <b>wxPython</b> are brought to you by
<b>Robin Dunn</b> and <b>Total Control Software</b>, Copyright
&copy; 1997-2006.</p>
</body>
</html>
'''
```

```
def __init__(self, parent):
    wx.Dialog.__init__(self, parent, -1, 'About Sketch',
                       size=(440, 400) )

    html = wx.html.HtmlWindow(self)
    html.SetPage(self.text)
    button = wx.Button(self, wx.ID_OK, "Okay")

    sizer = wx.BoxSizer(wx.VERTICAL)
    sizer.Add(html, 1, wx.EXPAND|wx.ALL, 5)
    sizer.Add(button, 0, wx.ALIGN_CENTER|wx.ALL, 5)

    self.SetSizer(sizer)
    self.Layout()
```

Most of this listing is taken up with the HTML string itself, which has some layout and font tags. The dialog is a combination of wx.html.HtmlWindow, and a button with the wx.ID_OK ID. Clicking the button automatically closes the window, as with any other dialog. A vertical box sizer is used to manage the layout.

Figure 6.8 displays the resulting dialog.

Figure 6.8
The HTML about box

To use this, wire up a menu item and a handler as in the following:

```
def OnAbout(self, event):
    dlg = SketchAbout(self)
    dlg.ShowModal()
    dlg.Destroy()
```

6.4.3 How do I build a splash screen?

Displaying a great splash screen with your application provides a professional look for your users. It can also distract the user while your application completes a time-consuming setup. In wxPython, it is easy to build a splash screen from any bitmap using the `wx.SplashScreen` class. The splash screen can be displayed for a specific length of time, and whether or not the time has been set, the screen always closes when the user clicks on it. The class consists almost entirely of its constructor as follows:

```
wx.SplashScreen(bitmap, splashStyle, milliseconds, parent, id,
    pos=wx.DefaultPosition, size=wx.DefaultSize,
    style=wx.SIMPLE_BORDER|wx.FRAME_NO_TASKBAR|wx.STAY_ON_TOP)
```

Table 6.10 defines the parameters for the `wx.SplashScreen` constructor.

Table 6.10   The parameters for the `wx.SplashScreen` constructor

Parameter	description
bitmap	A `wx.Bitmap`, this is exactly what is displayed on screen.
splashStyle	Another bitmap style, this can be any combination of the following: `wx.SPLASH_CENTRE_ON_PARENT`, `wx.SPLASH_CENTRE_ON_SCREEN`, `wx.SPLASH_NO_CENTRE`, `wx.SPLASH_TIMEOUT`, `wx.SPLASH_NO_TIMEOUT`, all of which are pretty descriptively named.
milliseconds	If `wx.SPLASH_TIMEOUT` is specified as the `splashStyle`, this is the number of milliseconds before it times out.
parent	Parent window. Generally `None`.
id	The window `id`, `-1` is usually fine.
pos	Position on screen if `wx.SPLASH_NO_CENTER` is the `splashStyle`
size	Size. Generally you don't need to specify this, since the size of the bitmap is used.
style	Ordinary wxPython frame style, the default is generally what you want

Listing 6.11 displays the code for a splash screen. In this case, we've replaced `wx.PySimpleApp` with a custom `wx.App` subclass.

Listing 6.11   The code for a splash screen

```
class SketchApp(wx.App):

    def OnInit(self):
        image = wx.Image("splash.bmp", wx.BITMAP_TYPE_BMP)
```

```
bmp = image.ConvertToBitmap()
wx.SplashScreen(bmp, wx.SPLASH_CENTRE_ON_SCREEN |
        wx.SPLASH_TIMEOUT, 1000, None, -1)
wx.Yield()

frame = SketchFrame(None)
frame.Show(True)
self.SetTopWindow(frame)
return True
```

Typically, the splash screen is declared in the `OnInit` method during application startup. The splash screen displays itself on construction and displays until it is clicked on, or until it times out. In this case, the splash screen displays in the center of the screen, and times out after one second. The `Yield()` call is important because it allows any pending events to be processed before continuing. In this case, it ensures that the splash screen receives and processes its initial paint event before the application continues startup.

6.5 *Summary*

- Most wxPython programs use common elements such as menus, toolbars, and splash screens. Using them helps the usability of your program and makes it look more professional. In this chapter we used a simple sketch application and enhanced it with a toolbar, status bar, menu bar, common dialogs, a complex layout, and an about and splash box.

- You can draw directly to the wxPython display by using a device context. Different kinds of displays require different device context classes, however, they all share a common API. Device contexts can be buffered for smoother display.

- A status bar can be automatically created at the bottom of a frame. It can contain one or more text fields, that can be sized and set independently.

- Menus can contain nested submenus, and menu items can have toggle states. Toolbars emit the same kinds of events as menu bars, and are designed to be easy to lay out groups of tool buttons.

- Opening and saving your data can be managed with the standard `wx.FileDialog`. Colors can be chosen using `wx.ColourDialog`.

- Complex layouts are created without explicitly placing each widget using sizers. A sizer automatically places its child objects according to a set of rules. Sizers include `wx.GridSizer`, which lays objects out in a two-dimensional grid, and `wx.BoxSizer`, which lays items out in a single line. Sizers can be nested, and can also control the behavior of their children when the sizer is stretched.

- An about box, or other simple dialog, can be created using `wx.html.Html-Window`. Splash screens are created using `wx.SplashScreen`.

In part 1, we've covered the basic concepts behind wxPython, and we've also covered some of the most common tasks. In part 2, we'll use the now familiar question-and-answer format, but we'll ask more detailed questions about the makeup and functionality of the wxPython toolkit.

Part 2

Essential wxPython

In this part of the book, we will explore the essential widgets that make up the core of the wxPython toolkit. These basics will be a critical part of any wxPython program you write. For each element, we'll show you the most important parts of the API for dealing with that element, as well as sample code and tips on how to use the element in actual programs.

Chapter 7, "Working with the basic controls," starts us off with the basic widget set. We'll cover text labels, text entry, buttons, and numerical and list choice widgets. We'll show you how to use each element, how to customize its look to match your application, and how to respond to user interaction. In chapter 8, "Putting widgets in frames," we'll move up the container hierarchy and talk about frames. We'll show you how to add widgets into a frame, and describe the available frame styles. We'll also cover the frame lifecycle from creation to destruction. In chapter 9, "Giving users choices with dialogs," we'll focus on dialogs, starting with the ways in which dialog containers differ from frames. We'll also show the range of predefined dialogs available in wxPython, as well as shortcuts for using them easily.

The focus of chapter 10, "Creating and using wxPython menus," is on menus. We'll discuss how to create menu items, which can be attached to menus, which can be placed on a menu bar. We'll also cover toggle menus, pop-up menus, and various ways to customize your menu display. In chapter 11, "Placing widgets with sizers," we demystify the art of the sizer. Sizers are used to simplify widget layout inside wxPython frames and dialogs. We'll cover the six kinds of predefined sizers, show you how they behave, and give some hints on when they are best used. Finally, in chapter 12, "Manipulating basic graphical images," we discuss the raw basics of drawing to the screen via a device context. This section lists the primitive drawing methods that you can use to draw your own widgets, or to support user drawing, or just for decoration.

7

Working with
the basic controls

This chapter covers

- Displaying text
- Working with buttons
- Entering and displaying numbers
- Providing the user with choices

The wxPython toolkit provides many different widgets, including the basic controls that are the topic of this chapter. We'll describe the wxPython starter kit, including static text, editable text, buttons, spinners, sliders, checkboxes, radio buttons, choosers, list boxes, combo boxes, and gauges. For each widget, we'll provide a brief example of how to use it, followed by a description of the relevant parts of the wxPython API.

7.1 Displaying text

This section begins with examples of displaying text on the screen, including static text fields that you use for labels, which come in both styled and unstyled varieties. You can also create text fields for single-line and multi-line user entry. In addition, we'll discuss how to choose a text font.

7.1.1 How do I display static text?

Perhaps the most basic task for any UI toolkit is drawing plain text on the screen. In wxPython, this is accomplished with the `wx.StaticText` class. Figure 7.1 displays the static text control.

In a `wx.StaticText`, you can change the alignment, font, and color of the text. A single static text widget can contain multiple lines of text, however, it cannot handle multiple fonts or styles. For multiple fonts or styles, use a more elaborate text control, such as `wx.html.HTMLWindow`, described in chapter 16. To display multi-

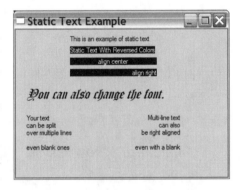

Figure 7.1   Samples of `wx.StaticText`, including font, alignment, and color changes

ple lines within a static text control, include a string with newline characters inside it, and make the control big enough to display all the text. One feature that you cannot see from just the figure is that the `wx.StaticText` window never receives or responds to mouse events, and never takes the user focus.

How to display static text

Listing 7.1 displays the code that produced figure 7.1.

Listing 7.1   A basic example of how to use static text

```
import wx

class StaticTextFrame(wx.Frame):
    def __init__(self):
        wx.Frame.__init__(self, None, -1, 'Static Text Example',
                size=(400, 300))
        panel = wx.Panel(self, -1)                              Viewing basic static text
        wx.StaticText(panel, -1, "This is an example of static text",   ◁
                (100, 10))
        rev = wx.StaticText(panel, -1,
                "Static Text With Reversed Colors",   ◁    Designating
                (100, 30))                                 reversed colors
        rev.SetForegroundColour('white')
        rev.SetBackgroundColour('black')
        center = wx.StaticText(panel, -1,
                "align center", (100, 50),
                (160, -1), wx.ALIGN_CENTER)   ◁    Designating
        center.SetForegroundColour('white')        center aligned
        center.SetBackgroundColour('black')
        right = wx.StaticText(panel, -1,
                "align right", (100, 70),     ◁    Designating
                (160, -1), wx.ALIGN_RIGHT)         right aligned
        right.SetForegroundColour('white')
        right.SetBackgroundColour('black')
        str = "You can also change the font."          Defining a
        text = wx.StaticText(panel, -1, str, (20, 100))   ◁   new font
        font = wx.Font(18, wx.DECORATIVE,
                wx.ITALIC, wx.NORMAL)
        text.SetFont(font)
        wx.StaticText(panel, -1,
                "Your text\ncan be split\n"    ◁   Displaying multi-lines
                "over multiple lines\n\neven blank ones", (20,150))
        wx.StaticText(panel, -1,
                "Multi-line text\ncan also\n"    ◁   Displaying aligned multi-lines
                "be right aligned\n\neven with a blank", (220,150),
                style=wx.ALIGN_RIGHT)

if __name__ == '__main__':
    app = wx.PySimpleApp()
    frame = StaticTextFrame()
    frame.Show()
    app.MainLoop()
```

The constructor for wx.StaticText is identical to the basic wxWidget constructors, as in the following:

```
wx.StaticText(parent, id, label, pos=wx.DefaultPosition,
        size=wx.DefaultSize, style=0, name="staticText")
```

Table 7.1 displays what the parameters are—most wxPython widgets have a similar set in their constructor. Refer to the widget discussion in chapter 2 for a more detailed description of constructor parameters.

Table 7.1   Parameters of the wx.StaticText constructor

Parameter	Purpose
parent	The containing widget
id	The wxPython identifier. To automatically create a unique identifier, use -1
label	Contains the text that you want to display in the static control.
pos	The position of the widget as a wx.Point object or a Python tuple
size	The size of the widget as a wx.Size object or a Python tuple
style	The style flag
name	Name used for finding the object

In the next section, we'll discuss style flags in more detail.

Working with the styles

All of the methods called on the static text instances in listing 7.1 belong to the parent wx.Window class; wx.StaticText defines no new methods of its own. A few style bits are specific to wx.StaticText, and they are listed in table 7.2.

Table 7.2   Style bit flags unique to the wx.StaticText class

Style	Description
wx.ALIGN_CENTER	Centers the static text within the size rectangle of the static text widget.
wx.ALIGN_LEFT	The text is left-aligned in the widget. This is the default.
wx.ALIGN_RIGHT	The text is right-aligned in the widget.
wx.ST_NO_AUTORESIZE	If this bit is used, the static text widget will not resize itself after the text is changed with SetLabel(). You would use this in conjunction with a center or right-aligned control to preserve the alignment.

The `wx.StaticText` control overrides `SetLabel()` in order to resize itself based on the new text, which happens unless the `wx.ST_NO_AUTORESIZE` style is set.

When creating a single line static text control with a center or right alignment, you should explicitly set the size of the control in the constructor. Specifying the size prevents wxPython from automatically sizing the control. The wxPython default size is the minimum rectangle surrounding the text. Since by default the text control is no larger than the text contained, and there is no blank space to show the alignment, it is irrelevant whether the control is left, right, or center aligned. To change the text in the widget dynamically during the program without changing the size of the control, set the `wx.ST_NO_AUTORESIZE` style. This prevents the widget from resizing itself back to a minimum rectangle after the text is reset. If the static text is inside a dynamic layout, changing its size may move other widgets on the screen, creating a distraction for the user.

Other techniques for text display

There are other ways of adding static text onto your display. One is the `wx.lib.stattext.GenStaticText` class, which is a Python-only reimplementation of `wx.StaticText`. It is more consistent cross-platform than the standard C++ version, and it receives mouse events. It's also preferable when you want to subclass and create your own static text control.

You can draw text directly to your device context using the `DrawText(text, x, y)` method or the `DrawRotatedText(text, x, y, angle)` method. The latter is the easiest way to add angled text to your display, although a subclass of `GenStaticText` that handles rotation is also available. Device contexts were covered briefly in chapter 6, and will be covered in more detail in chapter 12.

7.1.2 How can I get the user to enter text?

Moving beyond the mere display of static text, we'll begin discussing user interaction when entering text. The wxPython class for the text entry widget is `wx.TextCtrl`, which allows both single-line and multi-line text entry. It can also act as a password control, masking the keys pressed. If supported by the platform, the `wx.TextCtrl` also provides rich text display, with multiple text styles defined and

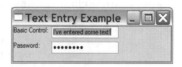

Figure 7.2 Examples of the single line text control, both plain and password

displayed. Figure 7.2 displays a sample of `wx.TextCtrl` as a single-line control, both with and without password masking.

In the next section, we'll illustrate how to create the text, then discuss the style options for text controls.

How to do it

Listing 7.2 displays the code used to generate figure 7.2.

Listing 7.2 The `wx.TextCtrl` single line example

```
import wx

class TextFrame(wx.Frame):

    def __init__(self):
        wx.Frame.__init__(self, None, -1, 'Text Entry Example',
                size=(300, 100))
        panel = wx.Panel(self, -1)
        basicLabel = wx.StaticText(panel, -1, "Basic Control:")
        basicText = wx.TextCtrl(panel, -1, "I've entered some text!",
                size=(175, -1))
        basicText.SetInsertionPoint(0)

        pwdLabel = wx.StaticText(panel, -1, "Password:")
        pwdText = wx.TextCtrl(panel, -1, "password", size=(175, -1),
                style=wx.TE_PASSWORD)
        sizer = wx.FlexGridSizer(cols=2, hgap=6, vgap=6)
        sizer.AddMany([basicLabel, basicText, pwdLabel, pwdText])
        panel.SetSizer(sizer)

if __name__ == '__main__':
    app = wx.PySimpleApp()
    frame = TextFrame()
    frame.Show()
    app.MainLoop()
```

The `wx.TextCtrl` class has a slightly more elaborate constructor than the `wx.Window` parent class, adding two arguments:

```
wx.TextCtrl(parent, id, value = "", pos=wx.DefaultPosition,
    size=wx.DefaultSize, style=0, validator=wx.DefaultValidator
    name=wx.TextCtrlNameStr)
```

The `parent`, `id`, `pos`, `size`, `style`, and `name` arguments are all identical to those in the `wx.Window` constructor. The `value` argument is the initial value of the text displayed in the control.

The `validator` argument is used for a `wx.Validator`. A validator is often used to filter data to ensure that only acceptable data is entered into the control. Validators are discussed in more detail in chapter 9.

Using single line text control styles

p 199   text events

In this section, we'll begin discussing some of the unique text control style bits. Table 7.3 describes the style flags that are used for a single-line text control.

Table 7.3 The style bits for a single line `wx.TextCtrl`

Style	Description
wx.TE_CENTER	The text is centered within the control.
wx.TE_LEFT	The text is left justified within the control. This is the default behavior.
wx.TE_NOHIDESEL	The name of this option parses to "no hide sel," in case you were having trouble decoding it. It's a Windows option to override a default behavior of the Windows text widget, namely that it doesn't highlight the selected text unless the widget has focus. With this option selected, the widget will always highlight the text. Has no effect on other systems.
wx.TE_PASSWORD	The text entered will not be displayed, but instead masked by asterisks.
wx.TE_PROCESS_ENTER	If this bit is specified, a text enter event is triggered when the user presses the enter key within the control. Otherwise, the keypress is managed internally by either the text control or the dialog.
wx.TE_PROCESS_TAB	If this bit is specified, a normal character event will be created for a tab key pressed (generally meaning a tab will be inserted into the text). If not specified, then the tab will be managed by the dialog, usually for keyboard navigation between controls.
wx.TE_READONLY	The text control is read-only, and cannot be modified by user input.
wx.TE_RIGHT	The text is right-justified within the control.

Like other style flags, these can be combined using the | operator, although the three alignment flags are mutually exclusive.

The text control automatically manages the user's keypress and mouse events to add text and to move the insertion point. The following common control combinations are included:

- <ctrl-x> cut
- <ctrl-c> copy
- <ctrl-v> paste
- <ctrl-z> undo

7.1.3 *How do I change the text without user input?*

In addition to changing the text of the display based on user input, wx.TextCtrl provides a number of methods that change the text in the display from within your program. You can change the text outright, or just move the insertion point to a different place in the text. Table 7.4 lists the text manipulation methods of wx.TextCtrl.

Table 7.4 Text manipulation methods of wx.TextCtrl

Method	Description
AppendText(text)	Appends the text argument to the end of the text in the control. The insertion point also moves to the end of the control.
Clear()	Resets the text value of the control to "". Also generates a text updated event.
EmulateKeyPress(event)	Given a keypress event, inserts into the control the character associated with the event, just as if the actual keypress had occured.
GetInsertionPoint() SetInsertionPoint(pos) SetInsertionPointEnd()	The position is the integer index of the current insertion point, or to put it another way, the index where the next inserted character would be placed. The beginning of the control is 0.
GetRange(from, to)	Returns the string between the given integer positions of the control.
GetSelection() GetStringSelection() SetSelection(from, to)	GetSelection() returns a tuple (start, end) with the indexes of the currently selected text. GetStringSelection() returns the string contents of that range. The setter takes the integer endpoints of the range.
GetValue() SetValue(value)	SetValue() changes the entire value of the control. The getter returns the entire string.
Remove(from, to)	Removes the given range from the text.
Replace(from, to, value)	Replaces the given range with new value. This can change the length of the text.
WriteText(text)	Similar to AppendText() except that the new text is placed at the current insertion point.

These methods are particularly useful when you have a read-only control, or if you want the text in the control to change based on events other than a user key press.

7.1.4 *How do I create a multi-line or styled text control?*

You can create a multi-line text control using the wx.TE_MULTILINE style flag. If the native widget has support for styles, you can change font and color styles within the text managed by the control, which is sometimes called rich text. For other platforms, the calls to set styles are simply ignored. Figure 7.3 displays an example of multi-line text controls.

Listing 7.3 contains the code used to create figure 7.3. Typically, creating a multi-line control is handled by setting the wx.TE_MULTILINE style flag. Later in this section, we'll discuss using rich text styles.

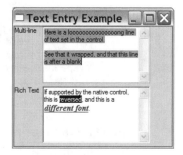

Figure 7.3 Examples of multi-line text controls, both with and without rich text

Listing 7.3 Creating a multi-line text control

```python
import wx

class TextFrame(wx.Frame):

    def __init__(self):
        wx.Frame.__init__(self, None, -1, 'Text Entry Example',
                size=(300, 250))
        panel = wx.Panel(self, -1)
        multiLabel = wx.StaticText(panel, -1, "Multi-line")
        multiText = wx.TextCtrl(panel, -1,      ←— Creating a text control
                "Here is a looooooooooooooong line "
                "of text set in the control.\n\n"
                "See that it wrapped, and that "
                "this line is after a blank",
                size=(200, 100), style=wx.TE_MULTILINE)
        multiText.SetInsertionPoint(0)       ←┐ Setting the cursor point

        richLabel = wx.StaticText(panel, -1, "Rich Text")
        richText = wx.TextCtrl(panel, -1,      ←— Creating a rich text control
                "If supported by the native control, "
                "this is reversed, and this is a different font.",
                size=(200, 100),
                style=wx.TE_MULTILINE|wx.TE_RICH2)
        richText.SetInsertionPoint(0)                Setting text styles
        richText.SetStyle(44, 52, wx.TextAttr("white", "black"))  ←┘
        points = richText.GetFont().GetPointSize()
        f = wx.Font(points + 3, wx.ROMAN,      ┐ Creating a font
                wx.ITALIC, wx.BOLD, True)     ←┘
        richText.SetStyle(68, 82, wx.TextAttr("blue",      Setting a style in
                wx.NullColour, f))            ←┘            the new font
        sizer = wx.FlexGridSizer(cols=2, hgap=6, vgap=6)
```

```
            sizer.AddMany([multiLabel, multiText, richLabel, richText])
            panel.SetSizer(sizer)

if __name__ == '__main__':
    app = wx.PySimpleApp()
    frame = TextFrame()
    frame.Show()
    app.MainLoop()
```

Using multiple or rich text styles

In addition to wx.TE_MULTILINE, there are other style flags that are only meaningful in the context of a multi-line or rich text control. Table 7.5 lists those window styles.

Table 7.5   The style bits for wx.TextCtrl, when used as a multiple line control

Style	Description
wx.HSCROLL	If the text control is multi-line, and if this style is declared, long lines will be horizontally scrolled instead of wrapped. This option is ignored in GTK+.
wx.TE_AUTO_URL	If the rich text option is set and the platform supports it, this style causes an event to be generated when the user mouses over or clicks on a URL in the text.
wx.TE_DONTWRAP	Another name for wx.HSCROLL.
wx.TE_LINEWRAP	A contrast to wx.TE_WORDWRAP. Lines which are wrapped can be wrapped at any character. Some operating systems may ignore this style.
wx.TE_MULTILINE	The text control will display multiple lines.
wx.TE_RICH	Under Windows, use the rich text control as the underlying widget. This allows the use of styled text.
wx.TE_RICH2	Under Windows, use the most recent version of the rich text control as the underlying widget.
wx.TE_WORDWRAP	Contrast to wx.TE_LINEWRAP, lines which wrap will only do so at word boundaries. This option is ignored on many systems.

Remember that style bits can be combined, so the multi-line rich text control in this example is declared with a style of wx.TE_MULTILINE | wx.TE_RICH2.

The text styles used in a wx.TextCtrl widget are instances of the class wx.TextAttr. A wx.TextAttr instance has a text color, a background color, and a font, all of which can be specified in the constructor as in the following:

```
wx.TextAttr(colText, colBack=wx.NullColor, font=wx.NullFont)
```

The text and background colors are wxPython `wx.Color` objects that can be specified with a string naming the color or a tuple with the (red, green, blue) values of the color. The `wx.NullColor` indicates that the existing background color of the control should be used. The font is a `wx.Font` object, which we'll discuss in the next subsection. The `wx.NullFont` object indicates that the current default font should be used.

The `wx.TextAttr` class has getter methods for the attributes `GetBackgroundColour()`, `GetFont()`, and `GetTextColour()`, as well as Boolean existence methods for `HasBackgroundColour()`, `HasFont()`, and `HasTextColour()`. If the attribute contains a default value, the existence methods return `False`. The `IsDefault()` method returns `true` if all three attributes contain default values. The class does not have setter methods, since instances of `wx.TextAttr` are immutable. To change the style of text, you must create an instance.

To use a text style, call `SetDefaultStyle(style)` or `SetStyle(start, end, style)`. The first method sets the current style of the control. Any text inserted into the control, either by typing or by using `AppendText()` or `WriteText()`, is displayed in that style. If any of the attributes of the style are default, the current value for that style is kept. However, if *all* of the attributes of the style are default, the default style is reinstated. The `SetStyle()` method is similar, but takes effect immediately on the text between the `start` and `end` positions. Default attributes in the style argument are resolved by verifying the current default style for the control. Listing 7.3 uses the following line of code to reverse the colors on several characters of text:

```
richText.SetStyle(44, 52, wx.TextAttr("white", "black"))
```

The background color becomes white, and the text color for those characters becomes black.

Table 7.6 lists the methods of `wx.TextCtrl`, which are useful in manipulating multi-line controls and rich text.

Table 7.6   Multi-line and style methods of `wx.TextCtrl`

Method	Description
GetDefaultStyle() SetDefaultStyle(style)	See the earlier part of this section for a description of default styles.
GetLineLength(lineNo)	Returns the integer length of the given line.
GetLineText(lineNo)	Returns the text of the given line

continued on next page

Table 7.6 Multi-line and style methods of `wx.TextCtrl` *(continued)*

Method	Description
GetNumberOfLines()	Returns the number of lines in the control. For a single-line control, returns 1.
IsMultiLine() IsSingleLine()	Boolean methods for determining state of the control
PositionToXY(pos)	Given an integer position within the text, returns a tuple with the (col, row) index of the position. The column and row indexes both start at 0.
SetStyle(start, end, style)	Immediately changes the style for the given range of text.
ShowPosition(pos)	Causes a multi-line control to scroll such that the given position is in view.
XYToPosition(x, y)	Inverse of `PositionToXY`—given a row and column, it returns the integer position.

Creating styles is much more flexible if you can use arbitrary fonts in the system. Next, we'll show you how to create and use font instances.

7.1.5 *How do I create a font?*

Fonts are specified as instances of the class `wx.Font`. You have access to any font that has been installed and is accessible to the underlying system. To create a font instance, use the following constructor:

```
wx.Font(pointSize, family, style, weight, underline=False,
    faceName="", encoding=wx.FONTENCODING_DEFAULT)
```

The `pointSize` is the font's integer size in points. The `family` is used to quickly specify a font without having to know the actual name of the font. The exact font chosen depends on the system and specific fonts available. A sample of available font families are displayed in table 7.7. The exact fonts you get will depend on your system.

Table 7.7 Sample of the existing font families

Font	Description
`wx.DECORATIVE`	A formal, old-English style font
`wx.DEFAULT`	The system default font
`wx.MODERN`	A monospace (fixed-pitch) font

continued on next page

Table 7.7 Sample of the existing font families *(continued)*

Font	Description
wx.ROMAN	A serif font, generally something like Times New Roman
wx.SCRIPT	*A handwriting or cursive font*
wx.SWISS	A sans-serif font, generally something like Helvetica or Arial

The style parameter indicates the italicized nature of the font, and is either wx.NORMAL, wx.SLANT, or wx.ITALIC. Similarly, the weight parameter indicates the boldness of the font, and is either wx.NORMAL, wx.LIGHT, or wx.BOLD. The constants here behave as expected based on their name. The underline parameter works only on Windows systems, and if set to True causes the font to be underlined. Use the faceName argument to specify the system name of the font you want to display.

The encoding parameter allows you to select one of several encodings, which are mappings between internal characters and font display characters. Encodings are *not* Unicode encodings, just different 8-bit encodings used by wxPython. For most usage, you can use the default encoding.

To retrieve a list of available fonts on the system, and make them available to the user, use the special class wx.FontEnumerator as in the following:

```
e = wx.FontEnumerator()
e.EnumerateFacenames()
fontList = e.GetFacenames()
```

To limit the list to only fixed-width, change the first line to e = wx.FontEnumerator(fixedWidth=True).

7.1.6 *Can I have styled text if my platform doesn't support rich text?*

Yes. There is a cross-platform styled text widget in wxPython, called wx.stc.StyledTextCtrl, that is a Python wrapper around the Scintilla rich text component. Since Scintilla is not part of wxWidgets, but rather a separate third-party component that has been incorporated into wxPython, it does not share the same API as the classes we have discussed. A full discussion of wx.stc.StyledCtrl is beyond our scope here, however, you can find documentation at http://wiki.wxpython.org/index.cgi/wxStyledTextCtrl.

7.1.7 *What if my text control doesn't match my string?*

When using a multi-line wx.TextCtrl, be aware of a small gotcha involving the way in which the text control stores the string. Internally, the multi-line string inside the wx.TextCtrl is stored using \n as the line separator. This is true no matter what the underlying operating system is, even though some systems use different character combinations as a line separator. When you retrieve the string using GetValue(), the native system's line separator is restored, so you don't have to worry about manual conversion backwards. The advantage is the text inside the control isn't dependent on any specific operating system.

The disadvantage is the line length and the line indexes inside the text control can be different than they are outside the text control. For example, if you are on a Windows system, where the line separator is \r\n, the length of the string as reported by GetValue() will be longer than the end of the string in the control as reported by GetLastPosition(). By adding the following two lines in listing 7.3,

```
print "getValue", len(multiText.GetValue())
print "lastPos", multiText.GetLastPosition()
```

we would get the following results from a Unix operating system:

```
getValue 119
lastPos 119
```

and the following results from a Windows operating system:

```
getValue 121
lastPos 119
```

The implication is that you should never use the position indexes of a multi-line text control to refer back to the original string, rather, they should only be used as arguments to other methods of wx.TextCtrl. For a substring of the text within the control, use GetRange() or GetSelectedText(). Also do not cross the indexes in reverse; don't use indexes of the original string to refer back into the text control. Following is an example of the incorrect way to get 10 characters immediately after the insertion point:

```
aLongString = """Any old
    multi line string
    will do here.
    Just as long as
    it is multiline"""
text = wx.TextCtrl(panel, -1, aLongString, style=wx.TE_MULTILINE)
x = text.GetInsertionPoint()
selection = aLongString[x : x + 10]  ### THIS WILL BE INCORRECT
```

The last line should be commented out for Windows or Mac systems because it uses x (the position of the insertion point in the text control) as an index for the original string. To return the correct characters in Windows or Mac systems, the last line should be written as follows:

```
selection = text.GetRange(x, x + 10)
```

7.1.8 How do I respond to text events?

There are a handful of command events generated by wx.TextCtrl widgets that you may want to use. All of these events are bound to the text widget in question, so you need to pass it to the Bind method to catch the event, as in the following:

```
frame.Bind(wx.EVT_TEXT, frame.OnText, text)
```

Table 7.8 describes these command events.

Table 7.8 Events of wx.TextCtrl

Event	Description
EVT_TEXT	Generated when the text in the control changes. This event is generated both in response to user input, and to the programmatic change via the SetValue() method.
EVT_TEXT_ENTER	Generated when the user presses Enter in a text control with the wx.TE_PROCESS_ENTER style set.
EVT_TEXT_URL	If on a Windows system, and wx.TE_RICH or wx.TE_RICH2 is set, and wx.TE_AUTO_URL is also set, then this event is triggered when a mouse event occurs over a URL within the text control.
EVT_TEXT_MAXLEN	If a maximum length is specified for the control using SetMaxLength(), then this event is triggered when the user attempts to enter a string longer than the maximum length. You might use this, for example, to display a warning message to the user.

Next, let's discuss controls that are designed primarily to take mouse input. The simplest of these is a button.

7.2 Working with buttons

There are numerous different types of buttons in wxPython. In this section we'll cover text buttons, bitmap buttons, toggle buttons, and generic buttons.

7.2.1 *How do I make a button?*

In part 1, we described several examples of buttons, so we will only briefly cover the basics here. Figure 7.4 displays a simple button.

Using a button is very straightforward. Listing 7.4 displays the code for this simple button example.

Figure 7.4 A simple button

Listing 7.4 Creating and displaying a simple button

```python
import wx

class ButtonFrame(wx.Frame):
    def __init__(self):
        wx.Frame.__init__(self, None, -1, 'Button Example',
                size=(300, 100))
        panel = wx.Panel(self, -1)
        self.button = wx.Button(panel, -1, "Hello", pos=(50, 20))
        self.Bind(wx.EVT_BUTTON, self.OnClick, self.button)
        self.button.SetDefault()

    def OnClick(self, event):
        self.button.SetLabel("Clicked")

if __name__ == '__main__':
    app = wx.PySimpleApp()
    frame = ButtonFrame()
    frame.Show()
    app.MainLoop()
```

The `wx.Button` constructor is similar to constructors we've already seen, as in the following:

```python
wx.Button(parent, id, label, pos, size=wxDefaultSize, style=0,
        validator, name="button")
```

The argument specific to `wx.Button` is the `label`, the text displayed on the button. It can be changed during the program with `SetLabel()`, and retrieved with `GetLabel()`. Two other useful methods are `GetDefaultSize()`, which returns the system suggested default button size (useful for consistency across frames), and `SetDefault()`, which sets that button as the default for the dialog or frame. The default button is often drawn differently than other buttons and is typically activated by pressing Enter while the dialog has focus.

The `wx.Button` class has one cross-platform style flag, `wx.BU_EXACTFIT`. If defined, the button does not use the system default size as a minimum, but instead is sized as small as possible while allowing the label to fit. If the native widget supports it, you can change the alignment of the label within the button using the flags wx.BU_LEFT, wx.BU_RIGHT, wx.BU_TOP, and wx.BU_BOTTOM. Each flag aligns the label to exactly the side you would expect based on its name. As we discussed in part 1, a wx.Button triggers one command event when clicked, with the event type EVT_BUTTON.

7.2.2 How do I make a button with a bitmap?

Occasionally, you'll want a picture on your button, rather than a text label, as in figure 7.5.

In wxPython, use the class wx.BitmapButton to create a button with a picture. The code to manage a wx.BitmapButton is very similar to the general button code, as displayed in listing 7.5.

Figure 7.5 A demonstration of a basic bitmap button. The left button is drawn with a 3D effect.

Listing 7.5 Creating a bitmap button

```
import wx

class BitmapButtonFrame(wx.Frame):
    def __init__(self):
        wx.Frame.__init__(self, None, -1, 'Bitmap Button Example',
                size=(200, 150))
        panel = wx.Panel(self, -1)
        bmp = wx.Image("bitmap.bmp", wx.BITMAP_TYPE_BMP).ConvertToBitmap()
        self.button = wx.BitmapButton(panel, -1, bmp, pos=(10, 20))
        self.Bind(wx.EVT_BUTTON, self.OnClick, self.button)
        self.button.SetDefault()
        self.button2 = wx.BitmapButton(panel, -1, bmp, pos=(100, 20),
            style=0)
        self.Bind(ex.EVT_BUTTON, self.OnClick, self.button2)

    def OnClick(self, event):
        self.Destroy()

if __name__ == '__main__':
    app = wx.PySimpleApp()
    frame = BitmapButtonFrame()
    frame.Show()
    app.MainLoop()
```

The primary difference is that for a bitmap button you need to supply a bitmap, rather than a label. Otherwise, the constructor and most of the code is identical to the text button case. A bitmap button emits the same EVT_BUTTON event when clicked.

There are a couple of interesting features related to bitmap buttons. First, there's a style flag, wx.BU_AUTODRAW, which is on by default. If the flag is on, the bitmap is surrounded by a 3D border to make it look like a text button (left button of figure 7.5), and the button is a few pixels larger than the original bitmap. If the flag is off, the bitmap is simply drawn as a button with no border. The right button in figure 7.5 shuts off the default by setting style=0, and it does not have the 3D effect.

By default, simply pass wxPython a single bitmap for the main display, and wxPython automatically creates standard derivative bitmaps when the button is pressed, has the focus, or is disabled. If the normal behavior is not what you want, you can explicitly tell wxPython which bitmaps to use with the following methods: SetBitmapDisabled(), SetBitmapFocus(), SetBitmapLabel(), and SetBitmap-Selected(). Each of these methods takes a wx.Bitmap object, and each has an associated getter function.

You cannot combine a bitmap and text by using the normal wxWidgets C++ library. You could create a bitmap that contains text. However, as we'll see in the generic button question, there is a wxPython addition that allows this behavior.

7.2.3 *How do I create a toggle button?*

You can create a toggle button using wx.ToggleButton. A toggle button looks exactly like a text button, but behaves more like a checkbox in that it gives a visual cue to a selected or unselected state. In other words, when you press a toggle button, it shows its state by continuing to look pressed until you click it again.

There are only two differences between a wx.ToggleButton and the parent wx.Button class :

- A wx.ToggleButton sends an EVT_TOGGLEBUTTON event when clicked.
- A wx.ToggleButton has GetValue() and SetValue() methods, which manipulate the binary state of the button.

Toggle buttons can be a useful and attractive alternative to checkboxes, especially in a toolbar. Remember, you cannot combine a toggle button with a bitmap button using the wxWidgets provided objects, but wxPython has a generic button class that provides this behavior, which we'll describe in the next section.

7.2.4 What's a generic button, and why should I use one?

A generic button is a button widget that has been completely reimplemented in Python, bypassing the use of the native system widget. The parent class is `wx.lib.buttons. GenButton`, and there are generic bitmap and toggle buttons.

There are several reasons for using generic buttons:

- The generic button look is more similar across platforms than native buttons. The flip side is that generic buttons may look slightly different from native buttons on a particular system.

- Using a generic button, you have more control over the look, and can change attributes, such as the 3D bevel width and color, in ways that the native control may not allow.

- The generic button family allows for combinations of features that the wxWidgets button does not. There is a `GenBitmapTextButton` which allows a text label and a bitmap, and a `GenBitmapToggleButton` which allows a toggle bitmap.

- If you are creating a button class, it's easier to use the generic buttons as a base class. Since the code and parameters are written in Python, they are more accessible for you to inspect and overwrite when creating a new subclass.

Figure 7.6 displays the generic buttons in action.

Listing 7.6 displays the code for figure 7.6. The second import statement, `import wx.lib.buttons as buttons`, is required for the generic button classes to be available.

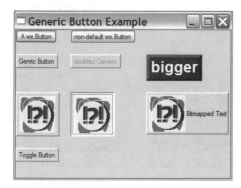

Figure 7.6
Generic buttons. The top row has regular buttons for contrast. This shows different color combinations, bitmap, bitmap toggle, and bitmap text buttons.

Listing 7.6 Creating and using wxPython generic buttons

```
import wx
import wx.lib.buttons as buttons

class GenericButtonFrame(wx.Frame):
    def __init__(self):
        wx.Frame.__init__(self, None, -1, 'Generic Button Example',
                size=(500, 350))
        panel = wx.Panel(self, -1)

        sizer = wx.FlexGridSizer(1, 3, 20, 20)
        b = wx.Button(panel, -1, "A wx.Button")
        b.SetDefault()
        sizer.Add(b)

        b = wx.Button(panel, -1, "non-default wx.Button")
        sizer.Add(b)
        sizer.Add((10,10))

        b = buttons.GenButton(panel, -1, 'Generic Button')        ◁─┘  Basic generic button
        sizer.Add(b)
                                                       Disabled generic button
        b = buttons.GenButton(panel, -1, 'disabled Generic')    ◁─┘
        b.Enable(False)
        sizer.Add(b)
                                                       A button with a
        b = buttons.GenButton(panel, -1, 'bigger')    ◁─┘  custom size and color
        b.SetFont(wx.Font(20, wx.SWISS, wx.NORMAL, wx.BOLD, False))
        b.SetBezelWidth(5)
        b.SetBackgroundColour("Navy")
        b.SetForegroundColour("white")
        b.SetToolTipString("This is a BIG button...")
        sizer.Add(b)

        bmp = wx.Image("bitmap.bmp", wx.BITMAP_TYPE_BMP).ConvertToBitmap()
        b = buttons.GenBitmapButton(panel, -1, bmp)    ◁─  Generic bitmap button
        sizer.Add(b)

        b = buttons.GenBitmapToggleButton(panel, -1, bmp)    ◁─  Generic bitmap toggle button
        sizer.Add(b)

        b = buttons.GenBitmapTextButton(panel, -1, bmp,    ◁─  Bitmap and text button
            "Bitmapped Text", size=(175, 75))
        b.SetUseFocusIndicator(False)
        sizer.Add(b)
                                                       Generic toggle button
        b = buttons.GenToggleButton(panel, -1, "Toggle Button")    ◁─┘
        sizer.Add(b)

        panel.SetSizer(sizer)

if __name__ == '__main__':
```

```
app = wx.PySimpleApp()
frame = GenericButtonFrame()
frame.Show()
app.MainLoop()
```

In listing 7.6, the use of a generic button is very similar to a regular button. Generic buttons emit the same EVT_BUTTON and EVT_TOGGLEBUTTON events as regular buttons. The generic button includes the GetBevelWidth() and SetBevel-Width() methods to change the amount of the 3D effect bevel. These are used in the large button in figure 7.6.

The generic bitmap button class GenBitmapButton works like the normal wxPython version. The GenBitmapTextButton takes first the bitmap and then the text in the constructor. The generics offer the GenToggleButton class, the GenBit-mapToggleButton, and the GenBitmapTextToggleButton. All three are the same as the non-toggle version, and respond to GetToggle() and SetToggle() to manage the toggle state of the button.

In the next section, we'll discuss options for allowing your user to enter or view a numerical value.

7.3 *Entering and displaying numbers*

At times, you want to display numerical information graphically, or you want the user to enter a numerical quantity without having to use the keyboard. In this section, we'll explore the slider, the spinner box, and the display gauge, tools in wxPython for numerical entry and display.

7.3.1 *How do I make a slider?*

A slider is a widget that allows the user to select a number from within a range by dragging a marker across the width or height of the control. In wxPython, the control class is wx.Slider, which includes a read-only text display of the current value of the slider. Figure 7.7 displays examples of a vertical and horizontal slider.

Basic slider use is fairly straightforward, but there are a number of events you can add.

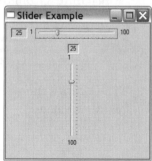

Figure 7.7   A vertical wx.Slider and a horizontal wx.Slider, which use the style flag wx.SL_LABELS

How to use a slider

As displayed in listing 7.7, a slider can manage a single value through the control.

| Listing 7.7 Displays code for the horizontal and vertical slider |

```python
import wx

class SliderFrame(wx.Frame):
    def __init__(self):
        wx.Frame.__init__(self, None, -1, 'Slider Example',
                size=(340, 320))
        panel = wx.Panel(self, -1)
        self.count = 0
        slider = wx.Slider(panel, 100, 25, 1, 100, pos=(10, 10),
                size=(250, -1),
                style=wx.SL_HORIZONTAL | wx.SL_AUTOTICKS | wx.SL_LABELS )
        slider.SetTickFreq(5, 1)
        slider = wx.Slider(panel, 100, 25, 1, 100, pos=(125, 50),
                size=(-1, 250),
                style=wx.SL_VERTICAL | wx.SL_AUTOTICKS | wx.SL_LABELS )
        slider.SetTickFreq(20, 1)

if __name__ == '__main__':
    app = wx.PySimpleApp()
    frame = SliderFrame()
    frame.Show()
    app.MainLoop()
```

Typically, when you use the wx.Slider class, all you'll need is the constructor, which differs from the other calls as in the following:

```python
wx.Slider(parent, id, value, minValue, maxValue,
        pos=wxDefaultPosition, size=wx.DefaultSize,
        style=wx.SL_HORIZONTAL, validator=wx.DefaultValidator,
        name="slider")
```

The value is the starting value of the slider, while minValue and maxValue are the extreme values.

Working with slider styles

The styles for a slider govern the placement and orientation of the slider, as listed in table 7.9.

Table 7.9 Styles for `wx.Slider`

Style	Description
wx.SL_AUTOTICKS	If set, the slider will display tick marks across it. The spacing is governed by the setter method `SetTickFreq`.
wx.SL_HORIZONTAL	The slider will be horizontal. This is the default.
wx.SL_LABELS	If set, the slider will display labels for the minimum and maximum value, and a read-only display of the current value. The current value might not display on all platforms.
wx.SL_LEFT	For a vertical slider, the ticks will be on the left of the slider.
wx.SL_RIGHT	For a vertical slider, the ticks will be on the right of the slider.
wx.SL_TOP	For a horizontal slider, the ticks will be on top of the slider.
wx.SL_VERTICAL	The slider will be vertical.

If you want changes in the slider value to affect another part of your application, there are several events you can use. These events are identical to those emitted by a window scroll bar, and are described in detail in the scrolling section of chapter 8.

Table 7.10 lists the setter properties you can apply to a slider. Each setter has an associated `Get` method—the descriptions in the table refer to the setter only.

Table 7.10 Settable attributes of a slider

Function	Description
GetRange() SetRange(minValue, maxValue)	Sets the boundary range of the slider
GetTickFreq() SetTickFreq(n, pos)	Sets the spacing between ticks, using the n argument. The pos argument is not actually used, but it's still required. Set it to 1.
GetLineSize() SetLineSize(lineSize)	Sets the amount by which the value changes if you adjust the slider by one line by pressing an arrow key.

continued on next page

Table 7.10 Settable attributes of a slider *(continued)*

Function	Description
GetPageSize() SetPageSize(pageSize)	Sets the amount by which the value changes if you adjust the slider by one page by pressing page up or page down.
GetValue() GetValue(value)	Sets the value of the slider.

Although sliders provide a quick visual representation of where the value lies along the possible range, they also have a couple of weaknesses. They take up a lot of space in their primary dimension, and it's difficult to set the slider exactly using a mouse, particularly if the range is quite large, or if the user has an accessibility issue. The spinner, which we'll discuss in the next section, resolves both of these issues.

7.3.2 How can I get those neat up/down arrow buttons?

A *spinner* is a combination text control and pair of arrow buttons that adjust a numeric value, and is a great alternative to a slider when you have minimal screen space. Figure 7.8 displays a wxPython spinner control.

Figure 7.8
A spinner control in wxPython

In wxPython, the `wx.SpinCtrl` class manages both the spinner buttons and the associated text display. In the next section, we'll create a spinner.

How to create a spinner

Use `wx.SpinCtrl` to change the value either by pressing the buttons or by typing in the text control. Non-numeric text typed into the control is ignored, although the control doesn't change back to the previous value until a button is pressed. A numeric value outside the control range is treated as the relevant maximum or minimum value, although that value doesn't revert to the end of the range until you press a button. Listing 7.8 displays the use of `wx.SpinCtrl`.

Listing 7.8 Using `wx.SpinCtrl`

```
import wx

class SpinnerFrame(wx.Frame):
    def __init__(self):
        wx.Frame.__init__(self, None, -1, 'Spinner Example',
                size=(100, 100))
```

```
        panel = wx.Panel(self, -1)
        sc = wx.SpinCtrl(panel, -1, "", (30, 20), (80, -1))
        sc.SetRange(1,100)
        sc.SetValue(5)

if __name__ == '__main__':
    app = wx.PySimpleApp()
    SpinnerFrame().Show()
    app.MainLoop()
```

Nearly all of the complexity of the spin control is in the constructor, which has several arguments as in the following:

```
wx.SpinCtrl(parent, id=-1, value=wx.EmptyString,
        pos=wx.DefaultPosition, size=wx.DefaultSize,
        style=wx.SP_ARROW_KEYS, min=0, max=100, initial=0,
        name="wxSpinCtrl")
```

The first part of this constructor is similar to all the other `wx.Window` constructors. However, the `value` argument here is a dummy. Set the initial value of the control using the `initial` argument, and use the `min` and `max` arguments to set the range of the control.

There are two style flags for `wx.SpinCtrl`. By default, `wx.SP_ARROW_KEYS` is declared because it allows the user to change the value of the control from the keyboard using the up and down arrow keys. The `wx.SP_WRAP` style causes the value of the control to wrap, meaning that if you go off the edge at one extreme, you wind up at the other extreme. Also, you can catch the `EVT_SPINCTRL` event, which is generated whenever the spin value is changed (even if it is changed via text entry). If the text is changed, an `EVT_TEXT` is fired, just as it would be if you were using a standalone text control.

As displayed in listing 7.8, you can set the range and value using the `Set-Range(minVal, maxVal)` and `SetValue(value)` methods. The `SetValue()` function can take either a string or an integer. To get the values, use the methods `GetValue()` (which returns an integer), `GetMin()`, and `GetMax()`.

When you need more control over the behavior of the spinner, such as spinning through floating point values, or a list of strings, you can put a `wx.Spin-Button` together with a `wx.TextCtrl`, and build plumbing between them. Put the two controls next to each other and catch `EVT_SPIN` events from the `wx.Spin-Button`, updating the value in the `wx.TextCtrl`.

7.3.3 How can I make a progress bar?

If you want to graphically display a numeric value without allowing the user to change it, use the relevant wxPython widget wx.Gauge. An example of this numeric value is a progress bar, displayed in figure 7.9.

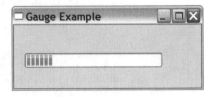

Figure 7.9 A wx.Gauge **displaying some progress**

Listing 7.9 displays the code that created this figure. Unlike many other examples in this chapter, in this example we added an event handler. The following code adjusts the value of the gauge during idle time, causing it to loop from start to finish and back again.

Listing 7.9 Displaying and updating a wx.Gauge

```
import wx

class GaugeFrame(wx.Frame):
    def __init__(self):
        wx.Frame.__init__(self, None, -1, 'Gauge Example',
                size=(350, 150))
        panel = wx.Panel(self, -1)
        self.count = 0
        self.gauge = wx.Gauge(panel, -1, 50, (20, 50), (250, 25))
        self.gauge.SetBezelFace(3)
        self.gauge.SetShadowWidth(3)
        self.Bind(wx.EVT_IDLE, self.OnIdle)

    def OnIdle(self, event):
        self.count = self.count + 1
        if self.count >= 50:
            self.count = 0
        self.gauge.SetValue(self.count)

if __name__ == '__main__':
    app = wx.PySimpleApp()
    GaugeFrame().Show()
    app.MainLoop()
```

The constructor for wx.Gauge is similar to the other numerical widgets:

```
wx.Gauge(parent, id, range, pos=wx.DefaultPosition,
        size=wx.DefaultSize, style=wx.GA_HORIZONTAL,
        validator=wx.DefaultValidator, name="gauge")
```

As you enter the numerical value using the `range` argument, it represents the upper bound of the gauge, while the lower bound is always 0. The default style, `wx.GA_HORIZONTAL` provides a horizontal bar. To rotate it 90 degrees, you use the style `wx.GA_VERTICAL`. If you are on Windows, the style `wx.GA_PROGRESSBAR` gives you the native progress bar from the Windows toolkit.

As a read-only control, `wx.Gauge` has no events. However, it does have properties you can set. You can adjust the value and range using `GetValue()`, `SetValue(pos)`, `GetRange()`, and `SetRange(range)`. If you are on Windows, and are not using the native progress bar style, you can use `SetBezelFace(width)` and `SetShadowWidth()` to change the width of the 3D effect.

7.4 Giving the user choices

Nearly every application requires a user to choose between a set of predefined options at some point. In wxPython, there are a variety of widgets to help the user in this task, including checkboxes, radio buttons, list boxes, and combo boxes. The following section will guide you through these widgets.

7.4.1 How do I create a checkbox?

A checkbox is a toggle button with a text label. Checkboxes are often displayed in groups, but the toggle state of each checkbox is independent. Checkboxes are used when you have one or more options that have clear on/off states, and the state of one option doesn't affect the state of the others. Figure 7.10 displays a group of checkboxes.

Figure 7.10
A group of wxPython checkboxes

Checkboxes are easy to use in wxPython. They are instances of the class `wx.CheckBox`, and can be displayed together by placing them inside the parent container together. Listing 7.10 provides the code that generated figure 7.10.

Listing 7.10 Inserting three checkboxes into a frame

```
import wx

class CheckBoxFrame(wx.Frame):
    def __init__(self):
        wx.Frame.__init__(self, None, -1, 'Checkbox Example',
                size=(150, 200))
        panel = wx.Panel(self, -1)
```

```
        wx.CheckBox(panel, -1, "Alpha", (35, 40), (150, 20))
        wx.CheckBox(panel, -1, "Beta", (35, 60), (150, 20))
        wx.CheckBox(panel, -1, "Gamma", (35, 80), (150, 20))

if __name__ == '__main__':
    app = wx.PySimpleApp()
    CheckBoxFrame().Show()
    app.MainLoop()
```

The `wx.CheckBox` class has a typical wxPython constructor:

```
wx.CheckBox(parent, id, label, pos=wx.DefaultPosition,
        size=wx.DefaultSize, style=0, name="checkBox")
```

The `label` argument takes the text that is displayed next to the checkbox. Check-boxes have no style flags which are unique to them, but they do trigger a unique command event, `EVT_CHECKBOX`. The toggle state of a `wx.CheckBox` can be retrieved with the methods `GetValue()` and `SetValue(state)`, and its value is a Boolean. The method `IsChecked()` is identical to `GetValue()` and is included to make the code clearer.

7.4.2 How can I create a group of radio buttons?

A radio button is a widget that allows the user to choose from among several options. Unlike checkboxes, radio buttons are explicitly deployed in groups and only one of the options can be selected at a time. When a new option is selected, the existing selection is switched off. The name radio button comes from the group of selection buttons on older car radios that exhibited the same behavior. Radio buttons are a bit more complex to use than checkboxes, because they need to be organized into a group in order to be useful.

In wxPython, there are two ways to create a group of radio buttons. One of them, `wx.RadioButton`, requires you to create the buttons one at a time, while `wx.RadioBox` allows you to deploy an entire group of buttons with a single object, displaying the buttons in a rectangle.

The `wx.RadioButton` class is simpler, and is preferred in the case where the radio buttons have a direct influence on other widgets, or where the layout of the radio buttons is not in a simple rectangle. Figure 7.11 displays an example of a few `wx.RadioButton` objects in a group.

Figure 7.11 Example of `wx.RadioButton` where radio buttons enable text control

We are using `wx.RadioButton` in this example because each radio button controls an associated text control. Since widgets outside the radio button group are involved, we can't just use a radio box.

How to create radio buttons

Listing 7.11 displays the code for figure 7.11, which manages the relationship between the radio buttons and the text controls.

Listing 7.11 Using `wx.RadioButton` to control another widget

```
import wx

class RadioButtonFrame(wx.Frame):
    def __init__(self):
        wx.Frame.__init__(self, None, -1, 'Radio Example',
                size=(200, 200))
        panel = wx.Panel(self, -1)                        Creating radio buttons
        radio1 = wx.RadioButton(panel, -1, "Elmo", pos=(20, 50),
            style=wx.RB_GROUP)
        radio2 = wx.RadioButton(panel, -1, "Ernie", pos=(20, 80))
        radio3 = wx.RadioButton(panel, -1, "Bert", pos=(20, 110))
        text1 = wx.TextCtrl(panel, -1, "", pos=(80, 50))
        text2 = wx.TextCtrl(panel, -1, "", pos=(80, 80))     Creating text
        text3 = wx.TextCtrl(panel, -1, "", pos=(80, 110))    controls
        self.texts = {"Elmo": text1, "Ernie": text2, "Bert": text3}
        for eachText in [text2, text3]:              Linking buttons and text
            eachText.Enable(False)
        for eachRadio in [radio1, radio2, radio3]:       Binding events
            self.Bind(wx.EVT_RADIOBUTTON, self.OnRadio, eachRadio)
        self.selectedText = text1

    def OnRadio(self, event):      Event handler
        if self.selectedText:
            self.selectedText.Enable(False)
        radioSelected = event.GetEventObject()
        text = self.texts[radioSelected.GetLabel()]    # map label ↦ text control obj
        text.Enable(True)
        self.selectedText = text

if __name__ == '__main__':
    app = wx.PySimpleApp()
    RadioButtonFrame().Show()
    app.MainLoop()
```

We've created radio buttons and text boxes, then initialized a dictionary containing the connections between them. A `for` loop disables two of the text boxes, and another one binds the radio button command event. When the event is clicked, the currently active text box is disabled, and the box matching the clicked button is enabled.

Using `wx.RadioButton` is similar to `wx.CheckBox`. The constructor is nearly identical, as in the following:

```
wx.RadioButton(parent, id, label, pos=wx.DefaultPosition,
        size=wx.DefaultSize, style=0,
        validator=wx.DefaultValidator, name="radioButton")
```

As in the checkbox, the `label` is used for the caption displayed next to the button.

The `wx.RB_GROUP` style declares the button to be the beginning of a new group of radio buttons. The definition of a group of radio buttons is important because it governs toggle behavior. When one button in the group is selected, the previously selected button in the group is toggled to the unchecked state. After a radio button is created with `wx.RB_GROUP`, all subsequent radio buttons added to the same parent are added to the same group. This continues until another radio button is created with `wx.RB_GROUP`, starting the next group. In listing 7.11, the first radio button is declared with `wx.RB_GROUP`, and subsequent ones are not. The result of this is that all the buttons are considered to be in the same group, and clicking on one of them toggles off the previously selected button.

Using a radio box

Typically, if you want to display a group of buttons, declaring them separately is not the best method. Instead, wxPython allows you to create a single object that encapsulates the entire group using the class `wx.RadioBox`. As displayed in figure 7.12, it looks very similar to a group of radio buttons.

To use the `wx.RadioBox` class, all you need is the constructor. Listing 7.12 displays the code that created figure 7.12.

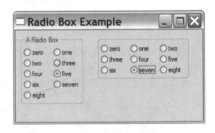

Figure 7.12   Two examples of `wx.RadioBox` built from the same underlying data with different configurations

Listing 7.12   Building a radio box

```
import wx

class RadioBoxFrame(wx.Frame):
    def __init__(self):
        wx.Frame.__init__(self, None, -1, 'Radio Box Example',
```

```
                 size=(350, 200))
        panel = wx.Panel(self, -1)
        sampleList = ['zero', 'one', 'two', 'three', 'four', 'five',
                      'six', 'seven', 'eight']
        wx.RadioBox(panel, -1, "A Radio Box", (10, 10), wx.DefaultSize,
                    sampleList, 2, wx.RA_SPECIFY_COLS)

        wx.RadioBox(panel, -1, "", (150, 10), wx.DefaultSize,
                    sampleList, 3, wx.RA_SPECIFY_COLS)

if __name__ == '__main__':
    app = wx.PySimpleApp()
    RadioBoxFrame().Show()
    app.MainLoop()
```

The constructor for wx.RadioBox is more complex than the simple radio button, since you need to specify the data for all the buttons at once, as in the following:

```
wx.RadioBox(parent, id, label, pos=wx.DefaultPosition,
       size=wxDefaultSize, choices=None, majorDimension=0,
       style=wx.RA_SPECIFY_COLS, validator=wx.DefaultValidator,
       name="radioBox")
```

There are a few arguments to the constructor that are unfamiliar or different. In this constructor, the label argument is the static text which is displayed on the border of the box. The buttons themselves are specified in the choices argument, which is a Python sequence of the string labels.

Like a grid sizer, you specify the dimensions of a wx.RadioBox by stating the size in one dimension, and wxPython fills as many slots in the other dimension as needed. The major dimension size is specified in the majorDimension argument. Which dimension is considered major depends on the style flag. The default value, which is also used for the example in listing 7.12 and figure 7.12, is wx.RA_SPECIFY_COLS. In the example, the number of columns is set to 2 (in the left box) or 3 (in the right box), and the number of rows is determined dynamically by the number of elements in the choices list. If you want the opposite behavior, set the style to wx.RA_SPECIFY_ROWS. If you want to respond to the command event when a radio box is clicked, the event is EVT_RADIOBOX.

The wx.RadioBox class has a number of methods to manage the state of the various radio buttons inside the box. For the methods that allow you to manage a specific internal button, pass the index of the button. The indexes start at 0 and proceed in the exact order that was used when the button labels were passed to the constructor. Table 7.11 lists the methods.

Table 7.11   Methods of wx.RadioBox

Method	Description
EnableItem(n, flag)	The `flag` argument is a Boolean which is used to enable or disable the button at index n. To enable the entire box at once, use `Enable()`.
FindString(string)	Returns the integer index of the button with the given label, or -1 if the label is not found.
GetCount()	Returns the number of buttons in the box.
GetItemLabel(n) SetItemLabel(n, string)	Returns or sets the string label of the button at index n.
GetSelection() GetStringSelection() SetSelection(n) SetStringSelection(string)	The `GetSelection()` and `SetSelection()` methods manage the integer index of the currently selected radio button. `GetStringSelection()` returns the string label of the currently selected button, while `SetStringSelection()` changes the selection to the button with the given string. Neither of the setter functions causes an `EVT_RADIOBOX` to be sent.
ShowItem(item, show)	The `show` argument is a Boolean used to display or hide the button at index `item`.

Radio buttons aren't the only way to give the user a choice of a series of options. List and combo boxes often take up less space, and can also be configured to allow the user to make multiple selections from the same group.

7.4.3 *How can I create a list box?*

A list box is another mechanism for presenting a choice to the user. The options are placed in a rectangular window and the user can select one or more of them. List boxes take up less space than radio boxes, and are good choices when the number of options is relatively small. However, their usefulness drops somewhat if the user has to scroll far to see all options. Figure 7.13 displays a wxPython list box.

In wxPython, a list box is an element of the class wx.ListBox. The class has methods that allow you to manipulate the choices in the list.

Figure 7.13   A wx.ListBox with a simple list of options

How to create a list box

Listing 7.13 displays the list box code that produced figure 7.13.

Listing 7.13 Using a `wx.ListBox`

```
import wx

class ListBoxFrame(wx.Frame):
    def __init__(self):
        wx.Frame.__init__(self, None, -1, 'List Box Example',
                size=(250, 200))
        panel = wx.Panel(self, -1)

        sampleList = ['zero', 'one', 'two', 'three', 'four', 'five',
                        'six', 'seven', 'eight', 'nine', 'ten', 'eleven',
                        'twelve', 'thirteen', 'fourteen']
        listBox = wx.ListBox(panel, -1, (20, 20), (80, 120), sampleList,
                wx.LB_SINGLE)
        listBox.SetSelection(3)

if __name__ == '__main__':
    app = wx.PySimpleApp()
    ListBoxFrame().Show()
    app.MainLoop()
```

(handwritten annotations: "pos" above (20, 20), "size" above (80, 120), "# starting selection" next to listBox.SetSelection(3))

The constructor for the `wx.ListBox` is similar to the one for a radio box, as in the following:

```
wx.ListBox(parent, id, pos=wx.DefaultPosition,
        size=wx.DefaultSize, choices=None, style=0,
        validator=wx.DefaultValidator, name="listBox")
```

The main difference between a radio box and a list box is that a `wx.ListBox` has no label attribute. The elements to be displayed in the list are placed in the choices argument, which should be a sequence of strings. There are three mutually exclusive styles which determine how the user can select elements from the list, as described in table 7.12.

Users often have problems with multiple and extended selections, because they usually expect to see a single selection list, and maintaining the multiple selections can be challenging, especially for users with accessibility issues. If you do use a multiple or extended list, we recommend that you clearly label the list as such.

Table 7.12   Selection type styles for a list box

Style	Description
wx.LB_EXTENDED	The user can select a range of multiple items by using a mouse shift-click, or the keyboard equivalent.
wx.LB_MULTIPLE	The user can have more than one item selected at a time. Essentially, in this case, the list box acts like a group of checkboxes.
wx.LB_SINGLE	The user can have only one item selected at a time. Essentially, in this case, the list box acts like a group of radio buttons.

There are three styles that govern the display of scroll bars in a wx.ListBox, as displayed in table 7.13.

Table 7.13   Scroll bar type styles for a list box

Style	Description
wx.LB_ALWAYS_SB	The list box will always display a vertical scroll bar, whether or not it is needed.
wx.LB_HSCROLL	If the native widget supports it, the list box will create a horizontal scrollbar if items are too wide to fit.
wx.LB_NEEDED_SB	The list box will only display a vertical scroll bar if needed. This is the default.

There is also the style wx.LB_SORT, which causes the elements of the list to be sorted alphabetically.

There are two command events specific to wx.ListBox. The EVT_LISTBOX event is triggered when an element of the list is selected (even if it's the currently selected element). If the list is double-clicked, the event EVT_LISTBOX_DCLICK is fired.

There are several methods specific to list boxes which that you to manipulate the items in the box. Table 7.14 describes many of them. All indexes start at zero, and represent the current list of items in the list from top to bottom.

Once you have a list box, it's only natural to want to combine it with other widgets, such as a pull-down menu, or a checkbox. In the next section, we'll explore these options.

Table 7.14 Methods of list boxes

Method	Description
Append(item)	Appends the string item to the end of the list.
Clear()	Empties the list box.
Delete(n)	Removes the item at index n from the list.
Deselect(n)	In a multiple select list box, causes the item at position n to be deselected. No effect in other styles.
FindString(string)	Returns the integer position of the given string, or -1 if not found.
GetCount()	Returns the number of strings in the list.
GetSelection() SetSelection(n, select) GetStringSelection() SetStringSelection(string, select) GetSelections()	Get selection returns the integer index currently selected (single list only). For a multiple list, use GetSelections(), which returns a tuple of integer positions. For a single list, GetStringSelection() returns the string at the selected index. The set methods set the given position or string to the state specified by the Boolean argument. Changing the selection in this way does not trigger the EVT_LISTBOX event.
GetString(n) SetString(n, string)	Gets or sets the string at position n.
InsertItems(items, pos)	Inserts the list of strings in the items argument into the list box before the position in the pos argument. A pos of 0 puts the items at the beginning of the list.
Selected(n)	Returns a Boolean corresponding to the selected state of the item at index n.
Set(choices)	Resets the list box to the list given in choices—that is, the current elements are removed from the list and replaced by the new list.

7.4.4 Can I combine a checkbox and a list box?

You can combine a checkbox with a list box using the class wx.CheckListBox. Figure 7.14 displays a checkbox and a list box together.

The constructor and most methods of wx.Check-ListBox are identical to wx.ListBox. There is one new event, wx.EVT_CHECKLISTBOX, which is triggered when one of the checkboxes in the list is clicked. There are two new methods for managing the checkboxes:

Figure 7.14 A check list box is very similar to a regular list box

Check(n, check) sets the check state of the item at index n, and IsChecked(item) returns True if the item at the given index is checked.

7.4.5 *What if I want a pull-down choice?*

A pull-down choice is a selection mechanism that only shows the choices when the pull-down arrow is clicked. A pull-down is the most compact way to display a choice of elements, and is most useful when screen space is tight. From a user perspective, a choice is most useful for a relatively large list of options, although they are also preferred when it's not necessary for the user to see all the options at all times. Figure 7.15 displays a closed choice. And figure 7.16 displays an open pull-down.

Figure 7.15
A pull-down choice, with no selection

Figure 7.16
A pull-down choice in the process of having an element selected

The use of a choice is very similar to a regular list box. Listing 7.14 displays how to create a pull-down choice.

Listing 7.14 Creating a pull-down choice

```python
import wx

class ChoiceFrame(wx.Frame):
    def __init__(self):
        wx.Frame.__init__(self, None, -1, 'Choice Example',
                size=(250, 200))
        panel = wx.Panel(self, -1)
        sampleList = ['zero', 'one', 'two', 'three', 'four', 'five',
                    'six', 'seven', 'eight']
        wx.StaticText(panel, -1, "Select one:", (15, 20))
        wx.Choice(panel, -1, (85, 18), choices=sampleList)

if __name__ == '__main__':
    app = wx.PySimpleApp()
    ChoiceFrame().Show()
    app.MainLoop()
```

The constructor for a choice is basically identical to the one for a list box:

```
wx.Choice(parent, id, pos=wx.DefaultPosition,
        size=wx.DefaultSize, choices=None, style=0,
        validator=wx.DefaultValidator, name="choice")
```

A `wx.Choice` has no specific styles, but it does have a unique command event, `EVT_CHOICE`. Almost all of the methods in table 7.14 that apply to single-selection list boxes also apply to `wx.Choice` objects.

7.4.6 *Can I combine text entry and a list?*

The widget that combines text entry and a list is called a combo box, and is essentially a text box bolted to a pull-down choice. Figure 7.17 displays a combo box.

On Windows, you can use the right-hand style, which is a text box bolted to a list box.

The code for creating a combo box is similar to the choice elements we have already seen. In this case the class is `wx.ComboBox`, which is a direct subclass of `wx.Choice`. Listing 7.15 displays the code details.

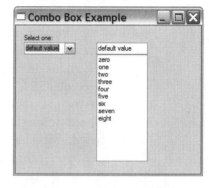

Figure 7.17 **A combo box showing the left box in the style** `wx.CB_DROPDOWN`, **and the right in** `wx.CB_SIMPLE`

Listing 7.15 Code for a demonstration of `wx.ComboBox`

```python
import wx

class ComboBoxFrame(wx.Frame):
    def __init__(self):
        wx.Frame.__init__(self, None, -1, 'Combo Box Example',
                size=(350, 300))
        panel = wx.Panel(self, -1)
        sampleList = ['zero', 'one', 'two', 'three', 'four', 'five',
                    'six', 'seven', 'eight']
        wx.StaticText(panel, -1, "Select one:", (15, 15))
        wx.ComboBox(panel, -1, "default value", (15, 30), wx.DefaultSize,
                    sampleList, wx.CB_DROPDOWN)
        wx.ComboBox(panel, -1, "default value", (150, 30), wx.DefaultSize,
                    sampleList, wx.CB_SIMPLE)

if __name__ == '__main__':
    app = wx.PySimpleApp()
    ComboBoxFrame().Show()
    app.MainLoop()
```

The constructor for `wx.ComboBox` should look familiar by now:

```
wx.ComboBox(parent, id, value="", pos=wx.DefaultPosition,
        size=wx.DefaultSize, choices, style=0,
        validator=wx.DefaultValidator, name="comboBox")
```

There are four styles for a `wx.ComboBox`. Two of them determine how the combo box is drawn: `wx.CB_DROPDOWN` creates a combo box with a pull-down list, and `wx.CB_SIMPLE` creates a combo box with a full list box. You can only use `wx.CB_SIMPLE` on Windows systems. Any combo box can be designated `wx.CB_READONLY`, which prevents the user from typing in the text area. When the combo box is designated read only, the selection must come from one of the elements in the choice list, even if you set it programmatically. Finally, there is `wx.CB_SORT`, which causes the elements of the choice list to be displayed alphabetically.

Since `wx.ComboBox` is a subclass of `wx.Choice`, all of the methods of `wx.Choice` can be called on a combo box, as displayed in table 7.14. In addition, a number of methods are defined to manipulate the text component, all of which behave the way they do for a `wx.TextCtrl` (see table 7.4 for details). The defined methods are `Copy()`, `Cut()`, `GetInsertionPoint()`, `GetValue()`, `Paste()`, `Replace(from, to, text)`, `Remove(from, to)`, `SetInsertionPoint(pos)`, `SetInsertionPointEnd()`, and `SetValue()`

7.5 *Summary*

In this chapter, we showed you how to use many of wxPython's most basic and commonly used controls. The generic version is somewhat more consistent across platforms.

- For the display of static text labels, you can use the `wx.StaticText` class. There is also a version implemented completely in wxPython, called `wx.lib.stattext.GenStaticText`.

- If you need a control that allows the user to enter text, the class to use is `wx.TextCtrl`. It allows both single and multi-line entry, as well as password masking and other effects. If the native widget supports it, you can use `wx.TextCtrl` to have styled text. Styles are instances of the class `wx.TextAttr`, and also use `wx.Font` to encapsulate font information. On all systems, you can use the class `wx.stc.StyledTextCtrl`, which is a wxPython wrapper around the open-source Scintilla text component, to achieve color and font styles in an editable text component.

- To create a button, use the `wx.Button` class, which also has a generic counterpart, `wx.lib.buttons.GenButton`. A button can have a bitmap instead of a text label (`wx.BitmapButton`), or have its state toggle between pressed and unpressed (`wx.ToggleButton`). There are generic equivalents to both bitmap and toggle buttons, which have a fuller range of features than the standard versions.

- There are a few ways to select or display numerical values. You can use the `wx.Slider` class to display a vertical or horizontal slider. The `wx.SpinCtrl` displays a text control with up and down buttons to change a numerical value. The `wx.Gauge` control displays a progress bar indicator of a number.

- You can choose from among a series of controls for letting the user pick from a list of options. The best control to use is based on the number of options, whether the user can select more than one, and the amount of screen space you want to use. Checkboxes are managed with the `wx.Check-Box` class. There are two ways to get radio buttons: `wx.RadioButton` gives a single radio button, while `wx.RadioBox` gives a group of buttons displayed together. There are several list display widgets that are used similarly. A list box is created with `wx.ListBox`, and you can add checkboxes by using `wx.CheckListBox`. For a more compact pull-down, use `wx.Choice`. `wx.Combo-Box` combines the features of a list and a text control.

Now that we've covered the basics of common widgets, in the next chapter we'll discuss the different kinds of frames that you can use to contain them.

Putting widgets in frames

This chapter covers

- Creating frames and applying styles
- Working with frames and scrollbars
- Creating alternative frame types
- Creating and manipulating splitter windows

All user interaction in your wxPython program takes place inside a widget container, which would commonly be called a window. In wxPython, that container is called a *frame*. In this chapter, we'll discuss several different styles of frames in wxPython. The primary `wx.Frame` class has several different frame style bits which can change its appearance. In addition, wxPython offers miniframes, and frames that implement the Multiple Document Interface (MDI). Frames can be split into sections using splitter bars, and can encompass panels larger than the frame itself using scrollbars.

8.1 The life of a frame

We'll start by discussing the most basic elements of frames: creating and disposing of them. Creating a frame involves knowing about all the style elements that can be applied; disposing of frames can be more complex than you might initially suppose.

8.1.1 How do I create a frame?

We've already seen numerous examples of frame creation in this book, but at the risk of repeating ourselves, we'll review the initial principles of frame creation.

Creating a simple frame

Frames are instances of the class `wx.Frame`. Listing 8.1 displays a very simple example of frame creation.

Listing 8.1 Basic `wx.Frame` creation

```
import wx

if __name__ == '__main__':
    app = wx.PySimpleApp()
    frame = wx.Frame(None, -1, "A Frame", style=wx.DEFAULT_FRAME_STYLE,
        size=(200, 100))
    frame.Show()
    app.MainLoop()
```

This creates a frame with the title A Frame, and a size of 200 by 100 pixels. The default frame style used in listing 8.1 provides the standard frame decorations like a close box and minimize and maximize boxes. Figure 8.1 displays the result.

Figure 8.1
The simple frame

This constructor for wx.Frame is similar to the other widget constructors we saw in chapter 7.

```
wx.Frame(parent, id=-1, title="", pos=wx.DefaultPosition,
        size=wx.DefaultSize, style=wx.DEFAULT_FRAME_STYLE,
        name="frame")
```

There are over a dozen style flags specific to wx.Frame, which we'll cover in the next section. The default style provides you with minimize and maximize boxes, the system pull-down menu, thick resizable borders, and a caption. This is suitable for most of your standard application window needs.

There are no event types tied to a wx.Frame beyond those that apply to any widget. However, since a wx.Frame is the one element on your screen that the user is most likely to close, you'll usually want to define a handler for the close event so that subwindows and data are properly managed.

Creating a frame subclass

You will rarely create wx.Frame instances directly. As we've seen in nearly every other example in this book, a typical wxPython application creates subclasses of wx.Frame and creates instances of those subclasses. This is because of the unique status of wx.Frame—although it defines very little behavior by itself, a subclass with a unique initializer is the most logical place to put information about the layout and behavior of your frame. Having to juggle your application-specific layouts and data without creating subclasses is possible, but is awkward in anything but the smallest application. Listing 8.2 displays an example of a wx.Frame subclass.

> **Listing 8.2 A simple frame subclass**

```
import wx

class SubclassFrame(wx.Frame):
    def __init__(self):
        wx.Frame.__init__(self, None, -1, 'Frame Subclass',
                size=(300, 100))
        panel = wx.Panel(self, -1)
        button = wx.Button(panel, -1, "Close Me", pos=(15, 15))
        self.Bind(wx.EVT_BUTTON, self.OnCloseMe, button)
        self.Bind(wx.EVT_CLOSE, self.OnCloseWindow)

    def OnCloseMe(self, event):
        self.Close(True)

    def OnCloseWindow(self, event):
        self.Destroy()
```

```
if __name__ == '__main__':
    app = wx.PySimpleApp()
    SubclassFrame().Show()
    app.MainLoop()
```

The resulting frame looks like figure 8.2.

We've seen this basic structure in many other examples, so let's discuss some of the frame-specific aspects of this code. The call to the `wx.Frame.__init__` method has the same signature as the `wx.Frame` constructor. The constructor for the subclass itself has no arguments, which

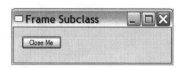

Figure 8.2 The simple frame as a subclass

allows you as the programmer to define the arguments that get passed to the parent, and keeps you from having to specify the same arguments repeatedly.

Also noteworthy in listing 8.2, is that the subwidgets of the frame are themselves placed inside a panel. A panel is an instance of the class `wx.Panel`, and is a simple container for other widgets with little functionality of its own. You should almost always use a `wx.Panel` as the top-level subwidget of your frame. For one thing, the extra level can allow greater code reuse, as the same panel and layout could be used in more than one frame. Using a `wx.Panel` gives you some of the functionality of a dialog box within the frame. This functionality manifests itself in a couple of ways. One is simply that `wx.Panel` instances have a different default background color under MS Windows operating systems—white, instead of gray. Secondly, panels can have a default item that is automatically activated when the Enter key is pressed, and panels respond to keyboard events to tab through the items or select the default item in much the same way that a dialog does.

8.1.2 *What are some different frame styles?*

The `wx.Frame` class has a multitude of possible style flags. Typically, the default style is what you want, but there are several useful variations. The first set of style flags that we'll discuss governs the general shape and size of the frame. Although not strictly enforced, these flags should be considered mutually exclusive—a given frame should only use one of them. Using a style flag from this group does not imply the existence of any decorators described in the other tables in this section; you'll need to compose the shape flag together with the other desired decorator flags. Table 8.1 describes the shape and size flags.

Table 8.1   Style flags for the shape and size of a frame

Style Flag	Description
wx.FRAME_NO_TASKBAR	A perfectly normal frame, except for one thing: under Windows systems and others supporting this ability, it will not display in the taskbar. When minimized, the frame will iconize to the desktop rather than to the taskbar. (This is the way that frames behaved in pre-95 versions of Windows).
wx.FRAME_SHAPED	The frame is nonrectangular. The exact shape of the frame is set with the `SetShape()` method. Shaped windows will be discussed later in this chapter.
wx.FRAME_TOOL_WINDOW	The frame has a smaller than normal title bar, typically used for auxiliary frames that contain a variety of tool buttons. Under Windows operating systems, a tool window will not display in the task bar.
wx.ICONIZE	The window will initially be shown minimized. This style only has an effect in Windows operating systems.
wx.MAXIMIZE	The window will initially be shown maximized (full-screen). This style only has an effect in Windows operating systems.
wx.MINIMIZE	The same as `wx.ICONIZE`

Out of this group, the style most in need of a screen shot is `wx.FRAME_TOOL_WINDOW`. Figure 8.3 displays a small sample of the `wx.FRAME_TOOL_WINDOW` with `wx.CAPTION` and `wx.SYSTEM_MENU` also declared. If you can't get the scale from the picture, let us assure you that the title bar of the tool frame is narrower than the other frame styles we've seen.

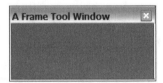

Figure 8.3   An example of the tool window style

There are two mutually exclusive styles that control whether a frame stays on top of other frames, even when the other frames gain the focus. This can be useful for small dialogs that don't remain visible for long. Table 8.2 describes the styles.

Finally, there are several decorations you can place on your window. These are not placed automatically if you abandon the default style, so you must add them, otherwise it's easy to end up with a window that doesn't close or move. Table 8.3 gives the list of decoration styles.

Table 8.2   Styles for frame floating behavior

Style Flag	Description
wx.FRAME_FLOAT_ON_PARENT	The frame will float on top of its parent, and only its parent. (Obviously, to use this style the frame needs to have a parent). Other frames will overshadow this frame.
wx.STAY_ON_TOP	The frame will always be on top of any other frame in the system. (If you have more than one frame designated as stay on top, the frames will overlap normally relative to each other, but will still be on top of all the other frames in the system.)

The default style is wx.DEFAULT_FRAME_STYLE and is equivalent to wx.MINIMIZE_ BOX | wx.MAXIMIZE_BOX | wx.CLOSE_BOX | wx.RESIZE_BORDER | wx.SYSTEM_MENU | wx.CAPTION. This style creates a typical window that you can resize, minimize, maximize, or close. It's a good idea when composing other styles to start with the

Table 8.3   Styles for decorating a window

Style Flag	Description
wx.CAPTION	Gives the window a title bar. You must include this style to have a place for the other elements that traditionally are placed here (the minimize and maximize box, the system menu, and context help).
wx.FRAME_EX_CONTEXTHELP	This is for Windows operating systems, and places the question mark Help icon in the right corner of the title bar. This style is mutually exclusive with wx.MAXIMIZE_BOX and WX.MINIMIZE_BOX. This style is an *extended* style, and must be added with the two-step creation process described later.
wx.FRAME_EX_METAL	On Mac OS X, frames with this style will have a brushed metal look. This is an extra style which must be set with the SetExtraStyle method.
wx.MAXIMIZE_BOX	Puts a maximize box in the normal place on the title bar.
wx.MINIMIZE_BOX	Puts a minimize box in the normal place on the title bar.
wx.CLOSE_BOX	Puts a close box in the normal place on the title bar.
wx.RESIZE_BORDER	Gives the frame a normal border with handles for resizing.
wx.SIMPLE_BORDER	Gives the frame a minimal border with no resizing or decorators. This style is mutually exclusive with all the other decorator styles.
wx.SYSTEM_MENU	Puts a system menu on the title bar. The exact contents of the system menu are consistent with the other chosen decorator styles—you have a "minimize" option only if wx.MINIMIZE_BOX is declared, for example.

default style to ensure that you have the right set of decorators. For example, to create a tool frame, you might use `style=wx.DEFAULT_FRAME_STYLE | wx.FRAME_TOOL_WINDOW`. Remember, you can use a ^ operator to remove the flag from a bitmask.

8.1.3 How do I create a frame with extra style information?

@47

The `wx.FRAME_EX_CONTEXTHELP` style is an extended style, which means that the value of its flag is too large to be set using the normal constructor (because of the specific limitations of the underlying C++ variable type). Normally you can set extra styles after the widget has been created using the `SetExtraStyle` method, but some styles, such as

Figure 8.4   A frame with the extended context help enabled

`wx.FRAME_EX_CONTEXTHELP`, must be set before the native UI object is created. In wxPython, this needs to be done using a slightly awkward method known as *two-step* construction. After using this construction, a frame is created with the familiar question mark icon in the title bar, as displayed in figure 8.4.

The flag value has to be set using the method `SetExtraStyle()`. Sometimes the extra style information must be set *before* the frame is instantiated, leading to the philosophical question of how you can call a method on an instance that does not yet exist. In the next sections, we'll show two mechanisms for performing this operation, with the second being a generic abstraction of the first.

Adding extra style information

In wxPython, extra style information is added before creation by using the special class `wx.PreFrame`, which is a kind of partial instance of a frame. You can set the extra style bit on the preframe, and then create the actual frame instance using the preframe. Listing 8.3 displays how two-step construction is done in a subclass constructor. Notice that it's actually a three-step process in wxPython (in the C++ wxWidgets toolkit, it is a two-step process, hence the name).

Listing 8.3   A two-stage window creation

```
import wx

class HelpFrame(wx.Frame):

    def __init__(self):                    ❶ The pre-construction object
        pre = wx.PreFrame()        ◁┘
        pre.SetExtraStyle(wx.FRAME_EX_CONTEXTHELP)
        pre.Create(None, -1, "Help Context", size=(300, 100),
            style=wx.DEFAULT_FRAME_STYLE        exclusive or.
```

```
                (wx.MINIMIZE_BOX | wx.MAXIMIZE_BOX))
        self.PostCreate(pre)
if __name__ == '__main__':
    app = wx.PySimpleApp()
    HelpFrame().Show()
    app.MainLoop()
```

❷ This call creates the frame

Transfer of underlying ❸ C++ pointers

❶ Create an instance of `wx.PreFrame()` (for dialog boxes, there's an analogous `wx.PreDialog()`—other wxWidgets widgets have their own preclasses). After this call, you can do whatever other initialization you need.

❷ Call the `Create()` method, which has the same signature as the wxPython constructor.

❸ This is the wxPython-specific line and is not done in C++. The `PostCreate` method does some internal housekeeping that makes your wxPython instance a wrapper around the C++ object you created in the first step.

Adding extra style information generically

The algorithm given earlier is a bit awkward, but it can be refactored into something a little easier to manage. The first step is to create a generic utility function that can manage any two-step creation. Listing 8.4 provides an example using Python's reflective ability to call arbitrary functions passed as variables. This example is meant to be called in the `__init__` method during the Python instantiation of a new frame.

 # defined at module level

> **Listing 8.4   A generic two-step creation function**

```
                   ✓ Frame instance being created
def twoStepCreate(instance, preClass, preInitFunc, *args,     # invoked as a class
        **kwargs):                                            # method: self is the
    pre = preClass()   # construct preClass instance          # first arg
    preInitFunc(pre)
    pre.Create(*args, **kwargs)
    instance.PostCreate(pre)
```

In listing 8.4, the function takes three required arguments. The `instance` argument is the actual instance being created. The `preClass` argument is the class object for the temporary preclass—for frames it is `wx.PreFrame`. The `preInitFunc` is a function object that would generally be a callback to an initialization method of the instance. After that, an arbitrary number of other optional arguments can be added.

The first line of the function, `pre = preClass()`, reflectively instantiates the pre-creation object, using the class object passed as an argument. The next line reflectively calls the callback function passed to the `preInitFunc`—in this context, that would usually set the extended style flag. Then the `pre.Create()` method is called, using the optional arguments. Finally, the `PostCreate` method is called to transplant internal values from pre to instance. At that point, the `instance` argument has been fully created. Assuming that `twoStepCreate` is imported, the utility function could be used as in listing 8.5.

Listing 8.5 Another two-step creation, using the generic method

```
import wx

class HelpFrame(wx.Frame):

    def __init__(self, parent, ID, title,
                 pos=wx.DefaultPosition, size=(100,100),
                 style=wx.DEFAULT_DIALOG_STYLE):
        twoStepCreate(self, wx.PreFrame, self.preInit, parent,
                      id, title, pos, size, style)    # Collected into args tuple

    def preInit(self, pre):
        pre.SetExtraStyle(wx.FRAME_EX_CONTEXTHELP)
```

The class `wx.PreFrame`, and the function `self.preInit` are passed to the generic function, and the `preInit` method is defined as the callback.

8.1.4 *What happens when I close a frame?*

When you close a frame, it goes away. Eventually. Unless the frame is explicitly told not to close. In other words, it's not completely straightforward. The purpose behind the widget closure architecture in wxPython is to give the closing widget ample opportunity to close documents or free any non-wxPython resources it might be holding onto. This is especially welcome if you are holding onto some kind of expensive external resource, such as a large data structure or a database connection.

Admittedly, managing resources is a more serious issue in the C++ wxWidgets world, since C++ does not manage cleanup of memory allocations for you. In wxPython, the explicit need for a multiple step closing process is lessened, but it can still be useful to have the extra hooks into the process. (By the way, the switch from the word *frame* to the word *widget* in this paragraph is deliberate—everything in this section is applicable to all top-level widgets, such as frames or dialogs).

When a user triggers the close process

The close process is most commonly triggered by a user action, such as clicking on a close box or choosing `Close` from the system menu or when the application calls the frame's `Close` method in response to some other event. When that happens, the wxPython framework causes an `EVT_CLOSE` event to be fired. Like any other event in the wxPython framework, you can bind an event handler to be called when an `EVT_CLOSE` happens.

If you do not declare your own event handler, the default behavior is invoked. This default behavior is different for frames and dialogs.

- By default, the frame handler calls the `Destroy()` method and deletes the frame and all of its component widgets.

- By default, the close handler for dialogs does not destroy the dialog—it merely simulates a cancel button press, and hides the dialog. The dialog object continues to exist in memory so the application can fetch values from its data entry widgets, if desired. The application should call the dialog's `Destroy()` method when it is finished with the dialog.

If you write your own close handler, you can use that handler to close or delete any external resources, but it's your responsibility to call the `Destroy()` method explicitly if you choose to delete the frame. Even though `Destroy()` is often called from `Close()`, just calling the `Close()` method does not guarantee the destruction of the frame. It's perfectly legitimate to decide to not destroy the frame under certain circumstances, such as when the user cancels the close. However, you'll still need a way to destroy the frame if you choose to. If you choose not to destroy the window, it's good practice to call the `wx.CloseEvent.Veto()` method of the close event, to signal to any interested party that the frame has declined the invitation to close itself.

If you choose to close your frame from somewhere within your program other than the close handler, such as from a different user event like a menu item, the recommended mechanism is to call the `Close()` method of the frame. This starts the process described previously in exactly the same way as a system close action would. If you must ensure that the frame is definitely deleted, you can call the `Destroy()` method directly; however, doing so may result in resources or data managed by the frame not being freed or saved.

When the system triggers the close process

If the close event is triggered by the system itself, due to system shutdown or something similar, there's one other place where you can manage the event. The `wx.App` class receives an `EVT_QUERY_END_SESSION` event that allows you to veto the application shutdown if desired, followed by a `EVT_END_SESSION` event if all running apps have approved the shutdown of the system or GUI environment. The behavior if you choose to veto the close is system-dependent.

Finally, it's worth noting that calling the `Destroy()` method of a widget doesn't mean that the widget is immediately destroyed. The destruction is actually processed when the event loop next goes idle—after any events that were pending when the `Destroy()` was called have been handled. This prevents certain problems that may occur if events are processed for widgets that no longer exist.

Over the next couple of sections we'll be switching from the lifecycle of a frame to discussing some things you can do with the frame while it's alive.

8.2 Using frames

Frames contain many methods and properties. Among the most important are the methods used to find arbitrary widgets inside the frame, and the ones used to scroll the content in your frame. In this section, we will discuss how these can be accomplished.

8.2.1 What are the methods and properties of wx.Frame?

The tables in this section contain the most basic properties of `wx.Frame`, and its `wx.Window` parent class. Many of these properties and methods are covered in more detail elsewhere in the book. Table 8.4 contains some of the publicly readable and modifiable properties of `wx.Frame`.

Table 8.4 Public properties of `wx.Frame`

Property	Description
GetBackgroundColor() SetBackgroundColor(wx.Color)	The background color of a frame is the color chosen for any part of the frame not covered by a child widget. You can pass a `wx.Color` to the setter method or you can pass a string with the color name. Any string passed to a wxPython method expecting a color is interpreted as a call to the function `wx.NamedColour()`.
GetId() SetId(int)	Returns or sets the wxPython identifier for the widget.
GetMenuBar() SetMenuBar(wx.MenuBar)	Gets or sets the menu bar object that is currently used by the frame, or `None` if there is no menu bar.
GetPosition() GetPositionTuple() SetPosition(wx.Point)	Returns the x, y position of the upper-left corner of the window, as a `wx.Point` or as a Python tuple. For top-level windows, the position is in terms of the display coordinates, for child windows, the position is in terms of the parent window.

continued on next page

Table 8.4 Public properties of `wx.Frame` (continued)

Property	Description
GetSize() GetSizeTuple() SetSize(wx.Size)	The C++ versions of the getter and setter are overloaded. The default getter and setter use a `wx.Size` object. The method `GetSizeTuple()` returns the size as a Python tuple. Also see `SetDimensions()` for other ways of accessing this information.
GetTitle() SetTitle(String)	The title string associated with a frame is displayed in the title bar of the frame if it was created with the `wx.CAPTION` style.

Table 8.5 displays some of the more useful nonproperty methods of `wx.Frame`. One to keep in mind is `Refresh()`, which you can use to manually trigger a redraw of a frame.

Table 8.5 Methods of `wx.Frame`

Property	Description
Center(direction=wx.BOTH)	Centers the frame (note that the non-American spelling `Centre`, is also defined). The argument can have the value `wx.BOTH` in which case the frame is centered in both directions, or `wx.HORIZONTAL` or `wx.VERTICAL`, in which case it centers in only one direction.
Enable(enable=true)	If the argument is `True`, the frame is enabled to receive user input. If the argument is `False`, user input is disabled in the frame. A related method is `Disable()`.
GetBestSize()	For a `wx.Frame`, returns the minimum size for the frame that fits all of its subwindows.
Iconize(iconize)	If the argument is `True`, minimizes the frame to an icon (the exact behavior is, of course, system-dependent). If the argument is `False`, an iconized frame is restored to normal.
IsEnabled()	Returns `True` if the frame is currently enabled.
IsFullScreen()	Returns `True` if the frame is being displayed in full screen mode, `False` otherwise. See `ShowFullScreen` for details.
IsIconized()	Returns `True` if the frame is currently iconized, `False` otherwise.
IsMaximized()	Returns `True` if currently in the maximized state, `False` otherwise.
IsShown()	Returns `True` if the frame is currently visible.
IsTopLevel()	Always returns `True` for top-level widgets such as frames or dialogs, and `False` for other widget types.

continued on next page

Table 8.5   Methods of `wx.Frame` *(continued)*

Property	Description
Maximize(maximize)	If the argument is `True`, maximizes the frame to fill the screen (the exact behavior is, of course, system-dependent). This will do the same thing as the user clicking on the Maximize box of the frame, which normally will enlarge the frame such that it fills the desktop but leaves the taskbar and other system components still visible.
Refresh(eraseBackground=True, rect=None)	Triggers a repaint event for the frame. If `rect` is none, then the entire frame is repainted. If a rectangle is specified, only that rectangle is repainted. If `eraseBackground` is `True`, the background of the window will also be repainted, if `False`, the background will not be repainted.
SetDimensions(x, y, width, height, sizeFlags=wx.SIZE_AUTO)	Allows you to set the size and position of the window in one method call. The position goes into the `x` and `y` arguments, the size into the `width` and `height` arguments. A value of `-1` passed to any of the first four parameters is interpreted based on the value of the `sizeFlags` argument. Table 8.6 contains the possible values for the `sizeFlags` argument
Show(show=True)	If passed a value of `True`, causes the frame to be displayed. If passed a value of `False`, causes the frame to be hidden. The call `Show(False)` is equivalent to `Hide()`.
ShowFullScreen(show, style=wx.FULLSCREEN_ALL)	If the Boolean argument is `True`, the frame is displayed in full screen mode—meaning it is enlarged to fill the entire display including covering the taskbar or other system components on the desktop. If the argument is `False`, the frame is restored to normal size. The `style` argument is a bitmask. The default value, `wx.FULLSCREEN_ALL`, directs wxPython to hide all style elements of the window when in full screen mode. The following other values can be composed using bitwise operations to suppress certain parts of the frame in full screen mode: `wx.FULLSCREEN_NOBORDER`, `wx.FULLSCREEN_NOCAPTION`, `wx.FULLSCREEN_NOMENUBAR`, `wx.FULLSCREEN_NOSTATUSBAR`, `wx.FULLSCREEN_NOTOOLBAR`.

The `SetDimensions()` method described in table 8.5 uses a bitmask of size flags to define default behavior if the user specifies `-1` as the value for a dimension. Table 8.6 describes those flags.

These methods do not cover the subject of locating specific children that are contained by a frame. This subject requires its own section to describe it fully.

Table 8.6   Size flags for the method `SetDimensions`

Flag	-1 interpreted as
wx.ALLOW_MINUS_ONE	a valid position or size
wx.SIZE_AUTO	converted to a wxPython default
wx.SIZE_AUTO_HEIGHT	a valid width, or a wxPython default height
wx.SIZE_AUTO_WIDTH	a valid height, or a wxPython default width
wx.SIZE_USE_EXISTING	the current value should be carried forward

8.2.2   *How do I find a subwidget of a frame?*

Occasionally, you'll need to find a specific widget on a frame or panel without already having a reference to that widget. A common application of this, as shown in chapter 6, is to find the actual menu item object associated with a menu selection (since the event doesn't hold a reference to it). Another use case is when you want an event on one item to change the state of an arbitrary other widget in the system. For example, you may have a button and a menu item that mutually change each other's toggle state. When the button is clicked, you need to get the menu item to toggle it. Listing 8.6 displays a small example taken from chapter 7. In this code, the `FindItemById()` method is used to acquire the menu item associated with the ID provided by the event object. The label from that item is used to drive the requested color change.

Listing 8.6   A function which finds an item by ID

```python
def OnColor(self, event):
    menubar = self.GetMenuBar()
    itemId = event.GetId()
    item = menubar.FindItemById(itemId)
    color = item.GetLabel()
    self.sketch.SetColor(color)
```

In wxPython, there are three methods for finding a subwidget, all of which act similarly. These methods are applicable to any widget that is used as a container, not just frames, but also dialogs and panels. You can look up a subwidget by internal wxPython ID, by the name passed to the constructor in the name argument, or by the text label. The text label is defined as the caption for widgets that have a caption, such as buttons and frames.

The three methods are:

- `wx.FindWindowById(id, parent=None)`
- `wx.FindWindowByName(name, parent=None)`
- `wx.FindWindowByLabel(label, parent=None)`

In all three cases, the `parent` argument can be used to limit the search to a particular subhierarchy (i.e., it's equivalent to calling the `Find` method of that argument). Also, `FindWindowByName()` looks first in the `name` arguments' if it does not find a match, it calls `FindWindowByLabel()` to look for a match.

8.2.3 *How do I create a frame with a scrollbar?*

In wxPython, scrollbars are not an element of the frame itself, but rather are controlled by the class `wx.ScrolledWindow`. You can use a `wx.ScrolledWindow` any place that you would use a `wx.Panel`, and the scrollbars move all the items that are inside that scrolled window. Figure 8.5 and figure 8.6 display a scroller in action, both in its initial state and after it has been scrolled. The top-left button scrolls off the viewport, and the lower-right button scrolls on.

In this section, we'll discuss how to create a window with a scrollbar and how to manipulate the scrolling behavior from within your program.

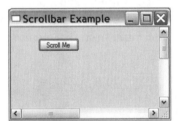 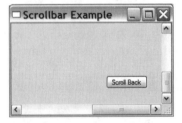

Figure 8.5 A `wx.Scrolled-Window` **after initial creation**

Figure 8.6 The same window after it has been scrolled

How to create the scrollbar

Listing 8.7 displays the code used to create the scrolled window.

Listing 8.7 Creating a simple scrolled window

```
import wx

class ScrollbarFrame(wx.Frame):
    def __init__(self):
        wx.Frame.__init__(self, None, -1, 'Scrollbar Example',
                size=(300, 200))
```

```
        self.scroll = wx.ScrolledWindow(self, -1)
        self.scroll.SetScrollbars(1, 1, 600, 400)
        self.button = wx.Button(self.scroll, -1, "Scroll Me",
                pos=(50, 20))
        self.Bind(wx.EVT_BUTTON, self.OnClickTop, self.button)
        self.button2 = wx.Button(self.scroll, -1, "Scroll Back",
                pos=(500, 350))
        self.Bind(wx.EVT_BUTTON, self.OnClickBottom, self.button2)

    def OnClickTop(self, event):
        self.scroll.Scroll(600, 400)

    def OnClickBottom(self, event):
        self.scroll.Scroll(1, 1)

if __name__ == '__main__':
    app = wx.PySimpleApp()
    frame = ScrollbarFrame()
    frame.Show()
    app.MainLoop()
```

The constructor for wx.ScrolledWindow is nearly identical to the one for wx.Panel:

```
wx.ScrolledWindow(parent, id=-1, pos=wx.DefaultPosition,
        size=wx.DefaultSize, style=wx.HSCROLL | wx.VSCROLL,
        name="scrolledWindow")
```

All of the attributes behave as you might expect, although the size attribute is the physical size of the panel within its parent, and not the logical size of the window for scrolling.

Specifying scroll area size

There are several automatic methods of specifying the size of the scrolling area. The most manual way, as displayed in listing 8.1, uses the method SetScrollBars:

```
SetScrollbars(pixelsPerUnitX, pixelsPerUnitY, noUnitsX, noUnitsY,
        xPos=0, yPos=0, noRefresh=False)
```

The key concept is that of *scroll unit*, which is the amount of space the window shifts for one movement of the scrollbar (often called a thumb shift, as opposed to a page shift). The first two parameters, pixelsPerUnitX and PixelsPerUnitY allow you to set the size of a scroll unit in both dimensions. The second two parameters, noUnitsX, and noUnitsY allow you to set the size of the scroll area in terms of scroll units. In other words, the size of the scroll area in pixels is (pixelsPerUnitX * noUnitsX, pixelsPerUnitY * noUnitsY). Listing 8.7 avoids any potential confusion by making the scroll unit one pixel. The xPos and yPos parameters allow you set the initial position of the scrollbars in terms of scroll units (not pixels), and the noRefresh argument, if true, prevents automatic refresh of the window after any scroll caused by the SetScrollbars() call.

There are three other methods that you can use to set the size of the scrolling area and then separately set the scroll rate. You might find these methods easier to use, because they allow you to specify dimensions more directly. You can use the scroll window method SetVirtualSize(), by setting the size directly in pixels, as in the following.

```
self.scroll.SetVirtualSize((600, 400))
```

Using the method FitInside(), you can set up the widgets inside the scroll area so that the scroll window bounds them. This method sets the boundaries of the scroll window to the minimum required to exactly fit all sub-windows:

```
self.scroll.FitInside()
```

A common use case for FitInside() is when there is exactly one widget inside the scroll window (like a text area), and the logical size of that widget has already been set. If we had used FitInside() in listing 8.7, a smaller scroll area would have been created, since the area would exactly match the edge of the lower-right button, rather than having additional padding.

Finally, if the scroll window has a sizer set inside it, using SetSizer() sets the scrolling area to the size of the widgets as managed by the sizer. This is the mechanism used most frequently in a complex layout. For more detailed information about sizers, see chapter 11.

With all three of these mechanisms, the scroll rate needs to be set separately using the method SetScrollRate(), as in the following.

```
self.scroll.SetScrollRate(1, 1)
```

The arguments are the scroll unit size in the x and y directions, respectively. A size greater than zero enables scrolling in that direction.

Scrollbar events

The button event handlers in listing 8.7 programmatically change the position of the scrollbars using the Scroll() method. This method takes the x and y coordinates of the scroll window, using scroll units and not pixels.

In chapter 7, we promised a listing of the events you can capture from a scrollbar, since they are also used to control sliders. Table 8.7 lists all scroll events handled internally by the scroller window. Typically, you won't use many of these events unless you are building custom widgets.

Table 8.7 Events of a scroll bar

Event Type	Description
EVT_SCROLL	Called when any scroll event is triggered.
EVT_SCROLL_BOTTOM	Triggered when the user moves the scrollbar to the maximum end of its range (the bottom or right side, depending on orientation).
EVT_SCROLL_ENDSCROLL	On MS Windows, triggered at the end of any scrolling session, whether it be caused by mouse drag or key press.
EVT_SCROLL_LINEDOWN	Triggered when the user moves the scrollbar down one line.
EVT_SCROLL_LINEUP	Triggered when the user moves the scrollbar up one line.
EVT_SCROLL_PAGEDOWN	The user has moved the scrollbar down one page.
EVT_SCROLL_PAGEUP	The scrollbar has moved up one page.
EVT_SCROLL_THUMBRELEASE	Called at the end of any scroll session that has been driven by the user actually dragging the scrollbar thumb with the mouse.
EVT_SCROLL_THUMBTRACK	Called repeatedly while the thumb is being dragged.
EVT_SCROLL_TOP	Triggered when the user moves the scrollbar to the minimum end of its range, which is either the top or left, depending on orientation.

The exact definition of line and page depends on the scroll units you've set, one line is one scroll unit and one page is the number of complete scroll units that fit in the visible portion of the scrolled window. For each of the EVT_SCROLL* events listed in the table there is a corresponding EVT_SCROLLWIN* event emitted by the wx.ScrolledWindow in response to the events from its scroll bars.

There is a wxPython-specific scrolled window subclass, wx.lib.scrolledpanel. ScrolledPanel, that allows you to automatically set up scrolling on panels that are using a sizer to manage the layout of child widgets. An added benefit of the wx.lib.scrolledpanel.ScrolledPanel is it allows the user to select the tab key to move between subwidgets. The panel automatically scrolls to put the newly focused widget in view. To use wx.lib.scrolledpanel.ScrolledPanel, declare it like a scrolled window, then, after all the sub-windows have been added, call the following method.

```
SetupScrolling(self, scroll_x=True, scroll_y=True, rate_x=20,
      rate_y=20)
```

The rate_x and rate_y are the scroll units of the window, and the class automatically sets the virtual size based on the size of the subwidgets as calculated by the sizer.

Remember, when determining the position of a widget inside a scrolled window, its position is always the physical position of the widget relative to the actual origin of the scroll window in the display frame, not the widget's logical position relative to the virtual size of the frame. This is true even if the widget is no longer visible. For example, after clicking on the Scroll Me button in figure 8.5, the button reports its position as (-277, -237). If this isn't what you want, switch between the display coordinates and the logical coordinates using the methods Calc-ScrolledPosition(x, y) and CalcUnscrolledPosition(x, y). In each case, after the button click moves the scroller to the bottom right, you pass the coordinates of the point, and the scroll window returns an (x, y) tuple, as in the following.

```
CalcUnscrolledPostion(-277, -237) returns (50, 20)
```

8.3 Alternative frame types

Frames are not limited to ordinary rectangles with widgets inside, they can assume other shapes. You can also create MDI frames which contain other frames inside. Or you can leave the title bar off the frame, and still allow the user to drag the frame around.

8.3.1 How do I create an MDI frame?

Remember MDI? Many people don't. MDI was an early '90s Microsoft innovation, that allowed multiple child windows in an application to be controlled by a single parent window, essentially providing a separate desktop for each application. In most applications, MDI requires all windows in the application to minimize together and maintain the same z-order relative to the rest of the system, which is limiting. We recommend using MDI only in cases where the user expects to see all of the application windows together, such as a game. Figure 8.7 displays a typical MDI environment.

MDI is supported in wxPython by using native widgets under Windows operating systems, and simulating the child windows in other operating systems. Listing 8.8 provides a simple example of MDI in action.

Figure 8.7
An MDI window

Listing 8.8   How to create an MDI window

```python
import wx

class MDIFrame(wx.MDIParentFrame):
    def __init__(self):
        wx.MDIParentFrame.__init__(self, None, -1, "MDI Parent",
                size=(600,400))
        menu = wx.Menu()
        menu.Append(5000, "&New Window")          # id specified
        menu.Append(5001, "E&xit")
        menubar = wx.MenuBar()
        menubar.Append(menu, "&File")
        self.SetMenuBar(menubar)
        self.Bind(wx.EVT_MENU, self.OnNewWindow, id=5000)   # id cited
        self.Bind(wx.EVT_MENU, self.OnExit, id=5001)

    def OnExit(self, evt):
        self.Close(True)

    def OnNewWindow(self, evt):
        win = wx.MDIChildFrame(self, -1, "Child Window")
        win.Show(True)    # child of self, an instance of MDI Parent Frame

if __name__ == '__main__':
    app = wx.PySimpleApp()
    frame = MDIFrame()
    frame.Show()
    app.MainLoop()
```

The basic concept of MDI is quite simple. The parent window is a subclass of `wx.MDIParentFrame`, and child windows are added just like any other wxPython widget, except that they are subclasses of `wx.MDIChildFrame`. The `wx.MDIParent-Frame` constructor is almost identical to `wx.Frame`, as in the following:

```
wx.MDIParentFrame(parent, id, title, pos = wx.DefaultPosition,
      size=wxDefaultSize,
      style=wx.DEFAULT_FRAME_STYLE | wx.VSCROLL | wx.HSCROLL,
      name="frame")
```

One difference is that a `wx.MDIParentFrame` has scrolling on by default. The `wx.MDIChildFrame` constructor is identical, except that it does not have the scrolling. As in listing 8.8, adding the child frame is accomplished by creating one, with the parent frame as the parent.

You can change the position and size of all child frames simultaneously by using the parent frame methods `Cascade()` or `Tile()`, which mimic the common menu items of the same name. Calling `Cascade()`, causes the windows to appear one on top of the other, as in figure 8.7, while `Tile()` makes each window the same size and moves them so they don't overlap. To programmatically move the focus among the child windows, use the parent methods `ActivateNext()` and `ActivatePrevious()`.

8.3.2 *What's a mini-frame and why would I use it?*

A mini-frame is just like a regular frame with two primary exceptions: it has a smaller title area, and it doesn't display in the window task bar under MS Windows or GTK. Figure 8.8 displays an example of a smaller title area.

Figure 8.8   A mini-frame in action

The code for creating the mini-frame is almost identical to creating a regular frame, the only difference is that the parent class is now `wx.MiniFrame`. Listing 8.9 displays the code.

Listing 8.9   Creating a mini-frame

```
import wx

class MiniFrame(wx.MiniFrame):
    def __init__(self):
        wx.MiniFrame.__init__(self, None, -1, 'Mini Frame',
                size=(300, 100))
        panel = wx.Panel(self, -1, size=(300, 100))
```

```
        button = wx.Button(panel, -1, "Close Me", pos=(15, 15))
        self.Bind(wx.EVT_BUTTON, self.OnCloseMe, button)
        self.Bind(wx.EVT_CLOSE, self.OnCloseWindow)

    def OnCloseMe(self, event):
        self.Close(True)

    def OnCloseWindow(self, event):
        self.Destroy()

if __name__ == '__main__':
    app = wx.PySimpleApp()
    MiniFrame().Show()
    app.MainLoop()
```

The constructor for `wx.MiniFrame` is identical to the constructor for `wx.Frame`, however the mini-frame supports additional style flags, listed in table 8.8.

Table 8.8   Style flags for `wx.MiniFrame`

Style	Description
wx.THICK_FRAME	Under MS Windows or Motif, draws the frame with a thick border.
wx.TINY_CAPTION_HORIZONTAL	Replaces `wx.CAPTION` to display a smaller horizontal caption.
wx.TINY_CAPTION_VERTICAL	Replaces `wx.CAPTION` to display a smaller vertical caption.

Typically, mini-frames are used in toolbox windows (i.e., Photoshop), where they are always available and they don't clutter up the task bar. The smaller caption makes them more space efficient, and visually separates them from normal frames.

8.3.3   *How do I make a non-rectangular frame?*

In most applications, frames are rectangles because rectangles have a nice regular shape and are relatively simple for an application to draw and maintain. Sometimes, though, you need to break out of the straight line straitjacket. In wxPython, you can give a frame an arbitrary shape. If an alternate shape is defined, the parts of the frame that are outside the shape are not drawn, and do not respond to mouse events; as far as the user is concerned, they are not part of the frame. Figure 8.9 displays a sample shaped window, displayed against a backdrop of the code in the text editor.

Events are set up so that a double-click toggles the non-standard shape on and off, and a right-click closes the window. This example uses the `images` module from the wxPython demo as the source of the image of Vippi, the wxPython mascot.

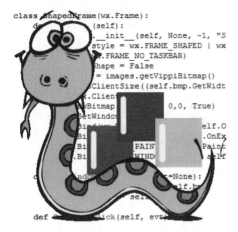

Figure 8.9
A window shaped into a
familiar non-rectangular shape

Listing 8.10 displays the code behind the non-rectangular frame (assuming that you can't read it behind the mascot in figure 8.9). This example is slightly more elaborate than some of the others we've seen, to display how to manage things like window closing in the absence of typical window interface decorations.

Listing 8.10   Drawing the shaped window

```
import wx
import images

class ShapedFrame(wx.Frame):
    def __init__(self):
        wx.Frame.__init__(self, None, -1, "Shaped Window",
                style = wx.FRAME_SHAPED | wx.SIMPLE_BORDER |
                wx.FRAME_NO_TASKBAR)
        self.hasShape = False                                    Acquiring
        self.bmp = images.getVippiBitmap()                       the image     ❶
        self.SetClientSize((self.bmp.GetWidth(), self.bmp.GetHeight()))
        dc = wx.ClientDC(self)                    Drawing
        dc.DrawBitmap(self.bmp, 0,0, True)      ❷ the image
        self.SetWindowShape()
        self.Bind(wx.EVT_LEFT_DCLICK, self.OnDoubleClick)
        self.Bind(wx.EVT_RIGHT_UP, self.OnExit)
        self.Bind(wx.EVT_PAINT, self.OnPaint)
        self.Bind(wx.EVT_WINDOW_CREATE, self.SetWindowShape)    Binding
                                                                the
    def SetWindowShape(self, evt=None):                         window
        r = wx.RegionFromBitmap(self.bmp)           Setting     create
        self.hasShape = self.SetShape(r)          ❹ the shape ❸ event

    def OnDoubleClick(self, evt):
        if self.hasShape:
```

```
        self.SetShape(wx.Region())
        self.hasShape = False
    else:
        self.SetWindowShape()

def OnPaint(self, evt):
    dc = wx.PaintDC(self)
    dc.DrawBitmap(self.bmp, 0,0, True)

def OnExit(self, evt):
    self.Close()

if __name__ == '__main__':
    app = wx.PySimpleApp()
    ShapedFrame().Show()
    app.MainLoop()
```

⑤ Resetting the shape

❶ After getting the image from the `images` module, we set the size of the inside portion of the window to the size of the bitmap. You can also create the wxPython bitmap from a regular image file, which will be discussed in more detail in chapter 16.

❷ In this case, we're drawing the image in the window. This is by no means an inevitable choice. You can place widgets and text inside a shaped window just like any other one (although they must be inside the shape region).

❸ This event, which forces a call to `SetWindowShape()` after the window is created, is redundant on most platforms. However, the GTK implementation requires that the native UI object for the window be created and finalized before the shape is set, so we use the window create event to be notified when that happens and set the shape in its handler.

❹ We use the global method `wx.RegionFromBitmap` to create the `wx.Region` object needed to set the shape. This is the easiest way to create an irregular shape. You can also create a `wx.Region` from a list of points that define a polygon. The transparent portion of the image's mask is used as the boundary for the purpose of defining the region.

❺ The double-click event toggles the shape of the window. To return the shape to the normal rectangle, call `SetShape()` with an empty `wx.Region` as the argument.

Except for the behavior around the edges and the fact that it doesn't have a normal close box or title bar, the shaped frame behaves like an ordinary frame. Any frame can change its shape, since the `SetShape()` method is part of the `wx.Frame` class, it would be inherited by any subclass. A shaped frame is particularly effective in a `wx.SplashScreen`.

8.3.4 *How can I drag a frame without a title bar?*

One obvious result of the previous example is that the frame is stuck—in the absence of title bar, there's no standard method of dragging the window. To resolve this problem, we need to add event handlers to move the window when dragging occurs. Listing 8.11 displays the same shaped window as before, with the addition of some events for handling left mouse clicks and mouse moves. This technique is applicable to any other frame, or even to a window inside a frame that you want to move (such as an element in a draw program).

Listing 8.11 Events to allow a user to drag a frame from the body of the frame

```
import wx
import images

class ShapedFrame(wx.Frame):
    def __init__(self):
        wx.Frame.__init__(self, None, -1, "Shaped Window",
                style = wx.FRAME_SHAPED | wx.SIMPLE_BORDER )
        self.hasShape = False
        self.delta = wx.Point(0,0)
        self.bmp = images.getVippiBitmap()
        self.SetClientSize((self.bmp.GetWidth(), self.bmp.GetHeight()))
        dc = wx.ClientDC(self)
        dc.DrawBitmap(self.bmp, 0,0, True)
        self.SetWindowShape()
        self.Bind(wx.EVT_LEFT_DCLICK, self.OnDoubleClick)
        self.Bind(wx.EVT_LEFT_DOWN, self.OnLeftDown)
        self.Bind(wx.EVT_LEFT_UP, self.OnLeftUp)          ❶ New
        self.Bind(wx.EVT_MOTION, self.OnMouseMove)            events
        self.Bind(wx.EVT_RIGHT_UP, self.OnExit)
        self.Bind(wx.EVT_PAINT, self.OnPaint)
        self.Bind(wx.EVT_WINDOW_CREATE, self.SetWindowShape)

    def SetWindowShape(self, evt=None):
        r = wx.RegionFromBitmap(self.bmp)
        self.hasShape = self.SetShape(r)

    def OnDoubleClick(self, evt):
        if self.hasShape:
            self.SetShape(wx.Region())
            self.hasShape = False
        else:
            self.SetWindowShape()

    def OnPaint(self, evt):
        dc = wx.PaintDC(self)
        dc.DrawBitmap(self.bmp, 0,0, True)
```

```
        def OnExit(self, evt):
            self.Close()

        def OnLeftDown(self, evt):
            self.CaptureMouse()                              Mouse down  ❷
            pos = self.ClientToScreen(evt.GetPosition())
            origin = self.GetPosition()
            self.delta = wx.Point(pos.x - origin.x, pos.y - origin.y)

        def OnMouseMove(self, evt):
            if evt.Dragging() and evt.LeftIsDown():          Mouse move  ❸
                pos = self.ClientToScreen(evt.GetPosition())
                newPos = (pos.x - self.delta.x, pos.y - self.delta.y)
                self.Move(newPos)

        def OnLeftUp(self, evt):
            if self.HasCapture():              ❹  Mouse
                self.ReleaseMouse()                up

if __name__ == '__main__':
    app = wx.PySimpleApp()
    ShapedFrame().Show()
    app.MainLoop()
```

❶ We're adding handlers for three events to make this work. Left mouse down, left mouse up, and mouse movement.

❷ A drag event starts when the left mouse is pressed. This event handler does two things. First, it captures the mouse, which prevents mouse events from being sent to other widgets until the mouse is released. Second, it calculates an offset between the position of the event and the upper left-hand corner of the window, which will be used to calculate the new position of the window as the mouse moves.

❸ This handler, called when the mouse moves, first checks to see if the event is a drag with the left button down. If so, it uses the new position of the mouse and the previously calculated offset to determine the new position of the window, and moves the window.

❹ When the left mouse button is released, ReleaseMouse() is called, which again allows mouse events to be sent to other widgets.

This drag technique can be refined to suit other needs. For example, if the mouse click should only start a drag if it is within is a defined region, you can do a test on the initial location of the mouse down event and only enable dragging if the click is in the right place.

8.4 *Using splitter windows*

A splitter window is a particular kind of container widget that manages exactly two sub-windows. The two sub-windows can be stacked horizontally or next to each other left and right. In between the two sub-windows is a *sash*, which is a movable border that changes the size of the two sub-windows. Splitter windows are often used for sidebars to the main window (i.e., a browser). Figure 8.10 displays a sample splitter window.

Splitter windows are useful when you have two panes of information and want the user to independently determine the size of each pane. Mac OS X Finder windows are an example of splitter window, and many text editors or graphics programs use something similar to maintain a list of open files.

8.4.1 *Creating a splitter window*

In wxPython, a splitter window is an instance of the class `wx.SplitterWindow`. Unlike most other wxPython widgets, splitter windows require further initialization after they are created before they can be used. The constructor is pretty straightforward.

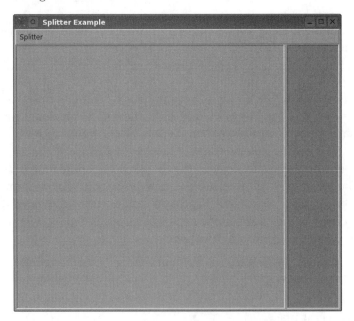

Figure 8.10   A sample splitter window after initialization

```
wx.SplitterWindow(parent, id=-1, pos=wx.DefaultPosition,
        size=wx.DefaultSize, style=wx.SP_3D,
        name="splitterWindow")
```

The parameters have the standard meanings—`parent` is the container for the widget, `pos` is the widget's location on its parent, `size` is its size.

After creating the splitter window, you must call one of three methods on the window before it can be used. If you want your splitter to initially display with only one sub-window, call `Initialize(window)`, where the `window` parameter is the single sub-window (typically a kind of `wx.Panel`). In this case, the window will split later on in response to some user action.

To display the splitter already split, use either `SplitHorizontally (window1, window2, sashPosition=0)` or `SplitVertically(window1, window2, sashPosition= 0)`. Both methods work similarly, with the `window1` and `window2` parameters containing the two sub-windows, and the `sashPosition` parameter containing the initial location of the sash. For the horizontal version, `window1` is placed on top of `window2`. If the `sashPosition` is a positive number, it represents the initial height of the top window (i.e., the sash is that number of pixels from the top). If `sashPosition` is a negative number, it defines the size of the bottom window, or the number of pixels from the bottom. If the `sashPosition` is `0`, then the sash goes in the exact middle of the splitter. In the vertical split method, `window1` is on the left, and `window2` is on the right. Again, a positive `sashPosition` sets the size of `window1` and is the number of pixels the sash is from the left border. A negative `sashPosition` similarly sets the size of the right window, and an `0` puts the sash in the center. If your sub-windows are complex, we recommend that you use sizers in the layout so that they react gracefully to the window resizing when the sash is moved.

8.4.2 A splitter example

The sample code in listing 8.12 displays how the splitter can be created in one sub-window and split later in response to a menu selection. This listing also uses some events that we'll talk about later. Notice how the sub-panel that we don't plan on making visible in the splitter right away is hidden by calling its `Hide()` method. We do this because we will not initially be telling the splitter to manage the size and placement of that sub-panel, so we hide it to get it out of the way. If we were to split the splitter and display both sub-panels at the beginning, we wouldn't have to worry about this.

Listing 8.12 How to create your very own splitter window

```python
import wx

class SplitterExampleFrame(wx.Frame):
    def __init__(self, parent, title):
        wx.Frame.__init__(self, parent, title=title)
        self.MakeMenuBar()
        self.initpos = 100
        self.sp = wx.SplitterWindow(self)           ◁┘ Creating a splitter window
        self.p1 = wx.Panel(self.sp, style=wx.SUNKEN_BORDER)   ◁┐ Creating
        self.p2 = wx.Panel(self.sp, style=wx.SUNKEN_BORDER)   ◁┘ sub-panels
        self.p2.Hide()                              ◁┐ Ensuring the spare
        self.p1.SetBackgroundColour("pink")            sub-panel is hidden
        self.p2.SetBackgroundColour("sky blue")
        self.sp.Initialize(self.p1)                 ◁┐ Initializing a splitter
        self.sp.SetMinimumPaneSize(10)

    def MakeMenuBar(self):
        menu = wx.Menu()
        item = menu.Append(-1, "Split horizontally")
        self.Bind(wx.EVT_MENU, self.OnSplitH, item)
        self.Bind(wx.EVT_UPDATE_UI, self.OnCheckCanSplit, item)
        item = menu.Append(-1, "Split vertically")
        self.Bind(wx.EVT_MENU, self.OnSplitV, item)
        self.Bind(wx.EVT_UPDATE_UI, self.OnCheckCanSplit, item)
        item = menu.Append(-1, "Unsplit")
        self.Bind(wx.EVT_MENU, self.OnUnsplit, item)
        self.Bind(wx.EVT_UPDATE_UI, self.OnCheckCanUnsplit, item)
        menu.AppendSeparator()
        item = menu.Append(wx.ID_EXIT, "E&xit")
        self.Bind(wx.EVT_MENU, self.OnExit, item)
        mbar = wx.MenuBar()
        mbar.Append(menu, "Splitter")
        self.SetMenuBar(mbar)

    def OnSplitH(self, evt):       ◁┘ Responding to a split horizontal request
        self.sp.SplitHorizontally(self.p1, self.p2, self.initpos)

    def OnSplitV(self, evt):       ◁┘ Responding to a split vertical request
        self.sp.SplitVertically(self.p1, self.p2, self.initpos)

    def OnCheckCanSplit(self, evt):
        evt.Enable(not self.sp.IsSplit())

    def OnCheckCanUnsplit(self, evt):
        evt.Enable(self.sp.IsSplit())

    def OnUnsplit(self, evt):
        self.sp.Unsplit()
```

@ 253

```
        def OnExit(self, evt):
            self.Close()

app = wx.PySimpleApp(redirect=True)
frm = SplitterExampleFrame(None, "Splitter Example")
frm.SetSize((600,500))
frm.Show()
app.SetTopWindow(frm)
app.MainLoop()
```

A splitter window can be split only one way at a time. An attempt to split a window that is already split will fail, resulting in the split method returning `False` (on success, it will return `True`). To determine if the splitter is currently split, call the method `IsSplit()`. This is done in listing 8.12 to ensure that the proper menu items are always enabled. @ 252

If you want to unsplit the window, use `Unsplit(toRemove=None)`. The `toRemove` parameter is the actual `wx.Window` object to remove, and must be one of the two sub-windows. If `toRemove` is `None`, the bottom or right window is removed, depending on the orientation of the splitter. By default, the removed window is not deleted by wxPython, so you can add it back later. The unsplit method returns `True` if the unsplit is successful. If the splitter is not currently split, or if the `toRemove` argument is not one of the splitter sub-windows, the method returns `False`.

To ensure you have an accurate reference to the sub-window you want, use the getter methods `GetWindow1()` and `GetWindow2()`. The `GetWindow1()` method returns the top or left sub-window, while `GetWindow2()` returns the bottom or right window. Since there isn't a direct setter, to change a sub-window, use the method `ReplaceWindow(winOld, winNew)`, where `winOld` is the `wx.Window` object you are replacing, and `winNew` is the new window to display.

8.4.3 *Changing the appearance of the splitter*

A number of style flags control the onscreen appearance of the splitter window. Note that since the splitter attempts to draw the sash in a manner that blends with the native platform controls, not all of the style flags listed will affect all systems. Table 8.9 describes the available flags.

As we'll see in the next section, you can also change the display of the splitter from your application, either in response to user action or on your own whim.

Table 8.9   Style flags for the splitter window

Style	Description
wx.SP_3D	Draw the border and sash with a 3D effect. This is the default style.
wx.SP_3DBORDER	Draws the border in a 3D style, but not the sash.
wx.SP_3DSASH	Draws the sash in a 3D style, but not the border.
wx.SP_BORDER	Draws a non-3D border around the window.
wx.SP_LIVE_UPDATE	Changes the default behavior for responding to a sash move. If this flag is not set, a line is drawn to indicate the new sash position while the user drags the sash. The sub-window sizes are not actually updated until the sash drag ends. If this flag is set, then the sub-windows are continually resized, repositioned, and redrawn as the sash is dragged.
wx.SP_NOBORDER	Does not draw any border at all.
wx.SP_NO_XP_THEME	Under Windows XP systems, does not use the XP theme for the sash, giving the window a more classic windows look.
wx.SP_PERMIT_UNSPLIT	If set, the window can always be unsplit. If not set, you can prevent the window from being unsplit by setting the minimum pane size greater than zero.

8.4.4   *Manipulating the splitter programmatically*

Once the splitter window is created, you can use window methods to manipulate the position of the sash. Specifically, you can use the method SetSashPosition(position, redraw=True) to move the sash. The position is the new position in pixels, defined from the top for a horizontal sash, or from the left for a vertical one. Negative indexes are used as in the split methods to indicate position from the other side. If redraw is True, the window updates immediately, otherwise it waits for a regular window refresh. The behavior of the set method is not defined if your pixel value is out of range. To get the current sash position, use GetSashPosition().

Under the default splitter behavior, the user can move the sash anywhere between the two borders. Moving the sash all the way to one border reduces the size of one sub-window to zero, causing a de facto unsplit of the window. To prevent this, you can specify the minimum size of the sub-windows using the method SetMinimumPaneSize(paneSize). The paneSize parameter is the minimum pixel size of a sub-window. The user is prevented from dragging the sash far enough to create a smaller sub-window, and programmatic changes to the sash position are similarly constrained. As mentioned earlier in this chapter, you can allow programmatic unsplitting even in a minimum sub-window size, by declaring the window with the style wx.SP_PERMIT_UNSPLIT. To get the current minimum sub-window size, use the method GetMinimumPaneSize().

Change the split mode of the window with the method SetSplitMode(mode), where the mode parameter is one of the constants wx.SPLIT_VERTICAL or wx.SPLIT_HORIZONTAL. If the mode changes, the top window becomes the left, while the bottom becomes the right (and vice-versa if the switch is the other way). This method does not cause a redraw of the window, instead, you must explicitly force a redraw. You can get the current split mode with GetSplitMode() which returns one of the two constant values. If the window is currently unsplit, GetSplitMode() returns the most recent split mode.

Typically, if the wx.SP_LIVE_UPDATE style is not set, the sub-windows only resizes at the end of a sash drag session. If you want to force a sub-window redraw at any other time, you can use the method UpdateSize().

8.4.5 *Responding to splitter events*

Splitter windows trigger events of type wx.SplitterEvent. There are four different event types of the splitter window, as listed in table 8.10.

Table 8.10 Event types of the splitter window

Event Type	Description
EVT_SPLITTER_DCLICK	Triggered when the sash is double-clicked. Trapping this event does not block the normal unsplit behavior of this action, unless you call the event Veto() method.
EVT_SPLITTER_SASH_POS_CHANGED	Triggered at the end of a sash change, but before the change is displayed on screen (so you can react to it). This event can also be halted with Veto().
EVT_SPLITTER_SASH_POS_CHANGING	Triggered repeatedly when the sash is being dragged. This event can be halted by using the event Veto() method, in which case the sash position does not change.
EVT_SPLITTER_UNSPLIT	This is triggered after the splitter has unsplit.

The splitter event class is a subclass of wx.CommandEvent. From the splitter event instance, you can get access to information about the current state of the splitter window. For the two events that concern the movement of the sash, call GetSash-Position() to recover the sash position relative to the left or the top, depending on the splitter orientation. In the position changing event, call SetSashPosi-tion(pos), and the XOR tracking line showing the expected position of the sash moves to the new position. In the position changed event, the same method will move the sash itself. For the double-click event, you can get the exact location of the click using the event's GetX() and GetY() methods. For an unsplit event, you can tell which window is going away using the GetWindowBeingRemoved() method.

8.5 Summary

- Most user interaction in a wxPython program takes place inside either a wx.Frame or a wx.Dialog. The wx.Frame class represents what a user would typically call a window. Instances of wx.Frame are created in much the same way as other wxPython widgets. A typical usage of wx.Frame involves creating a subclass which extends the base class, usually by defining subwidgets, layout, and behavior. Usually, a frame contains a single top level subwidget of type wx.Panel or some other container window.

- There are a variety of style flags specific to wx.Frame. Some of these flags affect the size and shape of the frame, others affect how it is drawn relative to other frames in the system, and others define what interface decorators are on the frame border. In some cases, a two-stage creation process is needed to define a style flag.

- A request can be made to close a frame by calling the Close() method. This gives the frame an opportunity to close any resources it might be holding. The frame can also veto a close request. Calling the Destroy() method forces a frame to go away without reprieve.

- A specific subwidget inside a frame can be found using its wxPython ID, its name, or its text label.

- Scrolling is managed by including a container widget of type wx.ScrolledWindow. There are several ways to set the scrolling parameters, the easiest is to use a sizer inside the scrolled window, in which case wxPython automatically determines the virtual size of the scroll panel. However, the virtual size can be set manually if desired.

- There are a couple of different frame subclasses that allow for different looks. The class wx.MDIParentFrame can be used to create an MDI, while a wx.MiniFrame can create a toolbox-style window with a smaller title bar. Frames can be made to appear non-rectangular using the SetShape() method. The region can be defined by any bitmap, with a simple color mask to determine the edge of the region. Non-rectangular windows are usually without the normal title bar allowing the frame to be dragged, but that can be managed by explicitly handling mouse events.

- A draggable sash between two sub-windows can be implemented using `wx.SplitterWindow`, which can be manipulated interactively by the user or programmatically if needed.

In the next chapter, we'll discuss dialog boxes, which behave similarly to frames.

Giving users choices
with dialogs

This chapter covers

- Creating modal dialogs and alert boxes
- Using standard dialogs
- Creating wizards
- Showing startup tips
- Creating validators and using them
  to transfer data

Where frames are used for long-term interactions with the user, a dialog is typically used to get a small amount of information from the user, and is then quickly dispatched. Dialog windows are often *modal*, which means that no other frame in the application can handle events until the dialog is closed. In this chapter we will discuss the many varieties of dialogs available in wxPython. In addition to allowing you to create your own dialog styles, wxPython provides you with several predefined dialog types. These predefined dialogs include both simple interactions, such as a basic alert box, and more complex dialogs that mimic system interactions, such as page layout or file selection.

9.1 Working with modal dialogs

Modal dialogs are used for quick interactions with the user or for any time that information in a dialog absolutely must be entered before the user can move forward in the program. Within wxPython, there are several standard functions to display basic modal dialogs. These dialogs include alert boxes, one line of text entry, and choosing from a list. In the following sections, we'll show you what these dialogs look like, and how using the predefined functions will make your life easier.

9.1.1 How do I create a modal dialog?

A *modal dialog* blocks other widgets from receiving user events until it is closed; in other words, it places the user in dialog mode for the duration of its existence. As you can see from figure 9.1, you can't always distinguish between dialogs and frames by their appearance. In wxPython, the difference between a dialog and a frame is not based on how they display, but is largely a matter of the way in which they handle events.

Figure 9.1
A sample modal dialog

A dialog is created and deployed somewhat differently from a frame. Listing 9.1 shows the code used to generate figure 9.1. After a dialog is displayed and a button is clicked, the dialog closes, and a message is printed to stdout.

Listing 9.1 Defining a modal dialog

```
import wx

class SubclassDialog(wx.Dialog):
    def __init__(self):                          ⟵┘ Initializing the dialog
        wx.Dialog.__init__(self, None, -1, 'Dialog Subclass',
                size=(300, 100))
```

```
        okButton = wx.Button(self, wx.ID_OK, "OK", pos=(15, 15))
        okButton.SetDefault()
        cancelButton = wx.Button(self, wx.ID_CANCEL, "Cancel",
                pos=(115, 15))

if __name__ == '__main__':
    app = wx.PySimpleApp()
    dialog = SubclassDialog()
    result = dialog.ShowModal()      ◁—  Showing the modal dialog
    if result == wx.ID_OK:
        print "OK"
    else:
        print "Cancel"
    dialog.Destroy()
```

Compared to the wx.Frame examples in the previous chapter, there are a couple of interesting things to note about this code. In the __init__ method, the button is added directly to wx.Dialog, rather than to a wx.Panel. Panels are used much less commonly in dialogs than in frames, partially because dialogs tend to be simpler than frames, but largely because the features of a wx.Panel (standard system background and tab key transversal through the controls) already exist by default in wx.Dialog.

To get the dialog to display modally, use the ShowModal() method. This has a different effect on program execution than the modeless Show() method used for frames. Your application will wait at the point of the ShowModal() call until the dialog is dismissed. The dialog being shown is the only part of the wxPython application that receives user events during that time, although system windows from other applications will still work.

The mode continues until the dialog method EndModal(retCode) is called, which closes the dialog. The retCode argument is an integer value, which is then also returned by the original ShowModal() method. Typically, the application uses the return value to learn how the user closed the dialog as a guide to future processing. However, ending the mode does not destroy or even close the dialog. Keeping the dialog around can be a good thing, because it means that you can store information about the user's selections as data members of the dialog instance, and recover that information from the dialog even after the dialog is closed. In the next sections, we'll see examples of that pattern as we deal with dialogs where the user enters data for use elsewhere in the program.

Since there are no event handlers defined in listing 9.1, you may be wondering how the dialog does anything in response to the button clicks. The behavior is already defined in wx.Dialog. There are two predefined wxPython ID numbers that have special meaning in dialogs. When a `wx.Button` with the ID `wx.ID_OK` is clicked in a dialog, the mode is ended, the dialog is closed, and `wx.ID_OK` is the return value of the `ShowModal()` call. Similarly, a button with the ID `wx.ID_CANCEL` does the same things, but returns the value `wx.ID_CANCEL`. It's up to the rest of the application to ensure that the semantics of OK and Cancel are appropriately enforced.

Listing 9.1 displays a typical method of dealing with a modal dialog. After the dialog is invoked, the return value is used as the test in an `if` statement. In this case, we simply print the result. In a more complex example, the `wx.ID_OK` branch would implement the actions that the user took within the dialog, such as opening the file or choosing the color.

Typically you should explicitly destroy a dialog when you are finished with it. This signals the C++ object that it should destroy itself which will then allow the Python parts of it to be garbage collected. If you wish to reuse the dialog later in your application without having to recreate it, perhaps to speed the response time for complex dialogs, you can keep a reference to the dialog and simply call its `ShowModal()` method when you need to activate it again. Be sure to destroy it when the application is ready to exit, otherwise `MainLoop()` will see it as a still existing top-level window and will not exit normally.

9.1.2 *How do I create an alert box?*

The three simplest ways of interacting with the user via a dialog box are `wx.MessageDialog`, which represents an alert box, `wx.TextEntryDialog`, which prompts the user to enter some short text, and `wx.SingleChoiceDialog`, which allows the user to select from a list of available options. The next three sections discuss these simple dialogs.

A message box dialog displays a short message and allows the user to press a button in response. Typically, message boxes are used to display important alerts, yes/no

Figure 9.2 A standard message box, in a yes/no configuration

questions, or to ask the user to continue with or cancel some action. Figure 9.2 displays a typical message box.

Using a message box is quite simple. Listing 9.2 displays two ways of creating a message box.

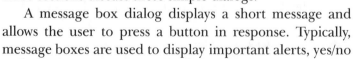

Listing 9.2 Creating a message box

```
import wx

if __name__ == "__main__":
    app = wx.PySimpleApp()
```

```
dlg = wx.MessageDialog(None, "Is this explanation OK?",
                       'A Message Box',
                       wx.YES_NO | wx.ICON_QUESTION)
retCode = dlg.ShowModal()
if (retCode == wx.ID_YES):
    print "yes"
else:
    print "no"
dlg.Destroy()

retCode = wx.MessageBox("Is this way easier?", "Via Function",
        wx.YES_NO | wx.ICON_QUESTION)
```

**Using
a class**

Using a function ①

Listing 9.2 creates two message boxes, one after the other. The first method creates an instance of the class wx.MessageDialog, and displays it using ShowModal().

Using the wx.MessageDialog class

Using the constructor for the wx.MessageDialog, you can set the message and buttons for the dialog, as in the following:

```
wx.MessageDialog(parent, message, caption="Message box",
    style=wx.OK | wx.CANCEL, pos=wx.DefaultPosition)
```

The message argument is the text that is actually displayed inside the body of the dialog. If the message string contains \n newline characters, there will be line breaks in the text. The caption argument is displayed in the title box of the dialog. The pos argument allows you to specify where the dialog is displayed on the screen—under MS Windows, this argument is ignored.

The style flags for a wx.MessageDialog split into two types. The first type controls the buttons that display in the dialog. Table 9.1 describes these styles.

Table 9.1 Button styles for a wx.MessageDialog

Button Style	Description
wx.CANCEL	Include a cancel button. This button will have the ID value of wx.ID_CANCEL.
wx.NO_DEFAULT	In a wx.YES_NO dialog, the No button is the default.
wx.OK	Include an OK button. This button will have the ID value of wx.ID_OK.
wx.YES_DEFAULT	In a wx.YES_NO dialog, the Yes button is the default. This is the default behavior.
wx.YES_NO	Include buttons labeled Yes and No, with the ID values of wx.ID_YES and wx.ID_NO, respectively.

The second set of style flags controls the icon displayed next to the message text. Those styles are listed in Table 9.2.

Table 9.2 Icon styles for a `wx.MessageDialog`

Style	Description
wx.ICON_ERROR	An icon indicating an error.
wx.ICON_EXCLAMATION	An icon indicating an alert.
wx.ICON_HAND	The same as `wx.ICON_ERROR`
wx.ICON_INFORMATION	The letter "i" information icon.
wx.ICON_QUESTION	A question mark icon.

Finally, you can use the style `wx.STAY_ON_TOP` to display the dialog above any other windows in the system, including system windows and wxPython application windows.

As you can see in listing 9.2, the dialog is invoked using `ShowModal()`. Depending on the displayed buttons, the result is either `wx.ID_OK`, `wx.ID_CANCEL`, `wx.ID_YES`, or `wx.ID_NO`. As with other dialogs, you'll typically use the response value to control program execution in response to the dialog.

Using the wx.MessageBox() function

Line ❶ of listing 9.2 displays a shorter method for invoking a message box. The convenience function `wx.MessageBox()` creates the dialog, calls `ShowModal()`, and returns, `wx.YES`, `wx.NO`, `wx.CANCEL`, or `wx.OK`. The signature of the function is simpler than the constructor for the `MessageDialog` object, as in:

```
wx.MessageBox(message, caption="Message", style=wx.OK)
```

In this example, `message`, `caption`, and `style` have the same meanings as in the constructor, and you can use all of the same style flags. As we'll see throughout this chapter, several of the predefined dialogs in wxPython also have convenience functions. As long as you are creating the dialogs for a single use, the mechanism you choose is a matter of preference. If you plan to hold onto the dialog to invoke it more than once, it may be preferable to instantiate yourself the object so you can hold onto the reference, although for simple dialogs such as these, the time saved is probably negligible.

To display a lot of text in your message box (i.e., an end-user license agreement display), you can use the wxPython-specific class `wx.lib.dialogs.Scrolled-MessageDialog`, which contains the following constructor:

```
wx.lib.dialogs.ScrolledMessageDialog(parent, msg, caption,
        pos=wx.wxDefaultPosition, size=(500,300))
```

This dialog doesn't use the native message box widget, it builds a dialog from other wxPython widgets. It only displays an OK button, and takes no further style information.

9.1.3 *How do I get short text from the user?*

The second simple type of dialog box is wx.Text-EntryDialog, which is used to get short text entry from the user. Typically, you'll see this used when requesting a username or password at the beginning of a program, or as a very rudimentary replacement for a data entry form. Figure 9.3 displays a typical text dialog.

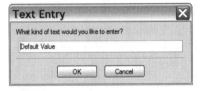

Figure 9.3
A text entry standard dialog

The code for this example is displayed in listing 9.3.

Listing 9.3 Code for text entry

```
import wx

if __name__ == "__main__":
    app = wx.PySimpleApp()
    dialog = wx.TextEntryDialog(None,
            "What kind of text would you like to enter?",
            "Text Entry", "Default Value", style=wx.OK|wx.CANCEL)
    if dialog.ShowModal() == wx.ID_OK:
        print "You entered: %s" % dialog.GetValue()
    dialog.Destroy()
```

As in the previous section, we create an instance of a dialog class, in this case wx.TextEntryDialog. The constructor for this class is a bit more complex than the simple message dialog:

```
wx.TextEntryDialog(parent, message, caption="Please enter text",
    defaultValue="", style=wx.OK | wx.CANCEL | wx.CENTRE,
    pos=wx.DefaultPosition)
```

The message argument is the text prompt that is displayed in the dialog, while the caption is displayed in the title bar. The defaultValue, if set, is displayed inside the text box. The style information can include wx.OK and wx.CANCEL, which displays the appropriate button.

Several of the styles from an ordinary `wx.TextCtrl` can also be set here. The most useful would be `wx.TE_PASSWORD`, which masks the input for securely entering a password. You can also use `wx.TE_MULTILINE` to allow the user to enter more than one line of text in the dialog, and `wx.TE_LEFT`, `wx.TE_CENTRE`, and `wx.TE_RIGHT` to adjust the justification of the entered text.

The last line of listing 9.3 displays another difference between the text box and the message box. The information entered by the user is stored in the dialog instance, and must be retrieved by the application afterwards. In this case, you can get at the value by using the dialog's `GetValue()` method. Remember, if the user presses Cancel to exit the dialog, it means they don't want you to use his entered value. You can also programmatically set the value with the `SetValue()` method.

The following are convenience functions for dealing with text dialogs:

- `wx.GetTextFromUser()`
- `wx.GetPasswordFromUser()`
- `wx.GetNumberFromUser()`

Most similar to the usage in listing 9.3 is `wx.GetTextFromUser`:

```
wx.GetTextFromUser(message, caption="Input text",
    default_value="", parent=None)
```

In this example, `message`, `caption`, `default_value`, and `parent` are all in the `wx.TextEntryDialog` constructor. If the user presses OK, the return value of the function is the user entered string. If the user presses Cancel, the function returns the empty string.

If you want the user to enter a masked password, you can use the `wx.GetPasswordFromUser` function.

```
wx.GetPasswordFromUser(message, caption="Input text",
    default_value="", parent=None)
```

In this example, the arguments mean what you'd expect. The user input is displayed as asterisks, and the return value is as in the previous function—the string if the user hits OK, an empty string if the user hits cancel.

Finally, you can request a number from a user with the `wx.GetNumberFromUserMethod`.

```
wx.GetNumberFromUser(message, prompt, caption, value, min=0,
    max=100, parent=None)
```

The argument names here are a bit different. The message is an arbitrarily long message displayed above the prompt string, which is directly above the text entry field. The value argument is a numeric long, and is the default value. The min and max arguments allow you to specify a valid range for user input. If the user exits with the OK button, the method returns the entered value, converted to a long. If the value cannot be converted to a number, or the value is outside the min and max range, the function returns -1, which means that if you use this function for a range of negative numbers, you may want to consider an alternate plan.

9.1.4 *How can I display a list of choices in a dialog?*

Figure 9.4   A single choice dialog

If allowing your users a blank text entry seems like too much freedom, you can restrict their options by using wx.Single-ChoiceDialog to give them a single choice out of a group of options. Figure 9.4 displays an example.

The essential code displayed in listing 9.4 is similar to the dialog examples we've already discussed in this chapter.

Listing 9.4   Displaying a dialog list of choices

```
import wx

if __name__ == "__main__":
    app = wx.PySimpleApp()
    choices = ["Alpha", "Baker", "Charlie", "Delta"]
    dialog = wx.SingleChoiceDialog(None, "Pick A Word", "Choices",
            choices)
    if dialog.ShowModal() == wx.ID_OK:
        print "You selected: %s\n" % dialog.GetStringSelection()
    dialog.Destroy()
```

The constructor for the wx.SingleChoiceDialog is as follows:

```
wx.SingleChoiceDialog(parent, message, caption, choices,
        clientData=None, style=wx.OK | wx.CANCEL | wx.CENTRE,
        pos=wx.DefaultPosition)
```

The message and caption arguments are as before, displaying the prompt in the dialog and the title bar, respectively. The choices argument takes a Python list of strings, and they are, as you might suspect, the choices presented in the dialog. The style argument has the three options that are in the default, allowing an OK button, a Cancel button, and the option to center the dialog on the screen. The centre option does not work on Windows operating systems, and neither does the pos argument.

If you want to set the dialog default before the user sees it, use the method SetSelection(selection). The argument to that method is the integer index of the selection, and not the actual string to be selected. After the user has made a selection, you can retrieve it by using either GetSelection(), which returns the integer index of the selected option, or GetStringSelection() which returns the actual selected string.

There are two convenience functions for single choice dialogs. The first, wx.GetSingleChoice, returns the string that the user selected.

```
wx.GetSingleChoice(message, caption, aChoices, parent=None)
```

The message, caption, and parent arguments are as in the wx.SingleChoiceDialog constructor. The aChoices argument is the list of items. The return value is the selected string if the user presses OK, and the empty string if the user presses Cancel. This means that if the empty string is a valid choice, you should probably not use this function.

Instead, you might use wx.GetSingleChoiceIndex.

```
wx.GetSingleChoiceIndex(message, caption, aChoices, parent=None)
```

This function has the same arguments, but a different return value. It returns the index of the user choice if OK, and -1 if the user hits Cancel.

9.1.5 How can I display progress?

In many programs, the program needs to go off and do something by itself unencumbered by user input. At that time, it's customary for the program to give the user some visual indication that it's actually doing something. In wxPython, that is often managed with a progress box, as displayed in figure 9.5.

The sample code to generate this progress box is displayed in listing 9.5.

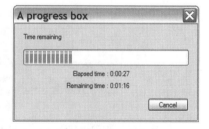

Figure 9.5   A sample progress box, joined in progress

> **Listing 9.5   Generating a sample progress box**

```
import wx

if __name__ == "__main__":
    app = wx.PySimpleApp()
```

```
progressMax = 100
dialog = wx.ProgressDialog("A progress box",
        "Time remaining", progressMax,
        style=wx.PD_CAN_ABORT | wx.PD_ELAPSED_TIME |
        wx.PD_REMAINING_TIME)
keepGoing = True
count = 0
while keepGoing and count < progressMax:
    count = count + 1
    wx.Sleep(1)
    keepGoing = dialog.Update(count)
dialog.Destroy()
```

All the options for the progress box are set in the constructor, which looks like this:

```
wx.ProgressDialog(title, message, maximum=100, parent=None,
        style=wx.PD_AUTO_HIDE | wx.PD_APP_MODAL)
```

The arguments are different than in other dialog boxes. The `title` is placed in the title bar of the window, and the `message` is displayed in the dialog itself. The `maximum` is the highest possible value of the counter you are using to display progress. As you can tell from figure 9.5, the user does not see this number, so feel free to make it any value that is convenient for your application.

Table 9.3 lists the six styles specific to the `wx.ProgressDialog` that affect its behavior.

Table 9.3 Styles for `wx.ProgressDialog`

Style	Description
wx.PD_APP_MODAL	If this flag is set, the progress dialog is modal with respect to the entire application, meaning that it will block all user events. If the flag is not set, the progress dialog is modal only with respect to its parent window.
wx.PD_AUTO_HIDE	The progress dialog will automatically hide itself when it reaches its maximum value.
wx.PD_CAN_ABORT	Puts a Cancel button on the progress box for the user to stop the process. How to respond to a cancel from this dialog will be explained later.
wx.PD_ELAPSED_TIME	Displays the elapsed time that the dialog has been visible.

continued on next page

Table 9.3   Styles for `wx.ProgressDialog` (continued)

Style	Description
wx.PD_ESTIMATED_TIME	Displays an estimate of the total time to complete the process based on the amount of time already elapsed, the current value of the counter, and the maximum value of the counter.
wx.PD_REMAINING_TIME	Displays an estimate of the amount of time remaining in a process, or (estimated time – elapsed time).

To use the progress dialog, make a call to its only method, `Update(value, newmsg="")`. The `value` argument is the new internal value of the progress dialog, and calling `update` causes the progress bar to be redrawn based on the proportion between the new value and the maximum value set in the constructor. The value argument can be higher, lower, or equal to the current value argument. If the optional `newmsg` argument is included, the text message on the dialog changes to that string. This allows you to give the user a text description of the current progress.

The `Update()` method usually returns `True`. However, if the user has canceled the dialog via the Cancel button, the next time you `Update()`, the method will return `False`. This is your chance to respond to the user's request to cancel, presumably by stopping whatever process you are measuring. Given this mechanism for detecting a user cancel, it is recommended that you update the progress bar as often as possible, so you can test for the cancel.

9.2   *Using standard dialogs*

Most operating systems offer standard dialog boxes for tasks like file choosing, font selection, and color picking. This enables users to see a consistent look and feel across the entire platform. You can use these dialogs from wxPython to give your application the same advantage. In addition, if you use wxPython, it provides similar dialogs even on platforms that don't have system dialogs for the feature.

9.2.1   *How can I use a file picker?*

File-choosing dialogs tend to be consistent from application to application. In wxPython, the `wx.FileDialog` uses the native OS dialog for the major platforms, and uses non-native look-alikes for other operating systems. The MS Windows version is displayed in figure 9.6.

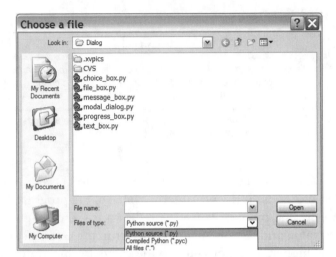

**Figure 9.6
The standard Windows
file chooser**

You can set up the file dialog to start in any directory, and you can also pass it a wildcard filter to limit the display to only certain file types. Listing 9.6 displays a basic example.

Listing 9.6   Using `wx.FileDialog`

```python
import wx
import os

if __name__ == "__main__":
    app = wx.PySimpleApp()
    wildcard = "Python source (*.py)|*.py|" \
            "Compiled Python (*.pyc)|*.pyc|" \
            "All files (*.*)|*.*"
    dialog = wx.FileDialog(None, "Choose a file", os.getcwd(),
            "", wildcard, wx.OPEN)
    if dialog.ShowModal() == wx.ID_OK:
        print dialog.GetPath()
    dialog.Destroy()
```

The file dialog is the most complex dialog we've seen in this chapter, in that it has several properties that can be programmatically read and written. The constructor allows you to set some of the properties, as in:

```python
wx.FileDialog(parent, message="Choose a file", defaultDir="",
        defaultFile="", wildcard="*.*", style=0,
        pos=wx.DefaultPosition)
```

The `message` argument appears in the title bar of the window. The `defaultDir` tells the dialog what directory to display initially. If the argument is empty or represents a directory that doesn't exist, the dialog starts in the current working directory. The `defaultFile` preselects a file, typically used when saving a file. The `wildcard` argument allows you to filter the list based on a given pattern, using the usual * and ? as wildcard characters. The wildcard can either be a single pattern, such as *.py, or a set of patterns in the format <description> | <pattern> | <description> | <pattern>—similar to the wildcard used in listing 9.6.

```
"Python source (*.py)|*.py|Compiled Python (*.pyc)|*.pyc|
    All files (*.*)|*.*"
```

If there is a pattern with multiple entries, they display in the familiar pull-down menu shown in figure 9.6. The `pos` argument is not guaranteed to be supported by the underlying system.

Selecting a file

The two most important style flags for `wx.FileDialog` are `wx.OPEN` and `wx.SAVE`, which indicate the kind of dialog and affect the behavior of the dialog.

A dialog used for opening a file has two flags that further affect behavior. The flag `wx.HIDE_READONLY` causes the dialog to gray out the checkbox that allows the user to open the file in read-only mode. The flag `wx.MULTIPLE` allows the user to select multiple files in a single directory for opening.

Save file dialogs have one useful flag, `wx.OVERWRITE_PROMPT`, that forces the user to confirm saving a file if the file already exists.

Either kind of file dialog can use the `wx.CHANGE_DIR` flag. When this flag is raised, a file selection also changes the application's working directory to the directory where the selection took place. Among other things, this allows the next file dialog to open in the same directory without requiring that the application store that value elsewhere.

Unlike the other dialogs we've seen so far in this chapter, these properties are all gettable and settable via methods. This is true for the properties `directory`, `filename`, `style`, `message`, and `wildcard`, all of which have getters and setters using the usual `Get`/`Set` naming convention.

After the user has exited the dialog, and after checking that it was exited with `wx.OK`, you can get the user's choice by using the method `GetPath()`, which returns the full pathname of the file as a string. If the dialog is an open dialog with `wx.MULTIPLE` selected, use `GetPaths()` instead. That method returns a Python list of path strings. If for some reason you need to know which of the pull-down filters was active when the user made her selection, you can use the `GetFilterIndex()` method, which returns an integer index into the list. To change the index programmatically, use `SetFilterIndex()`.

The following is a convenience function for using file dialogs.

```
wx.FileSelector(message, default_path="", default_filename="",
    default_extension="", wildcard="*.*'', flags=0, parent=None,
    x=-1, y=-1)
```

The `message`, `default_path`, `default_filename`, and `wildcard` arguments do what you'd expect from the constructor, despite being named differently. The `flags` argument is normally called `style`, and the `default_extension` adds an extension onto a selected file name that doesn't when you save a file. The return value is the string pathname if the user presses OK, or an empty string if the user presses Cancel.

Selecting a directory

If the user wants to select a directory rather than a file, use `wx.DirDialog`, which presents a tree view of the directory structure as shown in figure 9.7.

The directory selector is somewhat simpler than a file dialog. Listing 9.7 displays the relevant code.

Listing 9.7 Displaying a directory chooser dialog

```python
import wx

if __name__ == "__main__":
    app = wx.PySimpleApp()
    dialog = wx.DirDialog(None, "Choose a directory:",
        style=wx.DD_DEFAULT_STYLE | wx.DD_NEW_DIR_BUTTON)
    if dialog.ShowModal() == wx.ID_OK:
        print dialog.GetPath()
    dialog.Destroy()
```

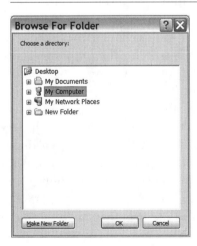

Figure 9.7
A directory selection dialog

Nearly all of the functionality of this dialog is in the constructor.

```
wx.DirDialog(parent, message="Choose a directory", defaultPath="",
    style=0, pos = wx.DefaultPosition, size = wx.DefaultSize,
    name="wxDirCtrl")
```

Because the message argument displays inside the dialog itself, you don't need a hook to change the title bar. The defaultPath tells the dialog what to select, and if it's empty, the dialog shows the root of the file system. The pos and size arguments are ignored under MS Windows, and the name argument is ignored in all operating systems. The style flag for this dialog, wx.DD_NEW_DIR_BUTTON, gives the dialog a button for creating a directory. This flag may not work in older versions of MS Windows.

The path, message, and style properties of this class have typical getters and setters. You can use the GetPath() method to retrieve the user selection after the dialog is dispatched. This dialog also has a convenience function.

```
wx.DirSelector(message=wx.DirSelectorPromptStr, default_path="",
    style=0, pos=wxDefaultPosition, parent=None)
```

All arguments are as in the constructor. The function returns the selected directory name as a string if OK is pressed, and the empty string if Cancel is pressed.

9.2.2 *How can I use a font picker?*

The font picker dialog in wxPython is different than the file dialog, because it uses a separate helper class to manage the information it presents. Figure 9.8 displays the MS Windows version of the font dialog.

Listing 9.8 displays the code used to generate figure 9.8, and should look somewhat different than previous dialog examples.

> **Listing 9.8   Sample code for a font picker dialog box**

```
import wx

if __name__ == "__main__":
    app = wx.PySimpleApp()
    dialog = wx.FontDialog(None, wx.FontData())
    if dialog.ShowModal() == wx.ID_OK:
        data = dialog.GetFontData()
        font = data.GetChosenFont()
        colour = data.GetColour()
        print 'You selected: "%s", %d points\n' % (
                font.GetFaceName(), font.GetPointSize())
    dialog.Destroy()
```

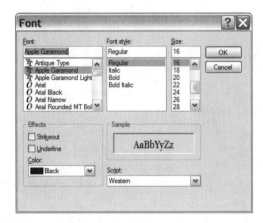

Figure 9.8
A sample font picker dialog

The constructor for `wx.FontDialog` is much simpler than the previous constructors.

```
wx.FontDialog(parent, data)
```

You cannot set a message or caption for this dialog, and the information that is ordinarily passed as style flags is instead contained in the `data` argument, which is of the class `wx.FontData`. The `wx.FontDialog` class has only one useful method of its own, which is `GetFontData()`, returning the font data instance.

The `wx.FontData` instance allows you to set the values that govern the display of the font dialog, and also contains the information entered by the user. For example, in listing 9.8 the code calls two getter methods of the `wx.FontData` instance to determine the details of the selected font. The constructor for `wx.FontData` takes no arguments—all properties must be set by using the methods in table 9.4

Table 9.4   Methods of `wx.FontData`

Method	Description
GetAllowSymbols() SetAllowSymbols(allowSymbols)	Determines whether symbol-only fonts (like dingbats) are displayed in the dialog. The argument is a Boolean. Only meaningful in Windows systems. The initial value of this property is `True`.
GetChosenFont() SetChosenFont(font)	Returns the font that the user has chosen as a `wx.Font` object. You should never need to call the setter for this property. If the user has selected Cancel, this property is `None`. The `wx.Font` class will be discussed in more detail in Chapter 12.

continued on next page

Table 9.4 Methods of `wx.FontData` *(continued)*

Method	Description
GetColour() SetColour(colour)	Returns the color selected in the color portion of the dialog. The setter allows you to preset the default value. The getter returns a `wx.Colour` instance. The setter can take one of those, or a string with the name of a color. The initial value of this property is `black`.
GetEnableEffects() EnableEffects(enable)	In the MS Windows version of the dialog, this property controls the appearance or nonappearance of controls to select color, strikeout, and underline features of the font.
GetInitialFont() SetInitialFont(font)	Returns the font which is the initial value of the dialog (i.e., the current application font). This property should be explicitly set by the application before the dialog is displayed. Its initial value is `None`.
SetRange(min, max)	Sets the available range for the point size of the font. Only used on MS Windows systems. The initial values are `0` and `0`, which means there are no limits on the range.
GetShowHelp() SetShowHelp()	If `True`, the MS Windows version of this dialog will display a Help button. The initial value is `False`.

A convenience function for the font dialog, which helpfully sidesteps the whole `wx.FontData` class, is as follows.

```
wx.GetFontFromUser(parent, fontInit)
```

The `fontInit` argument is an instance of `wx.Font` that is used as the initial value of the dialog. The return value of the function is a `wx.Font` instance. If the user closes the dialog with an OK, the method `wx.Font.Ok()` returns `True`, otherwise, it returns `False`.

9.2.3 *How can I use a color picker?*

The color picker dialog is similar to the font dialog, because it uses an external data class to manage its information. Figure 9.9 displays the MS Windows version of the dialog.

Listing 9.9 displays the code to generate the dialog, which is nearly identical to the code seen in the previous section for the font picker.

Listing 9.9 Code for a color picker dialog

```
import wx

if __name__ == "__main__":
    app = wx.PySimpleApp()
```

```
dialog = wx.ColourDialog(None)
dialog.GetColourData().SetChooseFull(True)
if dialog.ShowModal() == wx.ID_OK:
    data = dialog.GetColourData()
    print 'You selected: %s\n' % str(data.GetColour().Get())
dialog.Destroy()
```

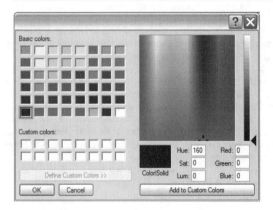

Figure 9.9
A standard wxPython color picker

The wxPython class for the color selector is `wx.ColourDialog`. Those of you in America will need to remember the non-USA spelling "colour." For those of you outside America, I'm sure this is a welcome change of pace. The constructor is simple, without many options to tweak, as in the following:

```
wx.ColourDialog(parent, data=None)
```

The `data` argument is an instance of the class `wx.ColourData`, which is simpler than its font data counterpart. It contains only the default no-argument constructor, and the following three properties:

- `GetChooseFull/SetChooseFull(flag)` A Boolean property that works under MS Windows only. When set, the color picker shows the full dialog, including the custom color selector. When unset, the custom color selector is not shown.

- `GetColour/SetColour(colour)` The property is of the type `wx.Colour`. This is the color value selected by the user. After the graph is closed, call this getter to see the user selection. Initially it is set to black. If it is set before the dialog is displayed, the dialog initially displays this color.

- `GetCustomColour(i)/SetCustomColour(i, colour)` returns or sets the element in the custom color array with index `i`. The index is between 0 and 15. Initially all of the custom colors are white.

A simple convenience function bypasses the `wx.ColorData` entirely:

```
wx.GetColourFromUser(parent, colInit)
```

Where `colInit` is a `wx.Colour` instance and is the initial value of the dialog when displayed. The return value is also a `wx.Colour` instance. If the user closes the dialog with an OK, the method `wx.Colour.OK()` returns `True`. If the user closes it with a Cancel, the method returns `False`.

9.2.4 *Can I allow the user to browse images?*

If you are doing graphics manipulation in your program, it's often useful to provide the user with thumbnails of the images while they're browsing the file tree. A wxPython dialog for this purpose is called `wx.lib.imagebrowser.Image-Dialog`. Figure 9.10 displays a sample.

Listing 9.10 displays the simple code for this image browser dialog.

Figure 9.10   A typical image dialog browser

Listing 9.10   Creating an image browser dialog

```python
import wx
import wx.lib.imagebrowser as imagebrowser

if __name__ == "__main__":
    app = wx.PySimpleApp()
    dialog = imagebrowser.ImageDialog(None)
    if dialog.ShowModal() == wx.ID_OK:
        print "You Selected File: " + dialog.GetFile()
    dialog.Destroy()
```

The `wx.lib.imagebrowser.ImageDialog` class is straightforward, and has relatively few options for the programmer to set. To change the dialog's behavior, review the Python source for changing the types of files displayed. The constructor takes just two arguments.

```
ImageDialog(parent, set_dir=None)
```

The `set_dir` argument is the directory in which the dialog when displayed. If it is not set, the application's current working directory is used. After the dialog is closed, `GetFile()` returns the complete path string of the selected file, and `Get-Directory()` returns just the directory portion.

9.3 *Creating a wizard*

A *wizard* is a series of simple dialogs chained together to force the user to step through them one by one. Typically, they are used to guide a user through installation or a complex setup procedure by breaking down the information into small pieces. Figure 9.11 displays a sample wizard, displaying Back and Next buttons.

Figure 9.11   A simple wizard sample

In wxPython, a wizard is a series of pages controlled by an instance of the class `wx.wizard.Wizard`. The wizard instance manages the events that take the user through the pages. The pages themselves are instances of either the class `wx.wizard.WizardPageSimple` or `wx.wizard.WizardPage`. In both cases, they are merely `wx.Panel` instances with the additional logic needed to manage the page chain. The difference between the two instances is manifested only when the user presses the Next button. An instance of `wx.wizard.WizardPage` allows you to determine dynamically which page to navigate to at runtime, whereas an instance of `wx.wizard.WizardPageSimple` requires that the order be preset before the wizard is displayed. Listing 9.11 displays the code for a simple wizard.

Listing 9.11   Creating a simple static wizard

```
import wx
import wx.wizard

class TitledPage(wx.wizard.WizardPageSimple):
    def __init__(self, parent, title):
        wx.wizard.WizardPageSimple.__init__(self, parent)
        self.sizer = wx.BoxSizer(wx.VERTICAL)
        self.SetSizer(self.sizer)
        titleText = wx.StaticText(self, -1, title)
        titleText.SetFont(
                wx.Font(18, wx.SWISS, wx.NORMAL, wx.BOLD))
        self.sizer.Add(titleText, 0,
                wx.ALIGN_CENTRE | wx.ALL, 5)
        self.sizer.Add(wx.StaticLine(self, -1), 0,
                wx.EXPAND | wx.ALL, 5)
```

❶ Creating sample pages

```
if __name__ == "__main__":
    app = wx.PySimpleApp()
    wizard = wx.wizard.Wizard(None, -1, "Simple Wizard")
    page1 = TitledPage(wizard, "Page 1")
    page2 = TitledPage(wizard, "Page 2")
    page3 = TitledPage(wizard, "Page 3")
    page4 = TitledPage(wizard, "Page 4")
    page1.sizer.Add(wx.StaticText(page1, -1,
            "Testing the wizard"))
    page4.sizer.Add(wx.StaticText(page4, -1,
            "This is the last page."))
    wx.wizard.WizardPageSimple_Chain(page1, page2)
    wx.wizard.WizardPageSimple_Chain(page2, page3)
    wx.wizard.WizardPageSimple_Chain(page3, page4)
    wizard.FitToPage(page1)

    if wizard.RunWizard(page1):
        print "Success"
```

Creating wizard instance

Creating wizard pages

❷ **Creating page chain**

❸ **Sizing the wizard**

❹ **Running the wizard**

❶ For the purpose of populating a wizard, we create a simple little page that contains a static text title. Typically, you'd have some form elements here, and probably some data for the user to enter.

❷ The function `wx.wizard.WizardPageSimple_Chain()` is a convenience method that mutually calls `SetNext()` and `SetPrev()` of the two pages passed as arguments.

❸ Calling `FitToSize()` sizes the wizard based on the page passed as an argument, and also all the pages reachable from that page in the chain. Call this method only after the page chain has been created.

❹ The argument to this method is the page to start the wizard on. The wizard knows to close when it reaches a page that has no Next page. The `RunWizard()` method returns `True` if the user goes through the whole wizard and exits by pressing the Finish button.

Creating the `wx.wizard.Wizard` instance is the first part of using a wizard. The constructor looks similar to the following:

```
wx.wizard.Wizard(parent, id=-1, title=wx.EmptyString,
    bitmap=wx.NullBitmap, pos=wx.DefaultPosition)
```

In this example, the `parent`, `id`, `title`, and `pos` are as in `wx.Panel`. If set, the `bitmap` argument displays on each page. There is one style flag, `wx.wizard.WIZARD_EX_HELPBUTTON`, that causes a Help button to display. This is an extended flag, and must be set using the two-step creation process outlined in chapter 8.

Typically, you'll manage the size of the window by calling `FitToSize()` as displayed in line ❸ of listing 9.11, however, you can also set a minimal size by calling SetPageSize() with a tuple or wx.Size instance. The GetPageSize() method returns the current size. In both cases, the size is only used for the part of the dialog reserved for individual pages, while the dialog as a whole will be somewhat larger.

You can manage the pages from within this class. The method GetCurrent-Page() returns the page currently being displayed, and if the wizard is not currently being displayed, the method returns None. You can determine if the current page has a next or previous page by calling HasNextPage() or HasPrevPage(). Running the wizard is managed with the RunWizard() method, as described in line ❹ of listing 9.11.

Wizards fire command events that you can capture for more specialized processing, as displayed in table 9.5. In all these cases, the event object itself is of the class wx.wizard.WizardEvent, which exposes two methods. GetPage() returns the wx.WizardPage instance which was active when the event was generated, rather than the instance that may be displayed as a result of the event. The method Get-Direction() returns True if the event is a page change going forward, and False if it is a page change going backward.

Table 9.5   Events of wx.wizard.WizardDialog

Event	Description
EVT_WIZARD_CANCEL	Fired when the the user presses the Cancel button. This event may be vetoed using Veto(), in which case the dialog will not be dismissed.
EVT_WIZARD_FINISHED	Fired when the user presses the Finished button.
EVT_WIZARD_HELP	Fired when the user presses the Help button.
EVT_WIZARD_PAGE_CHANGED	Fired after the page has already been changed, to allow for postprocessing.
EVT_WIZARD_PAGE_CHANGING	Fired when the user has requested a page change, but it has not yet occurred. This event may be vetoed (if, for example, there is a required field that needs to be filled).

The wx.wizard.WizardPageSimple class is treated as though it were a panel. The constructor for the class allows you to set the Previous and Next pages, as in the following:

```
wx.wizard.WizardPageSimple(parent=None, prev=None, next=None)
```

If you don't want to set them in the constructor, you can use the SetPrev() and SetNext() methods. And if that's too much trouble, you can use wx.wizard.

WizardPageSimple_Chain(), which sets up the chaining relationship between two pages.

The complex version of wizard pages, wx.wizard.WizardPage, differs slightly. Rather than setting the Previous and Next explicitly, it defines handler methods that allow you to use more elaborate logic to define where to go next. The constructor is as follows:

```
wx.WizardPage(parent, bitmap=wx.NullBitmap, resource=None)
```

If set, the bitmap argument overrides the bitmap set in the parent wizard. The resource argument loads the page from a wxPython resource. To handle the page logic, override GetPrev() and GetNext() to return whatever you want the wizard to do next. A typical usage may be to dynamically determine the Next page based on user response to the current page.

9.4 *Showing startup tips*

Many applications use startup tips as a way of introducing users to program features they otherwise may not see. There is a very simple mechanism in wxPython for showing startup tips. Figure 9.12 displays a sample tip window.

Listing 9.12 displays the code.

Figure 9.12 A sample tip window with a helpful message.

Listing 9.12 Displaying a startup tip in five lines or less

```python
import wx

if __name__ == "__main__":
    app = wx.PySimpleApp()
    provider = wx.CreateFileTipProvider("tips.txt", 0)
    wx.ShowTip(None, provider, True)
```

There are two convenience functions that govern the startup tips. The first creates a wx.TipProvider, as in the following:

```
wx.CreateFileTipProvider(filename, currentTip)
```

The filename attribute is the name of a file with the string tips. The currentTip is the index of the tip within the file to start with, and the first tip in the file is index 0. The application is responsible for storing that information between runs.

The tip file is a simple text file where each line is a new tip. Blank lines in the file are skipped, and lines beginning with # are considered comments, and are also skipped. Here is the tip file for this example.

```
You can do startup tips very easily.
Feel the force, Luke.
```

The tip provider is an instance of the class `wx.PyTipProvider`. If you need more elaborate functionality, you can create your own subclass of `wx.TipProvider` and override the function `GetTip()`.

The function that displays the tip is `wx.ShowTip()`.

```
wx.ShowTip(parent, tipProvider, showAtStartup)
```

The `parent` is the parent window, if any, and the `tipProvider` is usually created from `wx.CreateFileTipProvider`. The `showAtStartup` argument controls whether the Show Tips At Startup checkbox is selected. It does not control whether the tips are actually displayed at startup, that's up to you. The return value of this function is the Boolean state of the Show Tips At Startup checkbox so that you can use that value the next time your application starts.

9.5 *Using validators to manage data in a dialog*

A *validator* is a special wxPython object that simplifies managing data in a dialog. When we discussed events in chapter 3, we mentioned briefly that if a widget has a validator, the validator can be automatically invoked by the event system. We've also seen `validator` as a parameter in the constructor of several of the wxPython widget classes, but we haven't yet discussed them.

The validator has three unrelated functions:

- Validates the data in the control before the dialog closes
- Automatically transfers data to and from the dialog
- Validates the data as the user types

9.5.1 *How do I use a validator to ensure correct data?*

A validator object is a subclass of `wx.Validator`. The parent class is abstract, and isn't used directly. Although there are a couple of predefined validator classes in the C++ wxWidget set, in wxPython, you will need to define your own validator classes. As we've seen in other cases, your Python classes need to inherit from a Python-specific subclass, `wx.PyValidator`, to be able to override all the parent

methods. A custom validator subclass must also override the method Clone(), ✳
which should return an identical copy of the validator.

A validator is attached to a specific widget in your system. That can be accomplished in one of two ways. First, if the widget allows it, the validator can be ✳
passed as an argument to the widget constructor. If the widget does not have a
validator argument to its constructor, you can still attach a validator by creating a
validator instance and calling the widget's SetValidator(validator) method.

To validate the data in the control, start by overriding the method Vali- ✳
date(parent) in your validator subclass. The parent argument is the parent window of the validator's widget, either the dialog or a panel. Use this to get the
data from other widgets in the dialog if that's important, or you can ignore the
argument altogether. You can use self.GetWindow() to get a reference to the ✳
widget being validated. The return value of your Validate(parent) method is a
Boolean. A True value indicates to the rest of the system that the data in the validator's widget is valid. A False value indicates a problem. You are allowed to
use wx.MessageBox() to display an alert from the Validate() method, but you
shouldn't do anything else that could raise events in the wxPython application.

The return value of the Validate() method is important. It comes into play
when you attempt to close a dialog using the OK button, (the button with an ID of
wx.ID_OK). As part of the processing of the OK click, wxPython calls the Validate() function of any widget the dialog contains that has a validator. If any of
those methods return False, the dialog will not close. Listing 9.13 displays a sample dialog with a validator that checks to see that all text controls have data.

Listing 9.13   A validator checking that all text controls have data

```
import wx

about_txt = """\
The validator used in this example will ensure that the text
controls are not empty when you press the Ok button, and
will not let you leave if any of the Validations fail."""

class NotEmptyValidator(wx.PyValidator):      ⟵ Creating the validator subclass
    def __init__(self):
        wx.PyValidator.__init__(self)

    def Clone(self):
        """
        Note that every validator must implement the Clone() method.
        """
        return NotEmptyValidator()       # return another instance of instance's class
```

```
    def Validate(self, win):        ❶  Using the validator method
        textCtrl = self.GetWindow()    # find the widget this validator is attached to
        text = textCtrl.GetValue()

        if len(text) == 0:
            wx.MessageBox("This field must contain some text!", "Error")
            textCtrl.SetBackgroundColour("pink")
            textCtrl.SetFocus()
            textCtrl.Refresh()
            return False
        else:
            textCtrl.SetBackgroundColour(
                wx.SystemSettings_GetColour(wx.SYS_COLOUR_WINDOW))
            textCtrl.Refresh()
            return True

    def TransferToWindow(self):
        return True

    def TransferFromWindow(self):
        return True

class MyDialog(wx.Dialog):
    def __init__(self):
        wx.Dialog.__init__(self, None, -1, "Validators: validating")

        # Create the text controls
        about   = wx.StaticText(self, -1, about_txt)
        name_l  = wx.StaticText(self, -1, "Name:")
        email_l = wx.StaticText(self, -1, "Email:")
        phone_l = wx.StaticText(self, -1, "Phone:")

        name_t  = wx.TextCtrl(self, validator=NotEmptyValidator())
        email_t = wx.TextCtrl(self, validator=NotEmptyValidator())
        phone_t = wx.TextCtrl(self, validator=NotEmptyValidator())

                                            Using the validator  ❷
        # Use standard button IDs
        okay   = wx.Button(self, wx.ID_OK)
        okay.SetDefault()
        cancel = wx.Button(self, wx.ID_CANCEL)

        # Layout with sizers
        sizer = wx.BoxSizer(wx.VERTICAL)
        sizer.Add(about, 0, wx.ALL, 5)
        sizer.Add(wx.StaticLine(self), 0, wx.EXPAND|wx.ALL, 5)

        fgs = wx.FlexGridSizer(3, 2, 5, 5)
        fgs.Add(name_l, 0, wx.ALIGN_RIGHT)
        fgs.Add(name_t, 0, wx.EXPAND)
        fgs.Add(email_l, 0, wx.ALIGN_RIGHT)
        fgs.Add(email_t, 0, wx.EXPAND)
```

```
        fgs.Add(phone_l, 0, wx.ALIGN_RIGHT)
        fgs.Add(phone_t, 0, wx.EXPAND)
        fgs.AddGrowableCol(1)
        sizer.Add(fgs, 0, wx.EXPAND|wx.ALL, 5)

        btns = wx.StdDialogButtonSizer()
        btns.AddButton(okay)
        btns.AddButton(cancel)
        btns.Realize()
        sizer.Add(btns, 0, wx.EXPAND|wx.ALL, 5)

        self.SetSizer(sizer)
        sizer.Fit(self)

app = wx.PySimpleApp()

dlg = MyDialog()
dlg.ShowModal()
dlg.Destroy()

app.MainLoop()
```

(handwritten: Note button sizing)

❶ This method tests that the underlying control has some data. If it does not, the background color of the widget is changed to pink.

❷ In these lines, a new validator *(handwritten: is)* attached to each text field in the dialog.

Figure 9.13 displays the dialog after attempting to close it with a blank field.

The code that explicitly tells the dialog to check the validators is not in the listing—it is a part of the wxPython event system. Another difference between dialogs and frames is that dialogs have the validator behavior built-in and frames do not. If you would like to use validators for validating controls not located in a dialog, call the parent window's `Validate()` method.[1] If the `wx.WS_EX_VALIDATE_RECURSIVELY` extra style is set for the window, `Validate()` of all the child windows is also called. If any of the validations fail, `Validate` returns `False`. Next, we'll discuss how to use validators to transfer data.

(handwritten: © 71)

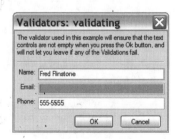

Figure 9.13   Attempting to close an invalid validator

(handwritten: ✗)

(handwritten bottom notes):
1 which you have overwritten in your [Frame, or...] derived parent class (?)
Should parent's Validate() be called from event handler?
Need to subclass wx.PyValidator?

9.5.2 *How do I use a validator to transfer data?*

The second important function of a validator is that it automatically transfers data into the dialog display when a dialog is opened, and automatically transfers data from the dialog to an external source when the dialog is closed. Figure 9.14 displays a sample dialog.

To accomplish this, you must override two methods in your validator subclass. The method `TransferToWindow()` is automatically called when the dialog is opened. You must use this method to put data into the validator's widget. The method `TransferFromWindow()` is automatically called when the dialog is closed using the OK button, after it has already been validated. You must use this method to move the data from the widget to some other source.

Figure 9.14   The transferring validator—this dialog will automatically display entered values when closed

The fact that a data transfer must happen implies that the validator must know something about an external data object, as displayed in listing 9.14. In this example, each validator is initialized with a reference to a global data dictionary, and a key within that dictionary that is important to that control. When the dialog is opened, the `TransferToWindow()` method reads from the dictionary at that key and places the data in the text field. When the dialog is closed, `TransferFromWindow()` reverses the process and writes to the dictionary. The example displays a dialog box to show you the transferred data.

Listing 9.14   A data transferring validator

```
import wx
import pprint

about_txt = """\
The validator used in this example shows how the validator
can be used to transfer data to and from each text control
automatically when the dialog is shown and dismissed."""

class DataXferValidator(wx.PyValidator):     ←— Declaring the validator
    def __init__(self, data, key):
        wx.PyValidator.__init__(self)
        self.data = data
        self.key = key

    def Clone(self):
        """
```

```
            Note that every validator must implement the Clone() method.
            """
            return DataXferValidator(self.data, self.key)

    def Validate(self, win):     ⟵ Not validating data
        return True

    def TransferToWindow(self):    ⟵ Called on dialog open
        textCtrl = self.GetWindow()
        textCtrl.SetValue(self.data.get(self.key, ""))
        return True

    def TransferFromWindow(self):    ⟵ Called on dialog close
        textCtrl = self.GetWindow()
        self.data[self.key] = textCtrl.GetValue()
        return True

class MyDialog(wx.Dialog):
    def __init__(self, data):
        wx.Dialog.__init__(self, None, -1, "Validators: data transfer")

        about   = wx.StaticText(self, -1, about_txt)
        name_l  = wx.StaticText(self, -1, "Name:")
        email_l = wx.StaticText(self, -1, "Email:")
        phone_l = wx.StaticText(self, -1, "Phone:")

        name_t  = wx.TextCtrl(self,     ⟵ Associating a validator with widget
                validator=DataXferValidator(data, "name"))
        email_t = wx.TextCtrl(self,
                validator=DataXferValidator(data, "email"))
        phone_t = wx.TextCtrl(self,
                validator=DataXferValidator(data, "phone"))

        okay    = wx.Button(self, wx.ID_OK)
        okay.SetDefault()
        cancel = wx.Button(self, wx.ID_CANCEL)

        sizer = wx.BoxSizer(wx.VERTICAL)
        sizer.Add(about, 0, wx.ALL, 5)
        sizer.Add(wx.StaticLine(self), 0, wx.EXPAND|wx.ALL, 5)

        fgs = wx.FlexGridSizer(3, 2, 5, 5)
        fgs.Add(name_l, 0, wx.ALIGN_RIGHT)
        fgs.Add(name_t, 0, wx.EXPAND)
        fgs.Add(email_l, 0, wx.ALIGN_RIGHT)
        fgs.Add(email_t, 0, wx.EXPAND)
        fgs.Add(phone_l, 0, wx.ALIGN_RIGHT)
        fgs.Add(phone_t, 0, wx.EXPAND)
        fgs.AddGrowableCol(1)
        sizer.Add(fgs, 0, wx.EXPAND|wx.ALL, 5)
```

```
            btns = wx.StdDialogButtonSizer()
            btns.AddButton(okay)
            btns.AddButton(cancel)
            btns.Realize()
            sizer.Add(btns, 0, wx.EXPAND|wx.ALL, 5)

            self.SetSizer(sizer)
            sizer.Fit(self)

    app = wx.PySimpleApp()

    data = { "name" : "Jordyn Dunn" }
    dlg = MyDialog(data)
    dlg.ShowModal()
    dlg.Destroy()

    wx.MessageBox("You entered these values:\n\n" +
                  pprint.pformat(data))

    app.MainLoop()
```

Calling of the transfer data methods of validators happens automatically for dialogs. To use validators for transferring data in non-dialog windows, call the parent widget's `TransDataFromWindow()` and `TransferDataToWindow()` methods as necessary. If the window has the `wx.WS_EX_VALIDATE_RECURSIVELY` extra style set, the transfer functions are also called on all of the child widgets.

In the next section, we'll discuss the most active use of a validator object, using it to evaluate data as the user enters it into the dialog box. This uses the validator and help from the wxPython event system.

9.5.3 *How do I validate data as it is entered?*

You can also use a validator to validate data entered into the dialog as the user enters it, before the data is passed to the widget. This is very powerful, since it can prevent bad data from getting into your application. Figure 9.15 displays an example, the dialog text explains the idea.

Figure 9.15 A validator verifying data on the fly

This method of validating data is less automated than other mechanisms. You must explicitly bind the character events from the validator's widget to a function, as in the following:

```
self.Bind(wx.EVT_CHAR, self.OnChar)
```

The widget assumes that the event source belongs to the validator. Listing 9.15 displays this binding in action.

Listing 9.15   Validating on the fly

```
import wx
import string

about_txt = """\
The validator used in this example will validate the input on the fly
instead of waiting until the okay button is pressed. The first field
will not allow digits to be typed, the second will allow anything
and the third will not allow alphabetic characters to be entered.
"""

class CharValidator(wx.PyValidator):
    def __init__(self, flag):
        wx.PyValidator.__init__(self)
        self.flag = flag
        self.Bind(wx.EVT_CHAR, self.OnChar)    ◁— Binding the character event

    def Clone(self):
        """
        Note that every validator must implement the Clone() method.
        """
        return CharValidator(self.flag)

    def Validate(self, win):
        return True

    def TransferToWindow(self):
        return True

    def TransferFromWindow(self):
        return True

    def OnChar(self, evt):
        key = chr(evt.GetKeyCode())
        if self.flag == "no-alpha" and key in string.letters:
            return
        if self.flag == "no-digit" and key in string.digits:
            return
        evt.Skip()

class MyDialog(wx.Dialog):
    def __init__(self):
        wx.Dialog.__init__(self, None, -1, "Validators: behavior
    modification")

        # Create the text controls
```

Viewing
the data
handler

```
about    = wx.StaticText(self, -1, about_txt)
name_l   = wx.StaticText(self, -1, "Name:")
email_l  = wx.StaticText(self, -1, "Email:")
phone_l  = wx.StaticText(self, -1, "Phone:")

name_t   = wx.TextCtrl(self, validator=CharValidator("no-digit"))
email_t  = wx.TextCtrl(self, validator=CharValidator("any"))
phone_t  = wx.TextCtrl(self, validator=CharValidator("no-alpha"))
okay     = wx.Button(self, wx.ID_OK)
okay.SetDefault()
cancel = wx.Button(self, wx.ID_CANCEL)
sizer = wx.BoxSizer(wx.VERTICAL)
sizer.Add(about, 0, wx.ALL, 5)
sizer.Add(wx.StaticLine(self), 0, wx.EXPAND|wx.ALL, 5)

fgs = wx.FlexGridSizer(3, 2, 5, 5)
fgs.Add(name_l, 0, wx.ALIGN_RIGHT)
fgs.Add(name_t, 0, wx.EXPAND)
fgs.Add(email_l, 0, wx.ALIGN_RIGHT)
fgs.Add(email_t, 0, wx.EXPAND)
fgs.Add(phone_l, 0, wx.ALIGN_RIGHT)
fgs.Add(phone_t, 0, wx.EXPAND)
fgs.AddGrowableCol(1)
sizer.Add(fgs, 0, wx.EXPAND|wx.ALL, 5)

btns = wx.StdDialogButtonSizer()
btns.AddButton(okay)
btns.AddButton(cancel)
btns.Realize()
sizer.Add(btns, 0, wx.EXPAND|wx.ALL, 5)

self.SetSizer(sizer)
sizer.Fit(self)

app = wx.PySimpleApp()

dlg = MyDialog()
dlg.ShowModal()
dlg.Destroy()

app.MainLoop()
```

Binding the validator ◁ (annotation pointing to the `name_t = wx.TextCtrl(self, validator=CharValidator("no-digit"))` line)

Because the OnChar() method is in a validator, it gets called before the widget responds to the character event. The method allows the event to pass on to the widget by using Skip(). You must call Skip(), otherwise the validator interferes with normal event processing. The validator performs a test to see if the character is valid for the control. If the character is invalid, Skip() is not called, and event processing stops. If necessary, events other than wx.EVT_CHAR can also be bound and the validator handles those events before the widget does.

Validators are a powerful and flexible mechanism for handling data in your wxPython application. Using them properly helps make the development and maintenance of your application smoother.

9.6 *Summary*

- Dialogs are used to handle interaction with the user in cases where there is a specific set of information to be obtained, and the interaction is usually over quickly. In wxPython, you can use the generic wx.Dialog class to create your own dialogs, or you can use one of several predefined dialogs. In many cases, commonly used dialogs also have convenience functions that make the use of the dialog easier.

- Dialogs can be displayed modally, meaning that all other user input within the application is blocked while the dialog is visible. A modal dialog is invoked by using the ShowModal() method, which returns a value based on whether the user pressed OK or Cancel to the dialog. Closing a modal dialog does not destroy it, and the same dialog instance can be used again.

- There are three generic simple dialogs available in wxPython. wx.MessageDialog displays an alert box or a yes/no question. wx.TextEntryDialog allows the user to enter text, and wx.SingleChoiceDialog gives the user a choice based on a list of items.

- When performing a long background task, you can use wx.ProgressDialog to display progress information to the user. The user can pick a file using the standard file dialog by using the wx.FileDialog class. There is a standard tree view which allows the user to pick a directory that is created using the wx.DirDialog class.

- You can access the standard font picker using wx.FontDialog and the standard color picker using wx.ColorDialog. In both cases, the dialog behavior and user response are controlled by a separate data class.

- To browse thumbnail images, use the wxPython-specific class wx.lib.imagebrowser.ImageDialog. This class allows the user to walk through her file system and select an image.

- You can create a wizard by using the wx.wizard.Wizard class to tie together a group of related dialog forms. The dialog forms are instances of either the class wx.wizard.WizardSimplePage or wx.wizard.WizardPage. The difference is that the page to page path for a simple page needs to be laid out before the wizard is displayed, while the standard page allows you to manage that logic at runtime.

- Startup tips can easily be displayed using the functions `wx.CreateFileTip-Provider` and `wx.ShowTip`.

- Validators are powerful objects that can automatically prevent a dialog from closing if the data entered is incorrect. They can also automatically transfer data between a dialog display and an external object, and can verify data entry on the fly.

10

Creating and using wxPython menus

This chapter covers
- Creating menus
- Working with menu items
- Adding submenus, pop-up menus, and custom menus
- Usability guidelines for menus

It's difficult to imagine an application without the familiar bar at the top starting with *File* and *Edit* and ending with *Help*. Menus are such a common part of the standard interface kit that they tend to fade into the background without drawing much attention. That's too bad, because the way that menus give the user access to all functionality quickly and easily was truly revolutionary.

In wxPython, there are three primary classes that manage menu functionality. The class wx.MenuBar manages the menu bar itself, while wx.Menu manages an individual pull-down or pop-up menu. A wx.MenuBar instance can, of course, contain multiple wx.Menu instances. The class wx.MenuItem represents one specific item within a wx.Menu.

In chapter 2 we provided a brief introduction to menus, in listing 5.5 we provided a mechanism for easily creating menu items, and in chapter 7 we introduced information on special menu effects. In this chapter, we will provide more detail on the creation and use of wxPython menus.

10.1 Creating Menus

First, we will discuss menu bars. To use a menu bar, perform the following actions:

- Create the menu bar
- Attach the menu bar to the frame
- Create the individual menus
- Attach the menus to the menu bar or to a parent menu
- Create the individual menu items
- Attach the menu items to the appropriate menu
- Create an event binding for each menu item

The order in which you perform these actions is somewhat flexible, as long as you create all items before use, and all actions are completed in the frame initialization method. You can manipulate the menus later in the process, but after the frame is visible, the order in which you do things may affect what the user sees. For example, it doesn't matter if you attach the menu bar to the frame right after creation, or if you wait until all other procedures are complete. For readability and maintenance purposes, we recommend that you keep related components together. For suggestions on how to organize menu creation, see the section on refactoring in chapter 5. In the next sections, we'll cover basic menu tasks.

10.1.1 How do I create a menu bar and attach it to a frame?

To create a menu bar, use the `wx.MenuBar` constructor, which takes no arguments.

```
wx.MenuBar()
```

Once the menu bar is created, attach it to a `wx.Frame` (or a subclass) using the `SetMenuBar()` method. Typically, you would do this inside the `__init__()` or `OnInit()` method of the frame:

```
menubar = wx.MenuBar()
self.SetMenuBar
```

You don't need to maintain a temporary variable for the menu bar, but doing so will make adding menus to the bar somewhat more straightforward. To get at the menu bar from someplace else in the program, use `wx.Frame.GetMenuBar()`.

10.1.2 How do I create a menu and attach it to the menu bar?

A wxPython menu bar consists of individual menus, each of which needs to be created separately. The following displays the constructor for `wx.Menu`.

```
wx.Menu(title="", style=0)
```

There is only one valid style for `wx.Menu` instances. Under GTK, the style `wx.MENU_TEAROFF` allows the menu to be detached from the menu bar and used as a stand-alone selector. Under other platforms, the style has no effect. If the platform supports it, a title can be given to the menu when it is created, which will add the text at the top of the menu above any regular menu items that are added to the menu. Figure 10.1 displays a blank window with three menus.

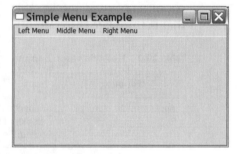

Figure 10.1
A blank window with three menus

Listing 10.1 displays the series of menus being added to a menu bar, without any items being added.

Listing 10.1   Adding menus to a menu bar

```python
import wx

class MyFrame(wx.Frame):
    def __init__(self):
        wx.Frame.__init__(self, None, -1, "Simple Menu Example")
        p = wx.Panel(self)
```

```
        menuBar = wx.MenuBar()      ◁—  Creating a menu bar
        menu = wx.Menu()      ◁—  Creating a menu
        menuBar.Append(menu, "Left Menu")      ◁┐
        menu2 = wx.Menu()                        ├ Appending the
        menuBar.Append(menu2, "Middle Menu")     ┘ menu to the bar
        menu3 = wx.Menu()
        menuBar.Append(menu3, "Right Menu")
        self.SetMenuBar(menuBar)

if __name__ == "__main__":
    app = wx.PySimpleApp()
    frame = MyFrame()
    frame.Show()
    app.MainLoop()
```

In the wxPython menu API, most of the manipulation of an object is managed by its container class. Later in this chapter, we'll discuss the specific methods of wx.Menu, since most of the methods concern manipulation of the menu items within the menu. In the remainder of this section, since we are talking about manipulating wx.Menu objects, we'll be listing the methods of wx.MenuBar that concern menus. Table 10.1 displays the four methods within wx.MenuBar that manipulate the contents of the menu bar.

Table 10.1   Methods of wx.MenuBar for manipulating the menus in the menu bar

Function	Description
Append(menu, title)	Appends the menu parameter to the end of the menu bar (the rightmost element displayed). The title parameter will be used to display the new menu. Returns True if successful, otherwise False.
Insert(pos, menu, title)	Inserts the given menu so that it is at the given pos (after this call, GetMenu(pos) == menu is true). As if inserting into a list, all the following menus are shifted to the right. The menu indexes are zero-based, so a pos of 0 is equivalent to putting the menu at the left of the menu bar. Inserting at GetMenuCount() as the pos is the same as using Append. The title is used for the display name. Returns True if successful.
Remove(pos)	Removes the menu at the position pos, shifting all other menus leftward. Returns the menu being removed.
Replace(pos, menu, title)	Replaces the menu at position pos, with the new menu passed in the menu parameter, and using the display name given by the title parameter. The other menus on the menu bar are unaffected. Returns the menu which was previously at the position pos.

The `wx.MenuBar` class contains a few other methods that manipulate the component menus in other ways, as displayed in table 10.2.

Table 10.2   Menu property methods of `wx.MenuBar`

Method	Description
EnableTop(pos, enable)	Sets the enable/disable state of the menu at position `pos`. If `enable` is `True`, then the menu is enabled, if `False`, then it is disabled.
GetMenu(pos)	Returns the menu object at the given position.
GetMenuCount()	Returns the number of menus in the menu bar.
FindMenu(title)	Returns the integer index of the menu in the menu bar with the given `title`. If there is no such menu, the method returns the constant `wx.NOT_FOUND`. The method will ignore decorations for keyboard shotcuts, if any.
GetLabelTop(pos) SetLabelTop(pos, label)	Getter and setter method for the display label of the menu at the given position.

10.1.3   *How do I add items to a pull-down menu?*

There are a couple of mechanisms for adding new menu items to a pull-down menu. The easier is to use the `Append()` method of `wx.Menu`, as in:

```
Append(id, string, helpStr="", kind=wx.ITEM_NORMAL)
```

The `id` parameter is a wxPython ID. The string argument is the string that will be displayed on the menu. The `helpStr`, if defined, will be displayed in the frame's status bar when the menu is highlighted. The `kind` argument allows you to set the type of the menu item to a toggle item. Later in this chapter we'll describe better ways of managing toggle items. The `Append` method places the new item at the end of the menu.

If you want to append a menu separator to the menu, the easiest way is the no-argument method `wx.Menu.AppendSeparator()`, which places a new separator at the end of the menu.

Listing 10.2 displays an example of using the `Append()` method to build a menu with two items and a separator.

Listing 10.2   Sample code for adding items to a menu

```python
import wx

class MyFrame(wx.Frame):
    def __init__(self):
        wx.Frame.__init__(self, None, -1,
                        "Menu Example with StatusBar")
```

```
        p = wx.Panel(self)
        self.CreateStatusBar()

        menu = wx.Menu()
        simple = menu.Append(-1, "Simple menu item",
            "This is some help text")
        menu.AppendSeparator()
        exit = menu.Append(-1, "Exit",
            "Selecting this item will exit the program")
        self.Bind(wx.EVT_MENU, self.OnSimple, simple)
        self.Bind(wx.EVT_MENU, self.OnExit, exit)

        menuBar = wx.MenuBar()
        menuBar.Append(menu, "Menu")
        self.SetMenuBar(menuBar)

    def OnSimple(self, event):
        wx.MessageBox("You selected the simple menu item")

    def OnExit(self, event):
        self.Close()

if __name__ == "__main__":
    app = wx.PySimpleApp()
    frame = MyFrame()
    frame.Show()
    app.MainLoop()
```

Figure 10.2 displays the menu with separators and status text.

Along with `Append()`, there are two other families of methods for menu item insertion. To put a menu item at the beginning of the menu, use one of the following methods:

- `Prepend(id, string, helpStr="",`
  `kind=wx.ITEM_NORMAL)`

- `PrependSeparator()`.

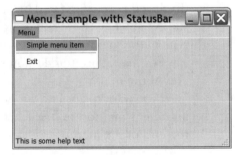

Figure 10.2 A sample menu, with separators and status text.

These two methods take the same arguments as their appending counterparts, with the only difference being the placement of the resulting menu item at the top of the menu rather than at the bottom.

To place the new item at an arbitrary place within the menu, use one of the following `Insert` methods:

- `Insert(pos, id, string, helpStr="", kind=wx.ITEM_NORMAL)`
- `InsertSeparator(pos)`

The new argument here, `pos`, is the index within the menu where the new item is displayed, so an index of `0` puts the new item at the beginning, and an index of the menu size puts the new item at the end. All menu items after the point of insertion are shifted downward.

All of these insertion methods implicitly create an instance of the class `wx.MenuItem`. You can also explicitly create an instance of that class using its constructor to set additional properties of the menu item besides just its label. For instance, you can set custom fonts or colors. The constructor for `wx.MenuItem` is as follows:

```
wx.MenuItem(parentMenu=None, id=ID_ANY, text="",
    helpString="", kind=wx.ITEM_NORMAL, subMenu=None)
```

The `parentMenu` argument, if specified must be a `wx.Menu` instance. The new menu item is not automatically added to the display of the parent menu when constructed. You must do this yourself. This behavior is different than the ordinary behavior of wxPython widgets and their containers. The `id` argument is the identifier for the new item. The trick of setting the `id` to `-1` to automatically generate an ID works the same for menu items as it does for windows. The `text` argument is the menu item's display string in the menu, and the `helpString` argument is the display string in the status bar, when highlighted. The `kind` is `wx.ITEM_NORMAL` for plain menu items; we'll see next that toggle menu items have different values. If the `subMenu` argument is not null, the new menu item is actually a submenu. We do not recommend that you use this mechanism to create submenus; instead use the mechanism described in section 10.3, Sprucing up your menus.

Unlike most widgets, creating the menu item does not add it to the specified parent menu. To add the new menu item to a menu, use one of the following methods of `wx.Menu`:

- `AppendItem(aMenuItem)`
- `InsertItem(pos, aMenuItem)`
- `PrependItem(aMenuItem)`

All three behave the same as their implicit counterparts described earlier.

To remove a menu item from the menu, use the method `Remove(id)`, which takes a wxPython ID, or `RemoveItem(item)`, which takes a menu item as the argument. Any subsequent menu items are shifted upward in the display. The `Remove()`

methods return the actual menu item that was affected. This allows you to store the item for later use. Unlike menu bars, menus don't have a method for direct replacement of menu items. A replacement must be managed as a removal and subsequent insertion.

The wx.Menu class also has two getters for obtaining information about its component menu items. GetMenuItemCount() returns the number of items in the menu, and GetMenuItems() returns a list of the menu items in the menu ordered by their position within the menu. This list is a copy of the actual list in the menu, meaning that changing the returned list does not change the menu itself. Therefore, you cannot use this list to bypass the methods for adding and removing menu items.

You can continue to add or remove menu items from a menu during runtime while the menu is active. Listing 10.3 displays sample code that adds menus during runtime. The OnAddItem() method, called when the button is pressed, inserts a new item at the end of the menu.

Listing 10.3 Adding menu items during runtime

```python
import wx

class MyFrame(wx.Frame):
    def __init__(self):
        wx.Frame.__init__(self, None, -1,
                          "Add Menu Items")
        p = wx.Panel(self)
        self.txt = wx.TextCtrl(p, -1, "new item")
        btn = wx.Button(p, -1, "Add Menu Item")
        self.Bind(wx.EVT_BUTTON, self.OnAddItem, btn)      ◁─┐ Binding the
                                                             │ button event
        sizer = wx.BoxSizer(wx.HORIZONTAL)
        sizer.Add(self.txt, 0, wx.ALL, 20)
        sizer.Add(btn, 0, wx.TOP|wx.RIGHT, 20)
        p.SetSizer(sizer)

        self.menu = menu = wx.Menu()
        simple = menu.Append(-1, "Simple menu item")
        menu.AppendSeparator()
        exit = menu.Append(-1, "Exit")
        self.Bind(wx.EVT_MENU, self.OnSimple, simple)
        self.Bind(wx.EVT_MENU, self.OnExit, exit)

        menuBar = wx.MenuBar()
        menuBar.Append(menu, "Menu")
        self.SetMenuBar(menuBar)
```

```
        def OnSimple(self, event):
            wx.MessageBox("You selected the simple menu item")

        def OnExit(self, event):
            self.Close()

        def OnAddItem(self, event):                              ┐ Adding
            item = self.menu.Append(-1, self.txt.GetValue())    ◁─┘ the item
            self.Bind(wx.EVT_MENU, self.OnNewItemSelected, item)  ◁─┐
                                                                    │ Binding
        def OnNewItemSelected(self, event):                        │ a menu
            wx.MessageBox("You selected a new item")               │ event

if __name__ == "__main__":
    app = wx.PySimpleApp()
    frame = MyFrame()
    frame.Show()
    app.MainLoop()
```

In this sample, `OnAddItem()` reads the value of the text in the text field, and uses `Append()` to add a new item to the menu. In addition, it binds a menu event so that the new menu item has functionality. In the next section, we'll discuss menu events.

10.1.4 *How do I respond to a menu event?*

In the last section, we displayed two code examples that respond to a menu selection. Like many of the widgets we saw in chapter 8, selecting a menu item triggers an instance of `wx.CommandEvent` of a specific type. In this case, the type is `wx.EVT_MENU`.

Menu item events vary from other command events in the system in two ways. First, the `Bind()` function that associates the menu item event with a specific function is called, not on the menu item instance or its containing menu or menu bar instances, but on the frame which contains the menu bar. Secondly, since the frame usually has multiple menu items responding to the same `wx.EVT_MENU` trigger, the `Bind()` method needs to take a third parameter, which is the menu item itself. This allows the frame to differentiate between menu events from different items.

So, a typical call to bind a menu event would look like this:

```
self.Bind(wx.EVT_MENU, self.OnExit, exit_menu_item)
```

where `self` is the frame, `self.OnExit` is the handling method, and `exit_menu_item` is the menu item itself.

Although the idea of binding the menu event through the frame may seem a little odd, there is a reason for it. Binding events through the frame allows you to transparently bind a toolbar button to the same handler as the menu item. If the toolbar button has the same wxPython ID as a menu item, the single `Bind()` call for `wx.EVT_MENU` will bind both the menu selection and the toolbar button click. This is possible because both the menu item event and the toolbar event get routed through the frame. If the menu item event was handled in the menu bar, it would never see the toolbar event.

Occasionally, you will have multiple menu items that need to be bound to the same handler. For example, a set of radio button toggle menus, all of which do essentially the same thing, may be bound to the same handler. To avoid having to bind each one separately, if the menu items have consecutive identifier numbers, use the `wx.EVT_MENU_RANGE` event type:

```
self.Bind(wx.EVT_MENU_RANGE, function, id=menu1, id2=menu2)
```

In this case, any menu item with an identifier between `menu1` and `menu2` (inclusive) would bind to the given function.

Although typically you'll only care about menu item command events, there are other menu events that you can respond to. In wxPython, the class `wx.MenuEvent` manages menu drawing and highlighting events. Table 10.3 details four event types for `wx.MenuEvent`.

Table 10.3 Event types of `wx.MenuEvent`

Event type	Description
EVT_MENU_CLOSE	Triggered when a menu is closed.
EVT_MENU_HIGHLIGHT	Triggered when a menu item is highlighted. Bound to a specific menu item ID. By default causes help text to be displayed in the frame's status bar.
EVT_MENU_HIGHLIGHT_ALL	Triggered when a menu item is highlighted, but not bound to a specific menu item ID—meaning that there's just one handler for the entire menu bar. You'd call this if you wanted any menu highlight change to trigger an action, no matter which items are selected.
EVT_MENU_OPEN	Triggered when a menu is opened.

Now that we've covered the basics of menu creation, we'll begin describing how to work with menu items.

10.2 *Working with menu items*

Although menus and menu bars are obviously vital to the structure of a menu system, most of your time and effort will be spent dealing with the menu items. In the next few sections, we'll talk about common menu item functions such as finding an item, enabling or disabling an item, creating toggle menu items, and assigning keyboard shortcuts.

10.2.1 *How do I find a specific menu item in a menu?*

There are a number of ways in wxPython to find a specific menu or menu item given a label or an identifier. You often use these methods in event handlers, especially when you want to modify a menu item or display its label text in another location. Listing 10.4 augments the previous dynamic menu example by using `FindItemById()` to get the appropriate menu item for display.

Listing 10.4   Finding a specific menu item

```
import wx

class MyFrame(wx.Frame):
    def __init__(self):
        wx.Frame.__init__(self, None, -1,
                          "Find Item Example")
        p = wx.Panel(self)
        self.txt = wx.TextCtrl(p, -1, "new item")
        btn = wx.Button(p, -1, "Add Menu Item")
        self.Bind(wx.EVT_BUTTON, self.OnAddItem, btn)

        sizer = wx.BoxSizer(wx.HORIZONTAL)
        sizer.Add(self.txt, 0, wx.ALL, 20)
        sizer.Add(btn, 0, wx.TOP|wx.RIGHT, 20)
        p.SetSizer(sizer)

        self.menu = menu = wx.Menu()
        simple = menu.Append(-1, "Simple menu item")
        menu.AppendSeparator()
        exit = menu.Append(-1, "Exit")
        self.Bind(wx.EVT_MENU, self.OnSimple, simple)
        self.Bind(wx.EVT_MENU, self.OnExit, exit)

        menuBar = wx.MenuBar()
        menuBar.Append(menu, "Menu")
        self.SetMenuBar(menuBar)

    def OnSimple(self, event):
        wx.MessageBox("You selected the simple menu item")
```

```
        def OnExit(self, event):
            self.Close()

        def OnAddItem(self, event):
            item = self.menu.Append(-1, self.txt.GetValue())
            self.Bind(wx.EVT_MENU, self.OnNewItemSelected, item)

        def OnNewItemSelected(self, event):
            item = self.GetMenuBar().FindItemById(event.GetId())   ◁─┐  Getting
            text = item.GetText()                                      │  the menu
            wx.MessageBox("You selected the '%s' item" % text)        │  item

    if __name__ == "__main__":
        app = wx.PySimpleApp()
        frame = MyFrame()
        frame.Show()
        app.MainLoop()
```

In this example, `FindItemById()` is used to get the item for the purpose of getting its text label for the display.

Both `wx.MenuBar` and `wx.Menu` have essentially the same methods for finding out information about specific menu items. The primary difference is that the `wx.MenuBar` methods will find an item anywhere on the menu bar, while the `wx.Menu` items will find an item only if it is in that particular menu. For most uses, the `wx.MenuBar` items are preferred, at least in part because the menu bar is easily accessible using the `wx.Frame.GetMenuBar()` method.

To find a top-level menu from the menu bar, use the menu bar method `FindMenu(title)`. This method returns either the index of the appropriate menu or the constant `wx.NOT_FOUND`. To get the actual menu, use `GetMenu()`:

```
    def FindMenuInMenuBar(menuBar, title):
        pos = menuBar.FindMenu(title)
        if pos == wx.NOT_FOUND:
            return None
        return menuBar.GetMenu(pos)
```

The `title` parameter of `FindMenu` matches the menu title with or without the decorator label characters discussed next. For example, `FindMenu("File")` still matches the menu item even if its label was instantiated as `&File`. All of the methods in these menu classes that find a menu item based on a label string share this functionality.

Table 10.4 specifies the methods of `wx.MenuBar` which can be used to find or manipulate a specific menu item.

Table 10.4 Menu item manipulation methods of `wx.MenuBar`

Method	Description
FindMenuItem(menuString, itemString)	Searches for a menu named `menuString` and a menu item named `itemString` within that menu. Returns the found menu item or `wx.NOT_FOUND`.
FindItemById(id)	Returns the menu item associated with the given wxPython identifier. If there is no such item, returns `None`.
GetHelpString(id) SetHelpString(id, helpString)	Getter and setter for the help string of the menu item with the given wxPython identifier. If there is no such menu item, then the getter returns `" "`. If there is no such menu item, the setter has no effect.
GetLabel(id) SetLabel(id, label)	Getter and setter for the display label of the menu item with the given wxPython identifier. Manages nonexistent ID the same way as the help string methods. These methods should only be used after the menu bar has been associated with a frame.

Table 10.5 displays a similar menu item API for `wx.Menu`. The methods behave similarly to the menu bar counterparts, except that the returned menu item must be in the invoked menu instance.

After the menu item is returned, you may want to do something useful, such as enable or disable the item. In the next section, we'll discuss enabling and disabling menu items.

Table 10.5 Menu Item methods of `wx.Menu`

Method	Description
FindItem(itemString)	Returns the menu item associated with the given `itemString`, or `wx.NOT_FOUND`
FindItemById(id)	As the menu bar method
FindItemByPosition(pos)	Returns the menu item associated with the given position in the menu
GetHelpString(id) SetHelpString(id, helpString)	As the menu bar methods
GetLabel(id) SetLabel(id, helpString)	As the menu bar methods

10.2.2 *How do I enable or disable a menu item?*

Similar to other widgets, menus and menu items can be enabled or disabled. A disabled menu or menu item usually displays as gray text, rather than black. A disabled menu or menu item does not trigger highlight or selection events, it's invisible to the event system.

Listing 10.5 displays sample code that toggles a menu item's enabled state, using the menu bar `IsEnabled()` and `Enable()` methods inside the button event handler.

Listing 10.5   Sample enable and disable item code

```python
import wx

ID_SIMPLE = wx.NewId()

class MyFrame(wx.Frame):
    def __init__(self):
        wx.Frame.__init__(self, None, -1,
                          "Enable/Disable Menu Example")
        p = wx.Panel(self)
        self.btn = wx.Button(p, -1, "Disable Item", (20,20))
        self.Bind(wx.EVT_BUTTON, self.OnToggleItem, self.btn)

        menu = wx.Menu()
        menu.Append(ID_SIMPLE, "Simple menu item")
        self.Bind(wx.EVT_MENU, self.OnSimple, id=ID_SIMPLE)

        menu.AppendSeparator()
        menu.Append(wx.ID_EXIT, "Exit")
        self.Bind(wx.EVT_MENU, self.OnExit, id=wx.ID_EXIT)

        menuBar = wx.MenuBar()
        menuBar.Append(menu, "Menu")
        self.SetMenuBar(menuBar)

    def OnSimple(self, event):
        wx.MessageBox("You selected the simple menu item")

    def OnExit(self, event):
        self.Close()

    def OnToggleItem(self, event):
        menubar = self.GetMenuBar()
        enabled = menubar.IsEnabled(ID_SIMPLE)
        menubar.Enable(ID_SIMPLE, not enabled)
        self.btn.SetLabel(
            (enabled and "Enable" or "Disable") + " Item")
```

```
if __name__ == "__main__":
app = wx.PySimpleApp()
frame = MyFrame()
frame.Show()
app.MainLoop()
```

To view or change the enable state of a menu item from the menu bar, from a specific menu, or from the menu item itself, call wx.MenuBar.IsEnabled(id), wx.Menu.IsEnabled(id), or wx.MenuItem.IsEnabled(). Menu bar and menu methods each take the wxPython identifier of a menu item. Both methods return True if the item exists and is enabled, and False if the item is disabled or does not exist. The only difference is that the wx.Menu method only searches within that particular menu, while the menu bar method searches the entire menu bar. The wx.MenuItem method takes no arguments, and returns the state of that particular menu item.

To change the enabled state, use wx.MenuBar.Enable(id, enable), wx.Menu.Enable(id, enable), or wx.MenuItem.Enable(enable). The enable parameter is a Boolean. If True, the menu item in question is enabled, if False, it is disabled. The scope of the Enable() methods is the same as the IsEnabled() methods. You can also enable or disable an entire top-level menu using the method wx.MenuBar.EnableTop(pos, enable). In this case, the pos parameter is the integer position of the menu within the menu bar, and the enable parameter is a Boolean.

10.2.3 *How do I associate a menu item with a keyboard shortcut?*

In wxPython you can set up keyboard navigation and shortcuts for menu items. Figure 10.3 displays a sample menu with keyboard decoration added. Notice that the menu names have an underlined character, and that next to the item labeled Accelerated is a Ctrl-A.

Studies have shown that keyboard shortcuts are not always the time saver that you think they are. However, they are standard interface elements, and your users will expect them to be there. Shortcuts are also helpful for users with accessibility issues. Listing 10.6 displays the code for adding keyboard shortcuts to menu items.

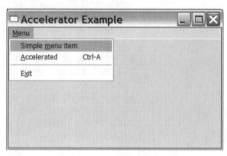

Figure 10.3
Menu items with keyboard shortcuts

Listing 10.6 Associating keyboard shortcuts to menu items

```python
import wx

class MyFrame(wx.Frame):
    def __init__(self):
        wx.Frame.__init__(self, None, -1,
                          "Accelerator Example")
        p = wx.Panel(self)
        menu = wx.Menu()
        simple = menu.Append(-1, "Simple &menu item")      ◁┘ Creating a
                                                              mnemonic
        accel  = menu.Append(-1, "&Accelerated\tCtrl-A")   ◁┐ Creating an
                                                              accelerator
        menu.AppendSeparator()
        exit = menu.Append(-1, "E&xit")

        self.Bind(wx.EVT_MENU, self.OnSimple, simple)
        self.Bind(wx.EVT_MENU, self.OnAccelerated, accel)
        self.Bind(wx.EVT_MENU, self.OnExit, exit)

        menuBar = wx.MenuBar()
        menuBar.Append(menu, "&Menu")
        self.SetMenuBar(menuBar)

        acceltbl = wx.AcceleratorTable( [   ◁┘ Using an accelerator table
                (wx.ACCEL_CTRL, ord('Q'), exit.GetId())
            ])
        self.SetAcceleratorTable(acceltbl)

    def OnSimple(self, event):
        wx.MessageBox("You selected the simple menu item")

    def OnAccelerated(self, event):
        wx.MessageBox("You selected the accelerated menu item")

    def OnExit(self, event):
        self.Close()

if __name__ == "__main__":
    app = wx.PySimpleApp()
    frame = MyFrame()
    frame.Show()
    app.MainLoop()
```

There are two kinds of keyboard shortcuts in wxPython; mnemonics and accelerators. Next, we'll be describing the differences between each type.

Using mnemonic shortcuts

A *mnemonic* is a single character that is used to access the menu item, and is represented visually by underlining that character. Mnemonics can be created by specifying the display text for the menu or menu item, and placing an ampersand before the character you want to use for the mnemonic, for example &File, &Edit, or Ma&cros. If you want an ampersand in your menu text, you must enter it as a double ampersand, for example, Font && Spacing.

Mnemonics are meant to be an alternate method for navigating a menu tree. They are only active when explicitly invoked by the user; under MS Windows this is done by pressing the alt key. Once the mnemonics are activated, the next keypress opens the top-level menu with the matching mnemonic. The key press after that opens the submenu or menu item within that menu, and so on until a menu item is selected, at which point a menu event is triggered as though the menu had been selected using the mouse. Mnemonic characters must be unique within the menu, but do not need to be unique across the entire menu bar. Typically, the first character of the menu display text is used as the mnemonic. If you have more than one menu item that starts with the same letter, there is no particular guideline governing which other character to use (the most common choices are the second letter or the last letter depending on which seems more reasonable). It's more important that the menu text be clear than to have the perfect mnemonic.

Using accelerator shortcuts

An *accelerator* in wxPython is a more typical keyboard shortcut, meaning a key combination that can be invoked any time which triggers the menu item. An accelerator can be created in two ways. The simpler way is to include the accelerator key combination in the display text of the menu or menu item when it is added to its parent. To do this, put a tab character \t after the text of your menu item. After the tab character, define the key combination. The first part of the key combination is one or more of Alt, Ctrl, or Shift, separated by either a + or a -, and followed by the actual key of the accelerator. For example: New\tctrl-n, Save As\tctrl-shift-s. Even if you only have one special key in the first part, you still use + or - to separate that part from the actual key. It does not matter if you use upper or lowercase for the key combination.

The actual key can be any number or letter or a function key, written as F1 through F12, plus one of the special words displayed in table 10.6 that represent other keys.

The wxPython methods ignore both mnemonics and accelerators for the purpose of finding a menu or menu item by its name. In other words, the call menubar.FindMenuItem("File", "Save As"), will still match the Save As menu item, even if that item's display name was entered as Save &As\tctrl-shift-s.

Accelerators can also be created directly using an accelerator table, which is an instance of the class wx.AccleratorTable. An accelerator table consists of a list of wx.AccelratorEntry objects. The constructor for wx.AcceleratorTable takes a list of accelerator entries, or it takes no arguments at all. In listing 10.6, we are taking advantage of the fact that wxPython will implicitly call the wx.AcceleratorEntry constructor with the list of arguments, (wx.ACCEL_CTRL, ord('Q'), exit.GetId()). The constructor for wx.AcceleratorEntry is as follows.

```
wx.AcceleratorEntry(flags,
    keyCode, cmd)
```

The flags parameter is a bitmask with one or more of the following constants: wx.ACCEL_ALT, wx.ACCEL_CTRL, wxACCEL_NORMAL, or wx.ACCEL_SHIFT. This parameter indicates which modifier keys need to be pressed to trigger the accelerator. The keyCode argument represents the

Table 10.6   Non-alphanumeric accelerator keys

Accelerator	Key
del	Delete
delete	Delete
down	Down arrow
end	End
enter	Enter
esc	Escape
escape	Escape
home	Home
ins	Insert
insert	Insert
left	Left arrow
pgdn	Page down
pgup	Page Up
return	Enter
right	Right arrow
space	Space bar
tab	Tab
up	Up arrow

regular key to be pressed to trigger the accelerator. It is either the ASCII number corresponding to a character, or one the special characters found in the wxWidgets documentation under Keycodes. The cmd argument is the wxPython identifier of the menu item which triggers its command event when the accelerator is invoked. As you can see from listing 10.6, declaring an accelerator in this way does not cause the key combination to be listed on the menu with the item display name. You still need to do that separately.

10.2.4 *How do I create a toggle menu item with a checkbox or radio button?*

Menu items are not only used for getting user input in the form of selections, they can also be used to display the state of the application. The most common mechanism for displaying state via a menu item is the use of a toggle menu item that emulates a checkbox or radio button (you can also just change the text of the menu item or use the enabled/disabled status to reflect application state). Figure 10.4 displays an example of both checkbox and radio menu items in action.

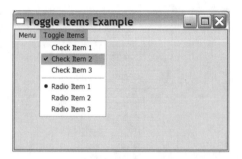

Figure 10.4 Sample toggle menus, showing both checkboxes and radio button menu items

As you might expect from its name, a checkbox toggle menu item changes from the off state to the on state and back every time it is selected. A radio toggle menu item allows exactly one menu item in a group to be in the on state. When another item in the group is selected, it moves to the on state and the item that was previously in the on state changes to the off state. Listing 10.7 displays how checkboxes and radio items are created.

Listing 10.7 Building toggle menu items

```python
import wx

class MyFrame(wx.Frame):
    def __init__(self):
        wx.Frame.__init__(self, None, -1,
                          "Toggle Items Example")
        p = wx.Panel(self)
        menuBar = wx.MenuBar()
        menu = wx.Menu()
        exit = menu.Append(-1, "Exit")
        self.Bind(wx.EVT_MENU, self.OnExit, exit)
        menuBar.Append(menu, "Menu")

        menu = wx.Menu()
        menu.AppendCheckItem(-1, "Check Item 1")
        menu.AppendCheckItem(-1, "Check Item 2")
        menu.AppendCheckItem(-1, "Check Item 3")
        menu.AppendSeparator()
        menu.AppendRadioItem(-1, "Radio Item 1")
        menu.AppendRadioItem(-1, "Radio Item 2")
```

```
            menu.AppendRadioItem(-1, "Radio Item 3")
            menuBar.Append(menu, "Toggle Items")

            self.SetMenuBar(menuBar)

        def OnExit(self, event):
            self.Close()

if __name__ == "__main__":
    app = wx.PySimpleApp()
    frame = MyFrame()
    frame.Show()
    app.MainLoop()
```

As you can see from the listing, a checkbox menu item is added using the method `AppendCheckItem(id, item, helpString="")`, which is similar to `Append()`. The arguments are the wxPython identifier, the display name in the menu, and the `Help` string to display in a status bar. Similarly, you can also use `PrependCheckItem (id, item, helpString="")` and `InsertCheckItem(pos, id, item, helpString="")`, both of which behave identically to their ordinary, non-checkbox, counterparts.

Radio button menu items can be appended using the `AppendRadioItem(id, item, helpString="")` method, and you can also use the methods `PrependRadio-Item(id, item, helpString="")` and `InsertRadioItem(pos, id, item, help-String="")`. Any set of consecutive radio menu items is considered a group, and only one member of the group can be toggled on at a time. The boundaries of a radio group are marked by the first non-radio menu item or menu separator in either direction. By default, the first member of a radio group is checked when the radio group is created.

Toggle menu items can be created using `Append()` by passing the `kind` parameter one of the constant values `wx.ITEM_CHECK`, `wx.ITEM_NORMAL`, `wx.ITEM_RADIO`, or `wx.ITEM_SEPARATOR`, each of which creates a menu item of the appropriate type. This is helpful if you are automating the creation of the menu items using some kind of data-driven process. All types of menu items can be created using the same method, although to make a separator by specifying a `kind` of `wx.ITEM_SEPARATOR` you must pass `wx.ID_SEPARATOR` for the `id` parameter.

You can also create a toggle menu item when you use the `wx.MenuItem` constructor, by passing one of the constant values mentioned earlier to the `kind` parameter of the constructor. The resulting menu item can be added to a menu using any of the `AppendItem()`, `PrependItem()`, or `InsertItem()` family.

To determine the toggle state of a menu item, use `IsCheckable()`, which returns `True` if the item is a checkbox or radio item, or `IsChecked()`, which returns

True if the item is a toggle and it is currently checked. You can set the toggle state of a menu item using the Check(check) method, which takes a Boolean argument, and sets the menu item appropriately. If the item is a radio button, the other items in the group are also changed.

You can also get the toggle state of a menu item from the menu or menu bar by using the method IsChecked(id), which takes the identifier of the menu item you wish to check. The usual restrictions apply—the menu bar item only works if it has been attached to a frame, and the menu version only finds menu items within that menu. You can set the state of the menu item from either the menu bar or menu using Check(id, check), which sets the state of the menu item with the given ID to the result of the Boolean.

10.3 *Sprucing up your menus*

Over the next few sections we'll discuss alternatives to make your menus more useful by making your menus more complex. First, we'll discuss nested submenus, then we'll talk about placing pop-up menus anywhere in your application. We'll close the section with thoughts on fancy styles for menu items.

10.3.1 *How do I create a submenu?*

If your application becomes too complex, you can create a submenu inside a top-level menu, which allows you to nest menu items and fit more items within a top-level menu. Submenus are particularly useful at grouping a set of options that belong together logically, especially when there would be too many options to fit comfortably at the top-level. Figure 10.5 displays a sample wxPython application with a submenu.

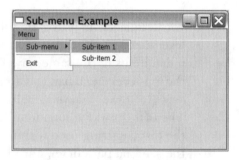

Figure 10.5   A submenu in wxPython

Listing 10.8 displays the code used to generate the figure.

Listing 10.8   Building a nested submenu

```
import wx

class MyFrame(wx.Frame):
    def __init__(self):
        wx.Frame.__init__(self, None, -1,
```

```
                              "Sub-menu Example")
        p = wx.Panel(self)
        menu = wx.Menu()

        submenu = wx.Menu()
        submenu.Append(-1, "Sub-item 1")
        submenu.Append(-1, "Sub-item 2")
        menu.AppendMenu(-1, "Sub-menu", submenu)    ◁─┐  Appending
                                                        the submenu
        menu.AppendSeparator()
        exit = menu.Append(-1, "Exit")
        self.Bind(wx.EVT_MENU, self.OnExit, exit)

        menuBar = wx.MenuBar()
        menuBar.Append(menu, "Menu")
        self.SetMenuBar(menuBar)

    def OnExit(self, event):
        self.Close()

if __name__ == "__main__":
    app = wx.PySimpleApp()
    frame = MyFrame()
    frame.Show()
    app.MainLoop()
```

You'll notice from listing 10.8 that a submenu is created in the same way as a top-level menu. You create an instance of the class wx.Menu, then populate it with menu items in the same way. The difference is that rather than appending it to the top-level menu bar, you append it to another menu using the method Append-Menu(id, text, submenu, helpStr). The arguments are very similar to Append(). The id is the wxPython identifier of the menu being added. The text argument is the display string used within the parent menu. The submenu itself is passed in the submenu parameter, and the text for the status bar goes in helpStr. In addition, there are also menu versions of the other insertion methods, Prepend-Menu(id, text, submenu, helpStr) and InsertMenu(pos, text, submenu, helpStr). These methods behave analogously to the menu item versions discussed earlier in this chapter.

Remember that the order of the steps for submenus is a little more important than for plain menu items, and it's recommended that you add the items to the submenu first, and then attach the submenu to the parent menu. This enables wxPython to correctly register keyboard shortcuts to the correct menu. You can nest submenus to arbitrary depth by appending to an existing submenu rather than the top-level menu, but you still need to create the new submenu before adding it to its parent.

10.3.2 *How do I create a pop-up menu?*

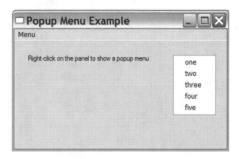

Figure 10.6 **A pop-up menu being popped up**

Menus don't just pull down from menu bars at the top of your frame. They can also pop up from anywhere in the frame. Most of the time, a pop-up menu is used to provide actions that are context-sensitive, and that relate to the object at the location where the user clicks. Figure 10.6 displays an example of pop-up menus in action.

Pop-up menus are created very similarly to standard menus, however, they are not attached to the menu bar. Listing 10.9 displays the code for a sample pop-up menu.

Listing 10.9   Code to create a pop-up menu in an arbitrary widget

```
import wx

class MyFrame(wx.Frame):
    def __init__(self):
        wx.Frame.__init__(self, None, -1,
                          "Popup Menu Example")
        self.panel = p = wx.Panel(self)
        menu = wx.Menu()
        exit = menu.Append(-1, "Exit")
        self.Bind(wx.EVT_MENU, self.OnExit, exit)

        menuBar = wx.MenuBar()
        menuBar.Append(menu, "Menu")
        self.SetMenuBar(menuBar)

        wx.StaticText(p, -1,
            "Right-click on the panel to show a popup menu",
            (25,25))

        self.popupmenu = wx.Menu()            ← Creating a menu    ┐ Populating
        for text in "one two three four five".split():   ←        ┘ the menu
            item = self.popupmenu.Append(-1, text)
            self.Bind(wx.EVT_MENU, self.OnPopupItemSelected, item)
        p.Bind(wx.EVT_CONTEXT_MENU, self.OnShowPopup)    ←  Binding a show
                                                            menu event
    def OnShowPopup(self, event):    ←  Displaying the pop-up
        pos = event.GetPosition()
```

```
            pos = self.panel.ScreenToClient(pos)
            self.panel.PopupMenu(self.popupmenu, pos)

        def OnPopupItemSelected(self, event):
            item = self.popupmenu.FindItemById(event.GetId())
            text = item.GetText()
            wx.MessageBox("You selected item '%s'" % text)

        def OnExit(self, event):
            self.Close()

if __name__ == "__main__":
    app = wx.PySimpleApp()
    frame = MyFrame()
    frame.Show()
    app.MainLoop()
```

The pop-up menu is created like any other menu (notice the use of a `for` loop to quickly create the menu items). Instead of being appended to the menu bar, it is stored in the instance variable `self.popupmenu`. Then the frame binds the method `OnShowPopup()` to the event `wx.EVT_CONTEXT_MENU`. The event `wx.EVT_CONTEXT_MENU` is triggered by whatever the standard mechanism is for triggering a pop-up menu on the underlying operating system. Under MS Windows and GTK, the mechanism is a right mouse click, under the Mac OS, it's a control click.

When the user performs a pop-up-triggering click on the frame, the `OnShowPopup()` handler method is called. The first thing this method does is determine the position to display the menu. The event position given in the `wx.ContextMenuEvent` instance passed to this method is stored in absolute screen coordinates, so we need to convert the coordinates to be relative to the panel which contains the pop-up, using the method `ScreenToClient()`.

After that the pop-up menu is invoked with the method `PopupMenu(menu, pos)` or you can use the related method `PopupMenuXY(menu, x, y)`. The `PopupMenu` function does not return until either a menu item has been selected or the menu is dismissed by pressing escape or clicking outside the menu region. If a menu item is selected, its event is processed normally (meaning that it needs to have a method bound to `EVT_MENU`), and the event processing is also completed before the `PopupMenu` method returns. The return value of `PopupMenu` is an uninteresting Boolean, so the only mechanism for responding to the selected item is the ordinary menu event mechanism.

A pop-up menu can have a title that displays at the top of the menu when it is activated. The title is manipulated with the properties `wx.Menu.SetTitle(title)` and `wx.Menu.GetTitle()`.

10.3.3 *How can I create fancier menus?*

If ordinary menu items aren't interesting enough for you, you can add a custom bitmap to be displayed next to the menu item (or used as a custom check symbol). Under MS Windows, you can also adjust the font and color of the menu item. Figure 10.7 displays a fancy menu example.

Listing 10.10 displays the code to produce the menu. To determine whether the program is running under Windows, you can check that `'wxMSW'` is in the `wx.PlatformInfo` tuple.

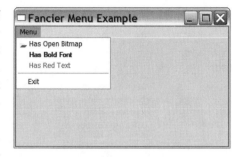

Figure 10.7   Menu items with custom bitmaps, colors, and fonts

---

Listing 10.10   Sample code for fancier menu items

```python
import wx

class MyFrame(wx.Frame):
    def __init__(self):
        wx.Frame.__init__(self, None, -1,
                          "Fancier Menu Example")
        p = wx.Panel(self)
        menu = wx.Menu()

        bmp = wx.Bitmap("open.png", wx.BITMAP_TYPE_PNG)
        item = wx.MenuItem(menu, -1, "Has Open Bitmap")
        item.SetBitmap(bmp)          ◁─┐ Adding a custom bitmap
        menu.AppendItem(item)

        if 'wxMSW' in wx.PlatformInfo:
            font = wx.SystemSettings.GetFont(
                wx.SYS_DEFAULT_GUI_FONT)
            font.SetWeight(wx.BOLD)
            item = wx.MenuItem(menu, -1, "Has Bold Font")
            item.SetFont(font)       ◁─┐ Changing the font
            menu.AppendItem(item)

            item = wx.MenuItem(menu, -1, "Has Red Text")
            item.SetTextColour("red")   ◁─┐ Changing the text color
            menu.AppendItem(item)

        menu.AppendSeparator()
        exit = menu.Append(-1, "Exit")
        self.Bind(wx.EVT_MENU, self.OnExit, exit)
```

```
        menuBar = wx.MenuBar()
        menuBar.Append(menu, "Menu")
        self.SetMenuBar(menuBar)

    def OnExit(self, event):
        self.Close()

if __name__ == "__main__":
    app = wx.PySimpleApp()
    frame = MyFrame()
    frame.Show()
    app.MainLoop()
```

Adding color or style to a menu item is primarily a matter of manipulating the properties that control the display. The only property that is applicable on a platform other than Windows is the bitmap, managed by `GetBitmap()`, that returns an item of type `wx.Bitmap`. There are two setters. The first, which works on all platforms, is `SetBitmap(bmp)`. This sets a bitmap displayed next to the menu item at all times. If you are on MS Windows and want to set custom bitmaps for a toggle menu, you can use `SetBitmaps(checked, unchecked=wx.NullBitmap)`, which creates one bitmap to be displayed when the item is checked, and one when it is unchecked. If the menu item is not a toggle, the `checked` argument is unused.

Under MS Windows, there are three other properties that you can change to affect menu item appearance, as listed in table 10.7. We recommend that you use these with caution, and only in cases where they would clearly enhance the user experience.

Table 10.7   Menu item appearance properties

Methods	Description
GetBackgroundColour() SetBackgroundColour(colour)	The property type is `wx.Colour`, the setter can also be passed a string which is the name of a wxPython color. Manages the background color of the item.
GetFont() SetFont(font)	The display font of the item. Type is `wx.Font`.
GetTextColour() SetTextColour(colour)	Manages the color of the text in the item display. Type as in background color.

Now that we've covered the functional aspects of using menus, we'll close the chapter with a brief discussion of how to use menus well and how to make your application easier for your users.

10.4 Usability guidelines for menus

For most complex applications, the menu bar is the user's primary point of contact with the application's functionality. Getting the menu right can go a long way toward making the application easier to use; getting it wrong can make your application impossible to navigate. With that in mind, here are some guidelines for usability in menu design.

10.4.1 Keeping menus uniform in length

Scanning the applications you use on a regular basis suggests that the upper bound on menu length is about 10-15 items before the user's eyes start to glaze over. Longer menus should definitely be split up. You should lean toward creating menus that are roughly the same length, keeping in mind that it's not always possible or desirable.

10.4.2 Creating logical item groups

You should never have a grouping of more than five items without a separator, unless there's a very strong logical reason to do so—such as a history list, or a list of plugins. Groups of more than five items tend to be very difficult for people to process. To have a larger group, the items would need to be very strongly linked together and have a reason why the user would expect the list to be longer than five items.

Adhere to standards when ordering menus

You should always stick to the accepted standard for menu ordering. The leftmost menu is FILE, and it contains new, open, save, print, and quit functionality, usually in that order, although other functionality is often added between printing and quitting. Nearly every application will use that functionality. The next menu is EDIT, and it contains undo, cut, copy, paste, and usually find, depending on what is appropriate for your application. The HELP menu is always rightmost, and a windows menu is frequently next to that. In between, you are generally on your own.

Provide easy access to commonly-used items

The user will always be able to access items that are higher in the menu more quickly than those at the bottom. The implication is that more commonly used options should be at the top. An exception is that most studies show that it's faster to hit the second item than the first.

Use informative menu names

Remember that the width of the menu target on the menu bar is proportional to the length of the name, and the width of the menu when it opens is proportional to the longest name of the items within it. Try to avoid giving top-level menus names shorter than four letters. Except for common names, we recommend that they be longer whenever possible, without being unclear. Don't be afraid to give a menu item longer text, although at about the 30-40 character range they become hard to read.

Remember the ellipsis when an item leads to a dialog

Any menu item that results in a dialog box being displayed should have a label that ends in an ellipsis (. . .).

Adhere to standard keyboard shortcuts

For keyboard shortcuts, always use the accepted standards for common functionality, as displayed in table 10.8.

There is no commonly accepted shortcut for Redo, you'll sometimes see `Ctrl-y`, `Alt-z`, or another combination. If you are providing many keyboard shortcuts beyond the common set, it's recommended that you provide the user with an option to change them. Keyboard shortcuts are most valuable in an application where the user is doing a lot of typing, such as a text editor. They are less valuable in an application where the user is doing a lot of mouse work.

Table 10.8   Common keyboard shortcuts

Shortcut	Function
Ctrl-a	Select all
Ctrl-c	Copy
Ctrl-f	Find
Ctrl-g	Find Again
Ctrl-n	New
Ctrl-o	Open
Ctrl-p	Print
Ctrl-q	Quit
Ctrl-s	Save
Ctrl-v	Paste
Ctrl-w	Close
Ctrl-x	Cut
Ctrl-z	Undo

Reflect the active toggle state

When creating a toggle menu item, there are a couple of things to be careful about. First, remember that an unchecked checkbox menu item looks identical to a normal menu item. If the item text says something like *fancy mode on*, the user may not know that selecting the menu item actually changes fancy mode. Another concern is having the item text reflect the state that is not currently active, rather than the one that is. This happens when you use the menu text to say what the selection does, for example saying *Turn fancy mode off* if fancy mode is on. There is no statement in the menu indicating what the state of fancy mode actually is, which can be confusing. To avoid this problem, it's a good idea to have a custom bitmap for unchecked menus (on platforms which allow this) to give the user a visual cue that the menu is a toggle. If you can't do that, text like *toggle fancy mode* or *switch fancy mode* (*now on*) can be clearer.

Use nesting cautiously

Nested hierarchical menus can be awkward to navigate, since they force the user to tunnel the mouse pointer through a narrow alley, then swerve at a 90-degree angle. You definitely want to avoid having more than one layer of nesting. If you are trying to map something that is genuinely tree-like, such as a directory tree, you may want to consider a separate dialog box with a tree control. Also, if you think your user population is going to have any kind of accessibility or coordination issues, try to avoid nested menus.

Avoid using font or color

Can you remember any application ever making use of font or color in its menu items? Neither do we (with the exception of menus whose purpose is to select a font or color). Definitely for use only in very rare cases.

10.5 *Summary*

- Menus are the most commonly used mechanism for allowing the user to trigger commands in a GUI application. Menus in wxPython are created using three primary classes, `wx.MenuBar`, which represents the menu bar and contains menus, represented by `wx.Menu`. The menu is made up of menu items, represented by `wx.MenuItem`. To build a menu bar, the menu bar item is created and attached to a frame. Each individual menu is created, and menu items are added to it. Then the menu is added to the menu bar. Items can be added at any place in the menu. An item can also be a menu separator, rather than a normal menu item. Menu item objects can be created explicitly or implicitly created when the item is added to the parent menu.

- Selecting a menu triggers a command event with the type `wx.EVT_MENU`. Menu events are bound via the containing frame, not via the menu item, menu, or menu bar. This allows toolbar buttons to trigger the same `wx.EVT_MENU` event as a menu item. If you have multiple menu items with consecutive identifiers that all have the same handler, they can be bound in one call using the event type `wx.EVT_MENU_RANGE`.

- Menu items can be found by ID or by label from either the containing menu or the containing menu bar. A menu item can also be enabled or disabled from its containing menu or menu bar.

- A menu can be attached to another menu rather than the menu bar, making it a nested submenu. There are specific methods of wx.Menu which allow you to add a submenu in the same way that a typical menu item is added.

- Menus can be associated with keys in two ways. A mnemonic is the keyboard menu navigation triggered when the user presses the ALT key. When in mnemonic mode, the key presses trigger the appropriate menu or menu item. Mnemonics are created by inserting an ampersand before the appropriate character when creating the menu. A true accelerator key can be created to bind a key combination to a menu item. This information can also be included when the menu item is created. The decorators for keyboard shortcuts are ignored for the purposes of finding a menu item by name.

- A menu item can have a toggle state. It can be a checkbox menu item, which switches from a checked to unchecked state and vice-versa when selected. The item can also be a radio menu item, in which case it is part of a group, only one of which can be in the checked state at a time. The checked state of a menu item can also be queried or changed via the menu bar or containing menu.

- A menu can be created to pop up on a click inside a wxPython widget, rather than pulling down from the menu bar. This is done by trapping the event type wx.EVT_CONTEXT_MENU, and using the method PopupMenu() to display the pop-up. Menu item events within the pop-up are handled normally.

- You can create a custom bitmap for a menu item, and under Windows operating systems, you can change the color and font of a menu item. Common sense should dictate the use of this feature.

Placing widgets
with sizers

This chapter covers

- Understanding sizers
- Spacing widgets in sizers
- Using the grid family of sizers
- Using box sizers
- Looking at sizers in action

Traditionally, one of the most vexing problems in programming a UI is managing the physical layout of the widgets within the window. In the beginning, there was absolute positioning, and the programmer would explicitly set the size and position of each widget on the screen. This is—to put it mildly—tedious, not to mention a pain in the neck. Even worse, absolute positioning only works if you have absolute control over the window size and number of widgets. If you allow the user to do something wild and crazy like make his text-entry widget bigger by resizing the window, you need to capture the window-resize event, then explicitly change the size and position of each widget. While you're doing that, make sure that the widgets still look good and don't overlap or fall off the edge of the window. This is even more of a pain in the neck and it gets worse if the user's interaction normally changes the number and type of widgets in the display. And, of course, if you or your client decide you want a different interface look, you have to go through the whole process all over again.

What you need is a structure that decides how to resize and move the widgets based on a predetermined pattern. There have been several solutions proposed to this problem. There is even a deprecated mechanism or two in the wxPython system. The recommended way to deal with complicated layout these days is by using a *sizer*. A sizer is an automated algorithm for laying out a group of widgets. A sizer is attached to a container, usually a frame or panel. Subwidgets that are created within a parent container must be separately added to the sizer. When the sizer is attached to the container, it then manages the layout of the children contained inside it.

The advantages of using a sizer are substantial. The sizer will automatically respond by recalculating the layout of its children when its container's size is changed. Similarly, if one of the children changes size, the sizer can automatically refresh the layout. Furthermore, sizers are easy to manage when you want to change the layout. The biggest downside is that the layouts sizers enforce can be somewhat restrictive. However, the most flexible sizers, the *grid bag* and *box*, will be able to do nearly everything you'll want them to.

11.1 What's a sizer?

A wxPython sizer is an object whose sole purpose is to manage the layout of a set of widgets within a container. The sizer is not a container or a widget itself. It is just the representation of an algorithm for laying out a screen. All sizers are instances of a subclass of the abstract class `wx.Sizer`. There are five sizers provided with wxPython, defined in table 11.1. Remember, sizers can be placed inside other sizers to give you even more flexibility.

Table 11.1   The predefined sizers in wxPython

Sizer Type	Description	
Grid	A very basic grid layout. Best used when the widgets you are placing are all exactly the same size and neatly fall into a regular grid.	326
Flex grid	A slight change from the grid sizer, allowing better results when the widgets are different sizes.	337
Grid bag	The most flexible member of the grid sizer family, allowing for more arbitrary placement of widgets in the grid. Useful for layouts where the display can be thought of as an irregular grid, with perhaps some items that take up more than one grid square.	341
Box	Either a horizontal or vertical box with widgets laid out in a line. Very flexible in controlling widget behavior when resized. Generally used in a nested fashion. Useful for nearly any kind of layout, although figuring out exactly how to nest the boxes can be tricky.	345
Static box	A standard box sizer with a line and a title around it.	349

If you want your layout to be grid- or box-like, wxPython can definitely accommodate; in practice almost any useful layout can be imagined as either a grid or a set of boxes.

All sizers know the minimal size of each of their children. Typically, the sizer also allows for additional information about the layout, such as how much space to place between widgets, how much it can increase the size of a widget to fill space, and how to align widgets when they are smaller than their allotted space. From these bits of information the sizer uses its layout algorithm to determine the size and position of each child. Each kind of sizer in wxPython will produce a different final layout from the same group of child widgets. You can see this throughout this chapter, as we use very similar layouts to demonstrate each sizer type.

There are three basic steps you take to use a sizer:

1   Add the sizer to a container. Connect the sizer to the widget whose children it is managing. A sizer is added to the container widget using the method SetSizer(sizer) of wx.Window. Since this is a method of wx.Window, this means that any wxPython widget can have a sizer, although a sizer is only meaningful for widgets which are containers.

2   Add each child widget to the sizer. All of the child widgets need to be separately added to the sizer. Merely creating child widgets with the container as a parent is *not* enough. The primary method for adding a widget

to a sizer is, appropriately enough, `Add()`. The `Add()` method has a couple of different signatures, which will be discussed in the next section.

3   (optional) Enable the sizer to calculate its size. Tell the sizer to calculate its size based on its children by calling either the `wx.Window` method `Fit()` on the parent window object or the `Fit(window)` method of the sizer. (The window method redirects to the sizer method.) In either case, the `Fit()` method asks the sizer to calculate its size based on what it knows about its children, and it resizes the parent widget to fit. There is a related method, `FitInside()`, which does not change the display size of the parent widget, but does change its virtual size—meaning that if the widget is inside a scrolled panel, wxPython would recalculate whether or not scroll bars are needed.

At this point we need to discuss both the behavior of specific sizers as well as the behavior common to all sizers. There's always a question whether to present the general or specific information first. Our solution is to start by presenting the grid sizer, which is the easiest to understand. After that, we'll discuss behavior common to all sizers, using the grid sizer as an example. (It helps that most of the common behaviors are very easy to visualize using the grid sizer as an example.) After that, we'll show the rest of the specific sizer types.

11.2 *Basic sizers with the grid sizer*

All of the following examples use a boring little widget whose goal is to take up space in a layout so you can see how the sizers work. Listing 11.1 gives the code for that widget, which is imported by the rest of the examples in this chapter. You'll see plenty of pictures of it throughout—it's basically a simple rectangle with a label.

> **Listing 11.1   The block window, used as a widget in later examples**

```
import wx

class BlockWindow(wx.Panel):
    def __init__(self, parent, ID=-1, label="",
                 pos=wx.DefaultPosition, size=(100, 25)):
        wx.Panel.__init__(self, parent, ID, pos, size,
                          wx.RAISED_BORDER, label)
        self.label = label
        self.SetBackgroundColour("white")
```

compare 538

```
        self.SetMinSize(size)
        self.Bind(wx.EVT_PAINT, self.OnPaint)

    def OnPaint(self, evt):
        sz = self.GetClientSize()
        dc = wx.PaintDC(self)
        w,h = dc.GetTextExtent(self.label)
        dc.SetFont(self.GetFont())
        dc.DrawText(self.label, (sz.width-w)/2, (sz.height-h)/2)
```

center text

We'll be placing several of these block widgets inside a frame using different sizers throughout this chapter. We'll start with the grid sizer.

11.2.1 *What is a grid sizer?*

The simplest sizer offered by wxPython is the grid. As the name implies, a grid sizer places its children in a two-dimensional grid. The first widget in the sizer's child list goes in the upper left corner of the grid, and the rest are laid out left-to-right and top-to-bottom, until the last widget is placed in the bottom right of the grid. Figure 11.1 shows an example, with nine widgets placed in a 3 x 3 grid. Notice that there is a slight gap between each widget.

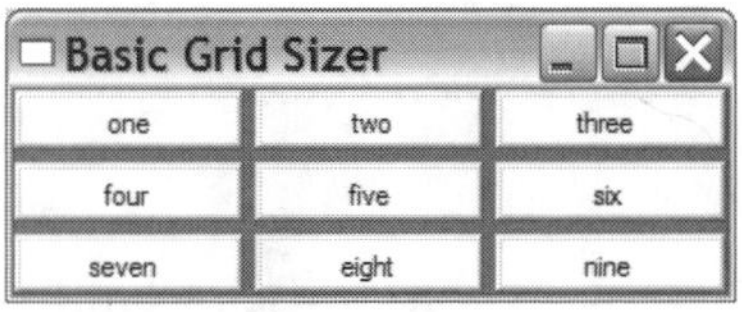

Figure 11.1
A simple grid sizer layout

When you resize the grid sizer, each slot gets bigger, but by default the widgets stay the same size, and stay attached to the top left corner of their assigned slot. Figure 11.2 shows the same window after being resized.

Listing 11.2 shows the code used to generate figures 11.1 and 11.2.

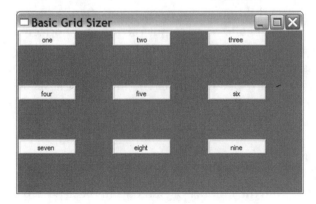

Figure 11.2
The grid sizer layout,
made bigger by the user

Listing 11.2   Using a grid sizer

```
import wx
from blockwindow import BlockWindow

labels = "one two three four five six seven eight nine".split()

class GridSizerFrame(wx.Frame):
    def __init__(self):
        wx.Frame.__init__(self, None, -1, "Basic Grid Sizer")
        sizer = wx.GridSizer(rows=3, cols=3, hgap=5, vgap=5)   ◁┐ Create the
        for label in labels:                                     │ grid sizer
            bw = BlockWindow(self, label=label)
            sizer.Add(bw, 0, 0)   ◁— Add widget to sizer
        self.SetSizer(sizer)   ◁┐ Associate sizer
        self.Fit()              │ with frame

app = wx.PySimpleApp()
GridSizerFrame().Show()
app.MainLoop()
```

As you can see from listing 11.2, a grid sizer is an instance of the class wx.Grid-Sizer. The constructor explicitly sets the four properties which are unique to the grid sizer:

```
wx.GridSizer(rows, cols, vgap, hgap)
```

In this constructor rows and cols are integers that specify the size of the grid—the number of widgets to be placed across and down. If either is set to 0, its value is inferred from the number of children in the sizer. For example, if the sizer created with the constructor wx.GridSizer(2, 0, 0, 0) has eight children, it will need to have four columns to fit the children in two rows, as specified.

The vgap and hgap parameters allow you to put vertical and horizontal space between the widgets. The vgap is the number of pixels to place between adjacent columns, and the hgap is the number of pixels to place between adjacent rows. These pixels are in addition to any pixels specified by the widget as its border, as we'll see in a couple more sections. The properties rows, cols, vgap, and hgap all have their getter and setter methods—GetRows(), SetRows(rows), GetCols(), Set-Cols(cols), GetVGap(), SetVGap(gap), GetHGap(), and SetHGap(gap).

The sizing and placement algorithm of the grid sizer is straightforward. It creates its initial grid layout when Fit() is first called. If necessary, the number of rows and columns are calculated from the number of elements in the list. Each space in the grid is the same size—even if the size of each widget is different. The largest dimension is used to calculate the size—each space in the grid is as wide as the widest child and as tall as the tallest child. Because of this, a grid sizer is best suited for layouts where the children are naturally all the same size (a calculator keypad is a classic example). A grid sizer with wildly different sized widgets tends to look a little odd. If you still want a grid-like layout, but you have different sized widgets, you will probably be better off looking at either the *flex grid sizer* or the *grid bag sizer*.

11.2.2 *How do you add or remove children from a sizer?*

The order in which child widgets are added to the sizer is very important. This is different from the general case of adding children to a parent widget. The typical layout algorithm for a sizer takes each child one at a time in order to determine its place in the display. The placement of the next item is dependent on where the previous items have already gone. For example, the grid sizer moves left to right and top to bottom based on the order of the widgets. In most cases, when you create the sizer in the parent widget constructor, you will be able to add the items in the correct order. However, in some cases, you'll need more flexibility, particularly if you are dynamically changing your layout at runtime.

Using the Add() method

The most common method for adding a widget to a sizer is `Add()`, which appends the new widget to the end of the sizer's child list. The exact meaning of being at the end of the list depends on the sizer type, but in general it means that the new widget will display toward the lower right of the display. The `Add()` method has three distinct styles:

```
Add(window, proportion=0, flag=0, border=0, userData=None)
Add(sizer, proportion=0, flag=0, border=0, userData=None)
Add(size, proportion=0, flag=0, border=0, userData=None)
```

The first version is the one you will use most often, and it allows you to append a widget to the sizer. The second version is used to nest one sizer inside another—this is most commonly done with box sizers, but you can do it with any sizer type. The third version allows you to add an empty space the size of the `wx.Size` object or `(width, height)` tuple to the sizer, generally used as a separator (for example, in a toolbar). Again, this is most often used in box sizers, but can be used in any sizer to make an area of the window blank or to enforce a separation between the other widgets.

The other parameters affect how the item is displayed within the sizer. Some of these items are only valid for certain sizers. The `proportion` element is only used by box sizers, and affects how much an item is stretched when the parent window changes size. This will be discussed, along with box sizers, later in this chapter.

The `flag` option is a place to put any of a number of bit flags which control alignment, border, and resizing. Those options will be discussed in a later section. The `border` parameter contains the width of the border, if a border is specified in the `flag` option. The `userData` parameter can be used to pass extra data if needed by a sizer for its algorithm. You might use this if you were designing a custom sizer.

Using the Insert() method

As you might expect if you've read the Menus chapter (chapter 10), there are related methods for inserting the new widget at other places in the sizer. The `Insert()` method allows you to place the new widget at an arbitrary index. It also has three flavors:

```
Insert(index, window, proportion=0, flag=0, border=0, userData=None)
Insert(index, sizer, proportion=0, flag=0, border=0, userData=None)
Insert(index, size, proportion=0, flag=0, border=0, userData=None)
```

Using the Prepend() method

There is also a `Prepend()` method, which adds the new widget, sizer, or space at the beginning of the sizer list, meaning that it will tend to display toward the upper left:

```
Prepend(window, proportion=0, flag=0, border=0, userData=None)
Prepend(sizer, proportion=0, flag=0, border=0, userData=None)
Prepend(size, proportion=0, flag=0, border=0, userData=None)
```

Figure 11.3 shows what the grid layout from listing 11.1 would look like if `Prepend()` had been used instead of `Add()`.

If you add new items to the sizer after it has already been displayed on screen, you need to call the sizer method `Layout()` to force the sizer to rearrange itself to accommodate the new item.

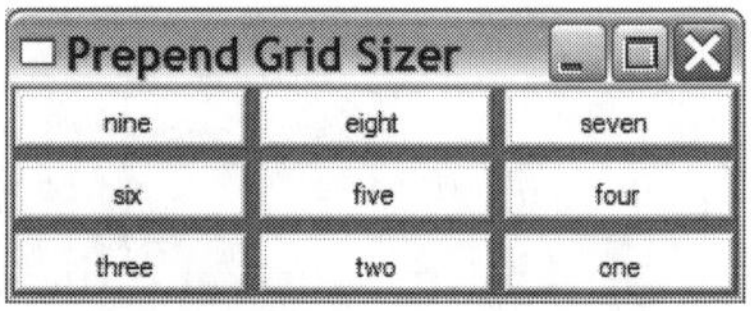

Figure 11.3
A grid layout with items prepended

Using the Detach() method

In order to remove an item from the sizer, you call the `Detach()` method, which removes the item from the sizer, but does not destroy it. This is especially useful if you want to hold on to the item you are removing for potential future use. There are three ways to use `Detach()`. You can pass it the window or sizer object that you want to detach, or you can pass it the integer index of the object:

```
Detach(window)
Detach(sizer)
Detach(index)
```

In all three cases, the `Detach()` method returns a Boolean representing whether the item was actually removed—it will return false if you try to detach an item that is not in the sizer. Unlike some other removal methods we've seen, `Detach()` does not return the item being removed, so if you want to keep it around, you need to already have a variable referencing the object.

Removing the item from the sizer does not change the on-screen display automatically. You need to call the `Layout()` method to force a resize and redraw.

You can always get a reference to the sizer that a window is in by using the `wx.Window` method `GetContainingSizer()`. The method returns `None` if the widget is not contained by a sizer.

11.2.3 How do sizers manage the size and alignment of their children?

When a new item is added to a sizer, the sizer uses either the initial size of the item, or the item's best size if there is no initial size set, in its layout calculations. In other words, the sizer does not adjust the size of an item until the sizer is asked to, usually in the context of a window being resized.

When the sizer parent widget is resized, the sizer needs to change the size of its components in response. By default, the sizer keeps the widget aligned to the top and left of its assigned space in the layout—although the exact specifics of what is considered to be its assigned space vary from sizer to sizer.

You can adjust the resize behavior of a specific widget by assigning specific values to the `flag` parameter when you add the widget to the sizer. Figure 11.4 shows the result of several different flags applied to the basic grid sizer example, after a user makes the window larger.

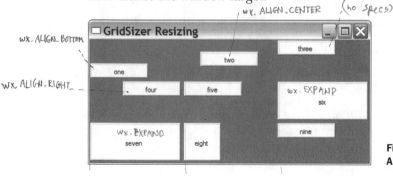

Figure 11.4
A grid with resizing widgets

Listing 11.3 shows the code used to generate figure 11.4. It is identical to the previous listing, except for the addition of a dictionary of flag values to be applied to the widgets as they are added. These values are shown in bold font.

Listing 11.3   A grid sizer with flags for aligment and sizing

```
import wx
from blockwindow import BlockWindow

labels = "one two three four five six seven eight nine".split()
flags = {"one": wx.ALIGN_BOTTOM, "two": wx.ALIGN_CENTER,
         "four": wx.ALIGN_RIGHT, "six": wx.EXPAND, "seven": wx.EXPAND,
         "eight": wx.SHAPED}                              Alignment flags

class TestFrame(wx.Frame):
    def __init__(self):
        wx.Frame.__init__(self, None, -1, "GridSizer Resizing")
        sizer = wx.GridSizer(rows=3, cols=3, hgap=5, vgap=5)
        for label in labels:
            bw = BlockWindow(self, label=label)
            flag = flags.get(label, 0)        φ is default if label not in dict
            sizer.Add(bw, 0, flag)
        self.SetSizer(sizer)
        self.Fit()

app = wx.PySimpleApp()
TestFrame().Show()
app.MainLoop()
```

Resizing, alignment management (margin note)

In this example, widgets "one," "two," and "four" change which part of the grid they align with using the flags wx.ALIGN_BOTTOM, wx.ALIGN_CENTER, and wx.ALIGN_RIGHT, respectively. You can see that as the window is resized, the widgets stay in contact with the side of their slot denoted by the flag (widget "three," which does not specify a flag, stays aligned to the top and left). Widgets "six" and "seven" both use the wx.EXPAND flag to tell the sizer to change their size to fill the available space, while widget "eight" uses wx.SHAPED to change its size while retaining a consistent proportion.

Table 11.2 shows the possible values of flag which are relevant for sizing and alignment.

Since these flags are a bitmask, they can be combined using |, in cases where that combination would be meaningful. So, wx.ALIGN_TOP | wx.ALIGN_RIGHT keeps the widget in the top right corner of its space. (Note that mutually exclusive values such as wx.ALIGN_TOP | wx.ALIGN_BOTTOM will always resolve to the non-default

Table 11.2   Size and alignment behavior flags

Flag	Description
wx.ALIGN_BOTTOM	Aligns the widget to the bottom of its allotted space.
wx.ALIGN_CENTER	Places the widget so that the center of the widget is in the center of its allotted space.
wx.ALIGN_CENTER_HORIZONTAL	Places the widget so that it is centered horizontally in its allotted space.
wx.ALIGN_CENTER_VERTICAL	Places the widget so that it is centered vertically in its allotted space.
wx.ALIGN_LEFT	Aligns the widget so that it is against the left edge of its allotted space. This is the default behavior.
wx.ALIGN_TOP	Aligns the widget so that it is against the top edge of its allotted space. This is the default behavior.
wx.EXPAND	Changes the size of the widget to fill its allotted space any time the size of the parent window changes.
wx.FIXED_MINSIZE	Causes the sizer to keep the minimum size of the item fixed, rather that checking if the item's best size has changed each time the sizer does a Layout().
wx.GROW	The same as wx.EXPAND but two whole characters shorter. Think of all the time you'll save!
wx.SHAPED	Changes the size of the widget such that it fills its allotted space along one dimension, and the other dimension is filled in proportion to the original shape of the widget. The proportional size of the smaller dimension cannot exceed the amount of space given to the widget by the sizer.

(also, wx.ALIGN_RIGHT)

← ?

value. This is because the default values are integer 0 and would not change the value of the other operand in a bitwise or operation.)

There are a few methods that you can use to manipulate the size and positioning of a sizer or its component widgets at runtime. You can obtain the current size and position of the sizer itself using the methods GetSize() and GetPosition()—the position is relative to the container that the sizer is associated with. This is most helpful if the sizer is nested inside another sizer. You can force a sizer to take on a specific size by calling the method SetDimension(x, y, width, height). After this method is called, the sizer recalculates the size of its children based on its new size and position.

11.2.4 *Can I specify a minimum size for my sizer or its children?*

Another important factor in the layout of widgets within a sizer is the ability to
specify a minimum size for the sizer itself or for any of its children. Often, you
don't want a control or a sizer to get smaller than a particular size, usually because
it will cause text to be cut off by the edge of the widget. Or, in the case of a nested
sizer, an entire widget might no longer be displayed inside the window. Given
their normal placement within a dialog, the OK and Cancel buttons are common
candidates for falling off the edge of a frame this way. Few things are more frus-
trating for a user than having the buttons for dismissing a dialog disappear. Luckily, you can use the specified minimum size to prevent this from happening.

Figure 11.5 shows an example of setting the minimum size for a specific widget. This window has not been resized by a user.

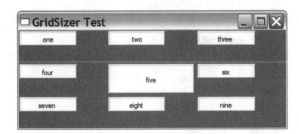

**Figure 11.5
A grid sizer with the size
of one item set explicitly**

Listing 11.4 shows the code to create this figure. It is similar to the basic grid code
with the addition of a single call to SetMinSize().

Listing 11.4   A grid sizer with a minimum size set

```
import wx
from blockwindow import BlockWindow

labels = "one two three four five six seven eight nine".split()

class TestFrame(wx.Frame):
    def __init__(self):
        wx.Frame.__init__(self, None, -1, "GridSizer Test")
        sizer = wx.GridSizer(rows=3, cols=3, hgap=5, vgap=5)
        for label in labels:
            bw = BlockWindow(self, label=label)
            sizer.Add(bw, 0, 0)
        center = self.FindWindowByName("five")
        center.SetMinSize((150,50))
        self.SetSizer(sizer)
```

```
        self.Fit()
app = wx.PySimpleApp()
TestFrame().Show()
app.MainLoop()
```

ie, widget or window (?)

When a sizer is created, it implicitly creates a minimum size based on the combined minimum size of its children. Most controls know their minimum "best size," and the sizers query that value to determine the defaults of the layout. If the control is created with a size explicitly set, that size overrides the control's default calculation of its minimum best size. The minimum size of a control can also be set using the window methods SetMinSize(width, height) and SetSizeHints (minW, minH, maxW, maxH)—the latter method allowing you to specify a maximum size as well. A widget will usually adjust its best size if attributes of that widget— typically the display font or label text—change.

✗ @353

The best size of a container window is determined from its sizer if the window has one. If not, the window's best size is whatever is required to be large enough to show all its children at their current size. If the window has no children, its minimum size is used if set. If all else fails, the current size of the container window is used as its best size.

✗

You can access the minimum size for the entire sizer with GetMinSize(). If you want to set a larger minimum size for the entire sizer, you do it using SetMinSize (width, height), which you can also invoke with a wx.Size instance—SetMin-Size(size), although in wxPython you'd rarely explicitly create a wx.Size. After the minimum size has been set, GetMinSize() returns either the explicit size or the combined size of the children, whichever is larger.

✗

If you want only to set the minimum size of a specific child within the sizer, use the SetItemMinSize() method of the sizer. Like Detach(), there are three ways to invoke SetItemMinSize(), with a window, a sizer, or an index:

330

(sizer methods)

```
SetItemMinSize(window, size)   # window is child of sizer being invoked
SetItemMinSize(sizer, size)    # sizer    "    "     "     "     "
SetItemMinSize(index, size)    # index identifies child in the list of sizer's children
```

In this case, the window or sizer being set must be a child of the sizer instance being invoked. The method will search through the entire nested tree of sizers looking for the specific subwindow or subsizer if needed. The index is the index in the list of the sizer's children. The size parameter, either a wx.Size object or a (width, height) tuple, is the explicit minimum size of the item within the sizer. If the minimum size as you set it is greater than the current size of the widget, it is automatically resized. You can't set the maximum size from the sizer, only from the widget using SetSizeHints().

11.2.5 *How do sizers manage the border around each child?*

A wxPython sizer can place a border around any or all of its children. The border is a consistent amount of empty space separating the widget from its neighbors. The size of the border is taken into account when the sizer calculates the placement of its children—the child is not made smaller to accommodate the width of the border. The size of the border does not change when the sizer resizes.

Figure 11.6 shows a 10-pixel border placed around all or part of the widgets in our basic grid layout. In each row, the middle element has the border around all four sides, while the other widgets have a border around only some sides. Adding the border does not make the widgets smaller; rather, it makes the frame larger.

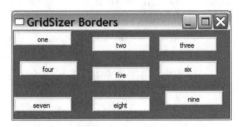

Figure 11.6 The grid sizer with a border

Listing 11.5 has the code relevant to figure 11.6. Again, it's similar to the basic grid sizer, but now we've added a dictionary of border values, and a 10-pixel border argument to the Add() statement.

Listing 11.5 The grid sizer code with borders

border management

```
import wx
from blockwindow import BlockWindow

labels = "one two three four five six seven eight nine".split()
flags = {"one": wx.BOTTOM, "two": wx.ALL, "three": wx.TOP,
         "four": wx.LEFT, "five": wx.ALL, "six": wx.RIGHT,           Border
         "seven": wx.BOTTOM | wx.TOP, "eight": wx.ALL,               flags
         "nine": wx.LEFT | wx.RIGHT}

class TestFrame(wx.Frame):
    def __init__(self):
        wx.Frame.__init__(self, None, -1, "GridSizer Borders")
        sizer = wx.GridSizer(rows=3, cols=3, hgap=5, vgap=5)
        for label in labels:
            bw = BlockWindow(self, label=label)
            flag = flags.get(label, 0)
            sizer.Add(bw, 0, flag, 10)         Adding widgets with
        self.SetSizer(sizer)                   border specified
        self.Fit()
```

```
app = wx.PySimpleApp()
TestFrame().Show()
app.MainLoop()
```

Putting a border around a widget inside a sizer is a two-step process. The first step is to pass additional flags to the `flags` parameter when the widget is added to the sizer. You can specify a border around the entire widget using the flag `wx.ALL`, or you can border on a specific side using `wx.BOTTOM`, `wx.LEFT`, `wx.RIGHT`, or `wx.TOP`. Naturally, the flags can be combined for any set of border sides you would like, such as `wx.RIGHT | wx.BOTTOM` which would give you a border on the right and bottom sides of the widget. Since border, sizing, and alignment information is all sent via the same `flags` parameter, you will often have to use the bitwise or operation to combine border information with sizing and alignment information for the same widget.

After you send the border information to the `flags` parameter, you also need to pass the width of the border, in pixels, to the `border` parameter. For example, the following call will add the widget to the end of the sizer list, placing a five pixel border around the whole thing:

```
sizer.Add(widget, 0, wx.ALL | wx.EXPAND, 5)
```

The widget will then expand to fill its available space, always leaving five blank pixels around it.

11.3 *Using the other sizer types*

Having covered the basics, we can move on to the more complicated and flexible sizer options. Two of these options—the flex grid sizer and grid bag sizer—are essentially variations on the grid theme. The other two—the box and static box sizers—use a different and more flexible layout structure.

11.3.1 *What's a flex grid sizer?*

A flex grid sizer is a more flexible version of a grid sizer. It is nearly identical to the regular grid sizer, with the following exceptions:

- It determines a separate size for each row and column.
- By default, it does not change the size of its cells when resized. You can specify which rows or columns should grow if needed.

- It can grow flexibly in either direction, meaning that you can specify proportional amounts for individual child elements, and you can specify the behavior in the non-flexible direction.

Figure 11.7 shows a flex grid sizer in action, using the same nine-cell layout as used for the basic grid sizer. In this case, the center cell has been made larger.

@ 334

Compare this image to figure 11.5, showing the same layout in an ordinary grid sizer. In the ordinary grid sizer, each cell is the same size as the middle object.

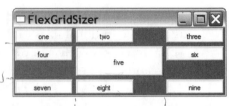

Figure 11.7 A simple flex grid sizer

In the flex grid sizer, cells are sized according to the row and column they are part of. They take the width of the widest item in their column and the height of the tallest item in their row. In this case, the cells for items "four" and "six" are taller, because they are in the same row as item "five," while the cells for "two" and "seven" are wider. The cells for "one," "three," "seven," and "nine" are the normal size, and are unaffected by the larger widget.

Figure 11.8 shows the default behavior of a flex grid sizer when resized, which is that the size of the cells is unchanged.

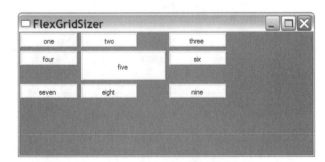

**Figure 11.8
A flex grid sizer being resized.**

Listing 11.6 shows the code for creating the image in figure 11.8.

Listing 11.6 Creating a flex grid sizer

```
import wx
from blockwindow import BlockWindow

labels = "one two three four five six seven eight nine".split()

class TestFrame(wx.Frame):
    def __init__(self):
```

```
        wx.Frame.__init__(self, None, -1, "FlexGridSizer")
        sizer = wx.FlexGridSizer(rows=3, cols=3, hgap=5, vgap=5)
        for label in labels:
            bw = BlockWindow(self, label=label)
            sizer.Add(bw, 0, 0)
        center = self.FindWindowByName("five")
        center.SetMinSize((150,50))
        self.SetSizer(sizer)
        self.Fit()               p 33

app = wx.PySimpleApp()
TestFrame().Show()
app.MainLoop()
```

A flex grid sizer is an instance of wx.FlexGridSizer. The class wx.FlexGridSizer is
a subclass of wx.GridSizer, so the property methods of wx.GridSizer are still
available. The constructor for wx.FlexGridSizer is identical to the parent class:

```
    wx.FlexGridSizer(rows, cols, vgap, hgap)
```

In order to have a row or column grow when the sizer grows, you need to
explicitly tell the sizer that the row or column is growable by using the appropriate method: 0-based

```
    AddGrowableCol(idx, proportion=0)
    AddGrowableRow(idx, proportion=0)
```

When the sizer grows horizontally, the default behavior is for the new width to be
allocated equally to each growable column. Similarly, a vertical resize is allocated
equally to each growable row. To change the default behavior and make rows or
columns grow at different rates, you use the proportion argument to the add
growable methods. If the proportion element is used, then the new space is allocated to the row or column relative to their proportion arguments. For example,
if you have two resizable rows, and their proportions are 2 and 1, then the first
row will get 2/3 of the new space, and the second row will get 1/3. Figure 11.9
shows the flex grid sizer with proportional spacing. In this case, the middle row
and column have proportion 2, and the end rows and columns have proportion 1.
Figure 11.9 shows what that looks like in practice.

As you can see, while all the cells have gotten larger, the middle row and column have gotten larger twice as fast as the ends. The widgets have not resized to
fill the cells, although they could if the wx.EXPAND flag had been used when they
were added to the sizer. Listing 11.7 shows the code used to create the flex grid
sizer—notice the use of the add growable methods.

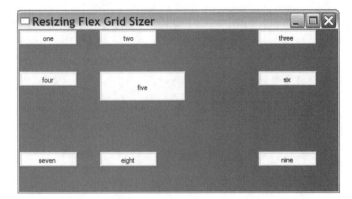

Figure 11.9
A flex grid sizer with a growable row and column

Listing 11.7   The flex grid sizer with growable elements

```python
import wx
from blockwindow import BlockWindow

labels = "one two three four five six seven eight nine".split()

class TestFrame(wx.Frame):
    def __init__(self):
        wx.Frame.__init__(self, None, -1, "Resizing Flex Grid Sizer")
        sizer = wx.FlexGridSizer(rows=3, cols=3, hgap=5, vgap=5)
        for label in labels:
            bw = BlockWindow(self, label=label)
            sizer.Add(bw, 0, 0)
        center = self.FindWindowByName("five")
        center.SetMinSize((150,50))
        sizer.AddGrowableCol(0, 1)
        sizer.AddGrowableCol(1, 2)
        sizer.AddGrowableCol(2, 1)
        sizer.AddGrowableRow(0, 1)
        sizer.AddGrowableRow(1, 5)
        sizer.AddGrowableRow(2, 1)
        self.SetSizer(sizer)
        self.Fit()

app = wx.PySimpleApp()
TestFrame().Show()
app.MainLoop()
```

 # row 0 : proportion 1
 # etc

If you use proportional sizing on one of your growable rows or columns, you need to specify a proportional amount on all the growables in that direction, otherwise you will get an odd flicker effect on resize as wxPython tries to deal with a proportion of zero.

There is one other mechanism to control widget growth in a flex grid sizer. By default, the proportional sizing applies to both directions of the flex grid; however, you can specify that only one direction should resize proportionally using the method `SetFlexibleDirection(direction)`, where the direction values are `wx.HORIZONTAL`, `wx.VERTICAL`, or `wx.BOTH` (the default). Then you specify the behavior in the other direction using `SetNonFlexibleGrowMode(mode)`. For example, if you call `SetFlexibleDirection(wx.HORIZONTAL)`, the columns behave as specified using `AddGrowableCol()`, and the call to `SetNonFlexibleGrowMode()` defines the behavior of the rows. Table 11.3 shows the available values for the `mode` parameter.

Table 11.3   Non-flexible grow mode values

Mode	Description
wx.FLEX_GROWMODE_ALL	The flex grid resizes all cells in the non-flexible direction equally. This overrides any behavior set using the add growable methods—all cells are resized regardless of their proportion or even whether or not they were specified as growable.
wx.FLEX_GROWMODE_NONE	Cells in the non-flexible direction are not resized, regardless of whether they were specified as growable.
wx.FLEX_GROWMODE_SPECIFIED	The sizer only grows those cells in the non-flexible direction that were specified as growable using the appropriate method. However, the sizer ignores any proportion information and grows all those cells equally. This is the default behavior.

Each of the methods discussed in the previous paragraph has an associated getter, `GetFlexibleDirection()` and `GetNonFlexibleGrowMode()`, which returns the integer flags. To emphasize the point made in the table, any setting specified using these methods supersedes the settings created by `AddGrowableCol()` and `AddGrowableRow()`.

11.3.2   What's a grid bag sizer?

A grid bag sizer is a further enhancement of a flex grid sizer. There are two innovations in the grid bag sizer.

- The ability to add a widget to a specific cell within the grid.
- The ability to have a widget span several cells of the grid (the way that a cell in an HTML table can).

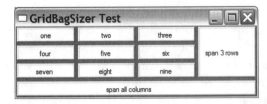

Figure 11.10
A sample grid bag sizer

Figure 11.10 shows a sample grid bag sizer. It's very similar to the example we've been using throughout this chapter, with the addition of new widgets to show a sample of a row span and a column span.

Listing 11.8 shows the code used to generate figure 11.10. Notice that the Add() method looks a little different than before.

Listing 11.8   Grid bag sizer sample code

```
import wx
from blockwindow import BlockWindow

labels = "one two three four five six seven eight nine".split()

class TestFrame(wx.Frame):
    def __init__(self):
        wx.Frame.__init__(self, None, -1, "GridBagSizer Test")
        sizer = wx.GridBagSizer(hgap=5, vgap=5)
        for col in range(3):
            for row in range(3):
                bw = BlockWindow(self, label=labels[row*3 + col])
                sizer.Add(bw, pos=(row,col))                        Widget
                                                                    spanning
        bw = BlockWindow(self, label="span 3 rows")                rows
        sizer.Add(bw, pos=(0,3), span=(3,1), flag=wx.EXPAND)

        bw = BlockWindow(self, label="span all columns")
        sizer.Add(bw, pos=(3,0), span=(1,4), flag=wx.EXPAND)       Widget
                                                                    spanning
        sizer.AddGrowableCol(3)      Make last row                 columns
        sizer.AddGrowableRow(3)      and col growable

        self.SetSizer(sizer)
        self.Fit()

app = wx.PySimpleApp()
TestFrame().Show()

app.MainLoop()
```

The grid bag sizer is an instance of wx.GridBagSizer, which is a child class of wx.FlexGridSizer. This means that all flex grid sizer properties apply here, including the adding of growable rows and columns.

The constructor for wx.GridBagSizer is a little different than its parent classes:

```
wx.GridBagSizer(vgap=0, hgap=0)
```

You don't need to specify the number of rows and columns in a grid bag sizer because you are adding child items directly into specific cells in the grid—the sizer will figure out the grid dimensions from there.

Using the Add() method on a grid bag sizer

The Add() method for grid bag sizers is different than for other sizers. It has four options:

1 Add(window, pos, span=wx.DefaultSpan, flag=0, border=0,
   userData=None)

2 Add(sizer, pos, span=wx.DefaultSpan, flag=0, border=0,
   userData=None)

3 Add(size, pos, span=wx.DefaultSpan, flag=0, border=0,
   userData=None)

4 AddItem(item)

These should look familiar, being operationally similar to the generic sizer methods. The window, sizer, size, flag, border, and userData parameters all behave the same way as in the generic sizer method. The pos element represents the cell within the sizer that the widget is assigned to. Technically, the pos element is an instance of the class wx.GBPosition, but through the magic of wxPython, you can just pass a tuple of the form (row, col), where the upper left of the grid bag is (0, 0).

Similarly, the span parameter represents the number of rows and columns that the widget should take up in the sizer. It is an instance of the class wx.GBSpan, but again, wxPython allows you to pass a tuple of the form (rowspan, colspan). If the span is not specified, the default value is (1, 1), meaning that the widget takes up one cell in each direction. For example, to place a widget in the second row, first column, and have it take up three rows and two columns, you would use the call Add(widget, (1, 0), (3, 2)) (the indexes are zero-based, so the second row has index one, and so forth).

The item parameter of the AddItem method is an instance of the class wx.GBSizerItem, which encapsulates all the information needed for a grid bag sizer to place the item. It's unlikely that you'll need to create a wx.GBSizerItem directly. If you do want to create one, its constructors have the same parameter signature as the other grid bag sizer Add() methods. Once you have a wx.GBSizer-Item, there are a number of getter methods that allow you access to properties of the item, perhaps the most useful of which is GetWindow(), which returns the actual widget being displayed.

Because items are added to a grid bag using the row and column index and spans, the order in which the items are added does not have to correspond to the display order the way that it does in other sizers. This can make it a bit of a headache to keep track of which item is actually displayed in which cell. Table 11.4 lists several ways the grid bag sizer makes it easier for you to track the items.

Table 11.4   Grid bag sizer methods for managing items

Method	Description
CheckForIntersection(item, excludeItem=None) CheckForIntersection(pos, span, excludeItem=None)	Compares the given item or given position and span with all other items in the sizer. Returns True if any of those items overlap the position of the item or the given position and span. The excludeItem is an optional item which is not included in the comparison (perhaps because it is item being tested against). The pos argument is a wx.GBPosition or a tuple. The span argument is a wx.GPSpan or a tuple.
FindItem(window) FindItem(sizer)	Returns the wx.GBSizerItem corresponding to the given window or sizer. Returns None if the window or sizer is not in the grid bag. This method will not recursively check inside subsizers.
FindItemAtPoint(pt)	The pt argument is a wx.Point instance or a Python tuple corresponding to the coordinate of the containing frame. The method returns the wx.GBSizerItem at that point. Returns None if the point is outside frame boundaries or if there is no sizer item at that point.
FindItemAtPosition(pos)	This method returns the wx.GBSizerItem at a given cell position, where pos is a wx.GBPosition or a Python tuple. Returns None if the position is outside the sizer bounds or if there is no item at that position.
FindItemWithData(userData)	Returns the wx.GBSizerItem for an item in the grid bag with the given userData object. Returns None if there is no such object.

Grid bags also have a couple of properties that can be used to manipulate cell size and item position. After the grid bag has been laid out and displayed onscreen you can use the method GetCellSize(row, col) to retrieve the on-screen display size of the given cell. This size includes the horizontal and vertical gap managed by the sizer itself. You can find the size of an empty cell using the method GetEmpty-CellSize(), and you can change that property with SetEmptyCellSize(sz), where sz is a wx.Size object or a Python tuple.

You can retrieve the position or span of an object that is already in the grid bag with the methods GetItemPosition() and GetItemSpan(). Each method will take a window, a sizer, or an index as the argument. The index argument corresponds to the index in the sizer's Add() list, which is unlikely to be meaningful in a grid bag context. Each method has a corresponding setter, SetItemPosition(window, pos) and SetItemSpan(window, span), in which the first argument can again be a window, sizer, or index, and the second argument is a Python tuple or a wx.GBPosition or wx.GBSpan object.

11.3.3 *What's a box sizer?*

The box sizer is the simplest and most flexible of the sizers provided by wxPython. A box sizer is a single vertical column or horizontal row, with the widgets being laid out in a line from left to right or top to bottom. Although this may sound too simplistic to be of any use, the real power of the box sizer comes from the ability to nest sizers inside each other, giving you the advantage of being able to easily place a different number of items in each row or column. And since each sizer is a separate entity, you have more flexibility in terms of layout. Despite the seeming simplicity, for most applications a vertical sizer with horizontal sizers nested inside will allow you to create your needed layout.

Figures 11.11–11.14 show several examples of simple box sizers. Each of these frames has been slightly resized by the user before the screen shot, to show how each sizer responds to the growth. Figure 11.11 shows a horizontal box sizer and figure 11.12 shows the same widgets in a vertical box sizer.

Figure 11.12
A vertical box sizer

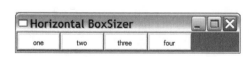

Figure 11.11   A horizontal box sizer

Figure 11.13 shows a vertical sizer with one widget that is set to expand and fill the available vertical space. Figure 11.14 shows a vertical sizer with two widgets set to grab the available vertical space in different proportions.

Figure 11.13
A vertical sizer
with one stretch
element

Figure 11.14
A vertical sizer
with two stretch
elements

The code to generate all four sizer frames is given in listing 11.9.

Listing 11.9 Generating a number of box sizers

```python
import wx
from blockwindow import BlockWindow

labels = "one two three four".split()

class TestFrame(wx.Frame):
    title = "none"
    def __init__(self):
        wx.Frame.__init__(self, None, -1, self.title)
        sizer = self.CreateSizerAndWindows()
        self.SetSizer(sizer)
        self.Fit()

class VBoxSizerFrame(TestFrame):
    title = "Vertical BoxSizer"

    def CreateSizerAndWindows(self):        # The vertical sizer
        sizer = wx.BoxSizer(wx.VERTICAL)
        for label in labels:
            bw = BlockWindow(self, label=label, size=(200,30))
            sizer.Add(bw, flag=wx.EXPAND)
        return sizer

class HBoxSizerFrame(TestFrame):        # The horizontal sizer
    title = "Horizontal BoxSizer"

    def CreateSizerAndWindows(self):
        sizer = wx.BoxSizer(wx.HORIZONTAL)
```

```
        for label in labels:
            bw = BlockWindow(self, label=label, size=(75,30))
            sizer.Add(bw, flag=wx.EXPAND)
        return sizer

class VBoxSizerStretchableFrame(TestFrame):
    title = "Stretchable BoxSizer"

    def CreateSizerAndWindows(self):
        sizer = wx.BoxSizer(wx.VERTICAL)
        for label in labels:
            bw = BlockWindow(self, label=label, size=(200,30))
            sizer.Add(bw, flag=wx.EXPAND)

        # Add an item that takes all the free space
        bw = BlockWindow(self, label="gets all free space", size=(200,30))
        sizer.Add(bw, 1, flag=wx.EXPAND)
        return sizer

class VBoxSizerMultiProportionalFrame(TestFrame):
    title = "Proportional BoxSizer"

    def CreateSizerAndWindows(self):
        sizer = wx.BoxSizer(wx.VERTICAL)
        for label in labels:
            bw = BlockWindow(self, label=label, size=(200,30))
            sizer.Add(bw, flag=wx.EXPAND)

        # Add an item that takes one share of the free space
        bw = BlockWindow(self,
                label="gets 1/3 of the free space",
                size=(200,30))
        sizer.Add(bw, 1, flag=wx.EXPAND)

        # Add an item that takes 2 shares of the free space
        bw = BlockWindow(self,
                label="gets 2/3 of the free space",
                size=(200,30))
        sizer.Add(bw, 2, flag=wx.EXPAND)
        return sizer

app = wx.PySimpleApp()
frameList = [VBoxSizerFrame, HBoxSizerFrame,
            VBoxSizerStretchableFrame,
            VBoxSizerMultiProportionalFrame]
for klass in frameList:
    frame = klass()
    frame.Show()
app.MainLoop()
```

◁─┐ **Horizontal with
    free space**

◁── **Proportional sizing**

After seeing the previous sizer examples, most of this code should make sense. Box sizers are instances of the class `wx.BoxSizer`, which is a direct subclass of `wx.Sizer`, adding almost no new methods. The constructor for `wx.BoxSizer` takes one argument:

```
wx.BoxSizer(orient)
```

The `orient` parameter represents the direction of the sizer, and can take either the value `wx.VERTICAL` or `wx.HORIZONTAL`. The only new method defined for box sizers is `GetOrientation()` which returns the integer constant value as it was set in the constructor. You cannot change the orientation of a box sizer once it has been created. All other functions of a box sizer use the common sizer methods discussed earlier in this chapter

The layout algorithm for a box sizer treats the sizer's primary direction (defined by its orientation when constructed) differently from its secondary direction. In particular, the `proportion` parameter only applies when the sizer is grown or shrunk along its primary direction, while the `wx.EXPAND` flag only applies when the sizer changes size in its secondary direction. In other words, when a vertical box sizer is stretched vertically, the `proportion` parameter passed to each of the `Add()` method calls determines how each item will grow or shrink vertically. The `proportion` parameter affects a horizontal box sizer the same way, except for affecting horizontal growth of the sizer and its items. On the other hand, growth in the secondary direction is controlled by using the `wx.EXPAND` flag for items, so items in a vertical box sizer will only grow horizontally if they have the `wx.EXPAND` flag set, otherwise the items remain at their minimum or best size. Figure 6.7 in chapter 6 illustrates this process graphically.

In box sizers proportional item growth works similarly to the way it works with flex grid sizers, with some exceptions. First, the box sizer proportional behavior is determined using the `proportion` parameter when the widget is added to the sizer—you do not need to separately specify it as growable the way that you would with a flex grid sizer. Second, the behavior of the sizer for proportions of 0 is different. In a box sizer, a proportion of 0 means that the widget will not be resized from its minimum or best size in the primary dimension, but it can still grow in the secondary dimension if the `wx.EXPAND` flag is used. When the box sizer calculates the layout of its items for the primary dimension it first adds up the space needed by the fixed size items, which are those with a proportion of 0. The remaining space is divided between the proportional items, with those with a larger proportion value getting the larger amount of the free space.

11.3.4 What's a static box sizer?

A static box sizer combines a box sizer with a static box. The static box provides a nice-looking border and text label around the sizer. Figure 11.15 shows three static box sizers in action.

Figure 11.15
Three static box sizers

Listing 11.10 shows the code used to create the static box sizers. There are two interesting things to notice here. The first is that you must create the static box object separately from the sizer, and the second is that this example shows how you might use nested box sizers. In this case, there are three vertical static box sizers placed inside a horizontal box sizer.

Listing 11.10 An example of a static box sizer

```
import wx
from blockwindow import BlockWindow

labels = "one two three four five six seven eight nine".split()

class TestFrame(wx.Frame):
    def __init__(self):
        wx.Frame.__init__(self, None, -1, "StaticBoxSizer Test")
        self.panel = wx.Panel(self)

        box1 = self.MakeStaticBoxSizer("Box 1", labels[0:3])      Make static
        box2 = self.MakeStaticBoxSizer("Box 2", labels[3:6])      boxes
        box3 = self.MakeStaticBoxSizer("Box 3", labels[6:9])

        sizer = wx.BoxSizer(wx.HORIZONTAL)    ←— Use sizer to manage others
        sizer.Add(box1, 0, wx.ALL, 10)
        sizer.Add(box2, 0, wx.ALL, 10)
        sizer.Add(box3, 0, wx.ALL, 10)

        self.panel.SetSizer(sizer)
        sizer.Fit(self)

    def MakeStaticBoxSizer(self, boxlabel, itemlabels):
        box = wx.StaticBox(self.panel, -1, boxlabel)    ←— Make static box
        sizer = wx.StaticBoxSizer(box, wx.VERTICAL)
```

326

```
        for label in itemlabels:
            bw = BlockWindow(self.panel, label=label)        ← ⌐ Add items
            sizer.Add(bw, 0, wx.ALL, 2)                        ⌐   to box

        return sizer               proportion   flag   border

app = wx.PySimpleApp()
TestFrame().Show()
app.MainLoop()
```

Static box sizers are instances of the class `wx.StaticBoxSizer`, which is a child class of `wx.BoxSizer`. The constructor takes the static box and the orientation:

```
    wx.StaticBoxSizer(box, orient)
```

In this constructor `orient` has the same meaning as it does for an ordinary `wx.BoxSizer`, and the `box` parameter is a `wx.StaticBox`. There is only one other method defined for static box sizers, `GetStaticBox()`, which returns the `wx.StaticBox` used to build the sizer. You cannot change the static box once the sizer is created.

The `wx.StaticBox` class has a typical constructor for wxPython controls, but in practice, many of the parameters have useful defaults and can be ignored.

```
    wx.StaticBox(parent, id, label, pos=wx.DefaultPosition,
            size=wx.DefaultSize, style=0, name="staticBox")
```

For use in a static box sizer, you do not need to set the `pos`, `size`, `style`, or `name` attributes, since the position and size will be managed by the sizer, and there are no unique style flags for a `wx.StaticBox`. This makes the constructor simpler:

```
    box = wx.StaticBox(self.panel, -1, boxlabel)
```

Now that we've shown you what the various kinds of sizers are, we're going to show you how you might use them in a real layout. See chapter 6 for another example of sizers being used to create a complex layout.

11.4 Can I see a real-world example of sizers in action?

So far, the sizer examples we've shown have been deliberately contrived to display the functionality of the sizers. However, you might be wondering how to use sizers to build a real layout, and we hope the following example will give you some ideas. Figure 11.16 shows a moderately complicated layout built with various sizers.

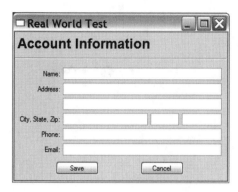

Figure 11.16
A more realistic sizer example

The code used to create figure 11.16 is shown in listing 11.11. The code looks complex, but we'll go through it piece by piece.

Listing 11.11 Using sizers to build the address form

```python
import wx

class TestFrame(wx.Frame):
    def __init__(self):
        wx.Frame.__init__(self, None, -1, "Real World Test")
        panel = wx.Panel(self)

        # First create the controls                              Creating  ❶
        topLbl = wx.StaticText(panel, -1, "Account Information")   widgets
        topLbl.SetFont(wx.Font(18, wx.SWISS, wx.NORMAL, wx.BOLD))

        nameLbl = wx.StaticText(panel, -1, "Name:")
        name = wx.TextCtrl(panel, -1, "");

        addrLbl = wx.StaticText(panel, -1, "Address:")
        addr1 = wx.TextCtrl(panel, -1, "");
        addr2 = wx.TextCtrl(panel, -1, "");
                    cszLbl
        cstLbl = wx.StaticText(panel, -1, "City, State, Zip:")
        city  = wx.TextCtrl(panel, -1, "", size=(150,-1));
        state = wx.TextCtrl(panel, -1, "", size=(50,-1));
        zip   = wx.TextCtrl(panel, -1, "", size=(70,-1));

        phoneLbl = wx.StaticText(panel, -1, "Phone:")
        phone = wx.TextCtrl(panel, -1, "");

        emailLbl = wx.StaticText(panel, -1, "Email:")
        email = wx.TextCtrl(panel, -1, "");

        saveBtn = wx.Button(panel, -1, "Save")
        cancelBtn = wx.Button(panel, -1, "Cancel")
```

```
# Now do the layout.

# mainSizer is the top-level one that manages everything
mainSizer = wx.BoxSizer(wx.VERTICAL)
mainSizer.Add(topLbl, 0, wx.ALL, 5)
mainSizer.Add(wx.StaticLine(panel), 0,
        wx.EXPAND|wx.TOP|wx.BOTTOM, 5)

# addrSizer is a grid that holds all of the address info
addrSizer = wx.FlexGridSizer(cols=2, hgap=5, vgap=5)
addrSizer.AddGrowableCol(1)
addrSizer.Add(nameLbl, 0,
        wx.ALIGN_RIGHT|wx.ALIGN_CENTER_VERTICAL)
addrSizer.Add(name, 0, wx.EXPAND)
addrSizer.Add(addrLbl, 0,
        wx.ALIGN_RIGHT|wx.ALIGN_CENTER_VERTICAL)
addrSizer.Add(addr1, 0, wx.EXPAND)
addrSizer.Add((10,10)) # some empty space
addrSizer.Add(addr2, 0, wx.EXPAND)
addrSizer.Add(cstLbl, 0,
        wx.ALIGN_RIGHT|wx.ALIGN_CENTER_VERTICAL)

# the city, state, zip fields are in a sub-sizer
cstSizer = wx.BoxSizer(wx.HORIZONTAL)
cstSizer.Add(city, 1)
cstSizer.Add(state, 0, wx.LEFT|wx.RIGHT, 5)
cstSizer.Add(zip)
addrSizer.Add(cstSizer, 0, wx.EXPAND)

addrSizer.Add(phoneLbl, 0,
        wx.ALIGN_RIGHT|wx.ALIGN_CENTER_VERTICAL)
addrSizer.Add(phone, 0, wx.EXPAND)
addrSizer.Add(emailLbl, 0,
        wx.ALIGN_RIGHT|wx.ALIGN_CENTER_VERTICAL)
addrSizer.Add(email, 0, wx.EXPAND)

# now add the addrSizer to the mainSizer
mainSizer.Add(addrSizer, 0, wx.EXPAND|wx.ALL, 10)

# The buttons sizer will put them in a row with resizeable
# gaps between and on either side of the buttons
btnSizer = wx.BoxSizer(wx.HORIZONTAL)
btnSizer.Add((20,20), 1)
btnSizer.Add(saveBtn)
btnSizer.Add((20,20), 1)
btnSizer.Add(cancelBtn)
btnSizer.Add((20,20), 1)

mainSizer.Add(btnSizer, 0, wx.EXPAND|wx.BOTTOM, 10)
```

② Vertical sizer

③ Columns for address

④ Row with empty space

⑤ Nested horizontal

⑥ Phone and email

⑦ Flex sizer added to main

⑧ Button row

```
    panel.SetSizer(mainSizer)

    # Fit the frame to the needs of the sizer. The frame will
    # automatically resize the panel as needed. Also prevent the
    # frame from getting smaller than this size.
    mainSizer.Fit(self)
    mainSizer.SetSizeHints(self)

app = wx.PySimpleApp()
TestFrame().Show()
app.MainLoop()
```

@ 335

❶ The first part of the code is the creation of the widgets used in the window, which begins at this line. We create them all before adding the sizers.

❷ The primary sizer in this layout is mainSizer, a vertical box sizer. The first elements added to mainSizer are the top static text label, and a static line.

❸ The next element in the sizer is addrSizer, which is a flex grid sizer with two columns that is used to hold the rest of the address information. The left column of addrSizer is designed for the static text captions, while the right one gets the text controls. This means that the labels and controls need to be added in an alternating order to keep the grid correct. You can see that nameLbl, name, addrLbl, and addr1 are the first four elements added to the flex grid.

❹ The next row is different, since the second address line has no caption. In that case, a (10, 10) sized chunk of empty space is added, and then the addr2 control.

❺ The next line is different again, as the "City, State, Zip" line take three different text controls, so a horizontal box sizer cstSizer is created. The three controls are added to cstSizer and then the box sizer is added to addrSizer.

❻ The phone and email lines are added to the flex sizer.

❼ The address flex sizer is officially added to the main sizer.

❽ The button row is added as a horizontal box sizer with some empty spacer elements to separate the buttons. Notice how the spacers are given a proportion of 1 and the buttons are left with the default of 0.

That ends the element layout, after that the sizer is fitted and given a size hint to prevent the frame from getting any smaller.

Before reading the next paragraph or running the example, try to figure out how this frame will respond to growth in the horizontal and vertical dimension.

If the window is resized vertically, none of the elements will move. This is because the main sizer is a vertical box sizer being resized in its primary direction, and none of its top-level elements were added with a proportion greater than zero. If the window is resized horizontally, the main sizer is a vertical box sizer being resized in the secondary direction, and therefore all its elements with the wx.EXPAND flag stretch horizontally. This means the label at the top doesn't grow, but the static line and the subsizers stretch horizontally. The flex grid sizer for the addresses specifies column 1 as growable, meaning that the second column containing the text controls will stretch. Within the "City, State, Zip" row, it is the city element which is given a proportion of 1, and will stretch, while the state and ZIP controls stay the same size. The buttons will stay the same size since they have a proportion of zero, but the empty space before, between, and after them will equally divide up the extra horizontal space since they each have a proportion of 1.

So, if you guessed that the grown window would look like figure 11.17, you were right.

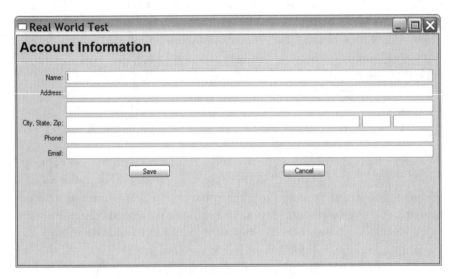

Figure 11.17 The account information, after the window was stretched

Notice how the elements that we wanted to stretch horizontally have, in fact, stretched, but the widgets are still displayed in basically the same position relative to each other. Despite the stretching, the window still looks good and is still usable.

11.5 *Summary*

- Sizers are a solution to the problem of managing layout in a wxPython program. Rather than manually specifying the size and position of each element in the layout, you can add the elements to a sizer, and the sizer is responsible for placing each element on the screen. Sizers are particularly good at managing layout when the user resizes the frame manually.

- All wxPython sizers are instances of a subclass of `wx.Sizer`. To use a sizer, you need to associate it with a container widget. Then, as child widgets are added to the container, you must also add them to the sizer. Finally, you call the sizer's `Fit()` method to trigger the sizer's algorithm for placement and layout.

- All sizers start with information about the minimal preferred size for each of its children. Each one uses a different mechanism for placing the widgets, so the same group of widgets will look different when placed inside a different sizer.

- Perhaps the simplest sizer in wxPython is the grid sizer (`wx.GridSizer`). In a grid sizer, elements are placed in a two-dimensional grid based on the order in which they are added to the sizer, starting with the top left and moving across and then down to the bottom right. Typically, you set the number of columns in the grid, and the sizer determines how many rows it needs, although you can specify both dimensions if you want.

- All sizers have various methods for adding widgets to the sizer. Since the order in which children are added to the sizer is important in the final layout, various methods are used to add a new widget to the front, back, or arbitrary spot in the list. When a widget is added to the sizer, other properties can be set which control how the child element changes when the sizer is grown or shrunk. The sizer can also be configured to place a border gap around some or all sides of the object.

Manipulating basic
graphical images

This chapter covers

- Loading images and creating image objects
- Creating device contexts
- Drawing to device contexts
- Drawing text to the context
- Managing drawing pens, drawing brushes, and device coordinates

The most fundamental action that any UI toolkit performs is the simple act of drawing on the screen. At its most basic level, every widget defined in wxPython consists of a series of draw commands sent to the screen. Whether those draw commands are in the wxPython codebase depends on whether the widget is native to the local operating system or completely defined by wxPython. In this chapter, we'll show you how to control wxPython at the level of basic drawing commands. We'll also show you how to manage and display other graphical elements like images and fonts.

The primary abstraction used by wxPython in drawing is the *device context*. The device context uses a standard API to manage drawing to devices such as the screen or a printer. The device context classes are where the most basic drawing functionality is located, such as drawing lines, curves, or text.

12.1 Working with images

Most applications need to load at least one image that is externally stored in a file. Examples would include toolbar graphics, cursors, icons, splash screens, or merely images used for decoration or to add some pizzazz. Traditionally, the complication in working with images is having to deal with all of the different graphical file formats that might be used to store an image. Fortunately, wxPython manages all of that for you—from inside wxPython. You'll use the same abstraction to deal with any image no matter its original format.

In the following sections, we'll talk about the abstractions that wxPython uses to manage images, which include large-scale images, as well as cursor images. You'll see how to load the images into your program, and then how to manipulate them.

12.1.1 How do I load images?

Image manipulation in wxPython is a dual-headed system where platform-independent image handling is managed by the class wx.Image, while platform-dependent image handling is managed by the class wx.Bitmap. In practice, what this means is that external file formats are loaded and saved by wx.Image, while wx.Bitmap takes care of displaying the image to the screen. Figure 12.1 displays the creation of different images and bitmaps, read in from different file types.

To load an image from a file use the wx.Image constructor:

```
wx.Image(name, type=wx.BITMAP_TYPE_ANY, index=-1)
```

File   359: handler type

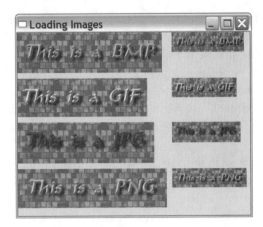

**Figure 12.1
Big and little images
of different types**

The name parameter is the name of the file to load from and the type is the handler type. The type ID is either wx.BITMAP_TYPE_ANY, or one of the type flags listed in Table 12.1. If you use wx.BITMAP_TYPE_ANY, then wxPython will attempt to automatically detect the file type. If you use a specific file type, wxPython will convert the file using that type. Listing 12.1 displays how images can be loaded using wx.BITMAP_TYPE_ANY.

359 [handwritten]

Listing 12.1 Loading and scaling simple images

```
import wx

filenames = ["image.bmp", "image.gif", "image.jpg", "image.png" ]

class TestFrame(wx.Frame):
    def __init__(self):
        wx.Frame.__init__(self, None, title="Loading Images")
        p = wx.Panel(self)

        fgs = wx.FlexGridSizer(cols=2, hgap=10, vgap=10)
        for name in filenames:
            img1 = wx.Image(name, wx.BITMAP_TYPE_ANY)          ❶ Loading images
                                                                  from a file
            w = img1.GetWidth()
            h = img1.GetHeight()                        ❷ Scaling
            img2 = img1.Scale(w/2, h/2)                    images

            sb1 = wx.StaticBitmap(p, -1, wx.BitmapFromImage(img1))
            sb2 = wx.StaticBitmap(p, -1, wx.BitmapFromImage(img2))

                                 Turning images into bitmap widgets ❸
            fgs.Add(sb1)
            fgs.Add(sb2)

        p.SetSizerAndFit(fgs)
        self.Fit()
```

337 wx. FlexGrid Sizer [handwritten]

p 363 [handwritten]

p 363 [handwritten]

id [handwritten]

parent (panel, here) [handwritten]

```
app = wx.PySimpleApp()
frm = TestFrame()
frm.Show()
app.MainLoop()
```

This listing should be rather straightforward. We start with a list of the image names that we want to load in. Looping over them, we first construct an instance of wx.Image, using the any type flag to direct wxPython to figure out the format without bothering us ❶. Then we scale the image to half size using the image methods ❷, and convert the image to a bitmap to be able to add the image to the display ❸.

Although this example defers the determination of the image format to wxPython, you can also specify the format explicitly. In the next section we'll show you what image formats are supported by wxPython.

Specifying an image file format

Images are managed with the use of *image handlers*. An image handler is an instance of wx.ImageHandler that provides a plug-in architecture for managing image formats. Under normal circumstances, you will not need to worry about the details of how image handlers work. All you need to know is that each handler has its own unique wxPython identifier to load a file in the associated format. Supported formats are listed in table 12.1. The type flag is the value used if you want to specify a type when loading an image.

Table 12.1 Supported file formats in wxPython

Handler class	Type flag	Notes
wx.ANIHandler	wx.BITMAP_TYPE_ANI	Animated cursor format. This handler only loads images, it does not save them.
wx.BMPHandler	wx.BITMAP_TYPE_BMP	Windows and OS/2 bitmap format
wx.CURHandler	wx.BITMAP_TYPE_CUR	Windows cursor icon format
wx.GIFHandler	wx.BITMAP_TYPE_GIF	Graphic Interchange Format. Due to copyright restrictions, this handler does not save images.
wx.ICOHandler	wx.BITMAP_TYPE_ICO	Windows icon format
wx.IFFHandler	wx.BITMAP_TYPE_IFF	Interchange file format. This handler only loads images, it does not save them.

continued on next page

[handwritten note:] After image img is created, it can be converted (back) to a bitmap (if of a supported type) with img.ConvertToBitmap() @ 379

Table 12.1 **Supported file formats in wxPython** *(continued)*

Handler class	Type flag	Notes
wx.JPEGHandler	wx.BITMAP_TYPE_JPEG	Joint Photographic Experts Group format.
wx.PCXHandler	wx.BITMAP_TYPE_PCX	PC Paintbrush format. When saving in this format, wxPython counts the number of different colors in the image. If possible, the image is saved as an 8-bit image (that is, if it has 256 or fewer colors). Otherwise, it saves as 24-bit.
wx.PNGHandler	wx.BITMAP_TYPE_PNG	Portable Network Graphics format.
wx.PNMHandler	wx.BITMAP_TYPE_PNM	Can only load ASCII or raw RGB images. Images saved by this handler are saved as raw RGB.
wx.TIFFHandler	wx.BITMAP_TYPE_TIF	Tagged Image File Format.
wx.XPMHandler	wx.BITMAP_TYPE_XPM	XPixMap format.
(auto)	wx.BITMAP_TYPE_ANY	Will try to autodetect the format to use and will then invoke the handler for it.

To use a MIME-type to identify the file, rather than a handler type ID, use the function `wx.ImageFromMime(name, mimetype, index=-1)`, where `name` is the filename, and `mimetype` is the string with the type of the file. The `index` parameter denotes the image to load in the case that the image file contains multiple images. This is only used by the GIF, ICO, and TIFF handlers. The default value (-1) means choose the default image, and is interpreted as the first image (index=0) by the GIF and TIFF handler and as the largest and most colorful one by the ICO handler.

Creating image objects

wxPython uses other global functions to create different kinds of `wx.Image` objects. To create an empty image with a specific size, use the function `wx.EmptyImage(width, height)`—all the pixels in the created image will be black. To create an image from an open stream or Python file-like object, use `wx.ImageFromStream(stream, type=wx.BITMAP_TYPE_ANY, index=-1)` Sometimes it's useful to create an image from raw RGB data, which can be done using `wx.ImageFromData(width, height, data)` where `data` is a string where each set of three consecutive characters represents a pixel's red, green, and blue components. The size of the string should always be `width*height*3`.

(Handwritten margin notes at top of page:)

wx. <bitmap maker> (
wx. Bitmap (Filename, <bitmap-type>)
wx. Empty Bitmap (width, height, depth = -1)
wx, Bitmap From Bits (bits, width, height, depth = -1)
wx, Bitmap form XPM Data (list of strings)

wx. Bitmap From Image (image, depth=-1)
wx. Image From Bitmap (bitmap)

Creating bitmap objects

There are several ways to create a bitmap object. The basic wx.Bitmap constructor is wx.Bitmap(name, type=wx.BITMAP_TYPE_ANY). The name argument is a filename and the type argument can be one of the types specified in the table 12.1. If the bitmap class is able to natively handle the file format then it does so, otherwise the image is automatically loaded via wx.Image and converted to a wx.Bitmap instance.

You can also create an empty bitmap with the method wx.EmptyBitmap(width, height, depth=-1)—the width and height parameters are, of course, the dimensions of the bitmap, and the depth is the color depth of the eventual image. There are two functions that allow you to create a bitmap from raw data. The function wx.BitmapFromBits(bits, width, height, depth=-1) creates a bitmap where the bits parameter is a Python list of bytes. The behavior of this function depends on the platform. On most platforms the bits are either 1 or 0 and the function creates a monochromatic bitmap. On Windows platforms, the data is passed directly to the Windows API function CreateBitmap(). The function wxBitmapFromXPM-Data(listOfStrings) takes as a parameter a list of Python strings, reading the strings as data in XPM format.

You can convert back and forth from an image to a bitmap by using the wx.Bitmap constructor wx.BitmapFromImage(image, depth=-1). The image parameter is the actual wx.Image object, and the depth is the color depth of the resulting bitmap. If the depth is not specified, the current display's color depth is used. You can convert the bitmap back into an image using the function wx.ImageFromBitmap(bitmap), passing an actual wx.Bitmap object. In listing 12.1, bitmap objects are created using the bitmap constructor and then used to construct wx.StaticBitmap widgets, which allows them to be placed into a container widget just like any other wxPython item.

12.1.2 What can I do with an image?

Once you have your image in wxPython, you can manipulate it in numerous useful ways, and use it to write some powerful image adjustment scripts.

You can query the size of the image with the methods GetWidth() and GetHeight(). You can also recover the color value at any pixel with the methods GetRed(x, y), GetGreen(x, y), and GetBlue(x, y). The return value of all these color methods is an integer with a value between 0 and 255 (in C terms, it's an unsigned int, but that distinction is not particularly meaningful in Python). Similary, you can set an individual pixel with SetRGB(x, y, red, green, blue), where x and y are the pixel coordinates, and the color values are between 0 and 255.

You can get all the data in one enormous lump with the method GetData(). The return value of the GetData() method is a big string where each character represents a member of an RGB triple, and each character can be considered an integer value between 0 and 255. The values are in order, with the first one being the red value of the pixel at (0, 0), the next one being the green value at (0, 0), and the next being the blue value at (0, 0). The next three are the color values at (0, 1) and so on. Algorithmically, it could be defined using the following Python pseudocode.

```
def GetData(self):
    result = ""
    for y in range(self.GetHeight()):
        for x in range(self.GetWidth()):
            result.append(chr(self.GetRed(x,y)))
            result.append(chr(self.GetGreen(x,y)))
            result.append(chr(self.GetBlue(x,y)))
    return result
```

[handwritten annotations: (1,0) ← (0,1); 1; # order (0,0), (1,0), (2,0)... (row by row) (0,1),(1,1); p.364 Set Alpha Data]

There are two things to be aware of when using the corresponding SetData(data) method that reads in similarly formatted string of RGB values. First, the SetData() method does not perform range or bounds checking to determine if your incoming string has values in the right range or if it is the correct length given the size of the image. If your values are incorrect, the behavior is undefined. Secondly, due to the way the underlying C++ code manages memory, it's a bad idea to pass a string returned by GetData() right back into SetData()—you should make a fresh string.

The image data string can easily be converted to and from other Python types that make it easier to access and manipulate the RGB values as integers, such as an array or a numeric type. For example, to make something that hurts the eyes if you stare at it too long, try this

```
import array
img = wx.EmptyImage(100,100)
a = array.array('B', img.GetData())
for i in range(len(a)):
    a[i] = (25+i) % 256      # work with unsigned 8 bit ints
img.SetData(a.tostring())    # convert array to string
```

*[handwritten annotations: w h; → string w 3 * 100 * 100 8-bit unsigned integers, each φ]*

Table 12.2 defines the many methods of wx.Image that perform simple image manipulations.

Those methods represent the starter set of image manipulation. In the next section we'll show you two ways to manage the more complex topic of a transparent or semitransparent image.

[handwritten annotations: colors = [[[r,g,b], [r,g,b], ..., [r,g,b]], ← row₀; [[r,g,b],], ← row₁; Use: colors[row][col][color]]

(handwritten margin notes at top):
img. Get Width ()
Get Height
Get Red (x, y)
Blue
Green

img. Get Data ()
imp. Set Data (s)
Set RGB (x, y, red, green, blue)

Table 12.2 Image manipulation methods of `wx.Image`

Method	Description
ConvertToMono(r, g, b)	Returns a `wx.Image` the same size as the original, where all pixels with the exact `r`, `g`, `b` color value are white, and all others are black. The original image is untouched.
Mirror(horizontally=True)	Returns a mirror image of the original. If the `horizontally` parameter is `True`, then the image is flipped around the horizontal axis, otherwise around vertical. The original image is unchanged.
Replace(r1, g1, b1, r2, g2, b2)	Changes the called image in-place. Every pixel with a color value of `r1`, `g1`, `b1` is reset to the color value `r2`, `g2`, `b2`.
Rescale(width, height)	Changes the size of the image to the new `width` and `height`. The original image is changed in-place, with pixel colors scaled to fit the new size.
Rotate(angle, rotationCentre, interpolating=True, offestAfterRotation=None)	Returns a new image created by rotating the original image. The `angle` parameter is a floating point indicating the amount of rotation in radians. The `rotationCentre` is a `wx.Point` around which the rotation occurs. If `interpolating` is True, a slower, more accurate algorithm is used. The `offsetAfterRotation` is a point indicating how much the image should be shifted after the rotation. Any blank pixels uncovered by the rotation will be set to black or to the mask color if the image has a mask.
Rotate90(clockwise=True)	Rotates the image 90 degrees in the direction governed by the Boolean `clockwise` parameter.
Scale(width, height)	Returns a copy of the orginal image scaled to the new `width` and `height`.

(handwritten notes beside Rotate row): offset after rotation X_delta, Y_delta · angle (rads) · rotation centre X_c, Y_c · black = (r, g, b) = (0,0,0)?

Setting image masks to specify a transparent image

(handwritten note): img. Set Mask Color (r, g, b)

An *image mask* is a special color set in the image which is rendered as transparent when the image is displayed on top of some other part of your display. A virtual greenscreen, so to speak, but you can set it to any color you want. You can set an image mask with the method `SetMaskColor(red, green, blue)`, where red, green, and blue define the colors of the mask for the image. If you want to turn off the mask, use `SetMask(False)`, and reset it with `SetMask(True)`. The method `Has-Mask()` returns a Boolean with the current state of the mask. You can also set the mask from another image of the same size using the method `SetMaskFrom-Image(mask, mr, mg, mb)`—in this case the mask is defined to be all the pixels in the `mask` `wx.Image` that have the color mr, mg, mb, regardless of what color those pixels are in the main image. This gives you a lot of flexibility in creating a mask, since you no longer have to worry about the color of the pixels in your original

(handwritten notes at bottom): main_img . Set Mask From Image (mask-img, mr, mb, mg)
main image: ↑ eg. create mask-img image with a white rect. area inside
transparent where mask-img is white

image. You can retrieve the mask color using the methods `GetMaskRed()`, `Get-MaskGreen()`, and `GetMaskBlue()`. If an image with a mask is converted to a `wx.Bitmap` then the mask is automatically converted to a `wx.Mask` object and assigned to the bitmap.

img . SetAlphaData(data)

Setting alpha values to specify a transparent image

An *alpha* value is another way to specify a transparent or partially transparent image. Each pixel has an alpha value, which is between 0 (if the image is totally transparent at that pixel) and 255 (if the image is completely opaque at that pixel). You set alpha values with the `SetAlphaData(data)` method, which takes a string of byte values similar to `SetData()`, but with only one value per pixel. Like `SetData()`, `SetAlphaData()` does no range checking. You can see if an alpha is set using `HasAlpha()` and you can recover the entire data set with `GetAlphaData()`. You can set the alpha value of a specific pixel with `SetAlpha(x, y, alpha)`, and recover that value with `GetAlpha(x, y)`.

In contrast to the image manipulation capabilities of `wx.Image`, you can do relatively little with a `wx.Bitmap`. Nearly all of the methods of the `wx.Bitmap` are simple getters of properties such as width, height, and color depth.

12.1.3 How can I change cursors?

The cursor is the most direct avatar of the user's presence on the screen. As such, it's used to provide immediate feedback to the user about the area being explored. Normally, it's a pointer to where the user's next mouse click will take effect, but depending on what widget the cursor is currently over, it can be a directional arrow, a text placement I-beam, or crosshairs. Typically, an application signals that it is too busy to accept input by changing the cursor to some kind of busy symbol, such as the classic hourglass.

You'll want to use the cursor to signal state in your application, and even though wxPython handles most of the basics for common widgets, you'll sometimes want to customize it, either because you have a custom widget or because your application needs to override the normal cursor behavior to signal a new state. Perhaps you just want your application to have its own unique cursor. In this section we'll show you how to use a cursor to signal state and how to customize cursors in wxPython.

You can create cursor objects in a variety of ways in wxPython. The cursor class is `wx.Cursor`, and there are two different ways of creating an instance. The simpler is the method `wx.StockCursor(id)`, that returns an instance of a predefined system cursor. As defined in table 12.3, the `id` parameter can be any number of flags.

wx. StockCursor ({cursortype})

Table 12.3   Predefined stock cursors

Cursor ID	Description
wx.CURSOR_ARROW	The normal arrow cursor.
wx.CURSOR_ARROWWAIT	A busy cursor showing both the normal arrow and an hourglass. Available on Windows systems only.
wx.CURSOR_BLANK	The invisible cursor. Useful when you want to trick the user.
wx.CURSOR_BULLSEYE	A bullseye cursor (small circle inside a larger cursor). Sometimes useful for precision pointing.
wx.CURSOR_CHAR	A character cursor. Not available on all platforms.
wx.CURSOR_CROSS	The ever-popular cross-hair cursor.
wx.CURSOR_HAND	Classic pointing hand cursor.
wx.CURSOR_IBEAM	The vertical I-beam cursor typically used inside a text edit field.
wx.CURSOR_LEFT_BUTTON	A cursor that depicts a mouse with the left button pressed—used to hint to the user that he should press that button. May not be available on all platforms.
wx.CURSOR_MAGNIFIER	Magnifying glass typically used to indicate zoom.
wx.CURSOR_MIDDLE_BUTTON	Depicts a mouse with the middle button pressed.
wx.CURSOR_NO_ENTRY	Cursor containing the arrow and a circle-with-a-slash no entry symbol. Used to indicate that an area of the screen is invalid (as the target of a drag and drop, for example).
wx.CURSOR_PAINT_BRUSH	A cursor that looks like a paint brush. Typically used in a paint program.
wx.CURSOR_PENCIL	The pencil cursor usually used in draw programs.
wx.CURSOR_POINT_LEFT	The cursor is a left-pointing arrow.
wx.CURSOR_POINT_RIGHT	The cursor is a right-pointing arrow.
wx.CURSOR_QUESTION_ARROW	The arrow with the question mark next to it usually used to indicate context-sensitive help.
wx.CURSOR_RIGHT_ARROW	Just like the normal arrow cursor, but in a mirror, so that it points to the right.
wx.CURSOR_RIGHT_BUTTON	A mouse with the right button pressed.

continued on next page

Table 12.3 **Predefined stock cursors** *(continued)*

Cursor ID	Description
wx.CURSOR_SIZENESW	One of the cursors usually used to indicate both direction resize, this one has arrows pointing from the lower left (southwest) to upper right (northeast).
wx.CURSOR_SIZENS	The vertical resize cursor, pointing up and down.
wx.CURSOR_SIZENWSE	The other dual-direction resize cursor, pointing from lower right to upper left.
wx.CURSOR_SIZEWE	The horizontal reize cursor, pointing left and right.
wx.CURSOR_SIZING	Generic sizing cursor, with arrows pointing in all four compass directions.
wx.CURSOR_SPRAYCAN	Another painting cursor.
wx.CURSOR_WAIT	The hourglass wait cursor.
wx.CURSOR_WATCH	The watch-shaped wait cursor.

Now that we've discussed predefined cursors, we'll show you how to create custom cursors using your own images.

Creating custom cursors

You can create a custom cursor from an image using the method wx.CursorFrom-Image(image). The image parameter is a wx.Image instance. The image is automatically resized to 32 x 32 (on MacOS 16 x 16). The mask color of the image becomes the transparent color of the cursor. By default, the hotspot is set to the (0,0) corner of the cursor image. To change that, you need to set an option in the image before you convert it:

```
image.SetOptionInt(wx.IMAGE_OPTION_CUR_HOTSPOT_X, 0)
image.SetOptionInt(wx.IMAGE_OPTION_CUR_HOTSPOT_Y, 22)
```

The actual wx.Cursor constructor is:

```
wx.Cursor(name, type, hotSpotX=0, hotSpotY=0)
```

The name parameter is the filename of the cursor to load. The type parameter is the icon type to load and uses the same wx.BITMAP_TYPE_ flags as wx.Image and wx.Bitmap. The hotSpotX and hotSpotY parameters set the hotspot of the icon. If the bitmap type used is wx.BITMAP_TYPE_CUR to load from a .cur file, then the hotspot is set automatically from the hotspot defined in the .cur file.

Once you have the cursor created, using it is a simple matter of calling the ✳
SetCursor(cursor) on any wxPython widget. This method causes the cursor to
be changed to the new shape when the cursor passes over the widget. There is
also a global wx.SetCursor(cursor) method that globally sets the cursor for the
entire application.

Images are great, but they only scratch the surface of what you can do graphically in wxPython. In the next section, we'll show how to send draw commands to
the screen, or a file, or other display objects.

12.2 *Dealing with device contexts*

simple   326   Block Window
*   538   Clock Window*

As we discussed earlier in this chapter, drawing to the screen is the most basic
thing that a UI toolkit does. Most of the drawing that wxPython does is encapsulated within the paint methods of each widget, because that encapsulation is perhaps the second most basic thing that a UI toolkit does. That won't always be
enough for you, though. Sometimes, as in chapter 6, you'll need to draw in
response to a user command. Sometimes you'll want some fancy animation. Sometimes you'll want to draw your screen to a nonstandard display like a printer.
Sometimes, you'll want a widget with a custom look, and sometimes you'll just
want to be decorative. In wxPython, all these tasks are managed by manipulating
an appropriate device context.

A device context is the abstraction that wxPython uses to allow you to draw on ✗
a graphical device, such as the screen or a printer, without knowing the details of
that device. This is managed by providing an abstract parent class, wx.DC, which
defines a common API used by a series of subclasses, each of which represents a
different graphic device. Chapter 6 presents device contexts, with an extended
example of how to use them. In the following sections we'll discuss device contexts in more detail.

12.2.1 *What is a device context, and how can I create one?*

There are ten subclasses of wx.DC in wxPython, split into the following three groups:

- Contexts used for drawing to a screen
- Contexts used for drawing to a location other than a screen
- Contexts used to buffer a device context until you are ready to draw it to
  a screen

Screen-based device contexts

The first group represents device contexts that draw to the screen. You'd think there would only need to be one of these, but in fact wxPython provides four of them, depending on exactly where you need to draw, and exactly when you are doing the drawing.

- `wx.ClientDC`
- `wx.PaintDC`
- `wx.WindowDC`
- `wx.ScreenDC`

Screen device contexts are meant to be created temporarily. This means you should only create them locally whenever you need one for drawing, and allow them to be garbage collected normally. You should never try to hold on to a screen device context as, say, an instance variable—this is unsafe and could lead to an unstable program.

Typically, you will draw to a window on the screen using either a `wx.ClientDC` or a `wx.PaintDC`. Which one you use depends on when you are performing the drawing. If you are drawing to the screen during a `EVT_PAINT` event handler you must use `wx.PaintDC`. At all other times, you must use `wx.ClientDC`. In fact, whenever you bind a handler to the `EVT_PAINT` event, you must create a `wx.PaintDC` [1] object in the handler method even if you don't use it (not creating a `wx.PaintDC` can cause the platform to assume that the event wasn't fully handled and so it will send another event). The reason that the paint events require a different kind of device context is that the `wx.PaintDC` instances are optimized to only draw within the area of the window that is actually being refreshed during the redraw event, making redrawing faster.

You create a client or paint device context via a simple constructor whose one argument is the wxPython widget that you wish to draw upon—`wx.ClientDC(window)` or `wx.PaintDC(window)`. When you use these contexts, you will only be able to draw within the client area of that widget. This means that in a frame you will not be able to draw over the border, the title bar, or other decorations.

If you need to draw on the entire area of a frame including the borders and decorations, you should use a `wx.WindowDC`. You create a `wx.WindowDC` in the same way you would a `wx.ClientDC`—the constructor is `wx.WindowDC(window)`. Like a `wx.ClientDC`, you should not create a `wx.WindowDC` during a paint event—the border-drawing behavior is not compatible with the clipping optimization of the paint device context.

1 Creating a wx.BufferedPaint DC does the trick   cf 538,

Occasionally, you won't want to be limited to merely drawing to a single window, and you need the whole screen to be your canvas. In that case, you can use a wx.ScreenDC. Again, you should not create one of these during a paint event. The constructor takes no arguments (since you don't need to specify a window for the drawing to take place within)—wx.ScreenDC(). After that, you can use it just like any other device context. The images you draw are displayed on top of all of the windows in your display.

Non-screen device contexts

The second group of device contexts are used to draw to items other than a screen. This is sort of a grab bag of different kinds of things that can be treated as logically equivalent to a screen display.

- wx.MemoryDC   *# draw to a bitmap stored in memory*
- wx.MetafileDC
- wx.PostScriptDC
- wx.PrinterDC

The first of these is wx.MemoryDC, which allows you to draw to a bitmap that is stored in memory and not being displayed. You create a wx.MemoryDC with a no argument constructor, wx.MemoryDC(), but you must associate it with a bitmap before using it. This is accomplished by calling the method SelectObject(bitmap) with an argument of type wx.Bitmap. Once that is done, you can draw to the memory device context, and the internal bitmap is changed. When you are done drawing, you can use the Blit() method to draw the bitmap to a window. We'll discuss memory device contexts in more detail in the following section.

The creation of MS Windows metafiles is simplified by using the wx.MetafileDC context. This context is only available on Windows systems—although it's hard to imagine all that much call for creating metafiles on other systems (frankly, it's hard to imagine there's all that much call for it on Windows systems, either). You create a metafile device context by passing a constructor with a file name, wx.MetafileDC(filename=""). If the filename is blank, the metafile is created in memory, but it's worth noting that there's not much you can do with it within wxPython. After creation, draw commands sent to this device context are written to the file. When you are done drawing, you can optionally call the method Close() which has no effect on the file itself, but does return a wxPython wx.Metafile object. With the current version of wxPython, the only thing you can do with a wx.Metafile object is send it to the clipboard with the SetClipboard(width=0, height=0) method.

Similar functionality that is of greater use across platforms is the `wx.Post-` `ScriptDC` object that creates Encapsulated PostScript files (`.eps`) files. You create a `wx.PostScriptDC` file from a print data object—`wx.PostScriptDC(printData)`. The `printData` argument is of the type `wx.PrintData`, which will be discussed in chapter 17. Once created, the PostScript device context can be used like any other DC. The filename you save to can be set in the `wx.PrintData` object. So, you can save the `.eps` file as in the following example.

```
data = wx.PrintData()
data.SetFileName("/tmp/test.eps")
data.SetPaperId(wx.PAPER_LETTER)
dc = wx.PostScriptDC(data)
dc.StartDoc("")
dc.DrawCircle(300,300, 100)
dc.EndDoc() # the file is written at this point
```

On Windows systems, you can access any Windows printer driver using the `wx.PrinterDC`. This class is also created from a print data object—`wx.PrinterDC` `(printData)`. We'll discuss printing further in chapter 17.

505

Buffered device contexts

The third group of device contexts allows you to buffer a device context until you are ready to draw it to a screen.

- `wx.BufferedDC`

- `wx.BufferedPaintDC`

Buffering allows you to perform individual drawing commands to the buffer, and then draw them all to the screen in one shot. This prevents screen flicker when you are doing several redraws at once. As a result, buffering is a common technique when doing animation or other screen intensive drawing techniques.

There are two buffered device contexts in wxPython—`wx.BufferedDC`, which can be used to buffer any device context (but is normally used just with a `wx.ClientDC`), and `wx.BufferedPaintDC`, which is specifically designed to buffer a `wx.PaintDC`. The buffered contexts both work in essentially the same way, as something of a simplified wrapper around a memory device context. The wxBufferedDC constructor takes a device context and an optional bitmap as parameters—`wx.BufferedDC(dc, buffer=None)`. On the other hand, `wx.BufferedPaintDC` takes a window and an optional bitmap—`wx.BufferedPaintDC(dc, buffer=None)`. The dc argument is the device context where you want the drawing to end up when finished, for the `wx.BufferedPaintDC` window argument is used to create a `wx.PaintDC` internally and the `buffer` argument is a bitmap that is used as the temporary buffer. If the `buffer` argument is not specified, the device context creates its own bitmap internally. Once the buffered device context is created, you use it just as though it was the device context that you intend to have as the final drawing. Internally, the buffer context uses a memory device context and the bitmap to store the drawing. The shortcut is that you don't have to do anything in particular to get the buffer to draw to the real device context. It happens automatically. When the buffered device context is garbage collected (typically when the method ends and it drops out of scope), the C++ destructor function triggers the `Blit()` which draws the final contents of the buffer to the actual device context, with no further work needed on your part.

12.2.2 *How do I draw to a device context?*

Now that you have your device context, you may want to actually draw some pictures of your own onto it. One advantage of the device context concept is that your program does not care which kind of device context is being used—the draw commands are the same no matter what.

Using wxPython, there are many ways to draw to a device context. The device context API defines about eighteen or so different methods that allow you to draw on the screen. Table 12.4 lists the first batch: methods that let you draw geometric shapes. Unless stated otherwise, all of these methods use the current pen to draw their lines, and the current brush to fill in their shape. We'll discuss more details about pens and brushes later in this chapter.

Table 12.4 Device context methods for drawing geometric shapes

Method	Description
CrossHair(x, y)	Draws a cross-hair along the entire extent of the context—a horizontal line at the given y coordinate and a vertical line at the given x coordinate, meeting at the point (x, y).
DrawArc(x1, y1, x2, y2, xc, yc)	Draws a circular arc, starting at the point (x1, y1) and ending at the point (x2, y2). The center of the circle whose arc is being described is the point (xc, yc). The arc is drawn counterclockwise from the first point to the second point. The current brush is used to fill in the wedge shape.
DrawCheckMark(x, y, width, height)	Draws a check mark, as you'd see inside a selected check box, inside the rectangle with the upper left corner (x, y), and the given width and height. The brush is not used to fill the background.
DrawCircle(x, y, radius)	Draws a circle centered on (x, y) with the given radius.

continued on next page

Table 12.4 Device context methods for drawing geometric shapes *(continued)*

Method	Description
DrawEllipse(x, y, width, height)	Draws an ellipse inscribed inside the rectangle with an upper left corner at (x, y) and with the given `width` and `height`.
DrawEllipticArc(x, y, width, height, start, end)	Draws an arc of an eclipse. The first four parameters are as in `DrawEllipse`. The `start` and `end` parameters are the start and end angles of the arc relative to the three-o'clock position from the center of the rectangle. Angles are specified in degrees (360 is a complete circle). Positive values mean counterclockwise motion. If `start` is equal to `end`, a complete ellipse will be drawn.
DrawLine(x1, y1, x2, y2)	Draws a line which starts at the point (x1, y1) and ends before the point (x2, y2). (By long-standing and inscrutable graphic toolkit convention, the endpoint is not drawn by this method).
DrawLines(points, xoffset=0, yoffset=0)	Draws a series of lines. The `points` parameter is a list of instances of `wx.Point` (or two-element tuples that are converted to `wx.Point`). The lines are drawn from point to point until the end of the list. If the offset is used, it is applied to each point in the list, allowing a common shape to be drawn at any point in the DC. The brush is not used to fill in the shape.
DrawPolygon(points, xoffset=0, yoffset=0 fillstyle= wx.ODDEVEN_RULE)	Draws a series of lines, similar to `DrawLines`, except that a line is also drawn between the last point and the first, and the brush is used to fill the polygon.
DrawPoint(x, y)	Fills in the given point using the current pen.
DrawRectangle(x, y, width, height)	The point (x, y) is the upper left-hand corner of the rectangle, and the `width` and `height` parameters are the dimensions.
DrawRoundedRectangle (x, y, width, height, radius=20)	Exactly like `DrawRectangle()`, but with the corners replaced by 90 degrees of a circle. The `radius` parameter governs the curvature. If positive, it is the radius of the circle used in pixels. If negative, the value size of the circle is made proportional to the whichever dimension of the rectangle is smaller. (The exact formula is - radius * dimension)
DrawSpline(points)	Takes in a Python list of points and draws the appropriate spline curve. This curve is not filled in by the brush.
FloodFill(x, y, color, style=wx.FLOOD_SURFACE)	Fills the space with the color of the current brush. The algorithm starts at the point (x, y). If the style is `wx.FLOOD_SURFACE`, then all touching pixels which match the given `color` are redrawn. If the style is `wx.FLOOD_BORDER`, then all pixels are drawn until a border in the given `color` is reached.

For all of the `Draw` methods that take just an x and y parameter, there is a corresponding `Draw...Point` method that takes a `wx.Point` instance instead; for example, `DrawCirclePoint(pt, radius)`. If the method has both an x, y and a width, height pair, then there is a method that takes both a `wx.Point` and a `wx.Size`, and is called `Draw...PointSize`, for example, `DrawRectanglePointSize(pt, sz)`. Those methods also have a corresponding `Draw...Rect` version, that takes a `wx.Rect` instance, `DrawRectangleRect(rect)`.

You can get the size of the device context using the method `GetSize()`, which returns a `wx.Size` instance. You can retrieve the color value at a specific pixel with the method `GetPixel(x, y)`, which returns a `wx.Color` instance.

Figure 12.2 displays a screen shot of the picture we're going to build using the draw methods and double buffering.

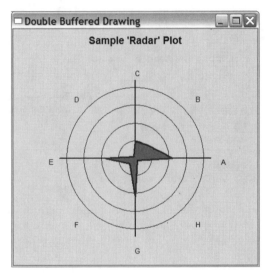

Figure 12.2
A sample radar graph

Listing 12.2 displays a simple radar graph that plots a collection of values in the range of 0-100 onto a polar coordinate system designed to easily show outliers. You may use this kind of graph to monitor some sort of resource allocation metrics, and a quick glance at the graph can tell you when conditions are good (within some accepted tolerance level), or approaching critical levels (total resource consumption). In this sample, the graph is continually refreshed with random data. This is a long example that demonstrates a number of things we've shown thus far.

Listing 12.2   Drawing a radar graph

```
import wx
import math
import random
```

(handwritten left margin: 538 digital clock)

```
class RadarGraph(wx.Window):          # Window subclass
    def __init__(self, parent, title, labels):
        wx.Window.__init__(self, parent)          list of strings
        self.title = title
        self.labels = labels
        self.data = [0.0] * len(labels)        eg [0.0, 0.0, ..., 0.0], length 8
        self.titleFont = wx.Font(14, wx.SWISS, wx.NORMAL, wx.BOLD)
        self.labelFont = wx.Font(10, wx.SWISS, wx.NORMAL, wx.NORMAL)

        self.InitBuffer()                    point size   family   style   weight

        self.Bind(wx.EVT_SIZE, self.OnSize)
        self.Bind(wx.EVT_PAINT, self.OnPaint)

    def OnSize(self, evt):
        # When the window size changes we need a new buffer.
        self.InitBuffer()

    def OnPaint(self, evt):
        dc = wx.BufferedPaintDC(self, self.buffer)
```

(handwritten: Fonts 196; ↑ point size family style weight)

❶ Refresh window from the buffer

❷ Creating the buffer

(handwritten left margin: 150: Similar use of buffer)

```
    def InitBuffer(self):
        w, h = self.GetClientSize()
        self.buffer = wx.EmptyBitmap(w, h)
        dc = wx.BufferedDC(wx.ClientDC(self), self.buffer)
        self.DrawGraph(dc)
        # dc goes out of scope: blit buffer to window
                            (During DrawGraph, draws made to a Memory DC)

    def GetData(self):
        return self.data

    def SetData(self, newData):
        assert len(newData) == len(self.data)
        self.data = newData[:]
        dc = wx.BufferedDC(wx.ClientDC(self), self.buffer)
        self.DrawGraph(dc)
```

Updating when data changes

```
    def PolarToCartesian(self, radius, angle, cx, cy):
        x = radius * math.cos(math.radians(angle))
        y = radius * math.sin(math.radians(angle))
        return (cx+x, cy-y)      # nice
```

*(handwritten above: h * 45)*

```
    def DrawGraph(self, dc):          ← Drawing the graph
        spacer = 10
        scaledmax = 150.0

        dc.SetBackground(wx.Brush(self.GetBackgroundColour()))
        dc.Clear()
        dw, dh = dc.GetSize()
```

(handwritten: lst = [[-,-,-,-],)

(handwritten diagrams of grids labeled dh and dw)

```
dc.SetFont(self.titleFont)
tw, th = dc.GetTextExtent(self.title)
dc.DrawText(self.title, (dw-tw)/2, spacer)
```
'Sample 'Radar' Plot' ↕ th

← tw →

←— **Drawing the title**

```
th = th + 2*spacer
cx = dw/2
cy = (dh-th)/2 + th
```
←— **Finding the center point**

| title & space | ↕ th + 2 * spacer |

← mindim

cx, cy

```
mindim = min(cx, (dh-th)/2)
scale = mindim/scaledmax
```
←— **Calculating the scale factor**

```
dc.SetPen(wx.Pen("black", 1))
dc.SetBrush(wx.TRANSPARENT_BRUSH)
dc.DrawCircle(cx,cy, 25*scale)
dc.DrawCircle(cx,cy, 50*scale)
dc.DrawCircle(cx,cy, 75*scale)
dc.DrawCircle(cx,cy, 100*scale)
```
←— **Drawing the ~~axes~~** *circles*

150 * scale ≐ mindim

```
dc.SetPen(wx.Pen("black", 2))
dc.DrawLine(cx-110*scale, cy, cx+110*scale, cy)
dc.DrawLine(cx, cy-110*scale, cx, cy+110*scale)
```
←— drawing the axes

horizontal

vertical

```
dc.SetFont(self.labelFont)
maxval = 0
angle = 0
polypoints = []
for i, label in enumerate(self.labels):
    val = self.data[i]
    point = self.PolarToCartesian(val*scale, angle, cx, cy)
    polypoints.append(point)
    x, y = self.PolarToCartesian(125*scale, angle, cx,cy)
    dc.DrawText(label, x, y)
    if val > maxval:
        maxval = val
    angle = angle + 360/len(self.labels)
```
['A', 'B',..., 'H']

Translating data values to polygon points

i ∈ [0, 1,..., 7]

←— **Drawing the labels**

determine maxval as we go

angle = angle + $\frac{360}{8}$

= angle + 45

```
c = "forest green"
if maxval > 70:
    c = "yellow"
if maxval > 95:
    c = "red"
dc.SetBrush(wx.Brush(c))
dc.SetPen(wx.Pen("navy", 3))
dc.DrawPolygon(polypoints)
```
←— **Setting brush color**

←— **Drawing the plot polygon**

```
class TestFrame(wx.Frame):
    def __init__(self):
        wx.Frame.__init__(self, None, title="Double Buffered Drawing",
                        size=(480,480))
        self.plot = RadarGraph(self, "Sample 'Radar' Plot",
                        ["A", "B", "C", "D", "E", "F", "G", "H"])
```

```
        # Set some random initial data values
        data = []    # for new plot vals
        for d in self.plot.GetData():    p362
            data.append(random.randint(0, 75))
        self.plot.SetData(data)

        # Create a timer to update the data values
        self.Bind(wx.EVT_TIMER, self.OnTimeout)
        self.timer = wx.Timer(self)          536
        self.timer.Start(500)
                        > ms; 50, ½ sec between timer events
    def OnTimeout(self, evt):
        # simulate the positive or negative growth of each data value
        data = []
        for d in self.plot.GetData():
            val = d + random.uniform(-5, 5)
            if val < 0:
                val = 0
            if val > 110:
                val = 110
            data.append(val)
        self.plot.SetData(data)

app = wx.PySimpleApp()
frm = TestFrame()
frm.Show()
app.MainLoop()
```

❶ This method does not need any drawing commands of its own. The buffered DC object automatically blits self.buffer to a wx.PaintDC when the device context is destroyed at the end of the method, Therefore, no new drawing needs to be done—we've already taken care of it.

❷ We create a buffer bitmap to be the same size as the window, then draw our graph to it. Since we use wx.BufferedDC whatever is drawn to the buffer will also be drawn to the window when the InitBuffer method is complete.

12.2.3 *How do I draw images to the context?*

Even with the existence of the image and bitmap objects mentioned at the beginning of this chapter, you will still need to use device context methods to draw images or copy from one device context to another, a process called a *blit*. One common use for this feature is to draw part of an image to the context. Historically, this was used to allow a program to deploy all of its peripheral images in one file, and use a partial blit to draw only the part that corresponded to a particular image or toolbar icon.

There are three device context methods used to draw images to the context, whether from another device context or from a preexisting image.

- `Blit()`
- `DrawBitmap()`
- `DrawIcon()`

Probably the most important method, and definitely the most complex one, is `Blit()`:

```
Blit(xdest, ydest, width, height, source, xsrc, ysrc,
     logicalFunc=wx.COPY, useMask=False, xsrcMask=-1,
     ysrcMask=-1)
```

[handwritten: srcdc]
[handwritten: destdc,]
[handwritten: # default logical operation # is overwrite]

Copying part of an image

The purpose of `Blit()` is to copy pixels rapidly from one device context to another. It's typically used when you want to copy part of one image to part of another image or to quickly copy pixel data to the screen. We've already seen that `Blit()` is used to manage buffered device contexts, for example. It is a very powerful and flexible method, with a number of parameters. Generally, it involves setting a rectangle on the destination context to be copied to, setting a rectangle on the source to copy from, and then a few parameters for the copy itself. The destination for a blit is the `wx.DC` instance whose `Blit()` method is being invoked. The `xdest` and `ydest` parameters are the location of the top left corner of the rectangle in the destination context where the data copy will begin. The `width` and `height` parameters set the size of the rectangle to be copied. The `source` is the other `wx.DC` where the pixels are coming from. This can be any other subclass of `wx.DC`. The `xsrc` and `ysrc` parameters denote the position on the source device context where the copying should start—obviously this will not necessarily be the same as `xdest` and `ydest`. However, the width and height parameters are shared between the source and destination—the two rectangles must be the same size.

The `logicalFunc` is the algorithm used to merge the old pixels and the new—the default behavior is to overwrite, but various kinds of XORish behavior can be defined. In table 12.6, we'll show a complete list of logical functions. If the `useMask` parameter is `True`, the blit is performed with a mask governing which pixels are actually copied. In this case, the selected source area must be a bitmap with an associated mask or alpha channel. If specified, the `xsrcMask` and `ysrcMask` parameters govern where on the mask the copy starts. If they aren't specified, then `xsrc` and `ysrc` are used. There is also a `BlitPointSize()` version of the method which replaces all three point pairs with wx.Point instances, and the width and height with a wx.Size.

Drawing a bitmap

Assuming you want to draw a complete image onto your device context, there are a couple of simpler methods you can use. To draw a bitmap, you have Draw-Bitmap(bitmap, x, y, useMask=False). The bitmap parameter is a wx.Bitmap object, which is drawn to the device context at the point (x, y). The useMask parameter is a Boolean. If it is False, the image is drawn normally. If True, and if the bitmap has a mask or alpha channel associated with it, then the mask is used to determine which parts of the bitmap are transparent. If the bitmap is monochromatic, the current text foreground and background colors are used for the bitmap, otherwise, the bitmap's own color scheme is used. Figure 12.3 displays that functionality.

(10, 10)

Figure 12.3
Drawing a face to the
screen multiple times

Listing 12.3 displays a simple example of using a device context to display a bitmap, as used to create figure 12.3.

Listing 12.3 Creating a device context and drawing a bitmap

```
import wx
import random
random.seed()
```

```
class RandomImagePlacementWindow(wx.Window):     # window subclass
    def __init__(self, parent, image):
        wx.Window.__init__(self, parent)
        self.photo = image.ConvertToBitmap()     ←— Getting the bitmap      @ 359
                                                  ensure at least one image in view
        self.positions = [(10,10)]   ←— Creating random locations
        for x in range(50):                                          ?
            x = random.randint(0, 1000)
            y = random.randint(0, 1000)
            self.positions.append( (x,y) )

        self.Bind(wx.EVT_PAINT, self.OnPaint)

    def OnPaint(self, evt):    — Window instance
        dc = wx.PaintDC(self)
        brush = wx.Brush("sky blue")
        dc.SetBackground(brush)
        dc.Clear()      ←— Clearing the DC with the background brush

        for x,y in self.positions:      ←— Drawing the bitmap
            dc.DrawBitmap(self.photo, x, y, True)

class TestFrame(wx.Frame):
    def __init__(self):
        wx.Frame.__init__(self, None, title="Loading Images",
                          size=(640,480))
        img = wx.Image("masked-portrait.png")
        win = RandomImagePlacementWindow(self, img)
                                  parent of our window is our frame
app = wx.PySimpleApp()
frm = TestFrame()
frm.Show()
app.MainLoop()
```

You may also draw a wx.Icon with DrawIcon(icon, x, y), which places the wx.Icon object at the point (x, y) in the device context. Any other image that you want to draw to the device context must first be converted to either a wx.Bitmap or a wx.Icon.

12.2.4 How can I draw text to the context?

To draw text into your device context, the method is DrawText(text, x, y). The string to draw is passed to the text parameter, and the x and y parameters mark the upper-left corner of the drawn text, meaning that the text is drawn below the y coordinate you pass. For angled text, use the DrawRotatedText(text, x, y, angle) method. The angle parameter is in degrees. A positive value rotates the text clockwise, and a negative value rotates it counterclockwise. The corresponding `DrawTextPoint(text, pt)` and `DrawRotatedTextPoint(text, pt, angle)` versions are also available.

You control the style of the text with features of the device context itself. The device context maintains a current font, text foreground color, and text background color. You can access this information with the getter and setter methods `GetTextForeground()`, `SetTextForegroud(color)`, `GetTextBackground()`, `SetTextBackground(color)`, `GetFont()`, and `SetFont(font)`. In wxPython you can specify whether text even has a background color with the method `SetBackgroundMode(mode)`. The legal values for `mode` are `wx.SOLID` if you want text to have a background color and `wx.TRANSPARENT` if you do not.

When putting text on the screen, it's useful to know in advance how much space it will take up. If you just want to know the general dimensions of the current font, you can use the methods `GetCharHeight()` and `GetCharWidth()` which return the average character height and width of the current font.

You can determine exactly how much space a specific string will take up with the method `GetTextExtent(string)`. This method returns a tuple (`width`, `height`) showing the exact dimensions of the rectangle bounding this text were it to be drawn in the current font. For more detail, use the method `GetFullTextExtent(string)`, which returns a tuple (`width`, `height`, `descent`, `externalLeading`). The `descent` value is the distance between the nominal baseline of the font and the actual bottom of the rectangle (where descending letters such as "y" are drawn), and the external leading is the (usually zero) amount of space added to the vertical dimension by the font itself. Often, what you really need to do with text extents is determine exactly where within the text a specific width is crossed (such as the right margin of your text display). The `GetPartialTextExtents(text)` method is a handy shortcut. It returns a list where each element is the width of the displayed string up to that point. The first element shows the display width of just the first character, the second element shows the width of the first two characters, and so on. To put it another way, it returns a list, `widths`, calculated as follows:

```
widths[i] = GetTextExtent(text[:i])[0]
```

The list can be used to determine how many characters you can draw in the available space.

All graphic operations are governed by the abstractions for pens and brushes to manage the characteristics of the foreground and background of your drawing. In the next section, we'll cover those objects.

12.3 *Graphics manipulation*

Graphics work is not limited to images and device contexts. There are other abstractions that allow you to control the drawings you make. In this section, we'll talk about the pen used for drawing lines, the brush used to paint backgrounds, pixel manipulation, and color names.

12.3.1 *How do I manage the foreground drawing pen?*

The color and style of the lines you draw on your device context are controlled by the current pen, which is an instance of the class wx.Pen. To get the current pen, use the device context method GetPen(). Not surprisingly, you can set the current pen with SetPen(pen).

The wx.Pen class is a simple structure with several properties related to drawing lines. The constructor for wx.Pen lets you set some of the properties.

```
wx.Pen(colour, width=1, style=wx.SOLID)
```

The colour parameter is either a wx.Colour object or any of the things that can be automatically converted to one—a tuple of RGB values, a string color name, or a string of RGB hex values such as "#12C588". The width is the width of the pen line, in pixels. The style controls the way in which the line is displayed. Table 12.5 displays the legal values of the style parameter—note that not all styles are supported on all platforms.

Table 12.5 Drawing styles of wx.Pen

Style	Description
wx.BDIAGONAL_HATCH	The pen will draw backward (northwest to southeast) hatch lines.
wx.CROSSDIAG_HATCH	A combination of wx.BDIAGONAL_HATCH and wx.FDIAGONAL_HATCH—in other words, it creates x shapes.
wx.CROSS_HATCH	Crosshatched + shapes.
wx.DOT	Small dots.
wx.DOT_DASH	Alternating between small dots and longer dashes.
wx.FDIAGONAL_HATCH	The pen will draw forward (southwest to northeast) hatch lines.
wx.HORIZONTAL_HATCH	Short, horizontal hash lines.
wx.LONG_DASH	Long dashes.

continued on next page

Table 12.5 Drawing styles of `wx.Pen` *(continued)*

Style	Description
wx.SHORT_DASH	Shorter dashes.
wx.SOLID	A solid line. This is the default.
wx.STIPPLE	Use a provided bitmap as the pen stroke.
wx.TRANSPARENT	Do not draw any lines.
wx.USER_DASH	Use the provided dash pattern.
wx.VERTICAL_HATCH	Vertical hash lines.

In addition to the complete constructor, there are a number of predefined pens, listed next. The description of the pens should be clear from the name—any attribute not specified in the pen name will be set the default value.

```
wx.BLACK_DASHED_PEN
wx.BLACK_PEN
wx.CYAN_PEN
wx.GREEN_PEN
wx.GREY_PEN
wx.LIGHT_GREY_PEN
wx.MEDIUM_GREY_PEN
wx.RED_PEN
wx.TRANSPARENT_PEN
wx.WHITE_PEN
```

The color, width, and style properties of the pen are accessible after creation with the normal property method names—`GetColour()`, `SetColour(color)`, `GetWidth()`, `SetWidth(width)`, `GetStyle()`, and `SetStyle()`. There are a couple of other properties that you can change in the pen. One is the end cap, the style that the pen uses at the end of a line. Typically, this is only visible for lines that are wider than one pixel. The methods are `GetCap()` and `SetCap(cap)`. The valid values for the cap are: `wx.CAP_BUTT`, which ends the line with a straight edge, `wx.CAP_PROJECTING`, which puts a square projection on the end of the line, and `wx.CAP_ROUND`, which rounds off the end of the line with a semicircle. The default is `wx.CAP_ROUND`. Similarly, you can define the join style, which is what the pen draws when two lines meet. The methods for this are `wx.GetJoin()`, and `wx.SetJoin(join)`. The legal join values are: `wx.JOIN_BEVEL`, where the outside corners of the two lines are merely connected with a straight line, `wx.JOIN_MITER`, where the outer edges of the two lines are continued until they meet at a point, and wx.JOIN_ROUND, which places a circular arc over the meeting points to round off the corner. The default is wx.JOIN_ROUND.

If you create the pen with the wx.USER_DASH style, you can set the specific style of the dash with the methods GetDashes() and SetDashes(dashes). The dashes parameter is a list of 16-bit strings of ones and zeroes. Each dash is interpreted with a 1 being a drawn pixel and a 0 being an undrawn pixel. The user dash pen style cycles through the provided dashes when drawing a pen line. If the pen has the wx.STIPPLE style, you can set a bitmap to be used as the stipple with Set-Stipple(stipple), and you can recover the bitmap with GetStipple().

When you are drawing with a pen (or blitting from another bitmap), the exact algorithm used to set the pixel in the destination context is called the *logical function*, and you can set it with SetLogicalFunction(function). The default value is wx.COPY, which places the source color as-is onto the destination. The other logical functions perform various bitwise operations using the color values of the source and destination. The most commonly used operations are wx.XOR and wx.INVERT, both of which can be used to manage *rubber-banding* or other graphic mechanisms where you need to set a pixel to another color temporarily, and then set it right back. Those are far from the only functions offered by wxPython, however. Table 12.6 displays the complete list, with the algorithms written out in Python bitwise operators.

Following is a quick just-in-time refresher on Python bitwise operators.

    &   bitwise and
    | bitwise or
    ^   bitwise exclusive or
    ~   bitwise complement

Table 12.6 Logical copy functions

Function	Algorithm
wx.AND	source & destination
wx.AND_INVERT	~source & destination
wx.AND_REVERSE	source & ~destination
wx.CLEAR	All pixels set to 0—black
wx.COPY	source
wx.EQUIV	~source ^ destination

continued on next page

Table 12.6 Logical copy functions *(continued)*

Function	Algorithm
wx.INVERT	~destination
wx.NAND	~source | ~destination
wx.NOR	~source & ~destination
wx.NO_OP	destination
wx.OR	source | destination
wx.OR_INVERT	~source | destination
wx.OR_REVERSE	source | ~destination
wx.SET	All pixels set to 1—white
wx.SRC_INVERT	~source
wx.XOR	source ^ destination

Again, the logical function applies any time pixels are drawn to the device context, whether using the draw functions or blit.

12.3.2 *How do I manage the background drawing brush?*

Any kind of fill operation, including flood fill or the fill of items created using the draw functions, is managed using the device context's current brush, which is an instance of wx.Brush. You can get the current brush using GetBrush(), and set one with SetBrush(brush). Calling the DC method Clear() redraws the entire device context using the current background brush.

The brush instances are a bit simpler than the pen. Here is the constructor for wx.Brush.

```
wx.Brush(colour, style=wx.SOLID)
```

The colour is, of course, the color used by the brush. As usual, it can be a wx.Colour instance, or an RGB-tuple, or a string. The style governs how the brush fills space, and can be one of the following, all of which have the same meaning as they do for wx.Pen.

```
wxBDIAGONAL_HATCH
wxCROSSDIAG_HATCH
wxCROSS_HATCH
wxFDIAGONAL_HATCH
wxHORIZONTAL_HATCH
```

```
wxSOLID
wxSTIPPLE
wxTRANSPARENT
wxVERTICAL_HATCH
```

The color and style can be manipulated via getter and setter—GetColour(), Set-Colour(colour), GetStyle(), SetStyle(). The only other thing you can do with a brush is set the stipple pattern with SetStipple(bitmap). If you create a stipple for the brush, then the style is also set to wx.STIPPLE for you. You can retrieve the stipple using GetStipple().

12.3.3 *How can I manage logical and physical device coordinates?*

In this section we'll talk about a variety of ways that wxPython allows you to manage coordinates, sizing, and the like. Let's start with coordinate axis management. Ordinarily, the coordinate system of a wxPython device context starts with (0, 0) in the upper-left, with the *y* coordinate getting larger as you move down, and the *x* coordinate getting larger as you move right. This is in keeping with the standard of nearly every graphics system since the beginning of time, and of course, the y-axis is flipped from the normal way a mathematical plane is drawn. Should the inconsistency with your geometry textbook bother you, you can change the orientation with the method SetAxisOrientation(xLeftRight, yBottomUp); both of the parameters are Boolean. If xLeftRight is True, then the x-axis increases from left to right, if it's False then the axis is flipped and increases from right to left. Similarly, if yBottomUp is True then the y-axis increases as it heads up, otherwise, it increases as it heads down.

The coordinate axis is measured in pixels. However, at times you'll want to store your dimension in some more useful real-world measurement. You can manage the conversion by setting a *map mode* with the method SetMapMode(mode). The map mode is a conversion that the device context will use between the physical coordinates of the screen and the logical coordinates in the measurement you specify. The legal values of the mode are displayed in table 12.7.

Table 12.7   Device context mapping modes

Mode	Logical Unit
wx.MM_LOMETRIC	0.1 millimeters
wx.MM_METRIC	1 millimeter

continued on next page

Table 12.7 Device context mapping modes *(continued)*

Mode	Logical Unit
wx.MM_POINTS	A point (as in the printing unit of measure—point size). Equal to 1/72nd of an inch.
wx.MM_TEXT	Default value. The unit is 1 pixel.
wx.MM_TWIPS	Printing unit, 20 to a point, or 1440 to an inch.

The accuracy of the logical to physical mapping depends on how well your system reports the dot pitch of the monitor in order to perform the conversion. You can see the value being used for the conversion with the method GetPPI(), which returns the value of pixels per inch. In practice, I wouldn't depend on a logical inch exactly matching a real inch.

The mapping mode conversions are automatically applied to your points and sizes when you use a device context method. Sometimes you will need to perform the conversion outside the device context. To convert from your logical coordinate to the device coordinate you use the methods LogicalToDeviceX(x) and LogicalToDeviceY(y). Both of these methods take in the integer measurements in the logical coordinates, apply the mapping mode, and return the measurement in device coordinates. There are related methods which use the mapping mode, but do not care about the current orientation of the axes, in essence taking an absolute value of the coordinate. Those methods are called LogicalToDevice-XRel(x) and LogicalToDeviceYRel(y).

The inverse set of methods take a location on the device axis and convert it to the logical coordinate system. Those methods, as you might guess, are called DeviceToLogicalX(x), DeviceToLogicalY(y), DeviceToLogicalXRel(x), and Device-ToLogcialYRel(y).

There are a series of device context methods that allow some information and control over the portion of the device context that you are drawing in. Often, you want to restrict drawing updates to a particular section of the device context. This is usually done for performance reasons, especially if you know that only one portion of a large or complex graphic needs to be redrawn. This kind of redraw is called *clipping*, and the method for setting it is SetClippingRegion(x, y, width, height). The four parameters specify a rectangle with the upper left corner, and the dimensions. Once set, only drawing actions taking place within the clipping region will be processed. To unset a clipping region, use the method Destroy-ClippingRegion(), which completely clears the clipping region. After that method is called, drawing actions are processed throughout the device context. To read the current clipping region, use the method `GetClippingBox()`, which returns a tuple `(x, y, width, height)`.

As you draw into a device context, wxPython maintains the value of the rectangle that would minimally surround all the drawing you have done to the context. This rectangle is called the *bounding box*, and is often useful in determining if the context needs to be refreshed. You can get the four sides of the bounding box with the methods `MaxX()`, `MaxY()`, `MinX()`, `MinY()`. These methods return the appropriate minimum or maximum value in device coordinates for the bounding box in the direction specifed. If there's a specific point on the screen that you want within the bounding box for some reason, you can add it with the method `Calc-BoundingBox(x, y)`, which recalculates the extent of the bounding box exactly as though you had drawn something at that point. You can start the bounding box calculations all over with the method `ResetBoundingBox()`. After that method is called, the bounding box reverts to its default state, as if nothing had been drawn to the context.

12.3.4 *What color names are predefined?*

The following color names are guaranteed to be recognized by wxPython:

aquamarine	black	blue	blue violet
brown	cadet blue	coral	cornflower blue
cyan	dark gray	dark green	dark olive green
dark orchid	dark slate blue	dark slate gray	dark turquoise
dim gray	firebrick	forest green	gold
goldenrod	gray	green	green yellow
indian red	khaki	light blue	light gray
light steel blue	lime green	magenta	maroon
medium aquamarine	medium blue	medium forest green	medium goldenrod
medium orchid	medium sea green	medium slate blue	medium spring green
medium turquoise	medium violet red	midnight blue	navy
orange	orange red	orchid	pale green
pink	plum	purple	red
salmon	sea green	sienna	sky blue

14×4 = 56

slate blue	spring green	steel blue	tan
thistle	turquoise	violet	violet red
wheat	white	yellow	yellow green

3×4 = 12   56+12 = 68 named colours

An additional set of color names and values can be loaded into the in-memory color database using the `updateColourDB` function located in the `wx.lib.colourdb` module.

12.4 Summary

- In wxPython, you can easily perform common graphics operations including image manipulation and drawing onto the screen. Images are managed via the class `wx.Image`, which handles platform-independent image tools, such as loading from common image file formats, and the class `wx.Bitmap`, which handles platform-dependent tasks such as drawing the image to the screen. Predefined image handlers exist for the most popular file formats. Once you have a `wx.Image` instance, you can do a variety of useful filtering operations on the data. You can define a transparent mask color, which causes a specific color in the image to be rendered as though it was transparent, allowing for chroma-key effects. You can also define a series of alpha values to make the image partially transparent on a pixel-by-pixel basis.

- A bitmap can be created from a bitmap file, or it can take in a `wx.Image` object and convert it to a bitmap. The only advantage of having your image in a `wx.Bitmap` instance is that wxPython needs an instance of `wx.Bitmap` in order to be able to draw your image to the screen.

- You can create your own cursor or use one of about two dozen stock cursors, including the most commonly used arrows and wait cursers, as well as some more obscure ones. You can also create your own cursor from a `wx.Image` instance.

- Actual drawing to the screen or to any of a number of other virtual devices is managed through the device context class `wx.DC`, which is an abstract class defining a common API for drawing. Various subclasses of `wx.DC` allow you to draw to the screen, directly to memory or to a file, or to a printer. Device contexts should only be created locally in your program, and should not be stored globally. When drawing to the screen, the type of device context you use depends on whether or not you are drawing within an `EVT_PAINT` handler. There also are separate device contexts which allow you to draw outside the normal client area of a window or on an arbitrary place on the screen, even if it is not inside your window.

- Other kinds of device contexts, such as `wx.MemoryDC` or `wx.BufferedDC`, allow you to draw directly to memory for the purpose of buffering draw operations until you are ready to show the completed image on screen. The `wx.BufferedDC` and `wx.BufferedPaintDC` classes allow a simple shortcut to managing buffered drawing.

- Several different methods allow you to draw lines or geometric shapes to a device context. Many of them have secondary forms allowing you to pass `wx.Size` or `wx.Point` instances to them directly rather than having to break them out into component pieces. You can draw text to the device context, either straight or rotated an arbitrary number of degrees. Helper methods allow you to manage the font, and determine how much space on the screen your text will cover.

- In addition to being able to draw a bitmap to the device context, you can perform a `Blit()` which allows you to rapidly copy part of the content of one device context to another. You can also draw an icon to the device context.

- You control the color and style of your drawing with a `wx.Pen` instance, which handles foreground drawing, and a `wx.Brush` instance, which handles background filling. In both cases, the device context maintains a current value for the object, which you can change at will. You can set the color and style for both objects, and for a pen you can also manage the width and dash pattern. The exact way in which the source pixel from the pen is combined with the color already existing in the device context is computed with the logical function—the default is to just copy the source over the destination, but there are a variety of other flavors to choose from.

- The device context draws in physical coordinates, meaning pixels, but you can set a parallel logical scale in inches or millimeters, and convert all your coordinates to their physical pixel values when you draw. You can also set the clipping region, which sets a rectangle in your device context as being the only area in which drawing should actually take place. The inverse of the clipping region is the bounding box, which is the rectangle representing the region of your device context in which drawing has already taken place.

Part 3

Advanced wxPython

In this part we start with three more complex widget objects, and move to features that won't be a part of every wxPython program, but are good to know for the times when you will need to, say, print something.

In chapter 13, "Building list controls and managing items," we cover the list control. More advanced than the simple list box, the list control allows a full Windows Explorer-like display, complete with different modes. You'll see how to switch between modes, add text and images to the list, and respond to user events. Chapter 14, "Coordinating the grid control," adds another dimension to the list, resulting in the grid control. Grids are very flexible, and we'll show you all the ways to manage your data in the grid, as well as the mechanisms for customizing grid display and editing. Chapter 15, "Climbing the tree control," deals with the tree control, which allows you to compactly display tree hierarchies. We'll show how to manage the tree data, traverse the tree, and customize the tree display.

In chapter 16, "Incorporating HTML into your application," we'll show how HTML is a convenient way to specify styles for text labels and for printing. We'll show you how HTML widgets work, and their limitations with respect to standard HTML. Chapter 17, "The wxPython printing framework," covers print issues, how to draw to a printer, as well as how to manage the standard print dialogs to communicate between wxPython and the underlying print system. We'll also show you how to add print preview functionality. Chapter 18, "Using other wxPython functionality," covers topics that didn't fit elsewhere. It covers passing data back and forth via the clipboard, then how to manage drag and drop operations. We'll also show you how to create periodic behavior using timers, and offer a few thoughts on threading in wxPython applications.

Building list controls
and managing items

This chapter covers

- Creating list controls in different styles
- Managing items in a list
- Responding to user selections from lists
- Editing labels and sorting lists
- Creating large list controls

Everyone has a list she needs to see, and wxPython programmers are no exception. In wxPython, there are two controls that you can use to display list-based information. The simpler is the list box, which is a plain single-column scrolled list similar to what you get from an HTML `<select>` tag. List boxes were discussed in chapter 8, and will not be discussed further in this chapter.

This chapter focuses on the more complicated list display, *list control*, a full-featured list widget. The list control displays `ListCtrl` multiple columns of information for each row, sorts based on any column, and can be displayed in different styles. You have a lot of flexibility over the detailed display of each part of the list control.

13.1 *Building a list control*

The list control can be created in one of four different modes:

- icon
- small icon
- list
- report

The basic idea of the modes should be familiar to you if you've ever used MS Windows Explorer or the Mac Finder—they correspond roughly to those programs' view options. We'll start our exploration of the list control by describing how to build a list control in each of the various modes.

13.1.1 *What is icon mode?*

A list control looks like the display panel of a file tree system like MS Windows Explorer. The control displays a list of information in one of four different modes. The default is *icon mode*, where each element in the list is displayed as an icon with the text for the item below. Figure 13.1 displays a sample list in icon mode.

The code for figure 13.1 is displayed in listing 13.1. Note that listing 13.1 depends on some .png files being in the directory with this module. These files are available at the book's website for you to run this example.

Listing 13.1   Creating a sample list in icon mode

```
import wx
import sys, glob

class DemoFrame(wx.Frame):
    def __init__(self):
        wx.Frame.__init__(self, None, -1,
```

```
                    "wx.ListCtrl in wx.LC_ICON mode",
                    size=(600,400))
    il = wx.ImageList(32,32, True)   ◁— Creating an image list
    for name in glob.glob("icon??.png"):
        bmp = wx.Bitmap(name, wx.BITMAP_TYPE_PNG)
        il_max = il.Add(bmp)            ◁—| Creating the list widget
    self.list = wx.ListCtrl(self, -1    ◁—|
            style=wx.LC_ICON | wx.LC_AUTOARRANGE)
    self.list.AssignImageList(il, wx.IMAGE_LIST_NORMAL)
    for x in range(25):         ◁—┐ Populating the list
        img = x % (il_max+1)      └
        self.list.InsertImageStringItem(x,
                "This is item %02d" % x, img)

app = wx.PySimpleApp()
frame = DemoFrame()
frame.Show()
app.MainLoop()
```

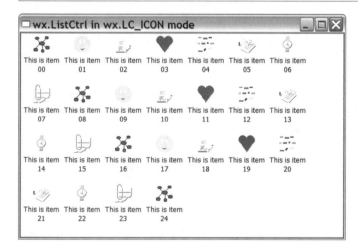

Figure 13.1
A sample list in icon mode

In listing 13.1, the demo frame creates an *image list* to hold references to the images to be displayed, then it builds and populates the list control. We'll discuss image lists later in this chapter.

13.1.2 *What is small icon mode?*

Small icon mode is like the regular icon mode, but with smaller icons. Figure 13.2 displays the same sample list, this time in small icon mode.

Small icon mode is most useful when you want to fit more items in the widget display, especially when the icons are not detailed enough to require being shown in full size.

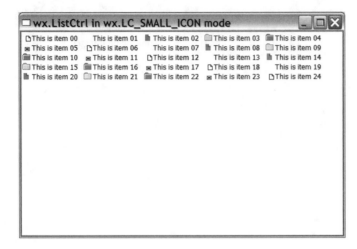

**Figure 13.2
A sample list control
in small icon mode**

13.1.3 *What is list mode?*

In *list mode*, the list displays in multiple columns, automatically wrapping from the bottom of one column to the top of the next as needed, as displayed in figure 13.3.

List mode has nearly all of the same strengths as small icon mode. The choice between them is largely a matter of whether column organization or row organization makes more sense for your data.

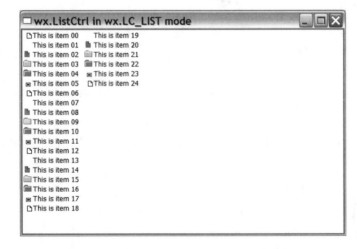

**Figure 13.3
A sample list
control in list mode**

13.1.4 *What is report mode?*

In *report mode*, the list is displayed in a true multi-column format, with each row able to have an arbitrary number of columns attached to it, as displayed in figure 13.4.

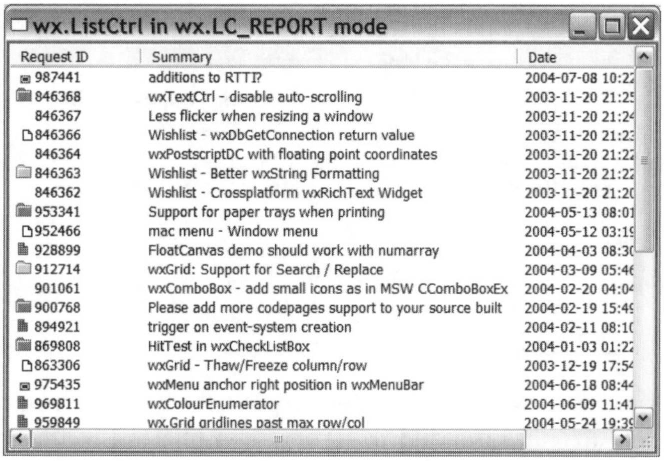

Figure 13.4
A sample list control in report mode

The report mode is different enough from the icon mode that it's worth presenting the sample code here as well. Listing 13.2 displays the code for creating a list in report mode.

> **Listing 13.2 Creating a sample list in report mode**

```
import wx
import sys, glob, random
import data

class DemoFrame(wx.Frame):
    def __init__(self):
        wx.Frame.__init__(self, None, -1,
                          "wx.ListCtrl in wx.LC_REPORT mode",
                          size=(600,400))

        il = wx.ImageList(16,16, True)
        for name in glob.glob("smicon??.png"):
            bmp = wx.Bitmap(name, wx.BITMAP_TYPE_PNG)
            il_max = il.Add(bmp)                          Creating the list
        self.list = wx.ListCtrl(self, -1, style=wx.LC_REPORT)   ◁┘
        self.list.AssignImageList(il, wx.IMAGE_LIST_SMALL)

        for col, text in enumerate(data.columns):     ◁── Adding columns
```

```
                        self.list.InsertColumn(col, text)

            for item in data.rows:        ⊲⏋ Adding rows
                index = self.list.InsertStringItem(sys.maxint, item[0])
                for col, text in enumerate(item[1:]):
                    self.list.SetStringItem(index, col+1, text)

                # give each item a random image
                img = random.randint(0, il_max)
                self.list.SetItemImage(index, img, img)

            self.list.SetColumnWidth(0, 120)     ⊲⏋ Setting column widths
            self.list.SetColumnWidth(1, wx.LIST_AUTOSIZE)
            self.list.SetColumnWidth(2, wx.LIST_AUTOSIZE)
            self.list.SetColumnWidth(3, wx.LIST_AUTOSIZE_USEHEADER)

app = wx.PySimpleApp()
frame = DemoFrame()
frame.Show()
app.MainLoop()
```

In the next sections, we'll discuss how the values are inserted into the proper locations. Report controls are not intended to be very complicated in their display logic. They are best suited for simple lists that contain one or two extra columns of data. If your list control is complex, or contains more data, it is recommended that you switch to a grid control, as described in chapter 14.

13.1.5 *How do I create a list control?*

A wxPython list control is an instance of the class wx.ListCtrl. The constructor is similar to the other widget constructors, as shown here

```
wx.ListCtrl(parent, id, pos=wx.DefaultPosition,
        size=wx.DefaultSize, style=wx.LC_ICON,
        validator=wx.DefaultValidator, name="listCtrl")
```

These parameters contain values from other widget constructors we have seen. The parent is the containing widget, the id is the wxPython identifier, with -1 indicating automatic creation. Explicit layout is managed by pos and size. The style controls the mode and other display options—we'll see those values throughout this chapter. The validator is used to validate specific inputs and is discussed in chapter 9. The name parameter is rarely used.

The style flag is a bitmask that manages a few different features of the list control. The first set of values that can be included in the style flag sets the mode in which the list displays. The default mode value is wx.LC_ICON. Table 13.1 displays the list control mode values.

Table 13.1 List control mode values

Style	Description
wx.LC_ICON	Icon mode, with large icons
wx.LC_LIST	List mode
wx.LC_REPORT	Report mode
wx.LC_SMALL_ICON	Icon mode, with small icons

In an icon or small icon list, there are three style flags that control the alignment of the icon relative to the list. The default value, wx.LC_ALIGN_TOP, aligns the icons to the top of the list. To get a left alignment, use wx.LC_ALIGN_LEFT. The style LC_AUTOARRANGE wraps the icons when reaching the right or bottom edge of the window.

Table 13.2 displays styles for a report list that affect the display.

Table 13.2 Display styles for a report list

Style	Default
wx.LC_HRULES	Display grid lines between rows of the list
wx.LC_NO_HEADER	Do not display the column headers.
wx.LC_VRULES	Display grid lines between columns of the list

Bitmask flags can be combined with the bitwise or operation. Use wx.LC_REPORT | wx.LC_HRULES | wx.LC_VRULES to get a list which looks very much like a grid. By default, all list controls allow multiple selection. To modify this so that only one item in the list can be selected at a time, pass the flag wx.LC_SINGLE_SEL.

Unlike other widgets we have seen, the list control adds a couple of methods to allow you to change style flags at runtime on an already existing list control. The method SetSingleStyle(style, add=True) allows you to add or remove one style flag, based on the contents of the add parameter. The call listCtrl.SetSingle-Style(LC_HRULES, True) adds horizontal rules, while the call listCtrl.SetSingle-Style(LC_HRULES, False) removes them. The call SetWindowStyleFlag(style) allows you to reset the whole window style, given an entire new bitmask, such as SetWindowStyleFlag(LC_REPORT | LC_NO_HEADER). These methods are useful for modifying the list control mode on the fly.

13.2 *Managing items in a list*

Once the control list is created, you can begin adding information to the list. In wxPython, this job is managed differently for textual information than it is for the images associated with each item in the list. In the following sections, we'll show you how to add images and text to your list control.

13.2.1 *What is an image list and how do I add images to it?*

Before we can talk about how information is added to the list control, we need to say a few words about how a list control manages images. Any image used within a list control must first be added to an image list, which is an indexed array of images stored with the list control. When associating an image with a specific item in the list control, the index of the image within the image list is used to refer to the image, rather than using the image itself. This mechanism ensures that each image is loaded only once, no matter how often it is used in the list. This serves to conserve memory in the case where an icon is repeated in several items in a list. It also allows for a relatively straightforward connection between multiple versions of the same image that can be used to denote different modes. For more information on creating wxPython images and bitmaps, see chapter 12.

Creating an image list

The image list is an instance of `wx.ImageList`, with the following constructor.

```
wx.ImageList(width, height, mask=True, initialCount=1)
```

The `width` and `height` parameters specify the pixel size of the images added to the list. Images larger than the specified size are not allowed. The `mask` parameter is a Boolean. If `True`, the image is drawn with its mask, if it has one. The `initialCount` parameter sets the initial internal size of the list. If you know that the list is going to be quite large, specifying the count initially may save memory allocations and time later on.

Adding and removing images

You can add an image to the list using the method `Add(bitmap, mask=wx.NullBitmap)`, where `bitmap` and `mask` are both instances of `wx.Bitmap`. The `mask` argument is a monochrome bitmap that represents the transparent parts of the image, if any. If the bitmap already has a mask associated with it, the associated mask is used by default. If the bitmap doesn't have a mask and you don't have a monochrome transparency map, but would rather set a specific color of the bitmap as the transparent color, you can use the method `AddWithColourMask(bitmap,` colour), where the colour is the wxPython color (or the name of one) to use as the mask. If you have a wx.Icon object to add to the image list, use the method AddIcon(icon). All of the add methods return the index where the new image has been assigned inside the list, which you can hold on to if you want to use the image later on.

The following code snippet displays an example of creating an image list (similar to listing 13.1).

```
il = wx.ImageList(32, 32, True)
for name in glob.glob("icon??.png"):
    bmp = wx.Bitmap(name, wx.BITMAP_TYPE_PNG)
    il_max = il.Add(bmp)
```

The image list must then be assigned to a list control using the following method call.

```
self.list.AssignImageList(il, wx.IMAGE_LIST_NORMAL)
```

To remove an image from the image list, use the Remove(index) method, where index is the integer index into the image list. This method modifies the index values for any image after that point in the image list, which might cause problems if you are dependent on specific index values elsewhere in the program. To remove the entire image list, use RemoveAll(). You can modify the bitmap at a specific index with the method Replace(index, bitmap, mask=wx.NullBitmap), where index is the index in the image list to modify, and bitmap and mask are as in Add(). If the item to modify is an icon, use the method ReplaceIcon(index, icon). There isn't a replace method that manages color masks.

Using the image list

You can get the length of the image list by using the method GetImageCount(), and the size of each individual image by using the method GetSize(), which returns a tuple (width, height).

While not directly relevant in the list control context, you can also draw an image from an image list onto a device context. For more information about device contexts, see chapters 6 and 12. The method is Draw, as in the following:

```
Draw(index, dc, x, y, flags=wx.IMAGELIST_DRAW_NORMAL,
     solidBackground=False)
```

In this call, the index parameter is the index of the item to draw within the image list and the dc parameter is a wx.DC device context to draw to. The x and y parameters are the starting position on the device context to draw the image. The flags control how the image is drawn, and bitmask of one or more of the constants `wx.IMAGELIST_DRAW_NORMAL`, `wx.IMAGELIST_DRAW_TRANSPARENT`, `wx.IMAGELIST_DRAW_SELECTED`, and `wx.IMAGELIST_DRAW_FOCUSED`. If `solidBackground` is `True`, the draw method uses a faster algorithm works only if the background being drawn on is solid.

Once you have an image list, you need to attach it to the list control. This is done using one of two list control methods, `AssignImage(imageList, which)` or `SetImage(imageList, which)`. The two methods take identical parameters, the first being the image list, and the second being an integer flag with the value `wx.IMAGE_LIST_NORMAL` or `wx.IMAGE_LIST_SMALL`. The only difference between the two is how the image list is managed on the C++ side. With `AssignImage()`, the image list becomes part of the list control and is destroyed when the list control is. With `SetImage()`, the image list retains a separate life, and is not automatically disposed of when the list control is destroyed, but will instead be disposed of when the Python object goes out of scope.

The list control can have two image lists assigned to it. The normal list, which is the one assigned with `wx.IMAGE_LIST_NORMAL`, is used in the display of regular icon mode. The small image list, assigned with `wx.IMAGE_LIST_SMALL`, is used in report and small icon mode. Under most circumstances, you only need to add one image list, but if you want the list to display in multiple modes (so the user can move from normal to small icon mode), you should provide both lists. If you do that, remember that the list control items will only know about images via the index into the image list, so the two image lists must match index for index. If the document icon is index two in the normal sized image list, it must also be index two in the small image list.

There is also an associated getter method for the list control, `GetImageList(which)`, that returns the image list associated with the `which` flag passed to the method.

13.2.2 *How can I add and delete items from a list?*

Before you can display a list, you need to add text information to it. In an icon list, you can add new items as icons, strings, or both. In a report view, you can also set information for the different columns in the row after you set the initial icon and/or string. The API and naming conventions for the item manipulation methods differ from those used by some of the other controls we've seen so far, so even if you already understand how menus or list boxes work, you still should read this section.

Adding text information to the list control is a one step process for an icon list, but a multi-step process for a report list. The first step, common to each list, is adding the first item in the row. For report lists, you must separately add the columns and the information in columns other than the leftmost one.

Adding a new row

To add a new row, use one of the `InsertItem()` methods. Which one you use depends on the kind of item you are inserting. If you are just inserting a string into the list, use `InsertStringItem(index, label)`, where the `index` is the row in the list where the new item will be displayed. If you just have an image, then use `InsertImageItem(index, imageIndex)`. In this case, the first index is the row in the list control, and the `imageIndex` is an index into the image list attached to the list control. To insert an image item, the image list must already have been created and assigned. If the image index you use is out of bounds in the image list, then you'll get a blank image. If you want to add an item that has both an image and a string label, use `InsertImageStringItem(index, label, imageIndex)`. This method combines the parameters of the previous two such that the `index` is still the index within the list control, `label` is the string display, and `imageIndex` is the index into the appropriate image list.

Internally, the list control manages information about its items by using instances of the class `wx.ListItem`. We mention that because the last method for inserting items to the list control is `InsertItem(index, item)`, where `item` is an instance of `wx.ListItem` that you have already created. We're not going into very much detail about list items here because it's unlikely you'll be using them much, and because the class is not very complicated—it's almost completely made up of getter and setter methods. Nearly all of the properties of a list item are exposed via methods in the list control itself.

Adding columns

To add columns to a list control in report mode, create the columns, then set the individual data cells for each row/column pair. Creating columns is done with the `InsertColumn()` method, which has the following signature.

```
InsertColumn(col, heading, format=wx.LIST_FORMAT_LEFT, width=-1)
```

In this method call, the `col` parameter is the index of the new column within the list—as with rows, you must supply this value. The `heading` parameter is the string text at the head of the column. The `format` parameter controls the alignment of the text in that column, acceptable values are `wx.LIST_FORMAT_CENTRE`, `wx.LIST_FORMAT_LEFT`, and `wx.LIST_FORMAT_RIGHT`. The `width` parameter is the initial display width of the column in pixels—the user can change that by dragging the column header edges around. To use a `wx.ListItem` object to set the column, there is also a version of this method named InsertColumnInfo(info), which takes a list item as the parameter.

Setting values in a multi-column list

You may have noticed that inserting an item using the row methods described earlier only sets the initial column of a multi-column report list. To set the strings in other columns, use the method SetStringItem().

```
SetStringItem(index, col, label, imageId=-1)
```

The index and col parameters are the row and column indexes for the cell you are setting. You can set the col parameter to 0 to set the first column, but the index must correspond to a row that already exists in the list control—in other words, you can only use this method on a row that has already been added. The label argument is the text to display in the cell, and the imageId is an index back into the appropriate image list, if you want to display an image in the cell.

The SetStringItem() method is technically a special case of the method SetItem(info), that takes a wx.ListItem instance. To use this method, set the row, column, and any other parameters on the list item instance before adding it to the list. You can also get the wx.ListItem instance at the cell by using the method GetItem(index, col=0), which returns the first column of a row by default, but takes the second parameter to allow you to select an item from a different column.

Item properties

There are a number of getter and setter methods that allow you to specify a part of an item. For the most part, these methods work on the first column of a row. To get at other columns, you might need to get the entire item using GetItem() and then use getter and setter methods of the item class. You can set the image for an item using SetItemImage(item, image, selImage), where the item parameter is the index of the item in the list, and image and selImage are both indexes into the image list, indicating the regular image and the image when selected, respectively. You can get or set the text of an item by using GetItemText(item) and SetItemText(item, text).

You can get or set the state of an individual item using GetItemState(item, stateMask) and SetItemState(item, state, stateMask). In this case, state and stateMask come from the values described in table 13.3. The state parameter (and the return value of the getter) is the actual state of the item, the stateMask is a mask of all possible values of current interest.

You can get a specific column with GetColumn(col), which returns the wx.ListItem instance for the column at the index col—meaning the header item for the

Table 13.3 Parameters for the state mask

State	Description
wx.LIST_STATE_CUT	The item is being cut. This state is only available under MS Windows.
wx.LIST_STATE_DONTCARE	The state doesn't matter. This state is only available under MS Windows.
wx.LIST_STATE_DROPHILITED	The item is highlighted because it is receiving a drop from a drag & drop. This state is only available under MS Windows.
wx.LIST_STATE_FOCUSED	The item has the cursor focus.
wx.LIST_STATE_SELECTED	The item is currently selected.

column. You can also set a column that has already been added using the method `SetColumn(col, item)`. You can programmatically get the width of a column using `GetColumnWidth(col)`, which returns the list width in pixels—obviously this is only useful for a list in report mode. You can set the column width using `SetColumn-Width(col, width)`. The width is either the integer width or one of the special values `wx.LIST_AUTOSIZE`, which sets the width to that of the longest item, or `wx.LIST_AUTOSIZE_USEHEADER`, which will set the width to that of the header text. Under non-Windows operating systems `wx.LIST_AUTOSIZE_USEHEADER` may just automatically set the column width to 80 pixels.

If you are getting confused about the indexes you've already added, you can query the list for the number of items already in it. The method `GetColumn-Count()` returns the number of columns defined in the list, and the method `Get-ItemCount()` returns the number of rows. If your list is in list mode, then the method `GetCountPerPage()` returns the number of items in each column.

To delete items from the list, use `DeleteItem(item)`, which takes the index of the item in the list. If you want to zap all the items at once, use `DeleteAllItems()`, or `ClearAll()`, both of which will manage the trick. You can delete a column with `DeleteColumn(col)`, which takes the column index of the doomed column.

13.3 Responding to users

Typically, the point of a list control is to do something when the user selects an item in the list. In the following sections, we'll show what events a list control can respond to, and present an extended example of using list control events.

13.3.1 How can I respond to a user selection in a list?

Like other controls, a list control triggers events in response to user actions. You can set handlers for these events using the `Bind()` method, as discussed in chapter 3. All of these event handlers receive an instance of `wx.ListEvent`, which is a subclass of `wx.CommandEvent`. The `wx.ListEvent` has a few getter methods specific to its class. Some of the properties are only valid for specific event types described in other sections of this chapter. The properties common to all event types are described in table 13.4.

Table 13.4 Properties of `wx.ListEvent`

Property	Description
GetData()	The user data item associated with the list item for the event
GetKeyCode()	In a keypress event, the key code for the key pressed
GetIndex()	The index of the affected item within the list
GetItem()	The actual `wx.ListItem` affected by the event
GetImage()	The image in the cell affected by the event
GetMask()	The bit mask in the cell affected by the event
GetPoint()	The actual mouse position of the event
GetText()	The text in the cell affected by the event

There are several different event types for `wx.ListEvent`, each of which can be given a different handler. Some of the events are discussed in later sections where they are more relevant. Table 13.5 lists all of the event types dealing with selecting items in the list.

Table 13.5 Event types for selecting items in a list control

Event Type	Description
EVT_LIST_BEGIN_DRAG	Triggered when the user begins a drag operation with the left mouse button
EVT_LIST_BEGIN_RDRAG	Triggered when the user begins a drag operation with the right mouse button
EVT_LIST_DELETE_ALL_ITEMS	Triggered by a call to a `DeleteAll()` method of the list
EVT_LIST_DELETE_ITEM	Triggered by a call to a `Delete()` method of the list
EVT_LIST_INSERT_ITEM	Triggered when an item is inserted into the list
EVT_LIST_ITEM_ACTIVATED	The item has been activated, by a user pressing enter or double click while the item is selected

continued on next page

Table 13.5   Event types for selecting items in a list control *(continued)*

Event Type	Description
EVT_LIST_ITEM_DESELECTED	Triggered when the item loses the user selection
EVT_LIST_ITEM_FOCUSED	Triggered when the item with the focus changes
EVT_LIST_ITEM_MIDDLE_CLICK	Triggered when the middle mouse button is clicked on the list
EVT_LIST_ITEM_RIGHT_CLICK	Triggered when the right mouse button is clicked on the list
EVT_LIST_ITEM_SELECTED	Triggered when an item is selected with a left mouse click
EVT_LIST_ITEM_KEY_DOWN	Triggered when a key is pressed while the list control has the focus

Listing 13.3 will provide examples of many of these event types in a running program.

13.3.2   *How can I respond to a user selection in a column header?*

In addition to events that are triggered by a user event within the main body of the list, there are events that are triggered by user activity in the column headers of a report list control. The wx.ListEvent objects created by a column event have another property, GetColumn(), that returns the index of the column in which the event takes place. If the event is a drag event of a column border, the index is for the column on the left side of the border being dragged. If the event is triggered by a click that is not inside a column, the method returns -1. Table 13.6 contains the list of column event types.

Table 13.6   List control column event types

Event Type	Description
EVT_LIST_COL_BEGIN_DRAG	Triggered when the user begins to drag a column border
EVT_LIST_COL_CLICK	Triggered by a click inside a column header
EVT_LIST_COL_RIGHT_CLICK	Triggered by a right click inside a column header
EVT_LIST_COL_END_DRAG	Triggered when the user completes a drag of a column border

Listing 13.3 displays some list event processing, and also provides examples of the methods described later in this chapter. Notice the various items triggered by menus in this program.

Listing 13.3 An example of many different list events and properties

```python
import wx
import sys, glob, random
import data

class DemoFrame(wx.Frame):
    def __init__(self):
        wx.Frame.__init__(self, None, -1,
                          "Other wx.ListCtrl Stuff",
                          size=(700,500))
        self.list = None
        self.editable = False
        self.MakeMenu()
        self.MakeListCtrl()

    def MakeListCtrl(self, otherflags=0):      ◁── Creating the list
        if self.list:
            self.list.Destroy()
        if self.editable:
            otherflags |= wx.LC_EDIT_LABELS

        il = wx.ImageList(16,16, True)      ◁─┘ Loading into image list
        for name in glob.glob("smicon??.png"):
            bmp = wx.Bitmap(name, wx.BITMAP_TYPE_PNG)
            il_max = il.Add(bmp)

        self.list = wx.ListCtrl(self, -1, style=wx.LC_REPORT|otherflags)
        self.list.AssignImageList(il, wx.IMAGE_LIST_SMALL)
        for col, text in enumerate(data.columns):      ◁── Adding the columns
            self.list.InsertColumn(col, text)
        for row, item in enumerate(data.rows):      ◁─┘ Adding the rows
            index = self.list.InsertStringItem(sys.maxint, item[0])
            for col, text in enumerate(item[1:]):
                self.list.SetStringItem(index, col+1, text)
            img = random.randint(0, il_max)      ◁── Assigning random images
            self.list.SetItemImage(index, img, img)
            self.list.SetItemData(index, row)      ◁─┐ Setting data item

        self.list.SetColumnWidth(0, 120)
        self.list.SetColumnWidth(1, wx.LIST_AUTOSIZE)            ⎫ Setting
        self.list.SetColumnWidth(2, wx.LIST_AUTOSIZE)            ⎬ column
        self.list.SetColumnWidth(3, wx.LIST_AUTOSIZE_USEHEADER)  ⎭ widths

        self.Bind(wx.EVT_LIST_ITEM_SELECTED, self.OnItemSelected,   ◁─┐
                  self.list)                          Binding user events │
        self.Bind(wx.EVT_LIST_ITEM_DESELECTED, self.OnItemDeselected,
                  self.list)
        self.Bind(wx.EVT_LIST_ITEM_ACTIVATED, self.OnItemActivated,
                  self.list)
        self.SendSizeEvent()
```

```
def MakeMenu(self):    <--  Creating a menu
    mbar = wx.MenuBar()
    menu = wx.Menu()
    item = menu.Append(-1, "E&xit\tAlt-X")
    self.Bind(wx.EVT_MENU, self.OnExit, item)
    mbar.Append(menu, "&File")

    menu = wx.Menu()
    item = menu.Append(-1, "Sort ascending")
    self.Bind(wx.EVT_MENU, self.OnSortAscending, item)
    item = menu.Append(-1, "Sort descending")
    self.Bind(wx.EVT_MENU, self.OnSortDescending, item)
    item = menu.Append(-1, "Sort by submitter")
    self.Bind(wx.EVT_MENU, self.OnSortBySubmitter, item)

    menu.AppendSeparator()
    item = menu.Append(-1, "Show selected")
    self.Bind(wx.EVT_MENU, self.OnShowSelected, item)
    item = menu.Append(-1, "Select all")
    self.Bind(wx.EVT_MENU, self.OnSelectAll, item)
    item = menu.Append(-1, "Select none")
    self.Bind(wx.EVT_MENU, self.OnSelectNone, item)

    menu.AppendSeparator()
    item = menu.Append(-1, "Set item text colour")
    self.Bind(wx.EVT_MENU, self.OnSetTextColour, item)
    item = menu.Append(-1, "Set item background colour")
    self.Bind(wx.EVT_MENU, self.OnSetBGColour, item)

    menu.AppendSeparator()
    item = menu.Append(-1, "Enable item editing", kind=wx.ITEM_CHECK)
    self.Bind(wx.EVT_MENU, self.OnEnableEditing, item)
    item = menu.Append(-1, "Edit current item")
    self.Bind(wx.EVT_MENU, self.OnEditItem, item)
    mbar.Append(menu, "&Demo")

    self.SetMenuBar(mbar)

def OnExit(self, evt):
    self.Close()

def OnItemSelected(self, evt):    <--  Item selected handler
    item = evt.GetItem()
    print "Item selected:", item.GetText()

def OnItemDeselected(self, evt):    <--  Item deselected handler
    item = evt.GetItem()
    print "Item deselected:", item.GetText()

def OnItemActivated(self, evt):    <--  Item activated handler
    item = evt.GetItem()
```

```
          print "Item activated:", item.GetText()

   def OnSortAscending(self, evt):
       self.MakeListCtrl(wx.LC_SORT_ASCENDING)       <⌐

   def OnSortDescending(self, evt):
       self.MakeListCtrl(wx.LC_SORT_DESCENDING)      <⌐

   def OnSortBySubmitter(self, evt):    <—  Sorting with nested function
       def compare_func(row1, row2):
           # compare the values in the 4th col of the data
           val1 = data.rows[row1][3]
           val2 = data.rows[row2][3]
           if val1 < val2: return -1
           if val1 > val2: return 1
           return 0

       self.list.SortItems(compare_func)

   def OnShowSelected(self, evt):    <⌐  Showing selected items
       print "These items are selected:"
       index = self.list.GetFirstSelected()
       if index == -1:
           print "\tNone"
           return
       while index != -1:
           item = self.list.GetItem(index)
           print "\t%s" % item.GetText()
           index = self.list.GetNextSelected(index)

   def OnSelectAll(self, evt):    <⌐  Selecting all items
       for index in range(self.list.GetItemCount()):
           self.list.Select(index, True)

   def OnSelectNone(self, evt):    <⌐  Deselecting selected items
       index = self.list.GetFirstSelected()
       while index != -1:
           self.list.Select(index, False)
           index = self.list.GetNextSelected(index)

   def OnSetTextColour(self, evt):
       dlg = wx.ColourDialog(self)
       if dlg.ShowModal() == wx.ID_OK:    <⌐  Changing text color
           colour = dlg.GetColourData().GetColour()
           index = self.list.GetFirstSelected()
           while index != -1:
               self.list.SetItemTextColour(index, colour)
               index = self.list.GetNextSelected(index)
       dlg.Destroy()

   def OnSetBGColour(self, evt):    <⌐  Changing background color
       dlg = wx.ColourDialog(self)
```

Rebuilding lists with sort style

```
        if dlg.ShowModal() == wx.ID_OK:
            colour = dlg.GetColourData().GetColour()
            index = self.list.GetFirstSelected()
            while index != -1:
                self.list.SetItemBackgroundColour(index, colour)
                index = self.list.GetNextSelected(index)
        dlg.Destroy()

    def OnEnableEditing(self, evt):        ⟵┘ Turning editing on
        self.editable = evt.IsChecked()
        self.MakeListCtrl()

    def OnEditItem(self, evt):        ⟵┘ Editing selected items
        index = self.list.GetFirstSelected()
        if index != -1:
            self.list.EditLabel(index)

class DemoApp(wx.App):
    def OnInit(self):
        frame = DemoFrame()
        self.SetTopWindow(frame)
        print "Program output appears here..."
        frame.Show()
        return True

app = DemoApp(redirect=True)
app.MainLoop()
```

Once you've entered the code and run it, you'll receive a demo of list control features, including items like sort that will be discussed in the next sections.

13.4 *Editing and sorting list controls*

In this section, we'll discuss editing, sorting, and finding items in list controls.

13.4.1 *How can I edit a label?*

Editing an entry in the list is simple, except in report lists, where the user can only edit the first column in each row. For other kinds of lists, that's not an issue; the regular label for each item is editable.

To make a list editable, include the style flag wx.LC_EDIT_LABELS in the constructor when the list is created.

```
list = wx.ListCtrl(self, -1, style=wx.LC_REPORT | wx.LC_EDIT_LABELS)
```

If the edit flag is set, the user can start an edit session by clicking on a list item that has already been selected (it doesn't have to be a quick double-click). The edit box is similar to editing within Windows Explorer. The user receives a small edit-in-place box where the text label was. Pressing Enter ends the edit session, and the new text becomes the text label. A mouse click elsewhere in the list control also ends the edit session (there can only be one edit session at a time). Pressing Escape cancels the edit session, and the new text is discarded.

The following two event types are triggered by an editing session.

- EVT_LIST_BEGIN_LABEL_EDIT
- EVT_LIST_END_LABEL_EDIT

Remember that if you want the normal processing to proceed in addition to your custom handler, you need to include a call to the event method Skip() in your event handler. A list event with the event type EVT_LIST_BEGIN_LABEL_EDIT is triggered when the user starts an edit session, and one with the event type EVT_LIST_END_LABEL_EDIT is triggered when the session ends (either by an Enter or an Escape cancel). You can veto the begin edit event, in which case the edit session does not start. Vetoing the end edit event prevents the list text from changing.

The wx.ListEvent class has a couple of properties that are only interesting when processing an EVT_LIST_END_LABEL_EDIT event. The method GetLabel() returns the new text of the list item label after the edit has been completed and okayed. If the edit was canceled via the escape key, then the method returns an empty string. This means that you cannot use GetLabel() to distinguish between a cancel and the user deliberately changing the item text to an empty string. If required, the method IsEditCancelled() returns True if the edit end was due to a cancel, and False otherwise. Use that method when you need to distinguish between a successful edit session and a canceled one.

If you want to have some other user event start an edit session, you can trigger an edit programmatically using the list control method EditLabel(item), where the item parameter is the index of the list item to be edited. This method triggers the EVT_LIST_BEGIN_LABEL_EDIT event, and the edit session continues just as though it had been initiated in the usual way.

If you would like to directly manipulate the text control being used for the editing, you can get it with the list control method GetEditControl(). The method returns the text control being used for the current edit. If there is no current edit, the method returns None. Currently, the method only works under Windows operating systems.

13.4.2 *How can I sort my list?*

There are three useful ways to sort a list control in wxPython, that we'll discuss in this section in ascending order of complexity

Telling the list to sort when created

The easiest way to sort a list control is by telling the list control in the constructor to sort items. You do this by using one of the style flags wx.LC_SORT_ASCENDING or wx.LC_SORT_DESCENDING. This flag causes the list to be sorted when initially displayed, and on MS Windows, the sorting continues to be honored when new items are added. The sort is based on the string text for each list item's data, and is a simple string comparison. If the list is in report mode, the sort is based on the string in column 0 (the left-most column) of each row.

Sorting based on data other than the display text

Occasionally, you'll want to sort your list based on something other than the string value of the list label. You can do that in wxPython, but it's a slightly more complicated process. First, you need to set item data for each item in the list, by using the SetItemData(item, data) method. The item is the index of the item within the (unsorted) list, and the data is whatever data you want to associate with that item. The data item must be an integer or a long value (due to the C++ expected data type), which limits the usefulness of this mechanism somewhat. To retrieve the item data for a row, use the method GetItemData(item).

Once you have the item data in place, you can use the method Sort-Items(func) to sort the items. The argument to the method is a Python callable object which takes in two integers. The function is called with the associated data of two list items to be compared—you don't get any reference to the rows themselves. The function should return a positive integer if the first item is greater than the second (meaning the first item should be earlier in the sorted list), a negative value if the first item is less than the second (meaning the first item is later in the sorted list), and zero if the two are equal. Although the most obvious way to implement this function is to just do a numerical comparison of the two items, that is by no means the only thing that you could do in the sort method. For instance, the data item could be a key in an external dictionary or list that has a more complex data item, which you could compare to determine sort order.

Column sorting with the mixin class

One common case for sorting a list control is to give the user the ability to sort a list in report view in any column by clicking on the column. You could do that

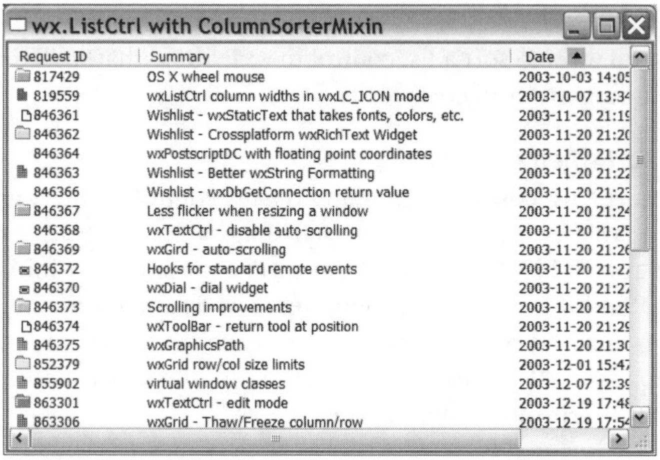

Figure 13.5
The column sorter mixin in action—notice the arrow in the date column indicating sort direction

with the SortItems() mechanism, but it would be somewhat complex to keep track of the columns. Fortunately, a wxPython mixin class, called ColumnSorter-Mixin, manages the information for you, and lives in the module wx.lib.mixins. listctrl. Figure 13.5 displays the column sorting using the mixin class.

Declare the mixin just like any other Python multiple inheritance declaration, as in the following.

```
import wx.lib.mixins.listctrl as listmix

class ListCtrlPanel(wx.Panel, listmix.ColumnSorterMixin):
    def __init__(self, parent, log):
        wx.Panel.__init__(self, parent, -1, style=wx.WANTS_CHARS)
        self.list = TestListCtrl(self, tID)
        self.itemDataMap = musicdata
        listmix.ColumnSorterMixin.__init__(self, 3)
```

Notice that the mixin is not extending the list control itself, although it could do that as well, but it's more likely that you are creating a custom panel. Instead, it's extending the containing panel. The panel gets code to manage the sorting and to bind the mouse click event in the column header. Listing 13.4 displays a completed column sorter example.

Listing 13.4   A report list with the column sorter mixin

```
import wx
import wx.lib.mixins.listctrl
import sys, glob, random
import data
```

```
class DemoFrame(wx.Frame, wx.lib.mixins.listctrl.ColumnSorterMixin):    ◁┐
    def __init__(self):                              Deriving from the mixin ┘
        wx.Frame.__init__(self, None, -1,
                          "wx.ListCtrl with ColumnSorterMixin",
                          size=(600,400))

        il = wx.ImageList(16,16, True)
        for name in glob.glob("smicon??.png"):
            bmp = wx.Bitmap(name, wx.BITMAP_TYPE_PNG)
            il_max = il.Add(bmp)

                                          ┌ Adding arrows to the image list
        self.up = il.AddWithColourMask    ◁┘
            wx.Bitmap("sm_up.bmp", wx.BITMAP_TYPE_BMP), "blue")
        self.dn = il.AddWithColourMask(
            wx.Bitmap("sm_down.bmp", wx.BITMAP_TYPE_BMP), "blue")

        self.list = wx.ListCtrl(self, -1, style=wx.LC_REPORT)
        self.list.AssignImageList(il, wx.IMAGE_LIST_SMALL) \
        for col, text in enumerate(data.columns):
            self.list.InsertColumn(col, text)
        self.itemDataMap = {}   ◁┐ Creating data maps
        for item in data.rows:
            index = self.list.InsertStringItem(sys.maxint, item[0])
            for col, text in enumerate(item[1:]):
                self.list.SetStringItem(index, col+1, text)
            self.list.SetItemData(index, index)      ◁┐ Associating data
            self.itemDataMap[index] = item            │ with maps
            img = random.randint(0, il_max)
            self.list.SetItemImage(index, img, img)

        self.list.SetColumnWidth(0, 120)
        self.list.SetColumnWidth(1, wx.LIST_AUTOSIZE)
        self.list.SetColumnWidth(2, wx.LIST_AUTOSIZE)
        self.list.SetColumnWidth(3, wx.LIST_AUTOSIZE_USEHEADER)

        wx.lib.mixins.listctrl.ColumnSorterMixin.__init__(self,   ◁┐
            len(data.columns))            Initializing the columns sorter ┘

    def GetListCtrl(self):
        return self.list

    def GetSortImages(self):
        return (self.dn, self.up)

app = wx.PySimpleApp()
frame = DemoFrame()
frame.Show()
app.MainLoop()
```

For the mixin to work, you need to perform the following in your own panel class:

1　The class that extends `ColumnSorterMixin` must have a method called `GetListCtrl()` which returns the actual list control to be sorted. This method is used by the mixin to get a reference to the control.

2　In the `__init__()` method of the extending class, you must create the list control referred to by `GetListCtrl()` before you call the `__init__()` method of the `ColumnSorterMixin`. The `__init__()` method of the mixin takes one argument, an integer representing the number of columns in the list control.

3　You must use `SetListData()` to set a unique data value for each row in the list. This can be (and most likely will be) nothing more than an index into a more complex data structure.

4　The extending class must have an attribute called `itemDataMap`. This attribute must be a dictionary. The keys to this dictionary are the data values set by `SetListData()`. The values are a tuple of the values you want to use to sort by each column. (Typically, this will just be the text in each column). In other words, the `itemDataMap` essentially replicates the data in the control in a form that is easy to sort.

In a typical usage of `ColumnSorterMixin`, you will either create the `itemDataMap` as you add items to your list control or you will create the `itemDataMap` first, and use that to build the list control itself.

Although the setup can be complex, the `ColumnSorterMixin` is a great choice for a common sorting use case.

13.4.3　*How can I learn more about list controls?*

Sometimes, you'll need to determine which item is selected in a list from someplace else in your program, or you'll need to change which item is currently selected programmatically in response to a user event, or to something happening internally in your program.

There are several related methods for finding the index of an item in the list, given some other piece of information about the item, as displayed in table 13.7.

Table 13.8 displays possible components of the `flags` return value from `Hit-Test()`. If applicable, more than one flag may be returned.

Table 13.7   Methods for finding items in a list

Method	Description
FindItem(start, str, partial=False)	Finds the first item whose label matches `str`. If the `start` index is `-1`, then the search starts at the beginning, otherwise the search starts at the `start` index. If `partial` is `True` then the test is a "starts with" test, rather than a whole string test. The return value is the index of the matching string.
FindItemAtPos(start, point, direction)	Finds the first item near `point`, a `wx.Point` referencing a position relative to the upper left corner of the list control. The `direction` parameter tells wxPython what direction to move in from the starting `point` to find the item. Possible values are `wx.LIST_FIND_DOWN`, `wx.LIST_FIND_LEFT`, `wx.LIST_FIND_RIGHT`, and `wx.LIST_FIND_UP`.
FindItemData(start, data)	Finds the item whose data (set with `SetItemData()`) matches the `data` parameter. The `start` parameter behaves as in `FindItem()`.
HitTest(point)	Returns a Python tuple of the form `(index, flags)`. The `index` is the item in the list control which is at the given `point`, or `-1` if there is no such item. The `flags` parameter contains further information about the point and the item. It is a bitmask with values described in table 13.8.

Table 13.8   Flags for the `HitTest()` method

Flag	Description
wx.LIST_HITTEST_ABOVE	The point is above the client area of the list
wx.LIST_HITTEST_BELOW	The point is below the client area of the list
wx.LIST_HITTEST_NOWHERE	The point is in the client area of the list, but not part of any item. Usually this is because it is after the end of the list.
wx.LIST_HITTEST_ONITEM	The point is anywhere in the bounding rectangle of the item returned in the `index` value.
wx.LIST_HITTEST_ONITEMICON	The point is specifically in the icon portion of the item returned in the `index` value.
wx.LIST_HITTEST_ONITEMLABEL	The point is specifically in the label portion of the item returned in the `index` value.
wx.LIST_HITTEST_ONITEMRIGHT	The point is in the blank area to the right of the item
wx.LIST_HITTEST_ONITEMSTATEICON	The point is inside the state icon of an item. This assumes that the list is in tree mode, and there is a user defined state.
wx.LIST_HITTEST_TOLEFT	The point is to the left of the client area of the list
wx.LIST_HITTEST_TORIGHT	The point is to the right of the client area of the list

To go in the other direction, there are a few methods that will give you information about the item, given the index. The methods GetItem() and GetItemText() were discussed earlier. Others are listed in Table 13.9.

Table 13.9   Item informational methods of the list control

Method	Description
GetItemPosition(item)	Returns the position of the item as a wx.Point. Only interesting in icon or small icon mode. The point returned is the upper left corner of the item placement.
GetItemRect(item, code= wx.LIST_RECT_BOUNDS)	Returns a wx.Rect with the bounding rectangle of the item at index item. The code parameter is optional. The default value is wx.LIST_RECT_BOUNDS, and causes wxPython to return the entire bounding rectangle for the items. Other values for the parameter are wx.LIST_RECT_ICON, which causes the return value to be only the bounding rectangle of the icon part, and wx.LIST_RECT_LABEL which returns the rectangle around the label.
GetNextItem(item, geometry= wx.LIST_ALL, state= wx.LIST_STATE_DONTCARE)	Returns the next item in the list after the given item index, based on the geometry and state parameters. The geometry and state parameters each have several values listed in tables which follow.
SetItemPosition(item, pos)	Moves the item at index item to the wx.Point passed in the pos parameter. Only meaningful for a list in icon or small icon view.

Table 13.10 lists values of the geometry parameter for GetNextItem(). The geometry parameter is only used under MS Windows.

Table 13.10   Values for the geometry parameter of GetNextItem()

Value	Description
wx.LIST_NEXT_ABOVE	Find the next item in the given state that is above the start item in the display.
wx.LIST_NEXT_ALL	Find the next item in the given state by index order in the list.
wx.LIST_NEXT_BELOW	Find the next item in the given state that is below the start item in the display.
wx.LIST_NEXT_LEFT	Find the next item in the given state that is to the left of the start item in the display.
wx.LIST_NEXT_RIGHT	Find the next item in the given state that is to the right of the start item in the display.

Table 13.11 displays the possible values of the state parameter from the GetNextItem() method.

Table 13.11   Values of the `State` parameter for `GetNextItem()`

Value	Description
wx.LIST_STATE_CUT	Find only items that are selected for a clipboard cut and paste.
wx.LIST_STATE_DONTCARE	Find any item, regardless of its current state.
wx.LIST_STATE_DROPHILITED	Find only items that are currently drop targets.
wx.LIST_STATE_FOCUSED	Find only items that have the focus.
wx.LIST_STATE_SELECTED	Find only items that are currently selected.

Table 13.12 displays the methods used for changing the text display of an item with a few getter and setter methods that control the font and color of the item.

Table 13.12   Display properties of the list control

Methods	Description
GetBackgroundColour() SetBackgroundColour(col)	Manages the background color for the entire list control. The `col` parameter is a `wx.Colour`, or the string name of a color.
GetItemBackgroundColour(item) SetItemBackgroundColour(item, col)	Manages the background color for the item at index `item`. This property is only used in report mode.
GetItemTextColour(item) SetItemTextColour(item, col)	Manages the text color for the item at index `item`. This property is only used in report mode.
GetTextColour() SetTextColour(col)	Manages the text color for the entire list.

Table 13.13 displays other methods of list controls that don't merit their own section, but are also useful.

Table 13.13   Other useful methods of the list control

Methods	Description
GetItemSpacing()	Returns a `wx.Size` item with the space in pixels between icons.
GetSelectedItemCount()	Returns the number of items in the list control that are currently selected.
GetTopItem()	Returns the index of the item at the top of the visible portion of the display. Only meaningful in list and report mode.

continued on next page

Table 13.13   Other useful methods of the list control *(continued)*

Methods	Description
GetViewRect()	Returns a `wx.Rect` corresponding to the smallest rectangle needed to span all items wthout scrolling. Only meaningful in icon and small icon mode.
ScrollList(dx, dy)	Causes the control to scroll. The `dy` parameter is the vertical amount in pixels. The `dx` parameter is the horizontal amount. For icon, small icon, or report view, the unit is pixels. If the list control is in list mode, then the unit is columns of the list display.

These tables cover much of the functionality of a list control. However, so far, all the list controls we've seen are limited by the fact that all their data must exist in the program memory at all times. In the next section, we'll discuss a mechanism for providing list data only as it is needed for display.

13.5 *Creating a virtual list control*

Let's assume that your wxPython application needs to display a list of all your clients. Initially you use a regular list control, and it works fine. Eventually your use of wxPython makes you more and more successful. Your client list gets longer and longer. Too many clients and your application starts to have performance problems. Perhaps it takes a longer amount of time to start up. Probably it starts using more and more memory. What can you do? You can create a virtual list control.

The problem is a result of the way list control data is managed. Typically, the data is copied into the list control from wherever the data is generated. This is potentially wasteful of resources, and while in a small list it is unlikely to make any difference, creating a larger list control could use a significant amount of memory as well as a lot of startup time.

To minimize the memory and startup requirements of a list control, wxPython allows you to declare a *virtual* list control, which means that the information about each item is only generated on demand when the control needs to display the item. This prevents the control from needing to store each item in its own memory space, and also means that the entire control isn't declared at startup. The drawback is that retrieval of the list items may be slower in a virtual list. Figure 13.6 displays a virtual list in action.

Listing 13.5 displays the entire code example that produces the virtual list control.

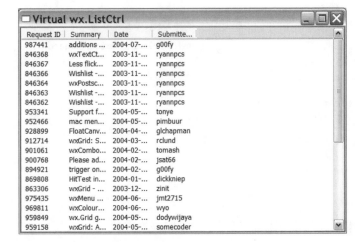

Figure 13.6
A virtual list control

Listing 13.5   A virtual list control

```
import wx
import sys, glob, random
import data

class DataSource:   ⟵— A data source

    def GetColumnHeaders(self):
        return data.columns

    def GetCount(self):
        return len(data.rows)

    def GetItem(self, index):
        return data.rows[index]

    def UpdateCache(self, start, end):
        pass
                                        ❶ Declaring the
class VirtualListCtrl(wx.ListCtrl):  ⟵—┘  virtual list
    def __init__(self, parent, dataSource):          Creating a list
        wx.ListCtrl.__init__(self, parent,          with virtual flag
            style=wx.LC_REPORT|wx.LC_SINGLE_SEL|wx.LC_VIRTUAL)  ⟵—
        self.dataSource = dataSource
        self.Bind(wx.EVT_LIST_CACHE_HINT, self.DoCacheItems)
        self.SetItemCount(dataSource.GetCount())  ⟵┐ Setting list size
        columns = dataSource.GetColumnHeaders()
        for col, text in enumerate(columns):
            self.InsertColumn(col, text)

    def DoCacheItems(self, evt):
```

```
            self.dataSource.UpdateCache(
                evt.GetCacheFrom(), evt.GetCacheTo())

    def OnGetItemText(self, item, col):   ◁⌐ Getting text on demand
        data = self.dataSource.GetItem(item)
        return data[col]

    def OnGetItemAttr(self, item):  return None
    def OnGetItemImage(self, item): return -1

class DemoFrame(wx.Frame):
    def __init__(self):
        wx.Frame.__init__(self, None, -1,
                          "Virtual wx.ListCtrl",
                          size=(600,400))

        self.list = VirtualListCtrl(self, DataSource())

app = wx.PySimpleApp()
frame = DemoFrame()
frame.Show()
app.MainLoop()
```

The data source class is a simple example that stores our sample data items. A real data source class would manage fetching items from a database or similar, but only needs to implement the same interface as our simple example.

To create a virtual list, the first step is to make the flag wx.LC_VIRTUAL one of the flags passed to the list control on initialization ❶. Typically, you need to create your virtual list control by subclassing wx.ListCtrl, rather than just using the constructor. This is because you need to override some methods of wx.ListCtrl in order to populate the virtual list. The declaration will look something like the following:

```
class MyVirtualList(wx.ListCtrl):

    def __init__(self, parent):
        wx.ListCtrl.__init__(self, parent, -1,
            style=wx.LC_REPORT|wx.LC_VIRTUAL)
```

The virtual list control must also call the SetItemCount() method sometime during its initialization. This tells the control how many data items exist in the data source so it sets appropriate limits and can manage the scrollbars. You can call SetItemCount() again if the number of items in the data source changes. Any of the On methods you override must be able to handle any value between 0 and SetItemCount() - 1.

Your virtual list control can override three methods of the parent class in order to determine what is displayed in the list control. The most important method to override is OnGetItemText(item, col). The item and col parameters are the row and column of the cell to be drawn and the return value is the string of the text to be displayed in that cell. For example, the following method just displays the coordinates of the cell.

```
def OnGetItemText(self, item, col):
    return "Item %d, column %d" % (item, col)
```

If you want an image to be displayed in a row, you need to override the method OnGetItemImage(item). The return value is an integer index into the list control's image list described earlier. If you do not override the method, the base class version returns -1, indicating no image to be displayed. If you want to change some of the display attributes of the row, then you can override the method OnGetItem-Attr(item), which again takes a row index as a parameter and returns an instance of the class wx.ListItemAttr. That class has a number of getters and setters that can be used to set the color, alignment, or other display settings for the row.

If the data on which you are basing the virtual list control changes and you wish to update the display, you can use the list control method RefreshItem(item) that forces a redraw of that particular row. The related method RefreshItems (itemFrom, itemTo) redraws all the rows between the two indexes.

To help you optimize fetching of data items in your data source, the virtual list control will send the EVT_LIST_CACHE_HINT event whenever it is about to display a new page of data. This gives your data source an opportunity to fetch several records at once from the database (or whatever) and save them. The subsequent OnGetItemText() calls for those items can be much quicker than having to go back to the database for each record.

13.6 *Summary*

- The list control is wxPython's widget for displaying lists of information. It is more complex and fully featured than the simpler list box widget. List controls are instances of the class wx.ListCtrl. A list control can be displayed in icon mode, with each item text displaying below an icon, or small icon mode with smaller icons. In list mode the elements display in columns, wrapping from the bottom of one to the top of the next and in report mode, the list displays in multi-column format with column headers and one row per item.

- The images for a list control are managed in an image list, which is an array of images accessible via an integer index. The list control can maintain separate image lists for different list modes, allowing for easy switching between, say, large and small icon mode.

- You insert text into the list using the method InsertStringItem(index, label), and an image using the InsertImageItem(index, imageIndex) method. To add both at once, you can use InsertImageStringItem(index, label, imageIndex). To add columns in report mode, you use the method InsertColumn(col, heading, format="wx.LIST_FORMAT_LEFT, width=-1). Once the column has been added you can add text to new columns using the method SetStringItem(index, col, label, imageId=-1).

- List controls generate several events that can be bound to program actions. The event items are of class wx.ListEvent. Common event types include EVT_LIST_INSERT_ITEM, EVT_LIST_ITEM_ACTIVATED, and EVT_LIST_ITEM_SELECTED.

- If the list control is declared with the flag wx.LC_EDIT_LABELS, then the user will be able to edit the text of list items when they are selected. The edit is accepted by pressing enter or clicking elsewhere in the control, it is canceled by pressing the escape key.

- You can sort lists by declaring them with the flag wx.LC_SORT_ASCENDING or wx.LC_SORT_DESCENDING. This will sort items based on their string order. In report mode, the strings in column 0 will be used. You can use the method SortItems(func) to create your own custom sorting method. For a list in report mode, the mixin class wx.lib.mixins.listctrl.ColumnSorterMixin can give you the ability to sort on a user-selected column.

- A list control declared with the flag wx.LC_VIRTUAL is a virtual list control. This means that its data is determined dynamically at runtime when items in the list are displayed. For a virtual list control, you must override the method OnGetItemText(item, col) to return the proper text to display in the given row and column. You can also override the methods OnGetItemImage(item) or OnGetItemAttr(item) to return the image or list display attributes for each row. If the underlying data changes, you can update a single row of the list using the method RefreshItem(item) and multiple rows with the method RefreshItems(itemFrom, itemTo).

Eventually, your data will become too complex to be stored in a mere list. You'll need something designed for a full two-dimensional spreadsheet style display, called the grid control, which we'll discuss in the next chapter.

14

Coordinating the grid control

This chapter covers
- Creating a grid
- Adding rows and cells and managing column headers
- Using a custom cell renderer
- Creating custom editors
- Capturing user events

The grid widget is perhaps the most complex and flexible single widget in wxPython. In this chapter, you'll get a chance to see and work with many of the grid widget's features. We'll talk about how you enter data into the grid control and how you manage the display attributes of the control, and we'll talk about custom editors and renderers. At base, the grid control allows you to display tabular data in a spreadsheet-like grid format. The widget allows you to specify labels for rows and columns, change the grid size by dragging grid lines, and specify font and color attributes for each cell individually.

In most cases, you will display your value as a simple string. However, you can also specify a custom renderer for any cell that allows you to display data differently; for example, displaying a Boolean value as a checkbox. You can edit a grid cell in-place in the table, and you can use different types of editors for different kinds of data. You can also create your own custom renderers and editors to give you nearly unlimited flexibility in the display and management of cell data. Grids also have a large amount of mouse and keyboard events that you can capture and use to trigger code in your application.

We'll start our discussion by showing two ways to create a wxPython grid.

14.1   *Creating your grid*

A grid control is a display of a two-dimensional data set. For the control to display useful information, you need to tell the grid control what data on which it should work. In wxPython, there are two different mechanisms for handling data in a grid control, each of which handles adding, deleting, and editing the data in a slightly different manner.

- The grid control can directly manage the values in each row and column.
- The data can be managed indirectly using a *grid table*.

The simpler is to have the grid control manage the values directly. In this case, the grid maintains its own copy of the data. This can be awkward if there is a lot of data or if your application already has an existing grid-like data structure. If so, you can use a grid table to manage the data for the grid. See chapter 5 to review how grid tables can be thought of as a model in an MVC framework.

14.1.1   *How do I create a simple grid?*

Although the grid control has a huge number of methods to control the precise display and management of its data, getting started with a grid control is

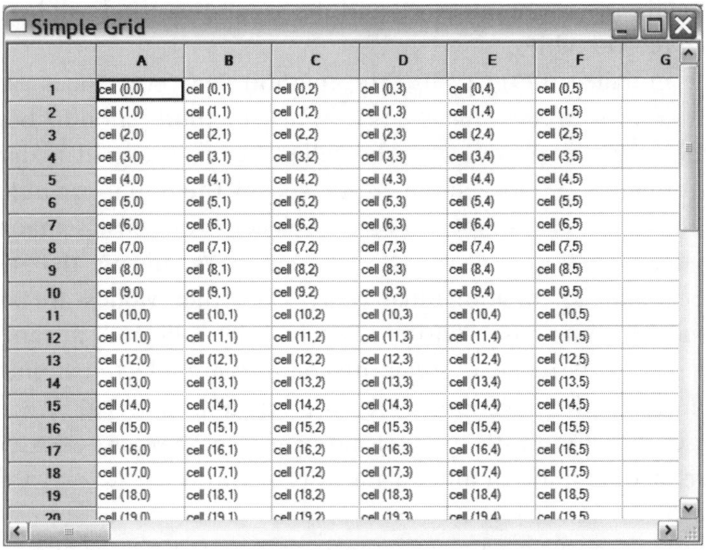

Figure 14.1
A basic grid control

straightforward. Figure 14.1 displays a sample grid, with some string data added to each cell.

Grid controls are instances of the class `wx.grid.Grid`. Because of the size of the grid class and related classes, and the fact that many programs do not use it, the wxPython grid classes are in their own module that is not automatically imported into the core namespace. The constructor for `wx.grid.Grid` is similar to the other widget constructors.

```
wx.grid.Grid(parent, id, pos=wx.DefaultPosition,
        size=wx.DefaultSize, style=wx.WANTS_CHARS,
        name=wxPanelNameStr)
```

All of these parameters are similar to the basic `wx.Window` constructor, and have the same meaning. The `wx.WANTS_CHARS` style is the default for a grid; beyond that, the `wx.grid.Grid` defines no specific style flags of its own. Since the grid class is so complex, a grid in your application is more likely than other widgets to be implemented as a custom subclass, rather than using an instance of `wx.grid.Grid` directly.

Unlike the other widgets we've seen, calling the constructor is not enough to create a usable grid. There are two ways to initialize the grid:

- `CreateGrid()`
- `SetTable()`

In this section we'll discuss one method, and the second method will be covered in the discussion of grid tables.

To explicitly initialize the grid, use the method `CreateGrid(numRows, num-Cols, selmode=wx.grid.Grid.SelectCells)`. This method should be called directly after the constructor, and must be called before the grid is displayed. The first two parameters, `numRows` and `numCols`, specify the initial size of the grid. The third parameter, `selmode`, specifies how selection of cells is managed in the grid. The default value, `wx.grid.Grid.SelectCells`, means that the user selection will be made up of individual cells. The other values are `wx.grid.Grid.SelectRows`, meaning that entire rows will be selected at once, and `wx.grid.Grid.SelectionColumns` where entire columns are selected at once. After creation, you can access the selection mode with the method `GetSelectionMode()` and you can reset the mode with the method `SetSelectionMode(mode)`. You can get the number of rows and columns using the methods `GetNumberCols()` and `GetNumberRows()`.

Internally, wxPython sets up a two-dimensional array of strings after the grid is initialized with `CreateGrid()`. Once the grid is initialized, you can place data using the method `SetCellValue(row, col, s)`. The `row` and `col` parameters are the coordinates of the cell to set, and the `s` is the string text to display at those coordinates. If you want to retrieve the value at a specific coordinate, you can use the function `GetCellValue(row, col)`, which returns the string. To empty the entire grid at once, you can use the method `ClearGrid()`. Listing 14.1 displays the sample grid code used to create figure 14.1.

Listing 14.1 A sample grid created using `CreateGrid()`

```
import wx
import wx.grid

class TestFrame(wx.Frame):
    def __init__(self):
        wx.Frame.__init__(self, None, title="Simple Grid",
                        size=(640,480))
        grid = wx.grid.Grid(self)
        grid.CreateGrid(50,50)
        for row in range(20):
            for col in range(6):
                grid.SetCellValue(row, col,
                               "cell (%d,%d)" % (row, col))

app = wx.PySimpleApp()
frame = TestFrame()
```

```
frame.Show()
app.MainLoop()
```

The use of `CreateGrid()` and `SetCellValue()` to set up your grid is generally limited to the case where your grid data is made up of simple strings. If your data is more complex, or if the table is particularly large, you're probably better off creating a grid table, as discussed next.

14.1.2 *How do I create a grid with a grid table?*

In more complicated cases, you can keep your data in a grid table, which is a separate class that stores the data and interacts with the grid control to display the data. The grid table is especially recommended where:

- the data from the grid is complex
- the data is already stored in other objects in your system
- the grid is large enough that it should not all be stored in memory at once

In chapter 5, we discussed grid tables in the context of the MVC design pattern, along with different ways of implementing a grid table in your application. In this chapter, we'll focus on the nuts and bolts of using a grid table. Figure 14.2 displays a grid created using a grid table.

To use a grid table, create your own subclass of `wx.grid.PyGridTableBase`. Your subclass must override a few of the methods of the parent `wx.grid.GridTableBase` class. Listing 14.2 displays the code used to create figure 14.2.

Listing 14.2   The code for using the grid table mechanism

```
import wx
import wx.grid

class TestTable(wx.grid.PyGridTableBase):      ◁— Defining the table grid
    def __init__(self):
        wx.grid.PyGridTableBase.__init__(self)
        self.data = { (1,1) : "Here",
                      (2,2) : "is",
                      (3,3) : "some",
                      (4,4) : "data",
                      }

        self.odd=wx.grid.GridCellAttr()
        self.odd.SetBackgroundColour("sky blue")
        self.odd.SetFont(wx.Font(10, wx.SWISS, wx.NORMAL, wx.BOLD))
```

```
            self.even=wx.grid.GridCellAttr()
            self.even.SetBackgroundColour("sea green")
            self.even.SetFont(wx.Font(10, wx.SWISS, wx.NORMAL, wx.BOLD))

    def GetNumberRows(self):
        return 50

    def GetNumberCols(self):
        return 50

    def IsEmptyCell(self, row, col):
        return self.data.get((row, col)) is not None

    def GetValue(self, row, col):        ⊲─┘ Providing data for the grid
        value = self.data.get((row, col))
        if value is not None:
            return value
        else:
            return ''

    def SetValue(self, row, col, value):
        self.data[(row,col)] = value

    def GetAttr(self, row, col, kind):
        attr = [self.even, self.odd][row % 2]
        attr.IncRef()
        return attr

class TestFrame(wx.Frame):
    def __init__(self):
        wx.Frame.__init__(self, None, title="Grid Table",
                          size=(640,480))

        grid = wx.grid.Grid(self)

        table = TestTable()
        grid.SetTable(table, True)        ⊲─ Assigning the table

app = wx.PySimpleApp()
frame = TestFrame()
frame.Show()
app.MainLoop()
```

In listing 14.2, all the application-specific logic has been moved to the grid table class, so there's no need to also create a custom subclass of wx.grid.Grid.

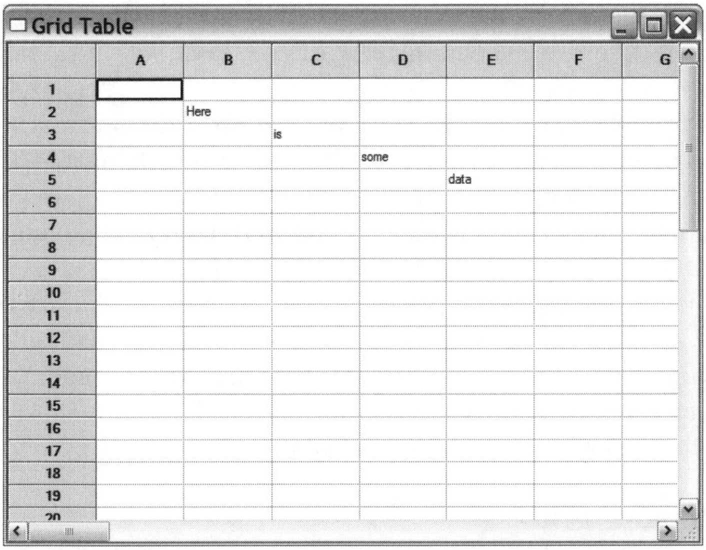

Figure 14.2
A simple grid using the grid table mechanism

For the grid table to be valid, there are five methods that you must override. Table 14.1 lists those methods. As we'll see in this chapter, there are other grid table methods that you can override to give your table more functionality.

To attach the grid table instance to your table instance call the method `Set-Table(table, takeOwnership=False, selmode=wx.grid.Grid.SelectCells)` instead of calling `CreateGrid()`. The `table` parameter is your instance of `wx.grid.PyGrid-TableBase`. The `takeOwnership` parameter causes the grid control to own the table.

Table 14.1   Methods to override in `wx.grid.GridTableBase`

Method	Description
GetNumberCols()	Returns the number of columns to display in the grid
GetNumberRows()	Returns the number of rows to display in the grid
GetValue(row, col)	Returns the value to display at the `row` and `col` coordinate passed as parameters
IsEmptyCell(row, col)	Returns `True` if the cell at the `row` and `col` coordinate is supposed to be empty. In many cases, this method will be hardwired to always return `False`.
SetValue(row, col, value)	Allows you to update your underlying data structure to match the user edit, if you want to. For a read-only table, you must still declare this method, but you can have it `pass` and do nothing. Automatically called when the user edits a cell.

If the parameter is set to `True`, the table is deleted by the wxPython system when the grid is deleted. The `selmode` parameter works the same way in `SetTable()` as it does in `CreateGrid()`.

There are a few other methods you may want to override to manage various parts of the grid other than the table data itself. Later in this chapter, we'll discuss some of those methods along with that different functionality. And, we'll see that in some cases a table created with `SetTable` behaves differently than one created with `CreateGrid()`.

One additional method that you can override is `Clear()`, which is called when the `ClearGrid()` is called on the grid—you would override this method to clean up the underlying data source, if appropriate. Now that you've gotten your data into the grid, you can start to do all sorts of fun stuff with it. In the next section, we'll show you how to manipulate the look of your grid.

14.2 *Working with your grid*

Once the grid is created and initialized, you can tweak it in a wide variety of ways. Cells, rows, or columns can be added and removed. You can add headers, change the size of a row or column, and programmatically change the visible or selected portion of the grid. Over the next few sections, we'll cover these grid manipulation features.

14.2.1 *How do I add and delete rows, columns, and cells?*

Even after the grid has been created, you can still add new rows and columns. Note that the mechanism works differently depending on how the grid was created. You can append a column at the right of your grid using the method `AppendCols(numCols=1)`. To append a row at the bottom of your grid, use the analogous method `AppendRows(numRows=1)`.

If you want to add a row or column other than the end of your grid, you can use the method `InsertCols(pos=0, numCols=1)` or `InsertRows(pos=1, numRows=1)`. In both cases, the `pos` parameter represents the index of the first of the new element being added. If the `numRows` or `numCols` is greater than one, further elements are added to the right of the start position (for columns), or below the start position (for rows).

To delete a row or column, you can use the methods `DeleteCols(pos=0, numCols=1)` and `DeleteRows(pos=0, numRows=1)`. In these methods, the `pos` parameter is the index of the first row or column to be removed, and any further elements are removed to the right or below that index as appropriate.

If the grid was initialized with CreateGrid(), the methods discussed previously always work, and any cells in the new rows or columns created start with an empty string as their value. If, however, the grid was initialized with SetTable(), the grid table object must approve the change to the table. This is because some table models may not be able to manage a change in table size (i.e., if the model is the display for a database table that you cannot modify).

To approve the change, your grid table must override the same change method. For example, if you call InsertCols() on your grid, the grid table must also declare an InsertCols(pos=0, numCols=1) method. The grid table method returns a Boolean True to approve the change or False to veto it. For example, to create a table that only allows rows to be appended to a limit of 50 rows, write the following method in your grid table base.

```
def AppendRows(self, numRows=1):
    return (self.GetRowCount() + numRows) <= 50
```

That method returns True to approve the change as long as the new total of rows is less than or equal to 50.

The contents of the new rows are dependent on the GetValue() methods of the grid table, so if you allow a size change in your table, you need to be sure that the GetValue() method can handle the new number of rows and columns.

Certain changes to a grid do not show up immediately, but instead wait for the grid to be refreshed. You can trigger an immediate refresh of the grid by using the method ForceRefresh(). In general, if you make a programmatic change to your grid that is not showing up, it's a good idea to try inserting a ForceRefresh() call to ensure that your change is displayed.

If you are doing a large set of changes to a grid and you don't want the grid display to flicker during the change, tell the grid to do the process as a batch by using the BeginBatch() method. This call increments an internal counter for the grid. You must balance the BeginBatch() call with a later call to EndBatch()—the EndBatch() call decrements the internal counter. While the counter is greater than zero; that is, between a begin and end call, the grid will not repaint itself. You may nest begin and end calls as necessary, they will increment and decrement the counter as called. As long as there is still an outstanding begin without an end, the grid will not repaint.

14.2.2 *How do I manage the row and column headers of a grid?*

In a wxPython grid control, each row and column has its own label. By default, rows are given numeric labels starting with 1 and columns are given alphabetical labels starting with A and continuing to Z, which is followed by AA, AB, and so on. If you're creating a spreadsheet, this is great, but not necessary for most other applications. For something a bit less generic, wxPython provides methods to change the labels. Figure 14.3 displays a sample grid with label headers.

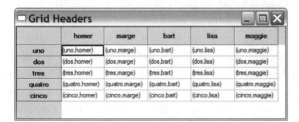

**Figure 14.3
A sample grid with
custom labels created**

Listing 14.3 contains the code used to build the figure—in this example, the grid was initialized with CreateGrid().

Listing 14.3   Code for a sample non-model grid with custom labels

```python
import wx
import wx.grid

class TestFrame(wx.Frame):

    rowLabels = ["uno", "dos", "tres", "quatro", "cinco"]
    colLabels = ["homer", "marge", "bart", "lisa", "maggie"]

    def __init__(self):
        wx.Frame.__init__(self, None, title="Grid Headers",
                          size=(500,200))
        grid = wx.grid.Grid(self)
        grid.CreateGrid(5,5)
        for row in range(5):
            grid.SetRowLabelValue(row, self.rowLabels[row])
            grid.SetColLabelValue(row, self.colLabels[row])
            for col in range(5):
                grid.SetCellValue(row, col,
                    "(%s,%s)" % (self.rowLabels[row], self.colLabels[col]))

app = wx.PySimpleApp()
frame = TestFrame()
frame.Show()
app.MainLoop()
```

As with adding and deleting rows, changing labels is done differently based on the type of grid. For grids that are created with `CreateGrid()`, set the label values using the methods `SetColLabelValue(col, value)` and `SetRowLabelValue(row, value)`. ❶ The `col` and `row` parameters are the index of the appropriate column or row, and the `value` parameter is the string to be displayed in that label. To get the labels for a row or a column, use the methods `GetColLabelValue(col)` and `GetRowLabelValue(row)`.

For a grid control using an external grid table, you can achieve the same effect by overriding the grid table methods `GetColLabelValue(col)` and `GetRowLabelValue(row)`. To clear up any confusion, these methods are called internally by the grid control when it needs to display a label and the grid has an associated table. Since the returned value is determined dynamically by the code you put in the overridden method, there's no need to override or call the setter methods. The setter methods still exist—still `SetColLabelValue(col, value)` and `SetRowLabelValue(row, value)`—but you would rarely use them, and only if you want the user to be able to change the underlying data. Typically, you don't need the setters. Listing 14.4 displays how to change labels in a table grid—this listing produces the same output as the previous listing.

Listing 14.4   Code for grid with a grid table that has custom labels

```python
import wx
import wx.grid

class TestTable(wx.grid.PyGridTableBase):
    def __init__(self):
        wx.grid.PyGridTableBase.__init__(self)
        self.rowLabels = ["uno", "dos", "tres", "quatro", "cinco"]
        self.colLabels = ["homer", "marge", "bart", "lisa", "maggie"]

    def GetNumberRows(self):
        return 5

    def GetNumberCols(self):
        return 5

    def IsEmptyCell(self, row, col):
        return False

    def GetValue(self, row, col):
        return "(%s,%s)" % (self.rowLabels[row], self.colLabels[col])

    def SetValue(self, row, col, value):
        pass
```

```
        def GetColLabelValue(self, col):    ⟵  Column labels
            return self.colLabels[col]

        def GetRowLabelValue(self, row):    ⟵  Row labels
            return self.rowLabels[row]

class TestFrame(wx.Frame):
    def __init__(self):
        wx.Frame.__init__(self, None, title="Grid Table",
                          size=(500,200))
        grid = wx.grid.Grid(self)
        table = TestTable()
        grid.SetTable(table, True)

app = wx.PySimpleApp()
frame = TestFrame()
frame.Show()
app.MainLoop()
```

By default, the labels are centered in their spaces; however, you can change that behavior by using the methods `SetColumnLabelAlignment(horiz, vert)` and `SetRowLabelAlignment(horiz, vert)`. In both cases, the `horiz` parameter controls the horizontal alignment and can have the values `wx.ALIGN_LEFT`, `wx.ALIGN_CENTRE`, or `wx.ALIGN_RIGHT`. The `vert` parameter controls the vertical alignment and can have the values `wx.ALIGN_TOP`, `wx.ALIGN_CENTRE`, or `wx.ALIGN_BOTTOM`.

The row and column label areas share a common set of attributes for color and font display. You can manage those properties with the setter methods `SetLabelBackgroundColour(colour)`, `SetLabelFont(font)`, and `SetLabelTextColour(colour)`, each of which modifies the property implied by its name. The `colour` attribute is an instance of `wx.Colour` or something that wxPython converts to a color, such as the string name of a color. The `font` property is an instance of `wx.Font`. The associated getter methods, `GetLabelBackgoundColour()`, `GetLabelFont()`, and `GetLabelTextFont()`, all exist.

14.2.3 *How can I manage the size of grid elements?*

The grid control offers several different methods to manage the size of cells, rows, and columns. In this section we'll discuss each of these methods. Figure 14.4 displays some of the ways to change the size of a specific cell.

Listing 14.5 displays the code for creating a grid with resized cells, rows, and columns.

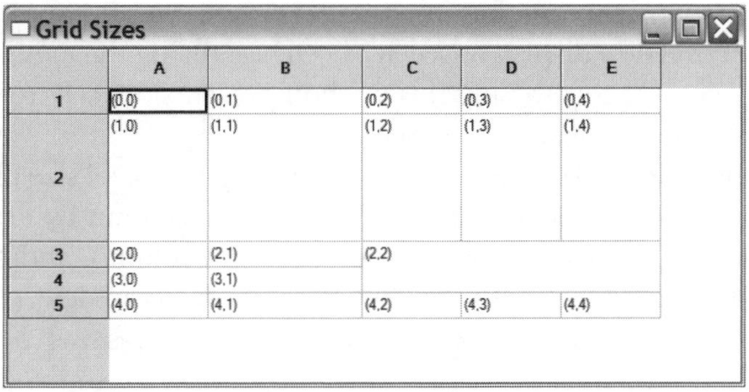

Figure 14.4
**A sample grid,
showing resized cells,
rows, and columns**

Listing 14.5   Code sample for resized cells

```python
import wx
import wx.grid

class TestFrame(wx.Frame):

    def __init__(self):
        wx.Frame.__init__(self, None, title="Grid Sizes",
                          size=(600,300))
        grid = wx.grid.Grid(self)
        grid.CreateGrid(5,5)
        for row in range(5):
            for col in range(5):
                grid.SetCellValue(row, col, "(%s,%s)" % (row, col))

        grid.SetCellSize(2, 2, 2, 3)
        grid.SetColSize(1, 125)
        grid.SetRowSize(1, 100)
app = wx.PySimpleApp()
frame = TestFrame()
frame.Show()
app.MainLoop()
```

Changing cell size

One basic way to affect the size of a cell is to make it span more than one row or column, analogous to the HTML rowspan and colspan attributes. To manage this in wxPython, use the method SetCellSize(row, col, num_rows, num_cols). This sets the cell at the coordinates row, col to flow over num_rows rows and num_col cols. Under normal circumstances, each cell takes up one row and one column, so to get the cell to overflow, you need to pass a value higher than one to those parameters. Passing a num_rows or num_cols value that is zero or less results in an error. If you set up a cell size that overlaps another cell's previously declared overflow size, the previously set cell has its size reset to one row and one column. You can also shut off overflow display on a cell by cell basis using the method `Set-CellOverflow(row, col, allow)`. Passing this method prevents the cell from overflowing even if its size has been set with `SetCellSize()`.

A more typical method of sizing a grid is by managing the pixel size on a row or column basis. You can set the size of a specific row or column by using the method `SetColSize(col, width)` to change the width of a column, and `SetRow-Size(row, height)` to change the width of a row. Naturally, you can determine the current size of a row or column using `GetColSize(col)` or `GetRowSize(row)`.

Setting default sizes

You can change the size of the entire grid by changing the default size of all rows or all columns. Following are the two methods for this.

```
SetDefaultColSize(width, resizeExistingCols=False)
SetDefaultRowSize(height, resizeExistingRows=False).
```

In both cases, the first parameter is the new size in pixels. If the Boolean second parameter is `True`, all the currently existing rows or columns are immediately resized to the new default. If the parameter is `False`, existing rows or columns are left untouched, and the new default is only applied to new rows or columns as they are added. In a typical use, you would most likely want to set this value at the beginning of your initialization, even before the call to `CreateGrid()` or `Set-Table()`. You can get the current default sizes using `GetDefaultColSize()` and `GetDefaultRowSize()`.

There is a performance implication to setting the default versus setting the sizes for individual rows or columns. To store the default values, wxPython only needs to store the two integer values. As soon as you set a single row or column to a non-default size, wxPython switches and stores the size of every row or column in an array. If your table is very large, this could use a significant amount of additional memory, so it's something to watch.

Occasionally, you'll want to set a minimum size for a row or column so that no matter what program methods are called or what the user does by dragging grid lines, the row or column can get no smaller. This may be the case if you have text that you don't want to be chopped in half, or a number that you don't want digits cut off from.

In wxPython, you can set the minimum value on a grid-wide basis or set it separately for individual rows and columns. To change the minimum value for the entire grid, use the method `SetColMinimalAcceptableWidth(width)` or `SetRow-MinimalAcceptableHeight(height)`. The parameter is the minimal size for all rows or columns in pixels. To set the minimum on a row-by-row basis, use `Set-ColMinimalWidth(col, width)` or `SetRowMinimalHeight(row, height)`. For these methods, the first parameter is the index of the item being sized and the second method is the new size in pixels. The minimal size of an individual row must be higher than the minimum grid-wide value, if that value is set. Existing rows or columns that happen to have a size smaller than the new minimum will not be automatically resized. Therefore, you probably want to call these methods early in the initialization process before data is added. For performance reasons, it's best to keep the minimum acceptable values close to the actual smallest size of a real cell as displayed. Each of these methods has one of the following associated getter functions.

- `GetColMinimalAcceptableWidth()`
- `GetRowMinimalAcceptableHeight()`
- `GetColMinimalWidth(col)`
- `GetRowMinimalHeight(row)`

Setting label sizes

The label area on the grid has a separate set of sizing functions. In this case, you are setting the width of the row labels, and the height of the column labels, which means you are treating the column labels as a special row, and the row labels as a special column. As an example, look at a spreadsheet and notice how the row and column labels are laid out. The setter methods are `SetRowLabelSize(width)`, which sets the width of the row labels, and `SetColLabelSize(height)`, which sets the width of the column labels. You can retrieve these sizes with the getter methods `GetRowLabelSize()` and `GetColLabelSize()`.

Often, you won't care about the actual pixel size of your cells, you'll want them to be auto sized big enough to display your data. In wxPython you can auto size the entire grid with the method `AutoSize()`. When that is called, all rows and columns are resized to minimally fit their contents. You can auto size on a more fine-grained basis using methods specific to rows and columns. The method `Auto-SizeColumn(col, setAsMin=True)` forces the column at the specified index to be automatically resized to minimally fit its contents. If the `setAsMin` parameter is `True`, the new auto size is made the minimum size of that column. Similarly, the method `AutoSizeColumns(setAsMin=True)` resizes all the columns in the grid. There are analogous methods for rows, `AutoSizeRow(row, setAsMin=True)` and `AutoSizeRows(setAsMin=True)`. Again, the `setAsMin` parameter allows you to simultaneously reset the minimum size of the row.

You can also allow the user to adjust the row size by dragging the cell label borders. The primary set of methods for doing this are:

- `EnableDragColSize(enable=True)`, governs whether the user can drag the column labels
- `EnableDragRowSize(enable=True)`, governs whether the user can drag the row labels
- `EnableDragGridSize(enable=True)` governs both dimensions at once

Using the enable methods without the parameter is a shortcut to enabling the dragging. Following are parallel methods that are shortcuts for disabling dragging:

- `DisableDragColSize()`
- `DisableDragRowSize()`
- `DisableDragGridSize()`

Following is a set of getter methods:

- `CanDragColSize()`
- `CanDragRowSize()`
- `CanDragGridSize()`

14.2.4 *How can I manage which cells are selected or visible?*

In a grid control, one or more cells can be selected by the user. In wxPython, there are several methods that allow you to manipulate the group of selected cells. You can also locate the exact cell containing the cursor, and the exact screen position of any specific cell in the grid.

At any given time, the selection in a grid control can be zero or more of the following:

- a collection of individually selected cells
- a collection of selected rows
- a collection of select columns
- a collection of selected blocks of cells

The user can select more than one group of cells by control- or command-clicking on cells, row or column labels, or dragging the mouse across cells. To determine whether there are any cells selected in the grid, use the method `IsSelection()` that returns `True` if there is a current selection in the grid of any kind. You can query whether any specific cell is in a current selection by using the method

IsInSelection(row, col), that returns True if the cell at the given coordinates is currently selected.

Table 14.2 displays several methods that allow you to get the current selection returned to you in different ways.

Table 14.2 Methods to return the set of currently selected cells

Method	Return Value
GetSelectedCells()	Returns a Python list of all the cells that were individually selected. Each item in the list is a tuple of (row, col) values.
GetSelectedCols()	Returns a Python list of the indexes of the columns that were selected by clicking the column labels.
GetSelectedRows()	Returns a Python list of the indexes of the rows that were selected by clicking the row labels.
GetSelectionBlockTopLeft()	Returns a Python list, each element of which is a (row, col) tuple of the top left corner of a currently selected rectangle.
GetSelectionBlockBottomRight()	Returns a Python list, each element of which is a (row, col) tuple of the bottom right corner of a currently selected rectangle.

There are also several methods for setting or modifying the selection. The first is ClearSelection() which removes any current selection. After this method is called, IsSelection() returns False. You can do the opposite action—make all the cells selected—with the method SelectAll(). You can select an entire column or row with the methods SelectCol(col, addToSelected=False) and Select-Row(row, addToSelected=False). In both cases, the first argument is the index of the row or column to select. If the addToSelected argument is True, all other currently selected cells remain selected and the row or column is added to the existing selection (simulating a control or command-click). If the addToSelected argument is False then all the other selected cells are deselected and the new row or column replaces them as the selection. You can similarly add a rectangular block with the method SelectBlock(topRow, leftCol, bottomRow, rightCol, addToSelected=False), where the first four arguments are the corners of the rectangle, and addToSelected behaves as in the previous methods.

You can tell whether a particular cell is visible in the current display by using the method IsVisible(row, col, wholeCellVisible=True). The method returns True if the cell at the given row and col attributes is currently displayed onscreen, as opposed to being in the hidden part of a scrolled container. If wholeCell-Visible is True, the entire cell must be visible for the method to return True, if the parameter is False, any part of the cell being visible is good enough. Conversely, the method `MakeCellVisible(row, col)` ensures that the cell at the given coordinates is visible with a minimal amount of scrolling.

In addition to the selected cells, the grid control also has a cursor cell that represents the cell with the current user focus. You can determine the current position of the cursor with the methods `GetGridCursorCol()` and `GetGridCursorRow()`, that return the appropriate integer index. You can place the cursor explicitly with the method `SetGridCursor(row, col)`. Not only does this method move the cursor, it implicitly calls `MakeCellVisible` on the new cursor location.

Table 14.3 describes grid control methods that help convert between grid coordinates and display coordinates.

Table 14.3   Coordinate conversion methods

Method	Description
BlockToDeviceRect (topLeft, bottomRight)	The `topLeft` and `bottomRight` parameters are cell coordinates—in wxPython, pass them as `(row, col)` tuples. The return value is a `wx.Rect` in device pixel coordinates of the rectangle bounded by the given grid coordinates. If necessary, the rectangle is clipped to the size of the grid window.
CellToRect(row, col)	Returns a `wx.Rect` with the coordinates relative to the container for the cell at grid coordinates `(row, col)`.
XToCol(x)	Returns the integer index of the column containing the given x coordinate in relation to the container. If there is no column at that coordinate, returns `wx.NOT_FOUND`.
XToEdgeOfCol(x)	Returns the integer index of the column whose right edge is closest to the given x coordinate. If there is no such column, returns `wx.NOT_FOUND`.
YToRow(y)	Returns the integer index of the row containing the given y coordinate. If there is no such row, returns `wx.NOT_FOUND`.
YToEdgeOfRow(y)	Returns the row whose bottom edge is closest to the given y coordinate. If there is no such row, returns `wx.NOT_FOUND`.

You could use these to convert the location of a mouse click to the grid cell that contains the click.

14.2.5   *How do I change the color or font of a grid cell?*

As with other controls, there are a set of properties that you can use to change the display attributes for each cell. Figure 14.5 displays some of what you can do with the attribute methods.

Listing 14.6 displays the code used to create figure 14.5. Notice the use of both grid methods aimed at a specific cell and of the creation of `wx.grid.Grid-CellAttr` objects.

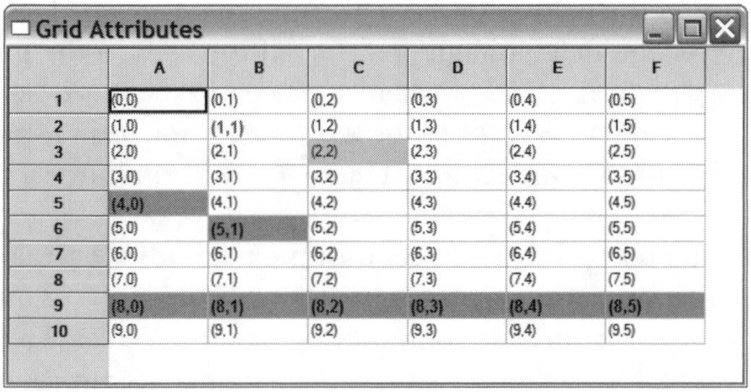

**Figure 14.5
A sample usage of the
grid attribute methods**

Listing 14.6 Changing the color of grid cells

```python
import wx
import wx.grid

class TestFrame(wx.Frame):

    def __init__(self):
        wx.Frame.__init__(self, None, title="Grid Attributes",
                          size=(600,300))
        grid = wx.grid.Grid(self)
        grid.CreateGrid(10,6)
        for row in range(10):
            for col in range(6):
                grid.SetCellValue(row, col, "(%s,%s)" % (row, col))

        grid.SetCellTextColour(1, 1, "red")
        grid.SetCellFont(1,1, wx.Font(10, wx.SWISS, wx.NORMAL, wx.BOLD))
        grid.SetCellBackgroundColour(2, 2, "light blue")

        attr = wx.grid.GridCellAttr()
        attr.SetTextColour("navyblue")
        attr.SetBackgroundColour("pink")
        attr.SetFont(wx.Font(10, wx.SWISS, wx.NORMAL, wx.BOLD))

        grid.SetAttr(4, 0, attr)
        grid.SetAttr(5, 1, attr)
        grid.SetRowAttr(8, attr)

app = wx.PySimpleApp()
frame = TestFrame()
frame.Show()
app.MainLoop()
```

We'll begin by discussing the methods used for setting the default values for the entire grid. You can set the default alignment for all the cells in the grid with `SetDefaultCellAlignment(horiz, vert)` where `horiz` is `wx.LEFT`, `wx.CENTRE`, or `wx.RIGHT`, and `vert` is `wx.TOP`, `wx.CENTRE`, or `wx.BOTTOM`. You can recover the default cell alignment with `GetDefaultCellAlignment()` which returns a tuple of `(horiz, vert)`.

The background and text color can be set with the methods `SetDefaultCellTextColour(colour)` and `SetDefaultCellBackgroundColour(colour)`. As usual, the color can either be a `wx.Colour` instance or the string name of a color. The getters are `GetDefaultCellTextColour()` and `GetDefaultCellBackgroundColour()`. Finally, you can manage the default font with `SetDefaultCellFont(font)` and `GetDefaultCellFont()`.

Using the following methods, you can set all of these attributes for an individual cell.

```
GetCellAlignment(row, col)
SetCellAlignment(row, col, horiz, vert)

GetCellBackgroundColour(row, col)
SetCellBackgroundColour(row, col, colour)

GetCellFont(row, col)
SetCellFont(row, col, font)

GetCellTextColour(row, col)
SetCellTextColour(row, col, colour)
```

Each method behaves as the default, with the addition of the `row` and `col` attributes that define the coordinates of the cell being discussed.

Selected cells have different background and foreground colors, which can be changed. The methods are `SetSelectionBackground(colour)` and `SetSelectionForeground(colour)`, with the associated getter methods `GetSelectionBackground()` and `GetSelectionForeground()`.

You can place extra space around the grid control by using the method `SetMargins(extraWidth, extraHeight)`—the parameters indicate the amount of pixels that are used to pad the grid within its container.

Internally, the `wx.grid.Grid` class uses a class called `wx.grid.GridCellAttr` to manage the attributes of each cell. That class has getter and setter methods for all of the properties discussed in this section. You can get the cell attr object for a specific cell by using the method `GetOrCreateCellAttr(row, col)`, which provides you with the cell attribute object for the appropriate cell, creating an object if necessary. A cell attribute object is only created if the cell has defined properties different from the grid default. Once you have the cell attribute object, you can use it to define display properties of the cell.

To create your own cell attribute object, the constructor is `wx.grid.GridCell-Attr()`. You can set some parameters, then pass the object to the methods `Set-ColAttr(attr)` or `SetRowAttr(attr)`, which applies the display attributes to every cell in that row or column, as displayed in listing 14.6.

If you are using a grid table, you can override the method `GetAttr(row, col)` to return a `wx.grid.GridCellAttr` instance specific to that particular cell, which is used by the grid in displaying that cell.

You can also change the color and display of the grid lines. The display of the grid lines is controlled with the method `EnableGridLines(enable)`. The `enable` parameter is a Boolean. If `True`, the lines are displayed, if `False` they are not displayed. You can change the color of the grid lines with `SetGridLine-Color(colour)`.

14.3 Custom renderers and editors

What makes the grid control so flexible and useful is the idea that the mechanism for displaying or editing a cell's contents can be changed on a cell-by-cell basis. In the following sections, we'll show how to use predefined renderers and editors, and how to write your own.

14.3.1 How do I use a custom cell renderer?

By default, a wxPython grid displays its data as a simple string, however, you can also display your data in a different format. You may want Boolean data to display as a checkbox, or a numerical value to display in a graphical format, or a list of data to display as a sparkline.

In wxPython, each cell can have its own renderer, which allows it to display its data differently. The following sections discuss a few renderers that come predefined in wxPython, and how to define your own if you so desire.

Predefined renderers

A grid renderer is an instance of the class `wx.grid.GridCellRenderer`, which is an abstract parent class. Typically, you would use one of its subclasses. Table 14.4 describes several predefined renderers that you can use in your cells. Each of these classes has a constructor and getter and setter methods.

To get the renderer for a specific cell, use the method `GetCellRenderer(row, col)`, which returns the renderer instance for the given cell coordinates. To set the renderer for a cell, use `SetCellRenderer(row, col, renderer)`, where the renderer

Table 14.4   Predefined grid cell renderers

Renderer class	Description
wx.grid.GridCellAutoWrapStringRenderer	Prints the textual data with word wrapping at the cell boundaries.
wx.grid.GridCellBoolRenderer	Renders Boolean data by using a checkbox in the middle of the cell—checked for `True`, unchecked for `False`.
wx.grid.GridCellDateTimeRenderer	Allows the cell to display a formatted date and/or time.
wx.grid.GridCellEnumRenderer	Renders a number as a textual equivalent. In other words, the data in the cell is in the list [0,1,2], but the cell would be rendered as one of ["John", "Fred", "Bob"].
wx.grid.GridCellFloatRenderer	Renders numerical floating point data with a specific width and precision. The constructor for this class takes two arguments (`width=-1, precision=-1`), where the `width` is the minimum number of digits to show, and the `precision` is the maximum number of digits displayed after the decimal point. The numbers displayed by this renderer are right justified by default.
wx.grid.GridCellNumberRenderer	Renders numerical data as entered. The numbers displayed by this renderer are right justified by default.
wx.grid.GridCellStringRenderer	Renders the cell data as a simple string. By default, data rendered by this renderer is left justified. This is the default renderer used by the grid for all cells.

argument is the new renderer for that cell. These methods simply set or get the renderer stored in the cell's attribute object, so you can also deal with the Grid-CellAttr directly if you prefer. You can get and set the default renderer for the entire grid by using the methods GetDefaultRenderer() and SetDefaultRenderer(renderer).

You can set the renderer for an entire column at once—the typical use case for this being a spreadsheet application where certain columns always display data of a particular type. The methods for doing this are SetColFormatBool(col), SetColFormatNumber(col), and SetColFormatFloat(col, width, precision). Each of these methods sets the column attribute to use the renderer with the same name, and is a shortcut for calling SetColAttr() with a custom attribute object.

Creating a custom renderer
To create your own custom cell renderer, create a subclass of wx.grid.PyGridCellRenderer—as with other wxPython classes, the Py version of the class allows for a Python class to subclass the base C++ class and properly reflect virtual method

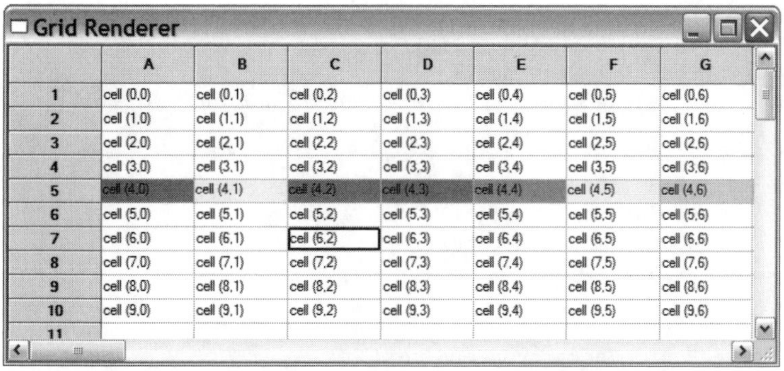

**Figure 14.6
A custom grid
renderer, setting
background colors**

calls to the Python methods. Creating a custom cell renderer allows you to do things like display a numerical value as a mini-bar graph or perform special formatting on a string or date.

Figure 14.6 displays a sample custom renderer that randomly draws a background color for the cell. The renderer is set for a specific row. You'll notice if you execute the code that the grid will flicker on redraw, as it reassigns the random color.

Listing 14.7 lists the code used to create the custom renderer, displaying the overridden renderer class and the overridden methods.

Listing 14.7   The code for a custom grid renderer that changes color randomly

```
import wx
import wx.grid
import random

class RandomBackgroundRenderer(wx.grid.PyGridCellRenderer):    ◁┘ Defining the
    def __init__(self):                                           renderer
        wx.grid.PyGridCellRenderer.__init__(self)

    def Draw(self, grid, attr, dc, rect, row, col, isSelected):   ◁┘ What to
        text = grid.GetCellValue(row, col)                           draw
        hAlign, vAlign = attr.GetAlignment()
        dc.SetFont( attr.GetFont() )
        if isSelected:
            bg = grid.GetSelectionBackground()
            fg = grid.GetSelectionForeground()
        else:
            bg = random.choice(["pink", "sky blue", "cyan",
                    "yellow", "plum"])
            fg = attr.GetTextColour()

        dc.SetTextBackground(bg)
        dc.SetTextForeground(fg)
```

```
                    dc.SetBrush(wx.Brush(bg, wx.SOLID))
                    dc.SetPen(wx.TRANSPARENT_PEN)
                    dc.DrawRectangleRect(rect)
                    grid.DrawTextRectangle(dc, text, rect, hAlign, vAlign)

            def GetBestSize(self, grid, attr, dc, row, col):
                text = grid.GetCellValue(row, col)
                dc.SetFont(attr.GetFont())
                w, h = dc.GetTextExtent(text)
                return wx.Size(w, h)

            def Clone(self):
                return RandomBackgroundRenderer()

    class TestFrame(wx.Frame):
        def __init__(self):
            wx.Frame.__init__(self, None, title="Grid Renderer",
                              size=(640,480))

            grid = wx.grid.Grid(self)
            grid.CreateGrid(50,50)

            attr = wx.grid.GridCellAttr()
            attr.SetRenderer(RandomBackgroundRenderer())
            grid.SetRowAttr(4, attr)        ◁┐ Assigning to row 4

            for row in range(10):
                for col in range(10):
                    grid.SetCellValue(row, col,
                                      "cell (%d,%d)" % (row, col))

    app = wx.PySimpleApp()
    frame = TestFrame()
    frame.Show()
    app.MainLoop()
```

Your renderer class must override three methods of the base class.

- `Draw()`
- `GetBestSize()`
- `Clone()`

The most important of these methods is `Draw(grid, attr, dc, rect, row, col, isSelected)`. The arguments to this method provide information about the grid that you will need to draw the cell. The `grid` argument is the grid instance containing this cell. The `attr` argument contains the grid attribute instance with the foreground and background color, among others. The `dc` argument is the device context to draw to if you need to use primitive drawing methods. The rect is the bounding rectangle of the cell in logical coordinates. The grid coordinates of the cell are given by the row and col elements, and isSelected is True if the cell is currently selected. Within your draw method, you are free to do whatever you want. You may find it convenient to call the super method of the base class, which draws the background color from the attr parameter and sets the foreground color and text font.

The second method to override is GetBestSize(grid, attr, dc, row, col). This method returns a wx.Size instance that represents the preferred size of the cell for that data, the size of which you can calculate on your own. The grid, attr, dc, row, and col attributes are defined exactly as they are in the Draw() method.

Finally, you should override the method Clone(), that returns a wx.grid.Grid-CellRenderer instance, which should be equal to the instance being called. Once the renderer is defined, you can use it just like the predefined renderer, by setting it as the renderer for specific cells.

14.3.2 *How do I edit a cell?*

A wxPython grid control allows you to edit cell values in place. For the grid as a whole, editing is on by default. Clicking on a selected cell, or beginning to type a new data value, opens a default string editor that lets you enter a different string. In this section, we'll discuss a number of ways to modify this default behavior.

You can shut off the editing for the entire grid with the method Enable-Editing(enable)—the enable parameter is a Boolean. If it is False, no cell in the grid can be editable. If editing is turned off using this function, then individual cells cannot have editing turned on. If the editing is on from this method, however, individual cells (or rows or columns) can be designated as read-only. You can determine if the grid is currently editable with the method IsEditable().

You can set the editing state for a specific cell with the method SetRead-Only(row, col, isReadOnly=True). A True passed to the isReadOnly parameter makes the cell read-only, a False makes the cell editable again. The SetRead-Only() method is a shortcut for the method of the same name in the class wx.grid.GridCellAttr. In other words, you could set a cell to be read-only using something like GetCellAttr(row, col).SetReadOnly(isReadOnly). The advantage of using the cell attribute mechanism is that you can combine it with the SetRow-Attr() and SetColAttr() methods to set entire rows or columns as editable or read-only at one time.

You can also manage the editable nature of the grid using the methods `EnableCellEditControl(enable=True)` and `DisableCellEditControl()`, the latter method is equivalent to `EnableCellEditControl(False)`. The enable method will create and show the cell editor in the currently selected cell. The disable method will hide the editor in the current cell, saving the edited data. The method `CanEnableCellControl()` returns true if the enable method will work on the current cell, meaning that the grid is editable and the cell has not been designated read-only. The method `IsCellEditControlEnabled()` returns true if the cell editor is active for the current cell.

There are also some methods that are used internally that you can use for more fine-grained control of the edit process. You can trigger an edit of the current cell (the cell at the cursor position) using the method `ShowCellEditControl()`, and you can end the edit with the method `HideCellEditControl()`. You can determine if the current cell is available for editing using the method `IsCurrentCellReadOnly()`. You can ensure that the new value entered in the editor is properly stored by the grid using the method `SaveEditControlValue()`. The grid control implicitly calls this method when focus moves away from the cell being edited, but it's a good idea to implicitly call it when you are doing something in your program that might cause a value to be lost (such as closing the window that encloses the grid).

Each individual cell has its own specific editor object. You can get a reference to that editor object with the method `GetCellEditor(row, col)`, the return value is an instance of the class `wx.grid.GridCellEditor`. You can set the editor with the method `SetCellEditor(row, col, editor)` where the `editor` parameter is a `wx.grid.GridCellEditor`. You can manage defaults for the entire grid with the `GetDefaultEditor()` and `SetDefaultEditor(editor)`. Just like the renderers, the editor object is stored as part of the `wx.grid.GridCellAttr` objects associated with the cell, row, or column.

14.3.3 *How do I use a custom cell editor?*

As with renderers, wxPython offers several standard editors for different types, and provides you the option to create your own.

Predefined editors

All wxPython editors are subclasses of the class `wx.grid.GridCellEditor`. Table 14.5 describes the standard editors.

In the next section, we'll show you how to create a custom cell editor.

Table 14.5   Cell editors in wxPython

Editor	Description
wx.grid.GridCellAutoWrapStringEditor	Uses a multi-line text control for editing the data value
wx.grid.GridCellBooleanEditor	An editor for Boolean cell data, consisting of a checkbox that the user can check or uncheck. It's visually slightly different from the checkbox used by the Boolean renderer. You do not have to have a Boolean renderer to use a Boolean editor—you could have the data display as 1 or 0 or on/off or something like that.
wx.grid.GridCellChoiceEditor	An editor for a specific list of options. When invoked, the user sees a pull-down list of the choices similar to a combo block. The constructor takes the parameters (choices, allowOthers=False). The choices parameter is the list of strings. If allowOthers is True, then the user can also type an arbitrary string in addition to selecting from the pull-down list.
wx.grid.GridCellEnumEditor	Derives from wx.grid.GridCellChoiceEditor and manages equating the numeric data value to the string presented to the user.
wx.grid.GridCellFloatEditor	An editor for entering floating point numbers with a specific precision. The constructor takes the parameters (width=-1, precision=-1), where the width is the minimum number of digits to show, and the precision is the maximum number of digits displayed after the decimal point. Numbers entered using this editor are converted to the appropriate width and precision.
wx.grid.GridCellNumberEditor	An editor for entering integer numbers. The constructor takes the parameter (min=-1, max=-1). If min and max are set, the editor does range checking and vetoes attempts to enter a number out of the range. If the editor is range checking, it also uses a spinner control on the right of the cell to allow the user to change the values via the mouse.
wx.grid.GridCellTextEditor	The default editor for entering string data.

Creating a custom editor

You may want to create a custom editor to do some custom processing on the value entered. To create your own editor, create a subclass wx.grid.PyGridCell-Editor. Subclassing an editor is a bit more complex than subclassing a renderer. Table 14.6 displays several methods that you are required to override.

Table 14.7 displays more methods of the parent class that you can override to improve the appearance or display of your custom editor.

Table 14.6 PyGridCellEditor methods that you must override

Method	Description
BeginEdit(row, col, grid)	The `row` and `col` attributes are the coordinates of the cell, and the `grid` is the containing grid. This method is called at the beginning of the edit request. In it, the editor is expected to fetch the value to edit, and do anything else needed to get ready for the edit.
Clone()	Return an equal copy of the editor.
Create(parent, id, evtHandler)	This method is expected to create the actual control used by the editor. The `parent` parameter is the containing widget, the `id` is the wxPython identifier of the control to create, and the `evtHandler` is the event handler bound to the new control.
EndEdit(row, col, grid)	Returns `True` if the edit has changed the value of the cell. Any other cleanup needed should be performed here.
Reset()	Called if the edit is canceled. Should return the value in the control to its original value.

Table 14.7 PyGridCellEditor methods that you can override

Method	Description
Destroy()	Perform any final cleanup when the editor is destroyed.
IsAcceptedKey(evt)	Return `True` if the key pressed in the `evt` should start the editor. The key F2 will always start the editor. The base class version assumes that any keypress will start the editor unless it's modified by a control, alt, or shift.
PaintBackground(rect, attr)	The two parameters are `rect`, a `wx.Rect` with the logical dimensions of the control on screen, and `attr`, the `wc.grid.GridCellAttr` associated with the cell. The purpose of this method is to draw any part of the cell not covered by the edit control itself. The base class version takes the background color from the attribute and fills the rectangle with that color.
SetSize(rect)	The `rect` attribute is a `wx.Rect` with the logical dimensions of the control on the screen. Use this method if needed to position the control within the rectangle.
Show(show, attr)	The `show` attribute is a Boolean determining whether the editor should be displayed, the `attr` is the cell attribute instance for the cell. Called to show or hide the control. In this method you would do anything needed behind the scenes to allow the display.
StartingClick()	When the editor is started by a mouse click on the cell, this method is called to allow the editor to use that click for its own purposes.

continued on next page

Table 14.7 PyGridCellEditor methods that you can override *(continued)*

Method	Description
StartingKey(evt)	If the editor is started by a key press, this method is called to allow the edit control to use the key, if desired (by using it as part of the actual edit, for example).

Once your editor is completed, you can set it as the editor for any cell using the SetCellEditor method. Listing 14.8 displays a sample custom editor that automatically converts the text you enter to uppercase.

Listing 14.8 Creating a custom uppercase editor

```python
import wx
import wx.grid
import string

class UpCaseCellEditor(wx.grid.PyGridCellEditor):     ←— Declaring the editor
    def __init__(self):
        wx.grid.PyGridCellEditor.__init__(self)

    def Create(self, parent, id, evtHandler):     ←— Called on creation
        self._tc = wx.TextCtrl(parent, id, "")
        self._tc.SetInsertionPoint(0)
        self.SetControl(self._tc)

        if evtHandler:
            self._tc.PushEventHandler(evtHandler)

        self._tc.Bind(wx.EVT_CHAR, self.OnChar)

    def SetSize(self, rect)
        self._tc.SetDimensions(rect.x, rect.y, rect.width+2, rect.height+2,
                               wx.SIZE_ALLOW_MINUS_ONE)

    def BeginEdit(self, row, col, grid):
        self.startValue = grid.GetTable().GetValue(row, col)
        self._tc.SetValue(self.startValue)
        self._tc.SetInsertionPointEnd()
        self._tc.SetFocus()
        self._tc.SetSelection(0, self._tc.GetLastPosition())

    def EndEdit(self, row, col, grid):
        changed = False
        val = self._tc.GetValue()
        if val != self.startValue:
            changed = True
            grid.GetTable().SetValue(row, col, val) # update the table
```

```
                self.startValue = ''
                self._tc.SetValue('')
                return changed

        def Reset(self):
            self._tc.SetValue(self.startValue)
            self._tc.SetInsertionPointEnd()

        def Clone(self):
            return UpCaseCellEditor()

        def StartingKey(self, evt):
            self.OnChar(evt)
            if evt.GetSkipped():
                self._tc.EmulateKeyPress(evt)

        def OnChar(self, evt):
            key = evt.GetKeyCode()
            if key > 255:
                evt.Skip()
                return
            char = chr(key)
            if char in string.letters:
                char = char.upper()
                self._tc.WriteText(char)         ⟵ Converting to upper case
            else:
                evt.Skip()

    class TestFrame(wx.Frame):
        def __init__(self):
            wx.Frame.__init__(self, None, title="Grid Editor",
                              size=(640,480))

            grid = wx.grid.Grid(self)
            grid.CreateGrid(50,50)
            grid.SetDefaultEditor(UpCaseCellEditor())    ⟵ Making a default editor

    app = wx.PySimpleApp()
    frame = TestFrame()
    frame.Show()
    app.MainLoop()
```

Refer to tables 14.6 and 14.7 to match the methods used in the editor class when they are called.

14.4 *Capturing user events*

The grid control gives a number of user events that you can respond to. We'll separate them into mouse events and keyboard events. This allows you fine-grained control over the user events, enabling your grid to be more responsive.

14.4.1 *How can I capture user mouse selections?*

For the grid control, not only are there several different mouse event types, there are also a few different event classes for those types. The most commonly used event class is `wx.grid.GridEvent`. The grid event class is a subclass of `wx.Command-Event`, and provides several methods to get at details of the event, as displayed in table 14.8.

Table 14.8   Methods of `wx.grid.GridEvent`

Method	Description
AltDown()	Returns true if the `alt` key was pressed when the event was triggered.
ControlDown()	Returns true if the `control` key was pressed when the event was triggered.
GetCol()	Returns the index of the column of the cell where the event occurred.
GetPosition()	Returns a `wx.Point` representing the logical coordinates in pixels where the event occurred.
GetRow()	Returns the index of the row of the cell where the event occurred.
MetaDown()	Returns true if the `meta` key was pressed when the event was triggered.
Selecting()	Returns `True` if the event is a selection and `False` if the event is a deselection of a cell.
ShiftDown()	Returns `True` if the shift key was pressed when the event was triggered.

There are several different event types associated with `wx.grid.GridEvent`. As in table 14.9, the names of the event types evoke the event being processed.

Table 14.9   Cell event types for grid mouse events

Event Type	Description
wx.grid.EVT_GRID_CELL_CHANGE	Triggered when the user changes the data in a cell via an editor.
wx.grid.EVT_GRID_CELL_LEFT_CLICK	Triggered when the user performs a left mouse click in a cell.

continued on next page

Table 14.9 Cell event types for grid mouse events *(continued)*

Event Type	Description
wx.grid.EVT_GRID_CELL_LEFT_DCLICK	Triggered when the user performs a left mouse double-click in a cell.
wx.grid.EVT_GRID_CELL_RIGHT_CLICK	Triggered when the user performs a right mouse click in a cell.
wx.grid.EVT_GRID_CELL_RIGHT_DCLICK	Triggered when the user performs a right mouse double-click in a cell.
wx.grid.EVT_GRID_EDITOR_HIDDEN	Triggered when a cell editor is hidden at the end of an edit session.
wx.grid.EVT_GRID_EDITOR_SHOWN	Triggered when a cell editor is shown at the beginning of an edit session.
wx.grid.EVT_GRID_LABEL_LEFT_CLICK	Triggered when the user performs a left mouse click in the row or column label area.
wx.grid.EVT_GRID_LABEL_LEFT_DCLICK	Triggered when the user performs a left mouse double click in the row or column label area.
wx.grid.EVT_GRID_LABEL_RIGHT_CLICK	Triggered when the user performs a right mouse click in the row or column label area.
wx.grid.EVT_GRID_LABEL_RIGHT_DCLICK	Triggered when the user performs a right mouse double click in the row or column label area.
wx.grid.EVT_GRID_SELECT_CELL	Triggered when the user moves the focus to a new cell, selecting it.

There are two event types that have an instance of wx.grid.GridSizeEvent. The event types are wx.grid.EVT_GRID_COL_SIZE, triggered when a column is resized, and wx.grid.EVT_GRID_ROW_SIZE, triggered when a row is resized. The grid size event has five of the same methods as wx.GridEvent—AltDown(), ControlDown(), GetPosition(), MetaDown(), and ShiftDown. The final method of wx.grid.Grid-SizeEvent is GetRowOrCol() that returns the index of the row or column changed, depending on the event type, of course.

There is one event that has an instance of wx.grid.GridRangeSelectEvent. The event type is wx.grid.EVT_GRID_RANGE_SELECT. It is triggered when the user selects a contiguous rectangle of cells. The event instance has methods to GetBottom-RightCoords(), GetBottomRow(), GetLeftCol(), GetRightCol(), GetTopRight-Coords(), and GetTopRow() of the rectangle selected, with the return value being either an integer index or a (row, col) tuple for the coordinate methods.

Finally, there is one event that has an instance of wx.grid.GridEditorCreated-Event with an event type of EVT_GRID_EDITOR_CREATED. As the name implies, the event is triggered when an editor is created by an edit session. The event instance has GetCol(), GetRow(), and GetControl() methods, which return the column index of the event, row index of the event, and the edit control being used, respectively.

14.4.2 How can I capture user keyboard navigation?

In addition to using the mouse, the user can navigate through the grid with the keyboard. You can also programmatically change the cursor with the move methods listed in table 14.10. Many of the methods take an expandSelection parameter. This parameter works the same in each method. If the parameter is True, the current selection is stretched to include the new cursor position. If the parameter is False, the current selection is replaced by the new cursor.

Table 14.10   Grid cursor move methods

Method	Description
MoveCursorDown(expandSelection)	Moves cursor down. Equivalent to a down arrow keypress (without expanding selection) or a shift-down keypress (with expanding selection).
MoveCursorDownBlock(expandSelection)	Moves the cursor down to one cell further than the current vertical extent of the selection. Equivalent to a ctrl-down keypress (without expanding selection) or a shift-control-down keypress (with expanding selection).
MoveCursorLeft(expandSelection)	Moves cursor left. Equivalent to a left arrow keypress (without expanding selection) or a shift-left keypress (with expanding selection).
MoveCursorLeftBlock(expandSelection)	Moves the cursor left to one cell further than the current horizontal extent of the selection. Equivalent to a ctrl-left keypress (without expanding selection) or a shift-control-left keypress (with expanding selection).
MoveCursorRight(expandSelection)	Moves cursor right. Equivalent to a right arrow keypress (without expanding selection) or a shift-right keypress (with expanding selection).
MoveCursorRightBlock(expandSelection)	Moves the cursor right to one cell further than the current horizontal extent of the selection. Equivalent to a ctrl-right keypress (without expanding selection) or a shift-control-right keypress (with expanding selection).

continued on next page

Table 14.10   Grid cursor move methods *(continued)*

Method	Description
MoveCursorUp(expandSelection)	Moves cursor up. Equivalent to an up arrow keypress (without expanding selection) or a shift-up keypress (with expanding selection).
MoveCursorUpBlock(expandSelection)	Moves the cursor up to one cell further than the current vertical extent of the selection. Equivalent to a ctrl-up keypress (without expanding selection) or a shift-control-up keypress (with expanding selection).
MovePageDown()	Moves the cursor selection down, such that the cells at the bottom of the display move to the top of the display.
MovePageUp()	Moves the cursor selection up, such that the cells at the top of the display move to the bottom of the display.

That covers nearly all of what you need to know about grids. In the next chapter, we'll tackle the next widget, the tree control.

14.5 *Summary*

- The grid control allows you to create spreadsheet-like grid tables with a great deal of control and flexibility. The grid control is an instance of the class wx.grid.Grid. Typically grid controls are complex enough that it's worthwhile to create your own custom grid subclass with its own __init__ method rather than just creating an instance of the base class and calling its methods elsewhere in your application.

- There are two ways to populate a grid control with data. The control can be built explicitly with the CreateGrid(numRows, numCols) method, after which individual cells can be set with the SetCellValue(row, col, s) method. Alternately, you can create an instance of a grid table, which acts as a model for the grid, and allows you to easily use data from another source in the grid display. A grid table is a subclass of wx.grid.PyGridTableBase with methods such as GetValue(row, col) which can be overridden to drive the grid behavior when displaying a cell. The table is connected to the grid control using the method SetTable(table). When a grid is created with a table, then the table gets veto power over changes to the grid's size with the row and column creation and removal methods.

- A grid has row and column labels that have default values similar to what you would expect in a spreadsheet. The display text and other display attributes of the labels can be changed with grid properties. The size of a row or column can be set explicitly for each item, or the grid can auto size based on the displayed data. The user can also be allowed to change the size of the grid by dragging the grid lines. You can set a minimum size for each row or column if desired, to prevent cells from becoming too small to display their data. In addition, specific cells can be set to overflow into other rows or columns using the SetCellSize(row, col, numrows, numcols) method.

- The user can select one or more rectangles of cells in the grid, and that process can be duplicated programmatically with a number of different Select methods. A grid cell that is scrolled off the screen can be moved onto the display with the MakeCellVisible(row, col) method.

- Much of the power and flexibility of the grid control comes from the ability to create custom renderers and editors for each cell. A renderer controls the display of information in the cell. The default renderer is just a simple string, but there are predefined renderers for Boolean, integer, and floating point data. You can create your own renderer by subclassing wx.Grid. PyGridCellRenderer and overwriting one method for drawing.

- By default, a wxPython grid allows in-place editing of the data. You can change that property on a cell-by-cell basis, or by row or column, or for the entire grid. The editor object governs what control the user sees when editing in place. The default is a normal text edit control for modifying strings. There are predefined editors for Boolean, integer, and floating point data, as well as one which gives users a finite choice of options. You can create your own custom renderer by subclassing wx.grid.GridCellEditor and overriding several of the base class methods.

- The grid control has a number of different events that you can capture, including separate events for mouse clicks in the cells and in the labels, and events triggered by changing the size of a cell. In addition, you can trigger navigation of the cursor in the grid programmatically.

Climbing the tree control

This chapter covers

- Creating a tree control and adding items
- Using styles to design the tree control
- Navigating the tree programmatically
- Managing the tree selection
- Controlling the visibility of items

The tree control is the last of the three wxPython controls for displaying complex data. In this case, the tree control is designed to show data with a strong hierarchy, where you can see that each piece of data has parent and child relationships. One standard example is a file tree, where directories have subdirectories or files inside them, leading to a nested hierarchy of files. Another example is a Document Object Model (DOM) tree of an HTML or XML document. Like the list and grid controls, the tree control provides some flexibility over the display of the items, and allows you to edit tree items in place. In this chapter, we'll show you how to edit tree items and how to respond to user tree control events.

15.1 Creating tree controls and adding items

A tree control is an instance of the class `wx.TreeCtrl`. Figure 15.1 displays a sample tree control.

Listing 15.1 shows the code used to generate that example. Notice that the tree is driven by an external structure stored in a file called `data.py`. We won't print that file here, but it is available at the book's web site. It consists of a nested list structure of the wxPython class hierarchy, a convenient data set for a tree control. Some of the mechanisms in this sample are discussed later in this chapter.

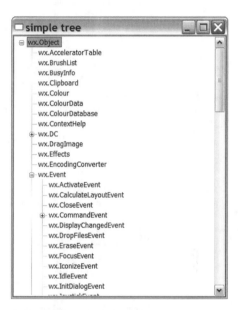

Figure 15.1   A basic tree control example

Listing 15.1   Sample code for the tree example

```
import wx
import data

class TestFrame(wx.Frame):
    def __init__(self):
        wx.Frame.__init__(self, None,
            title="simple tree", size=(400,500))
        self.tree = wx.TreeCtrl(self)              ←┘ Creating the tree
        root = self.tree.AddRoot("wx.Object")      ←— Adding a root node
        self.AddTreeNodes(root, data.tree)         ←┐ Adding nodes from the data set
```

```
            self.Bind(wx.EVT_TREE_ITEM_EXPANDED,
                self.OnItemExpanded,        ◁─┐  Binding some interesting events
                self.tree)
            self.Bind(wx.EVT_TREE_ITEM_COLLAPSED,
                self.OnItemCollapsed,
                self.tree)
            self.Bind(wx.EVT_TREE_SEL_CHANGED,
                self.OnSelChanged, self.tree)
            self.Bind(wx.EVT_TREE_ITEM_ACTIVATED,
                self.OnActivated, self.tree)
            self.tree.Expand(root)      ◁─┐  Expanding the first level

        def AddTreeNodes(self, parentItem, items):   ◁──  Building the tree nodes
            for item in items:
                if type(item) == str:
                    self.tree.AppendItem(parentItem, item)
                else:
                    newItem = self.tree.AppendItem(parentItem, item[0])
                    self.AddTreeNodes(newItem, item[1])

        def GetItemText(self, item):
            if item:
                return self.tree.GetItemText(item)
            else:
                return ""

        def OnItemExpanded(self, evt):
            print "OnItemExpanded: ", self.GetItemText(evt.GetItem())

        def OnItemCollapsed(self, evt):
            print "OnItemCollapsed:", self.GetItemText(evt.GetItem())

        def OnSelChanged(self, evt):
            print "OnSelChanged:   ", self.GetItemText(evt.GetItem())

        def OnActivated(self, evt):
            print "OnActivated:    ", self.GetItemText(evt.GetItem())

app = wx.PySimpleApp(redirect=True)
frame = TestFrame()
frame.Show()
app.MainLoop()
```

The following constructor for wx.TreeCtrl is typical of the wxPython widget
constructors.

```
wx.TreeControl(parent, id=-1, pos=wx.DefaultPosition,
        size=wx.DefaultSize, style=wx.TR_HAS_BUTTONS,
        validator=wx.DefaultValidator, name="treeCtrl")
```

The parameters are similar to the generic `wx.Window` object. The constructor provides you with an empty tree with no elements.

15.1.1 *How do I add a root?*

When you add items to the tree, the first item you add must be the root element. The method for adding the tree's root is `AddRoot()`, called with the following parameters:

```
AddRoot(text, image=-1, selImage=-1, data=None)
```

You can add a root only once. If you try to add a second root after one has been set, wxPython raises an exception. The `text` parameter of the method contains the display string for the root element. The `image` parameter is an index into the image list representing the image displayed next to the text in the tree. The image lists will be discussed in more detail in section 15.5, but for now it's enough to know that they behave similarly to the image list for a list control. The `selImage` is a similar index that is set into the image list for selected items. The `data` parameter is a data object that is associated with that item, mostly for purposes of sorting. However, as a wxPython programmer you do not want to use this mechanism for specifying the data object, because the C++ data type of the `data` parameter is a class called `wx.TreeItemData`. If you are programming in C++, use `wx.TreeItemData` as a wrapper around your data. If you are programming in Python, there's a shortcut that we'll discuss in section 15.3.

The `AddRoot()` method returns an ID for the root item. The tree control uses its own class to manage items, `wx.TreeItemId`. For the most part, you don't need to worry about the exact value of this ID. It's enough to know that each item has a unique `wx.TreeItemId`, and that the values can be tested for equality. The methods of the tree control class that take indexes to search or identify individual items of the tree all take instances of `wx.TreeItemId`. The `wx.TreeItemId` is not mapped to any simple type—its actual data value is not relevant, since you only use it to test for equality.

15.1.2 *How do I add more items to the tree?*

Once you have the root in place, you can begin to add elements to the tree. The method you'll use most frequently is `AppendItem(parent, text, image=-1, selImage=-1, data=None)`. The `parent` parameter is the `wx.TreeItemId` of the existing tree item which will be the parent of the new item. The `text` is the text string that is displayed for the new item. The `image` and `selImage` parameters are, as in the add root method, indexes into the appropriate image list for the image to be displayed with the new item. The `data` parameter is also used the same way as in the add root method. The result of this method is that the new item is placed at the end of the parent item's list of children. The method returns the `wx.Tree-ItemId` of the newly created item. You'll need to hold on to that ID if you want to add children to that item. A sample interaction may look like the following.

```
rootId = tree.AddRoot("The Root")
childId = tree.AppendItem(rootId, "A Child")
grandChildId = tree.AppendItem(childId, "A Grandchild")
```

This snippet provides you with a root item, gives the root item a child, and gives that child a child node of its own.

To add the child item at the beginning of the list of children rather than at the end, use the method `PrependItem(parent, text, image=-1, selImage=-1, data=None)`. With the exception of the placement of the new item, this method behaves identically to `AppendItem()`. The parameters have the same meaning, and it also returns the `wx.TreeItemId` of the new item.

If you want to insert an item into an arbitrary spot of your tree, you can use one of the two insert methods. The first is `InsertItem(parent, previous, text, image=-1, selImage=-1, data=None)`. The `parent`, `text`, `image`, `selImage`, and `data` parameters are identical to the append and prepend versions of this method. The `previous` parameter is a `wx.TreeItemId` corresponding to an item in the child list of the `parent`. The new item is placed in that child after the item passed in the `previous` argument.

If you want to put a new item before something in the list rather than after, use the method `InsertItemBefore(parent, before, text, image=-1, selImage=-1, data=None)`. As the name suggests, this method places the new item before the item passed in the `before` parameter. However, the `before` parameter is not a tree item ID. Rather, it is the integer index of the item in the child list. (Yes, this is confusing. No, there's no easy way to get at the index, you have to manage it yourself. Yes, this is the legacy of a rough patch in the original C++ code.) In any case, assuming you've passed in the correct value, this behaves as you would expect. The new item is added before the item at the given index, and the method returns a `wx.TreeItemId` for the new item.

15.1.3 *How do I manage items?*

To get rid of an item already in the tree, use the `Delete(item)` method, where the `item` parameter is the `wx.TreeItemId` of the item to be zapped. Calling this function causes a tree event to be triggered with the event type `EVT_TREE_DELETE_ITEM`.

Later in this chapter we'll discuss the details of this event type. To leave the item itself, but delete all of its child nodes, call the method `DeleteChildren(item)` where the `item` is again a `wx.TreeItemId`. This method causes all children of the given item to be deleted. Oddly, it does not generate a delete event. To clear the tree entirely, use the method `DeleteAllItems()`. As you might guess, this method deletes all the items in the tree. It is supposed to generate a separate delete event for each item, however, this does not work on some older MS Windows systems.

Once you've added an item to the tree, you can recover its display text using the method `GetItemText(item)`, where the `item` is a `wx.TreeItemId`, and the return value is the display text. If you want to change the text of an item, use the method `SetItemText(item, text)`, where `item` is again a `wx.TreeItemId`, and `text` is the new display text.

Finally, you can get the total number of items in the tree by using the method `GetCount()`. If you want the number of children under just one specific item, use `GetChildrenCount(item, recursively=True)`. The `item` parameter is the `wx.TreeItemId` of the parent. If `recursively` is `False` then the method returns only the number of immediate children of the parent, if it is `True`, the count is for all children no matter what their nested depth.

15.2 What styles control the display of the tree control?

The display styles for the tree control fall into four basic categories. The first set defines whether the tree control has explicit buttons displayed next to the text of a parent object as a target for expanding or collapsing the parent node. These are displayed in table 15.1.

Table 15.1 Button codes for the tree control

Style	Description
wx.TR_HAS_BUTTONS	The tree control has whatever buttons are typical for the platform. For example on MS-Windows a small (+) button is used to indicate that the item can be expanded and a small (-) button is used to indicate that it can be collapsed.
wx.TR_NO_BUTTONS	The tree control does not have buttons next to parent nodes.

The next set, displayed in table 15.2, determines where the tree control draws connecting lines.

Table 15.2   Line codes for the tree control

Style	Description
wx.TR_LINES_AT_ROOT	If set, the tree control will draw lines between the multiple root items. Note that you can only have multiple root items if wx.TR_HIDE_ROOT is set.
wx.TR_NO_LINES	If set, the tree control will not draw any vertical connecting lines between siblings. This item, if set, will supercede wx.TR_LINES_AT_ROOT.
wx.TR_ROW_LINES	The tree control will draw a border between rows.

The third set of styles, displayed in Table 15.3, controls the selection mode of the tree.

Table 15.3   Selection mode styles for the tree control

Style	Description
wx.TR_EXTENDED	Multiple disjoint items can be selected (by control-clicking or command-clicking, depending on your operating system). May not be implemented on all systems.
wx.TR_MULTIPLE	A range of consecutive items can be set, but only a single range.
wx.TR_SINGLE	Only one tree node can be selected at a time. This is the default mode.

Table 15.4 displays other styles that affect display properties of the tree.

Table 15.4   Other styles for the tree control

Style	Description
wx.TR_FULL_ROW_HIGHLIGHT	If set, the tree will highlight the entire horizontal width of the row being selected. By default, only the section actually containing the text is highlighted. On MS Windows systems this option is only valid if wx.NO_LINES is also set.
wx.TR_HAS_VARIABLE_ROW_HEIGHT	If set, the rows will be different height depending on their individual image and text components. Otherwise, all rows will have the same height, determined by the tallest row.
wx.TR_HIDE_ROOT	If set, the root element as determined by AddRoot() will not be displayed. Instead, all of the children of that node will be displayed as if they were roots. Use this option to give the appearance of a tree with multiple roots.

Finally, wx.TR_DEFAULT_STYLE provides you the default tree display based on whatever existing styles are closest to the native widget on your current operating system (i.e., different button types for Windows and Mac). You can change the styles for the widget on the fly during your program using the method SetWindowStyle(styles), where the styles parameter is the integer bitmask of the new styles you want.

To change the display characteristics of the tree, the tree control has several properties that are similar to those we've seen in other controls. In all cases, the item parameter is a wx.TreeItemId corresponding to the item you want changed. You can set the background color of the item with the method SetItemBackgroundColor(item, col), where col is a wx.Colour or something wxPython can convert to a color. You can change the text color with SetItemTextColour(item, col), with the col again representing a color. You can set the display font of the item with SetItemFont(item, font), where the font argument is a wx.Font instance. If you just want the text to display bold, you can use the method SetItemBold(item, bold=True), where the bold argument is a Boolean which determines if the item should be displayed in bold. These four methods each have an associated getter function. The getter functions are GetItemBackgroundColor(item), GetItemTextColour(item), GetItemFont(item), and IsBold(item). In each case, the item parameter is a wx.TreeItemId.

15.3 *Sorting elements of a tree control*

The basic mechanism for sorting elements of a tree control is the method SortChildren(item). The item parameter is, as you should expect by now, an instance of wx.TreeItemId. The method sorts the children of that item from the top of the list downward in alphabetical order of their display strings.

There's one quirk to sorting in a tree control. In order for a tree to sort, each tree item needs to have data attached, which is true even if you are going to use the default sort. In the default case, the attached data is merely None, but for sorting to work, you still need to explicitly set that in the tree control.

In section 15.1, we mentioned that the methods that allow you to create a tree item also allow you to associate the item with an arbitrary data object. We also told you not to use that mechanism. The data item is of the type wx.TreeItemData. If you were programming in C++, you'd create a subclass of wx.TreeItemData that wrapped your actual data item. Since you are not programming in C++, there's a predefined set of shortcuts in wxPython that you can use to associate a Python object with a tree item.

The shortcut setter method is `SetItemPyData(item, obj)`. You pass this method a `wx.TreeItemId` and an arbitrary Python object, and wxPython manages the association behind the scenes. When you want the data item back, you call `GetItemPyData(item)`, which returns the Python object.

ADVANCED NOTE There is a special wxPython constructor for `wx.TreeItemData` that takes a Python object: `wx.TreeItemData(obj)`. You can then use the `GetItemData(item)` and `SetItemData(item, obj)` methods to manage the Python data. This is the mechanism that the `SetItemPyData()` method uses behind the scenes. This information may be useful to you at some point, but for the most part you can get by with the py data methods.

To use the associated data for sorting your tree, your tree must be a custom subclass of `wx.TreeCtrl`, and you must override the method `OnCompareItems(item1, item2)`. The two parameters are `wx.TreeItemId` instances of the two items being compared. The return value is `-1` if `item1` should sort before `item2`, `1` if `item1` should sort after `item2` and `0` if the two items are equal. This method is automatically called by the tree control when it sorts to calculate each comparison. You can do whatever you want within the `OnCompareItems()` method. Specifically, you can call `GetItemPyData()` to get the associated data methods for each item, as in the following:

```
def OnCompareItems(self, item1, item2);
    data1 = self.GetItemPyData(item1)
    data2 = self.GetItemPyData(item2)
    return cmp(data1, data2)
```

This snippet sorts the tree based on whatever the Python comparison function returns for `data1` and `data2`.

15.4 *Controlling the image for each item*

The images for the tree controls are managed with an image list in much the same way as images are managed in list controls. For details on creating image lists, see chapter 13. Once you've created the image list, you assign it to the tree control using the method `SetImageList(imageList)` or `AssignImageList(imageList)`. The former allows the image list to be shared with other controls, and the latter gives ownership of the image list to the tree control. You can later get the image list using the method `GetImageList()`. Figure 15.2 displays a sample tree with some images.

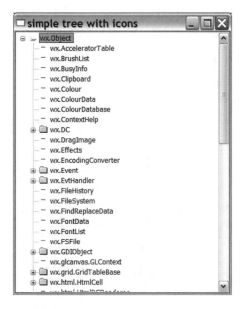

Figure 15.2
The sample tree with an image list assigned

Listing 15.2 provides the code used for figure 15.2. It uses the art provider object to provide common images.

Listing 15.2   A tree control with icons

```
import wx
import data

class TestFrame(wx.Frame):
    def __init__(self):
        wx.Frame.__init__(self, None,           Creating an image list
                title="simple tree with icons", size=(400,500))
        il = wx.ImageList(16,16)                 ←
        self.fldridx = il.Add(                   ←  Adding images
            wx.ArtProvider.GetBitmap(wx.ART_FOLDER,    to a list
                wx.ART_OTHER, (16,16)))
        self.fldropenidx = il.Add(
            wx.ArtProvider.GetBitmap(wx.ART_FILE_OPEN,
                wx.ART_OTHER, (16,16)))
        self.fileidx = il.Add(
            wx.ArtProvider.GetBitmap(wx.ART_NORMAL_FILE,
                wx.ART_OTHER, (16,16)))
        self.tree = wx.TreeCtrl(self)
        self.tree.AssignImageList(il)    ←  Attaching a list and tree
        root = self.tree.AddRoot("wx.Object")
        self.tree.SetItemImage(root, self.fldridx,   ←  Setting root images
                        wx.TreeItemIcon_Normal)
```

```
            self.tree.SetItemImage(root, self.fldropenidx,
                                   wx.TreeItemIcon_Expanded)

            self.AddTreeNodes(root, data.tree)
            self.tree.Expand(root)

        def AddTreeNodes(self, parentItem, items):
            for item in items:                          Setting data images
                if type(item) == str:
                    newItem = self.tree.AppendItem(parentItem, item)
                    self.tree.SetItemImage(newItem, self.fileidx,  ◄──┘
                                           wx.TreeItemIcon_Normal)
                else:
                    newItem = self.tree.AppendItem(parentItem, item[0])
                    self.tree.SetItemImage(newItem, self.fldridx,  ◄──┐
                                           wx.TreeItemIcon_Normal)
                    self.tree.SetItemImage(newItem, self.fldropenidx,
                                           wx.TreeItemIcon_Expanded)

                                                          Setting node
                    self.AddTreeNodes(newItem, item[1])       images

        def GetItemText(self, item):
            if item:
                return self.tree.GetItemText(item)
            else:
                return ""

app = wx.PySimpleApp(redirect=True)
frame = TestFrame()
frame.Show()
app.MainLoop()
```

As we've seen, when you add an item to the list, you have the option of associating two different images with the item—one for the unselected state and one for when the item is selected. As with list controls, you specify the index of the image you want within the image list. If you want to get the image assigned after the item is created, you can use the method GetItemImage(item, which=wx.TreeItemIcon_Normal). The item parameter is the wx.TreeItemId of the item. The which parameter controls which image you get back. With the default value wx.TreeItemIcon_Normal you get the index of the unselected image for the item. Other values for the which parameter are wx.TreeItemIcon_Selected which returns the image in the selected state, and wx.TreeItemIcon_Expanded, and wxTreeItemIcon_SelectedExpanded which return images used when the tree item is expanded. Note that the latter two images cannot be set using the add methods—if you want to set them, you have to do it with the method SetItem-Image(item, image, which=wx.TreeItemIcon_Normal). The item is, again, the wx.TreeItemId of the item under discussion, the image parameter is the integer index of the new image, and the which parameter takes the same values with the same meaning as in the getter method.

15.5 *Navigating the tree programmatically*

In section 15.1 we mentioned that there was no direct way to get a Python list of the children of a given item in the tree, let alone the index of a specific child. To do that, you need to walk the tree nodes yourself using the methods in this section.

To start walking the tree, get the root using GetRootItem(). This method returns the wx.TreeItemId of the root item of the tree. You can then use methods such as GetItemText() or GetItemPyData() to retrieve more information about the item.

Once you have an item, getting its children involves a kind of an iterator which lets you walk through the list of children one by one. You get the first child in the subtree with the method GetFirstChild(item) which returns a two-element tuple (child, cookie). The item is the wx.TreeItemId of the first child, and the second is a special token value. In addition to telling you what the first child is, this method initializes an iterator object that allows you to walk through the tree. The cookie value is just a token that allows the tree control to keep track of multiple iterators on the same tree at the same time without them interfering with each other.

Once you have the cookie from GetFirstChild(), you can get the rest of the children by repeatedly calling GetNextChild(item, cookie). The item is the ID of the parent tree item, and the cookie is the cookie as returned by GetFirstChild() or the previous call to GetNextChild(). The GetNextChild() method returns a two-element tuple (child, cookie). If there is no next child, you've reached the end of the child list, and the system returns an invalid child ID. You can test this by using the method wx.TreeItemId.IsOk(), or using the Python shortcut of just testing the item, since it has a magic __nonzero__ method. The following helper function returns a list of the text for each child of a given tree item.

```
def getChildren(tree, parent):
    result = []
    item, cookie = tree.GetFirstChild(parent)
    while item:
        result.append(tree.GetItemText(item))
```

```
      item, cookie = tree.getNextChild(parent, cookie)
   return result
```

This method gets the first child of the given parent item, adds its text to the list, then loops through the child items until it gets an invalid item, at which point it returns the result. The order in which items are displayed is based on the current display state of the tree—you will get the items in the exact order of the current display from top to bottom.

To cut right to the end and get the last child for a given parent, you can use the method GetLastChild(item), which returns the wx.TreeItemId of the last item in the list. Since this method is not used to drive an iterator through the entire child list, it does not need the cookie mechanism. If you have the child and you want the parent, the method GetItemParent(item) will return the tree ID of the parent of the given item.

You can walk back and forth between items at the same level using the methods GetNextSibling(item), and GetPrevSibling(item). These methods return the tree ID of the appropriate item. Since these methods are also not used to drive iterators, they do not need a cookie. If there is no next or previous item because you have reached the end of the list, the method returns an invalid item (i.e., item.IsOk() == False.

To determine if an item has any children, use the method ItemHasChildren(item) which returns a Boolean True or False. You can set whether an item has children using the method SetItemHasChildren(item, hasChildren=True). If an item has its children property set to True, it will display onscreen as though it had children, even if there are no actual children. This means that the item will have the appropriate button next to it, allowing it to be collapsed or expanded even if there is nothing to actually show by expanding the item. This is used to implement a virtual tree control where not all items logically in the tree have to physically be there, saving runtime resources. This technique is demonstrated in section 15.7.

15.6 *Managing the tree selection*

A tree control allows you to programmatically manage the set of selected items in the tree. The basic method for doing this is the method SelectItem(item, select=True). In a single selection tree control, this method takes a wx.TreeItemId and makes that item the current selection, and the previously selected item is automatically deselected. If the select parameter is False, then this method can be used to deselect the currently selected item. In a multiple or extended tree control, then the `SelectItem()` method changes the state of the item without changing the selected status of any other item in the tree. In a multiple or extended selection tree, you can also use the method `ToggleItemSelection(item)`, which just flips the select state of the `item` passed to the method.

There are three shortcut methods for deselecting items. The plain method `Unselect()` deselects the currently selected item of a tree in single select mode. In a multiple select tree, use the method `UnselectAll()`. If you only want to deselect one item within a multiple select tree, use the method `UnselectItem(item)`.

You can query the select state of an item with the method `IsSelected(item)`, which returns Boolean `True` or `False`. In a single selection tree, you can get the `wx.TreeItemId` of the current selection with the method `GetSelection()`. If it's a multiple selection list, use the method `GetSelections()`, that returns a Python list of the `wx.TreeItemId` of all selected items.

When the selection changes in a tree control, there are two events that are triggered that can be captured. The first event, `wx.EVT_TREE_SEL_CHANGING`, happens before the selection is actually changed. If you handle this event, you can use the event `Veto()` method to prevent the selection from changing. After the selection has changed, the event `wx.EVT_TREE_SEL_CHANGED` is triggered. The event class for these events is `wx.TreeEvent`, discussed more completely in section 15.8.

15.7 *Controlling which items are visible*

There are two mechanisms in the tree control that allow you to programmatically control various aspects of which items are visible on the screen display. You can specify whether a given tree item is expanded or collapsed with the methods `Collapse(item)` and `Expand(item)`. These methods change the display of the tree control, and have no effect if called on an item that does not have children. There is a convenience function, `CollapseAndReset(item)`, that collapses the item and deletes all of its children from the tree. In addition, the method `Toggle(item)` changes the state of the item from expanded to collapsed or vice versa. You can query the current expanding state of the item with the method `IsExpanded(item)`.

Expanding or collapsing a tree item triggers two events in much the same way that changing the selection does. Before the expand or collapse, the event `wx.EVT_TREE_ITEM_COLLAPSING` or `wx.EVT_TREE_ITEM_EXPANDING` is triggered. In your handler method, you can block the expansion or collapse with the event `Veto()` method. After the expansion or collapse takes place, the event `wx.EVT_TREE_ITEM_COLLAPSED` or `wx.EVT_TREE_ITEM_EXPANDED` is triggered, depending, of course, on whether the event was an expansion or collapse of the item. All four of these events are types of the wx.TreeEvent class.

A *virtual tree*

One interesting use of the expanding and collapsing items is to create a virtual tree where new items are only added when a parent is expanded. Listing 15.3 displays a sample tree with new items added.

Listing 15.3   A tree where new items are added dynamically on expansion

```
import wx
import data

class TestFrame(wx.Frame):
    def __init__(self):
        wx.Frame.__init__(self, None, title="virtual tree with icons",
  size=(400,500))
        il = wx.ImageList(16,16)
        self.fldridx = il.Add(
            wx.ArtProvider.GetBitmap(wx.ART_FOLDER, wx.ART_OTHER, (16,16)))
        self.fldropenidx = il.Add(
            wx.ArtProvider.GetBitmap(wx.ART_FILE_OPEN,   wx.ART_OTHER,
                (16,16)))
        self.fileidx = il.Add(
            wx.ArtProvider.GetBitmap(wx.ART_NORMAL_FILE, wx.ART_OTHER,
                (16,16)))
        self.tree = wx.TreeCtrl(self)
        self.tree.AssignImageList(il)
        root = self.tree.AddRoot("wx.Object")
        self.tree.SetItemImage(root, self.fldridx,
                          wx.TreeItemIcon_Normal)
        self.tree.SetItemImage(root, self.fldropenidx,
                          wx.TreeItemIcon_Expanded)

        self.tree.SetItemPyData(root, data.tree)      ◁— Creating a root
        self.tree.SetItemHasChildren(root, True)
                                                   Binding events
        self.Bind(wx.EVT_TREE_ITEM_EXPANDED, self.OnItemExpanded,   ◁┘
                  self.tree)
        self.Bind(wx.EVT_TREE_ITEM_COLLAPSED, self.OnItemCollapsed,
                  self.tree)
        self.Bind(wx.EVT_TREE_SEL_CHANGED, self.OnSelChanged, self.tree)
        self.Bind(wx.EVT_TREE_ITEM_ACTIVATED, self.OnActivated, self.tree)

        self.Bind(wx.EVT_TREE_ITEM_EXPANDING,
                  self.OnItemExpanding, self.tree)
        self.tree.Expand(root)

    def AddTreeNodes(self, parentItem):   ◁┘ Adding nodes to a parent
        items = self.tree.GetItemPyData(parentItem)
```

```
            for item in items:
                if type(item) == str:
                    # a leaf node
                    newItem = self.tree.AppendItem(parentItem, item)
                    self.tree.SetItemImage(newItem, self.fileidx,
                                           wx.TreeItemIcon_Normal)
                else:
                    # this item has children
                    newItem = self.tree.AppendItem(parentItem, item[0])
                    self.tree.SetItemImage(newItem, self.fldridx,
                                           wx.TreeItemIcon_Normal)
                    self.tree.SetItemImage(newItem, self.fldropenidx,
                                           wx.TreeItemIcon_Expanded)
                    self.tree.SetItemPyData(newItem, item[1])
                    self.tree.SetItemHasChildren(newItem, True)

        def GetItemText(self, item):
            if item:
                return self.tree.GetItemText(item)
            else:
                return ""

        def OnItemExpanded(self, evt):
            print "OnItemExpanded: ", self.GetItemText(evt.GetItem())

        def OnItemExpanding(self, evt):      ◁─┘ Creating nodes when expanding
            print "OnItemExpanding:", self.GetItemText(evt.GetItem())
            self.AddTreeNodes(evt.GetItem())

        def OnItemCollapsed(self, evt):
            print "OnItemCollapsed:", self.GetItemText(evt.GetItem())
            self.tree.DeleteChildren(evt.GetItem())      ◁─┐ Removing nodes
                                                             when collapsing
        def OnSelChanged(self, evt):
            print "OnSelChanged:    ", self.GetItemText(evt.GetItem())

        def OnActivated(self, evt):
            print "OnActivated:     ", self.GetItemText(evt.GetItem())

app = wx.PySimpleApp(redirect=True)
frame = TestFrame()
frame.Show()
app.MainLoop()
```

This mechanism could be expanded to read the data from any external source for viewing. We'll mention the possibility of the data being in a database, but this mechanism could also be used to build a file tree, preventing you from having to traverse areas of the file structure that users aren't interested in.

Controlling visibility

There are a number of methods that allow you to manage which items are visible within the display. An object may be not visible either because it has been scrolled off the visible part of its containing frame or because it is part of a child list that is collapsed. You can determine whether an item is visible on the screen with the IsVisible(item) method which returns True if the item is visible, and False if it is not. You can force an item to become visible by using the method Ensure-Visible(item). This method forces the item to become visible by expanding the item's parent (and its parent, and so on) if needed, and then scrolling the tree to put the item in the visible part of the control. If you only need to do the scrolling portion, use the method ScrollTo(item) to manage the task.

Iterate through the visible items in the tree starting with the method Get-FirstVisibleItem(). This method returns the wx.TreeItemId of the topmost item in the visible portion of the display. To iterate through the display, use the method GetNextVisible(item) passing it the previously used item returned from GetFirstVisibleItem() or GetNextVisible(). This method returns the wx.TreeItemId of the item following the one passed to the method (meaning the next lowest row in the display) regardless of nesting or depth. To move upward in the list, use the method GetPreviousVisible(item). If the item is not visible, then an invalid item is returned.

There are a few other methods that affect the visible display of items in the tree. The tree control has a property that sets the number of pixels that are indented by the control at each new level. Get the current value of that property with GetIndent(), and set it with SetIndent(indent), where indent is the integer value of the number of pixels to indent new levels.

Get information about the tree item at a specific point using the method Hit-Test(point), where point is a wx.Point of a location in the tree control. The return value is a tuple (item, flags) where item is the wx.TreeItemId of the item at that point, or None. If there is no item at that point, then an invalid item will be returned which can be tested by calling its IsOk() method. The flags portion of the result is a bitmask with several possible values giving extra information about the location being tested. Table 15.5 contains a complete list of flags.

There are a couple of methods that allow you to deal with the actual boundaries of the items on the screen. The method GetBoundingRect(item, text-Only=False) returns a wx.Rect instance corresponding to the bounding rectangle of the text item on the screen. The item parameter is the wx.TreeItemId of the item in question. If the textOnly parameter is True then the rectangle only includes the area covered by the item's display text. If the parameter is False,

Table 15.5   Valid hit test flags for the tree control

Hit Test Flag	Description
wx.TREE_HITTEST_ABOVE	The point is above the tree's client area and not part of any item.
wx.TREE_HITTEST_BELOW	The point is below the tree's client area and is not part of any item.
wx.TREE_HITTEST_NOWHERE	The point is within the tree's client area, but is still not part of any item.
wx.TREE_HITTEST_ONITEMBUTTON	The point is on the expand/contract icon button which is part of the item.
wx.TREE_HITTEST_ONITEMICON	The point is on the image portion of the item.
wx.TREE_HITTEST_ONITEMINDENT	The point is in the indent area to the left of the display text of the item.
wx.TREE_HITTEST_ONITEMLABEL	The point is in the display text of the item.
wx.TREE_HITTEST_ONITEMRIGHT	The point is to the right of the display text of the item.
wx.TREE_HITTEST_ONITEMSTATEICON	The point is in the state icon for the item.
wx.TREE_HITTEST_TOLEFT	The point is to the left of the tree's client area and is not part of any item.
wx.TREE_HITTEST_TORIGHT	The point is to the right of the tree's client area and is not part of any item.

then the rectangle also includes the image displayed with the rectangle. In neither case does the rectangle include the blank area from the edge of the tree control to the beginning of a nested display item. If the item is not currently visible, then the method returns None.

15.8   *Making a tree control user editable*

The tree control can be set up to allow the user to edit the text display of the various tree items. This allows you to make the control interactive, so the user can make changes to the data on the fly. This may be useful in a DOM or XML editor, allowing the user to change the document directly from the structured view.

This functionality is enabled by creating the tree control with the style flag wx.TR_EDIT_LABELS. With this flag set, the tree control behaves similarly to the editable list control. Selecting a tree item gives the user a text control to edit the text. Pressing escape cancels the edit without changing the item. Leaving the edit session in any other way (such as pressing Enter or clicking outside the text control) okays the edit and changes the tree item.

You can programmatically start an edit on a particular tree item with the method EditLabel(item). The item parameter is the wx.TreeItemId of the item you wish to edit, which triggers the edit process in exactly the same way as if the user had selected the item. To stop the edit from your program, use the method EndEditLabel(cancelEdit). As of this writing, EndEditLabel() only works under Windows systems. In this case, you don't need to pass the item ID—there can only be one active edit at a time, so that's the one that will be ended. The cancelEdit parameter is a Boolean. If it is True, the edit is canceled, and the tree item is not changed, if it is False, the edit is accepted normally. If for some reason you need access to the actual text edit control being used, call the method GetEditControl() which returns the wx.TextCtrl instance being used for the current edit, or None if there is no current edit. Currently, this method only works on Windows systems.

When an edit session begins, either by user selection or by a call to Edit-Label(), a wx.TreeEvent with event type wx.EVT_TREE_BEGIN_LABEL_EDIT is triggered. If this event is vetoed with the event Veto() method, the edit does not actually start. When the session ends, either by a user click or a call to EndEdit-Label(), an event of type wx.EVT_TREE_END_LABEL_EDIT is triggered. This event can also be vetoed, in which case the edit is canceled, and the tree item is not changed.

15.9 *Responding to other user events from a tree control*

In this section, we'll discuss the properties of the wx.TreeEvent class. Table 15.6 lists those properties.

Table 15.6   Properties of wx.TreeEvent

Property	Description
GetKeyCode()	Returns the integer key code of the key pressed. Only valid for the event type wx.EVT_TREE_KEY_DOWN. This property will not tell you if any modifier keys were also pressed.
GetItem()	Returns the wx.TreeItemId of the item which is the subject of the event.

continued on next page

Table 15.6 Properties of `wx.TreeEvent` *(continued)*

Property	Description
GetKeyEvent()	Only valid for `wx.EVT_TREE_KEY_DOWN` events. Returns the underlying `wx.KeyEvent` being wrapped by the `wx.TreeEvent`. This key event will be able to tell you if modifier keys, such as shift or command, were pressed during the event.
GetLabel()	Returns the current text label of the item. Valid for the `wx.EVT_TREE_BEGIN_LABEL_EDIT` and `wx.EVT_TREE_END_LABEL_EDIT`.
GetPoint()	Returns a `wx.Point` of the mouse position for the event. Only valid for the drag events.
IsEditCancelled()	Only valid for a `wx.EVT_TREE_END_LABEL_EDIT` action. Returns a Boolean— `True` if the current edit ended with a user cancel, and `False` otherwise.
SetToolTip(tooltip)	Only valid for the `wx.EVT_TREE_ITEM_GETTOOLTIP` event. Allows you to set the tooltip for the item. This property only works on Windows systems.

Table 15.7 lists a few event types for the `wx.TreeEvent` that didn't fit into any of the previous sections, but that may be useful at some point.

Table 15.7 Other event types for the tree control

Event type	Description
wx.EVT_TREE_BEGIN_DRAG	This event is triggered when the user starts to drag a tree item with the left mouse button pressed. In order for the drag to actually do anything, the event handler must explictly call the event method `Allow()`.
wx.EVT_TREE_BEGIN_RDRAG	This event is triggered when the user starts to drag a tree item with the right mouse button pressed (on Macintosh systems, this means a control-click). In order for the drag to actually do anything, the event handler must explictly call the event method `Allow()`.
wx.EVT_TREE_ITEM_ACTIVATED	Triggered when an item is activated by a user double-click.
wx.EVT_TREE_ITEM_GETTOOLTIP	This event is sent when the mouse hovers over an item in the tree, and can be used to set a tooltip that is specific to that item. Simply set the label parameter in the event object and the system will take care of the rest.
wx.EVT_TREE_KEY_DOWN	This event is sent when a key is pressed while the tree control has the focus.

That's most of what you need to know about the tree control proper. We'll close off the chapter with a useful variant of the control that you can also use.

15.10 *Using a tree list control*

In addition to the wx.TreeCtrl, wxPython provides the wx.gizmos.TreeListCtrl which is a combination of a tree control and a list control in report mode. In addition to the features of the wx.TreeCtrl discussed in this chapter, the TreeListCtrl is able to display additional columns of data for each row. Figure 15.3 displays a sample tree list control.

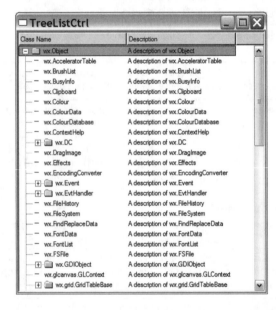

Figure 15.3
A sample tree list control

From the user's perspective the control looks like a list control in report mode with a tree control embedded in one of the columns, but from the programmer's perspective it is very similar to the tree control with some additional methods, parameters, and events borrowed from the list control for dealing with the extra columns. Listing 15.4 displays the code for a tree list control.

Listing 15.4   Using a tree list control

```
import wx
import wx.gizmos
import data

class TestFrame(wx.Frame):
    def __init__(self):
        wx.Frame.__init__(self, None, title="TreeListCtrl", size=(400,500))
```

```
        il = wx.ImageList(16,16)
        self.fldridx = il.Add(
            wx.ArtProvider.GetBitmap(wx.ART_FOLDER, wx.ART_OTHER, (16,16)))
        self.fldropenidx = il.Add(
             wx.ArtProvider.GetBitmap(wx.ART_FILE_OPEN,   wx.ART_OTHER,
(16,16)))
        self.fileidx = il.Add(
             wx.ArtProvider.GetBitmap(wx.ART_NORMAL_FILE, wx.ART_OTHER,
(16,16)))

        self.tree = wx.gizmos.TreeListCtrl(self, style =      ◁──┐ Creating
            wx.TR_DEFAULT_STYLE | wx.TR_FULL_ROW_HIGHLIGHT)         the control
        self.tree.AssignImageList(il)
        self.tree.AddColumn("Class Name")      ◁── Creating columns
        self.tree.AddColumn("Description")
        self.tree.SetMainColumn(0) # the one with the tree in it...
        self.tree.SetColumnWidth(0, 200)
        self.tree.SetColumnWidth(1, 200)

                                                        Adding text to
        root = self.tree.AddRoot("wx.Object")           another column
        self.tree.SetItemText(root, "A description of wx.Object", 1)   ◁──┘
        self.tree.SetItemImage(root, self.fldridx,
                               wx.TreeItemIcon_Normal)
        self.tree.SetItemImage(root, self.fldropenidx,
                                wx.TreeItemIcon_Expanded)
        self.AddTreeNodes(root, data.tree)
        self.Bind(wx.EVT_TREE_ITEM_EXPANDED, self.OnItemExpanded, self.tree)
        self.Bind(wx.EVT_TREE_ITEM_COLLAPSED, self.OnItemCollapsed,
                  self.tree)
        self.Bind(wx.EVT_TREE_SEL_CHANGED, self.OnSelChanged, self.tree)
        self.Bind(wx.EVT_TREE_ITEM_ACTIVATED, self.OnActivated, self.tree)
        self.tree.Expand(root)

    def AddTreeNodes(self, parentItem, items):
        for item in items:
            if type(item) == str:
                newItem = self.tree.AppendItem(parentItem, item)
                self.tree.SetItemText(newItem,                        ◁──┐
                               "A description of %s" % item, 1)
                self.tree.SetItemImage(newItem, self.fileidx,   Adding text
                               wx.TreeItemIcon_Normal)            to another
            else:                                                   column
                newItem = self.tree.AppendItem(parentItem, item[0])
                self.tree.SetItemText(newItem, "A description of %s" %   ◁──┘
                        item[0], 1)
                self.tree.SetItemImage(newItem, self.fldridx,
                                  wx.TreeItemIcon_Normal)
                self.tree.SetItemImage(newItem, self.fldropenidx,
                                  wx.TreeItemIcon_Expanded)

                self.AddTreeNodes(newItem, item[1])
```

```
        def GetItemText(self, item):
            if item:
                return self.tree.GetItemText(item)
            else:
                return ""

    def OnItemExpanded(self, evt):
        print "OnItemExpanded: ", self.GetItemText(evt.GetItem())

    def OnItemCollapsed(self, evt):
        print "OnItemCollapsed:", self.GetItemText(evt.GetItem())

    def OnSelChanged(self, evt):
        print "OnSelChanged:   ", self.GetItemText(evt.GetItem())

    def OnActivated(self, evt):
        print "OnActivated:    ", self.GetItemText(evt.GetItem())

app = wx.PySimpleApp(redirect=True)
frame = TestFrame()
frame.Show()
app.MainLoop()
```

Because of the similarities of the list control for the extra methods, we don't need to list all the methods here. The API for adding and modifying columns is essentially identical to the one in the list control.

15.11 *Summary*

- The tree control provides you with a compact display of nested, hierarchical data, such as a file tree, or an XML document. Tree controls are instances of the class wx.TreeCtrl. Occasionally, you'll want to subclass wx.TreeCtrl, particularly if you need to do custom sorting.

- To add items to the tree, start with the method AddRoot(text, image=-1, selImage=-1, data=None). The return value of this method is a wx.TreeItemId representing the root item of the tree. The tree control uses its wx.TreeItemId as its own identifier class, rather than using integer IDs, as most of the other widgets do. Once you have the root item, you can start adding child items with the method AppendItem(parent, text, ·image=-1, selImage=-1, data=None), passing it the ID of the parent item. The new item is added to the end of the child list of the parent item. The method returns the wx.TreeItemId of the new item. There are related items for prepending

0, 0, 0
       1

       2
_____

0 1 0
0 1 1
0 1 2

cols - 1

rows - 1

the item to the front of the list, or inserting it at an arbitrary location within the list. The method `Delete(item)` removes an item from the tree, and `DeleteChildren(item)` removes all the children of the given item.

- The tree control has several styles which change the visual display of the tree. One set controls the type of flip button next to the item for expanding or collapsing the tree item. Another set controls whether lines are drawn between items in the list. A third set controls whether the tree has single or multiple selection. You can also use styles to simulate a tree with multiple roots by hiding the actual root of the tree.

- By default, a tree can be sorted in alphabetical order of the display text. However, in order for this to work, you must attach data to each item. The easiest way to do this is with the method `SetItemPyData(item, obj)` which associates an arbitrary Python object with the item. You can recover the data with `GetItemPyData(item)`. If you want to use the data to write a custom sorting function, you must extend the `wx.TreeCtrl` class and override the method `OnCompareItems(item1, item2)` where the two arguments are the IDs of the items to be compared.

- The tree control manages images with an image list similar to the way that list controls manage it. You use `SetImageList(imageList)` or `AssignImage-List(imageList)` to attach an image list to the tree control. Then, when new items are added to the list, you can associate them with specific indexes within the image list.

- There is no specific method that allows you to recover the child list of a parent item. Instead, you need to iterate over the child list, starting with the method `GetFirstChild(item)`. This returns the item ID of the first child along with a cookie that you use to pass to `GetNextChild(item, cookie)` and which allows multiple iterations of the child list to be active at the same time. You can also go straight to the end of the list with `GetLastChild(item)`.

- You can manage the selection of the tree with the method `Select-Item(item, select=True)`. In a multiple selection tree, you can also use `ToggleItemSelection(item)` to change the state of the given item. You can query the state of an item with `IsSelected(item)`. You can expand or collapse an item with `Expand(item)` or `Collapse(item)`, or toggle its current state with `Toggle(item)`.

- The style `wx.TR_EDIT_LABELS` makes the tree control user editable. In an editable list, the user can select an item, and type in a new display label. Pressing escape cancels the edit without changing the item. You can also veto the edit by trapping the `wx.EVT_TREE_END_LABEL_EDIT` event type. Veto-ing the event forces a cancel without changing the item. The `wx.TreeEvent` class provides properties that allow access to the display text of the item being manipulated, as well as other properties of the event.

Incorporating HTML 16
into your application

This chapter covers
- Displaying HTML in a wxPython window
- Manipulating and printing HTML windows
- Using the HTML parser
- Supporting new tags and other file formats
- Using widgets in HTML

Originally intended as a simple semantic markup for a hypertext system used by physicists, HTML has since become more complex and widespread. Over time, HTML's document markup has proven useful outside of a web browser, and is now often used as a commonly understood minilanguage for general text markup (as in a text control), or to manage a series of hyperlinked pages (as in a help system). In wxPython, there are a number of features dedicated to managing your HTML needs within your application. You can display simple HTML in a window, follow hyperlinks, create your own HTML help pages, and even embed a more fully featured browser if you need more complexity.

16.1 Displaying HTML

The most important thing you can do with HTML in wxPython is display it in a window. Over the next two sections we'll discuss the HTML Window object and show how you can use it on your own local text or on a remote URL.

16.1.1 How can I display HTML in a wxPython window?

HTML within wxPython is a useful mechanism for quickly describing a text layout involving styled text or a simple grid, as we discussed in chapter 6. The wxPython `wx.html.HtmlWindow` class is used for this purpose. Its goal is to display HTML, making it a fancy static text control with hypertext links. Figure 16.1 displays a modest example.

Figure 16.1   A very simple `HtmlWindow`

Listing 16.1 displays the code used to create figure 16.1.

Listing 16.1   Displaying the simple `HtmlWindow`

```
import wx
import wx.html

class MyHtmlFrame(wx.Frame):
    def __init__(self, parent, title):
        wx.Frame.__init__(self, parent, -1, title)
        html = wx.html.HtmlWindow(self)
        if "gtk2" in wx.PlatformInfo:
            html.SetStandardFonts()

        html.SetPage(
            "Here is some <b>formatted</b> <i><u>text</u></i> "
            "loaded from a <font color=\"red\">string</font>.")
```

```
app = wx.PySimpleApp()
frm = MyHtmlFrame(None, "Simple HTML")
frm.Show()
app.MainLoop()
```

As you can see, the `wx.html.HtmlWindow` is declared and used the same way as every other wxPython widget, however, you must import the `wx.html` module, as `wx.html.HtmlWindow` is declared in a submodule of the `wx` package along with several HTML helper classes. The constructor is nearly identical to `wx.ScrolledWindow`.

```
wx.html.HtmlWindow(parent, id=-1, pos=wx.DefaultPosition,
        size=wx.DefaultSize, style=wx.html.HW_SCROLLBAR_AUTO,
        name="htmlWindow")
```

All of these parameters should look familiar by now. The most important difference is that the default style is `wx.html.HW_SCROLLBAR_AUTO`, which tells the HTML window to automatically add scrollbars as needed. The opposite style—never display scrollbars—uses the style flag `wx.html.HW_SCROLLBAR_NEVER`. One more HTML window style to use is `wx.HW_NO_SELECTION`, which prevents the user from making a text selection in the window.

When writing the HTML for display in the HTML window, remember to keep it simple. The widget is designed for simple styled text display, not for use as a full multimedia hypertext system. Most basic text tags are supported, but more advanced features like cascading style sheets and JavaScript are not. Highly complex tables and image setups may work, but you're setting yourself up for a fall. Table 16.1 contains the officially supported HTML tags. In general, tags and attributes behave as they would in a web browser, however, this is not a full-fledged browser, and there are likely to be cases that behave oddly. So that there is no confusion, table 16.1 is not in perfect HTML syntax—it's just the tag name followed by the list of supported attributes for that tag, if any. When using the HTML window you'll need to use proper HTML syntax.

Table 16.1   Valid HTML tags for the HTML window widget

Category	Valid tags
Document Structure Tags	<a href name target> <body alignment bgcolor link text> <meta content http-equiv> <title>

continued on next page

Table 16.1   Valid HTML tags for the HTML window widget *(continued)*

Category	Valid tags
Text Structure Tags	\<br\> \<div align\> \<hr align noshade size width\> \<p\>
Text Display Tags	\<address\> \<b\> \<big\> \<blockquote\> \<center\> \<cite\> \<code\> \<em\> \<font color face size\> \<h1\> \<h2\> \<h3\> \<h4\> \<h5\> \<h6\> \<i\> \<kbd\> \<pre\> \<samp\> \<small\> \<strike\> \<string\> \<tt\> \<u\>
List Tags	\<dd\> \<dl\> \<dt\> \<li\> \<ol\> \<ul\>
Image and Map Tags	\<area coords href shape\> \<img align height src width usemap\> \<map name\>
Table Tags	\<table align bgcolor border cellpadding cellspacing valign width\> \<td align bgcolor colspan rowspan valign width nowrap\> \<th align bgcolor colspan valign width rowspan\> \<tr align bgcolor valign\>

The HTML window uses wx.Image to load and display images, so it can support all the image file formats that wx.Image does.

16.1.2 How can I display HTML from a file or URL?

Once you have an HTML window created, the next challenge is to display the HTML text in the window. The following four methods are used to get HTML text into the window.

- SetPage(source)
- AppendToPage(source)
- LoadFile(filename)
- LoadPage(location)

The most direct is the method SetPage(source), where the source parameter is a string containing the HTML source that you want displayed in the window.

Once you have text in the page, you can append HTML to the end of text that is currently in the window with the method AppendToPage(source). For both the SetPage() and AppendToPage() methods, the code assumes that the source is

HTML, meaning that if you pass it plain text, the spacing is ignored in keeping with the HTML standard.

If you want your window to behave more like a browser by actually browsing external resources, you have two options. The method `LoadFile(filename)` reads the contents of a local file and displays them in the window. In this case, the window takes advantage of the MIME type of the file to load an image file or an HTML file. If it can't decide which type the file is, it loads the file as plain text. If the document that is loaded contains relative links to images or other documents, the base location used to resolve those links is the location of the original file.

Of course, a real browser isn't limited to mere local files. You can load a remote URL with the method `LoadPage(location)`, where the location is typically a URL, but could also be a pathname to a local file. The MIME type of the URL is used to determine how the page is loaded. Later in this chapter, we'll describe how to add support for new file types.

Figure 16.2 displays a page loaded into an HTML window.

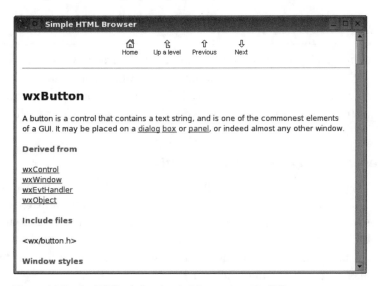

Figure 16.2   An HTML window loaded from a remote URL

Listing 16.2 displays the code used to display figure 16.2.

Listing 16.2   Loading the HTML window content from a web page

```
import wx
import wx.html
```

```
class MyHtmlFrame(wx.Frame):
    def __init__(self, parent, title):
        wx.Frame.__init__(self, parent, -1, title, size=(600,400))
        html = wx.html.HtmlWindow(self)
        if "gtk2" in wx.PlatformInfo:
            html.SetStandardFonts()

        html.LoadPage(
            "http://wxwidgets.org/manuals/2.5.4/wx_wxbutton.html")

app = wx.PySimpleApp()
frm = MyHtmlFrame(None, "Simple HTML Browser")
frm.Show()
app.MainLoop()
```

The key point in listing 16.2 is the `LoadPage()` method. A more full-featured window would probably display the URL in a text box, and change the window contents when the user enters a new URL.

16.2 *Manipulating the HTML window*

Once you have an HTML window, you can manage it in various ways. You can trigger actions based on user input, manipulate the contents of the window, automatically bind the containing frame to display information about the window, and print the page. In the following sections, we'll describe how to accomplish each of these.

16.2.1 *How can I respond to a user click on an active link?*

The use of a `wx.html.HtmlWindow` is not limited to display. You can also respond to user input. In this case, you do not need to define your own event handlers, as the C++ code comes with a set of predefined handlers that you can override in your own subclass of `wx.html.HtmlWindow`. This is the sort of thing you'd do to make your HTML window behave like an actual browser, including following hyperlinks, and displaying tooltips when the user hovers over a link.

Table 16.2 describes the defined handlers. The `wx.html.HtmlWindow` class does not define these events using the normal event system, so you must handle them with these overloaded member functions, rather than binding them as event types.

Again, if you want an HTML window that responds to user input, you must create your own subclass and override these methods.

Table 16.2 Event handlers of `wx.html.HtmlWindow`

Method	Description
OnCellClicked (cell, x, y, event)	Called when the user clicks inside the HTML document. The `cell` argument is a `wx.html.HtmlCell` object representing a portion of the displayed document, usually something like a run of same-styled text, a table cell, or an image. The `wx.html.HtmlCell` class is created by the HTML parser, and will be discussed later in the chapter. The `x` and `y` coordinates are the exact pixel location of the mouse click, and the `event` is the relevant mouse click event. The default version of this method simply delegates to `OnLinkClicked()` if the cell contains a link, otherwise it does nothing.
OnCellMouseHover (cell, x, y)	Called when the user rolls the mouse over an HTML cell, where a cell has the same definition as above. The arguments are as in `OnCellClicked()`.
OnLinkClicked(link)	Called when the user clicks on a hyperlink. The `link` argument is of the parser-created class `wx.html.HtmlLinkInfo`, and contains the information needed to load the linked resource. The default version of the method calls `LoadPage` on the URL in the link. A common use case for overriding this method is to use an `HtmlWindow` to make a fancy about box for an application. In that case you might change the behavior so the user clicks homepage to launch's the system's default browser using Python's `webbrowser` module.
OnOpeningURL (type, url)	Called when the user requests a URL to open, whether it is a page or an image that is part of a page. The type argument is `wx.html.HTML_URL_PAGE`, `wx.html.HTML_URL_IMAGE`, or `wx.html.HTML_URL_OTHER`. This method returns one of the following—`wx.html.HTML_OPEN` to allow the resource to load, `wx.html.HTML_BLOCK` to prevent the resource from loading, or a string that will be used as a `url` redirect, and this method is then called again on the redirected location. The default version of this method always returns `wx.html.HTML_OPEN`.
OnSetTitle(title)	Called when the HTML source has a `<title>` tag. Generally used to display that title elsewhere in the application.

16.2.2 *How can I change an HTML window programmatically?*

If you are displaying an HTML page, there's a good chance that your frame is behaving like a browser in one way or another. Even if it's not actually browsing the web, it could be browsing help files, or other kinds of linked data. If your user is browsing, the text being changed in your display also needs to change in response to user information.

There are a couple of ways to access and change information in the HTML window while it's running. First, you can get the URL of the currently opened page with the method `GetOpenedPage()`. This method only works if the current page was loaded using the `LoadPage()` method. If so, the return value is the URL of the current location (as a string). If not, or if there is no currently open page, the method returns an empty string. There's a related method, GetOpenedAnchor(), that returns the anchor within the currently opened page. If the page was not opened with LoadPage(), you get an empty string.

To get the HTML title of the current page, use the method GetOpenedPage-Title(), returning whatever value is contained in the current page's <title> tag. If the current page doesn't have a <title> tag, you get an empty string.

There are a few methods for changing the text selection within the window. The method SelectAll() changes the text selection to the entire body text of the opened page. You can make a more specific selection with SelectLine(pos) or SelectWord(pos). In both cases, the pos argument is the wx.Point of the mouse position, and selects either the entire line or just the word at that point. To extract the current selection as plain text you can use the SelectionToText() method, while the method ToText() returns the entire document as plain text.

The wx.html.HtmlWindow maintains a history list of the source pages loaded into it. Using the methods listed in table 16.3, that history list can be navigated as in a typical browser.

Table 16.3   History methods of `wx.html.HtmlWindow`

Method	Description
HistoryBack()	Loads the previous entry in the history list. Returns `False` if there is no such entry.
HistoryCanBack()	Returns `True` if there is a previous entry in the history list, `False` otherwise.
HistoryCanForward()	Returns `True` if there is a next entry in the history list, `False` otherwise.
HistoryClear()	Empties the history list.
HistoryForward()	Loads the next entry in the list. Returns `False` if there is no such entry.

To change the fonts being used, use the method SetFonts(normal_face, fixed_face, sizes=None). The normal_face argument is the string name of the font you want to use for the proportional font in the window display. If the normal_face is an empty string, the system default is used, otherwise, the exact font names used are dependent on the operating system. The fixed_face argument works similarly, and specifies the font used for monospaced text in your browser (for example, within <pre> tags). If specified, the sizes element is a Python list of seven integers representing the absolute font sizes that correspond to the HTML logical font sizes between -2 and +4 (as used in a <font> tag). If the argument is None or not specified, defaults are used. There are default constants for wx.html.HTML_FONT_SIZE_n, where n is between 1 and 7. These constants specify the default font used for the corresponding HTML logical font size. The exact values of the constants may differ depending on the underlying system. To select a set of fonts and sizes that are based on the user's system preferences (rather that the hard-coded defaults) call `SetStandardFonts()`. This is especially useful when running wxPython under GTK2, as it produces a better set of fonts.

If for some reason you need to change the distance between the edge of the window text and the edge of the window, the HTML window defines the method `SetBorders(b)`. The b argument is the integer pixel width between the edge of the window and the beginning of the text.

16.2.3 *How can I display the page title in a frame's title bar?*

One thing you've probably noticed in your web browser is that the display window is not the only element of the browser. Among the other elements of note are a title bar and status bar in the containing frame. Typically, the title bar displays the title of the HTML page being displayed, and the status bar displays information about links as they are moused over. In wxPython, there are a couple of shortcuts that allow you to set this relationship up quickly and easily. Figure 16.3 displays this relationship in action using a page from the wxWidgets online documentation. The title of the window display is based on the web page title, and the status bar text, also comes from the HTML window.

Listing 16.3 displays the code used to produce figure 16.3.

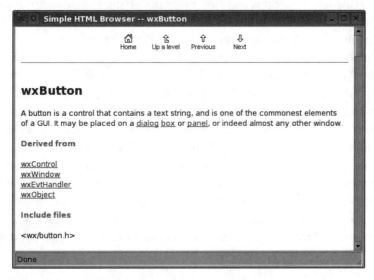

Figure 16.3   An HTML window with status and title bar caption

Listing 16.3   Loading the `HTMLWindow` content from a web page

```
import wx
import wx.html

class MyHtmlFrame(wx.Frame):
    def __init__(self, parent, title):
        wx.Frame.__init__(self, parent, -1, title, size=(600,400))
        self.CreateStatusBar()

        html = wx.html.HtmlWindow(self)
        if "gtk2" in wx.PlatformInfo:                    Associating the
            html.SetStandardFonts()                      HTML to the frame
        html.SetRelatedFrame(self, self.GetTitle() + " -- %s")
        html.SetRelatedStatusBar(0)    ◁   Associating the HTML to the status bar

        html.LoadPage(
            "http://wxwidgets.org/manuals/2.5.4/wx_wxbutton.html")

app = wx.PySimpleApp()
frm = MyHtmlFrame(None, "Simple HTML Browser")
frm.Show()
app.MainLoop()
```

To set up the title bar relationship, use the method `SetRelatedFrame(frame, format)`. The `frame` argument is the `wx.Frame` where you want the HTML window's title information to display. The `format` argument is the string you want to display in the title bar of that frame. It can be any string you want, as long as it contains the pattern "%s" somewhere—that pattern is replaced by the `<title>` of the HTML page being displayed in the HTML window. A typical `format` argument would be something like "My wxPython Browser: %s". When a page is loaded in the window, the frame title is automatically replaced with the new page information.

To set up the status bar, use the method `SetRelatedStatusBar(bar)`. This method must be called after `SetRelatedFrame()`, as it associates the HTML window with an element in the status bar of the related frame. The `bar` argument is the display slot in the status bar that should be used to display the status information. Typically, this will be 0, but it could be different if the frame has its status bar configured to display multiple slots. If the `bar` argument is -1, no messages are displayed. Once this relationship is created, when the mouse moves over an active anchor in the HTML display, the URL being linked to is displayed in the status bar.

16.2.4 *How can I print an HTML page?*

Once the HTML is displayed on the screen, the next logical thing to do is print the HTML. The class for this is `wx.html.HtmlEasyPrinting`. You create an instance of `wx.html.HtmlEasyPrinting` with a simple constructor,

```
wx.html.HtmlEasyPrinting(name="Printing", parentWindow=None)
```

The parameters aren't usually that important—the `name` parameter is just a string that is used for display in the various dialogs that the easy printing instance creates. If defined, the `parentWindow` is the parent window of those dialogs. If the `parentWindow` is `None`, the dialogs display at the top level. You should only create one instance of `wx.html.HtmlEasyPrinting`. Although this is not enforced by the wxPython system, the class is designed to be a singleton.

Using the class instance

With a name like `wx.html.HtmlEasyPrinting`, you'd expect that using the class would be easy. And it is. To start, you can show the user dialog boxes for settings with the methods `PrinterSetup()` and `PageSetup()`. Calling these methods causes the appropriate dialog to be displayed to the user. The easy printing instance stores these settings for later use, so that you don't have to. If you want to access those data objects for your own specific handling, use the methods `GetPrintData()` and `GetPageSetupData()`. The `GetPrintData()` method returns a `wx.PrintData` object, and `GetPageSetupData()` returns a `wx.PageSetupDialogData` object, both of which are discussed in more detail in chapter 17.

Setting fonts

You can set the fonts for the printing using the method `SetFonts(normal_face, fixed_face, sizes)`. This method behaves in the same way `SetFonts()` does for the HTML window (the settings in the print object do not affect the settings in the HTML window). You can set a page header or page footer to be printed on each page using the methods `SetHeader(header, pg)` and `SetFooter(footer, pg)`. The `header` and `footer` arguments are the strings to be displayed. In the string, you can use the placeholder `@PAGENUM@` which is replaced at runtime with the page number being printed. You can also use the placeholder `@PAGESCNT@` which is the total number of pages being printed. You can use either placeholder as many times as you want. The `pg` parameter is one of the three constants `wx.PAGE_ALL`, `wx.PAGE_EVEN`, or `wx.PAGE_ODD`. The constant controls on which pages the header or footer displays. By calling this method more than once with different `pg` settings, you can set separate headers and footers for odd and even pages.

Previewing output

If you want to preview the output before printing, you can use `PreviewFile(html-file)`. In this case the input is the name of a file local to your machine containing the HTML. Alternately, you can use the method `PreviewText(htmlText, base-path="")`. The `htmltext` is the actual HTML you want printed. The `basepath` is a path or URL to the location of the file which is used to resolve things like relative image paths. Both methods return Boolean `True` if the preview is successful, and Boolean `False` if not. If there is an error, the global method `wx.Printer.GetLast-Error()` will have more information about the error. More detailed information about that method is discussed in chapter 17.

Printing

Having read this far in the section about the easy printing method, you are probably wondering how to simply print an HTML page. The methods are `Print-File(htmlfile)` and `PrintText(htmlText, basepath)`. The arguments behave the same way as they do in the preview methods, with the exception that these methods actually print to the printer using the settings specified in the settings dialog. A `True` result indicates that, as far as wxPython was concerned, the printing was successful.

16.3   Extending the HTML window

In this section we'll show you how to handle obscure HTML tags in the HTML window, how to invent your own tags, how to embed wxPython widgets in the HTML, how to handle other file formats, and how to create a real HTML browser in your application.

16.3.1   How does the HTML parser work?

The HTML window has its own internal parser within wxPython. Actually, there are two parser classes, but one of them is a refinement of the other. In general, working with parsers is only useful if you want to extend the functionality of the `wx.html.HtmlWindow` itself. If you are programming in Python and want to use an HTML parser for other purposes, we recommend using one of the two parser modules that are distributed with Python (`htmllib` and `HTMLParser`), or an external Python tool like Beautiful Soup. We're only going to cover this enough to give you the basics needed to add your own tag type.

The two parser classes are `wx.html.HtmlParser`, which is the more generic parser, and `wx.html.HtmlWinParser`, which is a subclass of `wx.html.HtmlParser`, with extensions specifically created to support displaying text in a `wx.html.Html-Window`. Since we're mostly concerned with HTML windows here, we'll focus on the subclass.

To create an HTML parser, use one of two constructors. The basic one, `wx.html.HtmlWinParser()`, takes no arguments. The parent `wx.html.HtmlParser` class also has a no-argument constructor. You can associate a `wx.html.HtmlWin-Parser()` with an existing `wx.html.HtmlWindow` using the other constructor— `wx.html.HtmlWinParser(wnd)`, where `wnd` is the instance of the HTML window.

To use the parser, the simplest way is to call the method `Parse(source)`. The source parameter is the HTML string to be processed. The return value is the parsed data. For a `wx.html.HtmlWinParser`, the return value is an instance of the class `wx.html.HtmlCell`.

The HTML parser converts the HTML text into a series of *cells*, where a cell is some meaningful fragment of the HTML. A cell can represent some text, an image, a table, a list, or any other specific element. The most significant subclass of `wx.html.HtmlCell` is `wx.html.HtmlContainerCell`, which is simply a cell that can contain other cells within it, such as a table, or a paragraph with different text styles. For nearly every document that you parse, the return value will be an `wx.html.Html-ContainerCell`. Each cell contains a `Draw(dc, x, y, view_y1, view_y2)` method, which allows it to actually draw its information in the HTML window.

Another important cell subclass is `wx.html.HtmlWidgetCell`, which allows an arbitrary wxPython widget to be inserted into an HTML document just like any other cell. This can include any kind of widget used to manage HTML forms, but can also include static text used for formatted display. The only interesting method of `wx.html.HtmlWidgetCell` is the constructor.

```
wx.html.HtmlWidgetCell(wnd, w=0)
```

In the constructor, the `wnd` parameter is the wxPython widget to be drawn. The `w` parameter is a floating width. If it is not `0`, it is an integer between `1` and `100`, and then the width of the `wnd` widget is dynamically adjusted to be that percentage of the width of its parent container.

There are many other cell types that are used to display the more typical parts of an HTML document. For more information regarding these other cell types, refer to the wxWidgets documentation.

16.3.2 *How can I add support for new tags?*

The cells returned by the parser are created internally by *tag handlers*, a pluggable structure by which HTML tags are associated with the creation and manipulation of the HTML parser cells. You can create your own tag handlers and associate them with HTML tags. With this mechanism you can extend the HTML window to include standard tags not currently supported, or custom tags of your own invention. Figure 16.4 displays the use of a custom HTML tag.

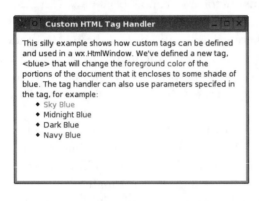

Figure 16.4
A wx.HtmlWindow using
a custom tag handler

Listing 16.4 displays the code used to produce figure 16.4.

Listing 16.4   Defining and using a custom tag handler

```
import wx
import wx.html


page = """<html><body>

This silly example shows how custom tags can be defined and used in a
wx.HtmlWindow. We've defined a new tag, &lt;blue&gt; that will change
the <blue>foreground color</blue> of the portions of the document that
it encloses to some shade of blue. The tag handler can also use
parameters specified in the tag, for example:

<ul>
<li> <blue shade='sky'>Sky Blue</blue>
<li> <blue shade='midnight'>Midnight Blue</blue>
<li> <blue shade='dark'>Dark Blue</blue>
<li> <blue shade='navy'>Navy Blue</blue>
</ul>

</body></html>
"""
```

<!-- no ending to li --> *(handwritten annotation)*

```
class BlueTagHandler(wx.html.HtmlWinTagHandler):        ◁─┐  Declaring the
    def __init__(self):                                     │  tag handler
        wx.html.HtmlWinTagHandler.__init__(self)

    def GetSupportedTags(self):       ◁─┐  Defining tags that
        return "BLUE"                     │  are handled

    def HandleTag(self, tag):     ◁─  Handling the tag
        old = self.GetParser().GetActualColor()
        clr = "#0000FF"
        if tag.HasParam("SHADE"):
            shade = tag.GetParam("SHADE")
            if shade.upper() == "SKY":
                clr = "#3299CC"
            if shade.upper() == "MIDNIGHT":
                clr = "#2F2F4F"
            elif shade.upper() == "DARK":
                clr = "#00008B"
            elif shade.upper == "NAVY":
                clr = "#23238E"

        self.GetParser().SetActualColor(clr)
        container = self.GetParser().GetContainer()
        container.InsertCell(wx.html.HtmlColourCell(clr))
        self.ParseInner(tag)
        self.GetParser().SetActualColor(old)
        container = self.GetParser().GetContainer()
        container.InsertCell(wx.html.HtmlColourCell(old))
        return True

wx.html.HtmlWinParser_AddTagHandler(BlueTagHandler)       ◁─┐  Telling the parser
                                                             │  about the handler
class MyHtmlFrame(wx.Frame):
    def __init__(self, parent, title):
        wx.Frame.__init__(self, parent, -1, title)
        html = wx.html.HtmlWindow(self)
        if "gtk2" in wx.PlatformInfo:
            html.SetStandardFonts()
        html.SetPage(page)

app = wx.PySimpleApp()
frm = MyHtmlFrame(None, "Custom HTML Tag Handler")
frm.Show()
app.MainLoop()
```

(handwritten annotation: # tag is a begin, end pair: <blue...> ... </blue> inner text)

The tags themselves are represented internally as methods of the class wx.Html. ✳
Tag, which is created by the HTML parser. Typically, you won't need to create your
own instances. Table 16.4 displays the wx.Html.Tag class with methods that are
useful to retrieve information about the tags.

Table 16.4 Some methods of `wx.Html.Tag`

Method	Description
GetAllParams()	Returns all the parameters associated with the tag as a string. For some purposes, it might be easier to parse this string rather than get each parameter individually.
GetName()	Returns the tag name, in uppercase text.
HasParam(param)	Returns `True` if the tag has the given parameter.
GetParam(param, with_commas=False)	Returns the value of the parameter `param`. If the `with_commas` parameter is `True`, you get a raw string including the quotation marks starting and ending the value, if any. Returns an empty string if the parameter doesn't exist. The related method `GetParamAsColour(param)` returns the parameter value as a `wx.Color`, and the method `GetParamAsInt(param)` returns the value as an int.
HasEnding()	Returns `True` if the tag has an ending tag, and false otherwise.

A tag handler used for extending the HTML window is a subclass of `wx.html.HtmlWinTagHandler`. Your subclass needs to override two methods, and needs to be aware of one further method. The first method to override is `GetSupportedTags()`. This method returns the list of tags that are managed by this handler. The tags must be in uppercase, and if there is more than one they are separated by a comma, with no spaces in between, as in the following example.

```
GetSupportedTags(self):
    return "MYTAG,MYTAGPARAM"
```

The second method that you need to override is `HandleTag(tag)`. Within the `HandleTag` method, you handle the tag by adding new cell elements to the parser (or alternately making changes to the container cell that the parser has open at that point). You get the parser by calling the `GetParser()` method of the tag handler.

To write a `HandleTag()` method, you should:

1 Get the parser.

2 Process the parameters to your tag as necessary, possibly making changes to or creating a new cell.

3 If the tag being parsed is a begin/end pair with inner text, parse the text in between.

4 Perform any cleanup needed to the parser.

As mentioned, you get the parser with GetParser(). To add or edit cells in the parser, you have three options. First, if you want to add another cell to the container, you can work with the current container. Next, you call the parser's Get-Container() method, then create your wx.html.HTMLCell subclass instance by whatever means you want, and add it to the container by calling the container's InsertCell(cell) method.

Occasionally, you'll want to create a container that is subordinate or nested within the currently open container. One example might be a table cell that is nested within a table row. To do this, you need to call the parser method OpenContainer(). This method returns your new container cell, into which you can insert display cells with the InsertCell(cell) method. For every container you open in your tag handler, you are expected to close it using the CloseContainer() method. If you do not have a balance between your OpenContainer() and Close-Container() calls, it will disrupt the parser behavior on the rest of the HTML text.

Another option is to create a container at the same level as the parser's current container, meaning that you aren't nesting containers. An example would be a new paragraph—it's not part of the previous paragraph, nor is it subordinate to it; it's a new entity in the page. In order to get that behavior in the parse, you need to close the existing container, open a new container, and reverse the process at the end of the method.

```
parser = self.GetParser()
parser.CloseContainer()
parser.OpenContainer()

# Do all your stuff

parser.CloseContainer()
parser.OpenContainer()
```

This has the effect of giving you a new container to put your information into, but ensuring that the parser has a clean container at the same nesting depth that existed at the beginning of the method.

16.3.3 *How can I support other file formats?*

By default, the HTML window can handle files with the MIME type text/html, text/txt, and image/* (assuming the wxPython image handlers are loaded). When confronted with a file that is not an image or HTML file, the HTML window attempts to display it as plain text. That may not be the behavior you want. If there is some file format that you want displayed in a custom way, you can create a `wx.html.HtmlFilter` to manage it. For example, you might want XML files to display as a source tree, or you could display Python source files with syntax coloring.

To create a filter, you must build a subclass of `wx.html.HtmlFilter`. This class has two methods, and you must override both of them. The first method is `Can-Read(file)`. The `file` parameter is an instance of `wx.FSFile`—the wxPython representation of an opened file. The `wx.FSFile` class has two properties that you would use to determine if your filter can read the file. The method `GetMimeType()` returns the file's MIME type as a string. The mime type is usually determined by the file's extension. The method `GetLocation()` returns a string with the absolute path or URL to the file location. The `CanRead()` method should return `True` if the filter will handle the file, otherwise it returns `False`. A sample `CanRead()` to handle Python source files may look like the following.

```
CanRead(self, file):
    return file.GetLocation().endswith('.py')
```

The second method you need to override is `ReadFile(file)`. This method takes in the same `file` parameter, and returns a string HTML representation of the file's contents. If you don't want to use the wxWidgets C++ file mechanisms to read the file, you can use the Python file mechanisms by simply opening a Python file at `file.GetLocation()`.

Once the filter has been created, it must be registered with the `wx.html.Html-Window` using the window's `AddFilter(filter)` static method. The `filter` parameter is an instance of your new `wx.html.HtmlFilter` class. Once it has registered the filter, the window uses it to manage the file objects that pass the `CanRead()` test.

16.3.4 How can I get a more fully featured HTML Widget?

Although the `wx.html.HtmlWindow` is not a fully featured browser pane, there are a couple of options for embedding a more fully featured HTML rendering window. If you are on a Windows platform, you can use the class `wx.lib.iewin.IEHtml-Window`, which is a wxPython wrapper around the Internet Explorer ActiveX control. This allows you to embed an Internet Explorer window directly into your application.

Using the Internet Explorer (IE) control is relatively straightforward and similar to using the internal wxPython HTML window. It has a widget-like constructor, as in the following.

```
wx.lib.iewin.IEHtmlWindow(self, parent, ID=-1,
        pos=wx.DefaultPosition, size=wx.DefaultSize, style=0,
        name='IEHtmlWindow')
```

Everything here is in keeping with wxPython widgets, the `parent` is the parent window, and the `ID` is the wxPython ID. There are no useful style flags for an IE window. To load HTML into the IE component, use the method `LoadString (html)`, where the `html` parameter is an HTML string to display. You can load from an open file, or anything that is a Python file object, using the method `Load-Stream(stream)`, or from a URL using the method `LoadString(URL)`. You can retrieve the text being displayed with the method `GetText(asHTML)`. The `asHTML` parameter is a Boolean. If `True`, the text is returned in HTML, otherwise, it's just returned as a text string.

On other platforms, you can try the wxMozilla project (http://wxmozilla. sourceforge.net), which attempts to create a wxPython wrapper around the Mozilla Gecko renderer. Currently, the project is still in beta. The wxPython extension for this project has an installer for Windows and Linux, with Mac OS X support in progress.

16.4 Summary

- HTML is not just for the Internet anymore. In wxPython, you can use an HTML window to display text with a simple subset of HTML markup. The HTML window is of the class `wx.html.HtmlWindow`. In addition to HTML text, the HTML window can manage any image that has a currently loaded image handler.

- You can give the HTML window its display information as a string, a local file, or a URL. You can respond to a user click either as a hypertext browser normally would, or with a custom response of your own. You can also connect the HTML window to its frame so that the title and status information automatically displays in the correct locations. The HTML window maintains a history list that you can access and manipulate. You can use the class `wx.Html.HtmlEasyPrinting` to print your page straightforward.

- There is an HTML parser in wxPython that you can use to create your own custom tags for your window. You can also set up custom file filters to render other file formats to an HTML window.

- Finally, if you get frustrated with the limitations of the HTML window, a wrapper around the Internet Explorer ActiveX control is available. If you aren't on Windows, there's a beta version of a wrapper around the Mozilla Gecko HTML renderer.

17

The wxPython printing framework

This chapter covers

- Printing in wxPython
- Creating and displaying the print dialog
- Creating and displaying the page setup dialog
- Printing from your application
- Performing a print preview

In chapter 16, we looked at one method of printing in wxPython—using wx.Html-EasyPrinting. This works fine if you are trying to print HTML (or something that can easily be converted to HTML), but is somewhat lacking as a complete printing solution. There is a more general printing framework in wxPython, which you can use to print anything and everything you want. Essentially, the wxPython framework allows you to draw your application to a printer, using device contexts and drawing operations. You can also create print previews that mimic your print display to the screen.

This chapter will cover the most important class in this framework, wx.Printout, which manages the actual graphics component. The printout instance can be managed either by a wx.Printer object representing the printer or a wx.PrintPreview object allowing for a screen-based rendering of the printout. We'll also look at a few classes that manage printer-related data, and the standard dialog boxes you can use to present that information to the user.

17.1 *How do I print in wxPython?*

We'll start with the wx.Printout class. Like frames, and unlike many of the widget classes, you'll create your own custom subclass of wx.Printout. Next, you will override methods of wx.Printout to define your custom printing behavior. There are seven methods of wx.Printout that you can override to customize how the printout object does its work. These methods are automatically called by wxPython during the course of a printing session. Figure 17.1 displays six of these methods

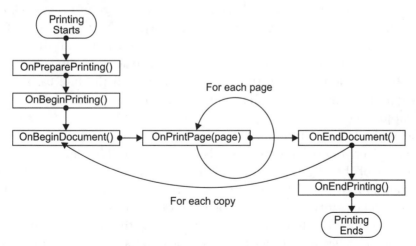

Figure 17.1 The lifecycle of a printout showing all the methods automatically called by wxPython

that are triggered by specific events. In most cases you will not need to overwrite all of them.

17.1.1 *Understanding the printout lifecycle*

You start a printing session by creating an instance of your printout object, and also an instance of the class `wx.Printer`.

```
wx.Printer(data=None)
```

The optional `data` parameter is an instance of `wx.PrintDialogData`. To start the actual printing, call the `Print(parent, printout, prompt=True)` method of `wx.Printer`. The `parent` parameter is the parent window for the printing (it's used as the parent window for any dialogs that are invoked). The `printout` parameter is your `wx.Printout` instance. If the `prompt` parameter is `True`, wxPython will display the printer dialog before printing, otherwise it will not.

After the `Print()` method starts, it calls the first of the overridable methods of `wx.Printout`, `OnPreparePrint()`. The prepare method is guaranteed to be called before the `wx.Printout` instance does anything else, so it's a good place to gather your data or do any calculations that need to be done before printing begins. The actual printing begins with the `OnBeginPrinting()` method, which you can also override for custom behavior if you want—by default, the method does nothing. The `OnBeginPrinting()` method will be called only once for the entire print session.

Each individual copy of the document that you wish to print triggers one call of `OnBeginDocument(startPage, endPage)`, where `startPage` and `endPage` are integer arguments telling wxPython what pages of the document to print. Both arguments are inclusive. If you override this method, you must call the base class method because it does some important accounting (such as calling `wx.DC.Start-Doc()`). In wxPython, you call the parent method with the line `base_OnBeginDocument(startPage, endPage)`. Returning `False` from `OnBeginDocument` will cancel the print job.

The method you are most likely to override is `OnPrintPage(pageNum)`, which is where you place your drawing commands for each page. The `pageNum` argument is the number of the page to print. Within this method, you call `GetDC()`, which returns an appropriate device context, depending on your current system platform. For actual prints, the instance you get is of the class `wx.PrinterDC` if you are on an MS Windows system. On any other system, the instance is of the class `wx.PostScriptDC`. If you are inside a print preview operation, you get a `wx.MemoryDC` for any operating system. Once you have the device context, you can make any device context drawing operations you want, and they will be printed or previewed appropriately.

After the pages are printed, the events unwind. At the end of each copy, a call to `OnEndDocument()` is triggered. Again, if you override this method, you must call the base class method with the line `base_OnEndDocument()`. This calls the `wx.DC.EndDoc()` method. And, when all your copies are done, the `OnEndPrinting()` method is called, finishing the print session.

There is one other overridable method of `wx.Printout`, which you will usually need to override and which is used by the printing framework for loop control. The method `HasPage(pageNum)` returns `True` if the integer `pageNum` is within the document and `False` otherwise. The default is to return `True` only when `pageNum == 1`.

17.1.2 *Print framework in action*

What follows is a code example to show you how the print framework works in practice. The example consists of a simple framework for printing text files, and an application that allows you to type a simple text file. Figure 17.2 displays the application.

Listing 17.1 displays both the print framework we've already discussed, as well as the dialog data mechanisms we'll get to shortly.

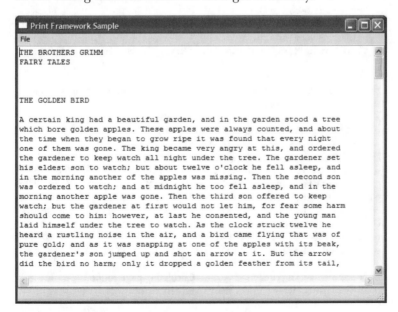

Figure 17.2 The simple printing framework in action

Listing 17.1   A long example of a print framework in action

```
import wx
import os


FONTSIZE = 10


class TextDocPrintout(wx.Printout):    ◁— Declaring the printout class

    def __init__(self, text, title, margins):
        wx.Printout.__init__(self, title)
        self.lines = text.split('\n')
        self.margins = margins

    def HasPage(self, page):    ◁—┘ How many pages?
        return page <= self.numPages

    def GetPageInfo(self):
        return (1, self.numPages, 1, self.numPages)

    def CalculateScale(self, dc):    ◁— Scaling the DC to screen size

        ppiPrinterX, ppiPrinterY = self.GetPPIPrinter()
        ppiScreenX, ppiScreenY = self.GetPPIScreen()
        logScale = float(ppiPrinterX)/float(ppiScreenX)

        pw, ph = self.GetPageSizePixels()    ◁— Adjusting scale
        dw, dh = dc.GetSize()
        scale = logScale * float(dw)/float(pw)
        dc.SetUserScale(scale, scale)
        self.logUnitsMM = float(ppiPrinterX)/(logScale*25.4)

    def CalculateLayout(self, dc):
        topLeft, bottomRight = self.margins    ◁— Determining margins
        dw, dh = dc.GetSize()
        self.x1 = topLeft.x * self.logUnitsMM
        self.y1 = topLeft.y * self.logUnitsMM
        self.x2 = (dc.DeviceToLogicalXRel(dw) -
                bottomRight.x * self.logUnitsMM)
        self.y2 = (dc.DeviceToLogicalYRel(dh) -                    Putting a buffer
                bottomRight.y * self.logUnitsMM)                   around page
        self.pageHeight = self.y2 - self.y1 - 2*self.logUnitsMM    ◁—┘
        font = wx.Font(FONTSIZE, wx.TELETYPE, wx.NORMAL, wx.NORMAL)
        dc.SetFont(font)
        self.lineHeight = dc.GetCharHeight()
        self.linesPerPage = int(self.pageHeight/self.lineHeight)

    def OnPreparePrinting(self):    ◁— Calculating page count
        dc = self.GetDC()
        self.CalculateScale(dc)
        self.CalculateLayout(dc)
```

```
        self.numPages = len(self.lines) / self.linesPerPage
        if len(self.lines) % self.linesPerPage != 0:
            self.numPages += 1

    def OnPrintPage(self, page):        ◁— Printing a page
        dc = self.GetDC()
        self.CalculateScale(dc)
        self.CalculateLayout(dc)
        dc.SetPen(wx.Pen("black", 0))    ◁⏌ Drawing an outline
        dc.SetBrush(wx.TRANSPARENT_BRUSH)
        r = wx.RectPP((self.x1, self.y1),
                      (self.x2, self.y2))
        dc.DrawRectangleRect(r)
        dc.SetClippingRect(r)

        line = (page-1) * self.linesPerPage    ◁— Drawing text
        x = self.x1 + self.logUnitsMM
        y = self.y1 + self.logUnitsMM
        while line < (page * self.linesPerPage):
            dc.DrawText(self.lines[line], x, y)
            y += self.lineHeight
            line += 1
            if line >= len(self.lines):
                break
        return True

class PrintFrameworkSample(wx.Frame):
    def __init__(self):
        wx.Frame.__init__(self, None, size=(640, 480),
                          title="Print Framework Sample")
        self.CreateStatusBar()

        self.tc = wx.TextCtrl(self, -1, "",
                              style=wx.TE_MULTILINE|wx.TE_DONTWRAP)
        self.tc.SetFont(wx.Font(FONTSIZE, wx.TELETYPE, wx.NORMAL, wx.NORMAL))
        filename = os.path.join(os.path.dirname(__file__), "sample-text.txt")
        self.tc.SetValue(open(filename).read())
        self.tc.Bind(wx.EVT_SET_FOCUS, self.OnClearSelection)
        wx.CallAfter(self.tc.SetInsertionPoint, 0)

        menu = wx.Menu()
        item = menu.Append(-1, "Page Setup...\tF5",
                           "Set up page margins and etc.")
        self.Bind(wx.EVT_MENU, self.OnPageSetup, item)
        item = menu.Append(-1, "Print Setup...\tF6",
                           "Set up the printer options, etc.")
        self.Bind(wx.EVT_MENU, self.OnPrintSetup, item)
        item = menu.Append(-1, "Print Preview...\tF7",
                           "View the printout on-screen")
        self.Bind(wx.EVT_MENU, self.OnPrintPreview, item)
        item = menu.Append(-1, "Print...\tF8", "Print the document")
```

```
            self.Bind(wx.EVT_MENU, self.OnPrint, item)
            menu.AppendSeparator()
            item = menu.Append(-1, "E&xit", "Close this application")
            self.Bind(wx.EVT_MENU, self.OnExit, item)

            menubar = wx.MenuBar()
            menubar.Append(menu, "&File")
            self.SetMenuBar(menubar)

            self.pdata = wx.PrintData()              ◁─┘  Initializing print data
            self.pdata.SetPaperId(wx.PAPER_LETTER)
            self.pdata.SetOrientation(wx.PORTRAIT)
            self.margins = (wx.Point(15,15), wx.Point(15,15))

    def OnExit(self, evt):
        self.Close()

    def OnClearSelection(self, evt):
        evt.Skip()
        wx.CallAfter(self.tc.SetInsertionPoint,
                     self.tc.GetInsertionPoint())

    def OnPageSetup(self, evt):
        data = wx.PageSetupDialogData()
        data.SetPrintData(self.pdata)
        data.SetDefaultMinMargins(True)
        data.SetMarginTopLeft(self.margins[0])
        data.SetMarginBottomRight(self.margins[1])
        dlg = wx.PageSetupDialog(self, data)        ◁─┐  Getting page
        if dlg.ShowModal() == wx.ID_OK:                │  setup data
            data = dlg.GetPageSetupData()
            self.pdata = wx.PrintData(data.GetPrintData())
            self.pdata.SetPaperId(data.GetPaperId())
            self.margins = (data.GetMarginTopLeft(),
                            data.GetMarginBottomRight())
        dlg.Destroy()

    def OnPrintSetup(self, evt):
        data = wx.PrintDialogData(self.pdata)
        dlg = wx.PrintDialog(self, data)
        dlg.GetPrintDialogData().SetSetupDialog(True)
        dlg.ShowModal();
        data = dlg.GetPrintDialogData()
        self.pdata = wx.PrintData(data.GetPrintData())
        dlg.Destroy()

    def OnPrintPreview(self, evt):     ◁─┘  Starting print preview
        data = wx.PrintDialogData(self.pdata)
        text = self.tc.GetValue()
        printout1 = TextDocPrintout(text, "title", self.margins)
        printout2 = TextDocPrintout(text, "title", self.margins)
```

```
                    preview = wx.PrintPreview(printout1, printout2, data)
                    if not preview.Ok():
                        wx.MessageBox("Unable to create PrintPreview!", "Error")
                    else:
                        frame = wx.PreviewFrame(preview, self, "Print Preview",
                                            pos=self.GetPosition(),
                                            size=self.GetSize())
                        frame.Initialize()
                        frame.Show()

        def OnPrint(self, evt):    ⬅ Starting print
            data = wx.PrintDialogData(self.pdata)
            printer = wx.Printer(data)
            text = self.tc.GetValue()
            printout = TextDocPrintout(text, "title", self.margins)
            useSetupDialog = True
            if not printer.Print(self, printout, useSetupDialog) \
                and printer.GetLastError() == wx.PRINTER_ERROR:
                wx.MessageBox(
                    "There was a problem printing.\n"
                    "Perhaps your current printer is not set correctly?",
                    "Printing Error", wx.OK)
            else:
                data = printer.GetPrintDialogData()
                self.pdata = wx.PrintData(data.GetPrintData()) # force a copy
            printout.Destroy()

app = wx.PySimpleApp()
frm = PrintFrameworkSample()
frm.Show()
app.MainLoop()
```

The printout class presented in listing 17.2 is able to print simple text documents, but doesn't handle page numbers or titles, and it assumes that no lines are longer than will fit within the page width. Those features are left as an exercise for the reader.

The most important code snippets are in the OnPreparePrinting() and OnPrintPage() methods of the framework and the OnPrint() method of the sample window. Notice how the draw commands in the OnPrintPage() are the same as if you were drawing to the screen.

17.1.3 *Working with wx.Printout methods*

There are a few getter-type methods in wx.Printout that allow you to retrieve information about the current print environment. Table 17.1 lists these information retrieval methods.

Table 17.1   Information retrieval methods of `wx.Printout`

Method	Description
GetDC()	This method returns the device context to be used for drawing the document for the printer or the print preview.
GetPageInfo()	Returns a 4-element tuple (`minPage, maxPage, pageFrom, pageTo`). The `minPage` and `maxPage` return values are the lowest and highest allowable page numbers, and they default to `1` and `32000`. The `pageFrom` and `pageTo` values are the range that must be printed, and those values default to `1`. You may override this method in your sublclass.
GetPageSizeMM()	Returns a tuple (`w, h`) of the width and height of a page in millimeters.
GetPageSizePixels()	Returns a tuple (`w, h`) of the width and height of a page in pixels. If the printout is being used for a print preview, the pixel count will reflect the current zoom level, meaning that the reported pixel count will change with the zoom level.
GetPPIPrinter()	Returns a tuple (`w, h`) of the pixels per inch of the current printer in both horizontal and vertical directions. In a preview, this value is consistent even if the zoom level of the preview changes.
GetPPIScreen()	Returns a tuple (`w, h`) of the pixels per inch of the current screen in both horizontal and vertical directions. In a preview, this value is consistent even if the zoom level of the preview changes.
GetTitle()	Returns the printout's title.

In the following sections, we'll discuss how to present the print dialog box to the user.

17.2   *How do I display the print dialog?*

Data about the print job, such as what pages to print and how many copies to make, is managed via the standard print dialog. The print dialog is similar to the font and color dialogs in that the dialog instance in wxPython is merely a thin wrapper around the native control and a separate data object that stores the dialog data.

17.2.1   *Creating a print dialog*

Figure 17.3 displays a sample print setup dialog.

In this case, the dialog is an instance of the class `wx.PrintDialog`, which you can get with the following constructor.

```
wx.PrintDialog(parent, data=None)
```

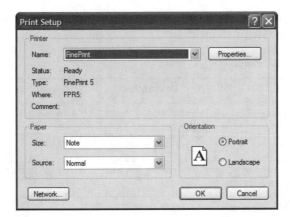

Figure 17.3
The print setup dialog

In this example, `parent` is the parent frame for the dialog, and `data`, if used, is a pre-existing `wx.PrintDialogData` instance that is used for the initial values of the dialog.

Using the methods

Once you have the dialog, you can display it using the standard `ShowModal()` method that will return `wx.ID_OK` or `wx.ID_CANCEL` depending on how the dialog is closed by the user. After you close the dialog, you can get to the data that the user entered with the method `GetPrintDialogData()`. You can also get to the printer device context associated with that data using the method `GetPrintDC()`, which will return `None` if no context has been created yet. The `OnPrintSetup()` method of the example in listing 17.1 displays how this dialog may be retrieved in practice.

Using the properties

The data object itself has several properties, one of which is a reference to an object of type `wx.PrintData`, which has even more properties. You can create your `wx.PrintDialogData` object using the constructor, `wx.PrintDialogData()`. This allows you to preset properties before you open the dialog.

The `wx.PrintDialogData` object has four properties that control whether various parts of the print dialog are enabled. The method `EnableHelp(enable)` turns the help feature of the dialog on or off. Other parts of the dialog are controlled by `EnablePageNumbers(enable)`, which covers the page number entry box, `EnablePrintToFile(enable)`, which manages the actual print button, and `EnableSelection(enable)`, which handles the toggle between print all and print selection only.

Table 17.2 displays other properties of the dialog data object that allow you to manage information about the print request.

Table 17.2 Properties of `wx.PrintDialogData`

Method	Description
GetAllPages()	Returns `True` if the user has selected the option to print the entire document.
GetCollate() SetCollate(flag)	Returns `True` if the user has selected the option to collate the printed pages.
GetFromPage() SetFromPage(page)	Returns the integer page number of the first page to print, if the user chooses to print a page range.
GetMaxPage() SetMaxPage(page)	Returns the maximum page number in the document.
GetMinPage() SetMinPage(page)	Returns the minimum page number in the document.
GetNoCopies() SetNoCopies()	Returns the number of copies that the user has chosen to print.
GetPrintData() SetPrintData(printData)	Returns the `wx.PrintData` object associated with this dialog.
GetPrintToFile() SetPrintToFile(flag)	Returns `True` if the user has chosen the option of printing to a file. The mechanism for printing to the file is managed by wxPython.
GetSelection() SetSelection(flag)	Returns `True` if the user has chosen the option of printing only the current selection. The exact definition of what is considered to be the current selection is up to your application.
GetToPage() SetToPage(page)	Returns the integer page number of the last page to print if the user specifies a range.

The `wx.PrintData` instance returned by the `GetPrintData()` method provides further information about the printing. In general, these items are in the printer settings subdialog of your print dialog. Table 17.3 lists the properties in the `wx.PrintData` object. The `wx.PrintData` object duplicates the collate and number of copies properties of `wx.PrintDialogData`.

The second useful print dialog contains the page setup data. In the next section we'll discuss the page setup data and its use.

Table 17.3   Properties of `wx.PrintData`

Method	Description
GetColour() SetColour(flag)	Returns true if the current print is for color printing.
GetDuplex() SetDuplex(mode)	Returns the current setting for printing on both sides of the page. The possible values are `wx.DUPLEX_SIMPLE` (no double-sided printing), `wx.DUPLEX_HORIZONTAL` (double-sided printing as though the pages were to be bound pad-style along the horizontal edge), and `wx.DUPLEX_VERTICAL` (double-sided printing as though the pages were to be bound book-style along the vertical edge).
GetOrientation() SetOrientation(orientation)	Returns the orientation of the page. Possible values are `wx.LANDSCAPE` and `wx.PORTRAIT`.
GetPaperId() SetPaperId(paperId)	Returns one of several identifiers matching the paper type. Space prevents a full listing. Common values are `wx.PAPER_LETTER`, `wx.PAPER_LEGAL`, and `wx.PAPER_A4`. See the wxWidgets documentation for a full listing of paper IDs.
GetPrinterName() SetPrinterName(printerName)	Returns the name used by the system to refer to the current printer. If the value is the empty string, the default printer is used.
GetQuality() SetQuality(quality)	Returns the current quality value of the printer. The setter only accepts the values `wx.PRINT_QUALITY_DRAFT`, `wx.PRINT_QUALITY_HIGH`, `wx.PRINT_QUALITY_MEDIUM`, or `wx.PRINT_QUALITY_LOW`. The getter can return any of these, or an arbitrary positive integer representing the dots per inch setting.

17.3   How do I display the page setup dialog?

Figure 17.4 displays how the page setup dialog allows the user to set data related to the page size.

Like the print data dialog, this dialog consists of a minimal dialog object that manages a data class of its own. In the next section, we'll discuss how to create a page setup dialog.

17.3.1   Creating a page setup dialog

You can create a page setup dialog by instantiating an instance of the class `wx.PageSetupDialog`.

```
wx.PageSetupDialog(parent, data=None)
```

The `parent` parameter is the parent window of the new dialog. The `data` parameter is an instance of `wx.PageSetupDialogData`—if you pass your own created

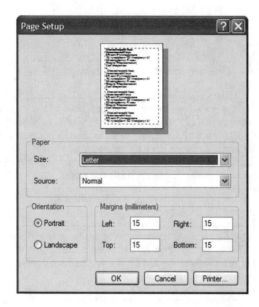

Figure 17.4
The wxPython page setup dialog box

instance in, the dialog starts off displaying the values of that instance. Once created, the dialog behaves like any other modal dialog, and you can display it using ShowModal(). As usual, the return value indicates whether the user closed the window with the wx.ID_OK or the wx.ID_CANCEL button. After the dialog has closed, you can gain access to the data object by calling GetPageSetupDialogData(), which returns an instance to the class wx.PageSetupDialogData.

17.3.2 *Working with page setup properties*

The wx.PageSetupDialogData class has several properties having to do with page setup. Table 17.4 shows properties that control the display of the dialog box itself. Unless otherwise specified, all of these properties default to True.

Table 17.4   Dialog control properties of wx.PageSetupDialogData

Property	Description
GetDefaultMinMargins() SetDefaultMinMargins(flag)	If this property is True and you are on the MS Windows system, the page setup will use the current properties of the default printer as the default minimum margin size. Otherwise, it will use a system default.

continued on next page

Table 17.4   Dialog control properties of `wx.PageSetupDialogData` *(continued)*

Property	Description
GetDefaultInfo() SetDefaultInfo(flag)	If this property is `True` and you are on an MS Windows system, the page setup dialog will not be shown. Instead all the defaults for the current printer will be put into the data object.
EnableHelp(flag) GetEnableHelp()	If `True`, the help portion of the dialog is enabled.
EnableMargins(flag) GetEnableMargins()	If `True`, the portion of the dialog dedicated to sizing the margins is enabled.
EnableOrientation(flag) GetEnableOrientation()	If `True`, the portion of the dialog for changing the orientation of the paper is enabled.
EnablePaper(flag) GetEnablePaper()	If `True`, the portion of the dialog which allows the user to change the paper type is enabled.
EnablePrinter(flag) GetEnablePrinter()	If `True`, the button allowing the user to setup a printer is enabled.

Table 17.5 displays the additional properties of the `wx.PageSetupDialogData` class that control the margin and paper size for the page.

Table 17.5   Margin and size properties of `wx.PageSetupDialogData`

Property	Description
GetMarginTopLeft() SetMarginTopLeft(pt)	The getter returns a `wx.Point` where the x value is the current left margin, and the y value is the current top margin. The setter allows you to change these values with a `wx.Point` or Python tuple.
GetMarginBottomRight() SetMarginBottomRight(pt)	The getter returns a `wx.Point` where the x value is the current right margin, and the y value is the current bottom margin. The setter allows you to change these values with a `wx.Point` or Python tuple.
GetMinMarginTopLeft() SetMinMarginTopLeft(pt)	As in `GetMarginTopLeft()`, only the value is the minimum allowable value for the left and top margins.
GetMinMarginBottomRight() SetMinMarginBottomRight(pt)	As in `GetMarginBottomRight()`, only the value is the minimum allowable value for the right and bottom margins.
GetPaperId() SetPaperId(id)	Returns the wxPython identifier for the current paper type. The same as the property of `wx.PrinterData`.
GetPaperSize() SetPaperSize(size)	The getter returns a `wx.Size` instance with the horizontal and vertical paper size. The unit is millimeters.
GetPrintData() SetPrintData(printData)	The getter returns the `wx.PrintData` instance associated with the current print session.

Now that we've described all of the data dialogs, we'll focus on printing something on the printer.

17.4 How do I print something?

Now that we've seen all of the print framework pieces, we need to print something. The actual printing part is controlled by an instance of the wx.Printer class. Having now explained all the other parts, the printing itself couldn't be simpler. Next, we'll provide you with the steps in the OnPrint() method that were included in listing 17.1.

Step 1 Get all your data in order

This would include at least the wx.Printout object with the printer commands, and will usually include a wx.PrintDialogData instance as well.

Step 2 Create a wx.Printer instance

To create the instance, use the constructor wx.Printer(data=None). The optional data parameter is an instance of wx.PrintDialogData. If included, the data in that instance governs the printing, so generally, you'll want to include one of those.

Step 3 Print with the wx.Printer method Print ()

The Print() method takes the following parameters:

```
Print(parent, printout, prompt=True).
```

The parent instance is a window to use as the parent window for any dialogs that are triggered while printing. The printout is your wx.Printout object to print. If prompt is True, the printer dialog box is displayed before printing, otherwise printing will start immediately.

The Print() method returns True if printing was successful. If not, you can call the printer method GetLastError() and get back one of the constants wx.PRINTER_CANCELLED (if the failure was due to the user canceling printing), wx.PRINTER_ERROR (if the failure occurred during the printing itself), or wx.PRINTER_NO_ERROR (if Print() returned True and nothing went wrong).

There are two other things you can do with a wx.Printer instance:

- You can display the abort dialog box with CreateAbortWindow(parent, printout), where parent and printout are as in the Print() method. If the user has aborted the print job, you can find out by calling the Abort() method, which will return True in that case.

- You can explicitly display the print dialog with `PrintDialog(parent)`, and you can retrieve the active print data object with `GetPrintDialogData()`.

17.5 How can I perform a print preview?

One of the advantages of the device contexts as they are implemented in wxPython is that it makes it easy to manage print preview, since most of the functionality comes from just replacing the printer device context with a screen device context. However, the print preview API is a bit different than for regular printing. For one thing, since print preview takes place on screen in a window, wxPython provides a frame class for previewing. The next three sections describe the print preview process.

Step 1 Create preview instance

The first step in a print preview is creating an instance of the class `wx.PrintPreview`, which is analogous to `wx.Printer`. Here is the constructor.

```
wx.PrintPreview(printout, printoutForPrinting, data=None)
```

Notice that where the `wx.Printer` instance took the parent window in the constructor, and the printout in the printing method, `wx.PrintPreview` handles the printout in the constructor. The first parameter to the constructor is `printout`, the `wx.Printout` object used to manage the preview. The `printoutForPrinting` parameter is another `wx.Printout` object. If it is not `None`, the print preview window, when displayed, contains a `Print` button that starts the print to the printer process. The `printoutForPrinting` printout object is used for the actual print. If the `printoutForPrinting` parameter is `None`, the button is not displayed. Of course, there is nothing preventing you from passing the same instance to both `printout` and `printoutForPrinting`, or from having both instances being identical versions of your custom printout class. The `data` parameter is either a `wx.PrintData` object or a `wx.PrintDialogData` object. If specified, it is used to control the print preview. In listing 17.1, we displayed an example of using a print preview in the `OnPrintPreview()` method of the window.

Step 2 Create preview frame

Once you have your `wx.PrintPreview`, you need the frame in which to view it. This is provided by the class `wx.PreviewFrame`, which is a subclass of `wx.Frame` providing the basic user interaction widgets for the preview. The constructor for `wx.PreviewFrame` allows you to pass it your `wx.PrintPreview` instance.

```
wx.PreviewFrame(preview, parent, title, pos=wx.DefaultPosition,
        size=wx.DefaultSize, style=wx.DEFAULT_FRAME_STYLE,
        name="frame")
```

The only really interesting parameter here is `preview`, which takes the `wx.Print-Preview` instance to be previewed. Everything else is standard `wx.Frame` boilerplate. The `wx.PreviewFrame` does not define any custom styles or events.

Step 3 Initialize the frame

Before you `Show()` your `wx.PreviewFrame`, you need to call the `Initialize()` method, which creates the internal pieces of the window and does other internal accounting. Once you `Show()` the frame, the buttons on the frame manage navigating through the preview and zooming and the like with no further intervention on your part. Should you want to intervene, you can look at the methods `CreateControlBar()` and `CreateCanvas()`, which create internal objects of the class `wx.PreviewControlBar` and `wx.PreviewCanvas`, respectively. Overriding those methods to create your own canvas and/or control bar objects, allows you to customize the look and feel of your print preview window.

17.6 *Summary*

- There is a general print framework in wxPython which goes beyond merely printing HTML to allow you to print anything that can be drawn to a device context. The main class in this framework is `wx.Printout`, but `wx.Printer` and `wx.PrintPreview` are also prominent.

- The `wx.Printout` class manages the graphical details of your print, and includes several lifecycle methods which can be overridden to customize the behavior and data used during your print session. The printing takes place during the method `OnPrintPage()`.

- The standard dialogs for printer setup and page setup are accessible from wxPython. The printer setup dialog is an instance of `wx.PrintDialog`, and the page setup dialog is an instance of `wx.PageSetupDialog`. Both dialogs have associated data classes that allow your program to manipulate all the values displayed in the dialogs.

- Once the data is in place, actually sending it to the printer is a relatively straightforward application of the `wx.Printer` class. You can use the `wx.PrintPreview` class to manage a print preview session, which includes a print preview frame, and the option to specify normal printing behavior from that frame.

18

Using other wxPython functionality

This chapter covers

- Placing objects on a clipboard
- Using the drop target
- Transferring and retrieving custom data objects
- Setting timed events using wx.Timer
- Writing multithreaded wxPython applications

After seventeen chapters and over five hundred pages, we still haven't covered everything that wxPython can do. In this chapter, we'll cover features that, while useful, aren't large enough to justify an entire chapter on their own. They include how to work with objects for clipboards, drag and drop operations, timers, and how to implement multithreading.

18.1 *Putting objects on the clipboard*

The clipboard and drag and drop features are closely related in wxPython. In both cases, the inter-window communication is mediated using an instance of wx.DataObject or one of its subclasses. The wx.DataObject is a special data object which contains metadata describing the formats that can be used to output the data. We'll start by discussing the clipboard, and then we'll talk about how drag and drop is handled differently.

There are three elements to a cut and paste operation.

- source
- clipboard
- target

If the source is in your application, your application is responsible for creating an instance of wx.DataObject and handing it off to the clipboard object. Often, the source for the clipboard data is external to your application.

The *clipboard* is a global object that holds onto the data and interacts with the underlying system clipboard as needed.

The *target* object is responsible for retrieving the wx.DataObject from the clipboard and converting it into some kind of useful data for your application.

18.1.1 *Getting data in the clipboard*

If you want your application to be a source for a clipboard event, meaning you want to be able to cut or copy data to the clipboard, place that data inside a wx.DataObject wrapper. The wx.DataObject wrapper class allows you to have metadata, meaning that the object also knows what kind of formats it can be read from or written as. This would be important if, for example, you were writing a word processing program and wanted to give the user the option of pasting in data as unformatted text or as formatted rich text. Most of the time, however, you don't need that much power or flexibility in your clipboard activity. wxPython provides three predefined subclasses of `wx.DataObject` for the most common use cases: plain text, bitmap image, and a filename. All of these derived objects are subclasses of `wx.DataObject` via the concrete subclass `wx.DataObjectSimple`. The data object simple class is specifically meant to be the parent class for data objects that have exactly one format.

To pass plain text, create an instance of the class `wx.TextDataObject`, using its constructor:

```
wx.TextDataObject(text="")
```

The `text` parameter is the text that you want to pass to the clipboard. If you don't know the text when you create the object, you can set the text with the `SetText(text)` method. You can recover the text using the `GetText()` method, and you can also find out how long the text is with the method `GetTextLength()`.

Having created the data object, you must then access the clipboard. The system clipboard is a global object in wxPython, named `wx.TheClipboard`. To use the clipboard, open it using the clipboard method `Open()`. The method returns a Boolean `True` if the clipboard has been opened, and `False` otherwise. It is possible for the clipboard open to fail if the clipboard is being written to by another application, so you should check the return value before using the clipboard. When you are done using the clipboard, close it by calling the clipboard method `Close()`. Leaving the clipboard open can block other clipboard users, so the goal is to have it open for as small an amount of time as possible.

18.1.2 *Manipulating data in the clipboard*

While you have the clipboard open, you can manipulate the data object it holds in a couple of different ways. You can place your object on the clipboard with `SetData(data)`, where the `data` parameter is any `wx.DataObject` instance. You can empty the clipboard with the method `Clear()`. If you want the data on the clipboard to survive after the close of your application, you must call the method `Flush()`, which instructs the system to hold on to your data. Otherwise, the wxPython clipboard object is cleared when your application exits.

Here is the code to add text to the clipboard:

```
text_data = wx.TextDataObject("hi there")
if wx.TheClipboard.Open():
    wx.TheClipboard.SetData(text_data)
    wx.TheClipboard.Close()
```

18.1.3 *Retrieving text data from the clipboard*

Recovering text data is also rather simple. Again, you need to retrieve and open the clipboard. Once you have the clipboard, call the method `GetData(data)`, where `data` is an instance of some concrete subclass of `wx.DataObject`. As we'll see in a moment, the `data` parameter should not have any actual data of its own when the method is called. This is an unusual getter, in that the return value of the method is not what you would expect—your data. Instead, the return value of this method is `True` if the data in the clipboard is able to be output in some format compatible with the data object passed in to the method. In this case, since we are passing in a `wx.TextDataObject`, a `True` result means that the clipboard data can be converted to plain text. Another way to look at it is if the method returns `True`, the clipboard data has been placed into the data object. If your data object is not compatible with the format of the data in the clipboard the method returns `False`. So, boilerplate code to retrieve text data from the clipboard looks like this.

```
text_data = wx.TextDataObject()
if wx.TheClipboard.Open():
    success = wx.TheClipboard.GetData(text_data)
    wx.TheClipboard.Close()
if success:
    return text_data.GetText()
```

Note that when you retrieve the data from the clipboard it does not matter which application placed it there. The data in the clipboard itself is managed by the underlying operating system, and wxPython's responsibility is to make sure that the formats match up behind the scenes to ensure that you get only data formats that you can handle.

18.1.4 *The clipboard in action*

In this section, we'll display a simple example that illustrates how to pass data to and from the clipboard. It's a frame with two buttons that allows the user to copy and paste text. When you run it, the example should look like figure 18.1.

Listing 18.1 displays the code used to produce figure 18.1.

Figure 18.1
An example frame that
uses the clipboard

Listing 18.1   A sample clipboard transaction

```python
import wx

t1_text = """\
The whole contents of this control
will be placed in the system's
clipboard when you click the copy
button below.
"""

t2_text = """\
If the clipboard contains a text
data object then it will be placed
in this control when you click
the paste button below. Try
copying to and pasting from
other applications too!
"""

class MyFrame(wx.Frame):
    def __init__(self):
        wx.Frame.__init__(self, None, title="Clipboard",
                          size=(500,300))
        p = wx.Panel(self)

        self.t1 = wx.TextCtrl(p, -1, t1_text,
                              style=wx.TE_MULTILINE|wx.HSCROLL)
        self.t2 = wx.TextCtrl(p, -1, t2_text,
                              style=wx.TE_MULTILINE|wx.HSCROLL)
        copy = wx.Button(p, -1, "Copy")
        paste = wx.Button(p, -1, "Paste")

        fgs = wx.FlexGridSizer(2, 2, 5, 5)
        fgs.AddGrowableRow(0)
        fgs.AddGrowableCol(0)
```

```
            fgs.AddGrowableCol(1)
            fgs.Add(self.t1, 0, wx.EXPAND)
            fgs.Add(self.t2, 0, wx.EXPAND)
            fgs.Add(copy, 0, wx.EXPAND)
            fgs.Add(paste, 0, wx.EXPAND)
            border = wx.BoxSizer()
            border.Add(fgs, 1, wx.EXPAND|wx.ALL, 5)
            p.SetSizer(border)

            self.Bind(wx.EVT_BUTTON, self.OnDoCopy, copy)
            self.Bind(wx.EVT_BUTTON, self.OnDoPaste, paste)

        def OnDoCopy(self, evt):     ◁─┘ Copy button event handler
            data = wx.TextDataObject()
            data.SetText(self.t1.GetValue())
            if wx.TheClipboard.Open():
                wx.TheClipboard.SetData(data)      ◁─┐ Placing data
                wx.TheClipboard.Close()               │ on clipboard
            else:
                wx.MessageBox("Unable to open the clipboard", "Error")

        def OnDoPaste(self, evt):    ◁── Paste button event handler
            success = False
            data = wx.TextDataObject()
            if wx.TheClipboard.Open():
                success = wx.TheClipboard.GetData(data)   ◁─┐ Getting data
                wx.TheClipboard.Close()                      │ from clipboard

            if success:
                self.t2.SetValue(data.GetText())   ◁─┐ Updating the
            else:                                      │ text widget
                wx.MessageBox(
                    "There is no data in the clipboard in the required format",
                    "Error")

app = wx.PySimpleApp()
frm = MyFrame()
frm.Show()
app.MainLoop()
```

In the next section, we'll discuss how to pass other data formats such as bitmaps.

18.1.5 *Passing other data formats*

Passing bitmaps back and forth via the clipboard is nearly identical to passing text. The data object subclass you use is wx.BitmapDataObject, and its getter and setter are called GetBitmap() and SetBitmap(bitmap). The data passed to and from the clipboard via this data object must be of the type wx.Bitmap.

The final predefined data object type is `wx.FileDataObject`. Typically, this data object is used in drag and drop (discussed in section 18.2), such as when you drop a file from your Explorer or Finder window onto your application. You can use this data object to receive filename data from the clipboard, and you can retrieve the filenames from the data object with the method `GetFilenames()`, which returns a list of strings where each string is one filename that has been added to the clipboard. You can place data onto the clipboard using this data object using the method `AddFile(file)`, which adds a filename string to the data object. There are no other methods to manipulate the list directly, so you're on your own if you want to perform other manipulations. Later in this chapter we'll discuss how to transfer custom objects via the clipboard, and how to drag and drop objects.

18.2 *Being the source of a drag and drop*

Drag and drop is functionally similar to cut and paste. In both cases, you are transferring data between various parts of your own application or between two different applications. Since the problem of managing data and formats is nearly identical, wxPython uses the same `wx.DataObject` hierarchy to ensure that formats are handled properly.

The biggest difference between drag and drop and cut and paste is that cut and paste relies on the existence of the centralized clipboard. Since the clipboard manages the data, the source application is done with the operation as soon as it passes it along—the source doesn't care what happens after that. Not so with a drag and drop. Not only does the source application need to create a drag manager object to serve the purpose of the clipboard, but it must also wait for the target application to respond. Unlike a clipboard operation, in drag and drop it is the target application that gets to decide whether the operation is a cut or a copy, so the source must wait to find out what it is expected to do with the transferred data.

Typically, you will start your drag source operation from inside an event handler, often a mouse down event, since the drag generally happens with the mouse down. Creating a drag source requires four steps:

1. Create data object
2. Create `wx.DropSource` instance
3. Execute drag operation
4. Cancel or accept drop

Step 1 Create a data object

The first step is to create your data object. This is done exactly as described earlier for a clipboard operation. For simple data, it is easiest to use the pre-defined subclasses of wx.DataObject. Data object in hand, you can create a drop source instance.

Step 2 Create drop source instance

The next step is to create an instance of wx.DropSource, which is the object that will play a transfer role analogous to that of the clipboard. The constructor for wx.DropSource is.

```
wx.DropSource(win, iconCopy=wx.NullIconOrCursor,
        iconMove=wx.NullIconOrCursor,
        iconNone=wx.NullIconOrCursor)
```

The win argument is the window object which initiates the drag and drop operation. The other three parameters allow you to customize the graphic used as the mouse is dragged for locations that will result in a copy, in a move, and where the drop is not allowed. If not specified, system defaults will be used. The graphics need to be wx.Cursor objects on MS Windows systems, but are wx.Icon objects on Unix—the Mac OS currently ignores your custom graphic.

Once you have your wx.DropSource instance, associate your data object to it with the method SetData(data). Next, we'll describe the actual drag.

Step 3 Execute the drag

The drag operation is begun by calling the drop source method DoDrag-Drop(flags=wx.Drag_CopyOnly). The flags parameter specifies which operations the target can perform on the data. Legal values are wx.Drag_AllowMove, which authorizes the target to perform either a move or a copy, wx.Drag_DefaultMove, which not only authorizes both a move or a copy, but makes the move operation the default, and wx.Drag_CopyOnly, indicating that the target can only specify a copy operation.

Step 4 Handle the drop

The DoDragDrop() method will not return until the drop is either canceled or accepted by a target. In the meantime, your application thread is blocked, although paint events will continue to be sent. The return value of DoDrag-Drop() is based on the operation requested by the target and consists of one of the following:

- `wx.DragCancel` for a canceled operation
- `wx.DragCopy` for a copy
- `wx.DragMove` for a move
- `wx.DragNone` on an error

It is your application's responsibility to respond to the return value appropriately. Typically, this means doing nothing in response to the copy, but deleting the dragged data in response to a move.

18.2.1 Dragging in action

Listing 18.2 displays a complete drag source control suitable for testing by dragging the arrow graphic to any application on your system that accepts text. Figure 18.2 displays that example.

Figure 18.2 The drop source control as it looks on screen

Listing 18.2 A small drag source control

```
import wx

class DragController(wx.Control):
    """
    Just a little control to handle dragging the text from a text
    control. We use a separate control so as to not interfere with
    the native drag-select functionality of the native text control.
    """
    def __init__(self, parent, source, size=(25,25)):
        wx.Control.__init__(self, parent, -1, size=size,
                            style=wx.SIMPLE_BORDER)
        self.source = source
        self.SetMinSize(size)
        self.Bind(wx.EVT_PAINT, self.OnPaint)
        self.Bind(wx.EVT_LEFT_DOWN, self.OnLeftDown)

    def OnPaint(self, evt):
        # draw a simple arrow
        dc = wx.BufferedPaintDC(self)
        dc.SetBackground(wx.Brush(self.GetBackgroundColour()))
        dc.Clear()
        w, h = dc.GetSize()
        y = h/2
        dc.SetPen(wx.Pen("dark blue", 2))
        dc.DrawLine(w/8,    y,   w-w/8, y)
        dc.DrawLine(w-w/8, y,   w/2,   h/4)
        dc.DrawLine(w-w/8, y,   w/2,   3*h/4)
```

```
        def OnLeftDown(self, evt):
            text = self.source.GetValue()
            data = wx.TextDataObject(text)
            dropSource = wx.DropSource(self)        ◁──┘ Creating the drop source
            dropSource.SetData(data)        ◁── Setting the data
            result = dropSource.DoDragDrop(wx.Drag_AllowMove)        ◁──┐ Performing
            if result == wx.DragMove:                                     the drop
                self.source.SetValue("")        ◁──┐
                                                   │ Deleting from
                                                   source if desired
    class MyFrame(wx.Frame):
        def __init__(self):
            wx.Frame.__init__(self, None, title="Drop Source")
            p = wx.Panel(self)
            label1 = wx.StaticText(p, -1, "Put some text in this control:")
            label2 = wx.StaticText(p, -1,
                "Then drag from the neighboring bitmap and\n"
                "drop in an application that accepts dropped\n"
                "text, such as MS Word.")
            text = wx.TextCtrl(p, -1, "Some text")
            dragctl = DragController(p, text)
            sizer = wx.BoxSizer(wx.VERTICAL)
            sizer.Add(label1, 0, wx.ALL, 5)
            hrow = wx.BoxSizer(wx.HORIZONTAL)
            hrow.Add(text, 1, wx.RIGHT, 5)
            hrow.Add(dragctl, 0)
            sizer.Add(hrow, 0, wx.EXPAND|wx.ALL, 5)
            sizer.Add(label2, 0, wx.ALL, 5)
            p.SetSizer(sizer)
            sizer.Fit(self)

app = wx.PySimpleApp()
frm = MyFrame()
frm.Show()
app.MainLoop()
```

Next, we'll show you what drag and drop looks like from the target side.

18.3 *Being the target of a drag and drop*

The steps required to be a drag and drop target roughly mirror the steps involved in being a source. The biggest difference is that on the source side you can use the class wx.DropSource directly; on the target side, you must first write your own custom subclass of wx.DropTarget. Once you have your target class, you'll need to create an instance of it and associate that instance with any wx.Window instance by using the wx.Window method SetDropTarget(target). With a target set, that wx.Window object, whether it's a frame, a button, a text area, or other widget, becomes a valid drop target. In order to receive data on your drop target you must also create a wx.DataObject instance of the desired type and associate it with the drop target with the drop target method SetDataObject(data). You need to pre-define the data object before the actual drop operation so that the drop target will be able to negotiate formats correctly. To retrieve the data object from the target, there's a getter method GetDataObject(). The boilerplate code displayed here allows the drop target to receive text, and only text. This is because the data object has been set to an instance of wx.TextDataObject.

```
class MyDropTarget(wx.DropTarget):

    def __init__(self):
        self.data = wx.TextDataObject()
        self.SetDataObject(data)

target = MyDataTarget()
win.SetDropTarget(target)
```

18.3.1 *Using your drop target*

The various event functions of your wx.DropTarget subclass get called when a drop occurs. The most important of these is OnData(x, y, default), which is the one event method that you must override in your custom drop target class. The x and y parameters are the location of the cursor at the time of the drop. The default parameter is the default result of the drop operation (i.e., copy or move), and is one of the four values listed earlier as possible return values for DoDrag-Drop(). Exactly which value gets passed as the default is based on the underlying operating system, the flags passed to DoDragDrop(), and the state of the modifier keyboard keys when the drop occurs. In practice, this usually means that if no keyboard keys are pressed, you get the default as specified by DoDragDrop(), but if the control or command key is pressed, you get the other operation if both are allowed by the call to DoDragDrop(). Within the OnData() method (and only within the OnData() method), you can call GetData(). The GetData() method takes the actual data from the drop source and puts it in the data object associated with your drop target object. Contrary to your probable expectation, GetData() does not return the data object, which is one reason why you would usually hold onto your data object as an instance variable. Here is the boilerplate code for MyDropTarget.OnData().

```
def OnData(self, x, y, default):
    self.GetData()
    actual_data = self.data.GetText()
    # Do something with the data here...
    return default
```

The return value of `OnData()` should be the resulting operation—you should return the `default` value, unless there is an error and you need to return `wx.Drag-None`. Once you have the data, you can do whatever you want with it. Remember, since `OnData()` returns information about the resulting operation, rather than the data itself, if you want to use the data elsewhere, you need to put it in an instance variable where it will still be accessible outside the method.

After the drop operation is either completed or canceled, the result value returned from `OnData()` is returned from `DoDragDrop()`, and the drop source's thread continues forward.

Within the `wx.DropTarget` class there are five `On...` methods that you can override in your subclass to provide custom behavior when the target invoked. We've already seen `OnData()`. Here are the others.

```
OnDrop(x, y),
OnEnter(x, y, default),
OnDragOver(x, y, default), and
OnLeave().
```

The meanings of the x, y, and `default` parameters are all as in `OnData()`. You do not need to override any of these methods, but you can if you want to provide custom feedback or functionality in your application.

The `OnEnter()` method is called first, when the mouse enters the drop target. You might use this to update a status window, for example. It returns the operation to be performed if a drop occurs (usually the one specified by the `default` parameter) or `wx.DragNone` if you will not accept the drop. The return value of this method is used by wxPython to specify which icon or cursor is used as the mouse glides over the window. The method `OnDragOver()` is called continuously as the mouse is inside the window, and again, it returns the desired operation or `wx.DragNone`. The method `OnDrop()` is called when the mouse is released and the drop occurs, and it calls `OnData()` by default. Finally, `OnLeave()` is called as the cursor exits the window in question.

As with data objects, wxPython provides a couple of predefined drop target classes to cover the most common cases. You still need to create a subclass and override a method to handle the data, but in this case the predefined class handles the `wx.DataObject` for you. For text, the class `wx.TextDropTarget` provides the overridable method `OnDropText(x, y, data)`. You would override this method instead of `OnData()`. The x and y are the drop coordinates, and the `data` parameter is the string being dropped, which you can use immediately without having to make further queries about data objects. Your override should return `True` if you accept the new text, and `False` otherwise. For file drops, the predefined class is `wx.FileDropTarget`, and the method to override is `OnDropFiles(x, y, filenames)`, where `filenames` is a list of the names of the files being dropped. Again, you can manipulate them as needed, and return `True` or `False` when done.

18.3.2 *Dropping in action*

The code sample in listing 18.3 displays how to create a frame that will accept file drops. You can test this code by dragging a file from your Explorer or Finder window onto the frame, and viewing the file information displayed in the frame. Figure 18.3 displays what the code looks like when it's running.

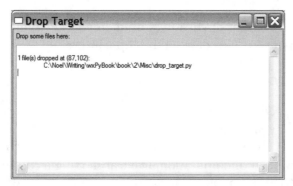

Figure 18.3
The drop target frame

Listing 18.3   The code for a file drop target

```python
import wx

class MyFileDropTarget(wx.FileDropTarget):          ◁─┐ Declaring the
    def __init__(self, window):                        │ drop target
        wx.FileDropTarget.__init__(self)
        self.window = window

    def OnDropFiles(self, x, y, filenames):          ◁─┘ Dropping file handler data
        self.window.AppendText("\n%d file(s) dropped at (%d,%d):\n" %
                               (len(filenames), x, y))
        for file in filenames:
            self.window.AppendText("\t%s\n" % file)

class MyFrame(wx.Frame):
    def __init__(self):
        wx.Frame.__init__(self, None, title="Drop Target",
                          size=(500,300))
        p = wx.Panel(self)
        label = wx.StaticText(p, -1, "Drop some files here:")
```

```
                    text = wx.TextCtrl(p, -1, "",
                                       style=wx.TE_MULTILINE|wx.HSCROLL)
                    sizer = wx.BoxSizer(wx.VERTICAL)
                    sizer.Add(label, 0, wx.ALL, 5)
                    sizer.Add(text, 1, wx.EXPAND|wx.ALL, 5)
                    p.SetSizer(sizer)
                    dt = MyFileDropTarget(text)      <— Making the text a target
                    text.SetDropTarget(dt)

        app = wx.PySimpleApp()
        frm = MyFrame()
        frm.Show()
        app.MainLoop()
```

So far, we've limited the data transfer discussion to predefined wxPython objects. Next, we'll discuss how to put your own data on the clipboard.

18.4 *Transferring custom objects*

Working with wxPython's predefined data objects limits you to plain text, bitmaps, or files. To be creative, you can allow any of your custom objects to be transferred between applications. In this section, I'll show you how to add more advanced features to your wxPython application, like transferring a custom data object and transferring an object in multiple formats.

18.4.1 *Transferring a custom data object*

Although the available data object options of text, bitmap, and list of filenames are flexible enough to cover a variety of uses, sometimes you will need to transfer a custom object, such as your own graphic format, or a custom data structure. Next, we'll cover a mechanism for transferring custom data objects, while retaining control over what kind of data your object will accept. The limitation on this method is that, for reasons that will be abundantly clear in a moment, it only works within wxPython. You cannot use this method to allow other applications to read your custom format. To send RTF to Microsoft Word, this mechanism won't work.

To do the custom data transfer, we're going to use the wxPython class wx.CustomDataObject, which is designed to handle arbitrary data. The constructor for wx.CustomDataObject is.

```
wx.CustomDataObject(format=wx.FormatInvalid)
```

The `format` parameter is technically an instance of the class `wx.DataFormat`, however, for our purposes, we can just pass it a string, and wxPython will take care of the data type. We only need the string to act as a label to differentiate one custom format from another. Once we have our custom data instance, we can put data into it using the method `SetData(data)`. The catch here is that in wxPython, the `data` parameter has to be a string. An annoying limitation, but there's a Python process for converting almost any Python object into a string—the `pickle` module. So, the boilerplate code will look something like this.

```
data_object = wx.CustomDataObject("MyNiftyFormat")
data = cPickle.dumps(my_object)
data_object.SetData(data)
```

After this snippet, you can pass the `data_object` to the clipboard or another data source to continue the data transfer.

18.4.2 *Retrieving a custom object*

To retrieve the object, perform the same basic steps. For a clipboard retrieve, create a custom data object with the same format, then get the data and unpickle it.

```
data_object = wx.CustomDataObject("MyNiftyFormat")
if wx.TheClipboard.Open():
    success = wx.TheClipboard.GetData(data_object)
    wx.TheClipboard.Close()
if success:
    pickled_data = data_object.GetData()
    object = cPickle.loads(pickled_data)
```

A drag and drop works similarly. Set the data object of the drop source to your custom data object with the pickled data, and the data target unpickles the data in its `OnData()` method and puts the data someplace useful.

Another way to create custom data objects is to build your own subclass of `wx.DataObject`. If you choose to go that route, you'll want to make your class a subclass of either `wx.PyDataObjectSimple` (for the generic object), or `wx.PyTextDataObject`, `wx.PyBitmapDataObject`, or `wx.PyFileDataObject`. That will enable you to override all the necessary methods.

18.4.3 *Transferring an object in multiple formats*

The big advantage of using wxPython data objects for data transfer is that the data objects are aware of their format. A data object can even manage the same data in multiple formats. For example, you may want your own application to receive your data in your own custom formatted text object, but you may still want other applications to be able to receive the data as plain text.

The mechanism for managing this functionality is the class wx.DataObject-Composite. All of the derived data objects we've seen so far have been subclasses of wx.DataObjectSimple. The purpose of wx.DataObjectComposite is to combine an arbitrary number of simple data objects into one data object. The combined object can deliver its data to a data object matching any of the component simple types.

To build a composite data object, start with the no-argument constructor wx.DataObjectComposite(), and then add the individual data simple objects with the method Add(data, preferred=False). To build a data object that combines your custom format with a plain text one, use.

```
data_object = wx.CustomDataObject("MyNiftyFormat")
data_object.SetData(cPickle.dumps(my_object))
text_object = wx.TextDataObject(str(my_object))
composite = wx.DataObjectComposite()
composite.Add(data_object)
composite.Add(text_object)
```

After this, pass the composite object to the clipboard or your drop source. If the target class requests the data using a data object in the custom format, it receives the pickled object. If it requests the data as plain text, it gets the string representation. The Add() method takes a second argument, preferred, which is a Boolean that marks the particular data object as the default if the target object does not specify a format (or specifies more than one). If no component is explicitly marked as preferred, the first object added is considered to be the preferred one.

In the next section, we'll show you how to use a timer to manage regularly scheduled events.

18.5 *Setting timed events using wx.Timer*

Sometimes you need your application to generate events based on the passage of a certain length of time. Games are certainly one usage, another might be giving a dialog a certain amount of time before it is automatically dismissed. To get this functionality, you can use the wx.Timer class in different ways.

18.5.1 *Generating EVT_TIMER events*

The most flexible and powerful way to use a wx.Timer class is to get it to generate EVT_TIMER events which you can bind to just like any other event.

Creating the timer

To create a timer, first create a `wx.Timer` instance using this constructor.

```
wx.Timer(owner=None, id=-1)
```

The owner parameter is some instance implementing `wx.EvtHandler`, meaning any wxPython widget or anything else that can receive event notifications. The optional `id` is used to differentiate this particular timer from any others. If it is not specified, wxPython will generate an ID number for you. If you don't want to set the owner and ID parameters when you create the timer, you can do so at any time using the method `SetOwner(owner=None, id=-1)`, which sets the same two parameters.

Binding the timer

After you've created the timer, you can bind the `wx.EVT_TIMER` event within your event handling widget with a line of code as in the following.

```
self.Bind(wx.EVT_TIMER, self.OnTimerEvent)
```

If you need to bind handlers for more than one timer to more than one handler function, you can either pass each timer's ID to `Bind`, or pass the timer object as the source parameter.

```
timer1 = wx.Timer(self)
timer2 = wx.Timer(self)                                    source
self.Bind(wx.EVT_TIMER, self.OnTimer1Event, timer1)
self.Bind(wx.EVT_TIMER, self.OnTimer2Event, timer2)
```

Just like all the other event code we've seen, this causes wxPython to react to the `wx.EVT_TIMER` event by passing control to the `OnTimerEvent()` method (or whatever method you put in that place).

Starting and stopping the timer

After the timer event is bound, all you need to do is start the timer, with the method `Start(milliseconds=-1, oneShot=False)`. The `milliseconds` parameter is, of course, the number of milliseconds that will elapse between the timer sending out the `wx.EVT_TIMER` events. Not all operating systems have system clocks with millisecond precision—if the operating system wxPython is running on does not, then the best timing available will be used. If the `milliseconds` parameter is -1, then the interval value when the timer was last started will be used (meaning that `milliseconds` actually is required the first time a `wx.Timer` is started). If `oneShot` is `True`, then the timer will fire its event once and then stop itself. Otherwise, you must explicitly stop the timer with the Stop() method. The Start() method returns a Boolean value indicating success or failure in starting the timer. Starting the timer may fail under unusual circumstances on systems where timers are a limited resource. Listing 18.4 uses this mechanism to drive a digital clock, updating the display once every second.

Listing 18.4   A simple digital clock

Blit 377

Compare
326
Block Window

373
radar graph

@ 370
ⓑ 368

```python
import wx
import time

class ClockWindow(wx.Window):
    def __init__(self, parent):
        wx.Window.__init__(self, parent)
        self.Bind(wx.EVT_PAINT, self.OnPaint)
        self.timer = wx.Timer(self)                          ←┘ Creating the timer
        self.Bind(wx.EVT_TIMER, self.OnTimer, self.timer)    ←  Binding a
        self.timer.Start(1000)    ←  Setting time interval      timer event

    def Draw(self, dc):    ←— Drawing current time
        t = time.localtime(time.time())
        st = time.strftime("%I:%M:%S", t)
        w, h = self.GetClientSize()
        dc.SetBackground(wx.Brush(self.GetBackgroundColour()))
        dc.Clear()
        dc.SetFont(wx.Font(30, wx.SWISS, wx.NORMAL, wx.NORMAL))
        tw, th = dc.GetTextExtent(st)
        dc.DrawText(st, (w-tw)/2, (h)/2 - th/2)

    def OnTimer(self, evt):    ←┘ Displaying the time event handler
        dc = wx.BufferedDC(wx.ClientDC(self))
        self.Draw(dc)

    def OnPaint(self, evt):                  # calls Draw() to do the work
        dc = wx.BufferedPaintDC(self)
        self.Draw(dc)

class MyFrame(wx.Frame):
    def __init__(self):
        wx.Frame.__init__(self, None, title="wx.Timer")
        ClockWindow(self)    # Add ClockWindow instance to self = frame instance
                             # I.e., tell ClockWindow instance that parent is self

app = wx.PySimpleApp()
frm = MyFrame()
frm.Show()
app.MainLoop()
```

Identifying current timer state

You can tell the timer's current state with the method `IsRunning()` and the current interval with the method `GetInterval()`. The method `IsOneShot()` will return `True` if the timer is running and is set to only fire once.

The `wx.TimerEvent` instance is nearly identical to its parent `wx.Event` class, but it does include a `wx.GetInterval()` method to return the interval of the timer in question. Using the event method `GetId()` returns the timer ID, in case you have bound events from multiple timers to the same handler and want to do different actions based on the specific timer which is firing.

18.5.2 Learning other timer uses

Another way to use the timer, preferable in the case where there's no obvious event target for the timer event, is to subclass `wx.Timer`. In your subclass you can override the method `Notify()`. That method is automatically called every time the timer interval passes—in the parent class, it's the `Notify()` method that triggers the timer event. Your subclass is under no obligation to trigger a timer event, however, and you can do anything you want in the `Notify()` method to respond to the timer's interval.

To trigger one specific action at some time in the future, there's a shortcut class called `wx.FutureCall`. Just about the only thing you need to know about `wx.FutureCall` is in this constructor.

```
wx.FutureCall(interval, callable, *args, **kwargs)
```

Once created, the `wx.FutureCall` instance waits an interval number of milliseconds, then calls the callable object passed to `callable` using any other positional or keyword arguments, which are passed to the callable using normal Python rules for argument passing. The interval is only triggered once, which is similar to a `wx.Timer` with `oneShot=True`. Once you've created the future call instance, you are done. Unless you plan to use the instance again, you don't need to keep a reference to it.

18.6 Creating a multithreaded wxPython application

In most GUI applications, it's useful for long-running processes to run in the background of the application so that they don't interfere with the user's interaction with the rest of the application. The mechanism for allowing background processing is typically to spawn a thread and allow the long process to run in that thread. And that's what you'll do in a wxPython program, with a couple of specific points that we'll describe in this section.

The most important point is that GUI operations must take place in the main thread, or the one that the application loop is running in. Running GUI operations in a separate thread is a good way for your application to crash in unpredictable and hard-to-debug ways. Technical reasons for this include the fact that many Unix GUI libraries are not thread-safe and issues involving the creation of UI objects under MS Windows. wxPython is not designed to have its own events take place in multiple threads, so we recommend that you not try it.

This prohibition includes any item that interacts with the screen, specifically, including wx.Bitmap objects. You're probably okay using wx.Image though, since that class does not typically deal with display issues.

Typically with wxPython applications, the background threads send messages to the UI thread for all UI updates, rather than taking care of the GUI updates themselves. Fortunately, there's no limit imposed by wxPython concerning the number of background threads you can have.

In this section, we'll look at a few ways you can effectively multithread your wxPython application. The most common technique is to use the wx.CallAfter() function, discussed next. Then, we'll look at how to set up a parallel event queue using Python's Queue object. Finally, we'll walk through how you can develop a customized solution for multithreading.

18.6.1 *Working with the global function wx.CallAfter()*

Listing 18.5 displays a sample use of threads, using the wxPython global function wx.CallAfter(), which is the easiest way to pass messages to your main thread. Simply, wx.CallAfter() allows the thread to call a function on a different thread when the current event processing completes. The functional object passed to wx.CallAfter() will always be executed in the main thread.

Figure 18.4 displays the resulting multithreaded frame.

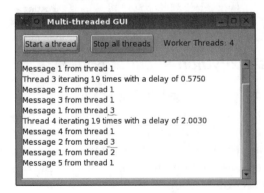

**Figure 18.4
Multithreading in the
background**

Listing 18.5 displays the code to produce this threading example.

Listing 18.5 A threaded example using wx.CallAfter() to pass messages to the main thread

```
import wx
import threading
import random

class WorkerThread(threading.Thread):
    """
    This just simulates some long-running task that periodically sends
    a message to the GUI thread.
    """
    def __init__(self, threadNum, window):        pynut2 : 344
        threading.Thread.__init__(self)
        self.threadNum = threadNum
        self.window = window
        self.timeToQuit = threading.Event()        pynut2 : 348
        self.timeToQuit.clear()
        self.messageCount = random.randint(10,20)
        self.messageDelay = 0.1 + 2.0 * random.random()

    def stop(self):
        self.timeToQuit.set()

    def run(self):        ◁┘ Running the thread
        msg = "Thread %d iterating %d times with a delay of %1.4f\n" \
                % (self.threadNum, self.messageCount, self.messageDelay)
        wx.CallAfter(self.window.LogMessage, msg)        ◁┐ Posting a call to
                                                             LogMessage
        for i in range(1, self.messageCount+1):
            self.timeToQuit.wait(self.messageDelay)
            if self.timeToQuit.isSet():
                break
            msg = "Message %d from thread %d\n" % (i, self.threadNum)
            wx.CallAfter(self.window.LogMessage, msg)        ◁┐ Posting a call to
        else:                                                    LogMessage
            wx.CallAfter(self.window.ThreadFinished, self)   ◁
                                                          Posting a call to
                                                          ThreadFinished
class MyFrame(wx.Frame):
    def __init__(self):
        wx.Frame.__init__(self, None, title="Multi-threaded GUI")
        self.threads = []
        self.count = 0

        panel = wx.Panel(self)
        startBtn = wx.Button(panel, -1, "Start a thread")
        stopBtn  = wx.Button(panel, -1, "Stop all threads")
        self.tc = wx.StaticText(panel, -1, "Worker Threads: 00")
```

```
        self.log = wx.TextCtrl(panel, -1, "",
                               style=wx.TE_RICH|wx.TE_MULTILINE)

        inner = wx.BoxSizer(wx.HORIZONTAL)
        inner.Add(startBtn, 0, wx.RIGHT, 15)
        inner.Add(stopBtn, 0, wx.RIGHT, 15)
        inner.Add(self.tc, 0, wx.ALIGN_CENTER_VERTICAL)
        main = wx.BoxSizer(wx.VERTICAL)
        main.Add(inner, 0, wx.ALL, 5)
        main.Add(self.log, 1, wx.EXPAND|wx.ALL, 5)
        panel.SetSizer(main)

        self.Bind(wx.EVT_BUTTON, self.OnStartButton, startBtn)
        self.Bind(wx.EVT_BUTTON, self.OnStopButton, stopBtn)
        self.Bind(wx.EVT_CLOSE,  self.OnCloseWindow)

        self.UpdateCount()

    def OnStartButton(self, evt):
        self.count += 1
        thread = WorkerThread(self.count, self)     <-- Creating a thread
        self.threads.append(thread)
        self.UpdateCount()
        thread.start()     <-- Starting the thread

    def OnStopButton(self, evt):
        self.StopThreads()
        self.UpdateCount()

    def OnCloseWindow(self, evt):
        self.StopThreads()
        self.Destroy()

    def StopThreads(self):     <-- Removing threads from pool
        while self.threads:
            thread = self.threads[0]
            thread.stop()
            self.threads.remove(thread)

    def UpdateCount(self):
        self.tc.SetLabel("Worker Threads: %d" % len(self.threads))

    def LogMessage(self, msg):     <-- Logging a message
        self.log.AppendText(msg)

    def ThreadFinished(self, thread):     <-- Removing a thread
        self.threads.remove(thread)
        self.UpdateCount()
```

1 when thread completes its iterations, it arranges to have its corpse removed from the Frame's thread list

2 The stop threads button was pushed; the Frame causes each thread to die and removes its corpse from the thread list

```
app = wx.PySimpleApp()
frm = MyFrame()
frm.Show()
app.MainLoop()
```

This listing uses Python's `threading` module. While the C++ wxWidgets toolkit does offer threading tools, we recommend you stick with the Python native ones. They are much simpler.

This code passes methods to the main thread using `wx.CallAfter(func, *args)`. Functionally, this posts an event to the main thread, after which the event is processed in the normal manner, and triggers the call `func(*args)`. So in this case, the thread calls `LogMessage()` during its lifecycle, and `ThreadFinished()` before it is through.

18.6.2 *Managing thread communication with the queue object*

Although using `CallAfter()` is the easiest way to manage thread communication, it's not the only mechanism. You can use Python's thread-safe `Queue` object to send command objects to the UI thread. The UI thread should be written to take commands from this queue in a `wx.EVT_IDLE` event handler.

Essentially, you will be setting up a parallel event queue for thread communication. The command objects can be whatever makes sense for the application, ranging from simple data values to thread objects whose `run()` method should be called when invoked. If you are using this method, the worker threads should call the global function `wx.WakeUpIdle()` when they add a command object to the queue to ensure that there will be an idle event as soon as possible. This technique is more complex than `wx.CallAfter()`, but it's a lot more flexible. In particular, this mechanism can help you to communicate between two different background threads, although all GUI manipulation should still be on the main thread.

18.6.3 *Developing your own solution*

You can also have your worker threads create instances of a wxPython event (standard or custom) and send it to a specific window in the UI thread using the global function `wx.PostEvent(window, event)`. The event is added to the internal pending event queue for that window, and `wx.WakeUpIdle` is automatically called. The advantage of this approach is that the event would then walk through the typical wxPython event facility, meaning you get a lot of event handling functionality for free. The disadvantage is that you have to manage all of the thread and event processing that the `wx.CallAfter()` function performs for you.

18.7 Summary

- Drag and drop and clipboard events are very similar, both use the meta-object `wx.DataObject` to mediate data formats. Default data objects exist for text, files, and bitmaps, but custom formats can be created. In using the clipboard, the global object `wx.TheClipboard` manages the data transfer and represents the underlying system clipboard.

- For a drag and drop operation, the drag source and drag target work together to manage the data transfer. The drag source event blocks until the drag target rules on whether the drag operation is valid.

- The `wx.Timer` class allows you to set events to happen at a set time in the future or periodically. The timer class can be explicitly set to trigger ordinary wxPython events, or one of a couple of wrapper functions can be used.

- Threading in wxPython is possible, but it's very important to make sure that all GUI activity takes place in the main thread. You can use the function `wx.CallAfter()` to manage interthread communication.

index

Symbols

__main__ 14

A

about box 147, 178, 182, 491
accelerator 308
    special keys 309
alert box 259, 261
alignment 189, 332
alpha value 364, 388
application 16
    crash 54
    lifecycle 34–35
    object 11, 30–31, 34, 54
    subclass 31
art provider 469
autocompletion 85, 87, 94,
        106, 112
automatic resizing 48

B

best size 335
Bind 60, 65–67, 80–81, 199,
        288, 301, 537
binder object 72, 78
bitmap 359, 369–370, 400
    button 201
    clipboard 526
    converting from image 361
    drawing 378
bitmap objects, creating 361

bitmask 44
bitwise operators 383
Blit 153, 369, 376–377, 389
    logical function 377
border 328, 336
box
    about 147, 178, 182, 491
    alert 259, 261
    bounding 387, 389
    checkbox 17, 211
    close 225
    combo 17, 221
    list 17, 58, 216
    sizer 174, 324–325, 348–349
box sizer 174, 325, 345
    layout algorithm 348
brush 371, 384
buffer 106, 151, 370
buffer device context 151, 153
buttons 17, 199
    arrow 208
    bitmap 201
    generic 203
    radio 17, 212
    toggle 162, 202

C

C++ 20–27, 44, 97–98, 103,
        130, 154, 189, 202, 235,
        464, 502
    adding a root 463
    bridging gaps with Python
        code 80

destructor 153, 371
different from Python 84
expected data type 413
interaction with Python 28
macros in 63
manages image list 402
manages memory 362
naming conventions 33–34
object names 9
overridden by Python 78
Python class subclasses 446
sorting a tree control 467
threading tools 543
toolkit 9–10
two-stage window creation
        230
user input 490
wxWidget set 282
calltips 85, 88, 94, 97, 106
CaptureMouse 152
cell
    editor 449–450
    span 437
checkbox 17, 211
    menu item 312
    toggle menu item 311
checked menu 158
child node 464
child widgets 329
children 325
choice dialog 266
clipboard 522
    bitmaps 526
    clearing 523

clipboard (*continued*)
 event 522
 example 524
 file object 527
 manipulating data in 523
 pasting from 92
 putting data in 522
 retrieving data 524
 transaction 525
clipping 386
 region 389
close box 225
close event 226
close process 232
color database 388
color names 387
color picker 169, 275
ColumnSorterMixin 416
combo box 17, 221
command event 74, 199
command line 84, 93
command prompt 84
command recall 91
constructor 43, 210, 250,
  368, 463
 message dialog 51
 pull-down choice 221
 spin control 209
 wx.Button 200
 wx.CustomDataObject 534
 wx.FlexGridSizer 339
 wx.Frame 40, 226
 wx.Frame parameters 41
 wx.grid.Grid 427
 wx.GridSizer 328
 wx.html.HtmlEasyPrinting
  495
 wx.html.HtmlWidgetCell
  497
 wx.html.HtmlWindow 487
 wx.Image 357
 wx.ImageList 400
 wx.ListBox 217
 wx.ListCtrl 398
 wx.MenuItem 299
 wx.MessageDialog 262
 wx.Pen 381
 wx.RadioBox 214
 wx.RadioButton 214

wx.Slider class 206
wx.SplitterWindow 251
wx.StaticText parameters
  188
wx.TextCtrl class 190
wx.TextEntryDialog 264
wx.TreeCtrl 462
container hierarchy 69, 73
controller 126–127
coordinate axis 385
coordinate, conversion 386
crust 107
cursor 359, 364, 388
 custom 366
 predefined 365
custom application class 33
custom events 62, 77
cut and paste
 elements 522
 Pycrust shell shortcuts 92
 See also drag and drop

D

design pattern 117
device context 148, 154, 357,
  367, 401, 519
 creation time 368
 dealing with 367
 drawing to 371
device coordinates 385
dialog 51, 55
 closing 260
 creation 259
dialog box 165
dialog data object 514
directory selector 272
dispatcher 98, 108
display 148
 gauge 205
docstring 13, 88, 97
doodle 147
drag and drop 522, 527,
  544
 return value 528
 target of 530
 See also cut and paste
drag manager 527
drag operation 528

drag source 527
 example 529
draw 148, 389
 See also device context
draw images 376
draw methods, varient types
  372
drop target 531
 drop 532
 entering 532
 exit 532
 mouse over 532
 return value 532
dropping, example 533
duplication 118

E

edit flag 411
edit session 412
editing, events 412
editor 109, 459
 custom 451
Encapsulated PostScript 370
encodings 197
EndModal 260
errors, troubleshooting guide
  53
event 57, 59, 70
 terminology 57
event binder 58, 60, 63–64
 names 63
event binding 64–65
 before wxPython 2.5 67
event driven 57–58, 61
 application 57
 architecture 59, 61
event handler 58, 60, 65, 69,
  73–74
event handling 57, 69, 76, 93
 cycle 59
event loop 86
event object 57, 62–64
event processing 69, 72–73
 enabling 71
event queue 58
event source 58
event triggers 62
event type 58, 60, 69

event-based 68
events, sequential ID 67
ExitMainLoop 39
extended style 230

F

file dialog 165
  opening 271
  saving 271
file format 357, 359, 501
file picker 269
file type 358
filling 110
fixed-width 197
flex grid sizer 325, 337
  comparison to grid sizer
    338
font 196
  for HTML printing 495
  picker 273
frame 9, 40, 225
  creating 225
  decoration 228
  dragging 248
  finding 237
  floating 229
  shaped 245
  statusbar 49
  widgets 42
functions 27

G

gauge 210
  display 205
GenBitmapTextButton 203
GenBitmapToggleButton 203
generic 121
  button 203
geometric shapes 371
GIF 359
Graphical User Interface.
    See GUI
greenscreen 363
grid 426
  adding elements 432
  auto size 439
  batch process 433

cell alignment 444
cell color 444
default size 438
direct initalization 428
display attributes 442
draggable size 440
editing 449
element size 438
event types 455, 459
header labels 435
headers 433
initialize 427
inserting elements 432
keyboard navigation 457
label size 439
labels 458
minimum size 438
refresh 433
selection 440, 459
setting cell values 428
visibility 441
grid bag sizer 325, 341
  dimensions 343
  empty cell 344
  span 344
grid control 426
  element size 436
grid coordinates 442
grid label, color and font 436
grid module 427
grid sizer 325, 327, 355
  layout algorithm 328
  resize behavior 327
grid table 426, 429
  adding elements 433
GTK 24, 244, 317–318
GUI 12, 40, 104
  unit-test 140

H

handler function 64, 72, 75
help 90
history 91
history list 492
horizontal box sizer 345
HTML 17, 179, 486
  cells 497
  displaying 486

including wxPython wid-
    gets 497
  loading file 489
  parser 496, 499, 503
  renderer 178
HTML window
  changing 491
  fonts 492
htmllib 496
HTMLParser 496
Hyper Text Markup Lan-
    guage. *See* HTML

I

icon 359
  alignment 399
  list 399
  mode 394
id 42
  in tree items 463
IDLE 85
idle
  event 153
  loop 59–60
image 16, 357, 400
  converting from bitmap 361
  creating from RGB 360
  handler 359
  loading 357
  manipulation 361, 388
  mask 363
  types 402
image list 395, 400, 423–424
  using 401
image objects, creating 360
imports 9
instance variables 122
intent 121
Internet Explorer 502–503
interpreter 110
inter-window communication
    522
introspect 111
introspection 14
item data 413
item, finding in list 416

J

Java 20
JavaScript 487
JPEG 360

K

keyboard interrupt 93
keyboard shortcut 307, 320
  PyCrust command recall 91
Keycodes 310
keypress 191

L

layout 118, 125, 170, 325
  code 117
list
  events 424
  insertion 424
list box 17, 216
  combining with checkbox
    219
  creating 216
list control 394, 398, 423
  adding columns 403
  adding rows 403
  attatching image list 402
  column header events 407
  column sorting 413
  data storage 420
  editing 411
  events 405
  information 416
  modes 394
  selection 399
  sort 413
  style flags 398
list event 412
list item properties 404
list item, state 404
list mode 396
ListBox 394
ListCtrl 394
logical function 383, 389
loop
  event 86
  main event 9, 12

M

Mac OS 6–8, 13, 24, 28, 229,
  250, 316, 503
magic literals 118, 122
main event loop 30, 77
main loop 59
MainLoop 32, 34, 54
managing resources 232
map mode 385
mapping, logical to physical
  386
mask 400
maximize 225
MDI 41, 225, 244, 256
  frame 242
menu 17, 158, 294
  creating 295
  design 319
  display string 299
  length 319
  manipulating 297
  ordering 319
  separator 51, 299
  status bar text 297
  tearoff 295
menu bar 49, 155
  creating 294
menu event 301
  binding 301
menu item 158, 303, 306, 322
  add bitmap 317
  adding 297
  adding dynamically 300
  binding multiple items 302
  disabling 306
  ellipsis 320
  enabling 306
  event 301
  finding 303
  groups 319
  information about 300
  insertion 299
  manipulating 304
  removal 299
  styles 318
  with mnemonic 309
meta-data 522
MIME-type 360

mini-frame 244
minimize 225
minimum size 334–335
mnemonic 308–309
modal dialog 259, 261
model 126–127, 133
  custom 136
Model/View/Controller.
  See MVC
modules
  crust 107
  dispatcher 98, 108
  editor 109
  filling 109
  grid 427
  interpreter 110
  introspect 111
  shell 111
  support 105–106
monochromatic 361
mouse click 62
mouse event 151
mouse pointer 4
Mozilla 503
MS Windows 267, 273, 309,
  317, 387, 412, 506, 540
multi-column, list control 397
multi-line 194
  text control 193
Multiple Document Interface.
  See MDI
multithreaded 539
MVC 117, 137, 140, 145
  compenents 126
  keeping model and view
    separate 126

N

namespace 95
naming conventions 33
nested list 461
nested menus 321
notebook 86

O

object, callable 88
OnExit 37–38

OnInit 11–12, 32, 34, 37–38, 54–55
orientation, axis 385
output, directing 35

P

page setup
  dialog 515
  properties 516
page title 493
paint events 368
panel 227, 241
password control 189
PCX 360
pen 371, 381
  predefined 382
Pending 77
pickle 535
PNG 317, 360, 395, 397, 401, 408, 415
PNM 360
pop up 322
pop-up menu 183, 293–294, 313, 315–317
post 60
pretty print 97
print 505
  dialog 512
  drawing 506
  framework 507
  HTML 495
print preview 519
  HTML 496
print request 514
printer 505
  dialog 506
  events 506
printing 506
  per copy 506
printing framework 507
printing session 506
printout lifecycle 505–506
ProcessEvent 72, 74, 78, 81–82
progress bar 210
  box 267
  dialog 267
prompt 84, 91
properties 33

proportion 339–340, 348
  single direction 341
pull-down 220
Py 115
  package 105
  support modules 105
PyAlaCarte 104, 109
PyAlaMode 104, 109, 111
PyCrust 84–87, 90–91, 93, 95, 102, 104, 108, 111–112, 115
  useful features 86
  wrapper 99
PyFilling 104
PyGridTableBase 128, 130–131, 133–134, 136
PyShell 104, 108, 111
Python 6, 21, 95
PYTHONPATH 53
PyUnit 140
PyWrap 99, 104

Q

queue
  event 58, 67
  object 543
Queue object 543

R

radio button 17, 212
radio button menu item, group boundaries 312
radio menu 158
radio toggle menu item 311
redirect 37
redirecting output 35
redraw 153
refactoring 117–118, 120–121, 125, 140, 231
reflection 231
ReleaseMouse 152
renderer 445, 459
  custom 446
  grid 445
  overridden methods 448
  predefined 445

report list
  editing 411
  setting values 404
report mode 397
  column width 405
resize
  automatic 48
  direction 174
rich text 189, 193–194

S

sash 250
Scintilla 89, 197
scroll unit 239
  size 240
scroll window 240
  position 242
scrollbar 177, 207, 218, 225, 238, 241, 326
  events 240
scrolling area 239
separator 297
session 98
SetTopWindow 32, 36, 38, 40
shebang 13
shell 84–86, 93, 102, 111
ShellFacade 111
ShowModal 52, 167, 260
shutdown 38
  emergency 39
Simplified Wrapper and Interface Generator. *See* SWIG
size flags 332
sizer 49, 170, 172, 240–241, 324, 350
  adding children 329
  calculate size 326
  changing size 331
  child list 329
  example 350
  inserting 330
  nesting 329
  prepend 330
  removing items 330
  static box 325, 349
Skip 71–72, 75–76, 80–81, 156
slider 17, 205
  styles 207

small icon
list 399
mode 395
spinner 208
splash screen 180
splitter 225
splitter window 250
manipulating 254
split 251
styles 253
startup tips 281
static text 186
status bar 49, 155, 493–494
multiple fields 156
status fields 157–158
stc.StyledTextCtrl 89
stretch factor 173
string, extent 380
style 45, 186
flags 227
submenu 158, 313
order of creation 314
subwidget 237
subwindow 47, 49, 55, 162
superdoodle 147
SWIG 10, 21, 28
syntax 118
highlighting 89
sys.stderr 35
sys.stdout 35

T

tabs
calltip 97
dispatcher 98
display 97
namespace 95
session 98
tag handler 498, 500
TestCase 141
TestSuite 141
text 17, 186
angled 379
dialog 264
drawing to device context 379
entry 189

metrics 380
style 380
text box 265
text control 412
string storage 198
thread 540
communication 543
threading module 543
TIFF 360
timer
events 536
notify 539
starting and stopping 537
state 539
tip window 281
title bar 248, 493
pattern 494
Tkinter 19
tkInter 86
toggle button 202
toggle menu item 297, 311, 320
toolbar 17, 49, 155, 161
tools 162
toolbox windows 245
tools, to run wxPython 6
tooltip 164
top window 14
top-level window 30, 34, 38–39, 54
transfer
custom data 534
multiple formats 535
transparent 364
mask 388
tree 272
adding elements 463
adding items 482
buttons 465
collapsing 473
connecting lines 465
data object 463
display attributes 467
display properties 466
editable 477, 483
expanding 473
image list 468
images 483
indent 476

iterating 483
iterator 471
managing items 464
navigating 471
root element 463
selection 472, 483
selection mode 466
sibling items 472
sorting 467, 483
styles 465, 483
virtual 474
visibility 476
visible 473
tree control 461, 482
tree item
data 467
images 470
specific point 476
tree list control 480
two-step construction 230–231

U

unable to import 53
unit test 117, 140
event 144
unittest 140–141
Unix 35, 54, 540
unpickle 535
update 137

V

validator 190, 282, 285
testing data as entered 288
transferring data with 286
using for correctness 282
vertical box sizer 345
veto 39, 233–234
view 126
virtual list control 420, 424
displaying text 423
image 423
update 423
virtual list, size 422

W

web page title 493
widgets
  adding to a sizer 325
  basic 17
  child 24, 288, 329
  controlling growth in
    sizer 341
  defined 9
  HTML 502
  laying out 170
Windows 24, 35, 54, 369
wizard 278
wx 9–10, 96, 102
wx.AccelratorEntry 310
wx.AccleratorTable 310
wx.App 11, 31, 38, 54, 64, 77,
  82, 180, 233
wx.App subclass 31–32
wx.App.MainLoop 59, 61
wx.Bitmap 153, 357, 361, 364,
  369, 388, 400, 540
wx.BitmapButton 201
wx.BitmapDataObject 526
wx.BoxSizer 171–173, 348
wx.Brush 152, 384, 389
wx.BufferDC 153
wx.BufferedDC 148, 152,
  370, 389
Wx.BufferedPaintDC 148
wx.BufferedPaintDC 370,
  389
wx.BufferPaintDC 153
wx.Button 62, 65, 68, 74–75,
  79, 200
wx.Button, 48
wx.CallAfter 540, 544
wx.CheckBox 211
wx.CheckListBox 219
wx.Choice 221
wx.ClientDC 149, 152–153,
  368
wx.Color 195, 373
wx.Colour 170, 381, 384,
  436, 444
wx.ColourData 169, 276
wx.ColourDialog 169, 276
wx.ComboBox 221

wx.CommandEvent 57, 62, 64,
  74, 81, 301, 406, 455
wx.ContextMenuEvent 316
wx.CreateFileTipProvider 281
wx.Cursor 364, 366, 528
wx.CursorFromImage 366
wx.CustomDataObject 534
wx.DataFormat 535
wx.DataObject 522–524,
  527–528, 535, 544
wx.DataObjectComposite 536
wx.DataObjectSimple 523,
  536
wx.DC 148, 153–154, 367, 377,
  388, 401
wx.DEFAULT_FRAME_
  STYLE 45
wx.Dialog 40, 74, 152, 260
wx.DirDialog 272
wx.DropSource 527–528
wx.DropTarget 530–531
  event handlers 532
wx.Event 57, 59–60, 62–63,
  71–72, 80–81
wx.EVT_BUTTON 60, 64
wx.EVT_MENU 64
wx.EvtHandler 58, 60, 64–65,
  67, 71, 81, 127, 537
  methods 67
wx.Exit 39
wx.FileDataObject 527
wx.FileDialog 165–166,
  269, 271
wx.FlexGridSizer 171, 339
wx.Font 195–196, 436
wx.FontData 274
wx.FontDialog 274
wx.FontEnumerator 197
wx.Frame 14, 40, 47, 55,
  225–227, 234–235, 494
  subclass 226
wx.FSFile 502
wx.FutureCall 539
wx.GBPosition 343
wx.GBSizerItem 343
wx.GBSpan 343
wx.GetFontFromUser 275
wx.GetNumberFromUser 265
wx.GetPasswordFromUser 265

wx.GetSingleChoice 267
wx.GetSingleChoiceIndex
  267
wx.GetTextFromUser 265
wx.gizmos.TreeListCtrl 480
wx.grid.Grid 128, 130, 427,
  430, 444, 458
wx.grid.GridCellAttr 442, 444
wx.grid.GridCellEditor 450,
  459
wx.grid.GridCellRenderer
  445, 449
wx.grid.GridEvent 455
wx.grid.GridTableBase 429,
  431
wx.grid.PyGridCellEditor 451
wx.grid.PyGridCellRenderer
  446, 459
wx.grid.PyGridTableBase 429,
  458
wx.GridBagSizer 172, 343
wx.GridSizer 171–172, 328,
  355
wx.html module 487
wx.html.HTMLCell 501
wx.html.HtmlCell 497
wx.html.HtmlContainerCell
  497
wx.Html.HtmlEasyPrinting
  503
wx.html.HtmlEasyPrinting
  495
wx.html.HtmlFilter 502
wx.html.HtmlParser 497
wx.html.HtmlWidgetCell 497
wx.html.HtmlWindow 178,
  487, 490, 503
  events 490
wx.html.HtmlWinParser 497
wx.html.HtmlWinTagHan-
  dler 500
wx.Html.Tag 499
wx.HtmlEasyPrinting 505
wx.HTMLWindow 186
wx.Icon 401, 528
wx.ID_ANY 42–43
wx.ID_CANCEL 42, 52, 261
wx.ID_HIGHEST 43
wx.ID_LOWEST 43

wx.ID_OK 42, 52, 261
wx.Image 357, 359–360, 362–364, 388, 488
wx.ImageHandler 359
wx.ImageList 400
wx.lib.buttons.GenButton 203
wx.lib.dialogs.ScrolledMessageDialog 263
wx.lib.evtmgr.eventManager 140
wx.lib.iewin.IEHtmlWindow 502
wx.lib.imagebrowser.ImageDialog 277
wx.lib.mixins.listctrl 414
wx.lib.pubsub 140
wx.lib.ScrolledPanel 241
wx.lib.stattext.GenStaticText 189
wx.ListBox 216, 218
wx.ListCtrl 398, 422–423
wx.ListEvent 406–407, 412
    event types 406
wx.ListItem 403–404
wx.ListItemAttr 423
wx.MDIChildFrame 244
wx.MDIParentFrame 244
wx.MemoryDC 149, 153, 369, 389, 506
wx.Menu 50, 158–159, 295–296, 299–300, 304, 314, 321
wx.MenuBar 294–296, 304, 321
wx.MenuEvent 302
wx.MenuItem 159, 294, 299, 321
wx.MessageBox 263
wx.MessageDialog 51, 261–262
wx.MetafileDC 149, 369
wx.MiniFrame 244
wx.MouseEvent 58, 63–64
wx.NewID 51
wx.NewId 42–43
wx.OK 52
wx.PageSetupDialog 515, 520
wx.PageSetupDialogData 515, 517
wx.PaintDC 149, 153, 368

wx.Panel 48, 55, 170, 227, 260
wx.Pen 151, 381
wx.Point 43, 378
wx.PostEvent 543
wx.PostScriptDC 149, 369–370, 506
wx.PreFrame 230, 232
wx.PreviewCanvas 520
wx.PreviewControlBar 520
wx.PreviewPane 519
wx.PrintData 513–514
wx.PrintDialog 512, 520
wx.PrintDialogData 506, 513, 518
    properties 513
wx.Printer 505–506, 518, 520
wx.PrinterDC 149, 369–370, 506
wx.Printout 505–506, 511, 518–520
    information retrieval 512
wx.PrintPreview 505, 519–520
wx.ProgressDialog 268
wx.PyCommandEvent 78
wx.PyDataObjectSimple 535
wx.PyEvent 78, 82
wx.PyEventBinder 63, 65, 81
wx.PyGridModel 128
wx.PySimpleApp 32, 180
wx.PyValidator 282
wx.RadioBox 212, 214–215
wx.RadioButton 212
wx.RealPoint 44
wx.RegisterId 42
wx.ScreenDC 149, 368–369
wx.ScrolledWindow 238
wx.ShowTip 282
wx.SingleChoiceDialog 53, 261, 266
wx.Size 43, 378
wx.SizeEvent 62–63
wx.Sizer 177, 324, 355
wx.Slider 205
wx.SpinCtrl 208
wx.SplashScreen 180, 247
wx.SplitterEvent 255
wx.StaticBoxSizer 172, 350
wx.StaticText 186
wx.StatusBar 50, 156, 158, 173

wx.stc.StyledTextCtrl 197
wx.StockCursor 364
wx.TextAttr 194
wx.TextCtrl 189–190, 192, 195, 198
wx.TextDataObject 523–524, 531
wx.TextDropTarget 532
wx.TextEntryDialog 52, 261, 264
wx.TheClipboard 523, 544
wx.Timer 536–537, 544
wx.TimerEvent 539
wx.TipProvider 281
wx.ToggleButton 202
wx.ToolBar 50, 161, 164
wx.TreeCtrl 461–462, 468, 480, 482
wx.TreeEvent 473, 478
wx.TreeItemData 467–468
wx.TreeItemId 463, 465, 467, 470–472, 476, 478
wx.Validator 190, 282
wx.WakeUpIdle 543
wx.Window 188, 234, 325–326, 427, 463, 530
wx.WindowDC 149, 368
wx.wizard.Wizard 278–279
wx.wizard.WizardEvent 280
wx.wizard.WizardPage 278, 281
wx.wizard.WizardPageSimple 278, 280
wxMozilla 503
wxPython 26, 57
    library 57
    package 10
wxWidgets 10, 20–22, 24, 33, 42, 63, 78, 230, 502

X

XML 123
XOR 383
XPM 360–361

Y

Yield 77

MORE TITLES FROM MANNING ...

Ajax in Action
> by David Crane and Eric Pascarello
> with Darren James
> ISBN: 1-932394-61-3
> 680 pages
> $44.95
> October 2005

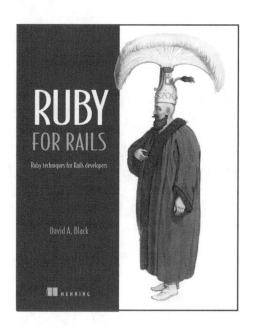

Ruby for Rails
> by David A. Black
> ISBN: 1-930114-69-9
> 600 pages
> $44.95
> May 2006

For ordering information go to www.manning.com

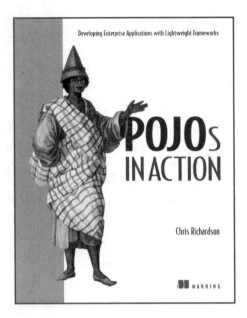